Learning C# Programming with Unity 3D

Learning C# Programming with Unity 3D

Second Edition

Alex Okita

CRC Press
Taylor & Francis Group
Boca Raton London New York

CRC Press is an imprint of the
Taylor & Francis Group, an **informa** business

AN A K PETERS BOOK

CRC Press
Taylor & Francis Group
6000 Broken Sound Parkway NW, Suite 300
Boca Raton, FL 33487-2742

© 2020 by Taylor & Francis Group, LLC
CRC Press is an imprint of Taylor & Francis Group, an Informa business

Printed on acid-free paper

International Standard Book Number-13: 978-1-138-33681-0 (paperback)
978-1-138-33682-7 (hardback)

Library of Congress Cataloging-in-Publication Data

Names: Okita, Alex, author.
Title: Learning C# programming with Unity 3D / Alex Okita.
Description: Second edition. | Boca Raton, FL : CRC Press/Taylor & Francis
Group, 2019.
Identifiers: LCCN 2019010020 | ISBN 9781138336810 (pbk. : acid-free paper) |
ISBN 9781138336827 (hardback : acid-free paper)
Subjects: LCSH: Computer games--Programming. | C# (Computer program language)
| Unity (Electronic resource) | Three-dimensional display systems.
Classification: LCC QA76.76.C672 O43 2019 | DDC 794.8/1526--dc23
LC record available at https://lccn.loc.gov/2019010020

**Visit the Taylor & Francis Web site at
http://www.taylorandfrancis.com**

**and the CRC Press Web site at
http://www.crcpress.com**

Contents

1

Introduction: What This Book Is About

This book was written as an answer for anyone to pick up a modern programming language and be productive. You will be able to start a simple game in Unity 3D from scratch. By the end of this book, you will have the basic skills to eventually become a capable unity game programmer, or at least know what is involved with how to read and write some code.

You should have general computer skills before you get started. Come prepared; you'll need a modern Windows or OSX computer capable of running modern software with an internet connection. After this book, you should be armed with the knowledge required to feel confident in learning more.

Each chapter has example code organized by chapter and section. We'll try to make a fun project starting with the basic functions of a typical game and we'll see how the basic game can be expanded upon and we'll learn a bit about what's involved with a larger project.

1.1 Why Read a Book: Why This Book May or May Not Be for You

You could go online and find videos and tutorials to learn; however, there is a disadvantage when it comes to learning things in order and in one place. Most internet video or tutorial websites may gloss over or dwell on a subject. You could skip ahead, but then what are you paying for?

Online content is often brief and doesn't go into much depth on any given topic. It is incomplete or still a work in progress. You'll often find yourself waiting weeks for another video or tutorial to come out.

Just so you know, you should find the act of learning exciting. If not, then you'll have a hard time continuing through to the end of this book. To learn any new skill, a lot of patience is required.

I remember asking an expert programmer how I'd learn to program. He told me to write a compiler. At that time, it seemed rather unfair, but now I understand why he said that. It is like telling someone who wants to learn how to drive Formula 1 cars to go compete in a race. In both cases, the "learning" part was left out of the process.

It is very difficult to tell someone who wants to learn to write code where to begin. However, it all really does start with your preparedness to learn. Your motivation must extend beyond the content of this book.

You may also have some preconceived notions about what programming is. I can't change that, but you should be willing to change your thoughts on the topic if you make discoveries contrary to your knowledge. Keep an open mind.

As a game developer, you should find the act of making a game, or simply learning how to make a game, is just as fun as playing a game. If your primary goal is only to make that game that you've had in your head for years, then you might have a problem. You may find this book a tedious chore if learning C# is just something in the way of making your game.

Computer artists often believe that programming is a technical subject that is incompatible with art. I find the contrary to be true. Programming is an art, much as literature and design are an art. Programming just has a lot of obscure rules that need to be understood for anything to work.

No, programming is not too hard to learn. Writing a massive multiplayer online role-playing game is quite hard. Learning how to write a simple behavior isn't hard; like drawing, you start off with the basics drawing spheres and cubes. After plenty of practice, you'll be able to create a real work of art. This applies to writing code, that is, you start off with basic calculations and then move on to the logic that drives a complex game.

1.1.1 Do I Need to Know Math?

With complex rules in mind, does programming require the knowledge of complex mathematics? Unless you are writing mathematical software, only a bit of geometry is required. Most of the examples here use only a tiny bit of math to accomplish their purpose. Mathematics and programming do overlap quite a lot in their methodology.

Math taught in schools provides a "best" solution. Programming results tend to behave a bit like a math proof, but the proof isn't just another bit of math. Rather, the proof of your code means that your zombies chase after humans. A considerable amount of math required has been done for you by the computer. It is just up to you to know what math to use, and then plug in the right variables.

1.1.2 Programming as a Form of Expression

There is a deeper connection between words and meaning in programming. This connection is more mechanical, but flexible at the same time. In relation to a programming language, programmers like to call this "expressiveness."

When you write words in literature, you infer most if not all of the meaning. When programming inference isn't implied, then you're free to define your own meanings for words and invent words freely.

One common merging of art and code appears within a video game. Anytime characters can react to each other and react to user interaction conveys a greater experience. An artist, an animator, or an environment designer should have some ability to convey a richer experience to the audience. A character artist can show a monster to his or her audience; but to really experience the creature, the monster should glare, grunt, and attack in reaction to the audience.

1.1.3 Games as a Stage with Lights

To do this, we're going to use Unity 3D, a game engine. If you were to write a play, you would not have to build the auditorium for your performance. Building lights and generating electricity to run them would distract you from writing your play. Playwrights don't often build lights and auditoriums from scratch, and there are plenty of venues you could use as your stage, which is where game engines come in.

Game engines such as Unity 3D, Unreal Engine, Crytek, and even Game Maker, or Godot have a lot of the basic game and math-related functions built for you. They are ready-built stages that allow you to focus on making your game. The necessary code for rendering and physics have been done for you.

1.2 Personal Information

I started in the 1990s cleaning up sprites for Atari. Back then the job qualifications were basically having Photoshop and a Wacom tablet. Oh, how times have changed!

I've worked for many different game studios, in both 2D and 3D, as an artist. I was exposed to many different software packages including Strata 3D on the Mac and Alias (PowerAnimator) on the SGI (Silicon Graphics International), among many others. I loved learning new 3D modeling, rendering, and animation applications. During my work as an artist, I used Maya, a popular 3D modeling package. While using Maya, I was introduced to the Maya Embedded Language (MEL) script. Today I use Modo with Python.

After working as a character rigger and technical artist, I learned many programming languages including MAXScript, MEL, and Python, which helped me to write tools for my fellow artists to use for speeding up production.

I eventually moved into the job of programmer as my primary job function. I wrote prototypes for Microsoft in Unreal using UnrealScript, a programming language much like JavaScript. This game studio was run by John Gaeta and Peter Oberdorfer, who are award-winning movie special effects directors.

I began my career path as an artist, then became a technical artist, and finally a programmer. This seems to be a common trend among a small variety of 3D artists like myself. I know quite a few folks who have followed the same career path.

During my transition from artist to programmer, I found that there was very little by way of help, documentation, web pages, or similar to complete the transition from an artist to a programmer. Many people assumed that you were either a programmer to begin with, or not interested in making that transition. After a long discussion, with my then girlfriend—now wife, about what a variable is, I decided it was time to write a book.

1.3 A Brief History of Computer Programming: How Programming Came to Be

Basic insight into the inner workings of your computer may help understand why and how some text gets converted into computer instruction. The words that make up C#, or any other programming language get converted into what is called byte code.

Skilled programmers tend to know more about the inner workings of their computer. Like any trade or learned skill, the more you know about how your tools work, the better understanding of the entire process you'll have.

To understand why programming tools work as they now do stems from knowing how they used to work. To understand how the current tools came about means knowing a bit of computer history and how computers used to work.

1.3.1 Mechanical Computers

The first programmable computer is arguably the Babbage machine built by Charles Babbage in the 1820s. Made of tens of thousands of moving parts and weighing several tons, it was a gigantic mechanical calculator that could display a 31-digit number. It was called the Difference Engine. in 1824 Babbage won a gold medal from the British Astronomical Society, by using his gigantic calculator, for correcting a set of tables used to chart the movement of planets through the sky.

In 1833, a countess named Augusta Ada King of Lovelace, commonly known as Ada Lovelace, met Babbage at a party where she was introduced to the Difference Engine. Several years later, it became evident that she understood the machine better than Charles himself. Despite being a housewife to the Earl of Lovelace, she wrote several documents on the operation of the Difference Engine as well as its upgraded version, the Analytical Engine. She is often considered to be the first computer programmer for her work with the Difference Engine and its documentation.

1.3.2 Logic

In 1848, George Boole gave us Boolean logic. It would take nearly a century between the Difference Engine and the first general programmable computer to make its appearance. Thanks to George, today our computers count in binary (1s and 0s), and our software thinks in terms of true or false.

In 1887, Dorr Eugene Felt built a computing machine with buttons; thanks to him, our computers have keyboards. In the 1890s, a tabulating machine used paper with holes punched in it representing 1s and 0s to record the US census. Back then it saved US$2 million and 6 years of work.

There was a moment in time where a trinary computer existed. In 1840, Thomas Fowler created a competing mechanical computer which worked with −1, 0, and +1. Even as late as 1958 an electronic version was created in the Soviet Union, but its usefulness lost out to binary which was easier to build and used less power.

In the 1900s, between Nicola Tesla and Alexander Graham Bell, modern computers were imminent with the invention of the transistor. In 1936, Konrad Zuse made the Z1 computer, another mechanical computer like that of Babbage, but this time it used a tape with holes punched in it like the tabulating machine. He'd later move on to make the Z3 in 1941.

1.3.3 Computer Science

In the 1940s, Alan Turing, a British computer scientist, designed and built an encrypted message decoder called the Bombe that used electromechanical switches for helping the Allied forces during World War II.

Between the 1930s and the 1950s, Turing informed the computer scientists that computers can, in theory, solve anything calculable, calling this concept *Turing completeness*. All of these components were leading toward our modern computer.

In the mid-1940s, John Von Neumann demonstrated, with the help of his theory, that the computer can be built using simple components. In this way, the software that controls the hardware can add the complex behavior. Thanks to Tesla and Bell, the Z3 was made completely of electronic parts. It included the first use of logic while doing calculations, making it the first complete Turing-complete computer. In 1954, Gordon Teal at Texas Instruments introduced the silicon-based transistor, a key component for building solid-state electronics that are used today in every computer.

1.3.4 The Origin of Software

The Z3 was programmed using Plankalkül, the first high-level programming language, invented by Zuse shortly after he finished building the machine. In 1952, Grace Hopper created the first compiler software that could translate human-readable words into machine operations. For the first time, the programmer didn't need to know how the transistors operated in the hardware to build software for the computer to run. This opened computer programming to a whole new audience.

Between the 1950s and 1970s, computers and computer languages were growing in terms of complexity and capability. In 1958, John McCarthy invented LISP (for LISt Processor) at the Massachusetts Institute of Technology (MIT). Object-oriented programming appeared in Simula 67 in 1967. Imperative and procedural programming made its appearance in Pascal in 1970.

1.3.5 Modern Computer Language

Bell Labs, started by Bell in the 1920s, hired Dennis Ritchie in 1967. In 1974, Ritchie published the C programming language that has become the most popular computer programming language. In 1983, Bjarne Stroustrup introduced C++ as "C with Classes."

In 2001, Microsoft released C#, a combination of several programming language paradigms taking the concepts from C, C++, LISP, Haskell, and others, and incorporating the ideas and concepts into a single language. Today, C# is in its seventh major revision, whereas C++ is in its seventeenth revision. C# is an evolving language having new features and concepts. Each revision makes the language more flexible and most important, more expressive.

1.3.6 The Future of Computer Languages

The International Business Machines Corporation (IBM), a US company founded in the 1920s, is currently engineering new technology using particle physics discovered nearly a century ago. Modern spintronics derived from the work of German physicists in the late 1920s.

Without particle physics and physicists such as Friedrich Hermann Hund, we wouldn't understand quantum tunneling, and the solid-state storage or universal serial bus (USB) thumb drive wouldn't exist. After the discovery and confirmation of the Higgs boson, you might ask "Why bother?" This question might not get a good answer for another hundred years, but it'll be worth it.

C# is not the last computer language; many others have been introduced just recently. Google has introduced Kotlin specifically for developing apps for Android and Apple has introduced Swift for their iOS platform. Microsoft, not to be outdone, introduced Q# for the future of quantum computing.

Using Q# for game development isn't likely, at least for now. Programming languages have advantages and disadvantages in different disciplines. The purpose of programming languages is to allow human readable text to be converted into instructions that run on a computer's CPU.

1.4 C#: A Flexible Programming Language

There are plenty of programming languages and each language was created to fulfill different roles. Modern programming languages in use today are often described by their paradigms. A paradigm can be explained as a sort of writing style; each style follows a different set of rules.

1.4.1 C# Paradigm

In poetry, a haiku follows a 5-7-5 syllable tempo. A sonnet follows an iambic pentameter with 10 syllables per line and rhymes in a specific pattern. Not all prose needs to end in rhyme like haiku, but many do. Rhyming and tempo are paradigms used in poetry.

Modern programming paradigms include object oriented, functional, imperative, and logic programming. Some programming languages use one or more of these paradigms together. For instance, F# is an imperative, object oriented, and functional language. However, Haskell is purely functional.

C# (pronounced "see sharp") is a combination of many different paradigms. As the name infers, C# is a C-style language and primarily expressed using the object-oriented paradigm. How C# expresses its different paradigms, and how you choose to write with it, is greatly up to you. Due to this flexibility, C# offers a variety of uses reaching far beyond game development.

You may have heard of C++, another multiparadigm language. It is often used by programmers who need detailed control over memory management and many other aspects of their final product. This attention to detail and design is required to produce a refined final product.

C# is an imperative language, that is to say, it carries out operations in order. It is also object oriented, so each object is allowed to do things on its own. Finally, it is also memory managed, aka garbage collected, so your computer's memory is organized for you. However, it does provide the flexibility to manage memory if you require that level of control. Just as well, C++ has recently added garbage collection features to match C#.

1.4.2 Unity 3D: A Brief History of Game Engines

A game engine is basically software that provides many of the basic functions that are commonly used to build a video game. Most game engines allow for rendering either 2D or 3D shapes by importing files generated in a third-party software such as Blender, or 3D Studio Max or Maya, if you can afford them. Another function often found in a game engine is the ability to write software for the game engine to run. Unity 3D allows you to write software to run your game in C#.

3D game engines have a relatively short history in general computing. Their evolution has been hot and fast. Starting around the 1990s, the 486 processor finally made its way into the general populace as a processor fast enough to allow for everyone to play 3D games. Or at least pseudo-3D, 2D images drawn in the shape of three-dimensional geometry. The technology for true 3D polygons would take a few more years to make it onto the average person's desktop.

Pseudo-3D was used to describe skewing and scaling flat sprites or 2D images to appear as though they were in 3D space. True vertex transformation wouldn't appear in popular video game engines on the PC with games such as Quake 1 until 1995. This was greatly with the help of faster and enhanced graphics processors. The modding community took Quake 1 and created many new additions and full conversions.

When powerful graphics processing units (GPUs) were introduced, it opened the floodgates for many more 3D games to make their appearance. At first, these games functioned only on million-dollar computers, but thanks to 3dfx, nVidia, Maxtrox, and ATi in the late 1990s, the GPU quickly took over being a requirement for any 3D game. At that time, id Software, run by John Carmack, quickly came to the forefront of the 3D gaming engine technologies that introduced many concepts such as spline surfaces, complex shadows, and lighting with Quake 2.

Around 1998, Epic Games' Unreal Engine and Valve Software's Source Engine took off with the launch of Unreal Tournament and Half-Life. More modding and conversions exploded onto the scene. Many successful game modifications including Counter-Strike would go on to be one of the most played online multiplayer games Valve Software would publish for years to come.

Before the availability of dedicated GPU and cheap RAM, computers didn't have enough free resources to support a game engine with editing tools. Often the game itself required so much of the computer that there was little room left for any extras, such as particle editors or just-in-time compiling.

The modding community influenced business, making Unreal 2 and Source more modder friendly. Garry's Mod and Unreal Editor changed how game engines were made by adding tons of user-friendly tools. Many users bought games specifically to "mod," or modify, and create new games.

It's no surprise that at this time many game engines would show up on the scene to cater to the modding community and the independent game developer. The large game engines found themselves top heavy by focusing on large publishers. Companies such as RenderWare and Gamebryo found themselves poorly positioned to compete against newcomers who focused on the independent developers such as Unity 3D.

With the independent game developer in mind, many game engines focused on affordability and cross-platform development. Tools such as Game Maker, Unreal Engine, and of course Unity 3D allowed for many more people to learn and build games without the multimillion-dollar investment formerly required for game production.

1.4.3 Why Use Unity 3D to Learn?

Making a game is more fun than making accounting software.

Having fun learning is more important as getting high test scores. After a test, you pretty much forget the anguish of studying all night and what it was for. So there is no reason to make learning menial work because studying should not be boring.

Once learning becomes entertainment, the lessons become something you want to remember. As a fun experience, you remember the experience longer. I've found that learning how to write game artificial intelligence (AI) and behavior is the best way to retain programming experience.

Programming lessons are often taught using stiff diagrams and simple math problems with little or no immediate or obvious applicable use. How often have you actually needed to know where trains would meet leaving two different cities at two different speeds? Experience shows that readers lose interest in any example involving grade-point averages or a train leaving from New York.

Unity 3D offers examples by blowing things up. Calculus and vector examples are usually explained using grids and lines. These concepts are lost by abstract pictures that lack meaning or application. In this case, we'll use math to solve for where a bad guy needs to throw a grenade in order to hit a moving target.

Finally, we'll end up with both the knowledge that will help build a game and the skills needed to write software outside of Unity 3D. With any luck, we'll also have fun while learning. Some of these examples may even help with your math classes.

Unity 3D also provides us with a complete set of tools we can use in our code quickly and easily. These tools are a part of the Unity 3D application programming interface (API). The Unity 3D API is filled with useful things such as commonly used routines, data structures, and classes. These parts of the API are often called a library. We'll learn what all that means in the remaining chapters.

1.4.4 How Does Unity 3D Use C#?

Not that long ago, Unity 3D supported three programming languages. First there was Boo, which was given an accompaniment with JavaScript followed by C#. As of the latest version of Unity 3D, C# is considered the primary, or first-class programming language. Both JavaScript and Boo have been phased out.

In general, C# is gaining more support across many open source projects and has a growing user base. The Dot Net Foundation which maintains .NET Core, is an open source project supported on multiple platforms.

You might be surprised to learn that programming languages have version numbers. With each new version of a language comes new features. As of the writing of this book, Unity 2018 and newer supports. NET 4.7 which is C# version 7.0. What does that mean? It's not so simple, actually. Microsoft created .NET (dot net): a framework or a standardized environment in which code can accomplish common tasks with fewer commands. Using software without a framework often means reinventing code that's been written many times. The framework is also intended to be easily extended. Unity 3D includes many game-related additions to help make building games easier.

The progression looks something like this table:

January 2002	C# 1.0	.NET 1.0	
April 2003	C# 1.2	.NET 1.1	
November 2005	C# 2.0	.NET 2.0	Unity 3D 4.1
November 2007	C# 3.0	.NET 3.5	
April 2010	C# 4.0	.NET 4.0	Unity 3D 5.6
August 2012	C# 5.0	.NET 4.5	
July 2015	C# 6.0	.NET 4.6	Unity 3D 2017.1
March 2017	C# 7.0	.NET 4.7	Unity 3D 2018.1
August 2017	C# 7.1	.NET 4.7.1	

As new versions of .NET were introduced, the language that went along with it was also upgraded, though with different version numbers. Confusing? Yes. Unfortunately, to add to the confusion there's also three versions of .NET that include .NET Standard, .NET Framework, and .NET Core. The differences between these have no effect on what we'll be learning in this book, so I'll leave that research up to you to do on your own. For now, we're not so concerned with the version of either so long as the features we learn about the C# language work within the context of Unity.

C# is used by a large community of general application programmers, not just game engineers. Unity 3D is also a cross-platform game engine, and a developer working on either OSX or Windows can both share and use files for Unity 3D. C# is the same on both Mac and PC as well as Android and iOS for mobile, so there is no concern over what operating system you're going to use.

1.4.4.1 *How to Tell Unity 3D What to Do*

Unity 3D and Microsoft Visual Studio are going to be our integrated development environment (IDE). IDEs come in many different forms. Many professional Windows programmers use Visual Studio, and Apple developers usually use Xcode in OSX. Microsoft has also made Visual Studio available for OSX. An IDE provides many tools that make programming easier by highlighting the lines of code and automatically completing many commonly repeated tasks.

When it comes to learning about the nuts and bolts of programming, you're basically learning about how your computer thinks, or in more general terms, how your computer does what it is told. Somewhere along the way you'll realize how unintelligent your computer is and how smart good programmers are.

Programming is basically writing detailed instructions on what to do and when. In short, get data then do something with the data. A big part of programming is figuring out where to get information; we'll call this data management. Then you use logic to determine what to do with the data once you have it. Programming logic is organized into algorithms found in statements organized into functions.

Unity 3D provides tools to move characters and objects with your code. These assets all live in the project directory as separate files or entities that you can control through code. Unity 3D provides scenes to give structure to your assets—3D models particle systems for explosions, fire, and other special effects—and tools to create and edit all these things. It is largely up to you to learn these different systems on your own, but this book covers the code part of things.

Unity doesn't provide a set of 3D modeling or 2D image editing tools. For this you'll want to find something like Blender 3D which is free or use another 3D modeling and texturing tools set. You'll also want to look into Gimp or Dogwaffle to paint 2D images to import into Unity.

1.5 What Is Programming?

It's all about writing code.

Programming is a process in which we organize data and use logic to do something with the data. The data is everything a computer can store; they can range from numbers to zombie characters in a video game. You do this by writing text into many files called source code. Source code written into text files replaces punch cards used by the computing machines half a century ago.

When data is combined with logic and then written into a single file, it's called a class. Classes are also data and, as such, can be managed with more logic. Classes are used to create objects in the computer's memory and can be duplicated to have a life of their own.

Classes are used to build objects. Each piece of data within the class becomes a part of that object. Different chunks of data inside of a class are called class members. Class members can also be chunks of logic called functions or methods. If that is not clear right now, don't worry we'll go into detail on that in Chapter 2.

Objects created from a class are called instances. In a game with a horde of zombies, each zombie is duplicated or instanced from a zombie class. Each zombie has unique values for each attribute or data element in the class. This means hit points and positions are unique for each duplicate zombie object.

Similar to families, objects can inherit properties from one another. The child, sometimes called a subclass, inherits attributes from its parent. For instance, the child created from a zombie may inherit the parent's hunger for brains. To be useful, the child zombie can also add new objects and change the objects it inherited from its parent class. As a result, now the child zombie might have tentacles that the parent didn't have.

Objects talk to each other through events and messages. Shooting at zombies can create an event, or in programmer terms, it "raises" an event. The bullet impact event tells the zombie class to then take necessary steps when hit by a bullet. Events command the class to take actions on its data, which is where functions come in.

Functions, also known as methods, are sections of logic that act on data. They allow your class to create additional events and talk to yet more objects. As the player presses the trigger and moves the joystick around, yet more events can be raised and messages can be sent. Events and messages allow the player to interact with your world; logic events and objects together build your game.

1.5.1 What Does C# Look Like?

A game in Unity 3D is made up of many different C# files. Each file can be referred to as a "class" and ends with the .cs file extension (which stands for C Sharp). This isn't a class like those that are taught. It is more akin to biology in which classes are categories that define different groups of organisms.

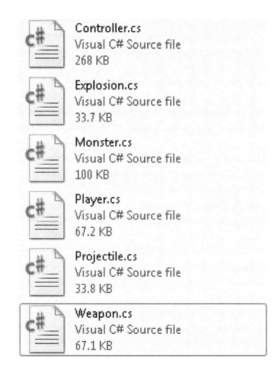

Controller.cs
Visual C# Source file
268 KB

Explosion.cs
Visual C# Source file
33.7 KB

Monster.cs
Visual C# Source file
100 KB

Player.cs
Visual C# Source file
67.2 KB

Projectile.cs
Visual C# Source file
33.8 KB

Weapon.cs
Visual C# Source file
67.1 KB

A basic game might have several different classes, each one named according to its purpose. Each one of these classes contains the text that is your actual C# code. Just so you know, by default Windows will hide the extensions of your files. As a result, if classes appear as simply Weapon or Monster and there is no extension.cs, then you should go into the Tools menu, select Folder Options/View, and enable file extensions.

As an exercise, we'll be building a simple game involving monsters and shooting. We'll start with a basic skeleton with simple object classes and simple movement behaviors. From this we'll build on some basic events when the player presses keys, moves the mouse, and shoots at targets.

1.5.2 Learning to Copy and Paste

> A good artist creates, a great artist steals.

Code examples exist for you to copy and paste into your project. The content for this book and all downloadable content are no different. You'll have to understand what the code does and fit it to your needs.

Every programmer copies code habitually. Whether it is from code written in a previous project, or code found on the internet. Programmers copy code to learn. Of course, it's still important to know how to write new code from scratch; most programming classes in school will prefer that you do this for all your assignments. With practice, being able to recognize what to copy and where to paste is something you'll only know from writing code to begin with.

Programming is a constant learning process. It is a language to command computers. Anytime you learn a new language, there will be plenty of words which you'll have to look up. Add to this the fact that every programmer gets to make up new words, and you've got a language that always needs a dictionary.

This is one reason why programmers are usually fast typists. This is also cause for programmers to be picky about what keyboard they prefer.

In most cases, the projects in this book will be in some state where you can read text that is already in place. Most of the projects are in a more complete state where you'll be able to run them and see an intended result.

As a programmer, I've gotten used to searching the internet for example code. Once I've discovered something that looks useful, I copy that code and paste it into a simple test case. After I've wrapped my head around what the code is doing, I rewrite it in a form that is more suited for my specific case.

Even if the code involves some fun trick, I'll learn from that code. As I learn new tricks, I grow as a programmer. The only way to learn new tricks is finding the necessity to solve a new problem for which I haven't already figured out a solution. Finding solutions to problems is a fundamental part of being a programmer.

1.5.3 Iteration

Programming is an iterative process. It's irregular to write an entire class or function without testing it many times. The general flow is to write a part of a function, test it, add a bit more, test again, and repeat until the function accomplishes its goal. Even then, many functions often work together in sequence. Often, you'll write a function, verify that it's working, write another function, and verify some more. Then you'll have them work with one another and test again, all the while you'll be changing and re-arranging your code to fix mistakes.

Most of the time you'll start off with a bunch of placeholders until you get around to finishing your code. As you're adding features and finishing code, you'll have chunks of work that aren't finished. This is a part of game development and a part of learning as well.

1.6 Compiling: Turning Words into Computer Instruction

To test and use your code, it is time to compile. Compiling is the process of taking all of your source files and building bytecode. Unity 3D uses .NET, as it is a compiler to generate the bytecode, but Unity 3D does this automatically. Mono is an open-source compiler that runs on many different processors and operating systems.

The combination of the central processing unit (CPU) and operating system is often called a platform. Each platform requires a unique native machine code to execute or run. Building code for each platform is called a target. Unity 3D converts the bytecode into a native machine code and can target Mac, PC, Android, and iOS.

Native machine code is the set of instructions that directly talk to the CPU and operating system (think of the holes punched into a card and fed to a machine). Unity 3D is a simple way to generate the complex set of instructions for your computer to run. Code that talks directly to the hardware is referred to as "low-level" programming.

There are layers of software between you and the computer's hardware. When writing C# for games using Unity 3D, your code is compiled by .NET. Unity 3D then takes the bytecode from .NET and compiles a target platform into a native machine code.

Both Unity 3D and .NET are the layers underneath your code and the computer's hardware, putting you on a higher level. This is often referred to as a computer layer abstraction. That is why C# is usually considered a high-level programming language.

Programming at a lower level requires much more knowledge of memory management and a wide variety of other APIs that might include graphic cards, physics, sound, and everything else that runs a game. Writing for a layer involves an in-depth knowledge of both the layers below and above the one you're writing for.

The computer hardware, such as CPU, graphics card, memory, and storage, live on the lowest level. Above them is the basic input/output system (BIOS) and software that starts the hardware when you press the Power button. Above that is your computer's operating system and drivers that talk to the hardware. Finally, Unity 3D lives above the operating system and your code lives above Unity 3D.

That is why we're going to use Unity 3D to write games and not start from scratch in raw C++. Otherwise, we'll have to spend a few years learning about physics, rendering, and assembly language or the instruction set that your CPU uses to operate.

1.7 What We've Learned

We should have an idea of what C# is, and what is required of you to learn it. If you haven't done so already, download and install the required software.

Unity 3D is free; there are no fees or royalties that need to be paid to the Unity 3D developers so long as you're not building any commercial product. Git is also free to use and you'll need that to follow the chapters on Git.

You're even allowed to deploy your projects on anything Unity can target. Until you're ready for a commercial launch, the free license is all you'll need for learning and sharing your game with your peers on your computer.

Optionally, you may also want to setup an account on the Unity 3D site if you want to download and use any of the assets from their Asset Store. A Visual Studio Community account and a GitHub account may also come in useful later.

1.8 Leveling Up: The Path Ahead

The computer systems in place today have evolved from machines with moving parts. Telling these machines what to do involved setting knobs and switches. Today, we use text organized into statements and logic.

It is difficult to imagine a time when computers were so slow that simple calculations involved waiting for clattering switches to finish moving around to produce an answer. Today, computers complete many billions of calculations in a single second. All too often, we take for granted that computers rely on the same concepts and systems engineered nearly a century ago.

Understanding how computers work puts into context how we write software. It is possible to write software without this understanding, but it is harder to appreciate how it works.

2

Before You Begin

This book focuses on learning C# and the fundamentals involved with programming a computer language. This book does not necessarily focus on the use of Unity 3D to complete a specific game. You're not required to make any purchases, since this book assumes that you're using the free version of Unity 3D and other software.

You will need an internet connection to download software. There are also some cases where you'll want to create an account for some websites. This is optional and not required. The services suggested are free and popular among game developers, so it's probably something a new game developer should learn how to use regardless.

Throughout the tutorials in the book are useful building blocks of code for game development. By no means will the final product be a finished game; at least one that's ready to ship. Access to free assets are included with this book. You're free to use them for any project you have in mind.

Along with Unity 3D you'll need to work with Git SCM, commonly known simply as "Git." Git is a source code manager, sometimes referred to as a Version Control System. This means you'll be able to store different versions of your project with revisions kept in history. Changes to files need to be organized to prevent the loss of effort. To coordinate, developers use git merged changes and track the history of every source file in a project.

As a new software developer, you'll be happy to have learned to use Git. Many millions of software developers rely on sites like GitHub.com or BitBucket.org to manage and share their code with both their team members and the rest of the world. Even as a solo developer, you'll see the benefits of source control indispensable.

2.1 What Will Be Covered in This Chapter

Before we get to know C#, we're going to need to make sure that you're ready with Unity Git and Visual Studio; otherwise you're not going to be able to follow along with the content of the rest of this book.

If you are already familiar with Unity and Git, then this chapter might be a review. If you think you already understand how a scene works and how to attach scripts to objects, then you can skip ahead to the next chapter. To ensure you've installed everything necessary, let's preview what we'll be covering in this chapter:

- Installing the Unity Editor
- What Git SCM aka "Git" is, and how it is used for this book
- Getting around in Unity Editor
- How to read C#
- GitHub and how to save code
- How to make use of C# within Unity 3D

The chapters that discuss Unity 3D will remain focused on how the code works and interacts with software that usually involves C#. There are plenty of books that focus on Unity 3D's game development tools for effects and art. It is recommended that you also obtain some reading materials to help you learn the rest of the Unity 3D tool set.

Microsoft Visual Studio is installed along with Unity 3D. Both the free and professional versions of Unity 3D use the same version. Visual Studio is commonly referred to as an integrated development environment, or IDE. You could use another text editor such as Notepad; examples found in later chapters will require Visual Studio for a complete experience.

Most of the elements of the Unity 3D tools such as particle systems, animation systems, and other components, such as lighting and sound, are not covered in this book. However, this book enables you to add any interactivity with those systems in the engine. By the time you finish this book, you should be able to intuitively know how to look up what's involved with playing a sound when the player clicks buttons and fires weapons.

We will be looking at a lot of source code. Source code is the term given to the text that is entered into a file by programmers. Fragments of source code, and in many cases a complete source, are provided as a part of completing the Git SCM tutorials. A sample of source code will look like the following:

```
1   using System.Collections;
2   using System.Collections.Generic;
3   using UnityEngine;
4
5   public class NewBehaviourScript : MonoBehaviour {
6
7       // Use this for initialization
8       void Start () {
9
10      }
11
12      // Update is called once per frame
13      void Update () {
14
15      }
16  }
```

If the sample makes no sense at all, don't worry; after just a few chapters you'll be more comfortable looking at the new punctuation and formatting. Each character, space, color, and words have a special meaning. To programmers, this formatting of characters is called *syntax*. If you've written something like HTML or even JavaScript, some of this might be familiar.

Unity calls the source code a script. Much like an actor in a play follows a script, the objects in Unity follow a script assigned to them. Web programmers write in JavaScript; before Unreal Engine 4, Unreal Engine used UnrealScript. Unity simply uses C# as its scripting language.

Don't make the mistake that C# is merely a scripting language and not a programming language. C# is used to write plenty of desktop and mobile apps from scratch. Unity calls C# a scripting language but it doesn't mean you're not programming.

It is important that you take care to notice the syntax—the placement of words and punctuation. Each curly brace, colon, and period is important. Forgetting a single period or a semicolon will stop all code from working.

The syntax is colored by Visual Studio with what is called syntax highlighting. The colors are chosen automatically based on the context in which the word or special character is used. The colors can also be customized to your personal preferences with settings found in Visual Studio. So, if you prefer a dark theme, that option can be found in the preferences.

We will spend a lot of time writing code and inspecting each line to understand what is going on. More importantly, we'll be thinking about why the code works and the alternate methods of accomplishing the same task. One important topic we'll also be looking at is how a line of code can break and how to fix it. There are many common mistakes all programmers make, which we may also get used to them early on.

Just as important, we'll look at how the code misbehaves and what common mistakes can take place. Error messages are not a problem, they are clues that inform where you need to fix your code. You can expect a lot of errors when you first get started; in many cases, a single line may have more than one error, so there might be multiple fixes before you're able to move on.

Alternate methods are important, you know that each task you approach isn't solved with a single solution. Approaching a problem is more important than memorizing and regurgitating the same solution when you see a similar problem again. In the real world, no two situations will be exactly alike. Each time you need to solve a problem, you'll need to invent a unique solution.

Programming is a creative process that allows for any number of different methods to accomplish a single task. Each variation of code has pros and cons. Each line of code may vary depending on the programmer; in this case, you may feel differently about what code to use and why you prefer it. Always use the version which you find easier to read and understand.

No doubt, if you're really going to get into making games with Unity 3D, you'll want to get an additional book that focuses on building assets, scenes, and effects. If you don't already know your way around Unity 3D, we should have a brief introduction to the Unity 3D interface that we're most concerned about when it comes to writing scripts.

2.2 Unity 3D Installation

There's a lot of software to install, so hopefully this won't take too long. Sometimes there are a lot of options, so it's best to double check with the book to make sure you don't miss something.

If you haven't already, download Unity 3D from https://store.unity.com/

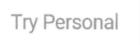

This will present a menu of options. Pick the free version on the following page then select the Download button, Unity Hub, for your operating system.

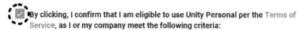

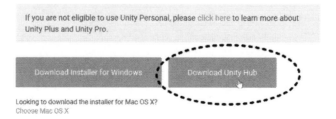

Unity Hub is a helper app that lists the latest builds of Unity. The list includes beta releases as well as different versions of Unity. Depending on your download speed, this might take a while to finish downloading. It is worth getting the latest version, as many features and options are always added with every new update.

Once the Unity Hub has finished installing, it's time to install Unity from the Unity Hub. When the Hub opens it will ask if you would like to sign into an existing account or if you'd like to create a new Unity ID. A third option exists if you're not connected to the internet. Follow any steps necessary to log into the Unity Hub. There's no fee required to install Unity, just a valid email address.

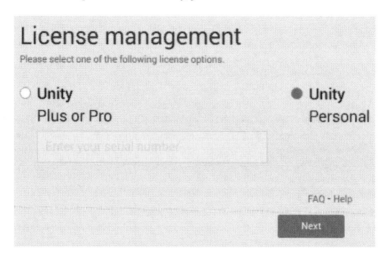

The License management panel will ask what version of Unity you will be using; select Unity Personal unless you've purchased a license. You'll be prompted with a dialog where you'll need to promise you are not using Unity in a professional capacity. You're allowed to download Unity once the personal license is activated. Under the Installs tab, you'll see options for "On My Machine," "Official Releases," and "Beta Releases."

Teams often settle on a specific version of Unity for compatibility. Some custom tools or plug-ins are targeted to a specific version of the Editor. So, upgrading the Editor may also mean upgrading plug-ins and fixing bugs between versions. To avoid forcing users to upgrade, Unity continues to support past versions of the Editor for developers who can't upgrade easily.

As a newcomer, you'll want all the latest features and that means picking the most recent version from the list of official releases. Aside from the Editor itself, you'll want to install the Dev tools: Microsoft Visual Studio Community as well as the official documentation. Be patient, we're just getting started.

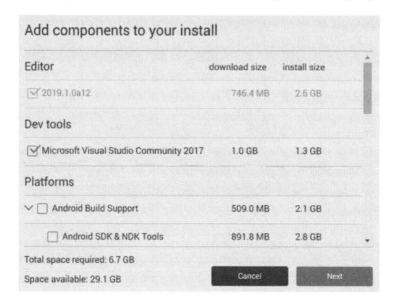

If you're on OSX you'll see the following:

To continue, allow the various installation pop-ups and agree to additional license agreements. Eventually, you'll see a progress bar replace the download button and the Unity Installation is officially underway. After the installation of the Unity Editor, the Visual Studio Install will automatically launch.

2.2.1 Visual Studio Installation

Visual Studio Installer opens on its own. When it's complete, the Unity 3D installer pops back to the front. With Visual Studio Community you'll also be able to write and build applications outside of Unity 3D! Visual Studio is not just an editor for Unity 3D alone. You'll be able to create practically any app from scratch for Windows, Android, and much more!

If your machine has problems with the installation, you'll be able to select one of the installations from the Hub and try again. There's also an "Add Component" option to try re-installing Visual Studio from the Hub as well.

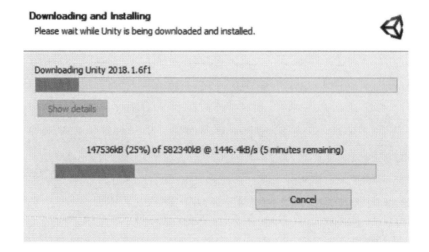

Once the installation is complete, start Unity 3D. If your splash screen looks different from the one below it's only because a newer version has been released and they updated the splash screen image. Don't worry, it's just cosmetic.

2.2.2 Unity Version Numbering

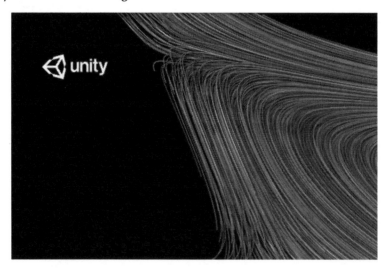

You might be wondering why there are so many different versions of Unity to download. The company keeps past versions around for various reasons. The latest version of Unity in the Official Releases list is going to be the recommended version. Older versions don't all support the same version of C# and the .NET framework, so some example code shown in this book might not work in older versions of Unity.

The Unity versions are numbered by year followed by a major and minor update version. You'll also see either a letter "a," "b," or "f" in the last part of the minor version number. This represents either an alpha, beta, or final release. Some versions are suffixed as LTS for Long Term Support; these are versions that are known to be the most stable.

Major updates often include engine changes that could interfere with custom plugins or may require some C# code changes between major versions. Minor updates usually don't include engine changes, but fix behaviors that might not have been working as expected by some users.

Alpha releases mean that the version is a work in progress or feature incomplete. Not all Alpha releases are available through the Hub. Unity often releases previews in their forums. Beta releases mean that the features require more testing before final release. Unity relies testing by their users to fully vet the functionality of their Editor before final release.

Final release updates mean bug fixes have been integrated, but no new features have been added. A new LTS version is released when most of the known bugs have been fixed. Of course, nothing is perfect, so as new bugs are found and fixed a new LTS version will be updated and released.

For the best experience it's a good idea to use the latest LTS version from the Official Releases list. Though for the most current features the newest final release in the Official Releases list is also safe. For all the coolest bleeding-edge tech, go for the Beta Releases. Upgrade notes and release notes accompany each release. In some cases, old features are removed as new ones take their place. In 2018, the MonoDevelop tool that used to be included is no longer supported as well as old programming features like Javascript and Boo support.

2.3 Git SCM Installation

For clarity, it's not necessary to download and install Git. Git is a stand-alone source code manager and it's great. GitHub, not to be confused with Git, is a free web service that facilitates sharing and storing a Git code repository. Signing up for a GitHub account is also not required. Both the Git software and the GitHub.com web service are fantastic resources and you're welcome to try them out, but neither are necessary.

Eventually, you will need to know your way around Git as a programmer. To the detriment of the curriculum, source code management is rarely, if ever, taught in a classroom setting. It's impossible to say how often source code management has saved a project. You will want Git if you write code.

Given a chance, I hope you'll follow along and learn a little Git. Some form of code management is used in every setting where programmers work together. At least some exposure to Git will help. Both personal and cooperative projects can leverage the power of Git.

If you want to skip out on Git, simply go to the "BookContents" URL and download the Zip file.

https://github.com/CSharpWithUnity/BookContents

Click the "Clone or Download" button, and then select Download ZIP from the following pop-up. This contains the Content, Unity projects and assets for each Chapter in this book. Unzip to somewhere on your computer and carry on.

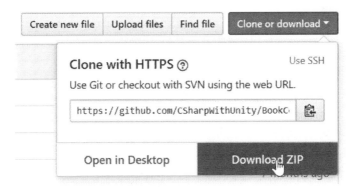

2.3.1 Git-SCM.com Git Software (Optional)

If you're interested in joining the millions of programmers who do use Git, download the Git SCM software. Navigate to:

https://git-scm.com/downloads

Download and install the software. No account is necessary to download and install the software. Just a few dialogs during the installation need to be clicked through with default settings and you're done.

Git changes how you'll want to save files. Without Git you'll often resort to saving a file as Character1.cs followed by Character2.cs and eventually Character2Final_Final_Final2.cs, hardly optimal. Also consider that the contents of the file can interfere with one another. Using Git you'll leave the file's name unchanged, but Git will retain the content history of each file. At any time, you'll be able to retrieve any version of any file.

2.3.2 GitHub.com Sign Up! (Also Optional)

To fully leverage the power of Git you'll want to start your own GitHub.com account. If for some reason you don't need GitHub, then you can skip to the next section and just get into the basics of the Git software.

GitHub is an independent service that integrates with Git. It's an on-line storage system that makes source code available on the internet and can act as a back-up for your projects. It's also a resource used by many programmers to share example code and open-source projects with the world. You'll find tens of thousands of Unity and C# projects on GitHub, the contents of this book are just some of them.

Visit https://github.com/ and fill in the new account form.

Make sure to write down your information since we'll need to match this up with the Git software we just installed in the previous chapter.

To start, select the Free option; this will give you unlimited private repos. Then, select Continue. You may need to wait for an email from GitHub to verify your humanity. After doing this, you'll be able to make a clone of the book contents to your own GitHub account.

Fill in the questionnaire with any response you feel comfortable with. These aren't going to change your interaction with the software, so the step is optional.

Next, you'll want to find the repo for this book. While you're logged in your new GitHub account, visit https://github.com/CSharpWithUnity/BookContents to find the contents for this book. On that page you'll have several options; the one we're looking for is called fork.

Clicking on this button will tell GitHub that you want to make a personal copy of the BookContents on the GitHub site. This means you'll have your own version, which you'll be able to edit and make changes to without disturbing the original.

Forking CSharpWithUnity/BookContents

It should only take a few seconds.

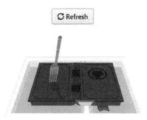

The above image indicates that GitHub is busy making a copy. Once complete, you'll have a new URL which points to your own copy of the contents for this book. This is your version; a completely independent copy of the contents of the book you're free to play with, modify, and share.

2.3.3 Git: The Basics

Git runs in what's called a console. A console is sometimes called a command line or, in OSX, a Terminal. The console looks like a text window, but it's a tool that uses text commands, which are usually referred to as shell commands, to carry out operations. Git Bash is a console window that uses Unix-like shell commands on a Windows machine. Examples of these commands will be following soon.

Mac users have the built-in Terminal. Windows users can also use the native Windows console or the Power Shell. For this book, we'll be using the Git Bash since the commands are the same in OSX's Terminal software.

A new window should pop up once Git has finished installing. There should also be a shortcut to Git Bash located either in your start menu, or desktop. This new window is a shell, or sometimes folks refer to it as a Terminal. The "$" symbol is called a "Prompt" and indicates the shell is ready for a shell command to execute. Our first command will be asking Git what version is running.

In the window type the following:

```
git --version
```

The start of the line "`git`" calls on the Git software. The double dash or perhaps minus-minus indicates the start of a command for Git to run. The enter key at the end tells Git to execute the command. When run, Git should reply with something like the following:

```
git version 2.18.0.windows.1
```

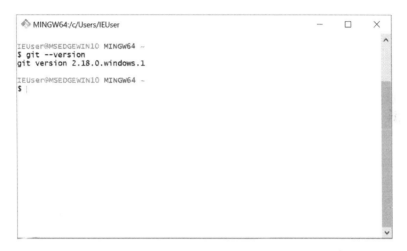

Git should reply with whatever version was installed. No doubt a newer version has come out since the writing of this chapter. Git gets updated often so expect a higher number than shown here.

Simply entering the following:

```
git
```

starts the Git software without any commands. Git replies with a list of commands it's able to run. In this list is "`clone`," which we will use to make a copy of the contents of the book.

Enter the shell command:

```
git clone
```

This will reveal the help text for the Git clone command. The first line is "`fatal: You must specify a repository to clone.`" Don't worry, nothing died; "fatal" is just a dramatic word Git uses when it stops doing something unexpectedly. From here you should also type in:

```
pwd
```

The "`pwd`" command is a regular shell command used to print out in what directory you're currently performing operations. When you want to know where you are in your computer the "`pwd`" command will tell you. For me I get "`/c/Users/alexokita`" indicating I'm in my user home directory. If you open your file browser, you can also find the same directory. Next, move into our Documents directory by using this command:

```
cd Documents
```

The letters "`cd`" is another regular Unix shell command that means "change directory" the following word is the directory you want to change to. This command also changes the prompt we've been seeing above the command prompt. You'll see your user name @ computer name followed by "~/Documents" this tells you that you're now running commands in your Documents directory. To get a list of what is in the Documents directory use the shell command:

```
ls
```

This will print out in text the names of the directories and files visible in the Documents directory. If there's nothing named BookContents then we'll make a clone of the Contents for the book here. If you have somewhere else that you'd prefer the "BookContents" go, then you can navigate there using the cd or change directory command. To go back a directory use cd.. or cd followed by a space and two dots.

```
git clone https://github.com/CSharpWithUnity/BookContents.git
```

This command begins downloading the repository to a directory in Documents and automatically creates a directory called "BookContents" named after the repo from Git.

```
alexokita@Buggy MINGW64 ~/Documents
$ git clone https://github.com/CSharpWithUnity/BookContents.git
Cloning into 'BookContents'...
remote: Enumerating objects: 91, done.
remote: Counting objects: 100% (91/91), done.
remote: Compressing objects: 100% (66/66), done.
remote: Total 2267 (delta 42), reused 60 (delta 22), pack-reused 2176
Receiving objects: 100% (2267/2267), 4.80 MiB | 1.45 MiB/s, done.
Resolving deltas: 100% (1403/1403), done.
Checking out files: 100% (725/725), done.
```

Your results might look a bit different, but you'll get the contents so long as you're connected to the internet and can reach GitHub.

2.3.4 Your First Repo

On your GitHub account with the book contents repo open, look for the Clone or Download button located to the right of the contents. This is how Git will locate the online version of your code. If you didn't create your own account and skipped creating a fork, you can clone directly from this URL instead: https://github.com/CSharpWithUnity/BookContents.

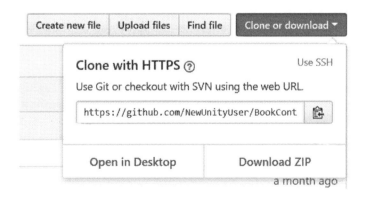

Copy the URL that's in the pop-up box. This works the same from your own fork as it does from the original repo you may have forked. You can do this by clicking on the clipboard icon on the right.

Now back to that Git Bash window.

If you're not in your ~/Documents directory, cd back to it. This is where we will create a clone of the contents for this book. This directory is the same as if you were to open your Documents folder in the Windows file explorer. If you're familiar with using the command line, then you're free to clone your GitHub repo to another directory if you like using the cd command.

When we copy the URL from the pop-up dialog, we can't use CTRL+V to paste that into Git Bash; instead we use the mouse middle click. This may seem unusual, yes, but that's just how Git Bash works.

Enter the command in the bash window:

git clone followed by the middle click which should look a bit like the following:

```
git clone https://github.com/NewUnityUser/BookContents.git
```

The NewUnityUser should be replaced with your own user name on GitHub.

```
MINGW64:/c/Users/IEUser/Documents                        —    □    ×

IEUser@MSEDGEWIN10 MINGW64 ~/Documents
$ git clone https://github.com/NewUnityUser/BookContents
Cloning into 'BookContents'...
remote: Counting objects: 103, done.
remote: Compressing objects: 100% (75/75), done.
remote: Total 103 (delta 25), reused 86 (delta 12), pack-reused 0
Receiving objects: 100% (103/103), 20.80 KiB | 519.00 KiB/s, done.
Resolving deltas: 100% (25/25), done.

IEUser@MSEDGEWIN10 MINGW64 ~/Documents
$
```

This will make a copy of the data from the remote data source on GitHub from your fork to your Documents directory. A new folder called BookContents stores all the files and project directories you'll need for this book. With your own GitHub account, you'll also be able to save your work on GitHub. If you've already cloned BookContents you should delete it before cloning your own repo.

The Git Bash is going to be our interface into GitHub. There are a lot of new useful GUI versions of Git and they all have their pros and cons. The command-line tool is the only version that's consistent and doesn't have different names and icons for each possible button. For consistency, we'll stick to the command-line version of Git.

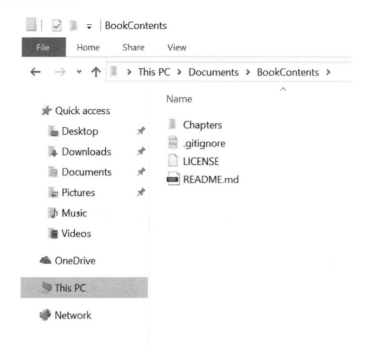

That's enough for now; done with all the setup!

A fork is a copy of the contents that has split away from the original content. You've created a unique and original version of the original contents of the book. You're free to make changes and modify the code in any way. None of the changes you make will accidentally get made to the original source of your fork.

This also means that if the original source gets updated, you'll need to "pull" those changes into your version to get the latest updates. Use the following command:

```
git add remote add upstream http://github.com/CSharpWithUnity/BookContents
```

This makes a connection from your fork of your repo to the original source that you originally split off from. As the command implies, there's a remote repo, something distant from your repo. You're adding something that's upstream of it. Upstream means that the remote source has updates that you may need to catch up with. The URL you're adding to is the source you want to make a remote connection.

To see if the remote has make progress, you use the following command:

```
git fetch upstream
```

This tells Git to collect the data that might be updated on the remote repository. This doesn't yet combine or update your local data to the remote version. This saves a local hidden preview of what's updated. To match your local data to the remote version use:

```
git merge upstream/master
```

This merges the data that's been updated on the remote repository into your local copy. If there have been a lot of updates, you might have a new text window pop open asking if you want to make a comment on what's been merged. Save and close the window, and the merge will proceed.

If all goes well, then your local stream has caught up to the upstream repo. Your local copy on your computer has updated, but your fork on Github is still behind. To update your fork on GitHub use the following:

```
git push
```

This sends your local data up to GitHub for safe keeping. Now, you've updated your repo!

2.3.5 Before Moving On

Visual Studio, like Unity and Git, sees regular updates. Like the Unity Hub, the Visual Studio Installer is a stand-alone app that checks for updates. In addition, when Visual Studio is open there's a little flag on the top right.

If you ever see the flag light up, it's time to upgrade or at least look at what upgrades are available by clicking on it. Built into Visual Studio is a list of updates and changes that are available.

Before getting too far ahead we should review what we have installed. We should also write down the user names and passwords for the new accounts we created. Here's a checklist of where you should be at before moving on:

- Unity 3D has been installed
- Visual Studio Community was installed with Unity 3D
- Git SCM with the Git-Bash shell has been installed (Optional)
- Your Github.com account has been created (Optional)
- You've obtained the BookContents by either:
- A fork of https://github.com/CSharpWithUnity/BookContents to your Github account (Optional)
- Cloned your fork of the BookContents to your local Documents directory
- Or you downloaded the Zip and decompressed it to BookContents

With a copy of the contents of the book source code and all the examples on your disk, and Unity 3D and Visual Studio installed, you're ready to continue. There's still a bunch of stuff to learn about Git, but we'll save that for later.

In case you wanted somewhere handy to keep this information, here's a place for you to write your information.

Unity 3D Account Info
User Name: _____
Password: _____
GitHub Account Info (Optional)
User Name: _____
Password: _____
Visual Studio Account Info (Optional)
User Name: _____
Password: _____

2.4 Unity General Overview

Let's start with a brief overview of the user interface (UI) for the Unity Editor. For each chapter there's a prepared Unity Project with C# files and scenes named after each chapter. The personal and professional versions of Unity interact with C# in the same way.

When you're starting the Unity Hub for the first time, you may be asked to sign in with your Unity User account. If you got through the previous chapter, then you should already have your login and password. Hopefully you wrote down your login information.

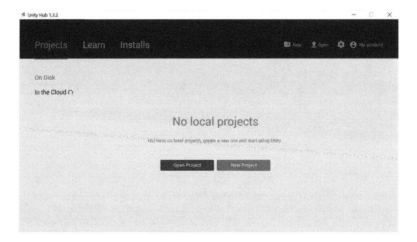

Across the top you'll see the menu tabs Projects, Learn, and Installs. These are the major tabs; on the right you'll also find New, Open, a gears icon, and an account icon. The Projects icon shows you a list of any local project, or if you're using the Unity Cloud project service, you'll see the projects listed there. The Learn tab will show some of the official Unity tutorials instructing you on how to use different tools that have been added to the Unity Editor. The Installs tab shows installers for different versions of Unity.

To get started Click on the Open Project icon and navigate to BookContents/Chapters/Chapter2 and select the folder.

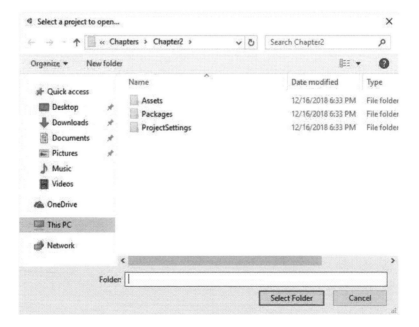

Upon opening a project, you may be asked if you want to upgrade. Specify the latest version of Unity and use the Current Build Target. Press Open and upgrade the project to the newer version of Unity. Unity updates the project and generates a few new directories with temp files used to build the game. Assets like textures, meshes, and sounds are all prepared for building a game. Once this is complete the main Editor view opens.

2.4.1 The Main Window

The default Unity Editor interface is divided into five major parts: (1) toolbar, (2) Hierarchy panel, (3) Scene and Game view, (4) Inspector panel, and (5) Project and Console panel.

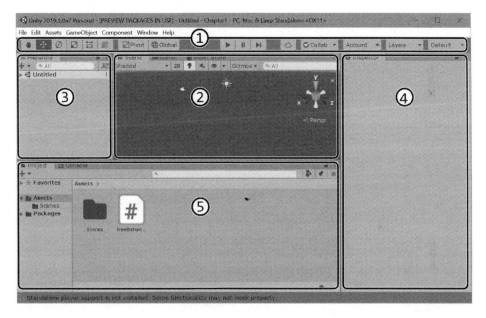

The tabs for any view can be dragged out and re-arranged in the Editor. Pulling a tab off detaches it from the main UI. The free tabs can remain a separate window, or they can be re-attached or grouped with other tabs. To restore the default layout, select Windows→Layouts→Default.

2.4.1.1 Toolbar

Label 1 in figure shows us the toolbar. The icons to the left are the navigation and manipulation tools. Toward the center of the tool bar are the Play, Pause, and Step Forward buttons. We will be using the Play-in-Editor button to test our code. On the right are various logins and view filters to help identify specific objects in the scene.

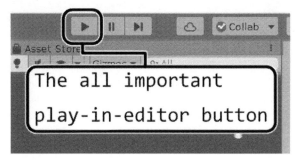

When the Play-in-Editor button is pressed, the Game view panel automatically comes to the front. Scripts attached to game objects in the open scene are executed and output is written to the Console panel. The contents of this book depend on opening a scene, examining code in the scene, and pressing the Play button to see what the code does. This pattern persists throughout the content of this book.

2.4.1.2 Scene, Game View, and Asset Store

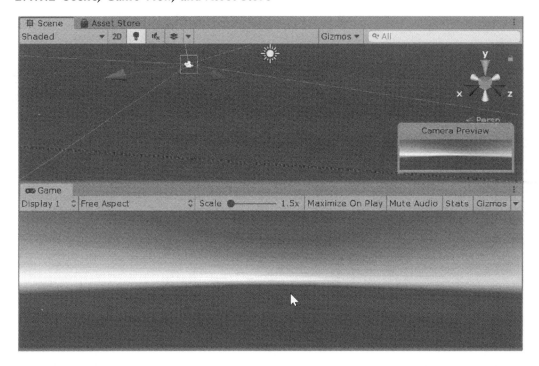

Label 2 shows us the Scene and Game view just mentioned. As the scene updates, the view from the Main Camera is shown through the Game view. The Scene tab falls to the background when the Game view comes forward. Clicking on the Scene tab allows us to see what's going on behind the scenes as the game updates. You're also able to move Game objects around using tools in the toolbar while the game is running. There are some exercises in this book which may require you to move game objects around as the game is being played.

The scene is more like a construction view of the game. The Game panel is the view of the game through the Main Camera. The difference here is that the Scene panel cannot be seen by the player, only you as the creator of the game can access the Scene view. With this view, you'll be able to arrange any object, light, or zombie the way you want.

2.4.1.3 Hierarchy Panel

Label 3 shows us the Hierarchy panel. In a new scene, you'll have a Main Camera and a Directional Light. The Hierarchy shows you all the Game objects that make your game scene. Any zombies, environments, cameras, lights, and sounds can be found in this panel after you add them. When any object is parented to another, it can be found by expanding the parent object with the triangle. In the following example, you'll find a piggy parented to a house.

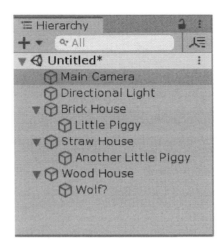

The hierarchy of the scene contains the Game objects in the currently open scene.

2.4.1.4 Inspector Panel

Label 4 shows us the Inspector panel. By selecting an object in either the Hierarchy or the Scene view, you'll be able to look at their various properties such as a Transform, which shows the object's position, rotation, and scale in the scene. Objects in the scene are updated with the Inspector.

   Take note of the Add Component button in this panel. This is one of the many ways in which we can assign a C# file to an object in the scene. If this seems a bit confusing, don't worry, we'll get back to what Components and Game objects are in a moment.

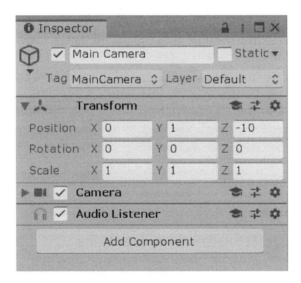

2.4.1.5 Project and Console Panel

Finally, label 5 shows us the Project and Console panels. The Project view shows us all the assets in the project. When we save a scene, it then turns into an asset for us to open from the Project view. As new C# files are added, they are shown here. To read the names of the files in the Project window use the slider located to the lower right of the window. Move the slider to the left to make the file names clearly readable.

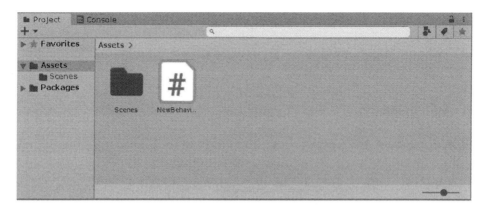

The last but most important part is the Console panel. By clicking on the Console tab, the Console view will be brought forward. This view displays the output text that is created by the C# code we write. Any problems, warnings, and errors will also be presented in the Console panel.

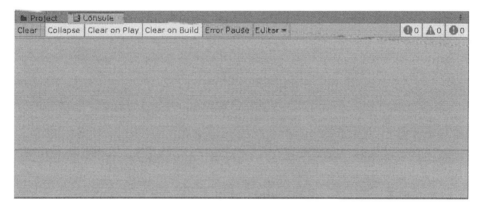

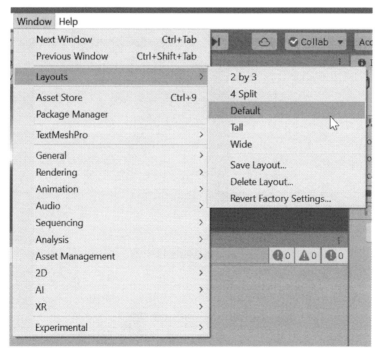

The Unity 3D installer also installed Visual Studio Community, the IDE used to edit code. We haven't written any C# yet, so we haven't gotten to Visual Studio, but that will come soon enough. Before that, we'll want to make sure that we're not too surprised by what we're about to get into.

2.4.1.6 Assets Directory

A Unity Project is a collection of many files and directories that store settings and assets used to build a game. Programming projects are made of many small text files called source files. In addition to these files, Unity includes 3D models, textures, sounds, and other resources used to build a game.

The primary location for all your C# files and assets is in the Assets directory. If you add a file outside this directory, your game will not be able to access it. When a project gets bigger, subdirectories in the Assets directory help keep your game organized. How you organize is up to you and your team; however, when you move or rename files it's best to do that from inside Unity 3D.

Living next to every file in the Assets directory is a .meta file. This meta file helps Unity 3D identify the file, as well as keep track of any settings related to that file. For instance, the SampleScene.unity generated with a new Unity Project has a neighboring .meta file that looks like the following:

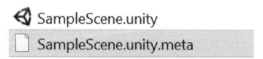

Open that meta file in Visual Studio and you'll see something like the following:

You should never need to directly edit a meta file, but it's important to know why it's there. When you share your game project, you'll want to include all the generated .meta files. Otherwise, your settings for each object in the scene might get lost!

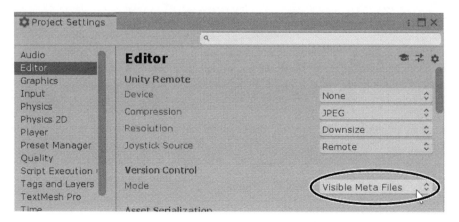

When starting your own projects double check that the Editor has the Visible Meta Files mode selected for Version Control in the Project Settings dialog. This will ensure that the files maintain their links between scenes and assets.

2.4.1.7 Project Settings Directory

The Editor itself has a lot of settings stored to prepare the environment to build to different platforms, Windows versus Android for instance. Global settings like those used by plugins, editor extensions, licenses, etc. are all stored in the Project Settings directory. Since many things like quality settings should be shared with your team, you should include the Project Settings directory when sharing your project.

2.4.1.8 Packages Directory

Next to the Assets directory in the computer's file browser is the Library directory. This contains the glue which Unity 3D uses to tie assets and logic together behind the scenes. Your editor preferences, platform settings, and many other bits that game engines need are placed here. It is very rare any user will need to go in here to make any modifications, so it is best to avoid messing with the contents of this directory.

2.4.2 Git Ignore

Several directories are created when Unity opens a project. When using Git, the generated files need to be left out when checking for changes to add. Git uses a text file called .gitignore as a template to filter out files to ignore.

The file uses patterns in text, if a file name or directory matches a pattern in the .gitignore file then it'll skip the file when searching for changes. If the .gitignore file contains log.txt then all files, anywhere, which the repo named log.txt will be ignored.

Thankfully, there are plenty of Unity users who also use Git and .gitignore examples are readily available. A quick search on the internet reveals something on GitHub called the Unity.gitignore. With a couple dozen contributors, it's promising, and it's also what I've included in the Git repo for the BookContents.

To inspect the .gitignore file use a text editor—Visual Studio would be good—and navigate to the root of the BookContents directory. Open the .gitignore and you'll see about 40 lines of text.

2.4.3 What We've Learned

Unity 3D has a diverse set of tools, all of which are useful once you've decided to go ahead and build a game. The engine has been used to create everything from 2D side-scrolling games to 3D first-person shooters. Fantasy role-playing games and top-down strategy games have all been produced and published using the Unity 3D game engine.

It is best for you to look around online for additional information on the Editor itself. There's plenty of cool stuff you can do once you follow some of the online tutorials that cover the basics of the Editor.

Topics on materials, particles, and animation will not be covered in this book. It's a good idea to get into the different aspects of the Editor to understand the most out of Unity 3D, once you've gotten through a portion of this book.

The Unity Project is a directory. In this directory are a few subdirectories generated by Unity when it's launched. Only the Assets, Project Settings, and Packages ever need to be backed up. New directories generated by Visual Studio and Unity when launched may include a hidden ".vs" directory, ".obj", and various other files, but they're updated when Unity or Visual Studio are launched, and these don't need to be backed up.

To be an independent game developer, you'll have to cover the breadth of skills that are usually taken on by different team members in a larger game production cycle. As a "lone-wolf" game developer, you must take on a variety of tasks, not just the code.

If you're an artist looking to add programming on top of your current skill list, then the rest of the Editor's functions will come more easily. It is still a good idea to know your way around Unity 3D if you're new to this game engine.

2.5 Sample Code

Throughout this book, samples of code will be shown in what is called a code fragment. Fragments, as the word infers, are small parts of a whole code sample. Complete code samples will be given when it is necessary to show how a completed source file will look like. If only one or two lines change in a complete file, only the changed lines will be shown as a code fragment. Here's an example of a complete source file:

```
Example.cs ⇗ ✕
Assembly-CSharp                               ▾  Example
   1    using System.Collections;
   2    using System.Collections.Generic;
   3    using UnityEngine;
   4
   5    public class Example : MonoBehaviour {
   6
   7        // Use this for initialization
   8        void Start () {
   9
  10        }
  11
  12        // Update is called once per frame
  13        void Update () {
  14
  15        }
  16    }
  17
```

The above example shows a new C# file generated by Unity 3D. We'll observe how it is created in a moment. What's important is that you could copy the text carefully into a new file named Example.cs and use it as is. First, let's see what a fragment will look like and then we'll go into how this is done.

2.5.1 Code Fragments

The following example shows a fragment of code taken from the completed source file:

```
  16        // Update is called once per frame
  17        void Update()
  18        {
  19
  20        }
```

You should be able to identify where the code was taken from, line numbers seen to the left of the code should help indicate where in the file to look. After identifying where its original is, you should be able to see what's changed or added. This means you should make the same changes in your version of the source code.

A fragment is intended to showcase smaller, more important components of a complete code sample. Rather than reading through the completed source file and looking for the change, a fragment will help you find the important differences when a new concept is shown.

Not all examples in the book will start with a complete source file. Often, the code fragment will require only one line to represent the concept being explained. The context of the code sample and your ability to understand the context should be sufficient by the time you begin to see those examples.

Most of the programming fragments will not make a visual impact in the scene inside of Unity 3D. There isn't a single command to make monsters appear or dragons breathe fire. Programming is the manipulation of data with logic, not magic.

If the changes are added correctly, your version will function the same way as described by the tutorial you're reading. A code fragment cannot function on its own. The rest of the code is required by Unity 3D to run without errors.

Once a concept has been introduced, you'll be required to remember how it is used. Later lessons will again reinforce the concept that learning how to program is a skill-building process. To program a complete game, you need to combine the different ideas taught here and write your own code. Building upon your own skill will not only expand your understanding of C#, but once concepts have been learned, you'll be able to apply them to other programming languages.

Occasionally, I'll refer to how C# differs from other programming languages. I'll leave it up to you to investigate what the other languages look like on your own. This provides a context as to why C# looks or acts in a particular way and how other programming languages solve the same problem. In most cases, you may find that many programming languages look and behave quite similar.

2.5.2 Are Errors Bad?

No, errors and warnings are there to help you. Don't be afraid to make mistakes. The code you write cannot break Unity 3D or your computer. At least nothing you'll learn from this book will enable you to do so.

As a matter of fact, it is often good to produce errors. The errors tell us what we can and cannot do. Programmers often ask themselves, "Will the compiler let me do this?," which may produce an error. If not, then the programmer will continue his thought with "Huh, I guess it will, so that means I can ...."

Creating and fixing errors tells us what the code expects from us. It is a sort of a conversation between the programmer and the computer; for example, the programmer asking questions in the form of a code statement and the computer replying with an error to the programmer who asks for things the computer can't do.

Many years ago, programming magazines used to share code in print. This meant that you'd have to copy word for word what was written in an article to get a program to run. Back then the compiler wouldn't tell you where the error was.

Hidden in your code could be a 1 (one) in place of an l (lower case L) and you'd have to find it yourself *after* typing in a few hundred lines of text. Be thankful for the modern IDE that tells you not only that there's an error, but often where the error is.

2.5.2.1 Compile-Time and Run-Time Errors

There are two general cases of errors: compile-time and run-time errors. Compile-time errors often include syntactical errors that are usually found right away by Unity 3D before the code is even run. These are shown in the Console panel which we saw in a previous chapter.

An error where specific words may be misspelled, or an incorrect character is placed in the code will result in an error in the syntax in your code.

There are many cases in which compile-time errors can pop up, far too many to list here. However, compile-time errors (sometimes called parsers) occur when the code itself is written incorrectly.

Run-time errors happen while the game is running and the code is executed. These errors are usually created by a misunderstanding of what the code can do. When Unity 3D comes across a statement that contains unexpected data or tries to do something mathematically impossible, for example, divide by zero, we get a run-time error. Such errors are usually a bit harder to fix as they only show up when there are specific conditions in the game. For these, we can mark the statement in Visual Studio and tell Unity 3D to stop when it gets there. Once that happens, we can inspect every bit of data and its value. This will help find and fix any problems that exist.

Errors simply stop Unity 3D from running your code. Some properly written code may follow correct syntax, but might require you to force Unity 3D to close using the task manager. However, this is rare and often easy to fix. Read the code samples carefully as you enter them into Visual Studio.

To fix the error, you find what character was mistyped and replace it with a correction. To test if the error is fixed, go back to Unity 3D from Visual Studio. If no errors or warnings are produced, then your code is clear of syntactical errors.

2.5.3 How to Follow Along

Many examples will require that you use both Visual Studio and read Unity 3D's console window. We'll be switching back and forth often for each section. When working in Unity 3D, you might need to have the Editor take up a lot of screen space to have access to all the different parts of the Unity 3D interface. Primarily we'll need to see both the Console and the Inspector panels. This is often why programmers like having multiple monitors. One monitor with their code and the other monitor with an editor open, showing them the resulting behaviors.

Each section may have a corresponding Unity 3D scene. Open the Unity Hub to open the different chapter exercises.

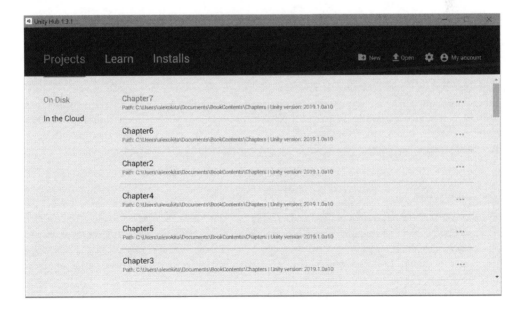

The Hub is a separate app from the Unity 3D Editor. It's used to install new and beta releases of Unity as well as create and open projects. From here, select the Open icon to the top right of the Hub app.

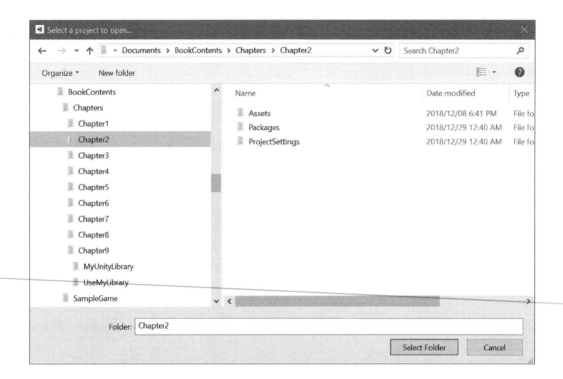

Select the directory of the chapter you're currently reading about and click on Select Folder. An additional window may open asking which version of Unity to use; select the latest version and continue. Select continue if any additional windows open asking about upgrading the project to the version of Unity you're using.

In each project for each chapter are Unity Scenes, each named by section. I'd suggest taking in a single chapter at a time and then letting the information sink in a bit. You should also conduct experiments on your own to gain a better understanding of what you just learned. If you can make assumptions about something you've learned and step beyond what was taught in the chapter, then I'd say you have a usable grasp of the chapter.

Without following each chapter and skipping around, you might find yourself reading terms that are unfamiliar. I try my best to build up from one chapter to the next. So, try not to skip too far ahead of yourself, unless you find yourself being bored and unchallenged; in that case, you skim through each chapter until you find something you're not already familiar with.

2.5.4 Comments: A First Look

In the code you'll see some marks that precede text in the IDE. Usually you'll see either // or /* with some text followed by */ at the end. These indicate what is called a Comment. A Comment makes the text invisible to the compiler.

If the compiler doesn't know the text is there, then what is it good for? Throughout the examples provided for this book comments are placed in the project near the example code. It's with the comments that additional help and information is presented.

```
7        // Use this for initialization
8        void Start () {
9            Debug.Log("Everything is working!");
10       }
```

Even the engineers at Unity leave helpful breadcrumbs in the code hinting at what the code in the file does. The image above shows the comment "// Use this for initialization" to indicate what the following code is used for. Comments are useful, and you should remember to use them to keep notes for yourself as you learn.

Comments are used like breadcrumbs in a deep forest. Comments help leave behind some of the thought process in why your code is written the way it is.

2.5.5 What We've Learned

We're going to have to do a lot of reading and writing. Sorry, that's just the case when it comes to code. If this doesn't detract from the experience of learning, then great! Otherwise you're going to have to just get over the fact that programming involves a lot of typing and thinking at the same time. If you're used to doing that sort of thing, then great!

2.6 Working with C#: Game Engines

Unity 3D is a game engine. You will be writing code that runs inside of this game engine. So, you're writing software that's run inside of another piece of software. What this means is that your code operates a layer further from your computer's hardware resources.

NOTE: What do I mean by further from the computer hardware resources? This is where the term "high-level programming" comes from. At the lowest level is the actual computer hardware. Programmers at this level are building silicon chips.

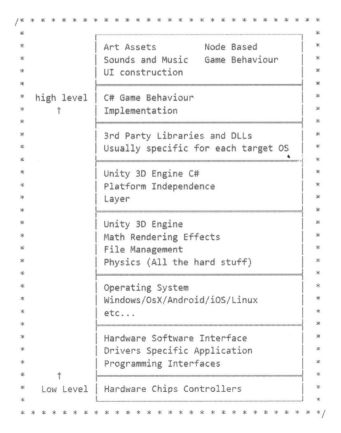

```
/* * * * * * * * * * * * * * * * * * * * * * * * * * *
 *                                                    *
 *                | Art Assets        Node Based    | *
 *                | Sounds and Music  Game Behaviour| *
 *                | UI construction                 | *
 *                |                                 | *
 *   high level   | C# Game Behaviour               | *
 *      ↑         | Implementation                  | *
 *                |                                 | *
 *                | 3rd Party Libraries and DLLs    | *
 *                | Usually specific for each target OS | *
 *                |                                 | *
 *                | Unity 3D Engine C#              | *
 *                | Platform Independence           | *
 *                | Layer                           | *
 *                |                                 | *
 *                | Unity 3D Engine                 | *
 *                | Math Rendering Effects          | *
 *                | File Management                 | *
 *                | Physics (All the hard stuff)    | *
 *                |                                 | *
 *                | Operating System               | *
 *                | Windows/OsX/Android/iOS/Linux   | *
 *                | etc...                          | *
 *                |                                 | *
 *                | Hardware Software Interface     | *
 *                | Drivers Specific Application    | *
 *                | Programming Interfaces          | *
 *      ↑         |                                 | *
 *  Low Level     | Hardware Chips Controllers      | *
 *                                                    *
 * * * * * * * * * * * * * * * * * * * * * * * * * * */
```

At one level above the silicon are things such as bus and motherboard where everything is either plugged into or soldered on. At another level above those are components that tell the motherboard what to do when power is turned on, how to look for data storage to launch operating systems, and just about everything else that happens when the computer is turned on.

Once this level finds an operating system, it hands over the tasks to the lowest level of your computer operating system where drivers and other hardware-to-software interfaces come into play to get your computer running. Once the computer gets booted and your operating system is properly talking to all the hardware components, it is ready for software applications to start running. At this level your software is usually not talking to any computer hardware directly, but it is talking to the software that runs the operating system.

Unity 3D is a software that talks to the operating system. When you write your game software your code usually talks directly to Unity 3D, but not to the operating system or computer hardware. Your code is being run with many other layers of software between you and the hardware. Similar to so many mattresses between you and the floor, there is more padding between you and any of the complexities that run your computer.

When your code is compiled, it turns into a machine language. The details here are simplified as there's a bit more going on under the hood than what we can explain here. The game code is made up of many different objects called classes. Classes are composed of data (also known as variables), logic (also known as functions or methods), and a name (also known as an identifier).

Functions and data work together inside of Unity 3D to make your game experience come to life. This coordinated effort can be packaged and turned into a new program that you can publish to any number of computer platforms including browsers, game consoles, and mobile devices.

C# has a few simple parts that we'll be studying later in this chapter. As a part of an exercise, we'll have to learn how to read a bit of code. Open the LineNumbers.cs class by double clicking on it in the Assets directory of the BookContents/Chapters/Chapter2 project.

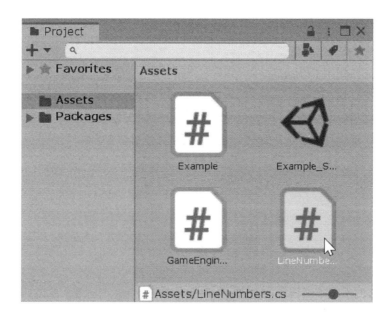

An underappreciated part of reading code is the line number. These numbers are found to the left of the code.

```
1   ☐using System.Collections;
2     using System.Collections.Generic;
3     using UnityEngine;
4
5   ☐public class LineNumbers : MonoBehaviour
6     {
7         public int SomeInt = 1;
8         public int OtherInt = 7;
9
10        // Use this for initialization
11        void Start () {
12            print(MyFunction(SomeInt, OtherInt));
13        }
14
15        // Update is called once per frame
16        void Update () {
17
18        }
19
20        int MyFunction(int a, int b)
21        {
22            return a + b;
23        }
24    }
25
```

Each line of code is numbered starting with 1 at the top and ascending as you scroll down. Here we can see that lines 1–3 of the code are required to access libraries or software that has already been written by many engineers to empower your code with a vast wealth of software.

At line 5, you'll find what is called a class declaration. This serves as a good overview of what to expect in the remaining chapters, so don't worry if this seems like a lot of unfamiliar information.

Continuing down you'll find some public variables at lines 7 and 8. At line 10, you'll find a comment describing the use of void Start(), which is the first line of code declaring a function. Inside the function at line 12, you'll find a statement that will be executed when the Start() function is called.

At lines 16–18, you'll find another function named Update() that doesn't do anything right now, and at line 20, you'll find another function named MyFunction(). At line 24, you'll find the closing curly brace that closes the LineNumbers class.

When Visual Studio comes across an error, the error list indicates both the type and the line the error appears. Place a random letter in the code and Visual Studio will be quick to indicate something is out of place.

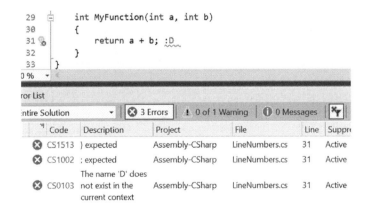

2.6.1 Creating and Assigning a New C# File: Now It's Your Turn

Let's start with the BookContents/Chapters/Chapter2 project we've been working with.

C# files are basic text files. It is possible to open Notepad or any other simple text editor and create a new file from scratch, but it is better to have Unity 3D create a clean, error-free starting file to work from. Right click on the Project panel and select Create→C# Script from the pop-up menu.

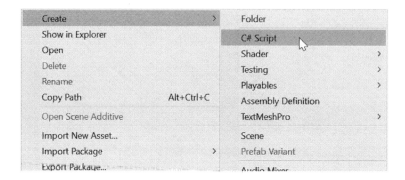

This will create a new C# file in the Assets directory in your project. We'll go into organizing these files with a bit more logic later, but for now we'll just leave it in the Assets directory. Alternatively, you can use the menu and select Assets→Create→C# Script to create a script in the Assets directory.

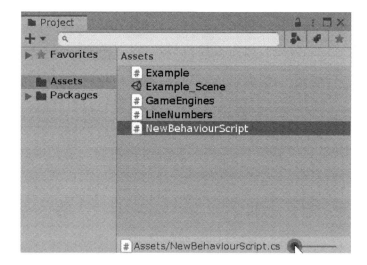

NOTE: You can resize the file display with the slider on the lower right. This will make longer file names easier to read.

This will create a file called `NewBehaviourScript`, which needs to be renamed as `MyScript` to follow along. If you unselect the file, it'll be created as `NewBehaviourScript`. This means you'll need to change the file name both in the Assets directory and in the class once it is opened in Visual Studio. We will cover how this is done in a moment. It's not necessary to add the .cs at the end of the file name when using the Asset Panel in Unity 3D; the Editor will keep track of the file types and add the correct file extensions.

To the right in the Inspector panel, you'll notice some code shown in the panel. This is a preview of the content in your new file. Selecting different objects both in the Assets panel and in the game scene will prompt different options to appear in the Inspector panel.

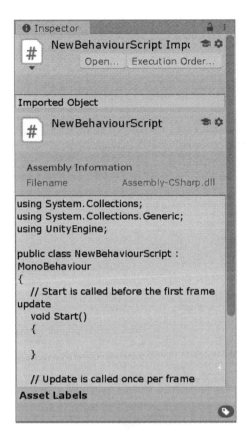

The Inspector panel will be useful for many different things, so we'll be using this quite a lot.

Don't bother trying to edit your code in the Inspector panel. This only serves as a preview to your code, so you might get a clue as to what the code is for. Editing the code is best done in an IDE which we'll jump into next.

Double click on the C# Example file in the Project panel to open Visual Studio.

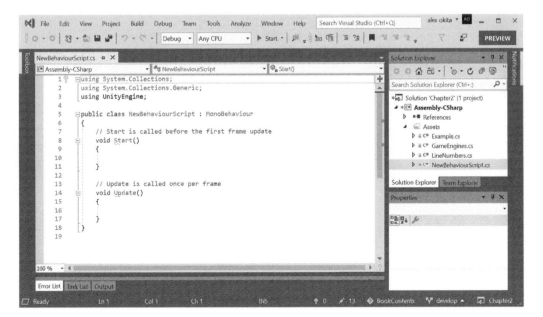

This is where we will be spending most of our time. An IDE is a software made specifically for editing code. Visual Studio is a popular IDE that has many modern features such as *automatic code completion* and *syntax highlighting*, and most importantly, the *debugger*. We'll get to know how to use these features as we read on.

2.6.2 Naming Your New File

Just to make sure we're off to a good start, the name of the C# file should match the name of the class. For example, if the file name was called PeanutButter.cs, you need to make sure that the class name matches.

Observe the line that reads as "public class Chocolate : MonoBehaviour {." When I mean the file name, I do mean the actual file located on the disk in your operating system. To get to these files, right click on the object in Unity 3D's Project panel to get to additional options. In Windows, select Show in Explorer from the right-click window.

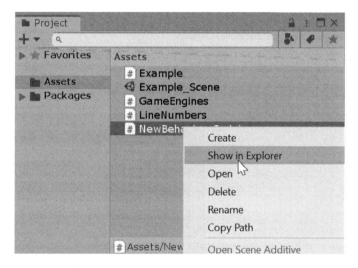

If the name of the file doesn't match the name of the class, you'll get a class definition error when the script is used in the game. Also, you can simply click on the name of the file in the Unity 3D's Project panel to rename it.

```
using System.Collections;
using System.Collections.Generic;
using UnityEngine;

public class Chocolate : MonoBehaviour
{
    // Start is called before the first frame update
    void Start()
    {

    }
```

If the name of the file matches the name of the class, we're in a good position to get started. Keep this file around as we're going to be using it in Chapter 3. Once the class name and the file name match up, you can move on. If the file is named NewMonoBehaviour, change its name to match the class name.

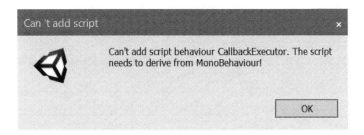

2.6.3 Using Your New File

To assign the C# file to an object in the scene, you can drag it from the Project panel onto an object in the scene. This seems to be simple, but the object might not be in view, or it might be too small to easily select.

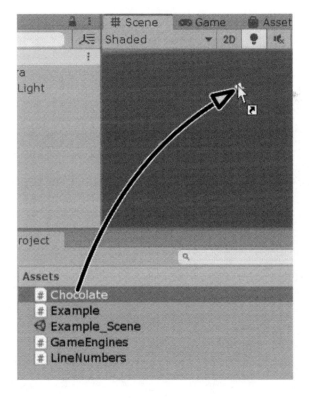

You can also drop it on an object in the Hierarchy panel. Everything in the scene is found in the Hierarchy panel.

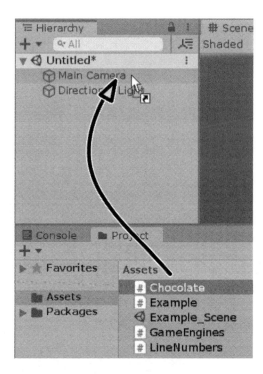

With a selected object in the scene, the Inspector panel will update its properties.

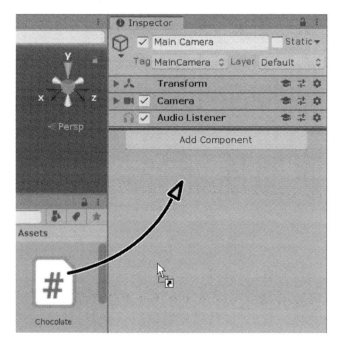

Dropping the Chocolate.cs file anywhere under the other properties in the Inspector panel will also add it to the selected object. If that's not enough, then you can press the Add Component button on a selected object in the scene and pick Scripts to select any scripts available in your project.

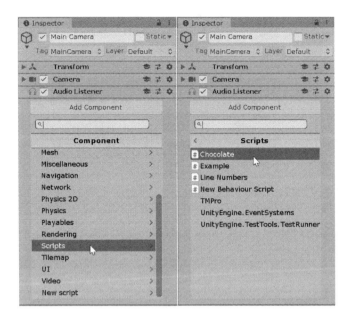

Using the Add Component button, you can even create, name, and add a script all at once! This has become my preferred system of creating and adding scripts to objects in a scene. It does everything all at once. After this it is just a matter of moving the script from the root of the Assets directory into a more organized directory.

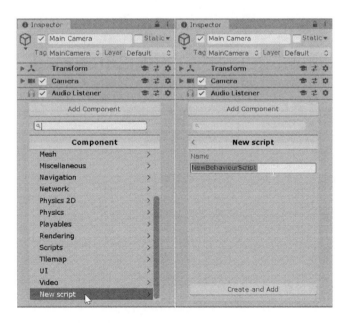

There are plenty of ways to use the Editor, but any one of the methods of assigning a script to an object in the scene will work just fine. The end result is that our script will be attached to an object in the scene. As soon as the Start Game button is pressed, your code will go live.

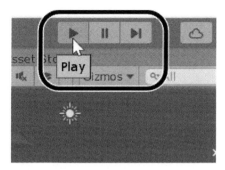

Press the button again to stop the game and your code from running.

After a script has been added to an object in the scene, it becomes a component of that object. All of the components of the object appear as additional rollouts in the Inspector panel. To edit a script component added to the object in the scene, you can double click on the component.

As an alternative you can click on the gear icon and select Edit Script from the pop-up menu.

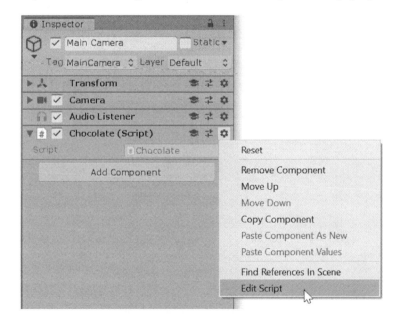

And finally, by clicking on the script attached to the component, the file in the Assets directory will highlight pointing out where the script lives in the project.

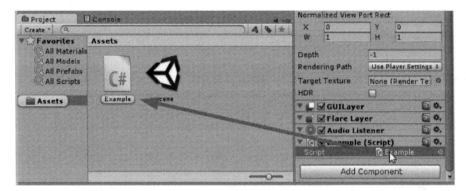

If a script becomes detached from a script component, the script can be replaced or changed by clicking on the little circle to the right of the script name.

Clicking on this little interface widget will open the following dialog showing you all of the available scripts in the project.

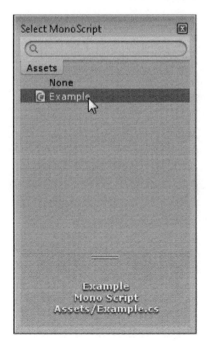

Selecting a script in the panel by double clicking will assign the script to the missing slot in the Inspector panel. To remove an unwanted script or script component, right click on the title of the component and select Remove Component.

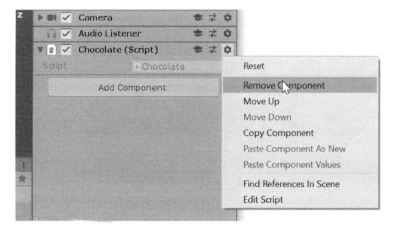

2.6.4 Additional Unity 3D Tools

To get an idea of what to expect in the remaining chapters, we can drop in a few simple shapes into the scene. Select GameObject→Create Other→Cube to drop a cube into the scene viewport. To pan around in the scene, press the Q button. Use the left mouse button in the scene viewport to pan around. The mouse wheel zooms the cube, and the right mouse button enables common "first person shooter style" navigation with WASD keyboard keys and mouse-look mode.

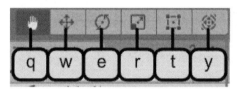

The W key enables the object translation mode. Select any tool aside from the View tool and you'll be able to box select or directly click on an object in the scene. Shift + Box select adds to your selection. Press the CTRL key while making a selection and you will unselect the next selected item.

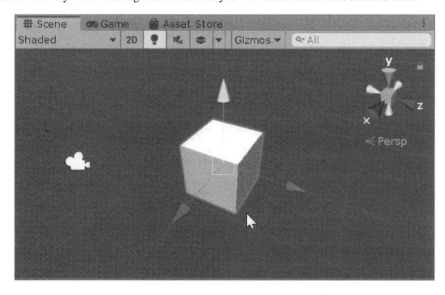

The Transform tool allows you to pick and drag the object around in the scene. Dragging left and right on a property in the Inspector will change the individual value.

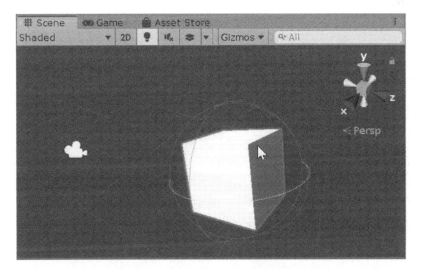

You can watch the Position values change under the Transform tab in the Inspector panel as you manipulate the cube. The numbers can also be entered directly into the X, Y, and Z fields of the Inspector panel if you want to have a precise control over an object's placement.

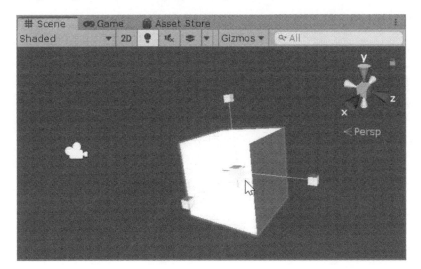

The E key will turn on the Rotation tool. Like the Transform tool, you can watch the object's rotation update in the Inspector panel as you manipulate the object in the scene.

The R key activates the Scale tool and you can change the size of an object or enter the values in the Inspector panel. All three of these tools allow you to pick and drag on various parts of the Manipulation tool in the scene. This changes the manipulation's behavior by constraining the action to one or two axes of freedom.

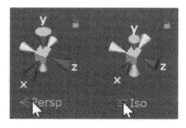

On the top right of the Scene viewport is a little widget that allows you to switch between various views of your scene. Top, front, and side views can be accessed quickly by clicking on one of the cones on the widget's cube. To change between a perspective and a parallel camera view, click on the Persp/Iso icon to toggle how the scene is rendered.

2.6.5 Working in a Live Scene

While the game is running, you're allowed to reach into the game through the Scene panel. You can select and move objects while the code is being updated. You can also use the Inspector panel to manipulate a selected object's parameters and variables.

Once you stop the game, any changes you made to anything in the scene are immediately reverted to whatever settings they had just before you started the game. This might mean losing some settings which you have tuned while playing the game.

If the settings were saved every time you stopped the scene, then testing a scene would be more troublesome. Going through a level shooting all of the zombies means that the next time you start the level again, everything would already be dead.

2.6.6 Saving a Scene

All the changes we've been doing have been created and applied to objects in a scene. After adding objects to a scene such as lights, cameras, and other objects, it is time to save the scene. The standard Save dialog instructs you to save and name the scene. The default location for a scene is the Assets directory in the project. It is possible to create a sub-directory in the Assets directory called Scenes or something similar; however, for our use, we'll save the scene in the Assets directory of the project.

2.6.7 Opening a Scene

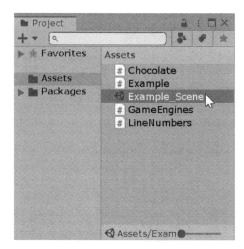

While working with each and every tutorial of this book, there's always going to be a scene file named Scene. Throughout the book, the tutorials will begin with the Scene file found in the downloaded project. To open the scene simply double click on the scene icon located in the Project panel under the Assets directory. You can also select File→Open Scene to open any scene in the project.

2.6.8 What We've Learned

Creating and assigning a new C# file to an object doesn't require so much work. There are plenty of ways to do this within the Unity 3D Editor. Once we add some code to the new C# file we're just a button press away from seeing our code in action. With some of the tutorials in this book, you'll be expected to create a new project, create new scripts, and assign the scripts to an object in a scene. With some of the more detailed tutorials, a completed version of the scene will be provided for you.

Amazingly enough, other professional tools for building things for Windows, Linux, or OSX all involve a similar process for creating desktop software. There's generally a lot more footwork involved with getting started. Templates, frameworks, and other IDE setup processes are required before even being able to get something to print out to a Console panel.

Learning C# with Unity 3D is one of the shortest routes from typing to execution that I can think of that has the most interactive results. The Editor itself allows you to interact with variables and values in real time. Selecting an object in the Scene editor and changing numbers in the Inspector panel allow you to have a direct connection to your code and see the changes in behavior in real time. This kind of interaction is only possible in the real-time nature of a game engine.

So far, we've gotten to do a bit of setup and preparation. Getting Unity 3D up and running is necessary, and if you've gotten stuck somewhere, make sure that you check the internet for any solutions. Naming files and classes correctly is also necessary to get your code to work. A single spelling error can break your code and nothing will work. Also remember that the upper- and lowercase letters matter a great deal. Naming your file the same as the contained class is also important, as a mismatch will also break your code and produce errors.

Programming is a highly rewarding endeavor. Don't let a small hitch bring you down. As you accumulate knowledge, writing code will only get easier. After you've learned one programming language, it is much easier to learn another.

I hope that after you've managed to wrap your head around C#, you'll be able to take the knowledge earned here, look at other programming languages, and feel a need to learn more. If you're an artist, adding the cool tricks that programming can offer to your palette of skills will only make you richer. And I mean richer in more than just the depth of skill.

2.7 Leveling Up: The Journey Has Just Begun

Get ready for some new concepts. Telling computers what to do and how to do it takes a lot of work. Computers aren't very bright; they're actually downright dumb. They do exactly what you tell them to do. If you get unexpected behaviors, it is up to you to make yourself clearer.

Of course, this all involves talking to a computer in its language, something that we should be able to do part way into this book. Once we've gone through the basics, we should be able to tell the computer simple commands and get expected results.

If you feel that you've gotten to a saturation point while reading this book, put this book aside for a bit and practice some of the concepts you've just learned. If you feel that you've explored all you can on your own, it is time to come back and pick up where you left off.

3

First Steps: Just Getting Started

This section will cover many basic terms and some of the basic ideas behind writing code. C# is among the many programming languages which share words and concepts to convey instructions to the computer. Once we get through the first few chapters you'll be introduced to some more of the basics which are directly related to reading and writing code.

Before we can get to that, we'll need to cover some terms and concepts that hold true for many different programming languages, not just C#. The methods and systems that allow converting words into executable code require strict rules.

When writing English or chatting online we tend to ignore formatting and punctuation. The brevity allows for faster communication; though only because we as humans have learned many new words and can use context to better interpret the contractions and acronyms in the written form of English used online or in text messages. Computers aren't so smart as to be able to interpret intent precisely.

Unity 3D is a 3D game engine. By 3D we mean three dimensions, which means we have an x, y, and z coordinate space. 2D or two-dimensional game engines like Game Maker only use x and y. This is the difference between a cube and a square. One has depth to each shape and the other does not.

Later, we will be working with three-dimensional vectors. Unity 3D uses Euclidian vectors to describe where objects are positioned in a 3D scene. When a position is described in terms of $x = 1$, $y = 2$, and $z = 3$, you should understand that this describes a position in 3D space. Unity 3D isn't limited to 3D space. Plenty of games use the x and y coordinates to make plenty of 2D games, but Unity 3D is by default a 3D game engine.

3.1 What Will Be Covered in This Chapter

We'll go over the specifics of the most basic concepts behind the C# programming language. C# has a great deal in common with other programming languages, so much of the knowledge here is transferable to many other programming languages. To get started on our journey toward an understading of C#, we'll investigate the following:

- Tokens, the smallest elements of C#
- How statements, give tokens meaning
- Keywords in C# with specific meaning
- How to use white space and proper formatting
- How statements are grouped together into a code block
- How classes are organized and what they're used for
- What a variable is and how it's used
- Types and how they behave when converted between one another
- Commenting on code and leaving messages to yourself and others within the code

Each section of this chapter will cover each new term in detail with some examples. There is a lot of vocabulary to learn. If you speak to a programmer, it may sound like they're speaking in a different language. The words they use have specific meaning in relation to programming. To continue through the rest of the book you'll need to learn what these new words mean in relation to writing code.

3.2 Review

In Chapter 2 we looked at what code looks like. Before going too much further, we want to make sure that we are able to open each of the different projects in Unity 3D to follow along.

Near the start of Chapter 2 you may have created a new GitHub account. In GitHub a fork of the book's repo was created to your account. From the fork the contents were pulled to your computer.

Your fork of the repo is visible to the public. You're the only one with access rights to make changes to your fork. If you discover a typo or any errors or "bugs," feel free to post a comment on the original repo.

If you didn't create a GitHub account and just downloaded a zip of the contents, that's fine too. Just be aware that there are a few chapters covering Git which you should still look at, since Git is indispensable even if you're not using it right now.

Before continuing you should be able to run Unity 3D, create and open C# files, and attach and remove the C# files to an object in a scene. You should also have the BookContents repo on your computer. Once all of this is done, you should be able to open a project from any of the chapters, then open a scene from the project. Finally, test the scene with the Play-in-Editor button and read the output in the Console window.

Double check by opening the BookContents/Chapters/Chapter2 project. Open the Sample Scene and press the Play-In-Editor button to make sure you've got everything working by looking for the output in the Console window.

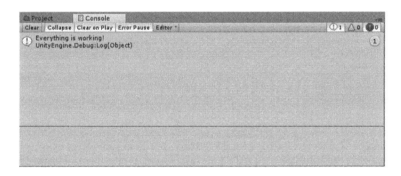

If any of this seems unfamiliar, go back and review Chapter 2; we'll be doing quite a lot here which depends on your being able to move objects and create and edit C# files. It's time to get into what code is, so keep calm and carry on!

3.2.1 Submitting Changes to Git

To make the most of Git you'll want to make some changes to files and submit them for safe keeping. At the root of BookContents is a README.md or markdown file. This is basically a text file with some clever formatting. Open this with Visual Studio and add in some information.

```
README.md ⊅ ✕
   1  # This is My version of the README
   2  Make sure to personalize it with your own welcome message!
   3
```

In the first line I've added the above two lines. Make sure you're more original than I am with your welcome message. Once you're done with your welcome message open Git Bash. Enter the following command:

```
git status
```

```
alexokita@Buggy MINGW64 ~/Documents/BookContents (master)
$ git status
On branch master
Your branch is up to date with 'origin/master'.

Changes not staged for commit:
  (use "git add <file>..." to update what will be committed)
  (use "git checkout -- <file>..." to discard changes in working directory)

        modified:   README.md

no changes added to commit (use "git add" and/or "git commit -a")

alexokita@Buggy MINGW64 ~/Documents/BookContents (master)
$
```

The status command asks Git to show you what's changed. The changes shown reflect any file modified throughout all the content in the BookContent repo. The line "Changes not staged for commit" show you which files have been modified, added, or deleted.

In the changes you'll see modified : README.md as well as instruction to discard changes if you would like to reset the file. To keep the changes, enter the command:

```
git add README.md
```

```
alexokita@Buggy MINGW64 ~/Documents/BookContents (master)
$ git add README.md
```

This adds the README.md to a list of files that will be included with a checkpoint of changes. In git terms this "stages" the file for commit. Think of this as a save point in a game. You can load your game from a checkpoint and start over if you mess up. Git grants your code with the same ability. To save the checkpoint we need to commit the changes with the following command:

```
git commit -m "adding changes to readme"
```

```
alexokita@Buggy MINGW64 ~/Documents/BookContents (master)
$ git commit -m "Adding changes to README.md"
[master 58a4fb7] Adding changes to README.md
 1 file changed, 5 insertions(+), 2 deletions(-)
```

The git commit command has two parts: the -m which indicates we'll add a note to our save point and the "Adding changes to README.md," which is the message to identify what the commit was created for.

This turns into a save point which we can come back to. You'll also notice the section that says [master 58a4fb7]; this is the code name for the save point. This is how Git remembers everything you've added to the repo. These numbers and letters are called hash codes. Your commit will have a different hash, so don't worry if it looks different. Every commit will be unique.

GitHub comes into play once you want to save your changes on your GitHub account. To upload the commit, use the command:

```
git push
```

```
alexokita@Buggy MINGW64 ~/Documents/BookContents (master)
$ git push
Enumerating objects: 5, done.
Counting objects: 100% (5/5), done.
Delta compression using up to 4 threads
Compressing objects: 100% (3/3), done.
Writing objects: 100% (3/3), 402 bytes | 402.00 KiB/s, done.
Total 3 (delta 2), reused 0 (delta 0)
remote: Resolving deltas: 100% (2/2), completed with 2 local objects.
To https://github.com/CSharpWithUnity/BookContents.git
   f016455..707a2f4  master -> master

alexokita@Buggy MINGW64 ~/Documents/BookContents (master)
$
```

Depending on how you've set your security settings you may need to enter a user name and password. Once that's done your commit will be pushed into GitHub. This means that even if your computer gets eaten by zombies, your work is safe on GitHub.

The pattern that we repeat is Add Commit Push. Every time you want to create a save point for your work, remember "Add, Commit, Push" to create a checkpoint.

To inspect your work, go to your GitHub page in a web browser.

The changes you've made to your README.md will appear in your fork of the repo.

3.3 Let's Build a Game—Part 1

An additional resource for you is a Unity "SampleGame" found in the SampleGame directory in the BookContents Git repo. A small set of free to use assets are ready for you to use in your own projects. This project also contains many helper objects that will show you how games are built.

Often, small game studios store their art assets in the Git repo along with the source code for the game. I've stored some asset files in the Art Assets directory next to the Unity Project. Feel free to inspect the 3D models in Blender and the 2D assets in Gimp. Both Blender and Git are open source and free to use for noncommercial use.

In the Unity Project directory called Unity-SampleGame you'll find that Assets has various directories to keep the Assets directory relatively organized. All the assets used specifically for the sample game are under the SampleGame sub-directory. In there, you'll find that Meshes, Prefabs, Materials, Textures, Scripts, and others have their own homes. Starting many projects in Unity 3D has formed a habit of organization. Your projects don't need to follow the same pattern, but anything similar will help in the future.

When an asset from the Unity asset store is downloaded, you'll usually find that it will live in its own directory, not unlike the one created for SampleGame. This convention of creating a directory in Assets for your own work is standard and should be followed to avoid conflicting files.

To get started with a new Unity 3D project you'll want to look at a checklist of a few settings before using source control. First are the meta files. Unity 3D creates additional text files that help link different assets to one another. To remember these associations in Git, you'll want to make them visible. Meta files allow the editor to restore the associations when a project is opened. Select Edit → Project Settings → Editor and find the drop-down menu with the Version Control section and set the Mode to Visible Meta Files.

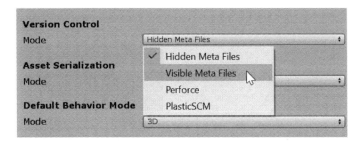

A game development cycle starts with a game design document. This includes what the player does and concept art as to what the game looks like as the player experiences your game. Often game designs also include some story and a world description. Assuming all of that is done, the engineering begins.

Programmers begin with the Unity Project and sometimes start some sort of technical document. A large game would often involve specific programming goals like database management for inventory, automatic loot box generation, or a multi-player match-making strategy. Before all of that comes prototyping and experimentation.

It's common for the experimentation to change the game design. Through experimentation unexpected game play experiences can emerge. New game play elements appear as code is written and unexpected results often appear either by accident or inspiration. Experimentation in Unity 3D means reading what Unity 3D has in its tool kit. Documentation available online often gives a general description of each Unity 3D function, but that hardly has meaning without seeing how the function works or what it does.

3.3.1 Movement Experiments

In the SampleGame Unity Project open the Assets/SampleGame/Scenes/Chapter3 Unity scene. A strange little object made of colored arrows should sit in the middle of the scene. This was created with a box collider and a rigid body attached. This gives the object physics properties that will make it fall and land on the ground under it without falling over.

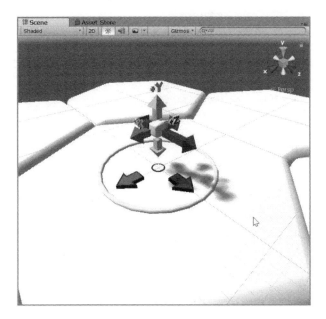

This object has been named TransformPrimitive to denote that we're going to use this to show us how to use the `Transform` Component of the Game Object. This little object has arrows pointing in each coordinate direction with a + sign pointing in the positive direction of that axis. Attached to this object is a script called MovementExperiment.cs which we'll open in Visual Studio to inspect. This can be found in the `Assets/SampleGame/Scripts` directory in the project.

The Start function contains a single line:

```
// Use this for initialization
void Start () {
    gameObject.transform.position = new Vector3(0, 0, 1);
}
```

This line tells the object to set the GameObject's `transform.position` to a new `Vector3` with the values for *x* and *y* set to 0 and *z* set to 1. As a hint, since we're new to Unity 3D most objects in a scene hierarchy are GameObjects. The GameObject is the fundamental type of "thing" that makes up the different elements that can interact within the game's scene. This is discovered by reading the Unity Documentation.

3.3.2 Reading Programmer Documentation

Programming documentation has become roughly standardized, to some extent programmers have come to use a similar format when it comes to sharing how their code is used. Unfortunately, it's still written by programmers, so for the uninitiated, definitions are obtuse.

Most of the time there's some type of outline with entries describing everything available in the API, or Application Program Interface. You can open the web page directly from Unity with the Help → Scripting Reference menu selection.

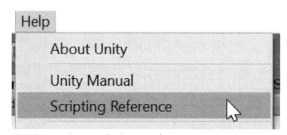

The following page is the Unity Scripting Reference. A column on the left shows you everything that the Unity 3D engineers have written anticipating what you might want to do in your game. This assumes you know what to do with the information.

Under the UnityEngine are most of the different systems that you'll eventually find useful for your game. In UnityEngine/Classes/GameObject you'll find an entry describing the GameObject.

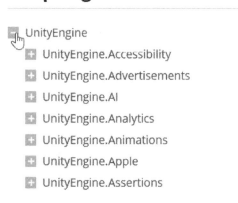

After the description you'll see the different things accessible inside of the object, or the object's members. Each one of the members is something that you can access, read, or ask the object to do. The members are separated as Properties, Constructors, Public Methods, etc.

Clicking on a member of the object will usually show you a similar page with the name of the function, sometimes followed by some example for using the member in question. The documentation for `GameObject` tells us that `Transform` is always added to a `GameObject` when created.

In addition to online documentation, Visual Studio has useful information built-in. Open the SampleGame/Chapter3/Scripts/MovementExperiment.cs script and Right click on the word `position` in Visual Studio and select `Peek Definition Alt+F12` from the pop-up menu. In Visual Studio for Mac you'll select `Go To Declaration ⌘D` to see a similar description.

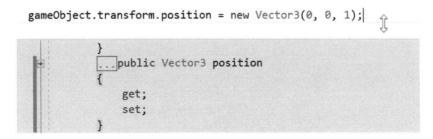

In Visual Studio for Mac

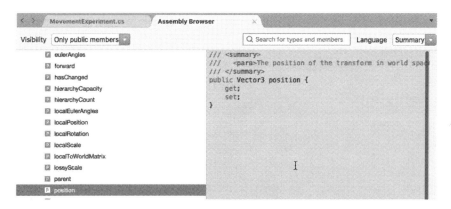

A new window, or part of a window appears beneath the line of code we're looking at. This window allows us to scroll through different members of the Transform class that position shares a relation with. As you scroll through the different listings you'll see a `get;` and a `set;` by some of the members and just `get;` listed under others. The members with `set;` mean this is a property you can change, ones with just `get;` you're only able to read.

Scrolling down even further you'll see some listings which end with `();` some of these have additional code in the parenthesis, these are called function members. Clicking on the small box with the + sign in the left margin expands a comment left by the programmer with a summary of what the function or property member is used for.

```
//
// Summary:
//      The position of the transform in world space.
public Vector3 position
```

Expanding the comment next to Position reveals the summary: `The position of the transform in world space.` The name of the member is preceded by `Vector3` indicating the type the property represents. With this you have the start of how to navigate around in Visual Studio just enough to begin experimenting. Press Escape to close the window or click on the close icon on the top right of the tab.

If we wanted to experiment with rotation, we might look at `localEulerAngles` see if we can change the transform primitive's rotation when the game starts. Pressing Play shows the transform primitive tipped up for a moment before falling. As we learn more vocabulary, the different sections in the documentation will have more meaning. The headings Static Methods, Inherited Members, and some others may not mean much right now, but as you read on they will.

The scripts you create for your game should live together in their own directory. When you download additional Unity Packages from the Asset store they will usually also live in their own respective project directories. Assets like your Materials, Prefabs, Scenes etc. should all live in their own directories to stay organized.

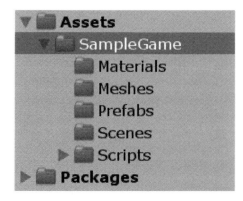

Unity 3D also has included a few of their own built-in packages for in-app purchases and analytics which live in their own sub-directories in the Packages directory in your projects next to the Assets directory.

When you feel more confident, continue some experiments on your own. If you can't get things working immediately don't let that put you off. As you learn more about C# you'll also have more knowledge to experiment with. As you feel more comfortable with the language, you'll also learn to read and understand what the comments left by the Unity 3D programmers mean.

For now, at least, we have a project setup in which we'll be able to construct our sample game.

3.4 Tokens

To get started open the BookContents/Chapters/Chapter3 Unity Project. To see the example code, look in the Assets and open the C# files named after each section. To follow along with this chapter you should open the Tokens.cs file in Visual Studio to see what the code looks like.

In written English the smallest elements of the language are letters, numbers, and punctuation. Individually, most letters and numbers lack specific meaning. The next larger element after the letter is the word. Each word has more meaning, but complex thoughts are difficult to convey in a single word.

To communicate a thought, we use sentences. The words in a sentence each have a specific contribution to the intent, as seen in the diagram below. To convey a concept, we use a collection of sentences grouped into a paragraph. And to convey a story we use a collection of many paragraphs organized into chapters and integrated into a book.

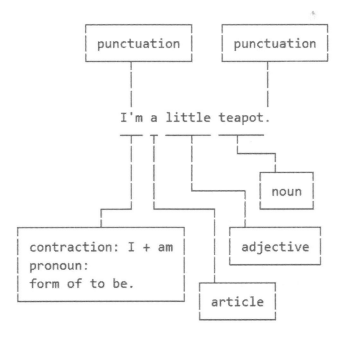

Programming has similar organizational mechanisms. The smallest meaningful element is a token, followed by statements, code blocks, and functions, followed by classes and namespaces, and eventually a program, or in our case the program is a game. Every file created in the process of writing C# is called a Compilation Unit, or source file.

We will begin with the smallest element and work our way up to writing our own classes. However, it's important to know the very smallest element to understand how all the parts fit together before we start writing complex code.

3.4.1 Writing C#

C# is an English-based programming language; like any other C-like programming language, it can be broken into tokens, the smallest meaningful fragment of text that the computer can understand. In a mechanical way of thinking, writing a story is the process of arranging words to convey meaning. In much the same way, writing code is arranging tokens to instruct the computer to carry out a process.

A token is made of a single character or a series of characters. For instance, in a simple statement like the following there are five tokens.

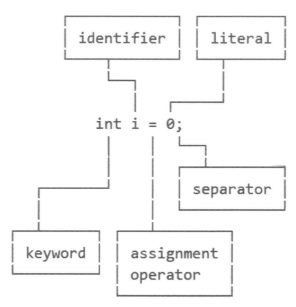

Tokens can be categorized as a *keyword, identifier, literal, assignment operator*, and *separator*. The above statement contains five tokens with spacing between each provided by white space. Together these tokens create an assignment statement.

The keyword `int` is followed by the identifier `i`. This is followed by an operator `=` which assigns the identifier on the left of the operator and the value of the literal `0` on the right. The last token `;` is a separator which ends the statement. White spaces and comments, which we have yet to cover, are not considered tokens, although they can act as separators. This is a lot to take in at once, but each one of these words will be further explained as we continue.

```
int j = 0; int k = 1;
```

The code shown above is two statements, the separator keeps the computer from misreading the code as a single statement. However, there are humans involved with writing code, and thus code needs to be readable by humans, or any other life form which might read your code. Proper code means following a specific formatting style. We'll dive into more about proper code style later in this chapter.

Each group of characters, or text, is converted by a *lexical analyzer*, sometimes called a *lexer*, in the computer and turned a *symbol*. This process is called *tokenization*, or as a computer scientist would say, a lexer tokenizes your code into symbols. Once tokenized, the symbols are *parsed*; this process organizes the tokens into instructions for the computer to follow. This unique vocabulary does frame programmers as a strange group of alien beings with a language all to themselves; I promise, however, conversations about lexical analyzers don't come up very often when talking with most programmers.

This may seem like a great deal of work and we are jumping ahead into more complex computer science topics, but all of this happens behind the scenes, so you don't need to see any of this taking place. It's important to understand what a compiler does and how it works, so you can write code in a way that the computer can understand. Therefore, a simple typo will stop the lexer from building code.

A computer can't interpret or guess at what it is you're trying to do. Therefore, if you mistype `int i = 0:` and not `int i = 0;` the last token cannot be converted by the lexer into a proper symbol, and thus this statement will not be parsed at all. This code results in an error before the code is even compiled.

3.4.2 Comments a First Look

In the Assets directory open the Comments script. One of the first types of tokens we'll want to investigate is the comment. Each section in the code will have a corresponding comment like the one below.

```
/* * * * * * * * * * * * * * * * * * * * *
 * Section 3.15 Comments a first look      *
 * * * * * * * * * * * * * * * * * * * * */
```

We'll go into more detail on various types of comments and how they're used in Section 3.14, but it's important to know what they look like before moving on. In each C# source file, you'll see various with // at the beginning of the line. This tells the lexical analyzer to ignore anything appearing after the // on that line.

```
//This is a single line comment.

// ← the two forward slashes make
// any line invisible to the lexer
```

Comments allow the author of the C# script to inform other readers of any information not included in the code itself. In addition to the // comment is the /* comment */ where anything between the start of the /* comment and the ending */ will also be invisible from the lexical analyzer.

```
/*
 ↑
 └ This is a multiline comment.
   everything between the opening
   token slash star stays hidden
   until you get to the closing
 ┌ slash star
 ↓
 */
```

Both types of comments are used extensively through all the code samples provided with each chapter.

```
/*          not hidden           */
/*              ↓                 */
/*hidden*/ int i = 0; /*hidden*/
```

In some cases, working code will be hiding behind a comment. To see how the code works, delete the // at the start of the line of code to reveal the statement to the lexical analyzer for compiling. To hide the code, simply put the // back at the beginning of the line. Programmers often leave code they're working on in comments to keep work in progress knowing that the code isn't fully functioning.

```
/* uncomment one of the three someInt lines
 * below by deleting the //
 * then make sure that only one
 * is visible to the lexer by commenting
 * the others out.
 */
int someInt = 0;//I print 0 through 10
//int someInt = 3; //starts at 3
//int someInt = 11; //this won't print
while (someInt < 10)
{
    System.Console.WriteLine(someInt);
    someInt++;
}
```

Single line comments that use // are used extensively throughout the code with the intent for you to uncomment them to see how code works. Uncommenting one line and commenting out another is a common strategy to test out various ways to solve a problem.

In a clean code base the code itself will speak clearly as to what it's doing. Comments would be kept to a minimum. If a function requires comments to explain how it works, then the function could be re-written to be easier to understand.

3.4.3 Separator Tokens

The most common separator is the semicolon (;). This mark of punctuation is used to end a code statement. Other separator tokens come in pairs. Curly braces are used in pairs to separate groups of code statements. The opening curly brace is the { with the pointy end pointed to the outside of the group; this is paired with the } which closes the curly brace pair.

```
/*  ┌ Opening                    *
 *  |              Closing ┐  *
 *  ↓                      ↓  *
 *  { Curly braces         }  *
 *  [ Square Brackets      ]  *
 *  ( Parenthesis          )  *
 *  < Angle Brackets       > */
```

Parentheses start with the (and end with the) while square brackets start with [and end with]. The different opening and closing braces, brackets, and parentheses have specific purposes that are used to help identify what they are being used for. There are angle brackets < and > as well; these are used to surround data types. And don't forget both single quotes ' and double quotes ", which are used in pairs as well to surround symbols called strings.

NOTE: In many word processors a beginning and an ending quote (" and ") are often used. The lexical analyzer doesn't recognize these smart quotes, so the text editor for programming uses straight quote marks (") instead. These subtle changes aren't so subtle once you realize that letters, numbers, and every other character used in programming are all parsed as American Standard Code for Information Interchange (ASCII) or unicode transformation format (UTF)-8, -16, or -32. Both ASCII and UTF are names given to the database of characters that the computer uses to read text. Computers don't use eyes to read. Rather, they use a database of numbers to look up each character being used. Therefore, to a computer " looks more like 0×201C and " like 0×0022 (the expected quotation mark), if we were using UTF-16.

Curly braces are used in code to separate statements. Parentheses are usually used to accept data. Square brackets are often used to help identify arrays. We'll get into arrays later; imagine something like a spreadsheet or a graph paper until we get to their explanation.

```
int[] arrayOfNumbers = { 1, (int)3.0, 9000 };
```

The above statement assigns three numbers to an array. The curly braces contain a pair of statements separated by a comma. The second statement in the curly braces is converting a number with a dot (.) into a number without a dot in it. This will take a bit of explanation, but it's good to get used to seeing this sort of thing. We'll get to what an array is soon enough, as well as a dot operator.

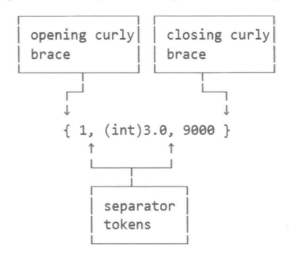

Often, when learning to program you'll see many strange tokens which might not seem to have any meaning. It's up to you to observe every token you come across and try to understand what it does. If none of the statements makes sense that's fine. At this point you're not expected to know what all this means yet, but you soon will.

3.4.4 Operator Tokens

Operators are like keywords but use only a few non-word characters. The colon or semi-colon is an operator; unlike keywords, operators change what they do based on where they appear, or how they are used. This behavior shifting is called operator overloading, and it's a complex subject that we'll get into later. It's also important to know that you can make up your own operators when you need to.

Commas in C# have a different meaning. A comma is used to separate different data values. Another special operator token is the semi-colon.

```
/*              semicolon operator   */
/*                    ↓              */
public class Example : MonoBehaviour
{
}
```

Here, the : was used following the name of the class to inform the compiler we're going to be adding to a pre-existing class called MonoBehaviour. In this case, : will tell our class to add new behaviors to MonoBehaviour. This means to build upon a class which already exists. We're creating a new child object related to MonoBehaviour; this is a class that was created by the developers at Unity 3D.

Here's a list of the various math related operators you can expect to find in C#.

=	Assignment Operator
+	Addition Operator
-	Subtraction Operatorr
*	Multiply Operator
/	Divide Operator
%	Remainder Operator

Operators provide our basic ability to do math in code. Operators are special characters that take care of specific operations between variables. Notation or the order in which operators and variables appear is normally taught with the following notation or mathematic grammar: a + b = c. However, in programming the following is preferred: c = a + b; the change is made because the = operator in C# works differently from its function commonly taught in math class.

```
result = operation
      c = a + b;
```

The left side of the = operator is the assignment side, and the right side is the operation side. This puts the emphasis on the value assigned rather than how it's assigned. The result is more important than how the problem is solved since the computer is doing the math. In programming the above example should be read as "c is assigned a plus b."

3.4.5 Literals

Literals are values which come in many different forms. Literals are things you assign to variables, or compare variables to. Literals can be considered tokens used in a literal manner. Numbers can be called numeric literals. Words like "This is a string" is also considered a literal.

Numbers are literals as well. The int or integer is a hole number like 1 or 100. We are used to seeing large numbers like 10,000 or ten thousand with a comma separating every thousand. However, commas have a different meaning in C#. To the compiler, 10,000 is a value 10 followed by a different value 000, a second number. This causes problems so large numbers need to be written without the comma. So, ten thousand in C# needs to be written as 10000 without the comma.

```
Vector3 vector = new Vector3()
{
    /* commas separate terms   */
    /*    ↓        ↓           */
    x = 1, y = 2, z = 3
};


/*        commas separate terms   */
/*             ↓              ↓    */
for (int i = 0, j = 1; ; i++, j++)
{
}
```

When assigning values to variables we often use literals to set a value for something specific. For example, if we wanted to convert radians to degrees we use the equation `degrees = (radians × π) / 180` to get an answer. In C# that would look like the following:

```
float degrees;
float radians = 3.14159f;

degrees = (radians * Mathf.PI) / 180;
Debug.Log("Degrees from 3.14
```

(constant) float Mathf.PI = 3.14159274
The infamous 3.14159265358979... value (Read Only).

The example shows `float radians = 3.14159f;` where `3.14159f` is the literal assigned to `radians`. Later `Mathf.PI` is not a literal but a different type of number called a const; more on that later. `radians` which is a variable that was assigned a literal. Then we divide that by `180` which is a literal.

When values like `180` are used in code directly it's sometimes called a "hard-coded" value. In cases where the math isn't going to change, like in the radian to degree conversion, this isn't a bad practice. However, in some cases like screen resolution a hard-coded value might work against you.

If you wanted to check where a mouse pointer was in relation to the center of a screen you might use half the screen width and half the screen height to get the center of the screen. Assuming you're on a computer with a 1920 pixel wide screen that's 1080 pixels tall you might use $x = 960$ $y = 540$ as the center of the screen. This would be wrong if the screen resolution were to change. You can't change a hard-coded value once you've built your project into a game to distribute.

When something is put into quotes, as in "I'm a literal," you are writing a string literal. Literals are common throughout nearly all programming languages and form the base of C#'s data types. Right now, we're dealing with only a few different types of literals, but there are many more we will be aware of soon.

3.4.6 Transitive and Non-Transitive Operations

In math class it's sometimes taught how some operations are transitive and others not. For instance, $2 + 3 + 4$ and $4 + 3 + 2$ result in the same values. Where each number appears between the operators doesn't matter, so the + operator is considered transitive. This concept holds true in C#. Results change when we start to mix operators.

```
int a = 1 + 2 - 4 + 7;
int b = 7 + 4 - 2 + 1;
int c = (7 + 4) - (2 + 1);
int d = (1 + 2) - (4 + 7);
```

This code fragment shows two different results using the same operators but with different number placement. We'll see how to overcome these problems later when we start using them in our game. Operator order is something to be aware of, and it's important to test each step as we build up our calculations to make sure our results end up with values we expect.

To ensure that the operations happen as you expect, either you can use parentheses to contain operands or you can do each calculation. We'll dive further into more detail with a second look at operators later, but this will have to wait until we have a much better understanding of the basics of C#.

3.4.7 Putting It All Together

The Unity 3D engineers have prepared many data types, functions, objects, and classes tailored specifically for game development. Classes often work together to share and manipulate data. There are exceptions to this rule, but C# allows for many different writing styles and paradigms.

Creating data produces components of an object. In general, you've created something that can be reused many times. Once you have created a zombie by adding brain-seeking logic and how many bullets are required to stop him, it's only a matter of duplicating that zombie to create a mob to terrorize your player.

As we proceed we'll become more familiar with what it means to use classes as objects; the tutorials will be aimed at making sure that this is all clear.

```
303        public void Start()
304        {
305            int i = 0;
306            while (i < 10)
307            {
308                Debug.Log(i);
309                i++;
310            }
311        }
```

In the Assets directory for Chapter 3 you'll find a Tokens_Scene Unity scene. Open this and press the Play-in-Editor button. Open the Console window and you'll see the following output.

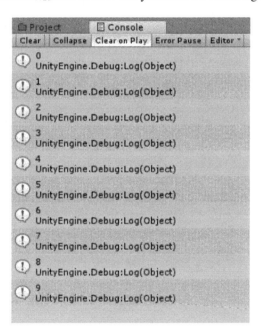

Let's break this code sample down. The first word is public, which is a keyword followed by void another keyword token. Start() is an identifier. A Tokens game object in the Unity scene has the Tokens.cs script attached and Unity executes the Start() function when the game begins.

The parentheses after the Start are operators used when we need parameters for our function. The parameters are discussed in Section 3.3.2. For now, take in the fact that both opening (and closing) parentheses are necessary after function identifiers. They're useful; trust me.

To begin the contents of the function we start with curly braces, the opening { and closing } curly braces. Everything that the function will do must be contained between the two braces. Any text appearing outside of them will not be part of the Start() function. The code contained in the curly braces becomes the function block of code, or code block.

The first statement in the function's code block is `int i = 0;` this is an assignment statement, where we declare `int i` and then use the = to assign `i` a literal value of 0. This is then separated from the next statement with the `;` operator.

The assignment statement is followed by `while (i < 10)`, which is called a looping condition. We'll read more on looping conditions later in Section 4.12. This looping statement is followed by an opening { curly brace. This indicates a code block specifically written for the while loop.

The code block contains the statement `Debug.Log(i);`, which is a function call using `i` as a parameter or argument. After the print function call is `i++;`, which applies the post-increment operator ++ to the variable `i`. This code block is ended with the closing } curly brace.

The `while` code block and the `int = 0;` are both within the `Start()` code block. To make the code more readable, tabs are added to indicate a separation between each section of code. Now bask in the knowledge that we've got words to describe everything presented in the above code sample. We may not understand everything that has been written, but we've got some vocabulary where we can get started.

3.4.8 What We've Learned

Programmers are meticulous about syntax. They have to be. The following two statements are very different: `int myint0 = -1;` and `Int my 0int = - 1:`. The first one will compile; the second one has at least five errors. You may not be able to spot the problems in the second statement, but by the end of the next section you will.

Internet forums are a great source for getting help when learning how to write code. When asking programmers for help it's best to limit your subject and consider your words carefully. Asking "How would I write a video game where you shoot zombies with a flame thrower" involves so many different concepts it's impossible for anyone to tell you where to start. At best you might get a link to a book on Amazon. In a single post, you're asking for too much.

If you formulate a smaller question like, "How do I attach flames to a zombie after it's been hit by a projectile?" you're more likely to get an answer. When talking to a programmer, using proper syntax, and providing context as to what you're code looks like and asking why it doesn't work, you are more likely you'll get the answer you were looking for.

3.5 Statements and Expressions

To continue, open the `StatementsAndExpressions.cs` file to follow along. When reading a book or story, you extract meaning from an ordered chain of words. In a similar way, computers extract commands from a chain of ordered instructions. In English we call this a sentence; programmers call this a *statement*. A statement is considered to be any chunk of code which accomplishes some sort of task separated by a semicolon.

At the center of any given task is the *algorithm*, not to be confused with a logarithm. An algorithm is a systematic process that accomplishes a task. In many ways you can think of it as a recipe, or rather a recipe is an algorithm for making food.

It could take one or two statements to accomplish a task, or it could take many hundreds of statements. This all depends on the difficulty of a given task. Each individual statement is a step toward a goal. This is the difference between spending a few minutes frying an egg, or spending an hour baking a soufflé. Each individual step is usually fairly simple; it's the final result that matters.

Like sentences, statements have different forms. Statements can declare and assign values to variables. These are called *declaration* and *assignment* statements. These statements are used to set up various types of data and give them names.

3.5.1 Expressions

The subjects of your statements are called *identifiers*. An *assignment statement* is used to give an identifier a value. When you read "The menu has kale for lunch and broccoli for dinner." The C# version might look a bit like the following:

```
private enum Food
{
    kale,
    broccoli
}
Food lunch = Food.kale;
Food dinner = Food.broccoli;
```

Assignment statements often incorporate some sort of operation. These are called *expressive statements*. Different from expressing an emotion, expressions in code look more like "x + y." Expressions process data. After processing, the result of an *expression* can be assigned to a variable. We'll learn more about variables and assignments in Section 3.10.2. Literals can also be used in an expression, for example myInt = x + 1; where 1 is a literal, but x may be a variable assigned before this expression. Together, x + 1; is an expressive statement, but x and 1 alone are not.

A collection of statements is called a *code block*, like a building block, something that's used to build. When writing a story, we call a collection of sentences a paragraph. The statements in a block of code work with each other to accomplish a task. An expression can also ask a block of code to execute. This is called an *invocation expression* or an expression that invokes a method.

3.5.2 How Unity 3D Executes Your Code

When a class is created, the contained instructions are not carried out at the same time. As it's been explained, each collection of parts in a class is made up of lines of text called *statements*. Each statement is carried out in order. Where the computer starts is usually dependent on which collection of statements it's told to start with. You're in charge of how the code is started.

Unity 3D provides us with a function called Start(), which we'll go into later. However, this is the preferred place to begin our code using Unity 3D. Once Start() is called, the computer goes to the first line in Start() and begins to carry out the instructions written there. As the computer gets to each statement the computer starts on the left of the statement and works its way to the right. Basically, a computer reads code like you're reading this sentence. In our examples we'll add code to the Start() method provided by Unity to run code when a scene is first started. If we want to repeat our code with every frame then we'll use the Update() method.

This is different from other development environments which often use Main() as their first place to begin running the code. When you start writing software in other environments you'll most likely start with Main(). We don't have to get into that right now, but it's good to know once you're done with this book.

3.5.3 Thinking in Algorithms

An algorithm is a step-by-step process. This lends itself to being written in an imperative programming language like C#, which executes operations one at a time and in order. Algorithms are written with statements starting at a beginning statement and finishing that statement before moving on to the next.

Just because we know what an algorithm is doesn't mean it's any easier to create one. Therefore, how do we go about writing the all-important algorithm? The first thing should be how you might accomplish any given task by hand.

As an example, say we're a computer surrounded by a mob of zombies. Thankfully, computers are very fast so we can do a lot before the zombies can get to us. With this in mind, we're going to want to focus on the zombie closest to us. Unfortunately, computers are also very dumb, so there's nothing which allows us to just guess at which one is the closest.

First, we're going to need to know how far away every zombie is from our point of view. Therefore, the computer would probably start with measuring the distance from itself to every zombie available to make a measurement to. After that we're going to have to compare zombies and distances, so we'll start with the first zombie we found and compare its distance to the next zombie we found.

If the next zombie is closer, we'll have to remember that one as being the closest one we've come across. Otherwise, if the next one is farther away, then we can forget about him and move on to the next zombie and compare numbers again. Once we've gone through all the zombies, we should have identified the zombie who is the closest one to us.

The process which we just thought through is an algorithm for finding the zombie closest to us. It's not complex, but we had to do a few steps to get to it. First, we needed to get a list of all the zombies we needed to sort through. After that it was an iterative process, by which we needed to remember one zombie as the closest one, then compare others against him to decide whether he would retain the status of being the zombie nearest to us. We'll be going over many of these problem-solving thought processes as we learn how to program.

This algorithm would look something like the following code block:

```
void Update()
{
    // Gather Data
    float closestDistance = Mathf.Infinity;
    GameObject closestGameObject = null;
    GameObject[] allGameObjects = FindObjectsOfType<GameObject>();

    // Process Data
    foreach(GameObject g in allGameObjects)
    {
        // Gather Data
        bool notMe = g != this.gameObject;

        // Process Data
        if (notMe)
        {
            // Gather Data
            Vector3 otherPosition = g.transform.position;
            Vector3 mPosition = transform.position;
            Vector3 difference = otherPosition - mPosition;
            float distance = difference.magnitude;

            // Process Data
            if(distance < closestDistance)
            {
                closestDistance = distance;
                closestGameObject = g;
            }
        }
    }

    // Gather Data
    Vector3 myPosition = transform.position;
    Vector3 closestPosition = closestGameObject.transform.position;
    Color red = Color.red;

    // Process Data
    Debug.DrawLine(myPosition, closestPosition , red);
}
```

We won't cover the entirety of how this code works, as we are yet to discuss the bulk of what's going on here, but in short, we gather data, then process data. We repeat the pattern of gathering data, then processing it. At the beginning, we gather data; a starting distance, a close game object and all the game objects in the scene. Then we process it with `foreach(GameObject g in allGameObjects)`. This happens again once in the foreach loop. You can see the pattern in this example, but this pattern exists throughout most programming tasks. Gather the data you need, then process it.

Just for a proof of concept we draw a line from the object. Because the script is attached to the object, we draw a line from the object the script is attached to toward the object selected as the closest. The scene will look something like this:

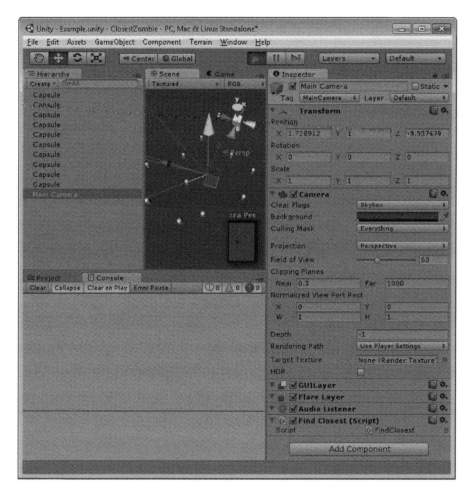

To view this open the `StatementsAndExpression_Scene` in the Editor and press the Play-in-Editor button, then switch over to the Scene panel. The `Debug.DrawLine` is not visible in the Game view and is only visible in the Scene editor. You can move some of the objects around the sphere to see the red line switch to different objects as they change distances. We put the code in the `Update()` method to make sure that the line is always visible, and the closest object can change if you move the objects around.

Programming is a lot more about a thought process than it is about processing. In other words, programming is less about how to do multiplication as it is about what to do with the result of a multiplication. In your everyday life we take for granted the everyday things we do on a regular basis. However, take a moment and really consider the complexity involved with something as simple as breathing.

Your diaphragm is receiving signals from your autonomic nervous system, causing several chemical reactions in the diaphragms muscle tissue, which then pull proteins toward one another causing it to contract. This in turn creates a lowered air pressure in your lungs, which pulls in air. A number of chemical processes allow the oxygen in the atmosphere to enter your blood stream. Thankfully, all of this happens without our thinking of it because of chemistry and physics. In programming, nothing is so automatic.

3.5.3.1 Wash, Rinse, Repeat

In our everyday life we see instructions written everywhere. However, if we follow instructions too closely we'd run into problems. If you interpreted, for example, the instructions on most shampoo labels like a computer we'd run out of shampoo the first time we used it.

To interpret the "wash, rinse, repeat" instructions like a computer we'd wash our hair, rinse it, then wash our hair, then rinse it, then wash our hair, then rinse it, ...; you get the picture. You'd continue the process until you run out of shampoo. Because there are no further instructions, once the shampoo has run out, a computer would send out an error of some kind. There wasn't a number given for how many times the instructions should be followed; there was no way to *terminate* the process, as a programmer would say. A computer would need to have the "shampooing" process killed to stop washing its hair. Simply put, computers lack common sense.

Here's a simple scenario: A spouse tells the programmer to go to the grocery store and says "Get some bacon, if there's milk get three." The programmer comes home with three packs of bacon, and no milk. If this makes sense, then you're thinking like a programmer. There are conditions to tell the programmer to get three packs of bacon if milk was available; just the fact that there was milk meant bringing home 3 × bacon.

3.5.4 What We've Learned

Programmers are often a group of literal thinkers. A programmer uses a different thought process from the artist. In terms of order of operation, programmers take things one step at a time. An artist tends to start with a broad picture, then refines detail where necessary. This process in programming terms is an imperative procedure, a step-by-step process where operations are carried out in a linear fashion.

As an artist or newcomer to programming, this imperative process can be a bit out of the ordinary. With some time and practice, however, this paradigm of thinking will become second nature. The approaches a programmer and an artist would take to solve a problem often diverge.

To learn how to write code is to learn how to think like a programmer. This may sound a bit awkward, but perhaps after some work, you'll understand why some programmers seem to think differently than everyone else.

3.6 Keywords

Keywords are special words, or symbols, that tell the compiler to do specific things. For instance, the keyword class at the beginning of a line tells the compiler you are creating a class. A *class declaration* is the line of code that tells the compiler you're about to create a new class.

```
class ClassName
{
}
```

The order in which words appear is important. English requires sentences and grammar to properly convey our thoughts to the reader. In code, C# or otherwise, programming requires statements and syntax to properly convey instructions to the computer.

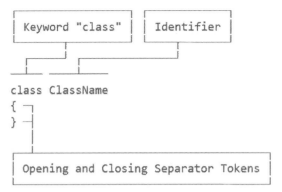

```
class ClassName
{
}
```

This creates a new class object called "ClassName"
Note: class needs to be all lower case.

Every class needs a name; in the above example we named our class ClassName, although we could have easily named the class Charles. When a new class is named the name becomes a new *identifier* This also holds true for every variable's name, though *scope* limits how long and where the variable's identifier exists. We'll learn more about variables and scope soon.

You can't use keywords for anything other than what C# expects them to be used for. These are called reserved keywords. Some keywords are only used in context with other keywords. There are exceptions, but in general, keywords inform the lexical analyzer of specific commands. Because keywords are reserved for a specific reason, you can't use them for anything other than the intended purpose. Altogether in C# there are roughly 80 keywords you should be aware of. We don't need to go over all of them now, so instead we'll learn them as we come across them.

```
int abstract = 0;
```

Because the word abstract is a reserved keyword, you can't use it as a variable name. The above class contains an error informing you on proper use of the abstract keyword.

3.6.1 The Class Keyword

To create a class named Charles we used the keyword class. The keyword commands C# to expect a word to identify the new class. The following word becomes a new identifier for the class. In this case Charles is used to name the class. Keywords often precede a word, and the computer uses the word following as its identifier.

The contents of Charles are defined between curly braces. After the class definition, the opening curly brace { is followed by any statements that Charles needs to be a proper Charles. When you're finished defining the contents of Charles, you use the closing curly brace } to indicate you're done with defining the Charles class.

```
class Charles { }
```

It's important to note that keywords start with lowercase letters. C# is a case-sensitive programming language, and as such, Class and class are two different things. In C# there is no keyword Class; only class starting with a lowercase c can be used. The same goes for every keyword in C#.

However, programming works this way: class Charles {} begins with the start of the class indicated with the open curly brace { and the end of the class indicated by the closing curly brace }, after which we go back and add the body later. Not everything works in this way, and it takes a bit of getting used to before you understand the flow. Certainly, however, this will come naturally after some practice.

Now we have a new class called Charles, which has no data and does nothing. This is to be expected since we haven't added any data or functions yet. You can also use the terminology this class is identified as Charles.

This class can't be used directly by Unity 3D. It lacks some of the necessary additions needed by the Unity 3D game engine to directly interact with this class. To be specific, this class doesn't have enough information to allow Unity 3D to know what to do with it. However, there are methods which make a minimal class, such as `Charles`, quite useful inside of Unity 3D, but we need to cover a great deal of ground before we can do that.

In Section 2.4 we looked at a complete source file, `Example.cs`, which is ready for use in Unity 3D. However, it's important to know what creates a minimal class before adding all the rest of the keywords and declarations which make it do anything in Unity 3D, our game engine.

Keep in mind, no two classes can share the same name. We'll go further into detail about class names and what's called a namespace later. The contents of the class are contained in the following pair of curly braces. All of the variables and functions that live between the opening curly brace { and the closing brace } become the contents of the class object.

Other keywords that we'll come across in this chapter include those that indicate a variables type. Some variable keywords which will be covered in the next few chapters are as follows:

```
int
```

```
float
```

```
string
```

These keywords indicate a type of variable. There are many more, but we're just going to look at these as an example. An int variable looks something like the following:

```
int i = 0;
```

A float looks like this:

```
float f = 3.14159f;
```

A string is used to store words like this:

```
string s = "some words in quotes";
```

If `int` and `float` seem similar, it's because they both deal with numbers, but as we will see, numbers behave quite differently when computers use them. Keywords are used quite often and they are case sensitive. Therefore, `int` and `Int` are different things, and thus using `Int i = 0;` will not work. Only `int` is recognized as a keyword, and there has been no definition written to tell C# what `Int` is. Keywords are also used to indicate special changes in code behavior. The keyword `if` is what is used to control code execution based on a conditional statement.

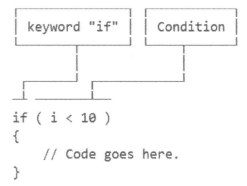

```
if ( i < 10 )
{
        // Code goes here.
}
```

As you are introduced to more and more keywords, you'll be expanding your ability to create new code as well. Keywords make up the complex vocabulary that is required to use C#.

3.6.2 What We've Learned

This was a short section, but it covered a fundamental component of a C# construct. Classes are both construction instructions and rules for objects to obey. Writing a complex class takes a step-by-step approach.

Keywords are an important component of any programming language. Some languages have very few keywords. LISP has a mere 18 keywords, C# has about 76, and COBOL has over 400 words reserved for special purposes.

Most programming languages use the same keywords for similar purposes. The `var` keyword is often used to indicate that a variable is being declared. Because of the similarities between programming languages, once you've learned one language, it's often easy to pick up and learn new languages.

3.7 White Space

Open the WhiteSpace.cs script found in the Assets of the Chapter3 Unity Project. White Space refers to the spaces between words and lines. When typewriters were still in fashion, new lines were entered by pushing on a lever which pushed the roller that held onto the paper to reposition the hammers with letters on them back to the beginning of the next line. This is the origin of the term "Carriage return character" where the mechanism holding the paper was referred to as the carriage. Now, these are called line feed character, next line character line separator, or paragraph separator. It's also interesting to note that these are unique Unicode characters. On Windows you'll find the option under Edit → Advanced → View White Space

In OSX with Visual Studio Community you'll find the option in the Preferences → Markers and Rulers → Show Invisible characters: and select Always

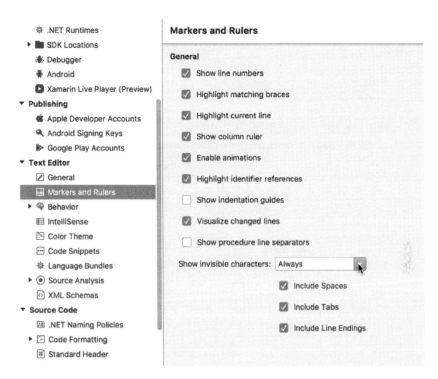

Like letters and numbers, white spaces are also characters entered in your code. In the editor you'll see faint dots arrows and on OSX you'll see \n marks spaced throughout your code.

```
1      //·Chapter·3.6·White·Space
2
3    ⊟class·WhiteSpace·{
4
5      ⇢   //·Use·this·for·initialization
6    ⊟ ⇢   void·Start·()·{
7      ⇢     ⇢
8      ⇢   }
9      ⇢
10     ⇢   //·Update·is·called·once·per·frame
11   ⊟ ⇢   void·Update·()·{
12     ⇢     ⇢
13     ⇢   }
14   }
15   □
```

In many cases the new lines and spaces and tabs are there only to help make the code more readable. And depending on what a programmer was taught, the white spaces will be used differently. For instance, adding white space after a function declaration is unnecessary, and the location of the curly braces can pretty much be moved anywhere before or after the contents of the function itself. Leaving the white spaces showing isn't necessary, but it's good to know what white space means when talking to a programmer. If none of this makes sense right now, it will later.

The placement of curly braces is easy to change; these decisions often lead to debates on standards among programmers. There's little difference either way. However, keeping your own code consistent helps you read your code and find errors faster.

It's important to remember that if you're going to be working with more classically trained programmers, they might get a headache when reading poorly formatted code. It's best to copy your programmer friends' style before coming up with your own way to format your classes and functions. No doubt, before the end of this book you will have formed opinions of your own when it comes to the use of white space and formatting your own code.

Normally, code might look a bit like the following:

```
    void MyFunction()
    {
        int i = 0;
        while (i < 10)
        {
            System.Console.Write(i);
            i++;
        }
    }
```

This looks like a readable collection of statements. However, the compiler could care less about how you use white space. Therefore, here is what would this code sample look like without the unnecessary white space:

There are still some necessary white space characters used to separate the different tokens in the function. There is the space between `void` and `MyOtherFunction`, and the space between `int` and `i`. In any case the white space is required after the use of a keyword. Keywords are unique words reserved for C#. If we used `voidMyFunction()` then there would be an error stating something about not knowing what a `voidMyFunction()` is. White space is also used to make code more readable. Without the white space the code becomes more difficult to interpret.

```
imagineforamomentwhatenglishwouldlooklikewithoutanyspacesorpunctuation
```

White space should also be used as needed. I once worked with a programmer who would put a few pages of white space between different functions. He said it made it easier to focus on what he was looking at when there was only one line of code on the screen at a time. Of course, this drove other programmers nuts. It's hardly a common practice.

Although he had a point, being able to focus on one code block at a time is important, but there's a thing called code folding that we'll learn about later on to help make your code more easy to organize.

3.7.1 Code Style

Between programmers there's often a discussion of code style. Many heated debates might flare up based on the use of white space. The differences are entirely based on style and in most cases have no effect on the efficacy of the code. In the following fragments the { is placed in different places.

```
    void SomeFunction() {
        // Some Code here...
    }

    void SomeOtherFunction()
    {
        // Some Other Code here...
    }
```

The execution of the two functions will perform equally, but the placement of the first curly brace { can make the code more or less readable depending on what you're comfortable with. Unity's developers offer us the first version, but for clarity we'll stick to the second version.

The finer points on where variables appear in a statement or how many statements can appear on a single line are usually dictated by how a programmer has learned to write code. Old school programmers prefer no line of code extending beyond 80 characters. This limit formed in 1928, when IBM punch cards had only 80 columns to poke holes in the paper. Though it's unlikely you'll have to work with an old curmudgeon, at least now you know why they might be grumpy.

Today, there's no physical limit other than what would make a statement difficult to read. If a single line of code spans several widths of your screen it's probably unreadable. In these cases it's better to break apart your statement into a few smaller statements. This will help keep the code more readable. Within the confines of this book we're somewhat more limited by space, so we too will be limiting the length of our statements based on the width of the margins of the book.

Likewise, if you've got a lovely 4k monitor you might be comfortable reading mile-long lines, but if you're stuck on a low-res laptop then you might hate having to scroll left and right just to read a single statement. Consider the fact that not everyone has a giant monitor.

Interpreting your own code several days or weeks after you've written it is just as important as handing your code off to someone else, with that person being able to read it. There are many times when I've come back to a project written several weeks ago and needed to spend a few minutes trying to figure out what I was thinking when I wrote the code. Sometimes, it takes only a few days for me to forget about the code I've written. Worse yet, if I write the code half asleep then I might forget what I was doing before I've even reached the end of a statement.

In the end it's up to you to pick what you'll stick to. However, it's considered rude to pick through someone else's code and reformat it. Code can sometimes become quite personal, and reformatting code might end up feeling like someone sneaking into your bedroom and reorganizing your sock drawer.

Another common debate rises between the use of tabs or spaces. In your IDE (integrated development environment) you can tell the editor how many spaces a tab is to represent, usually this number is either 4 or 2 spaces. Style guides often bring this up, and in large corporate environments some preference is usually enforced. This isn't something you need to immediately concern yourself with, but it's good to be aware that there are programmers out there with a strong opinion on what works best.

3.7.2 What We've Learned

White space and formatting are important to creating a clean easy-to-read class. Every large company will have a set of rules for their programmers to follow. These coding standards, as they are called, are usually maintained by a lead programmer and can vary from company to company.

Smaller teams of engineers can have a less restrictive set of rules, but this often leads to some confusion and large bodies of unreadable code. Everyone has his or her own coding style and preferences. If there is an established set of coding standards, then it's best to follow it.

So far as this book is concerned, it's best that you learn how to make your code work before concerning yourself with strict coding rules. Code formatting and style are important. How you express yourself through code is up to you, so long as it works. Getting your code to work is a big enough challenge; style and proper formatting will come naturally with time as you see the benefits of different code styles, and how they contribute to your code's readability.

3.8 Code Blocks

To follow along, open the CodeBlocks.cs file in the Chapter3 Unity Project. Code blocks, or a "block of code," are collections of statements grouped together. The block, or chunk is separated by a starting curly brace { then ended with a closing curly brace }. C# programmers often use tabs to indent the contents of a code block.

This makes the different blocks more readable. This becomes more apparent when we have blocks within blocks. Some languages like python rely on the tabs to indicate separate blocks of code. Code blocks help organize statements together in a continuous set of steps.

Getting used to how spacing is essential for writing readable code. Next, we'll use a logic control statement followed by a block of code. The block for this `if` statement is indented to the right to indicate it's confined within the logic control statement.

```
// im outside of the block of code below
if (true)
{
    // code goes here
    // im also in this block of code
}
// im outside of the block of code above
```

If we take a look at a more complex section of code we can see why it's important to differentiate code by using tabs. When looking at code it might not be apparent, but programmers are very fastidious about text layout. Each programmer has a preferred style, but it's safe to say that most, if not all, programmers hate seeing badly formatted code.

```
int i = 7;
int j = 13;
if (i < j){
j = 7;}
```

In the above example we can clearly see `int j` being set twice. What isn't obvious is why it's declared twice. All the lines start at the same position and look crowded. Programming tools offer many text layout options, so white space is used to separate different blocks of code.

```
int k = 8;
int l = 9;


if (k < l)
{
    l = 8;
}
```

By adding in some white space, we can make the `if` statement more visible. Adding white space around our blocks of code is important to maintain readability. There are also blocks of code that can live within another block of code. In general, it's all related to the same block. Blocks inside of a block are called nested code blocks. White space is used to separate the nested code from the block it's found in.

```
if (true)
{
    //code here
    if (true)
    {
        //another block of code.
    }

}
```

The block of code following the second if statement is considered to be nested inside of the first block of code. This is because of the placement of the first opening curly brace { and the related closing curly brace }. You form hierarchies by placing the different curly braces within one another.

```
if (true)
{//code here
if (true)
{//another block of code.
}
}
```

Poorly indented curly braces make for confusing code; the above code is still valid, but it's less readable compared to the previous version. Most code-editing tools will automatically add in the proper number of indents for you. It's something you'll have to get used to when writing your own code.

We'll go into further detail as to what this all means later. Just gather from this discussion that a bunch of statements appearing between a pair of curly braces is considered a block of code.

3.8.1 What We've Learned

Much of programming involves proper use of style and a great deal of white space to accomplish that style. So far we've just been covering vocabulary; yet, without that vocabulary we can't have a proper conversation about programming. This includes talking to other programmer friends, who will have a hard time understanding you if you can't speak their language.

3.9 Classes: A First Look

To follow along open the Classes.cs file found in the Chapter3 Unity Project. The most important part of any C# program is the class. Classes here are not the sort that students go to; rather, they are classes in terms of classification. Classes in C# appear in several different forms. Some are called partial classes, and some classes can even appear inside of another class; these classes are called nested classes.

A class is a collection of data and instructions. The instructions can be referred to as functions methods or, sometimes, procedures. The data stored in a class is called a field or property. Everything in a class together are members of the class. All the naming aside, what's important is what classes do and how they're used.

```
/* Class Stuff has Things,  */
/* and can Do A Thing.      */
class Stuff
{
    int Things;       /* ← Data member      */
    void DoAThing() /* ← Function member */
    {
        //Do the thing!
    }
}
```

Classes are flexible and easily changed, but this flexibility is not without some complexity. As we've seen before, the class declaration can contain a lot more than the following example. However, much of the complexity comes later in this book, when needed.

When you approach a game or any sort of programming task first gather data; then figure use of the data; last, act on the data. In most programming paradigms it's best to start off with variables at the beginning of your new class. For instance, in this pseudo code we might want to know what day it is before going out:

```
bool PartyTonight = false;/* ← Collect your */
void DoParty()/*            ┌─── data.       */
{   /*                  ●↓                  */
    DateTime today = DateTime.Now;
    /*      test your data                  */
    /*                  ●↓                  */
    if (today.DayOfWeek == DayOfWeek.Friday)
    {   /* act on your data                 */
        /*                  ●↓              */
        PartyTonight = true;
    }
}
```

We start off with getting a day, and then deciding what to do tonight based on the day. We should refrain from partying based on what the day is, unless we want to show up for work late. Almost every operation follows that pattern, get data, check data, set data. We'll go into more detail on this topic later, after we've learned about how to use a variable in a class properly.

3.9.1 Objects

Object oriented programming (OOP) was invented to associate data and logic into nicely packaged bundles of code. When you write a class in C# you're creating blueprints and instructions for a new object. Any number of objects can then be constructed based on your blueprints. Programmers use the term *instantiate* when talking about creating an object from the class blueprint.

Each instantiated object is an *instance* of the class from which it was constructed. The class is not itself one of the instances created by it. The newly created object contains all the functions and data written into the class.

```
            /*    ┌──────────────────┐  */
class Zombie/* ←──│This is the plan  │  */
{           /*    │to build a zombie │  */
}           /*    └──────────────────┘  */
            /*    ┌──────────────────┐  */
            /*    │this is an        │  */
void MakeZombie()/* │instance of     │  */
{   /*        ┌────────│a zombie      │  */
    /*        ↓    └──────────────────┘  */
    Zombie zombie = new Zombie();
}
```

To make this clear, a class in of itself is not an object, just a plan for making objects. We start with a C# class which contains instructions to build an instance of itself. Unity 3D hides a bit of this instantiation from you when you've attached a script to an object in the scene. A script attached to a GameObject in the scene tells Unity to instantiate the class at the start of the game.

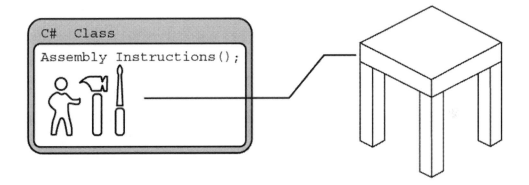

A class might be nothing more than a container for some data. As an example, our zombie shooter could have a hypothetical ammunition pick-up class. In the ammunition pick-up, we could store a type of ammo, along with how many rounds are stored in it. When a player discovers a stock-pile of ammunition, the variety and count can be randomized for any number of pick-ups.

```
class Ammunition
{
    AmmoType ammoType;
    int ammoCount = 10;
}
```

On the other hand, a class can also contain behaviors for a complex boss who plans to crash a comet into the earth, or any other instruction for world domination. The contents of which are a bit out of reach for this book.

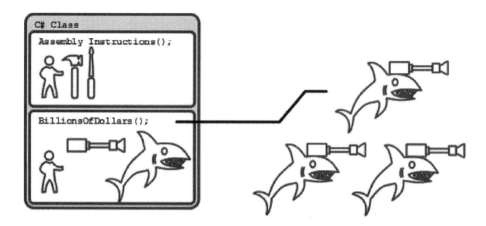

Just as important, a class can create more than one instance of an object. This process is called *instancing*. Each instance is created from the same blueprint and thus behaves the same as all the other instances of the same class. Each instance can have unique values. In Unity 3D, each instance of an object can have unique positions in 3D space.

OOP is particularly useful for video games. Individual classes can address different aspects of your game. A zombie class can be instanced many times to create a mob of mindless zombies. Likewise, a solitary class can be written to manage how to move your player's character around when keys or buttons are pressed. A separate class can manage inventory and how to deal with items.

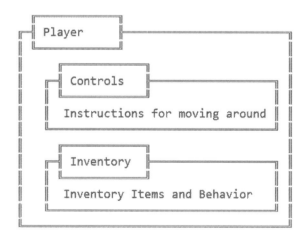

Monsters, bullets, cameras, and lights all have classes from which they are created. Almost every object you see in any level in Unity 3D can be instanced from a class. An instance of an object communicates to another object through *messages* and *events*.

When people in the real-world deal with household items they are rarely concerned with how they function. Knowing how a toaster works has little effect on the toaster's performance. We put bread in a toaster, push down on a button, and wait for a delicious toast.

A toaster, however, is more than a button and a receptacle for bread. It's a collection of wires, heating elements, transformers, and other electrical components which are hidden under a shiny cover. We interact with an *abstraction* of a toaster, never dealing with the insides ourselves.

Abstraction presents only the parts we need to accomplish a given task and hides the rest. To make toast we need a place to put bread and a button to start the machine. The toaster does its work and toast happens, or at least it should.

Messing with the insides of the toaster class isn't recommended; that's why there are labels telling us to keep forks out of the toaster. To protect a human class from fumbling around with the insides of a toaster class the toaster is protected by *encapsulation.*

Encapsulation is the term used to define to how classes hide data and functions from the outside world. To interact with the toaster we must use the toaster's *interface*, but there are other objects in the kitchen which have buttons, and the human class is very good at pushing buttons.

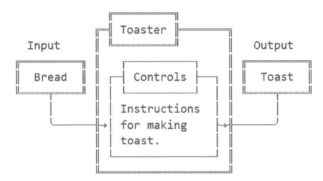

When you put bread into a blender and press a button you will get a very different result from the toaster, but they are both kitchen appliances and use the same power outlet. They're both made of metal and run on the same electricity, but they do different things.

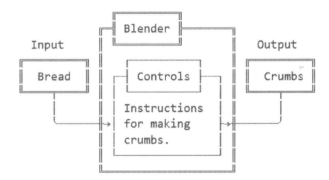

When and where it's possible, a programmer will reuse as much code as possible. A blender and a toaster could share similar components, only the operation carried out on a slice of bread is different when they are used. The capability to change the contents of an operation is described as *polymorphism.*

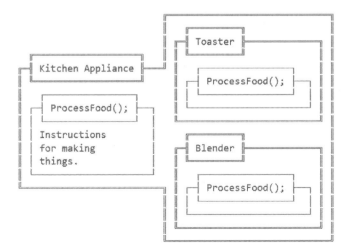

A generic kitchen appliance would be a place to put food and a button to press to process food. Each version of a kitchen appliance does different things to food. A wise programmer would make sure that all the appliances inherit from the generic kitchen appliance.

Inheritance allows many classes to share common attributes and behaviors. If you wanted a toaster with more than one slot and a knob to adjust the darkness of your toast you would want to inherit the original toaster's functions first. This means that the base of both toaster and blender is a kitchen appliance. A dual slot toaster inherits from toaster, which inherits from kitchen appliance. This in turn means that if any changes are made to kitchen appliance that change or addition is inherited by all of the subclasses inheriting from kitchen appliance.

This would mean inheriting the original toaster's electronic systems, casing, and original button. All of these components may also be made from other classes. This would mean only changing one electronic part to adapt a toaster for sale, say, in Europe.

Aggregating many different classes into a single class allows another layer of flexibility. By aggregating many separate components or classes into a single useful toaster or blender means you can more easily swap individual parts for new behaviors. A toaster is the aggregate total of many smaller parts.

You may find yourself writing code for a zombie or a toaster and see some similarities between those things and other objects in your game. When your player attacks a zombie or a toaster, they may both break apart. Both the zombie and toaster can share functions related to getting attacked.

As far as your code may be concerned, one object chases after you trying to eat your brains, and the other object turns bread into delicious toast. Keep this in mind when you start writing your own code. Even though some things may seem unrelated, maybe even humans and zombies can both enjoy toast.

3.9.2 What We've Learned

I'll let this sink in a little bit. Being new to programming is usually a very intimidating experience. Having to learn any new language is a daunting task. Because much of programming is taught in English we've got a slight advantage. At least the mentioned 80 keywords aren't written in a foreign language.

The main take away from this chapter is the fact that OOP is the process of building objects, instancing them, and then using them. Using objects involves reading data, using logic on the data, and then carrying out tasks based on the logic.

As we move on, feel free to jump back between chapters to refresh your memory if there are concepts which you might have forgotten. It's important to proceed at your own pace; jumping ahead before you're clear on a topic leads to confusion, then frustration, and leading to quitting altogether.

We're here to learn and have fun while learning. Building a game for modern gaming platforms is easy once you've got your head wrapped around this whole C# thing, so stick to it and you'll reap the rewards. Not only will you be able to write your own games from scratch, you'll also be able to write plenty of other apps using other development tools which use C#.

We've also come across a great deal of vocabulary related to classes. If you're not completely clear as to what these words mean we'll be covering chapters dedicated to these more complex concepts. When you're ready, it's time to continue learning and getting ready to make some games.

3.10 Variables

To follow along open the Variables.cs script from the Chapter3 Unity Project. Programming is only able to accomplish a task once it's able to read, manipulate and create data. Variables are the little bits of data or information which make up the game world. Everything you see in a game scene, and even things that are implicitly assumed, like gravity, can be interpreted as data that can be stored into a variable. Logic behavior can be controlled by comparing values stored in variables.

The concept of a variable is something we might take for granted in day-to-day life. When you save a contact in your phone you've assigned values to a name; you added "Mom" with a phone number to your address book.

A variable can be either something that's constantly changing or something you've set once and shouldn't change. For instance, an object's location should be updating if it's falling or getting pushed on by other forces in the world. This object's location is a variable, which the programmers at Unity have named transform.position. The Position value has three parts, an *x*, *y*, and *z* component.

Various numbers used in common math operations have been named with easy to remember identifiers. A value like PI, which doesn't need to change, lives in Unity 3D's API. It can be found as UnityEngine. Mathf.PI.

3.10.1 Identifiers

Identifiers, which are considered symbols or tokens, are words that you invent and then assign a meaning. Identifiers can be as simple as the letter i or as complex as @OhHAICanIHasIdentifier01. We'll get into properly creating names later, but *identifier* is the word that's used to name any function, variable, or type of data you create. From the address book example above, the entry "Mom" is the identifier and its value is the phone number you assigned.

With a GameObject or a Camera in a Unity Scene, a collection of variables can be seen in the Inspector panel. The Camera has a Transform Component, the Transform has a Position, Rotation, and Scale. Inside of each of these are X, Y and Z variables. The Camera component has a longer list of variables starting with Clear Flags and ending with Target Display. Each of the Identifiers name a different type of data you're able to modify and save in the scene.

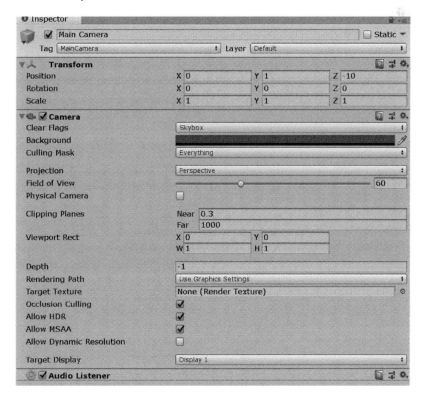

3.10.2 Data

Data, in a general sense, is sort of like a noun. Like nouns, data can be a person, place, or thing. Programmers refer to these nouns as objects, and these objects are stored in memory as variables. The word *variable* infers something that might change, but this isn't always the case. It's better to think of a variable as a space in your computer's memory to put information.

When you play word games like MadLibs you might ask for someone's name, an object, an adverb, and a place. Your result could turn out like "*Garth* ate a *jacket*, and *studiously* played at the *laundrymat*." In this case the name, object, adverb, and place are variable types. The data is the word you use to assign the variable with.

Programmers use the word *type* to denote what kind of data is going to be stored. Computers aren't fluent in English and don't usually know the difference between the English types noun and adjective, but they do know the difference between letters and a whole variety of numbers. There are many predefined types that Unity 3D is aware of. If you add that to the ability to create new types of data, the kinds of data we can store is practically unlimited.

The C# built-in types are sometimes called POD, or plain old data. The term *POD* came from the original C++ standard which finds its origin dating back to 1979. POD types have not fundamentally changed from their original implementation.

Programmers define the word *type* to describe the variety of data to be stored. Variables are created using declarations. Declaration is defined as a formal statement or announcement.

Each set of words a programmer writes is called a statement. In English we'd use the word *sentence*, but programmers like to use their own vocabulary. Declaration statements for variables define both the type and the identifier for a variable.

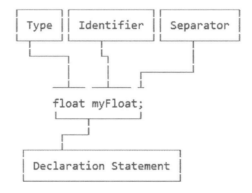

The Unity Inspector panel allows us to see variables in action. With the Variables GameObject in the Variables_Scene selected, the Inspector panel reveals three variables declared as seen in the example code below.

```
public float MultiplyBy;/*→      ①         */
public float InputValue;/*→   | values are */
public float Result;/*←       | assigned   */
void Update()        /*       |            */
{   /*                        |            */
    /*                        |            */
    /* ↑          ↓           ↓            */
    Result = InputValue * MultiplyBy;
    /* ↑          ↓           ↓            */
    /* |result is    | * |                 */
    /* ③updated        ② operation         */
    /*                   is performed      */
}
```

The Three identifiers `InputValue`, `MultiplyBy`, and `Result` are declared and made visible to the Editor. In the `Update()` function we assign `Result` by multiplying `InputValue` by `MultiplyBy`. If you change either `InputValue` or `MultiplyBy` you'll see the `Result` automatically Update the value seen to the right of the Identifier.

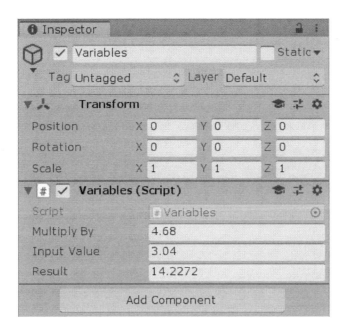

You may have noticed the keyword `public` before the `float`; we'll explain that later in Chapter 4 where we discuss access modifiers. In this case, this tells Unity 3D to show that variable in the Inspector panel with the attached script. By placing the `Result` calculation in the `Update()` function we ensure that the calculation is updated every frame.

3.10.3 Variable Manipulation

Declaring a variable creates space in the computer's memory for a value. The manifestation of this can be seen by the box to the right of the declared identifier in the Inspector panel in Unity 3D. In the previous example, we made space for three values. Unity 3D took the first two values and modified the value stored for `Result`.

Now that we know what parts are required to make a variable declaration, what can we do with them? Once a variable has been declared and assigned it can be reassigned at any time.

```
int i = 0;
System.Console.Write(i);
// i has been assigned 0

i = 1;
System.Console.Write(i);
// i reasssigned to 1
```

On the second line the variable i is no longer 0; it's 1 now. If we check what value is being stored at i we'd find a 1. So long as i is not assigned again, i will retain its value.

```
int i = 1;
```

```
[♥] (local variable) int i

A local variable or function named 'i' is already defined in this scope

The variable 'i' is assigned but its value is never used

Show potential fixes (Alt+Enter or Ctrl+.)
```

To create another declaration of i in the same block of code will produce an error as we're trying to create a declaration for i twice. A declaration for i has already been made the identifier cannot be declared more than once.

3.10.3.1 Declaration Placement Examples

A valid variable declaration can only appear in a few places in your code. Some of the conditions for valid placement of a variable declaration are related to something called scope which will be covered in further detail in Chapter 4. To ease into variable declaration, we'll confine our attention to declaring a variable to a single class. A declaration for someInt should appear between the opening and closing curly braces of a class.

```
int outterInt;
```

```
●ₐ (field) int <invalid-global-code>.outterInt

A namespace cannot directly contain members such as fields or methods

Show potential fixes (Alt+Enter or Ctrl+.)
```

```
class SomeClass
{
    int innerInt;
}
```

The code above shows a problem with the first outterInt declaration happening above the definition of class SomeClass. The declaration of int innerInt inside of SomeClass is allowed, as we have seen demonstrated before.

One common mistake many new and old programmers make is forgetting to add the semicolon to the end of a statement. Visual Studio helps a great deal with pop-ups like the one above. The red squiggle lines underline problems and highlight errors which keep Unity from running your code.

We've now completed two important tasks. We created a variable identifier giving the variable a way to access the contents of the variable. C# under the hood gave that variable some space in your computer's memory to put an integer. The int variable is now defined as SomeNumber, an object we can fill with a number with practically any int value.

When variables are declared for the first time, or initialized, in C# they are usually immediately given a value. This is not true with all types of variables, but number values are assigned 0 when they are created. For more complex data types their default value is null when they are initialized. This initialization behavior will become useful later when we start inspecting the values of variables.

3.10.4 Dynamic Initialization

When we both define and assign a variable we use the term *dynamic initialization*. Some data types automatically give themselves a default value when they are initialized without an assignment. For instance, a Boolean automatically assumes it's false when it's created.

```
bool SomeBool;
bool AnotherBool = false;
```

In this case, if we were to use SomeBool before assigning it then the result would act as though it were initialized false. In the above example both SomeBool and AnotherBool have the same value. Likewise, most numbers are initialized to 0 (zero).

```
int SomeInt;
int AnotherInt = 0;
```

So in this case both SomeInt and AnotherInt have the same value. However, this changes when we dynamically assign a value to a variable when initializing.

```
int OtherInt = 7;
int LastInt = 11;
```

When we assign a value to an int when it's initialized we skip the default initialization, and the value assumes its assignment when it's created.

3.10.5 What We've Learned

Variables are stored in your computer's memory. By defining a variable by its type, you instruct the computer to set aside a block of memory in the computer's RAM (Random Access Memory) to store data. To access the data you give it a name, or an identifier.

Once the identifier has been defined you can assign or read the data stored in memory through its identifier. In many cases the identifier needs to be unique. Depending on when it was created an identifier might have the same name as one created before it.

When this happens you get an error telling you that a variable has already been defined with that identifier. Changing one or the other's name solves the problem. When creating identifiers we need to consider what they're used for and how to name them.

Some code standards place rules on how an identifier should be named. For instance, a bool might always start with is to indicate how it's used. Therefore, a zombie might have isWalking or isRunning, indicating what it's doing. Other standards might use a prefix b for bools, so bWalking or bRunning could be used to indicate the same thing. How you decide to name variables is up to you, but it's good to know what we're about to get into so far as naming variables, which we'll be covering next.

3.11 Variable Names

Continuing in the Variables_Scene open the VariableNames.cs script in the Assets directory of the Chapter3 Unity 3D Project. It's important to know that variable identifiers and class identifiers can be pretty much anything. There are some rules to naming anything when programming. Here are some guidelines to help. Long names are more prone to typos, so keep identifiers short. A naming convention for variables should consider the following points:

- Short and easy to remember
- Succinct and to the point
- Meaningful but not long
- Unique
- Avoid special characters
- Describes what it's used for

The variable name should indicate what it's used for, or at least what you're going to do with it. This should be obvious, but a variable name shouldn't be misleading. Or rather, if you're using a variable named radius, you shouldn't be using it as a character's velocity. It's also helpful if you can pronounce the variable's name; otherwise, you're likely to have issues when trying to explain your code to another programmer.

```
public int SomeLongComplexHardToRememberVariableName;
```

If you were to use a long complex hard to remember variable name, Unity 3D wouldn't be able to show you the entire name in the Inspector panel.

There is an advantage to keeping names as short as possible, but still quite clear. Your computer screen, and most computers for that matter, can only fit so many characters on a single line. You could make the font smaller, but then you run into readability issues when letters get too small.

Consider the following function, which requires more than one variable to work.

```
SomeCleverFunction(TopLeftCorner - SomeThickness + OffsetFromSomePosition,
BottomRightCorner - SomeThickness + OffsetFromSomePosition);
```

The code above uses many long variable names. Because of the length of each variable, the statement takes up multiple lines making a single statement harder to read. We could shorten the variable names, but it's easy to shorten them too much.

```
CleverFunc(TL-Thk+Ofst, LR-Thk+Ofst);
```

Variable names should be descriptive, so you know what you're going to be using them for; too short and they might lose their meaning.

```
int a;
```

While short and easy to remember, it's hard for anyone else coming in to read your code and know what you're using the variable a for. This becomes especially difficult when working with other programmers. Variable naming isn't completely without rules.

```
int 8;
```

A variable name can't be a number. This is bad; numbers have a special place in programming as much of it has other uses for them. MonoDevelop will try to help you spot problems. A squiggly red line will appear under any problems it spots. And speaking of variable names with numbers, you can use a number as part of a variable name.

```
int varNumber2;
```

The above name is perfectly valid, and can be useful, but conversely consider the following.

```
int 13thInt;
```

Variable names can't start with any numbers. To be perfectly honest, I'm not sure why this case breaks the compiler, but it does seem to be related to why numbers alone can't be used as variable names.

```
int $;
int this-that;
int (^_^);
```

Most special characters also have meanings, and are reserved for other uses. For instance, in C# the minus or dash character (-) is used for subtraction; in this case C# may think you're trying to subtract that from this. Keywords, you should remember, are also invalid variable names as they already have a special meaning for C#. In MonoDevelop, you might notice that the word this is highlighted, indicating that it's a keyword. Spaces in the middle of a variable are also invalid.

```
int spaces are bad;
```

Most likely, adding characters that aren't letters will break the compiler. Only the underscore and letters can be used for identifier names. As fun as it might be to use emoticons for a variable, it would be quite difficult to read when in use with the rest of the code.

```
int ADifferenceInCase;
int adifferenceincase;
```

The two variables here are different. Case-sensitive languages like C# do pay attention to the case of a character; this goes for everything else when calling things by name. Considering this: A is different from a.

NOTE: Trained programmers are often taught a variation of naming conventions, which yields easier-to-read code. Much of this is dependent on scope, which we will discuss in Section 4.4.4. There are also conventions which always prefix variable names with an indication of what sort of data is stored by that variable.

As a programmer, you need to consider what a variable should be named. It must be clear to you and anyone else with whom you'll be sharing your work with. You'll also be typing your variable name many times, so they should be short and easy to remember and type.

The last character we discuss here is the little strange @ or at. The @ can be used only if it's the first character in a variable's name.

```
int @home;
int noone@home;
int nobodyhome@;
```

In the second variable declared here we'll get an error. Some of these less regular characters are easy to spot in your code. When you have a long list of variables it's sometimes best to make them stand out visually. Some classically trained programmers like to use an underscore to indicate a class scope variable. The underscore is omitted in variables which exist only within a function.

You would find the reason for the odd rule regarding @ when you use int, which is reserved as a keyword. You're allowed to use int @int, after which you can assign @int any integer value. However, many programmers tend to use MyInt, mint, or _int instead of @int based on their programming upbringing.

Good programmers will spend a great deal of time coming up with useful names for their variables and functions. Coming up with short descriptive names takes some getting used to, but here are some useful tips. Variables are often named using nouns or adjectives as they describe an attribute related to what they're used for.

A human character can often have a health attribute. Naming this `HealthPoints` or `NumberOfHealthPoints` is sometimes considered too wordy, or even redundant. However, if you and your friends are accustomed to paper role-playing games, then perhaps HitPoints would be preferred.

In the end, once you start using the name of the variable throughout the rest of your code, it becomes harder to change it as it will need to be changed everywhere it's used. Making a global change like this is known as refactoring. Visual Studio can help change the name of a class, variable, or function throughout a project by refactoring your code.

NOTE: You may also notice the pattern in which uppercase and lowercase letters are used. This is referred to as either BumpyCase or CamelCase. Sometimes, the leading letter is lowercase, in which case it will look like headlessCamelCase rather than NormalCamelCase.

Many long debates arise between programmers as to which is correct, but in the end either one will do. Because C# is case sensitive, you and anyone helping you should agree whether or not to use a leading uppercase letter.

These differences usually come from where a person learned how to write software or who taught that person. The use of intermixed uppercase and lowercase is a part of programming style. Style also includes how white space is used.

When you name variables in Unity 3D the use of CamelCase or BumpyCase will automatically separate the different words indicated by an uppercase letter in the Inspector panel. This doesn't actually affect how the declaration was written. This will only change how your variable's name appears in the Unity 3D Editor.

3.11.1 Useful Variables in Unity 3D

Open the UsefulVariables_Scene in Chapter3/Assets. Open the UsefulVariables.cs script attached to the game object of the same name in the scene.

Unity 3D is a great way to demonstrate what variables look like and how they act. When variables of different types are added to a script the Inspector represents the data type in various different ways.

```
public bool MyBool;
public int MyInt;
public int MyOtherInt = 700;
public float MyFloat;
public string MyString;
public Vector3 MyVector3;
```

Adding the keyword `public` before the type and the identifier informs the Unity 3D Editor to expose the variable to the Inspector panel. The different types change how the variable is represented in the Inspector. You may also notice that `MyBool` has a space added to show "My Bool" next to the checkbox. Unity 3D formats bumpy text into different words for readability, but it doesn't actually change the text in your code.

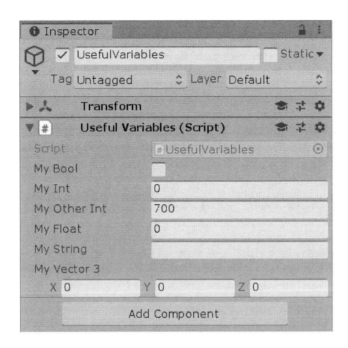

By setting values in the Inspector panel, we tell the script what values to start with when the script is run. The `Int` and `Float` we declared are by default initialized to 0 when they appear in the Inspector.

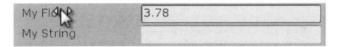

Dragging on the `My Float` item left and right adjusts the value stored on the object in the scene. Many variable types are initialized with a default value if nothing is provided when they are declared.

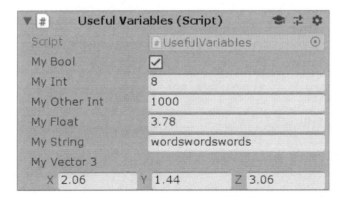

Initialization is the process by which variables and other chunks of data are created and stored for the first time in a class object. Initialization can be either automatically declared, like `MyInt` or `MyFloat`, or declared as variables are initialized. Or they can be dynamically assigned like `MyOtherInt` where we assigned 700. The default values will be overwritten when they are edited in the Inspector panel.

If you make changes to the default values and save the scene, the changes will be saved to the scene where the script is used. To bring the defaults back, right click on the script's component title bar and select Reset to revert the values to those declared in the script.

Integers or int are whole numbers. Numbers which have a decimal in them are not integer values. Such numbers, having values with fractions, have several different names, for example, float, or double. We'll go into some more depth as to what number types mean in Chapter 4. You'll notice you're not able to change MyInt to 0.1 or any number with a decimal point in it. The fields provided for each parameter is limited to the type of value that's allowed to be entered. We'll study why this is in the next chapter.

3.11.2 Variable Assignment

We stepped through some basic guidelines regarding assignment of variables, but what happens when we change the assignment? The variables' assignment happens one line at a time. The computer starts at the top of the code and works its way down one line at a time. What this means is, the value of a variable shows its changes only after the assignment is made.

For instance, in the following code sample we'll start off with one variable and change its assignment several times and print the results.

```
/* int declares a new thing        */
/* assignment operator = assigns    */
/* the new int thing a value        */
/*                                  */
/*              =                   */
/*         ↓         ↑              */
int MyVariable = 7;
/*         ↓                        */
/*                                  */
/*         ↓                        */
Debug.Log(MyVariable);
/* Debug.Log prints to the console  */
/* what is in it's argument list () */
// 7
/*            MyVariable            */
/*  ↓         ↑ gets a new value    */
MyVariable = 13;
Debug.Log(MyVariable);
// 13
/* the new value is printed         */

MyVariable = 3;
Debug.Log(MyVariable);
// 3
MyVariable = 73;
Debug.Log(MyVariable);
// 73
```

With the code included in a new C# script named Variables assigned to the GameObject in the scene of the same name, we'll get the following output in the Console panel.

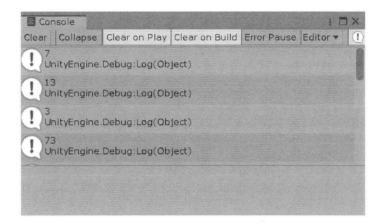

Using the same variable named MyVariable and after assigning it different values, we get different numbers printed to the Console panel. This is because the identifier MyVariable is nothing more than its value; it's just a number. In other words, we could use the following code fragment and get the same result from both print outputs.

```
int MyVariable = 7;
/* terms are                    then the */
/* evaluated    ① ( 7 + 7 ) result is*/
/* first        ②=( 14 )      printed  */
Debug.Log(MyVariable + MyVariable);
// 14            ③ 14 appears in the console
/* this is functionally the same as */
Debug.Log(7 + 7);/* this               */
// 14
```

If we want to mix variables together, we can do that too. Because MyVariable is an integer value, we can treat it like any other integer, or whole number. This can be demonstrated best with another int variable.

```
int MyVariable = 7;
int MyOtherVariable = 3;

/*  terms are    ( 7 * 3 )           */
Debug.Log(MyVariable * MyOtherVariable);
// 21
/* the same as   ( 7 * 3)            */
Debug.Log(MyVariable * 3);
// 21
```

Here we'll get an expected 21 printed out to the Console panel from both Debug.Log functions. To be clear, MyVariable * MyOtherVariable and MyVariable * 3 are equivalent. Next, let's consider what happens when we assign a variable to another variable:

```
int MyVariable = 7;
int MyOtherVariable = 3;
Debug.Log(MyVariable * MyOtherVariable);
// 21
/*      ┌──←=(3)┐ MyVariable              */
/*      ↓        ↑ gets a new value       */
MyVariable = MyOtherVariable;

/*  terms are     ( 3 * 3 )              */
Debug.Log(MyVariable * MyOtherVariable);
// 9
```

Now we have `MyVariable` being assigned the value that is `MyOtherVariable`. Therefore, let's think through this logic. `MyOtherVariable` is assigned a value of 3, so if we assign `MyVariable` a value of 3 the second print function will return `MyVariable * MyOtherVariable`. This means it's actually just 3 * 3, which means 9 will be printed out to the Console panel.

3.11.3 Putting It Together: Using the Variables

We've named variables and given them assignments. It's about time we start to consider how to apply these new concepts to something useful in Unity 3D. Open the UsingTheVariables_Scene in the Chapter3 Unity Project.

We'll start off with a basic scene with a handy TransformPrimitive; we'll be seeing this gizmo quite often. Next, open the `UsingTheVariables` script attached to the TransformPrimitive in Visual Studio. To start with, we're going to add in a `public` variable at the class level. We will be getting to what this all means in Section 4.4.3, but for now what we're doing is making this variable available to the rest of the functions as well as the Editor.

```
public float RotationSpeed;
public float Rotation;
```

Your code should look like the one above. Now, hopping back into Unity 3D you should see both `RotationSpeed` and `Rotation` in the Inspector panel.

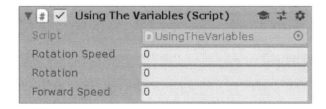

This little thing has a 0 in it; that's what we want. We'll be making use of this variable in the `Update()` function found in the class. Let's add the following code to the `Update()` function and see how it works.

```
Rotation += RotationSpeed * Time.deltaTime;
```

The `Time.deltaTime` object is a useful value. The calculation of the value comes from the amount of time that passes between updates. The `Update()` method is run once per frame. Slow computers struggle to update as often as faster computers.

More time passes between updates on a slow machine. If you want a value to update at the same speed on both slow and fast machines `Time.deltaTime` is a good way to regulate how much a value is changed when it's updated. As an example, if you have a machine that runs at 100 frames per second then 1/100th of a second passes between `Update()` calls. On a machine that runs at 10 frames per second 1/10th of a second passes between frames. You can't rely on `Update()` to increment a value at the same speed in both situations.

When the Play-in-Editor button is pressed we see the `Rotation` value increment up based on `Rotation Speed` values.

With this we can plug the `Rotation` value into the object's rotation with the following code:

```
transform.localEulerAngles = new Vector3(0, Rotation, 0);
```

Small values in `RotationSpeed` will rotate the object very slowly. In the Inspector you can watch the `Y` of the `Rotation` in the `Transform` component update with the same value as seen in `Rotation`. Also try assigning negative values to rotate the transform primitive the other way.

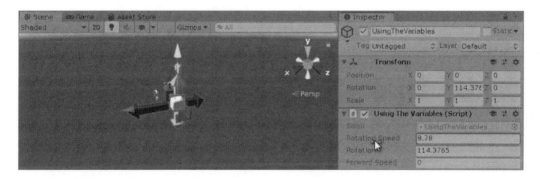

Play with this for a little bit; just make sure `RotationSpeed` is a value other than 0.

To make this more interesting, we'll add `public float ForwardSpeed;` after the `Rotation Speed` and the `Rotation` variables.

```
public float RotationSpeed;
public float Rotation;
public float ForwardSpeed;
```

With this we could modify the position of the Transform primitive object.

```
transform.position += transform.forward * (ForwardSpeed * Time.deltaTime);
```

The line above should appear after the `transform.localEulerAngles` are updated. With three lines of code and two inputs, a `ForwardSpeed` and a `RotationSpeed` variable we've created a small sort of steerable object.

We haven't quite created a driving simulator, but we've only written three lines of code to move around a funny looking colored arrow mesh. Altogether, there is actually quite a lot of interesting things to play with here.

3.11.4 What We've Learned

We're taking very small steps to start off. There's a great deal of new concepts for you to absorb and many questions to be asked. If there is anything unclear then take a moment to go back and review.

So far, we've mostly covered terms related to writing C#. Learning about programming is somewhat about learning new vocabulary, and we've covered keywords and a few operators and variables. We just wrote variables to a C# class object and added it to an object in our Unity 3D scene.

C# is an OOP paradigm. Every class is an object. Once we learn how to write our own objects, we'll learn how to read other objects and possibly even begin to understand the complexity laid out in Unity 3D's library.

3.12 Types: A First Look

For this chapter we'll look at the Types script found in Chapter3 Project Assets directory. When we assign a variable a value such as int i = 1; we're making an interesting assumption. We assume using 1 automatically infers a value type that matches the variable type. Computers use a wide variety of different types of data for storing numbers.

We've been seeing the keyword int being thrown around as though you know what an int is. In our everyday lives we hardly think there's any difference between numbers 1 and 1.0 or even the word *one*. As humans we can easily conceptualize numbers as units of measure and converting between them. The conversion between the word *one* and the number 1 isn't so easy for a computer.

The keyword int is short for integer. Integers are whole number values. The integer is a C# built-in type, as mentioned before it's considered plain old data. Basically, this means that integers are a fundamental part of C#. Other built-in types include float, double, string, bool, and object. Less commonly used built-in types are char, short, and byte. Altogether, there are 15 different built-in types. All of these, except object and string, are value types.

Every type of data you're able to build must be based on built-in types. The system which creates floats, doubles, and bools is rooted in the origin of computing. Remember the punch tapes and pieces of paper with holes in them? Those were records of 1s and 0s which were fed into computers for storing in the form of mechanical switches, either on or off. The patterns represented numbers or instructions and logic.

Today, we still use the same system of 1s and 0s, or binary, only we don't need to punch holes in paper to tell the computer what to do. The methods of creating and storing the instructions have become many times more complex, but nonetheless the principle of the 1 and 0 are the same. These are called bits; one possible origin for that name is the little bits of paper that were left over from punching holes in the paper cards.

3.12.1 Value and Reference Types

The int, float, double, and bool are commonly used value types. The basics of this usage pattern relate to the system that stores and organizes the computer's memory. When you talk about computer storage you use the word *megabyte* or *gigabyte*. Value types are stored with a very specific purpose in mind: to keep track of a numeric value.

NOTE: The word *mega* refers to how many millions of bytes a component in your computer can store. *Giga* indicates how every many billions of bytes are being stored. Have you ever thought about what a byte actually is?

A byte is what's called an 8-bit unsigned integer, or a system of using 8 bits to form a number. What this means is, it's a whole number like 0, 7, or 32,767. The word *unsigned* indicates that the number cannot be negative, like –512.

A 1 or 0 in computer terms is called a bit. We won't go into detail on how computers use bits to count, and it's a rather fun thing to learn on your own. However, it's important to know that a byte has a limited range, from 0 to 255. I'll just leave you with the idea that you could count up to 1023 on your 10 fingers if you used binary rather than decimal. Your fingers can be used to represent a 10-bit unsigned integer. The computer's calculation capabilities used to be far more limited than they are today. An 8-bit game console made in the 1980s had a limited number of colors, 256 to be exact. This limitation was based on the number of bits that the processor could handle. The processor had a limited number of transistors which could be used at any one time. Shortly after, floating point co-processors were introduced, which had a much larger numeric range allowed, by having closer to 32 bits to work with.

In all of these cases, when you use a value type, that number is actually stored as 1s and 0s in your computer's RAM. This should be considered remarkable. In the past you'd have to go through flaming hoops to store a value. Now you just type in `float f = 3.1415926535;` and you can measure the circumference of the galaxy accurately to within the width of a single atom.

What all these types have in common is that they are stored as a single element. Large values like `double gigawatts = 1210000000.0` and `double mint = 2.0` use the same amount of memory.

Your computer doesn't assign one double or the other more space in memory. These types are referred to as *primitive types*. The only difference between an `int` and a `float` is the number of bits they use at a time, 8 and 32 respectively; `doubles` use 64 bits.

The `string` and `object` types differ a bit in how they are stored. These types are a composite of any number smaller elements. The bigger a string or object the bigger chunk of memory the computer opens to place that object or string. These are called *reference types* or sometimes called *nullable types* because C# doesn't look to a single element in memory to get data from it.

We will explain nullable types in Section 4.4.1.2, but in short, a nullable type is a space in memory which is reserved for data that has yet to be fulfilled. Primitive or value types are commonly reserved and assigned at the same time. There are systems which allow this to be changed, but we're getting ahead of ourselves for now.

In Unity 3D, a commonly used type is the Vector3. Vectors, in the math world, are directions in *x*, *y*, and *z* with a length. Unity 3D uses vectors to keep track of a position in 3D space. The `Vector3` type is a composite of three `float` variables. This means that a Vector3 is made up of different components. From this, we may infer that a `Vector3` is a *nullable* type. Each float is labeled x, y, and z. However, unlike the primitive types the `Vector3` needs to be instanced. This means that you can't simply use the following syntax.

```
int i = 0;//a valid initialization of an int.
Vector3 v1 = (x = 0, y = 0, z = 0);//not valid initialization.
Vector3 v2 = new Vector3();//this is how it's done.
```

Nullable types need to be initialized; that is, they need some form of initial value. We'll go into further detail on this later. It's important to remember there are differences between types when they are being initialized. Later on, as you begin to create and use objects and variables it'll be important to remember how to initialize the different variable types.

3.12.2 What We've Learned

There are many different forms which data can take. Each form is called a type. The different forms depend on how they are organized and how they are initialized. Reference or nullable types require some form of initial parameters before they can be used. Value or primitive types usually have an initial value when they are created.

When variables are declared, they are assigned a type. The type changes how the variable behaves and what values it's allowed to store. As we move forward, remembering how types behave is important. C#, and many other C-like programming languages, has specific rules with how to deal with data of differing types.

3.13 Strong Typing

Continue with the same Types script from the previous chapter. Strong typing has nothing to do with how hard you type on the keyboard! C# sees a difference between numbers in how they are written. A whole number like 1 is different from 1.0, even though we can think of them as having the same value. Some of these differences can be added by adding a letter. Therefore, 1.0 and 1.0f are different numbers as well.

C# is a *strongly* typed programming language. When a programming language uses strong types, you're expected to keep the different types separated. This means that a 1 + 1.0f can create a problem. Because the two numbers are actually different types of numbers we must convert one of them to match the other before the operation can take place.

To convert from one type to another we must tell C# that we intend to make that conversion from a 1 to a 1.0 by using what's called a *cast operator.* Thus, 1 + 1.0 will either become 1 + 1 or 1.0 + 1.0 depending on what operation you choose. Aside from changing how memory is used, types also limit any problems which might come about when working in a team of programmers.

If one programmer is new to your game and has made assumptions about hit points being in floating point values, he'd quickly find out as soon as he looked that you're using integer values and change how he intends to use those numbers. Value types not only store a value assigned to them but also provide a great deal of information to be inferred by the programmer reading the code.

```
Vector3 vec = new Vector3(1.0, 1.0, 1.0);
```

In Unity, the statement Vector3 vec = new Vector3(1.0, 1.0, 1.0) will throw an error. The number 1.0 is called a double, which uses 64 bits, whereas 1.0f, which is a float, uses 32 bits. The difference means float 1.0f is half the size of the double 1.0 in memory. A Vector3 is made up of three float values, not three doubles.

```
float f = 1.0f;
double d = 1.0;
```

Therefore, in terms of declaring a variable and assigning it float f = 1.0f and double d = 1.0; the same type problems exist as with assigning a Vector3 (), which is made of three different float values. To properly tell C# you mean a 32-bit version of 1.0 would be to add an f after the number: 1.0f means you want to use the 32-bit version of 1.0 and not the 64-bit version of 1.0. Therefore, to declare Vector3 vec = new Vector3 (1.0f, 1.0f, 1.0f); is the correct way to assign a proper Vector3().

Confused? I'd imagine so; we'll clear things up in a bit. Just hang in there.

For our purposes of learning how to code, knowing anything about bits may not mean a lot. However, if you ever talk to a programmer it'll be very important that you know the difference. Before getting too far ahead we should know that Unity 3D uses floats and ints quite often. There is also a difference between the different data types in that they cannot be simply used interchangeably without consequence.

3.13.1 Dynamic Typing

Not all programming languages are so strict with types, but it's a good idea to get used to working with strict types before learning more lazily typed programming languages, like Lua (http://www.lua.org/). These are sometimes called "Duck"-typed languages; this refers to the proverb "if it looks like a duck and it sounds like a duck, it's probably a duck." Type conversion is important for learning more complex languages like C, or C++. These languages offer a wider number of platforms and a more detailed level of control.

With dynamically typed languages like Lua or UnrealScript, you can run into strange hard-to-track-down bugs. However, when it comes to a type we might see something like this:

```
var i = 1; // int?
if(i) // bool?
{
    Console.WriteLine("is " + i + "i true or a 1?"); // int string or a bool?
    i = i * 0.1; // now is i a double?
}
```

In the above it's not clear what the variable i is supposed to be, is it a bool or an int or a double? When var above starts off as an integer, but we use it as a bool and then multiply it by a floating point value, what is i? What have we turned it into if we want to use it as something else, or how do we turn it back?

As we will see in Section 7.14.4, we are allowed to make some exceptions to the type of a variable. The keywords var and dynamic do mean you're expecting an unexpected type to be coming, but once it's there, you had better know what to do with it.

3.13.2 What We've Learned

We have glossed over the specifics of how numbers work in the computer's memory, but we'll get into that in Section 6.20.2. Superficially, we should know that not all numbers are the same. A byte is 8 bits, a nibble is 4. An int is 32 bits, and an int64 is 64 bits, but that's not all. A float is also 32 bits and a double is 64 bits, but these can't hold the same values as an int or int64.

The float and double use some of their bits called a mantissa to hold the numbers after the decimal. Therefore, 1.01 requires some of the bits to represent the 1, and these are called the significant digits. The mantissa uses some bits to represent the other 1 in the number. Then there are more bits set aside to tell C# where the dot (.) goes in the number, and these bits are called the exponent. Therefore, with 1.02, the exponent tells the mantissa 2 to move an extra zero after the dot, so 1.02 is the final result.

We take for granted the work going on under the hood to store a simple number. All of this happens thanks to many computer scientists who have worked in the last several decades. Konrad Zuse and John von Neumann introduced a system of floating point representation to computing in the 1940s, with the Z1 and later the Z3. Their system is roughly the same system in use today.

3.14 Type Casting, Numbers

Continue with the Types script from the previous chapter. Data in C# comes in various forms. Not just number type, but a class or any object for that matter becomes a new type of data. At least, numbers can be thought of as having comparable value. Casting is a tricky topic which we'll come back to a few more times.

The following is a simple exercise, but an important one nonetheless. When you start to deal with keeping score, or recording injuries to a monster, it's important that behaviors are predictable. Many problems begin to show up if the math you're using involves mixing numbers with decimal values like floats or doubles, or with integers which have no fractional value.

```
int hundredInt = 100;
```

Decimals are not allowed on an int value. In this case, 100.2 is not an int data type.

```
float hundredFloat = 100.0f;
double hundredDouble = 100.0;
```

Decimals are allowed for both float and double. The only caveat is that a float requires an f post fixed to the number when it's assigned.

Converting types between one another is simple when you need to deal with numbers. When we start creating our own classes the task of casting becomes a bit more detailed, but not necessarily more difficult; there's just a bit more work involved. We'll get to that soon enough.

When we go between number types or the built-in value types (POD), we work with things which seem to come with C#. So far we've seen things like int and float. Integer values like 1, 7, and 19 are useful for counting. We use these for counting numbers of items in an array, or how many zombies are in a scene, for instance. Integers are whole numbers, even though we might be counting zombies whole or not.

Once we start needing numbers with fractions we need to use float values. To get an object's speed or *x*, *y*, and *z* coordinates in space we need to use values like 12.612f, or x = 13.33f, to accurately place an object in space. If not, objects would move around in a scene as though they were chess pieces locked to a grid.

When a float value exists as 0.9f we lose some values after the decimal when converting the floating point value to an integer.

```
float a = 0.9f;
int b = (int)a;
Debug.Log(b);
```

If we observe the above code in the Types_Scene in Unity 3D running by pressing the Play-in-Editor button, we'll see the following output in the Console panel.

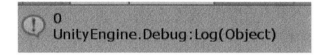

Without the cast operator int b = a; we get an error telling us we need to cast the value before assigning it.

```
Assets/Types.cs(75,17): error CS0266: Cannot implicitly convert type `float'
to `int'. An explicit conversion exists (are you missing a cast?)
```

The first part of the error message says "Cannot implicitly convert type," which has a very specific meaning that we'll get to before the end of this chapter, but first let's cover explicit type casting.

3.14.1 Explicit versus Implicit Casting

As we have seen, in the Start () function where we declared float a = 0.9f; a was converted to 0. Even though we were only 0.1f away from 1f to 0.9f away from 0 we're left with a 0 instead assigned to int b. To do these conversions we use the explicit casting method, as shown with (int) a;, which explicitly tells C# to convert the value stored at a to a float value. When we are required to use an explicit cast, we're also warned that there may be some data lost in the conversion.

Casting is a process by which C# changes the type of a variable to another type. This may or may not involve a loss of information. In some cases, the conversion doesn't require the explicit cast operator. The following code casts an int to a float.

```
int c = 3;

float d = c;

Debug.Log(d);
```

With the above code we get a 3 printed out to the Console panel. We didn't need to use an explicit casting operator. This is because when we cast from an int, in this case 3, there would be no data loss when it's cast to a float. This is possible through an implicit cast. Implicit casts are allowed only when there is no data lost in the process of converting from one type to another.

There are no integer values which will result in a loss of any value when it's converted to a float. Technically, there are more float numbers between 0 and 1 than there are integer numbers between 0 and 1, or any other sequence of two numbers for that matter.

3.14.1.1 A Basic Example

Continuing on with the Types script we've been using for the last few chapters.

```
int mInt = 1;
double mDub= 0.9;
int c = mInt * mDub;
```

If we look at what is going on here we'll want to think for a moment about what it means. The integer mInt is assigned 1 and double mDub has 0.9 assigned. We should assume that 0.9 will be assigned to c after the multiplication, but this assignment is stopped by a type conversion error. C# usually gives us pretty clear reasons for its errors. In this case we know there's a cast missing between an int and a double. We get the "Cannot implicitly convert type 'double' to 'int'." error.

The error states we can't implicitly convert a double to an int. Why not? 1 certainly looks like 1.0, or so it seems. However, 0.9 can't be turned into an integer. There's no integer between 0 and 1. Even though 0.9 is very close to being 1, it's not.

```
int c = mInt * (int)mDub;
```

We use type conversion to tell C# to explicitly change b from a double to an int by preceding the b with (int). What value is going to be assigned to c if it can't be 0.9? The (int) operator is an explicit cast. Casting with the explicit operator works by using the destined type surrounded by the () operators.

If we read the cast value for (int)mDub is 0, which means we've lost data going from the double value to an integer value. Even though 0.9 is almost a 1, the first int value is 0, followed by values that are cut off by the type conversion. Now we see why type conversion matters.

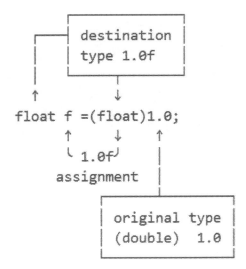

In a simple case, observe the type double 1.0 preceded by the (float) operator. The type assigned to the operator matches the destination float f. We will find other casts which look like this in Sections 6.14 and 6.20, but we're introducing the concept early on as it's a very common problem to come across. The syntax (int) turns a number following this operator into an int. Likewise int i = 0; double d = (double) i; is a way to cast an int into a double. However, this isn't always necessary.

Some conversions take place automatically as an implicit cast. In the above example we can use the following code without any problems.

```
int anotherInt = 1;
double anotherDouble = 0.9;
int yetAnotherInt = anotherInt * (int)anotherDouble;
Debug.Log("yetAnotherInt: " + yetAnotherInt);
double yetAnotherDouble = yetAnotherInt;

// this doesn't need a cast
Debug.Log("yetAnotherDouble: " + yetAnotherDouble);
```

Here we assign double d = a; where a is int 1, which we know isn't a double. This produces no errors. The same goes if we add another line float f = a;. In this case f is a float. These are called implicit casts. An integer value doesn't have a mantissa or an exponent. Both the double and float do have these two possibly large and important values. These two terms were explained at the end of Chapter 2.

When mashing a double into an int we lose the mantissa and exponent. By using an explicit cast, we tell C# that we don't mind losing the data. This doesn't mean that an implicit cast will not lose any data either. An int can hold more significant values than a float. We can observe this with the following lines of code added to the Start () function.

```
int largeInt = 2147483647;
Debug.Log("largeInt: " + largeInt);
float largeFloat = largeInt;
Debug.Log("largeFloat: " + largeFloat);
int backAgain = (int)largeFloat;
Debug.Log("backAgain: " + backAgain);
```

This code produces the following console output, after a bit of cleaning up:

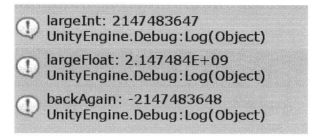

When we start with the value 2147483647 assigned to int we're at one extreme of the integer value. This is the biggest number the int can hold, for reasons discussed in Section 3.11.1, but in short, it's because it's using only 32 bits to store this number.

If we cast this into largeFloat we can use an implicit cast, which converts the value from int to float. In this case, we see only 2.147484 followed by the exponent E+09, which tells us that the dot (.) is actually nine places over to the right.

When we convert the float back into an int with an explicit cast we get a −2147483648, which is certainly not what we started with. This tells that there's some significant information lost in the conversion from float to int, but there were also numbers lost in the implicit cast from int to float.

This still happens if we remove a digit from the end.

```
int largeIntAgain = 214748361;
Debug.Log("largeIntAgain: " + largeIntAgain);
float largeFloatAgain = largeIntAgain;
Debug.Log("largeFloatAgain: " + largeFloatAgain);
int backAgainAgain = (int)largeFloatAgain;
Debug.Log("backAgainAgain: " + backAgainAgain);
```

This sends the following numbers to the Console:

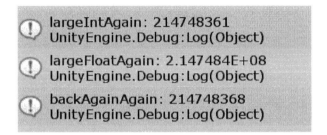

The last digit is changed from 1 to 8. The 8 is coming from some strange conversion when we go from int into float. Even if we look at the numbers being stored in the float value we can tell that there's already a change in value. This tells us that in general, we need to be very careful when converting from one type into another.

Logically, another difficult problem is converting from a string to a number value. When you use string s = "1"; you're not able to use (int)s to convert from a string to an int. The types of data are very different since strings can also contain letters and symbols. The conversion of (int) "five" has no meaning to the computer. There's no dictionary which is built into C# to make this conversion. This doesn't mean that there are no options.

```
string s = "1";
int fromString = int.Parse(s);
Debug.Log("fromString: " + fromString);
```

The code added to the Start () function will produce the following number:

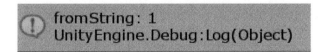

There are plenty of options when faced with dealing with significantly different types. The int.Parse() function is an option that we can use to convert one value into another. Again, we might be getting a bit ahead of ourselves, but it's important to see that there are different ways to convert between different types.

3.14.2 What We've Learned

In this chapter we used some syntax which has not been formerly introduced. For the sake of seeing what happens to numbers between casting we needed to do this. In Section 6.20, we will cover the details of what happened in this chapter, so don't worry. Everything in this chapter will be explained in detail soon enough.

We've still got a lot to cover about types. It's a bit early to see how they relate to one another and why there is a difference. Once we move into evaluating numbers we'll start to see how the different types interact. Accuracy is one place where we begin to see the effects of type conversion. A float with the value of 0.9 turns into 0 when it's converted to an int.

This chapter is just a cursory look at types. There's a lot more to conversion than just losing some numbers. Later on we'll see what happens when we need to convert between different game play characters like zombies and humans. Many attributes need to have specific conversions but then they're both bipedal creatures.

3.15 Comments

We've already been seeing plenty of comments in the code. All of the text between /* and */ are comments as well as text following // are comments. Comments are left as breadcrumbs to help keep notes in your code. Once a new line is started the // no longer applies and the next line is becomes visible to the lexical analyzer.

```
//these are not the lines you are looking for...
```

Programmers use comments for many reasons. Mostly, comments are used to describe what a function is used for. Quite often, comments are left as notes for both the person who wrote the code and for others. Sometimes, when a function is confusing, or isn't always working, a comment can be left as a "to do" list.

To facilitate the programmer, Visual Studio even has a window that reads comments and looks for the notation //TODO: and adds them to a list of tasks. You can find this in the View → Task List window. Where you might see the following:

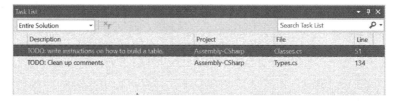

If you check in the window, you'll be able to jump to the line in the highlighted file by double clicking on the Task List item. Whatever text appears on that line will show up in the Task List.

Once we start writing our own functions, we'll want to leave comments to help remember what we were thinking when we wrote them. Sometimes, if we need help, we can indicate to our friends our intentions. You can leave comments like //I'm still working on this, I'll get back to it tomorrow... if you're still working on some code.

Or you can ask for help: //help, I can't figure out how to rotate the player, can someone else do this?! is a simple short comment. Even professional programmers leave comments for their co-workers, letting everyone who may be looking at their work a clue as to what was going on in their code.

In more than one case, the comments in a large code base needed to be cleaned up before releasing to the public. The engineers responsible needed to remove foul language from the comments to avoid any public ridicule. In some instances, the comments in the code were also defaming competing game engines.

When a comment requires more than a single line, use the following notation:

```
/* this is a multiline comment
   which can carry on to other lines
   you can keep on writing anything
   until you get to the following */
```

There are various styles which you can follow with multi-line comments.

```
/* this is also a multiline comment
 * but we have little * at the start
 * of each line and we finish this
 * with the closing comment on it's
 * own line
 */
```

Anything between the /* and the */ will be ignored by the C# compiler. It's often a good habit for a programmer to introduce a class by leaving a comment at the top of the file. For instance, it's common to see the following in a class written for other people to edit.

```
/* Player class written by Alex Okita
 * This class manages the player's data and logic
 */
```

The use of comments isn't limited to simple statements. They are often decorated by extra elements to help them stand out.

```
/*********************************************
 * This comment was written by Alex Okita *
 *********************************************/
```

Comments have several other uses which will come in handy; for instance, when testing code you can comment a section of code that you know works and test out new code next to the code commented out. If your test doesn't work you can always clear it out and un-comment the code that does work. We'll play with this idea later in this chapter.

Using comments on the same line of code is also a regular practice.

```
void MyFunction()
{
    int someInt = 0; // declaring some regular int as 0
}
```

We can inform anyone reading our code what a specific statement is doing. Although we want to be smart with how our comments are written, if we add too many comments in our code the actual statements that matter get lost between a bunch of words that don't matter.

Comments are also useful for testing different collections of code. When you're learning about how different behaviors affect the results of your functions it's often useful to keep different versions of your code around. This is often the case when trying to debug a problem and eliminate lines of code without having to completely get rid of them.

```
void MyOtherFunction()
{
    int someInt = 0;//I print 0 through 10
    //int someInt = 3; //starts at 3
    //int someInt = 11; //this won't print
    while (someInt < 10)
    {
        System.Console.WriteLine(someInt);
        someInt++;
    }
}
```

It's possible to test out various test cases using comments to allow you to pick and choose between different statements. In the above code fragment, we've got someInt declared three different ways. Depending on which line is left un-commented we can choose between different values.

We can leave another comment on the line after the statement, reminding us what the result was. For covering an entire section of code it's easier to use the /* */ form of commenting.

```
void AnotherFunction()
{
    int someInt = 0;//I print 0 through 10
                   //int someInt = 3;//starts at 3
                   //int someInt = 11;//this won't work, so leave me out.
                   //trying out new code here
    for (int i = 0; i < someInt; i++)
    {
        System.Console.WriteLine(someInt);
    }

    //the code below will do the same thing.
    /*
    while(someInt < 10) {
    System.Console.WriteLine(someInt);
    someInt++;
    }
    */
}
```

In the above code, we've commented out the while loop following the for loop which accomplishes the same task. In this way we can easily switch between the two different loops by switching which loop is commented out. Programmers often leave sections of code in their functions commented out so they verify the validity of the new code they've added in.

The /* */ notation for comments can also be used in smaller places. Anytime the // notation appears everything on the same line is commented out. Using the /* */ notation we can hide a segment of a line of code.

```
void InLineComment()
{
    int someInt = 0;

    while (someInt </*10*/100)
    {
        System.Console.WriteLine(someInt);
        someInt++;
    }
}
```

For instance, we can hide the 10 in the while loop and replace it with another number altogether. The /*10*/ is hidden from the computer so the 100 is the only part of the condition that's seen by the computer. This can easily get a bit uglier as a single statement can begin to stretch out and become unreadable.

```
Vector3(/* this is the x variable */1.0f,
    2.0f/* <- that was the Y variable*/,
    /* the z */3.0f/*variable is here*/);
```

Although the above code is perfectly valid, it's not recommended that something like this appear in your code. When mixing in too many comments a simple declaration can get ugly.

3.15.1 Line Numbers

Each line of code in Visual Studio is indicated in the margin of the Editor to the left. When Unity 3D or Visual Studio comes across a typo or some unexpected character it's indicated in the Console panel or the Visual Studio Error List.

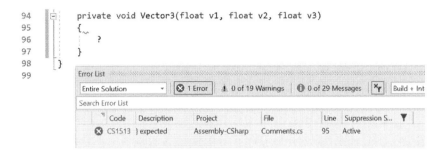

The Error List in Visual Studio tells us where an error may have occurred in our code. There's an expected } at line 95. Right after the line with the red squiggle you'll see a lonely ? in the middle of the function. Unity shows us a similar error.

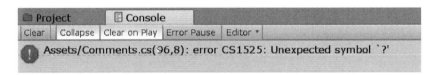

The error tells us: `Comments.cs(96,8): error CS1525: Unexpected symbol '?'`. The `(96,8)` tells us the position where the error is occurring. The first number is the line number. In the source code mentioned, we added in the ? on the 96th line. The 8 tells us that the character is on column 8, or the 8th character position from the left. If you were to count the number of spaces from the left you'd reach 8 and find the ?, which Unity 3D is erroring on.

This is a more precise example of an error, but we may not always be so fortunate. In general, the line number indicated is more or less a starting place where to start looking for an error. It's difficult to say when and how various errors take place in code, but in general, syntax errors tend to be fairly easy to fix. Difficulties arise when the code itself is using proper syntax but the result is erroneous or deviates from expected behavior.

When this happens we'll have to use other techniques to track down the bugs. We'll save those techniques for when we're ready for them. For now we'll just stick to learning proper syntax and comments.

3.15.2 Code Folding

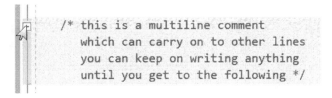

When you add in a long comment using the /* */ notation, MonoDevelop recognizes your comment.

Clicking on the little box in the number column will collapse the comment into a single line. This feature comes in most of the modern IDEs meant for writing in C#. This feature is also handy when you're rewriting large segments of code, in that it reduces any distractions.

```
void FunctionsCanFold()
{
    int someInt = 0;
    while( someInt < /*10*/ 100)
    {
        someInt++;
    }
}
```

We can collapse many blocks of code into a single line. If you look at the line numbering following the Update () function you'll see the numbers jump from 79 to 93. This process of collapsing has hidden three lines of code; moreover, this feature will be particularly handy when you need to see two different functions which might have a great deal of code between them.

```
void FunctionsCanFold()[...]
/* clickint on the [+] in the left margin next
 * to the function above will turn the function into
 * void FunctionsCanFold()[...]
 */
```

This also works for any instance where the opening curly brace { is followed by the closing curly brace }. This folds the for statement into a more compact form, so we don't have to look at what it's doing. This allows us to focus on the code block we're most interested in focusing on.

A special type of comment is the region. This uses the # character followed by the word region to create a foldable area of text. The words following the start of a region indicate a starting point of a foldable area of text.

```
#region Special Area of Interest
void SomeFunction()
{
    // doing things in area of interest
}
int SomeInt = 0;
class SomeClass
{
    int SomeClassesInt = 1;
}
#endregion
```

The end of the region is indicated by #endregion to close off the foldable text area. When the region is folded the first line of text remains visible to identify the folded region's content.

```
Special Area of Interest
```

Regions can also have other regions within them. Visual Studio will help highlight hierarchies of regions when you leave the cursor on one of the beginnings or ends of the region.

```
#region Special Area of Interest
void SomeFunction()
{
    // doing things in area of interest
}
int SomeInt = 0;
#region Sub Section in the area
class SomeClass
{
    int SomeClassesInt = 1;
}
#endregion
#endregion
```

A large C# file can be made a bit easier to navigate by adding regions. These are intended to help collapse groups of functions or variables to make other parts of the same file easier to read. To focus on a smaller section of code it's often useful to create regions to hide away sections you're less interested in.

```
#region Special Area of Interest
void SomeFunction()
{
    // doing things in area of interest
}
int SomeInt = 0;
Sub Section in the area
#endregion
```

Often regions are setup around parts of a class that serve a specific function. This affords the engineer a clever and elegant way to help organize code. In a way, the fussy organizational skills of a good programmer are expressed through comments, regions and function grouping.

The code examples for this book have regions to delineate sections of code for each chapter.

3.15.3 Summary Comments

```
/// <summary>
/// A Vector3 function of my own!
/// </summary>
/// <param name="v1"></param>
/// <param name="v2"></param>
/// <param name="v3"></param>
private void Vector3(float v1, float v2, float v3)
{
    //?
    /* uncomment the ? above to see the error
     * produced in the book.
     */
}
```

If you type in three slashes (/s) over a function, Visual Studio will automatically add in a summary comment. Like the other comments the summary comments are also collapsible. Visual Studio also recognizes many different forms of comment tags.

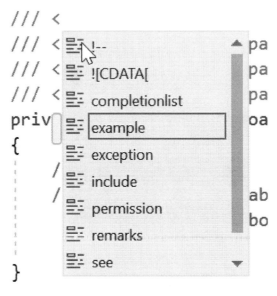

When you add in a < the above automatic code completion pop-up dialog appears. You can add in description examples and other tags. This feature of Visual Studio demonstrates how important comments are in a well-written source file. Comments and comment tags have many different options. To avoid writing the rest of this book about comments I'll leave experimenting with the comment tags to you. They are important, but not essential, to learning how C# works.

3.15.4 Navigating in Code

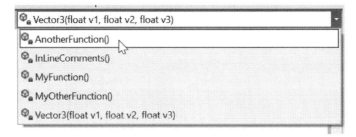

There are also clever ways to get around in a source file. Up at the top of the panel in Visual Studio is a handy drop-down menu which has a list item for every function in the class. You'll also notice an icon next to each listing.

Add in a `public` keyword before the `void MyPublicMethod()` function and the lock icon goes away. This indicates that the `CleverComments()` function is `public`. Selecting the item jumps the cursor to the beginning of the function. This comes in particularly handy when dealing with large source files which might have many different functions in them.

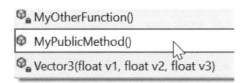

3.15.5 What We've Learned

Comments are a necessary part of any good source file. Available online tools will parse your source files, find summary comments, and generate an entire website documenting your code. Organized code and comments are parts of your code style. The more organized your code is the more readable it becomes.

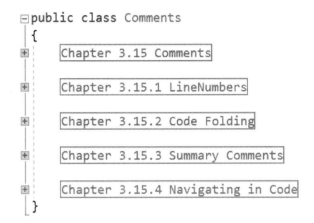

When you've written several dozen different C# files you'll find that code written months ago might look alien. I often find myself thinking to myself "What was I thinking when I wrote this?" when I open a file from many months before.

In these cases, I hope I wrote in detailed comments, leaving myself at least some clue as to what was going on to lead to the code that has been written;. Usually, however, I haven't and I need to read through the rest of my code to come up with an understanding of what was going on.

It's time to get back to Unity 3D and start writing something more interesting than comments. We spent a great deal of time in this chapter writing things that are ignored by the computer. It's time to get to writing code that matters.

3.16 Leveling Up: Moving on to Basics

At this point we've looked at the components that make up C#. We should be able to look at code and identify the different tokens and roughly what they do. The ; is a separator token which ends a code statement. Likewise, we should understand that a : and a ; have different roles in code and cannot be used interchangeably.

Variables have a type, and this type determines how the variable can be used. We should also know that different types cannot interact without explicit conversions between them. Converting between different types can result in loss of data, and thus we should be mindful when doing so.

When we look at a statement, we should be able to identify the different tokens which the statement is composed of. In a statement like int a = 6; we should be able to see that we're using five different tokens.

What the different tokens are used for may not be clear, but that information will be presented as we continue. Learning a programming language is just as involved as learning any other language. Just like any language has grammar and vocabulary, C# has syntax, keywords, and structure.

3.16.1 Git Revision History

Using Git to save the history of a file is its main strength. With every commit and push you create a new checkpoint for the files updated with the commit. The changes don't need to include every file affected in the commit.

With the Git Bash open you can browse the history of each file. The revisions for the README.md file can be seen with

```
git log README.md
```

The command prints out a commit followed by a long hash value followed by the author, date, and comment from the commit. If there are a lot of commits then using:

```
git log --oneline README.md
```

will produce an easier to read history of the file. The shorter hash also makes it easier to pick a version of the file.

```
git checkout 38cd1c9 README.md
```

This will revert the README.md to its initial commit version. Open the file in a text file to confirm.

```
git status
```

```
alexokita@Buggy MINGW64 ~/Documents/BookContents (master)
$ git status
On branch master
Your branch is up to date with 'origin/master'.

Changes to be committed:
  (use "git reset HEAD <file>..." to unstage)

        modified:   README.md


alexokita@Buggy MINGW64 ~/Documents/BookContents (master)
$ █
```

This will show the status of the README.md as modified. To get the latest version of the README.md file again use:

```
git checkout HEAD README.md
```

The file will be back to the latest version checked in. Git log and checkout are simple commands to remember. With the add commit and push commands you'll be able to keep track of your files and see what's changed between revisions. Git is great!

4

Basics: The Building Blocks of Code

After covering the small parts that make up code, it's time to start learning how all the parts come together to create a behavior. Creating data is easy; keeping the data organized is harder. Adding logic to do something with the data is harder still. That said, it's not impossible; otherwise, no one would write code.

This chapter covers how a statement of code works and where the power that drives the code originates. Programming is much less enigmatic when you understand the mechanisms that drive it. To understand why code behaves the way it does, it's important to know your way around the language.

4.1 What Will Be Covered in This Chapter

This chapter is about getting past the simple details and going into the structure of code. This process is somewhat comparable to learning the grammar of the C# programming language. We'll cover the basics about the different types of logic statements and looping statements.

Logic allows you to pick different actions based on the result of a calculation. If you want to tell a human to run away from a zombie or run to a human for help, you'll need logic, to control that human's behavior. Logic takes data, makes a comparison, and chooses which section of code to execute.

Looping statements can read and react to more than one data set. If you're in a room with any number of zombies, you'll want to take them into account all at once. Looping statements are an integral part of any programming language. We'll see why they're so useful in this chapter, in which we discuss the following topics:

- Building a game starting with input
- Creating a new class
- Directives: The keyword `using`
- Functions
- Order of operation
- Scope
- Keyword `This`
- Logic and operators
- Loops
- Warnings and errors

4.2 Review

Before getting ahead of yourself, it's important to remember some of what we just covered. We will be learning many new tokens in this chapter. A token, as we know, is the smallest element that makes up a statement.

Statements are tokens organized to accomplish a task. Tokens can be keywords, or words reserved by C# for special purposes. Some tokens are used to separate statements, and others are used to assign values to variables.

A keyword cannot be used for anything other than what it has been reserved for. Some keywords can be used only in a specific context. Several keywords are used only if you've defined a specific library, where they have been defined; we'll discuss some of these topics later in this chapter.

When you create a variable, you've created a new token. Some variables exist only in the context they were created in; the control of this existence is called scope, something which is coming up in this section as well. As a reminder, when you invent a word to identify a variable that word becomes a new token.

Once created, the token can be used in many ways; you can apply an operation to a token and use it to assign values to other variables. These operations all happen in a very specific order. Create a variable, execute an operation or an expression, assign the value. This is what makes C# an imperative language.

4.3 Building a Game—Part 1

Building an entire game is a large undertaking, to say the least. Creating a core game play mechanic is something that should be prototyped in different forms. In short when you're learning, it's better to make many simple small games or test cases that explore a single mechanic. Then the classes you write for Input, navigation, inventory, score etc. It's best to write code that can be copied to a larger project.

Designing a complete game with backstory, character development can be done in parallel with the core functionality of what the player does from moment to moment. Often, what you're able to accomplish as an engineer influences the kind of story you're able to convey. A vast open world with many different stories would take hundreds of hours to build content. Narrowing the scope of your project is important.

At the beginning of almost every game development project, the input. It's also quite interesting since Unity 3D has a lot of options on how to deal with getting Input. Keyboards, Game Controllers, the Mouse, Touch Screens, and any number of alternative systems count as "Input" in a broad sense. But let's just get something simple working first.

In the Unity-SampleGame project, open the Scenes/Section 4.3 unity scene. In the hierarchy, find the game object called TransformPrimitive with a DirectMousePosition script attached. Open the DirectMousePosition.cs in Visual Studio to follow along. This is about as simple as it can get.

```
// Update is called once per frame
void Update () {
    gameObject.transform.position = Input.mousePosition;
}
```

This may not be the most useful of input systems, but it's useful to see what `Input.mousePosition` is doing. After pressing the Play-In-Editor button you might be able to observe the TransformPrimitive in the unity scene moving around rather quickly as the mouse moves around over the Game window. Select the game object and take a look at the Inspector panel's transform values. The x and y values increase as the mouse gets further away from the lower left corner of the game window.

The lower left of the Game window puts lower numbers into the Transform of the GameObject, the top right puts larger numbers in there. If the game camera is only looking at what is near the center of the world, then you'll rarely see the TransformPrimitive in view unless your mouse is near the lower left of the game view; truly not a useful input system.

We learned something, you can move an object with the mouse, though erratically. Mouse X and Y turn into game object X and Y. The game view's origin or x = 0 y = 0 coordinate is at the lower left and the maximum values are at the top right.

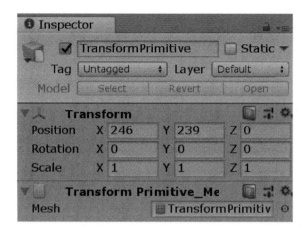

The above image shows some values assigned to the Transform of the TransformPrimitive in the Inspector. The cursor moved toward the middle of the view of the game while being played in the editor shows values in the hundreds taken from the mouse coordinates. As to be expected, the X and Y values change as the mouse moves around on the game view. The Z is left at 0 since the screen is a 2D image.

4.3.1 Mouse Point

To make better use of the input values we'll want to use the mousePosition data. Open the Section 4.3.1 unity scene to observe a better way to use the mouse position. Selecting objects, pointing at a position, and drawing lines need mouse positions translated into world coordinates to work. Many common tasks have starting points built into Unity 3D.

Our Unity scene to follow has a MousePointController object with MousePoint.cs script attached. To start, the code gets the camera used to see the game. One quick way is to use the Main Camera, or in this case the code myCamera = Camera.main; does this for us. To move the transform primitive to where the mouse cursor is pointing, we use myTransformObject = GameObject.Find("TransformPrimitive"); to find the object in the scene.

```
myCamera = Camera.main;
myTransformObject = GameObject.Find("TransformPrimitive");
```

Now that we have a reference to the two objects being updated in each frame; we'll start to use them in the Update() function provided by Unity. In the Update() function we'll use what's called a ray, a mathematic type that is basically a starting point in 3D space with a direction. That ray will start with the Main Camera in the scene, and point at the mouse point in the screen to the world.

Once the ray is cast, Unity provides a physics system that takes the ray and checks if it collides with anything in the world. That method is called Physics.RayCast(); and that updates what is called a RaycastHit with the outcome from the Physics.RayCast();. Physics uses the mousePosition to create a line from the center of the game camera through the mousePosition on the screen and into the game world. If Physics tells is we've intersected with something, then we put the TransformPrimitive at the location where the hit occurs.

```
Ray ray = myCamera.ScreenPointToRay(Input.mousePosition, Camera.MonoOrStereoscopicEye.Mono);
RaycastHit hit;
if (Physics.Raycast(ray, out hit))
{
    myTransformObject.transform.position = hit.point;
}
```

The position of the transform primitive is assigned to the hit.point when updated by Physics. Raycast();. This happens on every frame; when we run the game at this point we'll see the transform primitive act like a cursor under the mouse as it's move around in the Game view.

Games don't usually move a character around in the scene as quickly as you can move a mouse. But the world position is important. If we want a character to move to the cursor we will need to know where in the world the mouse is pointed.

4.3.2 Move to Point

The Unity scene Section 4.3.2 has the same setup as the previous section with the addition of a little character with a MoveToPoint.cs script attached. This will point the little robot to the point in the world where the transform primitive is. When we click the left mouse button the robot will move to the trans form primitive's position.

First we'll need a Vector3 that represents the direction that we need to point the robot in. This is done by subtracting the position of the robot from the position of the transform primitive.

```
Vector3 lookTarget = myTransformObject.transform.position - transform.position;
```

With this Vector3 we need to get a rotation value. Rotations in Unity are stored as Quaternion, a type of math that stores angles of directions. Quaternions can be tricky, but the engineers at Unity have provided us with a way to calculate the proper quaternion values with Quaternion.LookRotation();. This is calculated with the look target's position and the upward angle of the robot. The upward direction comes from transform.up so we know what axis to rotate the robot around and the lookTarget gives us what direction to rotate to.

To use the direction value we want to rotate the robot with Quaternion.Slerp() which means Smooth Linear-interpolate. Interpolation means we'll use time to step with small values from one value, the transform.rotation of the robot to a goal rotation, in this case the direction we got from the LookRotation() function.

```
Quaternion direction = Quaternion.LookRotation(lookTarget, transform.up);
transform.rotation = Quaternion.Slerp(transform.rotation, direction, Time.deltaTime * 5f);
```

This rotation is updated on every frame by virtue of being in the Update() function. Now we'll use the Input.GetMouseButton(0) to let us know when the left mouse button is pressed. GetMouseButton(1) would be the right mouse button. With use of an if() statement to update the movement target called moveToPosition.

When the left mouse button is down we set the value of the moveToPosition to the position of the transform primitive with myTransformObject.transform.position; as seen in the code.

```
if (Input.GetMouseButton(0))
{
    moveToPosition = myTransformObject.transform.position;
}
```

This now updates so long as the left mouse button is down. To get the robot to actually move to that position we'll assign the robots `transform.position` to the result of another interpolation position with `Vecter3.Lerp()` where we use the current position and the target position as values.

Now when we run the game we'll have a robot that faces the position of the mouse in the world and will move to it so long as the left mouse button is pressed.

This counts as a very simple system of navigation for a character to move in a scene. This acts as our starting point. As we come across new systems we'll be able to understand more about the functions we just used and add new systems to make the robot navigate a more complex environment.

4.3.3 What We've Learned

We're just getting started. Our road toward zombie destruction needs a great deal of footwork and studying. Some of what we're about to get into might seem a bit mundane, but it's only the beginning.

We're learning a new language with new words and concepts. With the help of Unity 3D we're going to have a foundation on which pretty much any game can be built. Stick to it and you'll be writing lots of code in no time.

The intent of the direct input experiment is to discover how data is presented to you. In a similar fashion, systems like touch and gyro from mobile devices may present data in an unexpected format. You can't necessarily change how data is given to you, but you can change how to use the data.

4.4 Class Construction

The class object is the focus as a new Unity C# engineer. In the previous chapter we saw a `MousePoint` and `MoveToPoint` class, but how were these classes created? As a Unity 3D engineer all of work goes into building the contents of a class. This was mentioned in Section 3.8, but we didn't look at what's involved with writing a new class. To see the creation of a class in action, The ClassConstruction_Scene and the ClassConstruction script in the scene on the object of the same name.

To get our heads around what a class is, we're going to write a class declaration inside of a class. This is what is called a nested class. To write a class you start with a *class declaration*.

A class declaration is basically the keyword `class` followed by an identifier. As a reminder, an identifier is simply a word you use to name any data you've created. Once a class has been declared, it's a matter of filling it with all the useful things that classes can do.

```
/*
 * A nested class can appear down below this comment.
 *
 *
 *      ┌─────────┐   ┌────────────┐
 *      │ keyword │   │ Identifier │
 *      └─────────┘   └────────────┘
 *         │              │
 *         │          ┌───┘
 * class MyNewClass
 * {
 * }
 * └
 *
 *      ┌────────────┐
 *      │ separators │
 *      └────────────┘
 *
 * Don't forget the { and } separators following the class declaration.
 *
 */
```

Where did ClassConstruction.cs come from? Much of this work is done for you by the Unity 3D Editor when you have Unity create a C# script for you. Alternatively, you can have Visual Studio create a script for you.

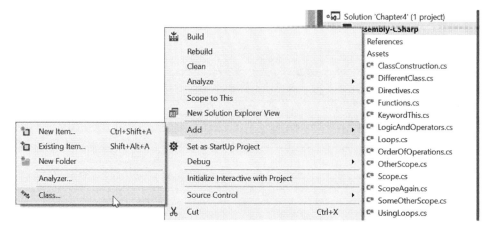

The right-click popup from the Assembly-CSharp item in the Solution Explorer window will bring up a menu to select Add→Class… item. This opens the following Dialog:

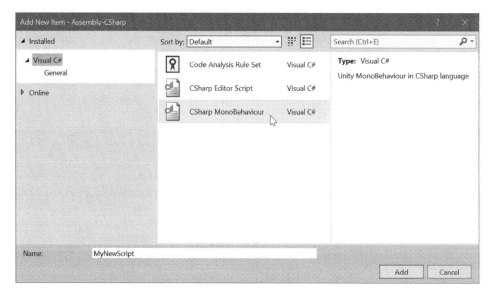

From here you can select a new CSharp MonoBehaviour or Editor script to build new scripts on. By default a file is called NewBehaviourScript.cs. In here, Unity 3D wrote some directives, declares a class called NewBehaviourScript, then adds in some base functions to get started. We'll go through the same steps to understand why the file is written like it is. And we'll start with the class declaration. Compare the NewBehaviourScript with the ClassConstruction script to see what the differences are.

```
Debug.Log(dataOne.myNumber);
// 1
Debug.Log(dataTwo.myNumber);
// 7
Debug.Log(dataThree.myNumber);
// 11
```

4.4.1 Class Declaration

A "class declaration" makes an announcement to tell Unity 3D that your object exists. In the preceding example we the MyNewClass object with the keyword class followed by the identifier MyNewClass. Together the class MyNewClass{} declared to your entire project that there's an object called MyNewClass. This declaration also means that MyNewClass as an identifier is special, and if you were to reuse the name for another object you'll create an error.

```
class MyNewClass
{
}
```

Classes are objects that could contain more objects called members, or *class members*. Often words like attributes, fields, properties, and components can also be used to describe a member of a class. In all cases each member of the class is given identifiers as well.

When you add a contact to your phone, you add a name, number, and email address into empty boxes; programmers often refer to these as fields. They are open spaces in your computer's memory into which you put data.

The sections of a class that contain logic and code statements are called *function members*. These are also accessed by their identifiers. Depending on what a function does for the class, it can be categorized as a *method, constructor, destructor, indexer, operator, property*, or *event*. How these functions differ from one another will be discussed in Sections 4.7.1.1, 5.4.3, 7.5, 7.13, and 7.15.

Classes need to talk to one another for any number of reasons. Zombies need to know where humans are, and bullets need to take chunks out of zombies. Suppose a zombie has several chunks left before slain, and the human has a position in the world where the zombie needs to chase him; this information needs to be shared. The availability of the information is called *accessibility*.

Data and function members can be made accessible to each other using the *public* keyword. We'll observe how this works in a moment. In a class that inherits from MonoBehaviour, making a variable public makes an identifier visible to the Inspector panel in the Editor. Inheritance is something coming in Section 5.3, so there's a bit to cover until then. However, it's important to know that accessibility has various effects with how classes interact with one another.

4.4.1.1 A Basic Example

Consider the class declaration shown for MyNewClass(). This is a nested class inside of the ClassConstruction class. A nested class encapsulates the purpose of the declaration for a specific purpose within its parent class. A Zombie and a Player class may have independent nested inventory classes. This would allow the inventory in each to behave differently.

Look just below that and you'll find a line that has the statement void Start(); this statement creates a function that is a member of the Example class. To create an instance of this class we add MyNewClass mClass = new MyNewClass(); to the Start() function.

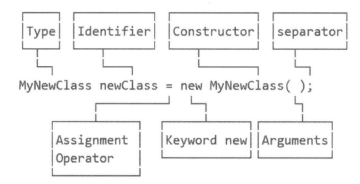

Let's examine the first two words, or tokens. The first token MyNewClass indicates the type of object we intend to create. The class we created is now a new type of data. Once MyNewClass has been declared as a class, it becomes an instruction to create a new type of data known by its identifier.

We know a variable is declared by a keyword followed by an identifier like int i; a class variable is declared in a similar way: MyNewClass mClass. However, unlike an int a class *cannot* be assigned with plain old data.

What differentiates an int from a class is how the type is created and then assigned. We'll have to go into detail a bit later when we would have a deeper understanding about data types, but for now, we'll consider an int as a fundamental type.

In practice, nearly every new behavior you create will begin with a new class. At the start of your project you'll likely create a unique classes for each game item, character, effect, etc. That's not to say you'll create a different class for similar items. For instance, a blue key and a red key might act in a similar way with their only distinction being color. In cases like this your class can contain options to be any color required.

4.4.1.2 Value and Reference Types

Although we declared class MyNewClass we have yet to give it anything to do. For now, there's nothing written in MyNewClass. Once we start adding features to MyNewClass the task of assigning a value to the class becomes ambiguous. In context:

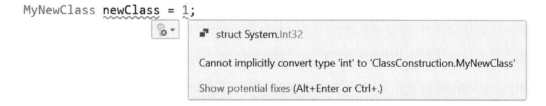

What would that mean if MyNewClass was a zombie? Is the 1 his name? How many hit points does he have? or what is his armor rating? Because C# can't be sure, the computer has no hope of making a guess.

This differentiates a *value type*, like an int, over a *reference type*, such as MyClass. However, before we go into a chapter about types we need to know more about classes, so we'll get back to the topic at hand.

Therefore, when creating a new instance of a reference type we need to use the form new MyNewClass(); to assign a variable of type MyNewClass. Thus, MyNewClass newClass = new MyNewClass(); is used to create a variable for MyNewClass and assign the variable newClass a new instance of the correct class.

To make things clear, `int i` can be assigned in the exact same way we assign `newClass`.

```
int i = new System.Int32();
```

We can use the above statement if we want to make our int declarations look the same as our class declarations. This is unorthodox and unnecessary, but it's possible. It's important to know that things like this do exist and that C# is flexible enough to allow us to do this.

4.4.2 Adding Data Fields

A data field is any type of information that lives inside of a class. We'll cover what data type really means in Section 6.5.3 but for now we'll assume that data can be pretty much anything, including a number. When a class has data fields added to it, we're giving the class a place that holds onto information and allows the class to remember, or store, some data. For instance, were we to write a zombie for a game we'd need the zombie to know, or store, how many brains it has eaten, or how many whacks it has taken from the player.

```
class DataFields
{
    int myNumbers;
}
```

To add a data field to a `DataFields` class we use the same declaration as we would for any other variable. This should be obvious, but since we're writing a class inside of a class this might be a bit confusing. However, when this is declared as `int myNumbers;` we're not allowed to use it yet.

4.4.3 Access Modifiers and the Dot Operator

To see to members of a class we use the *dot operator* (.) to tell C# we want to access a member of a class. When a new data field is added to a class it's assigned a type and an identifier. The identifier turns into the word we use after the dot to request access to that data or function.

```
class DataFields
{
    int myNumber;
}

void TestAccess()
{
    DataFields data = new DataFields();
    data.
            ┌─────────────────────┐
            │ ⊗ │Equals           │
            │ ⊗   GetHashCode     │
            │ ⊗   GetType         │
            │ ⊗   ToString        │
            └─────────────────────┘
```

If we try to find the `myNumber` data field when using Visual Studio we won't see the `myNumber` data field in the list of members. To make the `int myNumber` accessible we need the `public` keyword. The `public` keyword is like several other keywords that change the accessibility of a variable within a class; such keywords are called *access modifiers*. There are several access modifiers we'll come to use, but for now we'll just get familiar with the `public` access modifier.

```
void TestAccess()
{
    DataFields data = new DataFields();
    data.
```

```
    ⊗  Equals
    ⊗  GetHashCode
    ⊗  GetType
    ●  myNumber
    ⊗  PrintMyNumber
    ⊗  ToString

    ●   ⊗
```

Adding the keyword `public` before the `int myNumber` changes the accessibility to the classes outside of `DataFields` and allow for other objects to see the data field. The data fields that can be changed this way are called *instance variables* that are unique to each instance of the class.

An instance is a unique version, or object, based on the class from which it was created from. Each instance stands on its own as a new object created from the class it's based on. All the class members are unique to each instance. There are systems that circumvent this behavior, but we'll get to that in Section 5.5.

To observe this point, we'll create a few instances of the class and set the data fields to different values.

```
DataFields dataOne = new DataFields();
dataOne.myNumber = 1;
DataFields dataTwo = new DataFields();
dataTwo.myNumber = 7;
DataFields dataThree = new DataFields();
dataThree.myNumber = 11;
```

Here, we created three instances of `DataFields`. Each one has its own `myNumber` data field and each one can be assigned a unique value. To check this, we use A Unity `Debug.Log` to print out the value of each instance of `DataFields myNumbers` field.

```
Debug.Log(dataOne.myNumber);
// 1
Debug.Log(dataTwo.myNumber);
// 7
Debug.Log(dataThree.myNumber);
// 11
```

Add in these three lines after `dataThree.myNumber` is assigned. We could do something useful by adding a function into the class that does this for us. Class members can include more than variables. Functions as members are accessible through the dot operator.

```
class DataFields
{
    public int myNumber;

    public void PrintMyNumber()
    {
        Debug.Log(myNumber);
    }
}
```

A function to print with `Debug.Log(myNumber);` added into the `PrintMyNymber()` function, is made `public` in the same way as `myNumber`. We'll get a better look at functions in Chapter 5, but this example serves as a quick and dirty introduction come back to a simple function nonetheless.

The `PrintMyNymber` function and the `myNumber` field both live together in the `DataFields` class and share the same scope. The dot operator is only necessary to access members inside of an object. The members of `DataFields` are next to one another inside of the class.

```
DataFields firstData = new DataFields();
firstData.myNumber = 3;
firstData.PrintMyNumber();
// 3
```

The instance of `firstData`, in the example above *contains* the `myNumber` and `PrintMyNumber()` members. To access the members inside of `firstData` you do need the dot operator. The dot operator allows you to use the specific member of a specific object. Each instance of the object is unique. This allows you to specify what happens to each unique instance of a `DataFields` object.

4.4.4 Class Scope

Members of a class may appear in any order within the class definition. The arrangement of data and function depends on style and practice. One practice might be to keep data fields next to the functions that use them.

```
class DataFunctionPairGrouping
{
    public int MyCounter;
    public void UseMyCounter()
    {
        MyCounter += 1;
        Debug.Log(MyCounter);
    }

    public float MyFloat;
    public void UseMyFloat()
    {
        MyFloat += 1.0f;
        Debug.Log(MyFloat);
    }
}
```

With the above example we can see that `MyCounter` lives next to `UseMyCounter()`, and likewise for `MyFloat` and `UseMyFloat()`. Here we see the data and function are grouped together.

```csharp
class DefineVariablesFirst
{
    public int FirstInt;
    public int SecondInt;
    public int ThirdInt;

    public void UseFirstInt()
    {
        Debug.Log(FirstInt);
    }
    public void UseSecondInt()
    {
        Debug.Log(SecondInt);
    }
    public void UseThirdInt()
    {
        Debug.Log(ThirdInt);
    }
}
```

C# allows for functions and variables to appear in any order within the class definition. C# ignores how the different members are arranged. This doesn't always hold true, especially once we get into how code itself is executed, but at the class level, or at the class scope, as programmers like to say, the ordering isn't as important.

Not all programming languages will allow this. UnrealScript, for example, enforces all variables live at the beginning of a function. Declaring them anywhere else raises an error. C# understands that formatting is less important than clarity. Declaring variables close to where they are used, however, is important for readability.

4.4.5 Class Members

As we add functions and variables to a class, we're adding *members* to the class. In the previous example, num is a member of `MyClass`. So too are `PrintNum()` and any other functions or variables included in the class. We can refer to some of the members as public, which means that other classes can access them, while the inaccessible members are private.

In most cases, if public is not used then you can assume the member belongs to private. Private members cannot be accessed from outside of the class, at least not directly. However, functions on the inside or local to the class can modify them freely.

4.4.6 What We've Learned

We just covered some of the very basic concepts of what makes up a class. There are plenty of other keywords and some complex concepts that we have yet to touch on. Later, we'll get into some additional clever tricks that classes allow for.

On your own, you should practice creating different data fields and add more functions to your class to get a feel for how they work. As you learn how to use more keywords, you should add them to your own classes to check that you understand how the keywords work.

In this chapter, we created `MyNewClass` as well as a few others inside of the `ClassConstruction` class. `MyNewClass` is an example of a nested class, or a class inside of a class. Multiple nested classes are allowed in C#, and nested classes are allowed inside of nested classes, should you really want to go there.

Using the dot operator we gain access to fields and functions inside of a class. C# relies on the features of classes and class members. We'll see how to access the many functions available to us in Chapter 5.

We've been working in a nested class all this time. To show how this works in another class, we can go back to Unity 3D and create a new class next to ClassConstruction.cs called DifferentClass.cs.

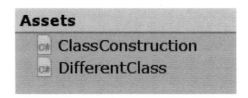

The above class is the automatically visible to `ClassConstruction` in Visual Studio. The `AccessOtherClass()` function in the `ClassConstruction` script sees the `DifferentClass` and can access it just like a nested class.

```
void AccessOtherClass()
{
    DifferentClass someOther = new DifferentClass();
    someOther.myInt = 1;
}
```

With these basic concepts we'll want to explore the different classes which Unity 3D and Microsoft have created to allow us to access the various abilities that are contained in the Unity 3D game engine. Accessing the classes and fields which Unity 3D has provided is quite simple, as we will see in Chapter 5.

4.5 Directives

Let's open the Directives.cs script in the Chapter 4 project. When you start writing code in Unity 3D, or any other programming environment, you consider the tools you must have to begin with. For instance, with the .NET (read as "dot net") framework we get things like `int`, `bool`, `float`, and `double`. These tools are given to us by adding `using System;` to our code.

We also have been taking for granted the use of `using UnityEngine;` this function gives us another massive set of tools to work with including a ton of work that allows us to use functions and events that are triggered by the Unity 3D game engine itself.

All these classes, functions, and events are stored in the `library` software. Basically, this is code that has been written to enable your code to communicate with Unity 3D. These resources provide a gigantic foundation to build your game on. Much of the difficult math and data management functions in relation to Unity 3D has been written for you.

Knowing what they are and how they are used is important. It's like knowing what tools you have in your toolbox. In Chapter 5, we'll go over their basic use and how to find out more about what they offer.

Directives provide the connection between your class and a selected library. Many hundreds of classes, written by the programmers who created Unity 3D, allow you to communicate between the player, the characters, and every other object in the game. In short, a library is software for your software. When we have Unity 3D create a new C# class the generated file has several blocks of code.

```
1    using System.Collections;
2    using System.Collections.Generic;
3    using UnityEngine;
```

In the first three lines of the class we had Unity 3D prepare for us are the directives we needed to get started. The connection between Unity 3D and your code is made, in part, by using directives. A directive makes a connection to outside or external resources called libraries.

Directives are required to appear at the beginning of a file before the class they're to be used in. This is different from how a variable can be used inside the scope of a class. Though there are some ways to bend the rules a little bit, but we'll leave that for Section 6.10 where we cover namespaces in a bit more detail.

The libraries that the directives call upon are connected to compiled code. Unity 3D is also connected to the libraries that your code uses. The connection is made by identifying the name of the library after the keyword `using` is entered.

Libraries live in paths, like a file in a folder on your computer, only they are compiled into a few tightly bundled binary files.

NOTE: The initialism *DLL* refers to *dynamically linked library*, which is a complete set of software compiled ahead of time for your use. Pretty much every software released these days include many different DLLs that allow the software to be updated and modified by only updating the DLLs they come with. Often some DLLs are located in your computer's operating system's directory, but depending on the software involved it too will bring along its own DLLs.

The first line, `using UnityEngine;`, pulls all of the resources that deal with specific Unity 3D function calls. For instance, moving an object, playing sounds, and activating particle systems are found inside of the `UnityEngine` library. The functions necessary for making bullets and magic spells work are built into `UnityEngine`.

As the resources that make up your game are imported into Unity 3D, they're made available to your code. The libraries provided by Unity 3D expose all the imported assets in such a way that they can be found like files on your computer.

The programmers at Unity 3D have taken on the bulk of these complex tasks for you so you don't have to deal with all the physics and PhD-level science of rendering 3D graphics. The keyword `using` is how we tell C# that we're going to ask for a specific library to access.

Many other programming languages do the same thing; for instance, Python uses the statement `import module` to do the same thing; JavaScript is more wordy, by requiring a path like `src = "otherScripts/externalLibrary.js"` to access external code.

C++ and C both do the same as C# with the keyword `using` to access external libraries. In the end, your code can work with pre-existing code stored in nicely packaged libraries. For Unity 3D, this is pretty much necessary.

4.5.1 Libraries

Libraries are collections of classes and data that have been bundled into a convenient package with Unity 3D. You can consider them to be like a compiled application. A library contains classes that are all accessible through the dot operator, like the classes we wrote in Chapter 3. Inside of Visual Studio you can look at some of the other libraries we can use.

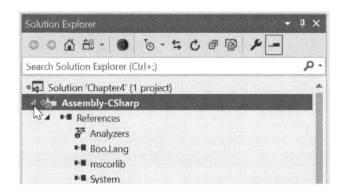

Inside of MonoDevelop, expand the References icon in the Solution Explorer. In case the Solution Explorer panel isn't open, then use the following menu to show the panel: View → Solution Explorer.

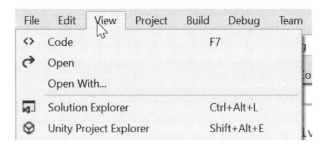

Scroll through the list to read the numerous entries listed. These are the tools written into Unity 3D at your disposal. In the Directives.cs class, entering the `using UnityEngine.` will prompt a pop-up. The pop-up window shows you the many different libraries available to Unity 3D.

We won't go too far into how to use these other functions. We are just now getting to know the functions we already have. Between both `UnityEngine` and `System.Collections` we've got quite a large set of tools already. Later, we'll be able to create our own libraries. Within our own libraries, we'll be able to write useful functions that can be used like anything found in `UnityEngine`.

In our Directives.cs class, we'll use the `Start()` function and look for a `StreamWriter` function. A StreamWriter is a class that will help us write some text to a new text file. However, the auto-complete pop-up shows "No Completions Found" as we start to enter the class we're looking for.

```
// Use this for initialization
void Start () {
    StreamWriter
}
```

The name 'StreamWriter' does not exist in the current context

Show potential fixes (Alt+Enter or Ctrl+.)

```
// Update is
void Update () {
```

Click on the helper icon to the left will expand some options to fix the problem. Select the second option where we have Visual Studio write `System.IO.StreamWriter` in place of `StreamWriter`.

Optionally we can have Visual Studio add the `using Stream.IO;` at the beginning of our class definition.

```
14    public class Directives : MonoBehaviour {
15
16        // Use this for initialization
17        void Start () {
18            StreamWriter
```

using System.IO;
System.IO.StreamWriter
Generate property 'Directives.StreamWriter'
Generate field 'Directives.StreamWriter'
Generate read-only field 'Directives.StreamWriter'
Generate local 'StreamWriter'

CS0103 The name 'StreamWriter' does not exist in the current context

```
...
using System.Collections.Generic;
using System.IO;
using UnityEngine;
...
```

Preview changes

Adding using SystemIO; to our class provides us with a connection to all of the contents of the System.IO libraries. StreamWriter is used to write to a text file.

```
// Use this for initialization
void Start () {
    StreamWriter writer = new StreamWriter("MyFile.txt");
    writer.WriteLine("This is a new file...");
    writer.Flush();
}
```

Using the StreamWriter we create a new object called writer. When the StreamWriter is instanced we pass a parameter with a string used for the file name; in this case, "MyFile.txt" is given to the new writer object.

With the object instanced as writer, we use the object and call upon the WriteLine member function and give it some text to write into the new file. The text "This is a new file..." will appear in the MyFile.txt file that Unity 3D will write for us. After that we need to use the Flush(); call to tell the writer to finish its work.

Press the Play button with Directives_Scene open to execute the Start() function in the C# class. To find the file, right click on the Assets directory in the Project view and select Show in Explorer from the pop-up menu.

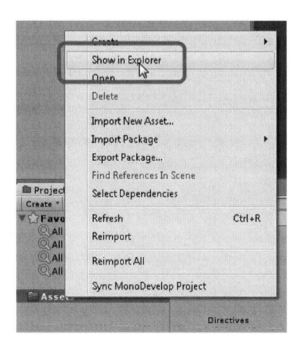

This action should bring up the directory where the new MyFile.txt has been written.

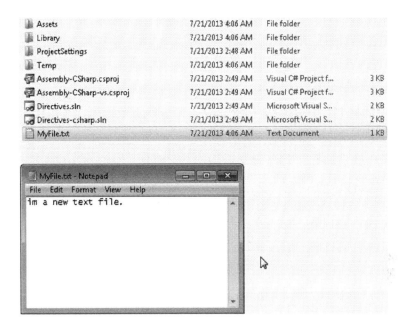

Opening the `MyFile.txt` will open the file in your usual text editor; in my case, it was Notepad. You could imagine writing various bits of information in this, or even begin to read from a text file into your game! This might make writing dialog for an RPG (role-playing game) game a bit easier. You wouldn't have to write all of the text into each object or even code in your game. Reading from a text file would make more sense.

Of course, we'll have to do more work to get the most out of reading and writing to text files, but this is just the beginning. We'll move on to more sophisticated tricks later on. This is just a glimpse into what we can do by accessing the different parts of the libraries available to us.

4.5.2 Ambiguous NameSpaces

The names of functions from libraries, should have unique names for each function. However, what happens if Unity 3D and System used the same name?

One of the many tools is a simple random number generator. The `Random.Range();` function was written by the Unity 3D programmers and requires a minimum and a maximum number. There's also a Random provided inside of System written by Microsoft which does a similar thing.

```
using UnityEngine;
using System;
```

However, if we add `using System;` to the list of directives, as in the above code sample, we'll get an error telling is there's an ambiguous reference between `UnityEngine.Random` and `System.Random`.

```
int rand = Random.Range(0, 10);
```

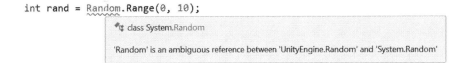

This means that there's an identically named `Random` function in `System` as well as `UnityEngine`. To resolve this error, we need to be more specific when we use `Random`. Since we might need to use other parts of the `System;` library, we'll want to keep this included; otherwise, we wouldn't have this problem at all.

```
int randUnity = UnityEngine.Random.Range(0, 10);
```

If we change `Random.Range()` to `UnityEngine.Random.Range()`, we'll fix the problem of conflicting functions. There will be many times where you might have to change the names of a specific library as well.

A Namespace is a system of creating reserved spaces for the names of variables and functions. The system doesn't always work, but you're still able to work around conflicting names by writing out the full path to a name you're want to use.

By expanding the References tab in the Assembly-CSharp project in the Solution Explorer in Visual Studio you can read a long list of namespaces that are included with a Unity Project.

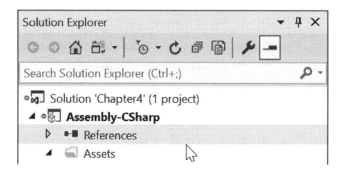

Only a few of these are ever included with a new MonoBehaviour script generated by Unity. Dozens of tools ranging from networking to file systems, diagnostics to security are included in the .NET framework alone. Unity also includes tools from Sprites path finding and terrain to vehicle physics lighting and particles.

Keeping a class specified to a single purpose means to use digression when picking what tools to use to accomplish a task. The available tools are separated into different categories to avoid including unrelated code.

4.5.3 What We've Learned

Knowing where to look for these functions is something that can be done only by having an investigative hunch. Usually, a quick search on the Internet can drum up a few clues as to what function you need to search for to get a specific task done.

Different libraries provide us with systems which help us add additional functionality to our classes. By default, we're given a rich set of tools to build into our game. It's also possible to write your own DLLs creating libraries for your game. This might allow you to add in platform-specific functions to accelerate various aspects of the game outside of the abilities of the built-in Unity 3D tools or engine.

The .NET frameworks as a whole have a number of namespaces that section off different sets of tools.

4.6 Functions

To follow along open the Functions_Scene and the corresponding Functions.cs script. Functions, sometimes called methods, contain statements which can process data. The statements can or cannot process data. Methods can be accessed by other statements. This action is referred to as *calling a function* or *making a function call*. In this chapter we touch on the `Start()`, but we've yet to figure out why the `Start()` functions work.

So far we've created a class and we gave the class some places to store data. We've even used some of those variables in Unity 3D. Then we exposed some variables to the editor to update when manipulated in the Inspector panel. We also wrote a simple function to print a number, but we really didn't get into how that worked or why the syntax looked the way it did.

To add useful behavior to our game, we'll need to add in logic. The logic needs to process data for anything in the game to happen. To coordinate this merging of data and logic, we'll need to write some functions.

4.6.1 What Are Functions?

In Chapter 3, we talked about the process of shampooing. A second look at the idea of a function is to comprehend the words *wash*, *rinse*, and *repeat* in more depth. If you've never heard of the word *wash* before then you're probably dirty, or a computer. Computers need every word defined for them before they understand it.

```
void Wash()
{
}
void Rinse()
{
}
void Repeat()
{
}
```

On a superficial level, we've used the above code to define the three words used to shampoo hair. However, none of the definitions contains any actions. They define the words or identifiers, but when they're used nothing will happen. However, the computer will be able to `Wash();` `Rinse();` `Repeat();` without any problems now.

In the previous chapter we wrote in `DataFields`:

```
public void PrintMyNumber()
{
    Debug.Log(myNumber);
}
```

`PrintMyNumber()` which is a simple function. Now that we can write some functions for use in Unity 3D let's get to some real coding.

NOTE: Functions may look different in different programming languages, but the way they work is mostly the same. The usual pattern is taking in data and using logic to manipulate that data. Functions may also be referred to by other names, for example, methods.

The major differences come from the different ways the languages use syntax. Syntax is basically the use of spaces or tabs, operators, or keywords. In the end, all you're doing is telling the compiler how to convert your instructions into computer-interpreted commands.

Variables and functions make up the bulk of programming. Any bit of data you want to remember is stored in a variable. Variables are manipulated by your functions. In general, when you group variables and functions together in one place, you call that a class.

In Chapter 3, we discussed a bit about writing a class starting with a declaration and the opening and closing curly braces that make up the body. Functions are written in a similar fashion.

We start with the declaration void MyFunction; then we add in both parentheses () and the curly braces {}, indicating to ourselves that we may or may not fill this in later. The first pair of parentheses (), doesn't necessarily always require anything to be added. However, the curly braces {}, or the body of the function, do need code added for the function to have any purpose.

When writing a new function, it's good practice to fill in the entirety of the function's layout before continuing to another task. This puts the compiler at ease; leaving a function in the form void MyFunction and then moving on to another function leaves the compiler confused as to what you're planning on doing.

The integrated development environment, in this case Visual Studio, is constantly reading and interpreting what you are writing, somewhat like a spell checker in a word processor. When it comes across a statement that has no conclusive form, like a variable, function, or class definition, its interpretation of the code you're writing will raise a warning or an error. Visual Studio might seem a bit fussy, but it's doing its best to help.

4.6.2 Unity 3D Entry Points

The Unity 3D developers provided us with MonoBehaviour which is a class that grants our C# classes to have direct access to the inner workings of the Unity 3D game scene. The MonoBehaviour class is a collection of every function and data type available to Unity 3D. We'll learn how to use these parts of Unity 3D in the following tutorials.

NOTE: It's also important to know that when learning the specifics of Unity 3D, you should be aware that these Unity 3D-specific lessons can be applied to other development environments. When you use C# with Windows or OSX, you'll be able to write applications for other operating systems for software other than Unity 3D.

Think of MonoBehaviour as a set of tools for talking to Unity 3D. Other systems have different sets of tools for making apps for other purposes. Learning how to use the other systems should be much easier after reading this book and learning how to talk to Unity 3D.

When dealing with most other C# applications, you'll need to use Main() as the starting point for your C# application. This is like many other development environments using C++ and C.

When Unity 3D creates a class it automatically added in void Start() and void Update() to the body of the class. These two functions are called *entry points*. Basically, the base MonoBehaviour class has several functions, that include Start() and Update(), which are called based on events that happen when your game is running.

There are other functions that are also automatically called when MonoBehaviour is used: Awake(), OnEnable(), Start(), OnApplicationPause(), Update(), FixedUpdate(), and LateUpdate(); these functions are commonly called when the object is created and your game is running. When the object is destroyed, OnDestroy() is called. There are also various rendering functions that can be called, but we don't need to go over them here.

To better understand what happens during each frame of the game it's best to imagine the game operating a bit like a movie. At the very beginning of the game, when the player presses Start, every actor in the scene with a script based on MonoBehaviour has its Start() function called.

Calling a function basically executes the lines of code that live inside of the curly braces that follow the function's declaration. Before the end of the first frame, the Update() functions of each script in the scene are called in no particular order.

At the beginning of the next frame, if there are no new scripts in the scene, the Start() functions are not called. Only Update() functions are called from that point on. Only if new scripts are introduced to the scene are Start() functions called on scripts new to the scene. If there is no code in the Start() function or if there is no Start() function in the script, then nothing happens.

To benefit from anything happening on each frame you'll need to put code into the Update() function. When a class is first introduced into the game world you need to add code into the Start() function. There are several other entry points that we'll be working with. And you'll be able to make use of them all as you see fit. It's important to know that without these entry points your class will be functioning on its own.

Functions all have specific names or identifiers. So far we've seen `Start()` and `Update()`, but there are many more functions which we'll make use of throughout this book. The first function we'll make use of the `Log();`, which is a function found inside of the `Debug` class. We'll return in a moment to how this function is used, but first we'll demonstrate how it's used.

If `Debug` is a class, this means that `Log()` is a member of `Debug`. The dot operator allows us to access the `Log()` function found in the `Debug` class.

```
Debug.Log("Start");
```

Inside of the `Start()` function add in `Debug.Log("Start");`, as seen in the example above. When the game is started, the class will execute the code found inside of the `Start()` function. This means that the `Debug.Log("Start");` statement is executed.

Continuing in the Functions_Scene, click on the Play button and then click on the Console panel to bring it to the top. You should see the following lines of text in the Console panel.

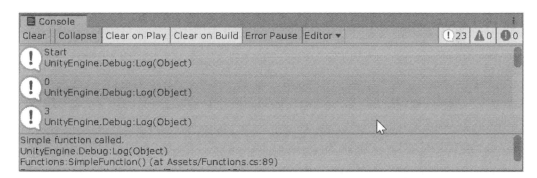

The first line says `Start`, followed by `UnityEngine.Debug:Log(Object)`, which is the expected result. If not, then double check a few different things. First check that the line of code you wrote ends with a semicolon (`;`) and is not left empty. Next, make sure that you're using quotes around the word: `"Start."`

Then, check that your spelling and case are correct: `Debug` and `Log`. Also make sure you didn't forget the dot operator (`.`) between `Debug` and `Log`. The punctuation matters a great deal. Missing any one of these changes the outcome of the code. Syntax is important for programming. Missing one detail breaks everything.

There are a few important things happening here, though many details left out for now. By the end of this chapter everything should be clear.

4.6.3 Writing a Function

A function consists of a declaration and a body. Some programmers like to call these *methods,* but semantics aside, a function is basically a container for a collection of statements. Let's continue with the Functions.cs script in the Chapter 4 Assets directory.

```
/*  ┌──────────────────────┐  ┌────────────┐ */
/*  │function declaration│  │parameters│ */
/*  └──────────────────────┘  └────────────┘ */
/*                                         */
/*                                         */
void MyFunction()
{
    // Function Body
}
```

Here is a basic function called MyFunction. We can add in additional keywords to modify the function's visibility. One common modifier we'll be seeing soon is public. We'll get further into the public keyword in Section 4.13 on accessibility.

```
public void MyPublicFunction()
{
}
```

The public keyword needs to appear before the return type of the function. In this case, it's void, which means that the function doesn't return anything. Return types are something else that we'll get into in Section 6.3.3, but functions can act as a value in a few different ways. For reference, a function that returns an int would look like this. A return statement of some kind must always be present in a function that has a return type.

```
public int MyIntFunction()
{
    return 1;
}
```

The public modifier isn't always necessary, unless you need to make this function available to other classes. If this point doesn't make sense, it will soon. The last part of the function that is always required is the parameter list. It's valid to leave it empty, but to get a feeling for what an arg, or argument in the parameter list, looks like, move on to the next example.

```
public void MyArgFunction(int i)
{
}
```

For the moment, we'll hold off on using the parameter list, but it's important to know what you're looking at later so it doesn't come as a surprise. Parameter lists are used to pass information from outside of the function to the inside of the function. This is how classes can pass information between one another.

We've been passing an argument for a while now using the Debug class. The Log member function of the Debug class takes a single argument. In Debug.Log("start"); the "start" is an argument we've been passing to the Log function. The Debug class is in the UnityEngine library and made available because of the using UnityEngine; statement.

We'll see how all these different parts of a function work as we get to them. Functions are versatile but require to be set up. Luckily, code is easy to build up one line at a time. It's good to know that very few people are capable of writing more than a few lines of code at a time before testing them.

To use a function, you simply enter the identifier followed by its argument list.

```
void SimpleFunction()
{
    Debug.Log("Simple function called.");
}

// Update is called once per frame
void Update ()
{
    SimpleFunction();
}
```

The placement of `SimpleFunction()` in the class has no effect on how it's called. For the sake of argument we can use `SimpleFunction()` anywhere in the class as long as it's been declared at the class scope.

For a function to work, we need to give it some instructions. If we declare an `int a` and set it to 0, we'll have some data to start with. In a function called `SetAtoThree()`, we set a to 3. If we call `CheckOnA()` a in the `Start()` function we'll get 0, the value which a was set to in the beginning. Then the function `SetAtoThree()` is called, which sets a to 3, so when a is logged again its new output is 3.

```
0
UnityEngine.Debug:Log(Object)

3
UnityEngine.Debug:Log(Object)
```

4.6.4 More on White Space and Tabs

Tabs are used to delineate the contents of a function. So far, we've been seeing each function written with its contents tabbed to the right with a single tab.

```
120    void·MoreTabs()
121    {
122        //tabbed·over·once!
123        int·i·=·0;
124        //while·statement·tabbed·over·as·well
125        while·(i·<·10)
126        {
127            //tabbed·over·even·more
128            Debug.Log(i);
129            i++;
130        }
131    }
```

The contents of the function are tabbed over once. The contents of the `while` statement inside of the function are tabbed over twice, as indicated by more spaces. This presentation helps to clarify that the contents of the `while` statement are executed differently from the rest of the function.

To help understand how the previous code fragment is read by the computer, we will step through the code one line at a time. This emulates how the function is run when it's called upon. Of course, a computer does this very quickly, but it's necessary for us to understand what the computer is doing many millions, if not billions, of times faster than we can comprehend.

NOTE: For a moment imagine your central processing unit (CPU) was made of gears spinning more than 2 billion times per second. The 2.4 GHz means 2,400,000,000 cps. A cycle is an update of every transistor in the silicon on the chip: over 2 billion pulses of electrons running through the silicon, every second turning on and off various transistors based on your instructions. Of course, not all the updates are dedicated to your game; many of the cycles are taken up by the operating system running Unity 3D, so performance isn't always what it should be.

The first line void `MoreTabs()` is identified by the computer and is used to locate the code to execute. Once the function is started the contents of the code begin at the first statement. In this case we reach `//tabbed over once!`, which is a comment and ignored.

Next we reach `int i = 0;`, which is a declaration and assignment of a variable that is identified as `i`, an identifier commonly used for integers. This declaration tells the computer to create a small place in memory for an integer value and it's told that we're going to use `i` to locate that data.

Following the variable declaration, we get to another comment that is also ignored by the computer. The `while (i < 10)` line of code follows the comment and this opens another space in memory for some operations. This also creates a connection to the i variable to check if the while statement will execute. If i is a value less than 10 then the statements in the following {curly braces} will be executed; otherwise, the contents of the while statement are ignored.

Another important character the computer finds is the opening curly brace ({) that tells it to recognize a new context for execution. The computer will read and execute each line in the while statement till it finds a closing curly brace (}). In this new context we'll return to the first curly brace until the while statement's condition is false.

Because i is less than 10, the while statement's condition is true, so we will proceed to the first line of the while statement. In this case, it's a comment that is ignored. This is followed by a Debug.Log() function, which also has a connection to the i variable. Therefore, this line prints to the console the value which is being stored at i. Once the value has been printed to the console the computer moves to the next line down.

The i++; statement tells the computer to look at the contents of i, add 1 to that value, and assign that new value back to i. This means that the new value for i is 1 since we started at 0. Once the computer reaches the closing curly brace, we jump back to the top of the while statement.

The contents of the curly braces are repeated until the value for i reaches 10; once the iteration returns 11, the condition of the while statement changes from *true* to *false*. Because 11 is not less than 10, the statements found between the curly braces will not be read. Therefore, the code in the while statement will be skipped. Once the computer reaches the closing curly brace of MoreTabs(), the computer stops running the function.

Computers do exactly what they're told and nothing more. The compiler runs using very explicit rules which it adheres to adamantly. Because of this, any strange behavior, which you might attribute to a bug, should point to how you've written your code. In many cases, small syntactical errors lead to errors which the computer will not be able to interpret.

It's greatly up to you to ensure that all of your code adheres to a format the computer can understand. When you write in English, a great deal of the sentiment and thought you put into words can be interpreted by each reader differently. For a computer there's only one way to interpret your code, so either it works or it doesn't.

4.6.5 What We've Learned

Function declaration is a bit like class declaration. Functions are the meat of where logic is done to handle variables. How variables make their way into and out of a function is covered in Section 6.18. There are many different ways to handle this, but we'll have to handle them one at a time.

On your own experiment with functions like the following:

```
void ATimesA()
{
    a = a * a;
}
```

You might want to set int a to a value other than 0 or 1 to get anything interesting out of this. Later, we'll be able to see how logic and loops can be used to make functions more powerful.

4.7 Order of Operation: What Is Calculated and When

Variables and functions work together to make your class operate as a part of your game. As an example, we're going to move an object through space using some simple math. To use numbers correctly, we need to be very specific. Remember, computers do exactly what they're told and nothing more.

Code is executed only when the function the code lives in is called. If the function is never called then nothing in the function will run. Once a function is called, the operation starts with evaluating the code at the top and works its way down to the end of the function one line at a time.

```
int a = 1;
Debug.Log(a); // 1
a = a + 3;
Debug.Log(a); // 4
a = a * 7;
Debug.Log(a); // 28
```

The first order which we've been working with so far is by line number. When code is evaluated each line is processed starting at the top; then it works its way down. In the following example, we start off with an integer variable and perform simple math operations and print the result.

As you might expect the first line prints 1, followed by 4, and then by 28. This is a rather long-handed method to get to a final result. However, things get a bit strange if we try to shorten this to a single line, as math operators work in a different order than we just used them.

```
int b = 1 + 3 * 7;
Debug.Log(b); // 22
```

After shortening the code to a single line like in this example, we get a different result, 22, which means 3 and 7 were multiplied before the 1 was added. Math operators have a priority when being evaluated, which follows the order of precedence. The multiply and divide operators have a higher precedence than add and subtract.

When evaluating int a, C# looked at the math operators first, and then did the math in the following order. Because the * is more important than the +; 3 * 7 was computed, turning the line into 1 + 21; then, the remaining numbers around + were evaluated, resulting a being assigned to 22, and then ultimately printing that to the Console output.

We'll observe the other behaviors and learn to control how math is evaluated. This section might not be so exciting, but it's worth the while to have this section as a reference. When your calculations begin to have unexpected results, it's usually because of order of operation coming into play and evaluating numbers differently from what you expected.

4.7.1 Evaluating Numbers

Calculation of variables is called *evaluation*. As we had mentioned before, each object added to the scene in Unity 3D's Editor has several components automatically added when it's first created. To make use of these components, you simply use their name in your code. The first component we'll be using is transform attribute. Transform contains the position rotation and scale of the object. You can see how these are changed when you select the object in the scene and move it around.

You can also enter numbers using the Inspector panel, or even click on the variable name and drag left and right as a slider to modify the data in the field. Moving objects around with code works in a similar manner as entering values in the Inspector panel. The position of the object is stored as three float values called a Vector3.

Operators in C# are the tools that do all of the work in your code. The first set of operators we'll discuss is arithmetic operators.

4.7.1.1 Math

+ −/* and %

The + and − do pretty much what you might expect them to: 1 + 3 = 4 and 1 − 3 = −2; this doesn't come as a surprise. Divide uses the /, putting the first number over the second number. However, the number *type* is important to sort out before we get too much further.

```
Debug.Log(10 / 3);
Debug.Log(10f / 3f);
Debug.Log(10.0 / 3.0);
```

The first line above is a 10/3, which might not return what you would expect. Writing a number without any decimal tells the compiler you're using integers, which will give you an integer result. Therefore, the result is simply 3, with the remaining one-third cut off since it's rounded down. The second line has an f after the number, indicating we want a float value. The third line without the f indicates a double value. This has twice the number of digits as a float.

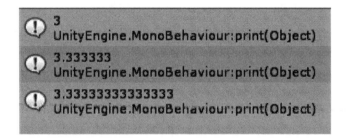

The result here shows the different number of trailing 3s after the decimal. We mentioned in Section 4.4.1.2 that there are different types of numbers. Here is an example of what that really means. An integer is a whole number without any decimal values. A float is a decimal type with only 7 digits in the number; a double is quite a lot bigger, having a total of 15 digits in the number.

```
28      // Use this for initialization
29      void Start ()
30      {
31          Debug.Log (10 / 3);
32          Debug.Log (10f / 3f);
33          Debug.Log (10.0 / 3.0);
34          Debug.Log (10000000.0f / 3.0f);
35          Debug.Log (1000000000000000.0 / 3.0);
36      }
```

Doing this experiment again with larger numbers exposes how our numbers have some limitations.

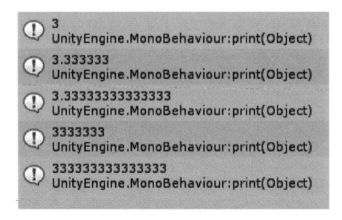

Like the integer, the large doubles and floats only have so many places where the decimal can appear. The number for the double is huge to begin with, but we should have more 3s after the number than are shown with a decimal. Where did they go? Keep in mind there *should* be an indefinite number of trailing 3s, but computers aren't good with indefinite numbers.

NOTE: Computers without special software can't deal with numbers with an unlimited number of digits. To show bigger numbers, computers use scientific notation like E+15 to indicate where significant numbers begin from the decimal point. Games, in particular, rarely ever need to deal with such large numbers. And to keep processes running fast, numbers are limited.

Software applications designed to deal with particularly huge numbers tend to work more slowly as they need to run with the same limitations, but instead perform operations on the first part of a number and then another operation on the second half of a number. This process can be repeated as many times as necessary if the number is even bigger. Scientific computing often does this and they have special number types to compensate. There are some additional number types, as well as other data types that aren't numbers. We'll leave the other data types for later (Section 5.3.4). The operators we're dealing with here are mainly for numbers.

Next up is the multiply operator (*). All the limitations that apply to the divide operator apply to the multiply operator as well. One important thing to consider here is that multiplication is technically faster than division. Therefore, in cases where you want to do 1000/4, the computer is going to be faster if you use 1000 * 0.25 instead.

This difference is a result of how the computer's hardware was designed. To be honest, modern CPUs are so much faster than they used to be, so using a / versus a * will usually make no noticeable difference. Old school programmers will beg to differ, but today we're not going to need to worry about this technicality, though I feel every classically trained programmer wants to scratch out my eyes right now.

Last up is the %, which in programming is called modulo, not percent as you might have guessed. This operator is used in what is sometimes called clock math. An analog clock has 12 hours around it. Therefore, a clock's hours can be considered %12, or modulo twelve, as a programmer might say.

To use this operator, consider what happens when you count 13 hours on a 12-hour clock and want to know where the hour hand will be on the 13th hour. This can be calculated by using the following term: 13%12; this operation produces the value 1 when calculated. Modulo is far easier to observe in operation than it is to describe.

The output from the code below here repeats from 0 to 11 repeatedly. Clocks don't start at 0, but computers do. Therefore, even though i is not being reset and continues to increase in value. On each update i is not being reset to 0, instead it continues to increment until you stop the game. A programmer would say "int i mod twelve" to describe i%12 shown here.

```
// Update is called once per frame
int mod = 1;
void Update ()
{
    int mod12 = mod % 12;
    Debug.Log(mod + " mod 12 = " + mod12);
    mod++;
}
```

Programmers are particular about their vocabulary and syntax, so it's best to understand how to think and talk like one. Programmers will usually assume you already know something like this, but it is worthwhile elaborating on the topic. Compilers, however, don't all think in the same way. Therefore, if you're curious and feel like learning other programming languages in the future, you might find that other languages will behave differently.

4.7.1.2 *Operator Evaluation*

As we saw before with 1 + 3 * 7 you may end up with different results, depending on the order in which you evaluated your numbers. To prevent any human misinterpretation of a calculation you can reduce the preceding numbers to 4 * 7 or 1 + 21. To make our intent clear we can use parentheses.

To gain control, we use the open and close parentheses to change the order of evaluation. For example, we can do this: 1 – 2 – (3 + 4), which turns into 1 – 2 – 7; a whole different result: –1 – 7 yields –8. A simple change in the order of operation can result in a completely different number when evaluated. This sort of thing becomes more important once we start shooting at zombies and dealing out damage. Some monsters might have thicker skin, and you'll want to reduce the damage done by a specific amount based on where he was shot.

4.7.1.2.1 *A Basic Example*

As we saw before, 1 + 3 * 7 will result in 22. We could use the long-winded version and start with a, then add 1 to it, then add 3 to that, and then multiply that by 7 to get 24. There's an easier way.

```
int c = (1 + 3) * 7;
Debug.Log(c);
```

By surrounding a pair of numbers with parentheses, we can tell the compiler to evaluate the pair within the parentheses before the multiplication. This results in 28, like the long-handed version of the same math. To elaborate we can add in another step to our math to see more interesting results.

```
int d = 1 + 3 * 7 + 9;
Debug.Log(d);
```

The code above results in 31 printed to the Console panel. We can change the result to 49 by surrounding the 7 + 9 with parentheses, like in the following.

```
int e = 1 + 3 * (7 + 9);
Debug.Log(e);
```

The complier computes the 7 + 9 before the rest of the math is computed. Parentheses take precedence over multiplication, regardless of where they appear. It doesn't matter where the parentheses appear, either at the beginning or at the end of the numbers: The parentheses are computed first.

Adding another set of parentheses can change the order of computation as well. Parentheses within parentheses tell the computer to start with the innermost pair before moving on. For instance (11 * ((9 * 3) * 2)) starts with 9 * 3; this turns into (11 * ((27) * 2), which then yields 27 * 2, which turns into (11 * (54)); 11 * 54 turns into 594. This can be switched round by shifting the placements of the parentheses to a different number. Try it out!

```
int f = (11 * ((9 * 3) * 2));
Debug.Log(f);
```

At this point, you will need to be very careful about the placement of the parentheses. For each opening parenthesis, there needs to be a corresponding closing parenthesis. If you're missing one, then Unity 3D will let you know. It's important to have a sense of what sort of math to use and when to use it.

In this case, where the parentheses encapsulate the entire expression their presence is redundant. Taking out the first and last parentheses will have no effect on the final result. This is true for most operations, but for clarity it's useful to know that they are indeed optional. To be clear about this, we can add any number of extra parentheses to the operation and there will be no other effect to the result, though it may look a bit strange.

```
int g = (((((11 * ((9 * 3) * 2)))))));
Debug.Log(g);
```

To make things clearer, we can rearrange this expression to be a lot more readable by setting up different variables. For each set of operations, we can create a new variable. The operations begin with the first variable; then, after the value is stored, the value is carried to the next time it's used. Just remember, a variable cannot be used until it's been created.

```
int h = 9 * 3;
int i = h * 2;
int j = i * 11;
Debug.Log(j);
```

In this example, we've created a different variable for each part of the math operation. First, we created a 9 * 3 variable assigned to h. After that we multiplied h by 2 and assigned that to i. Finally, we multiplied i by 11 and assigned that result to j. To view the result, we printed out j to get 594, the same result as the long, fairly obscure operation we started with. This example shows a simple use of variables to make your code more readable.

This seems like we're back to where we started with, at the beginning of this section. To be honest, both methods are perfectly valid. The decision to choose one system over another is completely dependent on which you find easier to understand.

What we should take away from this is the order in which the lines are read. The operations start at the top and work their way line by line to the bottom of the function. As variables are assigned new values, they are kept until they are reassigned.

It's important to note that by creating more than one variable, you're asking the computer to use more space in your computer's memory. At this point we're talking about very small amounts of memory. A classically trained programmer might want to fix this code upon reading it, and then convert it to a single line. To be honest, it does take up more space and not only visually.

When starting a new set of operations, it's sometimes helpful to use a more drawn-out set of instructions, using more variables. When you're more comfortable that your code is doing what you expect it to, you can take the time to reduce the number of lines required and do a bit of optimization. There's nothing wrong with making things work first and cleaning them up later.

4.7.2 What We've Learned

Therefore, you've been introduced to variables and you've learned about functions, two big components of programming needed to make a game. Directives will allow your code to talk with Unity 3D and put meaning behind your variables and functions.

We're using C# and .NET, which is an object-oriented programming environment. We just learned objects are all the little bits of information that make up your different C# classes. When we're done with writing some code, Unity 3D will automatically interpret your code for your game.

At this point, we've got a pretty strong grasp of the basics of what code looks like and the different parts of how code is written. We've yet to make use of any logic in our functions, but we should be able to read code and know what is and isn't in a function.

It would be a good idea, by way of review, to make a few other classes and get used to the process of starting new projects, creating classes, and adding them to objects in a Unity 3D Scene. Once you're comfortable with creating and using new classes in Unity 3D you'll be ready to move on.

4.8 Scope: A First Look

Encapsulation is the term given to where data can be accessed from. The amount of accessibility is called scope. The visibility of a variable to your logic changes depending on where it appears.

Encapsulation can hide, or change the accessibility of data between statements, functions, and classes. Another way to think about it is keeping data on a need-to-know basis. This invisibility is intended for several reasons. One reason is to reduce the chances of reusing variable names.

```csharp
// Use this for initialization
void Start ()
{
    for (int i = 0; i < 10; i++)
    {
        Debug.Log(i);
    }
}
```

4.8.1 Class Scope

To get a better look at how scope and encapsulation work together, Open the Scope_Scene in the Chapter 4 Unity Project. Attached to the Scope GameObject is the Scope script. When the scene is run, the code attached to the Scope GameObject will run as normal.

```csharp
// Use this for initialization
void Start ()
{
    for (int i = 0; i < 10; i++)
    {
        Debug.Log(i);
    }
}
```

The `MyInt` variable exists at the class scope level. `MyInt` can be used in any function that lives in the class scope. The example code you're looking at will produce the following Console output:

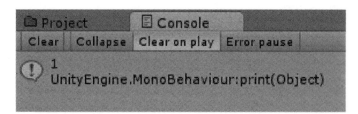

Both `Start()` and `Update()` live in the class scope so both can see the `MyInt` variable. Therefore, the following code will send a 1 to the console. Both `Start()` and the `Update()` functions will keep sending 1s to the Console window.

```
int myInt = 1;

void Start ()
{
    Debug.Log(myInt);
}

void Update ()
{
    Debug.Log(myInt);
}
```

Placement of a variable at the class scope has little effect on where it's used. The code above can be rearranged easily. The code below will behave the same as the code above.

```
void Start ()
{
    Debug.Log(myInt);
}

void Update ()
{
    Debug.Log(myInt);
}

int myInt = 1;
```

The functions and variables act in the same way, irrespective of where they appear in the class. However, class scope is easy to override with other variables of the same name. This is called *variable collision*, the effects of which you should be aware of, as discussed in Section 7.4.

```
int myInt = 2;|
Debug.Log(myInt);
```

[●] (local variable) int myInt

If we declare a variable of the same name in more than one place then it will be overridden by the newest version of our variable. If you were to run this script in your scene, you'd have the Console printout 2 because of the line that preceded the print function call.

There are problems with how variables can collide with one another. And the best way to avoid this problem would be to come up with good names for your variables. What happens if we try to use both versions of myInt?

```
Debug.Log(myInt);
int myInt = 2; // stomps on class scoped myInt
Debug.Log(myInt);
```

The scope in which the new myInt declaration appears wipes out the existence of myInt defined at the class scope. The result of such a declaration will be an error: "A local variable myInt cannot be used before it is declared." You may have expected the first print function to print out the class scope version of myInt, but this isn't the case.

Variables named at the class scope still exist even if you reuse the name with new variables named in a function. The word "this" is a keyword. If "this" preceeds a variable, C# understands to use the variable named in the class scope and not the variable named in the function scope.

```
Debug.Log(this.myInt);
int myInt = 2; // stomps on class scoped myInt
Debug.Log(myInt);
```

By creating an int myInt inside of the Start() function in your class you have effectively hidden the class scoped myInt from the function. Although it can be accessed as this.myInt, the function scoped version of myInt in the function takes precedent.

This example should also highlight that a variable can be used only after it's been initialized. This is a situation best avoided, so it's good to remember what variable names you've used so you don't use them again.

To elaborate, a function starts from the first curly brace ({) and computes one line at a time, working its way from the top, moving toward the bottom until it hits the closing curly brace (}). An error occurs if a variable is used in a statement before the variable is declared.

```
int myInt = 1;
float myInt = 1; //nope.
```

Something that might be obvious but should be mentioned is the fact that you can't reuse a variable name. Even if the second variable is a different type, we'll get the following error in MonoDevelop explaining our error.

Another effect of creating a variable inside of a function is the fact that another function can't see what's going on. In the following code we declare a StartInt in the Start() function. After that we try to use it again in the Update() function, which results in an error.

```
void Start ()
{
    int declaredInStart = 1;
    Debug.Log(declaredInStart);
}


void Update ()
{
    Debug.Log(declaredInStart);
}
```

C# is telling us that we can't use a variable before it's declared. Of course, we did declare it once, but that was in a different function. The Update() function can't see inside of the Start() function to find the declatedInStart variable declared in the Start() function.

You'll have to keep this in mind once you start writing your own functions. There are two common ways to work with declaring variables. The first is to place all your variables at the top of the function.

This way you ensure that everything you may need to use is already declared before you need them. The second method is to declare the variable just before it's needed.

```
int firstInt = 100;
int secondInt = 200;
Debug.Log(firstInt);
Debug.Log(secondInt);
```

In this case, we're being very clear inside of this function about what variables we may use. For short functions this can sometimes be a lot easier to deal with. You can easily sort your variables and change their values in one place. It's also easier to check if you're accidentally reusing a variable's name.

```
int thirdInt = 300;
Debug.Log(thirdInt);
int fourthInt = 400;
Debug.Log(fourthInt);
```

In this second case, we're using the variable only after it's created. When writing long functions you may find the second method a bit more clear as you can group your variables together near the logic and functions that will be using them.

This is a small example of code style. When reading someone else's code, you'll have to figure out how they think. In some cases, it's best to try to match the style of existing code. However, when you're writing everything on your own, it's best to keep to your own style and decide how you want to arrange your code.

If we declare a variable at the class scope, all functions inside of the class can see, and access, that variable. Once inside of a function, any new variables that are declared are visible only to that function. Some statements can declare variables as well, and those variables are visible only inside of the statement they are declared. Once we get to know about more statements, we'll see how they work, but we'll need to keep scope in mind when we get there.

4.8.2 Function Scope

Variables often live an ephemeral life. Some variables exist only over a few lines of code. Variables may come into existence only for the moment a function starts and then disappear when the function is done. Variables in the class scope exist for as long as the class exists. The life of the variable depends on where it's created.

In a previous exercise, we focused on declaring variables and showing them in the Unity 3D's Inspector panel. Then we observed when variables need to be declared to be used without any errors. The placement and `public` keywords were necessary to expose the variables to the Unity 3D editor.

The `public` keyword can be used only at the class scope. This is called class scope as the variable is visible to all of the functions found within the class. Making the variable `public` means that any other class that can see this class can then also have access to the variable as well. We'll go into more detail on what this means and how it's used in a bit.

```
void SomeFunction()
{
    public int fifthInt;
}
```

Adding the `public int` within the a function will produce an error. You're not allowed to elevate a variable to the class scope from inside of a function. Visual Studio will not give you the most informative error message, but Unity will have a different message for you. `Unexpected symbol "public";` the reason is that variables within a function cannot be made accessible outside of the function.

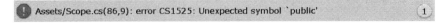
Assets/Scope.cs(86,9): error CS1525: Unexpected symbol `public'   ①

There are systems in C# to make data within a function accessible, but using the keyword `public` is not it. We'll look into how that's done in Section 6.1. A variable declared inside of a function exists only as the function is used. The functions declared in the class are also a part of the class scope, and at the same level as the variables declared at the class scope level. If a function in a class is preceded by the `public` keyword, it's accessible by name, just like a variable. Without the `public` keyword the function will remain hidden. We'll make use of `public` functions in Section 6.3.2, but it's important to know that a function can be made publicly available, like variables.

Referring to the Scope script created for this chapter, we're going to make use of the functions given to us by the programmers at Unity 3D. The location of a variable in code changes where it can be seen from and how it can be used.

As noted, limiting accessibility of any variable is called encapsulation. The curly braces, {}, and parentheses, (), have a specific context. This context can keep their contents hidden from other sections of code. This means that `Start()` can have one value for `myInt`, and if you a different `myInt` in `Update()`, it will not be affected by the `myInt` in `Start()`.

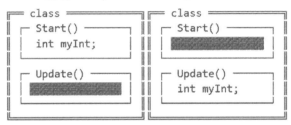

If we look at the above figure we can visualize how scope is divided. The outer box represents who can see `ClassInt`. Within the `Start()` function we have a `StartInt` that only exists within the `Start()` function. The same is repeated for the `UpdateInt`, found only in the `Update()` function. This means that `Start()` can use both `ClassInt` and `StartInt` but not `UpdateInt`. Likewise, `Update()` can see `ClassInt` and `UpdateInt` but not `StartInt`.

In the diagram below the boxes represent different levels of scope.

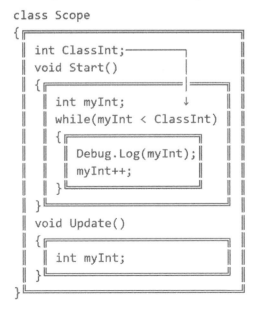

Within the Start() function is a while loop. The while() loop can use both ClassInt and myInt. The following Update() function can see ClassInt but not myInt, which exists in the Start() function. The variable ClassInt was declared in the class scope, whereas the myInt variable was only declared inside of the Start() function's scope and isn't accessible outside of the Start() function.

4.8.3 Blank Scope

Blank Scope is obscure and not often used, but worth mentioning. Curly braces are used to encapsulate code, we've observed plenty of how that works with classes and functions. However, a pair of curly braces can encapsulate code without a specific reason.

```
void BlankScope()
{
    int a = 0;
    {
        int b;
        Debug.Log(a);
    }
    Debug.Log(b);
}
```

The name 'b' does not exist in the current context

Show potential fixes (Alt+Enter or Ctrl+.)

In the code above, we have a function named BlankScope but there's also a pair of curly braces where int b; has been declared. This is called a *blank scope*. The Debug.Log(b); cannot see int b outside of the blank scope. This does help in cases where working on a particularly tricky code might require some isolation.

```
{
    int b = 0;
    Debug.Log(b);
}
{
    int b = 1;
    Debug.Log(b);
}
```

With blank scope you can declare variables with identifiers that were already used elsewhere in the code. If you were testing out different algorithms you might want to use blank scope to isolate different ideas.
    If you're using blank scope you're also able to fold code bracketed by the curly braces.

```
{
    Debug.Log("blank scope...");
}// put a label of what the code is doing here.
```

One clever trick is to put a comment at the bottom of the curly braces.

```
⊞          ...// put a label of what the code is doing here.
```

With the comment at the bottom, when your code is folded it will have a title so you can identify what the code does. Organizing your code is something that comes after quite a lot of practice. Eventually you'll end up coming up with schemes of your own to help keep your code organized. No suggestions on *how* to organize code have been made. Tools and systems have been introduced, but no style has been recommended. I'll leave the specific style up to you to make your own decisions on.

4.8.4 What We've Learned

Encapsulation describes a system by which a variable's scope is defined. Depending on where a variable is declared, the scope of the variable changes. Encapsulation prevents variables from overlapping when they're used. Encapsulation, therefore, allows one function to operate independently from another function without our needing to worry about a variable's name being reused.

We'll cover more situations where scope becomes a useful tool to help classes message one another. Encapsulation and scope define a major principle of object oriented programming, and understanding this concept is important to learning how to write C#.

4.9 This

What happens when a class needs to refer to objects in itself? In most cases, a class can use its own properties and fields and not get confused what variable is being referred to. For instance, we can take a look at a basic class that has the following.

```csharp
int someInt = 0;
void AssignInt(int i)
{
    someInt = i;
}
```

Here, we have someInt defined at the class scope. We've have a function that assigns the someInt to i. There are no problems with this setup. On the other hand, should the AssignInt be modified to look like the following:

4.9.1 A Basic Example

In the KeywordThis_Scene open the KeywordThis script found on the KeywordThis object. Looking at the AssignInt function, there's no confusion with the assignment of someInt. The situation changes when the parameter name in AssignInt changes to someInt.

```csharp
void AssignSomeInt(int someInt)
{
    someInt = someInt;
}
```

The `AssignSomeInt(int someInt)` function has no errors, and the project builds. The expectation is that `someInt` will be assigned the value that was coming into the function through the parameter. However, we get a different result.

```
private void Start()
{
    Debug.Log(someInt); // 0
    AssignSomeInt(3);
    Debug.Log(someInt); // still 0?
}
```

If we use this to assign someInt in the `Start()` function we get the Log output of 0 both before and after using the function. Hover over the assignment in the `AssignSomeInt` function and you'll observe the message "Assignment made to same variable; did you mean to assign something else?" To solve this problem, we'll look at the simple solution.

```
void AssignThisSomeInt(int someInt)
{
    this.someInt = someInt;
}
```

This assigns the class scoped `someInt` the value of the incoming parameter `someInt`. This is because in the function `AssignThisSomeInt`, where we assign the parameter `someInt` variable `this.someInt`. Without the keyword `this`, the local scope of the function overrides the class scope use of `someInt`.

4.9.2 When This Is Necessary

With the addition of the keyword `this` to the function above, we can specify which version of the `someInt` variable we're talking about. It's easy to avoid the requirement of the `this` keyword. Simply use unique parameter names from the class's variables and you won't need to use the `this` keyword.

There is no unexpected behavior if we superfluously use the `this` keyword anytime we want to.

```
void AssignThisInt(int i)
{
    this.someInt = i;
}
```

The use of `this` can help make the code more readable. In a complex class where we have many different variables and functions, it sometimes helps to clarify if the variable being assigned is something local to the function we're reading or if the variable is a class scoped variable. Using this we can be sure that the variable is assigned to a class variable, and not something only in the function.

Getting into something somewhat obscure, but worth mentioning is self-referencing. In some cases, an object may need to look to itself as a variable. To do this you'd have an object store itself as a variable.

```
class ThisThing
{
    ThisThing myThing;
    public void AssignThing()
    {
        myThing = this;
    }
}

void AssignAThingToItself()
{
    ThisThing thing = new ThisThing();
    thing.AssignThing();
}
```

The example above shows a class called ThisThing. Inside of it there's a variable declaration called myThing that's the same type as itself. To assign the class itself to the myThing variable there's a function called AssignThing() where the contents of that function assigns this to myThing.

The function AssignAThingToItself() executes the code and creates a thing and has it assign itself to the myThing variable. With some data types where objects need to reference to both themselves and similar components you'll create what's called a linked list. One of the components of a linked list is being able to reference itself among other objects it might be linked to.

We may be jumping ahead into some complex data structures, so we'll hold off more complex subjects for now. It's not too common for an object needing to reference itself in this way, but C# lets you do it.

4.9.3 What We've Learned

In general, this is a somewhat awkward keyword. The necessity of using the keyword this arises in very few use cases.

When naming variables and functions, it's best to keep to a consistent pattern. In general, many people use longer names at the class scope. For instance, the following code uses a pattern of shorter and shorter variable names depending on the variable's scope:

```
class MyClass
{
    int MyInt;
    void MyFunction(int mInt)
    {
        int m = mInt;
        MyInt = m;
    }
}
```

At the scope of the entire class the `int` is `MyInt`. Within the function `MyFunction` in `MyClass` a local variable visible to `MyFunction` in the argument list is called `mInt`. The variable defined inside of the function is simply `m`.

There are obvious limitations to using a convention like shortening variable names. It's very easy to run out of letters and end up with unclear variable names, but it's a simple place to get started.

This isn't a common practice convention by any means; it's one that I've personally become used to using. These sorts of personal conventions are something that everyone needs to invent for his or her individual use. I'd expect you to find your own convention for naming variables.

The flexibility of C# allows everyone to have a personal style of writing code. Identifiers aren't the only place where one can find self-expression through code. Another way to express one's self through code is deciding to use a `for-while` or `do-while` loop. Both can be used for the very similar tasks, but the decision is ultimately left to the programmer writing the code.

For any reason should you feel like you prefer one method over another you should follow your own intuition and write how you like to. Programming is a creative process and writing expressive code is a process just like any other form of art.

4.10 Building a Game—Part 2

Previously we worked to get at a little robot character moving with a point and click system. Unity 3D allows us to attach more than one script to a GameObject in a scene. The additional components attached to the game object append additional behaviors.

An entity with behaviors is a conceptual relationship or Entity Component Model. Programmers, like scientists, use categorization to classify work. Words like Domain Driven Design (DDD), or Model-View-ViewModel (MVVM), or Component Object Model (COM) are techniques. Design patterns are intended to help organize what classes contain what functions and where to store data.

Most game engines, Unity 3D included, follow the Entity Component Model where an object in the scene has various components attached to it. The components include sounds, particle effects, 3d models, and so forth. Each component can in turn, also have more components attached to them. Weapons can have sounds effects and models which are then attached to a character. Where the division of work splits a component into multiple parts is dependent on the engineer coming up with the systems that drive the game. Split things up too small and you've got numerous classes with different interfaces and functions that can be confusing. Too few components and classes can grow into large masses of complex code.

Decisions like when to split a class into multiple components only comes with experience. After writing a few different games, the natural lines of delineation between components becomes more apparent. We have yet to write one game, though, so let's get back to that.

If we want to add some shooting behavior to our character, we should use the right mouse button. The previous exercise used the left mouse button to tell the character to move toward the mouse position. Lots of projectiles are more fun than one so right click down should start spraying a bunch of projectiles at the mouse point and when we release the shooting stops.

We should also have some targets to shoot at, so we'll also want to have a system to pop up something to shoot at. When the targets take enough hits, we'll have them explode and go away. This means we'll need to build some sort of target damage system.

4.10.1 Additional Components

Layers of behaviors added to an entity in a scene makes creating complex behavior easier. The alternative is to create a single script that manages every entity in the scene at once. Let's avoid that and write a system to allow our little guy some target practice.

Continuing with the Unity-SampleGame, open the Section 4.10 scene to review what's going on.

The process begins with needing to fire projectiles from the character. Projectiles will originate from the Robo character, so the script should start there.

Following the logic we'll want a way to determine how and when the projectiles should be created. Weapons in games often have a rate of fire, or how many projectiles are created per minute.

```
// convert RPM to tenthsOfSeconds
float NextShot(float rpm)
{
    // 600 rounds per minute
    //÷ 60 minute
    //——
    //= 10 rounds per second
    float perSecond = rpm / 60;

    // tents of a second
    // between each round
    //
    //   1 second
    //÷ 10 rounds per second
    //——
    //=0.1 seconds

    float tenths = 1 / perSecond;
    return tenths;
}
```

To use this in Unity we need to convert rounds per minute into tenths of seconds. The conversion in the example takes a supposed 600 rpm and converts that into 0.1f seconds with some basic math.

```
if (Input.GetMouseButton(1) && Time.time > NextTime)
{
    // calculate how soon we can fire the next shot
    NextTime = Time.time + NextShot(RateOfFire);
```

In the Update function we check for `GetMouseButton(1)` for the right mouse button. We use the `NextShot` function to set `NextTime` to regulate how often the weapon will fire. To give ourselves a bullet to create we use `GameObject ProjectileObject` and assign a Prefab of a projectile to the Robo in the scene. Prefabs are assemblies of game objects that have been stored in the Assets directory. These are GameObjects that have components added so they can function on their own.

```
public GameObject ProjectileObject;
public GameObject ProjectileStart;
public AudioClip BlasterShotClip;
```

The projectiles need to have a transform to be instantiated with. An instantiated object without a position and orientation to start with will appear at the origin of the scene. To provide the projectile with a position in front of Robo, an empty GameObject named "ProjectileStart" has been added. This gets assigned to the ProjectileWeapon script. Last is a SoundClip that will play when the weapon is fired. To play the audio, the Robo has an AudioSource component attached, so the audio clip has a something to play from.

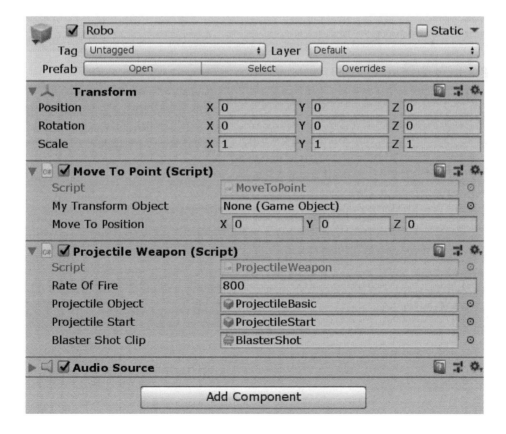

Now the rest of the Update() function can be filled in.

```
// get the position of the "barrel" of the weapon
Vector3 pos = ProjectileStart.transform.position;
// get the rotation of the "barrel" of the weapon
Quaternion rot = ProjectileStart.transform.rotation;

// create a new projectile with the barrel position
// and rotation.
Instantiate(ProjectileObject, pos, rot);

// make a pew! noise
GetComponent<AudioSource>().PlayOneShot(BlasterShotClip);
```

We get a Vector3 and a Quaternion from the ProjectileStart object and assign it to the Instantiate function that uses the "Original" as a template to create a new projectile. Once the object is created we play a "Pew!" sound. So what is the projectile?

4.10.2 The Projectile

The projectile has three features. First, it has a travel speed; second, it's got a life time; and last, it's got a damage value. To ensure that the world doesn't get populated with too many bullets that never hit anything we assign a number to terminate a projectile after a time limit.

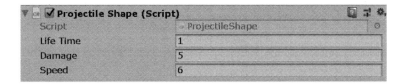

In the Start() function we use the Life Time's value to both Get and Set a time limit.

```
LifeTime = Time.time + LifeTime;
```

Here, imagine that if time was 3, it's just assigned 3 + the Current Time which might be 21 seconds into the game. With that math, Life Time of 3 becomes Current Time 21 + Life Time 3. This sets the end of life to 24. So in Update we check the following:

```
if (Time.time >= LifeTime)
{
    Destroy(this.gameObject);
}
```

When the current time is past the Life Time of the Projectile GameObject, the projectile destroys itself. The speed value is used to set its initial Velocity when it's created.

```
GetComponent<Rigidbody>().velocity = transform.forward * Speed;
```

When the projectile is instantiated, it's given a position and orientation to start with. Velocity of `transform.forward` multiplied by its `speed` will simply shove the projectile forward. Making the physics in Unity a bit easier to work with, we turn off gravity on the rigid body attached to the Projectile GameObject.

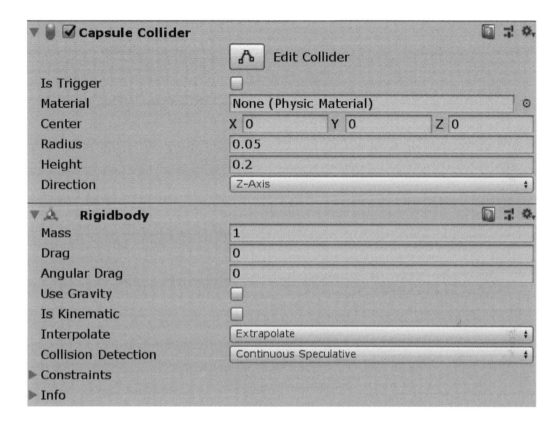

Features like Interpolate and Collision Detection are set to Extrapolate and Continuous Speculative, as recommended by the Unity documentation for fast moving projectiles. This ensures that the projectile doesn't pass through stationary objects without collision detection. If an object is moving fast enough the `Update()` function might miss a collision. Our projectile also has a colorful contrail attached to it for added visual effect.

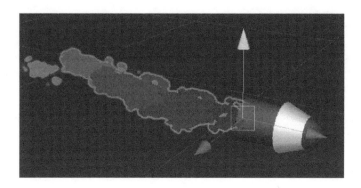

4.10.3 The Target

We need something to shoot at. The large red boxes populating the scene have a DamageSystem script attached. This has three values as well, a damage number, and Two GameObjects that are spawned when it's hit with a projectile.

```csharp
public int Damage;
// Prefabs to instantiate when a hit is recorded
public GameObject ExplosionSmall;
public GameObject ExplosionLarge;
```

The first explosion is instantiated when we record a hit, but the target is not destroyed. The second explosion will be instantiated when the target is destroyed. The damage value is decremented by the projectile.

```csharp
private void OnCollisionEnter(Collision collision)
{
    ProjectileShape other = collision.gameObject.GetComponent<ProjectileShape>();
    if (other != null)
    {
        // make the projectile go away.
        Destroy(other.gameObject);
        Vector3 pos = collision.contacts[0].point;
        Vector3 dir = collision.contacts[0].normal;
        Quaternion rot = Quaternion.LookRotation(dir);

        Damage -= other.Damage;
        if (Damage <= 0)
        {
            Instantiate(ExplosionLarge, pos, rot);
            // make this thing go away.
            Destroy(this.gameObject);
        }
        else
        {
            Instantiate(ExplosionSmall, pos, rot);
        }
    }
}
```

To record collision events we use the MonoBehaviour OnCollisionEnter event delegate. To check what collided with the target we use ProjectileShape other. Everything that touches the target will trigger the OnCollisionEnter delegate. By using GetComponent() on anything touching the target, we can check if the colliding object is a projectile. The statement if (other != null) is true when the collision occurs with an object that has the ProjectileShape script attached.

We reduce the target damage by the projectile's damage value and check if the value is less than or equal to 0. If we are not at or below 0, we create a small explosion, otherwise we create a large explosion and destroy the target game object. The large and small explosions are particle systems with the sound source attached to them to play the explosion sound. When the particle system is finished, the object is set to destroy itself.

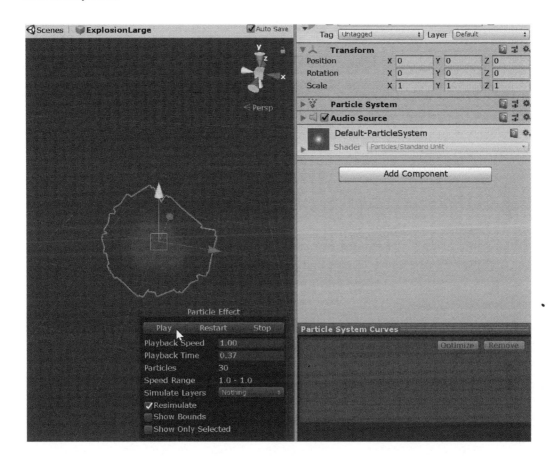

You might ask why the target doesn't play the sound. The audio source component needs to be in the scene for the audio to be heard. If the target destroys itself, it takes the audio source away with it. An audio clip never gets played on an object that doesn't exist.

4.10.4 What We've Learned

Here's where we get a tad philosophical. With the idea in mind that the explosion object plays the explosion sound, does that mean that the projectiles should play the blaster shot sound? The current setup has the weapon playing the blaster shot sound, but we could easily change the responsibility of the audio source. To change things completely, we could have a third object in the scene that plays all the sounds. A sound management object could be marked to not be destroyed, so this ensures that all the sounds will be played when objects are destroyed.

Quite a lot has been accomplished with very simple behaviors. We rely on events and options Unity 3D has built. Unity 3D is a game engine after all, so we should leverage all the features prepared for making games.

We've invested some time in seeing how to pool together simple language features to make complex behavior, so let's continue to see how C# works to understand more about what we just looked at in this chapter.

4.11 Logic and Operators

Logic allows you to control what part of a function is evaluated based on changes to variables. Using logic, you'll be able to change which statements in your code will run. Simply put, everything you write must cover each situation you plan to cover. Logic is controlled through a few simple systems, primarily the if keyword and variations of "if."

4.11.1 Booleans

Open the LogicAndOperators.cs script in Visual Studio along with the LogicAndOpetarors_ Scene in the Unity Editor. Using George Boole's logic is a basic tool in nearly every programming paradigm. This is a rather detailed section, since there's a lot to cover. So let's dig in!

In programming booleans, or bools for short, are values that represent either true or false, in some cases 1 or 0. It's easiest to think of these as switches in either on or off position. To declare a variable as a bool, you use something like the following.

```
public class LogicAndOperators : MonoBehaviour
{
    /* This value appears in the Inspector */
    /* panel.                            */
    public bool someBool;
```

By using public you'll expose the boolean variable to Unity 3D's Editor. This declaration will make the variable appear in the Inspector panel. The boolean needs to appear here to be seen by the rest of the class in Unity 3D. We'll learn why this is so in Section 4.13 on scope, but we'll digress for now.

The value for `Some Bool` appears in the Inspector as an empty check box. This means that you can set the `bool` as either true or false by checking it on or off, checked or unchecked. Your code can also set your `public` variables by running the game.

```
void Start()
{
    someBool = (1 == 1);
}
```

NOTE: C# does a pretty good job of automatically initializing many of its built-in types. Number values are always initialized to 0 when they are not given a value. Bools are initialized as false when not given a value. This is handy to know since not all languages do this.

For instance, Lua, another commonly used game programming language, assumes nothing about the value until it's given one. Therefore, when any variable is first declared, it's initialized as nil, which is like C#'s behavior when creating a variable of a more complex data type. Though C# calls this uninitialized state `null`, this means the same as nothing. For good measure, UnrealScript uses the keyword none to mean the same as `null`.

Changes made before the game is run will be saved on that object. For making a game, for example, you can place treasure chests throughout a dungeon and set the amount of gold in each one. This is great since you will not need to make a different script for each treasure chest.

```
public int Gold;
```

For instance, setting a number for gold in the treasure chest will allow you to change the gold in each instance placed in a scene.

4.11.2 Equality Operators

Equality operators create boolean conditions. There are many ways to set a boolean variable. For instance, comparisons between values are a useful means to set variables. The most basic method to determine equality is using the following operator: `==`.

There's a difference between use of a single and a double equal symbol. `=` is used to assign a value, whereas `==` is used to compare values. Another way to read the `==` is to say the left value "is equivalent to" the right value.

When you need to compare two values you can use the following concept. You'll need to remember that these operators are called equality operators, if you need to talk to a programmer. The syntax here may look a bit confusing at first, but there are ways around that.

```
/*
 * value 1 compared to value 1
 * 1 == 1 is true
 */
someBool = (1 == 1);
```

There are other operators to be aware of. You will be introduced to the other logical operators later in the chapter. In this case, we are asking if two number values are the same. When the game is started, you'll be able to watch the someBool check itself to true if not then the operator returns false. This is the same as the following.

```
someBool = true;
someBool = false;
```

To explain how this works, we'll need to look at the order of operation that just happened. First, the right side of the first single = was calculated. 1 == 1 is a simple comparison, asking if 1 is the same as 1, which results with a true value. Test this out and check for the result in Unity 3D.

To make this a clearer, we can break out the code into more lines. Now, we're looking at a versus b. Clearly, they don't look the same; they are different letters after all. However, they do contain the same integer value, and that's what's really being compared here.

```
/* values in a and b are compared   */
/* ● a is assigned 1                 */
/* ● b is assigned 1                 */
int a = 1;/*1 == 1 is true           */
int b = 1;/*↓      ↓ ●               */
someBool = (a == b);
/*   ↑           true                */
/*   └─────●─────┘                   */
/*   someBool is assigned            */
/*   true                            */
```

Evaluations have a left and a right side. The single equal to operator (=) separates the different sides. The left side of the = is calculated and looks to the value to the right to get its *assignment*. Because 1 == 1, that is to say, 1 is equivalent to 1, the final result of the statement is that someBool is true. The check box is turned on and the evaluated statement is done.

```
/* values in a and b are compared   */
/* ● a is assigned 1                 */
/* ● b is assigned 3                 */
int a = 1;/*1 == 3 is false          */
int b = 3;/*↓      ↓ ●               */
someBool = (a == b);
/*   ↑           false               */
/*   └─────●─────┘                   */
/*   someBool is assigned            */
/*   false                           */
```

As you might expect, changing the value in one of the variables will change the outcome of this equality test. someBool will be clicked off because the statement is no longer true. Or in plain language, Is a equal to b? The answer is no, or as far as someBool is concerned, false.

4.11.3 Logical Not!

If we compare values that are equal, we get a value that's `true`. If we need a value that's `false` the `!` symbol flips the result. As we saw with the above statement, 1 is 3 is `false`, we can also use 1 is not 3 to be `true`.

```
bool a_IsNot_b;
/* values in a and b are compared      */
/* ➊ a is assigned 1                    */
/* ➋ b is assigned 3                    */
int a = 1;/* 1 != 3 is true            */
int b = 3;/* ↓      ↓ ➋                 */
a_IsNot_b = (a != b);
/* ↑            true                    */
/* └──────➋──────┘                      */
/* a_IsNot_b is assigned                */
/* true                                 */
Debug.Log("a_IsNot_b:" + a_IsNot_b);
// a_IsNot_b:true
```

The operator `!=` means not equal. In the `(1 != 3)`, we get true since 1 is not equal to 3. Logically this also means that `1 != 1` is `false`. It is not `true` that 1 is not equal to 1.

```
/* values in a and b are compared      */
/* ➊ a is assigned 1                    */
/* ➋ b is assigned 1                    */
bool a_IsNot_b;
int a = 1;/* 1 != 1 is false           */
int b = 1;/* ↓      ↓ ➋                 */
a_IsNot_b = (a != b);
/* ↑           false                    */
/* └──────➋──────┘                      */
/* a_IsNot_b is assigned                */
/* false                                */
Debug.Log("a_IsNot_b:" + a_IsNot_b);
// a_IsNot_b:False
```

The not operator `!` can also be assigned to a value after it's been calculated. After an evaluation comes in as either `true` or `false`, the `!` can be applied to the value to flip the result from `true` to `false`.

```
bool not_a_is_b;
int a = 1;/*   1 == 1 is true          */
int b = 1;/*   ↓      ↓                 */
not_a_is_b = !(a == b);
/* ➋↑          ↑  true                  */
/* └──────────➋──────┘                  */
/* ➋ not true                           */
/* ➋ false is assigned                  */
Debug.Log("not_a_is_b:" + not_a_is_b);
// not_a_is_b:false
```

In the above, the `1 == 1` value returns `true`. Before it's assigned to not_a_isNot_b the `!` is applied to the `true` resulting in not_a_isNot_b set to `false`. This can be applied to any other value as well.

```
bool not_a_isNot_b;
int a = 1;/*       1 != 1 is false      */
int b = 1;/*         ↓    ↓              */
not_a_isNot_b = !(a != b);
/* ●↑              ↑ false              */
/*   └──────────●──┘                    */
/*   ● not false                        */
/*   ● true is assigned                 */
Debug.Log("not_a_isNot_b:" + not_a_isNot_b);
// not_a_isNot_b:true
```

The logic of `1` is not `1` evaluates as false, then not is applied so false becomes true. Applying the not `!` operator to a not equals operation makes the statement hard to read. It's important to simplify how and when the operators are used. The fewer operators you can use the better.

4.11.4 Greater and Less than Operators

To further empower the comparisons, we can use the `>` and `<` operators. These are the greater than and less than operators. This operator compares values. In the statement `(3 > 0)` we ask if 3 is greater than 0 which evaluates `true`.

```
/* this compares the values of numbers  */
/* -5 -4 -3 -2 -1 ±0 +1 +2 +3 +4 +5      */
/*├──────────────┼───────┼──────┤        */
/*               0       3               */
bool greaterThan = (3 > 0);
Debug.Log("greaterThan:" + greaterThan);
// greaterThan:true
```

The order around the operator is important and evaluates as you would expect. If you reverse the terms of the operation where we ask if `(0 > 3)` zero is greater than 3, we get false.

```
/* this compares the values of numbers  */
/* -5 -4 -3 -2 -1 ±0 +1 +2 +3 +4 +5      */
/*├──────────────┼───────┼──────┤        */
/*               0       3               */
bool greaterThan = (0 > 3);
Debug.Log("greaterThan:" + greaterThan);
// greaterThan:false
```

This can be modified by the ! not operator as with the previous == operations. This does the same thing to the operation as before.

```
bool greaterThan = !(0 > 3);
/*                 ↑ not operator          */
Debug.Log("greaterThan:" + greaterThan);
// greaterThan:true
```

In contrast we can also use the < operator to see if the left operand is less than the right operand.

```
bool lessThan = (0 < 3);
Debug.Log("lessThan:" + lessThan);
// lessThan:true
```

As with the greater than operator the less than functions in the same way with the left value compared to the right value. What may be less expected is if the values are the same.

```
/* -5 -4 -3 -2 -1 ±0 +1 +2 +3 +4 +5     */
/*├─────────────────────┼─────────┤     */
/*                      3 vs 3 ?    */
bool lessThan = (3 < 3);
Debug.Log("lessThan:" + lessThan);
// lessThan:false
bool greaterThan = (3 > 3);
Debug.Log("greaterThan:" + greaterThan);
// greaterThan:false
```

Both (3 < 3) and (3 > 3) are false. The result of the evaluations only checks if the values are greater or less than when making a comparison. If the values are equal, then the value of the operation is false. To check for greater than or equal to or for less than and equal to we use the >= and <= operators.

```
bool lessThanOrEqual = (3 <= 3);
Debug.Log("lessThanOrEqual:" + lessThanOrEqual);
// lessThanOrEqual:true
bool greaterThanOrEqual = (3 >= 3);
Debug.Log("greaterThanOrEqual:" + greaterThanOrEqual);
// greaterThanOrEqual:true
```

By changing the < and > to <= and >= the same check of 3 versus 3 returns true since the value evaluates as equal to. The <= and >= operators combine the > or < and the == operators into a single operator. There are operators that enable further logical combinations.

4.11.5 Logical And and Or Operators

When we use the <= and the >= operators we are asking is less than or equal to. This is an abbreviation of using a < || == where || is the logical "or" operator. This can also be read as "double bar" but, "or operator" is preferable.

```
bool lessThanOrEqual = (3 < 3 || 3 == 3);
Debug.Log("lessThanOrEqual:" + lessThanOrEqual);
// lessThanOrEqual:true
bool greaterThanOrEqual = (3 > 3 || 3 == 3);
Debug.Log("greaterThanOrEqual:" + greaterThanOrEqual);
// greaterThanOrEqual:true
```

The logical or operator returns true if any one of the operands returns true. The above shows that the left 3 > 3 is false, but the 3 == 3 is true. The assignment of lessThanOrEqual is true since the right side of the || operator is true. This is clearer if we use a combination of true false statements.

```
/* logical || or operator              */
bool logicalOr = (false || true);
Debug.Log("logicalOr:" + logicalOr);
// logicalOr:True
bool logicalOrs = (false || false || false || true);
Debug.Log("logicalOrs:" + logicalOrs);
// logicalOr:True
bool oneFalse = (false || true || true || true);
Debug.Log("oneFalse:" + oneFalse);
// oneFalse:True
```

The evaluation of a logical or requires at least one true value in the statement to return a true evaluation. In the second statement shown you can see four different values where only the far right one is true, but the logicalOrs value is assigned true. Any number of || operators can be used in a statement.

```
/* logical && and operator             */
bool falseTrue = (false && true);
Debug.Log("falseTrue:" + falseTrue);
// falseTrue:False
bool falseFalse = (false && false);
Debug.Log("falseFalse:" + falseFalse);
// falseFalse:False
bool trueTrue = (true && true);
Debug.Log("trueTrue:" + trueTrue);
// trueTrue:True
bool notTrueEnough = (false && true && true && true);
Debug.Log("notTrueEnough:" + notTrueEnough);
// notTrueEnough:False
```

The logical && and operator requires all values of a statement to be true to return true. If any one value in the statement is false then the final evaluation is false. Using the logical operators in practice is usually for comparing a range of values.

```
/* this compares the values of numbers  */
/* -5 -4 -3 -2 -1 ±0 +1 +2 +3 +4 +5      */
/*├───────────┼───────────┼───────────┤  */
/*            ├───────────┤              */
/*           -3 < x        x < 3         */
int x = -5;
while(x < 5)
{
    bool inRange = (-3 < x && x < 3);
    Debug.Log(x + " inRange:" + inRange);
    x++;
}
/* -5 inRange:False
 * -4 inRange:False
 * -3 inRange:False
 * -2 inRange:True
 * -1 inRange:True
 *  0 inRange:True
 *  1 inRange:True
 *  2 inRange:True
 *  3 inRange:False
 *  4 inRange:False
 */
```

Using a statement like "-3 is less than x and x is less than 3" we can create a range from -2 to 2 to return true and every other number to return false. The while loop also uses the < operator to control the termination of the statement. We'll get into loop statements in more detail in the next chapter. In any case, there's no restriction on how the values can be checked.

```
bool ranges = (x < 3 && -3 < x) &&
              (x > -3 && 3 > x) &&
              (x > -3 && x < 3) &&
              (x < 3 && x > -3);
```

The above statement returns the same values as the previous form. The range is a bit harder to read, but the same result comes out. Each one of the variations on checking the range between -2 and 2 as True.

4.11.6 If and Branching

The boolean values allow functions to make decisions based on a true false condition. The "if" statement controls when a block of code is invoked based on the contained condition.

```
if(true)
{
    Debug.Log("Do the thing!");
}

if(false)
{
    // unreachable code.
    Debug.Log("Won't do a thing.");
}
```

The condition in the parameter for the "if" statement controls whether the code following the statement is invoked. This also shows us that unreachable code can result if a statement is never true. To use what we had just seen in action we'll generate a grid of cubes. Then we'll use an "if" statement to set the color of each cube based on its distance from the LogicAndOperators game object.

```
// change the color with the if statement
if (2 < distance && distance < 4)
{
    mat.color = Color.red;
}
else
{
    mat.color = Color.white;
}
```

The above statement uses an "if" statement to set the color of the cube to red when the distance to the cube is more than 2 and less than 4. The else statement changes the color to white where the "if" statement isn't true.

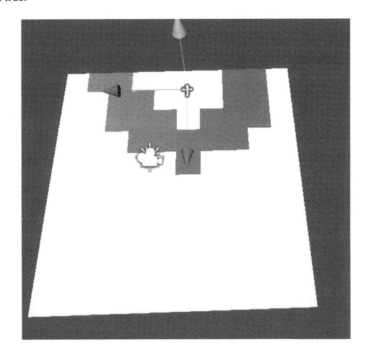

The if-else statement is used often. The else case occurs where the if statement is not true. We can expand this to include additional "if" statements. Checking the position of the cube's x value against the LogicAndOperators.position.x we set the color to blue.

```
if(cubePos.x > myPos.x)
{
    mat.color = Color.blue;
}
```

If the cube's x value is greater than myPos.x then the cube is blue, otherwise the previous statements values are left alone.

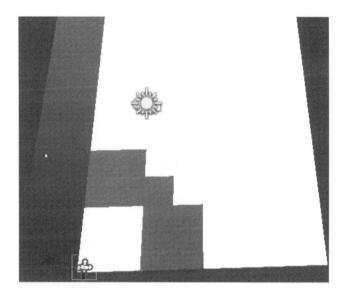

As the game object orbits around the center of the world, the blue divide can be seen traveling across the white cube objects. The else statement cannot stand alone, it can only appear after a valid if statement. Adding if-else-if after the blue creates another pattern.

```
if(cubePos.x > myPos.x)
{
    mat.color = Color.blue;
}

if(cubePos.z > myPos.z)
{
    mat.color = Color.green;
}
else if(cubePos.x < myPos.x)
{
    mat.color = Color.yellow;
}
```

The above changes the coloring of the cubes to yet another pattern:

Experimenting with different values in the "if" statements dramatically changes the colors of the cube array. Unreachable code can easily creep into nested if-else statements.

```
if (2 < distance && distance < 4)
{
    mat.color = Color.red;
}
else
{
    mat.color = Color.white;
    if (cubePos.x > myPos.x)
    {
        mat.color = Color.blue;
        if (cubePos.z > myPos.z)
        {
            mat.color = Color.green;
        }
        else if (cubePos.x < myPos.x)
        {
            mat.color = Color.yellow;
        }
    }
}
```

If you look closely, in the second "else" statement we have a condition if(cubePos.x > myPos.x) where we also ask inside of that else if(cubePos.x < myPos.x). The second statement will never be true. The second statement is excluded by the first. Unfortunately, this isn't caught by Visual Studio, and isn't flagged as unreachable code.

Playing with different combinations of the `if-else` statements for the colored cubes can be fun and interesting. The results turn into color patterns revolving around the LogicAndOperators game object. An interesting challenge would be to split the colors into red blue green and white with the red circle. Think that's something you can do?

4.11.7 What We've Learned

Thinking through logic is one of the most difficult parts of programming in general. For now, the logic has been straightforward, but logic can get quickly very fast. Once things get more difficult, it may be easier to set and calculate values ahead of when they're used. Rather than chain long if-else statements it's sometimes easier to use one at a time and layer the effects rather than multiple embedded if-else statements.

4.12 Loops

To follow along, we'll be using the Loops script found on the object of the same name in the Loops_ Scene in the Chapter 4 Unity Project.

This section is something you may need to return to several times for reference. Learning these different loops is all very different. Most of them accomplish the same thing, but with subtle differences. In general, the `for(;;)` loop is the easiest to use, and sometimes the fastest.

The `Update()` function is run once every frame. Within that function, our logic is evaluated, starting at the top moving toward the bottom. Once the function is complete, the next frame begins, and the `Update()` function is called again to restart the evaluation at the top. This process is then repeated for every frame while the game is running.

To further understand how this process affects our code, we should be able to count the number of frames and thus the number of times the `Update()` function has been called. To do this, we'll simply create a `public int` to count the number of times the `Update()` function has been called.

4.12.1 Unary Operators

The term *unary operator* means there's only one operation required. In C#, and many other programming languages, unary operators work only on integers. Integers are best at counting whole values. In this case, we're going to keep track of how many times the `Update()` function has been called.

Integers are whole numbers, like 1, 2, and 1234. Unlike how numbers are commonly used in written English, in code, no commas are used: "1,234," for example, should be written "1234." Commas are special characters in C#, so the computer will look at 1,234 as a 1 followed by a different number 234. We'll go further into the differences between numbers, but we need to know a bit about integers before proceeding. In a new project in Unity 3D start with the Loops project.

```
// Update is called once per frame
void Update () {
    counter = counter + 1;
}
```

To start, we should look at how the process looks like in long hand. Adding `counter = counter + 1` means we're going to take the previous value of `counter` and add 1 to it. Some programming languages require this counting method. Lua, for example, needs to increment variables in this manner.

More complex languages like C# can shorten this to a single statement with the use of a unary operator.

```
counter++;
```

The unary operator ++ works the same as the long-hand version from the previous statement. When you run the game you can watch the counter value update in the Inspector panel in Unity 3D. After only a few seconds, you can see the counter running up very quickly. Each time the Update() function is called, the counter is incremented by 1.

Another unary operator is the --, which decrements a value rather than increments. Replace ++ with -- and you can watch the counter running down into negative numbers. Each one of these has important uses.

4.12.2 While

If we want to run a specific statement more than once in a loop, we need another method. To do this, C# comes with another couple of keywords, while and for. The while() statement is somewhat easier to use. It needs only one bool argument to determine if it should continue to execute.

This statement is somewhat like the if() statement, only that Unity 3D returns to the start of the while() statement checks if the contained statement is true and repeats the code block again.

```
void Update ()
{
    while (counter < 10)
    {
        Debug.Log(counter);
        counter++;
    }
}
```

We start again with public int counter. The while() loop checks if the counter is less than 10. While the counter is less than 10, then we run the contents of the while statement that increments the counter. Once the counter is larger than 10, the while statement doesn't evaluate its contents. As a programmer might say, the while loop's code block will not be executed.

There is one danger using while statements. If the while statement remains true, it will not stop. In this case, it means that the Update() function will not finish and the game will freeze on the frame until while(false). This also means that any input into Unity 3D will respond very slowly as it's still waiting for the Update() function to end. We'll observe how runaway loops behave later in this chapter.

One important observation to make is that counter++ lives inside the while with the above code sample. This means that the Update() no longer increments the counter value. The while loop increments the value.

```
void Update ()
{
    counter++;
    int i = 0;
    while (i < 10)
    {
        Debug.Log(i);
        i++;
    }
    Debug.Log(counter);
}
```

The form above creates an int i = 0; just before the while() statement. Inside of the while() statement the value of i is incremented as before. After the loop the counter value is printed to the Unity Console. The output for the above sends a string of numbers 0 to 9, then a number from counter. This means that counter is incremented with the start of the Update() function, the while() loop executes 10 times, then the counter is incremented.

4.12.3 For

To gain a bit more control over the execution of a loop, we have another option. The for() loop requires three different statements to operate. The first statement is called an initialization, the second is a condition, and the third is an operation.

```
for( initialization ; condition ; operation )
{
    code goes here...
}
```

The first argument allows us to set up an integer. After that, we need to have some sort of boolean condition to inform the for loop when to stop. The last argument is something that operates on the initialized variable from the first statement in the for loop. The following code block is a typical example of the for() loop statement.

```
for (int i = 0; i < 10; i++)
{
    Debug.Log(i);
}
```

Inside of the Update() loop, the for() statement contains int i = 0; restricted to its own scope. The three arguments, are separated by a semicolon (;). The first part, int i = 0, is the initialization. The condition checks if i < 10 to return true or false. The operation of the for() loop uses a unary operator and increments the value for i.

```
for (int i = 0; i < 10; i++)
{
    Debug.Log(i);
}
Debug.Log(i);
```

The variable i we wrote into the for loop is gone once you leave the for loop. The attempt to Debug. Log(i); after the for() statement fails since i no longer exists outside of the context of the for() statement.

At the same time, you're not going to want to declare an int i before using one in the for loop.

```
int i = 0;
for (int i = 0; i < 10; i++)
{

}
```

The second part of the for loop is i < 10, the condition letting the for loop know when to stop running. This is similar to the while loop we just took a look at. The for loop offers alternative uses of its arguments, some uses may seem awkward. This is unorthodox, but you can leave out the initialization section if an int value has been declared before the loop.

```
int i = 0;
for (; i < 10; i++)
{
    Debug.Log(i);
}
```

There's not much of a reason for this but it's not going to break anything. The last argument of the for loop is an operation which runs after the first two arguments are evaluated. If the second part of the for loop is true, then the contents of the curly braces are evaluated. The last part of the expression is i++ that can also be moved around.

```
int i = 0;
for (; i < 10;)
{
    Debug.Log(i);
    i++;
}
```

Unlike the while loop that relies on an external variable, the for loop contains everything it needs to operate, although, as we've just seen, we can still move the parts of the for loop around. If only the condition argument of the for loop is used then the for loop acts the same as a while loop. Although rearranging the parts of a for loop like this is not recommended, this does serve as a way to show how flexible C# can be.

```
int i = 0;
bool loop = true;
for (; loop;)
{
    Debug.Log(i);
    i++;
    if (i > 10)
        loop = false;
}
```

Just so you know, a classically trained programmer might have a migraine after looking at this for() statement, so give him or her a break and just do things normally.

The while loop runs only once after the counter reaches 10 after the first time it's evaluated. Each time the Update() function is called, the for loop starts over again. We can use a slight variation of this using float values, though this isn't any different from using integers. Again, it's best to use integer values in a for loop, and this is only to show how C# can be changed around freely.

```
for (float f = 0; f < 10f; f = f + 1.0f)
{
    Debug.Log("float: " + f);
}
```

Try not to be too clever with your loops. Yes, you can do quite a lot and C# is very lenient and will let you get away with the code above. I would never recommend you use float values in a for() statement. However, I will not tell you to *never* use a float in a for() loop. I would just be curious as to why.

4.12.4 Do-While

Do-while is another loop to add to our toolbox. We saw the for() and the while() looping statements in Section 4.12.3. The for() and while() loops are the most common and the simple to use. There are, however, variations on the same theme that might come in handy.

The great majority of the tasks can be handled by the simple for() loop. However, variations in looping statements are created either to support different programming styles or to conform to changing requirements in different programming styles or to allow for different conditions to terminate the loop.

The while() and the for() loops both check various conditions within their parameter list before executing the contents of the loop. If we need to check after the loop's execution, then we need to reverse how the loop operates.

```
int i = 0;
do
{
    Debug.Log(i);
    i++;
} while (i < 10);
```

The do-while loop has some subtle differences. For most programmers, the syntax change has little meaning and, for the most part, do-while can be rewritten as a simple while loop.

It's worth noting that most programming languages use the same keywords for the same sort of task. Lua, for instance, uses for in a similar fashion:

```
for int i = 1, 10 do
    print(i)
end
```

However, Lua likes to shorten the conditions of the for loop by assuming a few different things in the condition and the operation of i. Other languages like Java, or JavaScript, use for and while more like C#. Things get really strange only if you look at something like F#:

```
for I = 1 to 10 do
printfn "%d" i
```

Syntax aside, once you know one version of the for loop, it's easier to figure out how another language does the same thing. The more basic concepts like booleans and operators also behave the same across languages. Therefore, you won't have to relearn how to use operators now that you know how they're used in C#.

4.12.5 Postfix and Prefix Notation

The placement of a unary operator influences when the operation takes place. Placement, therefore, has an important effect on how the operator is best used. This is a difficult concept to explain without seeing in use, so we'll skip right to some sample code.

```
int i = 0;
Debug.Log(i);          // 0
while (i < 1)
{
    Debug.Log(i++); // 0
    Debug.Log(i);    // 1
}
```

For various reasons, the i++ is the more standard use of the unary operator. When this code is executed, the first Debug.Log(i);, before the while() loop, will produce a 0, just as when i was first initialized. The first time the Debug.Log(i++); inside of the while loop is called, another 0 is produced in the Unity 3D Console panel. Where things become interesting is at the third Debug.Log(i); statement, where we have a different number.

The statement where i++ appears will use the value which i held before it was incremented. After the statement where i++ appears, the value of i will have been incremented. This is the difference between postfix and prefix, where i++ is a postfix notation and ++i is prefix notation. To illustrate this difference, observe the change when we use a prefix notation:

```
int i = 0;
Debug.Log(i);          // 0
while (i < 1)
{
    Debug.Log(++i); // 1
    Debug.Log(i);    // 1
}
```

The first version, with postfix notation, produces two 0s and a single 1 before the while loop terminates. The second version produces one 0 and two 1s before the while loop terminates. The choice of which notation to use depends mostly on what value you need i to take when you use it. The syntax difference is subtle, but once it's understood, the effects can be controlled. To make the difference more drastic, we can move the placement of where the unary operation occurs.

```
int i = 0;
Debug.Log(i);
while (++i < 1)
{
    Debug.Log(i); //unreachable code
}
```

The above statement will produce a single 0 in the Unity 3D's Console panel. The condition to execute the while loop begins as false, where the value for i is not less than 1, thus the Debug.Log() statement is never called. However, if we change things around, we'll get a 0 and a 1 printed to the Console panel.

```
int i = 0;
Debug.Log(i);
while (i++ < 1)
{
    Debug.Log(i); // 1
}
```

This code block means that the while loop started off true, since the value of i was 0 when evaluated, and only after the evaluation was complete was i incremented. Using the while loop in this way is unconventional, and it might be best avoided even though it's clever.

4.12.6 Using Loops

To continue to follow along, we'll open the UsingLoops_Scene In the Chapter 4 Unity Project. In the scene open the UsingLoops script. Loops are used to complete repetitive tasks. In the following use of the while loop, we count up the number of cubes. To see results from the while loop, we'll create a new cube for each execution of the while loop. To do this, we'll create a new GameObject named box.

To initialize the box, we start with GameObject.CreatePrimitive(PrimitiveType.Cube). This initialization has a couple of new concepts. The first is the GameObject.CreatePrimitive() function. CreatePrimitive()is a function found inside of the GameObject class.

To let `CreatePrimitive` know what to make, we're using the `PrimitiveType.Cube`, which is of `PrimitiveType`; technically, it's an enum, but more on that later. Then, as we've seen before in the `while` loop, we're incrementing the `numCubes` variable to make sure that the `while` loop doesn't run uncontrolled.

```
public class UsingLoops : MonoBehaviour
{
    int numCubes = 0;
    private void Start()
    {
        while (numCubes < 10)
        {
            GameObject box = GameObject.CreatePrimitive(PrimitiveType.Cube);
            box.transform.position = new Vector3(numCubes * 2.0f, 0, 0);
            numCubes++;
        }
    }
}
```

To tell where each cube is created, we move each cube to a new position by setting the box to new `Vector3`. In `Vector3()`, we'll take the value of `numCubes` and multiply it by `2.0f`, making sure that each cube is moved to a different x location. Logically, each iteration of `numCubes` will increment by 1. Therefore, on the first execution, we'll have `0 * 2.0f` that ends with 0. Then, the second time through the `while` loop, the result will be `1 * 2.0f`, then `2 * 2.0f`, and so on, until `numCubes` is larger than 10.

Each time the `while` loop is evaluated, the box points to a new instance of a cube primitive. The previous iteration of the `while` loop forgets about the previous instance of the box, which instance box is referencing becomes very important as we don't necessarily want to deal with every instance of the box game object we're thinking about.

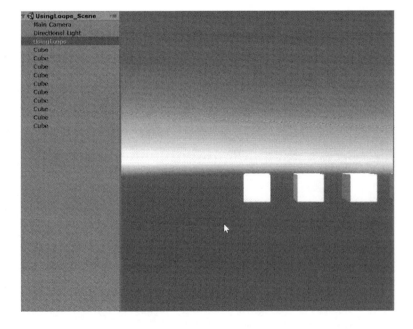

Running the code in the scene results in a long chain of 10 cubes.

An inquisitive person should be asking, "Where did `CreatePrimitive` come from?" The answer to that is found inside of the `UnityEngine.dll.GameObject` is going to be the primary focus of creating any object in the game, as the name might suggest. Peek at the definition by right clicking on the `GameObject` found inside of the Solution Explorer in Visual Studio, we find a promising `CreatePrimitive()` function. This is related to how we found `Vector3()` in an earlier section.

```
GameObject box = GameObject.CreatePrimitive(PrimitiveType.Cube);
                                                    GameObject [from metad
269         // Parameters:
270         //   type:
271         //     The type of primitive object to create.
272         [FreeFunction("GameObjectBindings::CreatePrimitive")]
273         public static GameObject CreatePrimitive(PrimitiveType type);
274         //
```

The `CreatePrimitive()` function expects a `PrimitiveType` as an argument. Clicking on the `PrimitiveType` found in the Assembly Browser window, you are presented with the following set of code.

```
GameObject box = GameObject.CreatePrimitive(PrimitiveType.Cube);
                                            PrimitiveType [from meta
7       //
8       // Summary:
9       //     The various primitives that can be created using the GameObje
10      //     function.
11      public enum PrimitiveType
12      {
13          //
14          // Summary:
15          //     A sphere primitive.
16          Sphere = 0,
17          //
18          // Summary:
19          //     A capsule primitive.
20          Capsule = 1,
21          //
22          // Summary:
```

Here is an enum called `PrimitiveType`. Inside this is `Sphere`, `Capsule`, `Cylinder`, `Cube`, and `Plane`. Each one is a value inside of the `PrimitiveType`. Enums are another generic type that C# makes extensive use of, which we'll introduce in Section 6.6.1. The `CreatePrimitive` function inside of the `GameObject` class is followed by: `GameObject`. This means that it's creating a `GameObject` for you to access. We'll learn about this once we start writing our own classes and functions with return types.

NOTE: Looking things up on the internet is also a huge help. There are many people asking the same questions as you. If you don't find what you're looking for, then you might just be asking the wrong question, or phrasing it in an obscure way. To find information on CreatePrimitive, search Google using "CreatePrimitive Unity" to get some quick possible answers.

In most cases, the answers are going to be brief and obscure, but they at least serve as an example for what you might need to look for in your own code to complete the task you're trying to complete.

This discussion might be a bit much to swallow right now, so we'll stick with the small bite we started with and get back to the deeper picture later. For now, let's get back to figuring out more on loops.

4.12.7 Loops within Loops

We've created a line of cubes, but how would we go about making a grid of cubes?

We'll write two `for` loops, one within the other. The first `for` loop will use `int i = 0` and the second will use `int j = 0` as their initialization arguments. Then we'll leave the numCubes as a `public int` we can change in the editor. If we set the `numCubes` in the inspector to 10, then each `for` loop will iterate 10 times.

```
public int numCubes = 10;
private void Start()
{
    [...]
    {
        for (int i = 0; i < numCubes; i++)
        {
            for (int j = 0; j < numCubes; j++)
            {
                GameObject box = GameObject.CreatePrimitive(PrimitiveType.Cube);
                box.transform.position = new Vector3(i * 2.0f, j * 2.0f, 0);
            }
        }
    }
}
```

Only in the second `for` loop do we need to create a box; then, in the x and y values of the Vector3, we will do some of the same math we did before. This time we'll use the int i variable for x and j for y to create a grid. This declaration creates a row and column relation between the two `for` loops. As one iterates through the row, the other inside of the row fills in the column with cubes.

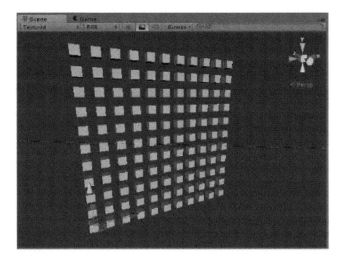

Hop to the Scene panel in the Unity 3D Editor to look at the grid of cubes that was produced when you pressed the Play button. When the first `for` loop begins, it gets to the second `for` loop inside of it. Only after the second `for` loop is done with its statements of creating 10 boxes will it go back to the first `for` loop that moves on to the next iteration. Also since we changed numBoxes to 10, the first `while()` loop we wrote will get skipped run since numCubes is not less than 10. Also worth noting, the numCubes++ that appears in the `while()` loop isn't in the `for()` loop. The line in the `for()` loop would create a runaway loop since the condition `for` loop termination would never be met.

4.12.8 Runaway Loops

Loops can often lead to runaway functions. A `while` loop without any condition to stop it will make Unity 3D freeze. The following shows some conditions that will immediately make Unity 3D stop on the line and never finish the frame. Adding any of these will halt Unity 3D, and you'll have to kill the Unity 3D app though the Task Manager.

```
while (true)
{
}


for (; ; )
{
}
```

In some cases, these conditions are used by some programmers for specific reasons, but they always have some way to break out of the function. Using either `return` or `break` can stop the loop from running on forever. These keywords are referred to as Jump Statements. It's worth mentioning that the keyword `return` is usually used to send data to another function. If there isn't a function waiting for data, it's better to use `break`.

```
while (true)
{
    return;
}


for (; ; )
{
    break;
}
```

There is a specific behavioral difference between `return` and `break`. With `return` you're stopping the entire function. With `break` you're stopping only the block of code the `break` is in.

```
Debug.Log("Starting");
for (; ; )
{
    Debug.Log("before break");
    break;
    Debug.Log("after the break");
}
Debug.Log("Ending");
```

First of all, we'd get a couple of warnings informing us of some unreachable code. However, that doesn't keep us from testing out the results printed on the Console panel.

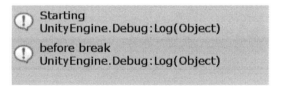

We do get the first line of the just before the `for()` loop function as well as the line before the `break` command. However, the line following `break` is not reached. This behavior changes if we replace `break` with `return`.

```csharp
Debug.Log("Starting");
for (; ; )
{
    Debug.Log("before break");
    //break;
    return;
    Debug.Log("after the break");
}
Debug.Log("Ending");
```

We get only one warning of unreachable code, but we do get a third line printed to the Console window.

```
Starting
UnityEngine.Debug:Log(Object)

before break
UnityEngine.Debug:Log(Object)
```

We do not to see "Ending" printed to the Console. We'll go into more detail on the specifics of how these functions are used later, which provides a very short example for break; For instance, we can use the following code to see how a `while (true)` can be stopped with a specific instruction.

```csharp
int counter = 0;
while (true)
{
    counter++;
    if (counter > 10)
    {
        Debug.Log("Break!");
        break;
    }
}
```

The counter builds up while we're trapped in the while loop. Once the counter is above 10, we break out of the while loop with the break keyword.

4.12.9 Breakpoints: A First Look

To have a better understanding on what we're seeing here, we're going to use a very important feature of an IDE. With the code we just entered in the previous Update() function, we have a while (true) and a counter++ incrementing away inside of it.

```
74          while (true)
75          {
76              counter++;
77              if (counter > 10)
78              {
79                  Debug.Log("Break!");
80                  break;
81              }
82          }
```

There's a narrow margin to the left of the numbers. The margin is for adding breakpoints. Breakpoints are small bookmarks that help you see exactly what's going on inside of your code. Click in the margin on the line with the counter++; and you'll see the line highlight.

In Visual Studio select Debug→Attach Unity Debugger. This action will open a dialog box with a list of Unity 3D game engines you might have open. In most cases, you would have only one.

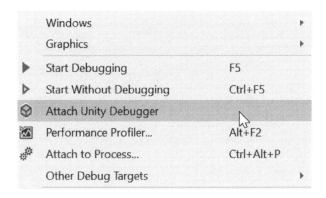

Select Unity in the following dialog and click on OK. Back in Unity press the Play-in-Editor button and wait for Visual Studio to hit the breakpoint.

```
74          while (true)
75          {
76              counter++;
77              ▶  if (counter > 10)
78              {
79                  Debug.Log("Break!");
80                  break;
81              }
82          }
```

You'll see that the line in Visual Studio is now highlighted, and a new set of windows has appeared at the bottom of the panel. Select the Locals panel and take a look at the `counter`. There are three columns: Name, Value, and Type, which tell you the `counter` is at 0, which will tell you the value for `counter` and that it's an `int`.

Press F5 to release the `break` and you'll see the `count` increment by 1. As soon as the code gets back to the breakpoint, it will stop again. What you're looking at is your code being updated only when you press the F11 key. This is called *stepping through code*. And it's a very important reason why Visual Studio is to be used with Unity 3D, and not something like Notepad.

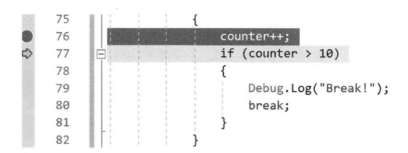

By tapping F11 a few times you can watch the code execute one line at a time. You can hover over each value with the cursor and watch their values change.

Debugging code is a major part of observing how your code is actually working. Breakpoints, and debugging tools like this and tools like the Locals tab are indispensable when it comes to writing complex code.

To stop debugging the code, and let Unity 3D go about its normal work, press the Stop button.

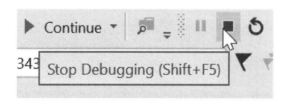

Pressing the little Stop icon will unlink Visual Studio from Unity 3D and the information that we were watching will stop updating. Unity 3D will also return to regular working order.

4.12.10 What We've Learned

The `for` loop is a tight self-contained method to iterate using a number. The `while` loop may be shorter, and use fewer parameters, but its simplicity requires more external variables to control. When faced with different programming tasks, it can be difficult to choose between the two loops.

In the end, each loop can be used to do the same thing using various techniques we have yet to be introduced to. Don't worry; we'll get to them soon enough. At this point, though, we have learned enough to start thinking about what we've learned in a different way.

The last major concept we learned was the breakpoint, used to inspect what's going on inside of a loop. Breakpoints can be set anywhere and bits of information can be picked out and inspected while your code is running.

Debugging code is a part of the day-to-day routine of the programmer. Using a debugger that allows you to step through your code's execution allows for a greater understanding of what your code's activity involves. The debugger shows you what your code is actually doing.

4.13 ScopeAgain

Scope was explored for a bit in Section 4.8, but there is some explaining left to do. We know that some variables exist only for the scope they were declared in. Other variables end up being shown in the Unity 3D Properties editor. This point doesn't explain how one class can talk to another class through a variable, or even whether this was even possible.

4.13.1 Visibility or Accessibility

Normally, variables and class definitions are considered private. This is usually implied and if you don't tell C# otherwise, it will assume you mean every variable to be private information.

```
private
public
protected
internal
```

There are only four keywords used to change the accessibility of a variable. Each one has a specific use and reason for being. For now, we'll examine the first two keywords in more depth. The keywords `private` and `public` are the two most-simple-to-understand ways to change a variable's accessibility.

We've used `public` before when we wanted a `bool` to show up in the Inspector panel in Unity 3D.

```
public bool SomeBool;
private void Start()
{
    SomeBool = true;
}
```

We have a `public bool SomeBool;` declared at the beginning of this ScopeAgain script. Because `private` is assumed, we can hide this by simply removing the `public` keyword. At the same time, we can be very explicit about hiding this `bool` by adding the `private` keyword.

```
private bool hiddenBool;
bool alsoHidden;
```

To the editor, there's no real difference between `hiddenBool` and `alsoHidden`. The differences will come in later when we look at *inheritance*. It's important to know about the other keywords that can precede both class and variable statements.

4.13.1.1 A Basic Example

For a better observation of a variable's scope, we're going to want to start with a scope project different from before. This time, we'll start with the MoreScope project. In this project, we have a scene file where our Main Camera has the `MoreScope` component added. On a cube in the same scene, we have another script component added called `OtherScope`.

Here's where things get interesting. From the camera, we're able to see the `OtherScope` class. This is indicated by MonoDevelop allowing us to access the `OtherScope` class as we type.

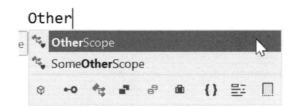

As we begin to type Other, the class OtherScope appears in the Autocomplete pop-up. This tells us that there are accessible objects, which we can access from class to class. This is referred to as the global scope.

4.13.2 Global Scope

When each class is created in Unity 3D, C# is used to make additions to the global scope of the project. This means that throughout the project, each class will be able to see every other class. This also means we can't have two class files with the same name. If we manage to create two scripts with the same name, we'll get the following error.

```
Assets/OtherScripts/OtherScope.cs(4,14): error CS0101: The namespace
"global::" already contains a definition for "OtherScope"
```

By creating two classes with the same name each class is added to the global namespace. This would happen should we define two variables with the same name in a class. Changing the name of one of the classes resolves the problem. There are other work arounds involving namespace, but we'll get to that later in Section 6.10.

Going back to the ScopeAgain script form the beginning of the tutorial we added an OtherScope other; variable. Next we want to assign a variable within other a value. In the game scene assign the OtherScope.cs class to a new Cube GameObject before running the game. In the MoreScope's Start() function, use the following statement.

```
OtherScope other;
private void Start()
{
    SomeBool = true;
    other = (OtherScope)GameObject.FindObjectOfType(typeof(OtherScope));
    Debug.Log(other.gameObject.name);
}
```

Unity's GameObject class has a function called FindObjectOfType() that will search the scene for any object of the type we're requesting. The statement following the assignment to other is Debug. Log(other.gameObject.name);, which prints the name of the gameObject that the component is attached to in the Console panel. When the game is run, we get the following output.

> ⚠ ArrowCube
>   UnityEngine.Debug:Log(Object)

This output indicates that we've correctly found and assigned the variable other to the component attached to the cube object in the scene. Now let's add some meaningful variables to OtherScope.

```
public float Size;
Vector3 mScale;
```

In the OtherScope class, we'll create two variables, one public float named Size and a Vector3 called mScale. The "m" notation is commonly used by programmers as a short version of "my." Thus "mScale" refers to "MyScale." In the Update() function of the OtherScope class, we'll add the following statements:

```
private void Update()
{
    mScale = new Vector3(Size, Size, Size);
    transform.localScale = mScale;
}
```

This will set the size of the cube object's transform.localScale to the public Size variable on the *x, y,* and *z* axes. In the a new public variable called otherScale is used to update the size in.

```
public float otherScale;
private void Update()
{
    other.Size = otherScale;
}
```

Because the size variable in the OtherScope class was made public, it's now accessible through the dot operator. When the scene is run, the size of the cube is controlled by the otherScale variable assigned to ScopeAgain class in the Inspector panel.

You can click-drag on the otherScale variable that has been exposed to the Inspector panel with the ScopeAgain game object selected. This action directly affects the size of the cube in the scene. Even though there's no visible connection between the two objects, their variables have been connected to one another through a global connection.

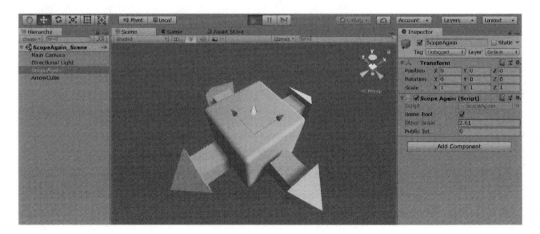

Accessing a variable is not the only way a class can manipulate another class. Functions can also be accessed by another class, if they've been made public.

The importance here is that ScopeAgain can see properties in OtherScope. Once they can see each other, the variables inside one another are accessible if they're made public. Could it be possible to declare variables that are accessible globally?

We could try to put a variable outside of a class. This might make it visible to any class that might want to access it. This, unfortunately, won't work. However, it doesn't mean that there are no systems that can make a variable globally accessible. However, we'll have to leave off here for now. The systems that allow for globally accessible variables require some steps along the way to fully understand, so we'll get to that stuff soon enough.

4.13.3 What We've Learned

Defining public variables allows for interobject communication, which is one of the principles behind object-oriented programming. This enables objects to communicate to one another in many unique ways.

Scope and object-oriented programming are related. Variable scope is related to object-oriented programming. By defining and maintaining scope, you're better able to control how other objects can communicate.

When working with a team of programmers, it's important to inform all on how your code behaves. You should communicate which variables in your class can be modified by how they are defined. Making variables public informs everyone that these are the variables allowed to be altered.

By protecting them, you're able to tell others which variables they are not allowed to touch. Much of the time, it's simple to leave things public while testing and making decisions on what needs to be made public. Once you've isolated what can and cannot be altered, it's best to hide variables that shouldn't be changed by outside objects.

4.14 Warnings versus Errors

There are two basic events that we will encounter early on in C#. The first are errors, and then we will get to the many warnings. Compile-time errors will stop all your classes from compiling. Because one class can look at and interact with another class, we need to make sure that every class is free from errors before our code can be compiled.

Most of these compile-time errors occurs from typos or trying to do something with the code that can't be interpreted by the lexer. Most of these errors deal with syntax or type-casting errors, which will prevent the rest of the code from working, so it's best to fix these errors before moving on.

At the same time, we'll get many warnings. Some of these warnings can be considered somewhat harmless. If you declare a variable and don't do anything to either assign something to it or use it in any way, then the lexer will decide that you're wasting resources on the variable. This produces a simple unused variable warning.

In some cases, code can still be compiled, but there will be some minor warnings. Warnings usually inform us that we've either written unused code, or perhaps we've done something unexpected. Code with a few warnings will not stop the compilation process, but it will let us know we've done something that might not necessarily work with Unity 3D.

4.14.1 Warnings

Open up the Warnings_Scene and find the Warnings script attached to the Warnings GameObject in the scene. The most common warning is an alert bringing to your attention a variable declaration without any use. This is something you may have been seeing from the previous projects. The Visual Studio IDE is quite good at reading your code and interpreting how it's used. A function like the following will produce a warning:

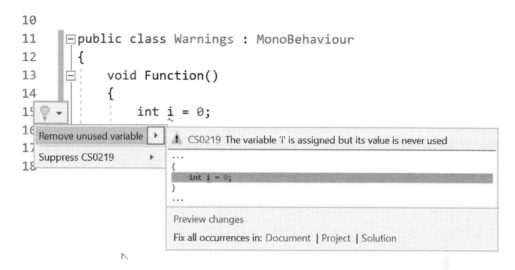

```
10
11    public class Warnings : MonoBehaviour
12    {
13        void Function()
14        {
15            int i = 0;
16
17
18
```

Visual Studio even gives you a helper to remove the unused variables. This simply states that i is unused, which is true. Nothing is doing anything with it, so is it necessary? Often, while you code, you'll be gathering and preparing data for later use. When we do this, we might forget that we created some data that might have been useful but never did anything with it.

In this case, we might do something with it later, so it's sometimes useful to comment it out.

```
void MyFunction()
{
    //int j = 0;
}
```

This leaves the variable around in case we need to use it, but it also clears out the warning. Most warnings don't lead to any serious problems.

4.14.2 Errors

One most common error occurs when we are dealing with missing variables or incorrect types. These errors show up often when we first start off writing our own functions and aren't used to working with different data types or know how they interact.

```
float f = 1.0;
```

This is a commonly written statement that produces the following error:

> ❌ CS0664   Literal of type double cannot be implicitly converted to type 'float'; use an 'F' suffix to create a literal of this type

The fix for the error is included in the error message. The message includes "Add suffix 'f' to create a literal of this type," which means we need to do the following.

```
float f = 1.0f;
```

This fixes the error. Many of the error messages give a clue as to what's going on and how to fix the error. Many of these errors show up before the game is run. These are called compile-time errors. Errors that show up while the game is running are called run-time errors.

Run-time errors are harder to track down. Often, this requires a debugging session to figure out where and why an error is happening.

4.14.3 Understanding the Debugger

Writing code that works is hard enough. To make sure that the code works, it's often easier to make it readable. To understand how the code works, we often need to add in additional statements to make it easier to debug as well.

We haven't covered declaration of multiple variables in one line; this is because it's bad form, but it's not illegal. We can declare both a and b in one statement. In the above, a remains unassigned, and b is now storing 0.

```
int a, b = 0;
Debug.Log(a);
```

This now produces an error, where a is used before it's assigned; however, the error might not be clear because in the line there certainly is a declaration and an assignment. The assignment is harder to read since it's all happening on one line.

```
int a = 0, b = 0;
Debug.Log(a + b);
```

This is also valid, but we've done nothing for readability or debugging.

```
52
● 53         int a = 0, b = 0;
54           Debug.Log(a + b);
55
```

Setting a breakpoint on this line highlights both the first variable, but doesn't help if we want to highlight the second declaration on the same line. This creates a problem if we're trying to find a problem with just one of the variables. This also highlights why we need to change our writing style to help debug our code.

```
61           int a = 0;
● 62         int b = 0;
63           Debug.Log(a + b);
```

Breaking up the declaration across multiple lines allows for setting a breakpoint on a specific statement rather than a multiple declaration statement. Likewise, debugging a statement like the following is no better.

```
int c = a; int d = b;
```

This line has two statements, but does not have a line break between them. This creates the problem of both readability and debuggability. When you're trying to isolate a problem, it's important to keep each statement on its own line so a breakpoint can be applied to it.

If we continue this exercise, we can take a look at an `ArrayList` that contains different types of data.

```
ArrayList list = new ArrayList();
list.Add(1);
list.Add(1.0f);
list.Add(1.0);
list.Add("1");
/* Lists can have pretty much anything
 * added to them. The foreach loop
 * doesn't know what is in the list.
 */
foreach (int i in list)
{
    Debug.Log(i);
}
```

In the list, we have an int of 1, a string this, a float 1.0f, and a double 1.0 and a string "1". The foreach loop assumes int and this works fine with the first iteration. Setting a breakpoint here shows in the Locals panel an int i with a value of 1. So far so good. When we step through the code by pressing F11 to get to the next item in the list, we get an error.

> ⓘ **InvalidCastException:** Cannot cast from source type to destination type.
> Warnings.Start () (at Assets/Warnings.cs:93)

`InvalidCastException` shows up in the Unity Console panel. Since `float` this isn't `int`, we get an error telling us what error was raised and in what line the error occurred on. This sort of debugging is only a contrived example setup to fail in a known location.

In most instances, problems like this aren't so easy to spot. The warnings and errors are often described with a line number, but it's not always easy to know why the exception was raised. Stepping into the code and checking out values is the only tool we really have to search for problems. To make things easier on yourself, it's sometimes better to break things out even more.

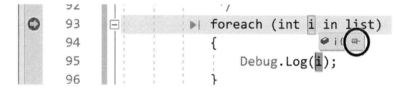

To get a better look at each variable in play, highlight the i in the `foreach` loop. This "pins" the variable to the window. If we step into each step of the code Visual Studio will open the following pop-up.

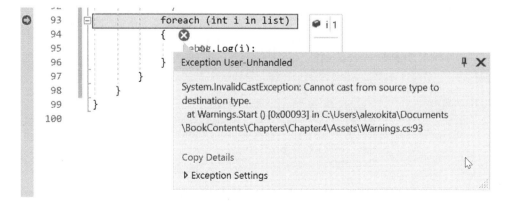

We can see that i is storing the value this that cannot be cast to an int. Stepping through code in the debugger should be a regular practice. Anytime anything remotely confusing comes up your first move past re-reading your code should be to start the debugger.

4.14.4 What We've Learned

Working through problems takes a step-by-step approach. Setting your code up for debugging requires some formatting changes to your code to help the debugger do its work. Once the code has been laid out for debugging, it's sometimes easier to read but our code can lose some efficiency.

It's always a good idea to keep your code clean and readable, but it's just as important to help your debugger do its work as well. Seeing the debugger step through your code also helps you understand how your own functions do their work.

When you have a chance to observe your code in operation, it's sometimes easier to see where code can be optimized—for example, when you see the same data being used over and over again. Passing values between variables in a visual sense can help reveal patterns. Once the patterns are seen, it can be easier to produce code that creates and reuses the same value less often.

4.15 Leveling Up: Fundamentals

At this point, I can say that you've gained enough of the basic skills to feel confident in your ability to read code and begin to ask the right questions. Just as important, the basics we've covered are shared among most programming languages.

Coming up with clever systems to control data is only a part of the task of programming. A great deal of work is coming up. It's also important to think of clear and concise names for variables. One thing is for sure: There have been plenty of pages written by people trying to wrangle in rampant names for identifiers.

At worst, you might have a situation where humans use health points, zombies hit points, vampires blood units, werewolves silver damage, and each one is simply a record of how many times they take damage before going down. It would be unfortunate for you to have to write functions for each human to shoot at every other type of monster and vice versa.

If someone offers help with your game, looks at your code, and you never hear back from that person again, it's surely due to the confused mess of code he or she got to look at. Some simple guidelines to help with naming have been outlined a number of times by various groups.

4.15.1 Style Guides

When faced with the fact that your code will have to eventually be seen by other programmers, it's best to try to avoid some of the embarrassment of explaining every identifier you've written. Furthermore, as a beginner, it's important that you gain some insight into the common practices that classically trained programmers have used throughout their careers. With any luck, books will help you keep up.

A style guide is a reference that often involves preferences involving everything from the placement of white space to naming conventions of identifiers. Official Microsoft style guides for C# provide details on how to name every different type of identifier. This enables us to tell identifiers apart from one another based on their use for variables, functions, or any other construct that C# uses.

As we learn about the different things that identifiers are used for, we'll also want to know how to best name the construct we're creating. A simple internet search for "C# style guide" will bring up various links, for example, coding standards, guidelines, and coding guidelines.

Once you start working with any number of programmers, it's best to come to some agreement on the practices you'll choose to follow. Everyone learned slightly different methods and ideologies when he or she was introduced to a programming language, even if C# wasn't the first programming language that person learned. This leads to many different styles and conventions.

5

Fundamentals: Building a Foundation

We've covered many of the basic concepts and terms that are commonly taught to new programmers. It's time to learn some of the fundamental concepts that are required for functioning code. By now, you should know what code looks like; now it's time to start writing it.

It is important that you compare C# to other programming languages. This comparison helps to contrast C# against languages that might do a similar task in a slightly different way. With such comparison results in mind, we're better able to understand why C# looks the way it does, and we'll be better prepared to understand a concept if we look something up on the Internet exemplified in a different language. Examples found on the Internet may be in another language. Armed with a bit of knowledge, you'll have a better chance of translating the discovery into C#.

A few assets available on the Unity 3D Asset Store are might still be written in JavaScript. This might be a good indication that it's not seen an update in a long time. When necessary, you might want to read the code to understand how to use one of the downloaded assets. If you've never seen JavaScript before, you might notice how some of the code will seem familiar, but you might also find much of it to be quite alien.

The internet provides us example code in many languages. A search for "how do I sort a list" would show examples in many programming languages. It's not a bad idea to be able to read all sorts of programming languages, get the gist of what it's trying to do and then translate that into C# for your own use.

5.1 What Will Be Covered in This Chapter

Learning how to add complexity to your code takes time. We'll cover how to make classes communicate with one another on a more global scope. Then we'll learn how to control the flow of our data in more comprehensive ways. Finally, we'll want to understand one of the more useful constructs in C#, the array, and all its related forms. To make use of the concepts we've learned so far, we'll want to investigate the following points:

- Review of classes
- Class inheritance
- The keyword *static*
- Jump statements, return, continue, break
- Conditional operators
- Arrays of various types, array lists, jagged arrays, dictionaries
- Strings

Some of the specifics in this chapter will require using the latest version of the .NET set up in Unity. To avoid compatibility issues with built-in packages, the player settings and packages directories are not included with each chapter. When a project is opened for the first time the Unity Editor creates new directories. When Visual Studio is launched after that, even more directories are created. To change the .NET version in Unity, open the Player Settings panel found in Edit -> Project Settings.

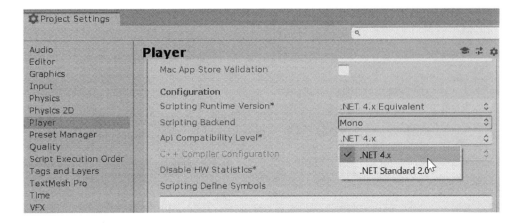

In here change API (application programming interface) Compatibility Level to .NET 4.x to enable the use of the latest features of the C# programming language. If there are errors in a project this may be one of the causes. Just make sure to double check this before continuing in each chapter.

It's likely that support for older versions of .NET will be phased out and this won't be an issue. Unity will eventually deprecate or exclude the option all together. Until then, you'll need to check on the Project Settings option to make sure you're using the correct version of the .NET API.

5.2 Review

For review open the Chapter 5 Unity Project, find the Review script in the Review_Scene attached to the Review game object. The topics covered thus far have a lot in common with programming languages like JavaScript, UnrealScript, Lua, and Java, to name a few. Some of the syntax might look different, but the basic operation of how variables are created and assigned mechanically works the same. For instance, in C#, we understand assigning a variable to look like the following statement.

```
int a = 10;
```

In Lua, another commonly used game programming language, you might see something more like

```
local a = 10
```

In JavaScript, we might see something like the following:

```
var a = 10;
```

A language might not use some of the tokens we're used to seeing in C#, but use of a keyword, an identifier, and an assignment operator with a value is the same. This rule also goes for something like a for loop. In C#, and many other C-style languages, we're used to using the following:

```
for (int i = 0; i < 10; i++)
{
    // Code Here
}
```

Javascript changes the above statement, using var in place of int, but the rest remains the same. However, in Lua, again, we would see something more like the following:

```
for i = 0, 10, i++
do
     // Code Here
end
```

Some programming languages like Lua tend to omit many of the tokens used to help show how code statements are encapsulated; some prefer the brevity of the language. For a C-style language, the use of curly braces helps visually separate the statements more clearly.

Often, getting to this point is a difficult and unforgiving task. I hope you had some classmates, coworkers, friends, or family members to help you work out some of the exercises. If you're still a bit foggy on some of the concepts, you may want to go back and review. We've covered many cool things so far. For instance, you should be able to identify what the following code is. To follow along with this section open the SomeNewClass script attached to the SomeNewClass GameObject in the Review_Scene.

```
class SomeNewClass
{

}
```

If you understood this to be a class declaration for SomeNewClass, then you'd be right. We should also know that for a class to be useful to Unity 3D, we need to add some directives that will look like the following. To add in directives, we start before the class declaration. We use the keyword using followed by a library path and add in both UnityEngine and System.Collections.

```
using UnityEngine;
using System.Collections;
class SomeNewClass
{

}
```

Directives allow our class to have access to the tools that .NET has to offer. For an app to have access to data storage on disk, you need to use similar directives. If you wanted to open an internet connection to a server and ask for a web page, you would include System.Net.Sockets. Once you get some data if you wanted to save it to a file on disk you'd add System.IO.

```
using System.IO;
using System.Net.Sockets;
```

We're still a couple keywords away from a usable class in Unity 3D, though. First, we need to make this class visible to the rest of Unity 3D. To change a class's visibility, we need to add some accessibility keywords.

```
using UnityEngine;
using System.Collections;
using System.IO;
using System.Net.Sockets;
public class SomeNewClass
{

}
```

We're almost there, and now we get to a part that might be confusing.

```
using UnityEngine;
using System.Collections;
using System.IO;
using System.Net.Sockets;
public class SomeNewClass : MonoBehaviour
{

}
```

What is this: MonoBehaviour stuff that's coming in after our class identifier? You should be asking questions like this. We'll get around to answering this in mode depth in Chapter 6. MonoBehaviour is another class that the programmers at Unity 3D have written. SomeNewClass is now inheriting from the class MonoBehaviour; we'll dive into what this all means in Chapter 6.

A class is the fundamental system for C#. You're allowed to write classes with nothing in them; for instance, class NothingClass{} is a complete class structure. You can add a single type of data in a class and give it an identifier. In this case, class MyData{int SomeNumber;} is an entire object with one integer value called SomeNumber in it. On the other hand, a file without anything other than int NothingInParticular; is meaningless.

A class can also be a complex monster, with many different behaviors. It's not uncommon for a class to contain several hundred or even a few thousand lines of code. The general practice is for a class to be as small as possible. Once a class grows past a few hundred lines, it's often time to consider breaking the class into several smaller classes of reusable code.

The intent is to reduce the amount of code that could cause an error. Complex code means difficult code to debug.

What all of this means in relation to Unity 3D is that we need to write several short classes and add them to the same GameObject. The same goes for any other programming project. The more modular your code is, the easier it is to create complex behavior by creating different combinations of code.

A search on Microsoft's .NET Framework API Reference will help you look for functionality you would like to add to a class. The using UnityEngine; directive gives you access to Unity specific functions. The using System.IO; gives you access to reading and writing data to local storage. The online reference will show you many hundreds of namespaces you can include in your Unity project. The API Browser is located at:

https://docs.microsoft.com/en-us/dotnet/api/

You'll want to navigate to the latest .NET Framework to see what tools are available, it's a long list!

5.2.1 Modular Code

Many different game types use a game controller to move around a character on the screen. You might want to re-use some of that code to move around the player's foes. A more modular approach provides a chance to reduce the amount of code you need to re-write.

The same goes for functions. Rather than having a long algorithm operating in the Update() function, it's better to modularize the algorithm itself. First, you might have some sort of initialization where you obtain the character's mesh and animation system. This should be done in a separate function call rather than being repeated at the beginning of every frame. We'll look at a better way to do this later in Section 7.18.

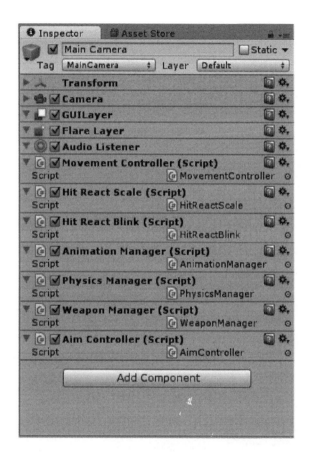

For now, we're reviewing all the different things we've learned. Next, we are going to want to add in the an entry point created by the Unity 3D programmers called Start() and to do this, we'll simply add them into the class code block.

```
public class SomeNewClass : MonoBehaviour
{
    private void Start()
    {
    }
}
```

The UnityEngine library has within it an EventSystem that is a part of the MonoBehaviour class you're inheriting from. That EventSystem then sends messages at appropriate times to every class instance of MonoBehavior to invoke various methods, so long as they are named correctly. In this case, Start() is the method we can rely on being invoked as a child of MonoBehaviour.

To review our understanding of the functions that will be called by the MonoBehaviour EventSystem, let's look at what void Start()   {} means. The keyword void implies that the function returns no values when it is done being invoked. You should note that the Start() begins with an upper case letter, the letter case matters as C# is case sensitive thus start and Start are different. The () open and closed parenthesis mean that Start() requires no arguments to be provided to be invoked.

```
private void Start()
{
    Debug.Log(MyFunction(7));
}


int MyFunction(int inPut)
{
    return inPut;
}
```

If we examine the function we added, we would find we created a new function called MyFunction. This function returns an int, and accepts an arg or argument with type int. In our Start() function, we're using a Debug.Log() function that comes from the Debug class in the UnityEngine library. The Start() function then passes an int 7 to MyFunction() argument list. The MyFunction returns a value inPut, which is then sent back up to the Debug.Log(), which sends 7 to the Console panel in Unity 3D.

If any of the return and argument list information is confusing we'll be going into further detail on that in Section 5.7.

Before moving on, we'll add in one last for loop. If you can guess that this code will print out a 0 through 10 in the Console output panel in Unity 3D, then you're doing great. If you were able to follow along with this example, then you've come quite a long way in understanding the basics behind C#.

```
void MyLoopFunction(int loops)
{
    for (int i = 0; i < loops; i++)
    {
        Debug.Log(i);
    }
}
```

Now that we've got most of the basics under our belt, it's time to move onto more interesting things that make C# a powerful language. What differentiates C# from older programming paradigms is the fact that it's an object oriented programming language. Objects make programming powerful, and—if you're not fully informed—confusing.

Modularity refers to the ability of code to be reused, or shared between objects. This means that you could have a generalized helper class where functions exist that you intend to use elsewhere. Going back to the Review script we can use the from there as well.

```
private void Start()
{
    SomeNewClass newClass = (SomeNewClass)FindObjectOfType(typeof(SomeNewClass));
    Debug.Log(newClass.MyFunction(11));
}
```

There are a few strategies to make this modularity more formal, but we've just got started with the basics. Each MonoBehaviour could also take on a more direct approach to modularity.

```
public class RotateX : MonoBehaviour
{
    void Update ()
    {
        transform.Rotate(new Vector3(1f * Time.deltaTime, 0, 0));
    }
}
```

```
public class RotateY : MonoBehaviour
{
    void Update ()
    {
        transform.Rotate(new Vector3(0, 1f * Time.deltaTime, 0));
    }
}
```

```
public class RotateZ : MonoBehaviour
{
    void Update ()
    {
        transform.Rotate(new Vector3(0, 0, 1f * Time.deltaTime));
    }
}
```

The three scripts above, attached to the same object, would effect the rotation of an object each in their own way.

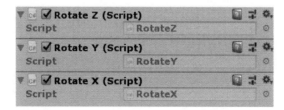

The object would tumble as though all three were applied in one script. This means you can layer multiple effects with multiple scripts. Each one can make modifications to the same GameObject in the scene.

From here on out, you're going to get into the more interesting capabilities behind C#. The basics we've covered have similar utility in most programming languages. Declaring functions and variables will look the same in many different languages. Order of operation and logic both behave similarly in most modern programming languages.

Try not to limit yourself to learning a single programming language. The science of computers is always changing. New languages are being written, and new business models rely on people who know about the latest developments.

5.3 Inheritance: A First Look

Once we've written a new class, we should be thinking toward generalizing what a class can do. When we started our class declarations, we always had the following ": MonoBehaviour" added after the class name. This means that our class is inheriting from another class named MonoBehaviour.

A pop-up with some interesting options appears over the word. Selecting "Go To Definition," opens the MonoBehavior assembly file. The word declaration is used here with the same meaning as when we use a declaration statement to create a new identifier. A declaration statement is used to assign a variable a new identifier.

```
⊞using [...]

⊟namespace UnityEngine
 {
     [...]public class MonoBehaviour : Behaviour
     {
         public MonoBehaviour();

         [...]public bool useGUILayout { get; set; }
         [...]public bool runInEditMode { get; set; }

         [...]public static void print(object message);
         [...]public void CancelInvoke(string methodName);
         [...]public void CancelInvoke();
         [...]public void Invoke(string methodName, float time);
         [...]public void InvokeRepeating(string methodName, float time, float repeatRate);
         [...]public bool IsInvoking(string methodName);
         [...]public bool IsInvoking();
         [...]public Coroutine StartCoroutine(string methodName);
         [...]public Coroutine StartCoroutine(IEnumerator routine);
         [...]public Coroutine StartCoroutine(string methodName, [DefaultValue("null")] object value);
         [...]public Coroutine StartCoroutine_Auto(IEnumerator routine);
         [...]public void StopAllCoroutines();
         [...]public void StopCoroutine(IEnumerator routine);
         [...]public void StopCoroutine(Coroutine routine);
         [...]public void StopCoroutine(string methodName);
     }
 }
```

This indicates that MonoBehaviour is a class that programmers at Unity 3D wrote for us to use. A closer look into MonoBehavior you'll see it inherits from Behavior. We can dive even deeper.

```
⊞using [...]

⊟namespace UnityEngine
 {
     [...]public class Behaviour : Component
     {
         public Behaviour();

         [...]public bool enabled { get; set; }
         [...]public bool isActiveAndEnabled { get; }
     }
 }
```

Seeing Behavior we can see that it too is inheriting from another object called Component. Component then inherits from Object. And Object doesn't inherit anything. Programmers like to call classes who form the foundation for many other classes a base class.

You'll also see that in each class there are functions described in each one. For instance, in Behavior, you'll see two functions called enabled and isActiveAndEnabled. These are things that Behaviour does that Component doesn't.

This might be a bit too much information right now, but this is showing you all the public members that you can access within the class MonoBehaviour. More interestingly, everything that Behavior, Component, and Object do MonoBehaviour also has. Each new child class inherits the important functions of its parent, this includes all of its ancestors.

MonoBehaviour is a class that is tucked away in a DLL (dynamically linked library). A DLL is a container of referenceable code shared between Unity 3D and you. In this case, the code was written by the engineers at Unity.

The keyword using allows us access to the contents of the library where MonoDevelop is living inside of. To allow us to inherit from MonoBehaviour, we need to add in the UnityEngine library with the statement using UnityEngine;.

In Visual Studio open the Solution Explorer under View -> Solution Explorer.

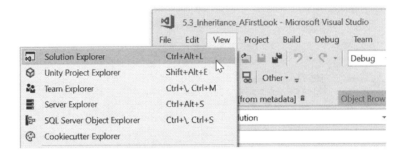

Then expand the References hierarchy, and select UnityEngine by double clicking it. An Object Viewer panel opens with a long list of objects living in the UnityEngine library. Change to the NameSpaces view of the object viewer by right clicking on the UnityEngine object and expand the UnityEngine object to reveal all of the different object types contained in UnityEngine.

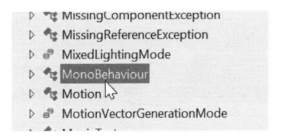

To summarize, UnityEngine is a library written by Unity's programmers. This library contains MonoBehaviour, a class that is required for our C# code to communicate with Unity's game object related functions. To use the MonoBehaviour functions, we tell our class to inherit from it.

The gameObject with your behavior will then connect to the rest of Unity through the code in the MonoBehaviour class.

5.3.1 Class Members

To see how classes and inheritance works together to make something useful, we'll look at building a simple character class. One important reason to create a base class for a character is to reduce the necessity of writing redundant code. If all characters will have a name, then it's certainly useful for all characters to use the same string variable to store their names.

To use programmer nomenclature, start with a "BaseCharacter.cs" to store attributes common among all the characters in the game. You'll find this in the Assets directory of the Chapter 5 Unity Project.

```
public class BaseCharacter : MonoBehaviour
{
}
```

This BaseCharacter.cs is now an object. When you declare a class, its identifier is an important name to identify the class by. The keyword class tells the computer to hold onto the following word as a new type of data. Each class's identifier basically becomes a new reserved word, much like a keyword, with special meaning.

In addition to the name of the class, all contained variables and functions should be considered special components of that new object. Encapsulation and accessibility determine how easily these contained objects can be used.

One interesting system that is offered by Visual Studio is in the Project view. You can display the members of the class you are writing.

Members of a class are not restricted to its functions. Any public variable or function becomes an accessible member of that class. To see how all of this works, we'll need to write some really simple classes in Visual Studio. We'll come back to this in a moment.

5.3.1.1 Inheriting Members

To begin open the InheritingMembers script in the Chapter5 Unity Project.

```
public class InheritingMembers : MonoBehaviour
{
    public class Cat
    {
    }

    public class PianoCat : Cat
    {
    }

}
```

The PianoCat class that inherits from Cat. In programming terms, PianoCat inherits from the base class Cat. So far, nothing interesting is happening, at least anything worthy of posting to the Internet.

To see what it means to inherit properties, we need to add some properties to Cat. Let's give our base Cat the ability to meow. Start with Debug.Log("Meow"); in our Cat class. Since this is happening as a nested class in InheritingMembers class Cat and PianoCat are both able to reference the libraries that are declared at the beginning of this file.

```
public class Cat
{
    int paws = 4;
    public void Meow()
    {
        Debug.Log("Meow");
    }
}

public class PianoCat : Cat
{
    public void PlayPiano()
    {
        Meow(); // inherited from Cat
    }
}
```

So while PianoCat plays piano in a new function, he can also meow Meow();, which is a function inherited from Cat. Both PianoCat and any other class inheriting from Cat are Cats. PianoCat is a Cat.

The terms "is-a" and "has-a" relate to component model and inheritance model object-oriented programming. The PianoCat object "is-a" Cat. In Unity you can observe a game object in the scene has a "Transform" component. So you can say a GameObject "has-a" Transform component.

The PianoCat objects can do things that Cat can do like Meow().

5.3.1.2 Is-A and Has-A

In the creation of a class you create a new Object. Objects can inherit from another object. An object can have any number members. Each member counts as something the Class has, but they do not count as something the class is.

```
public class LaptopComponent : Component
{
}


/* ComputerCat Is-A Cat      */
public class ComputerCat : Cat
{
    /* ComputerCat Has-A LaptopComponent */
    LaptopComponent Laptop;
}
```

The is keyword allows you to check if a PianoCat is a Cat.

```
Cat cat = new Cat();
PianoCat pianoCat = new PianoCat();
ComputerCat computerCat = new ComputerCat();

bool pianoCatIsCat = pianoCat is Cat;
Debug.Log("PianoCat is a Cat?" + (pianoCatIsCat ? "True" : "False"));
// PianoCat is a Cat? True

bool pianoCatIsComputerCat = pianoCat is ComputerCat;
Debug.Log("PianoCat is a ComputerCat?" + (pianoCatIsComputerCat ? "True" : "False"));
// PianoCat is a ComputerCat False
```

The above shows that bool can be set by checking if an instance of a `pianoCat is Cat`. This doesn't mean that a PianoCat object is a ComputerCat which returns false. Visual Studio also flags this knowing that a pianoCat will never be a ComputerCat.

Checking if a Cat has various properties is possible, but we'll need to wait for a chapter on reflection to comb through the members of a class.

5.3.2 Instancing

To make use of these two classes, we're going to need to do something useful with them. In the first part of our IneritingMembers.cs class, we've still got our void `Start()` that we can begin to add code to. When we start to enter PianoCat, the auto complete pop-up provides us with a PianoCat option.

```
private void Start()
{
    PianoCat famousCat = new PianoCat();
    famousCat.PlayPiano();
}
```

To make use of a class, we need to create an instantiation of the class. Instancing a class means to construct it from a blueprint. Each instance is a new object created from the class; any changes you do to the instanced version is unique to that instance.

We've created a `famousCat` with the properties of a `PianoCat`. To make this new cat (famous-Cat) play piano, we call on the member function found in the `PianoCat` class. `famousCat`.

PlayPiano(); is easily added through the handy pop-ups that Visual Studio gives us. As soon as we add in the dot operator after famousCat, we're given several options, one of which is PlayPiano, but we also get Meow() function which originated in Cat.

```
PianoCat famousCat = new PianoCat();
famousCat.PlayPiano();
famousCat.Meow();
```

The Meow() is a member function of PianoCat because PianoCat inherited from Cat. Likewise, if we made a NyanCat or HipsterCat based on Cat, they would also inherit the Meow() function from Cat. Running the code in Unity 3D returns an expected meow in the Console panel.

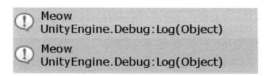

We also had a number of paws on Cat; we can access that value through famousCat. In our Start() function, in the first class we started with, we can use Debug.Log() to show how many paws the famousCat inherited from Cat. However, we forgot to add something.

Change the accessibility of the paws value in Cat to public. And the Debug.Log will be able to access the paws value from the Start() function in the IneritingMembers script.

```
public int paws = 4;
```

In our Start() function, in the InheritingMembers class we started with, we can use Debug.Log() to show how many paws the famousCat inherited from Cat.

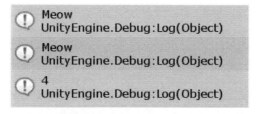

When any class you create has the notation : MonoBehaviour added to the class declaration you inherit a great number of functions and properties. This inheritance works in the same way PianoCat inherited paws and Meow() from Cat with the :Cat notation.

We've gotten to a point where we'd like to search the entire scene for a specific object. In this case, we should look for every player in the scene. Useful functions definitions are found in the GameObject class.

We can find an object using its name or tag. If we want to find any object that happens to have a player. cs component, we need to know which GameObject it's attached to first. It's hard to know the name of the object we're looking for if we only know one thing about it. However, there is a more general way to find things.

Of course, we could just use Unity 3D's Editor and assign tags, but we wouldn't learn how to do things with code alone. In a more realistic situation, we could just have our game designers assign tags to everything, use the `FindWithTag()` function, and be done with it.

To give ourselves a better understanding of objects and types, we should go through this process without tags. This way, we will gain a bit more understanding as to what defines objects and types, and how to use null. The null keyword basically means "nothing"; we'll see how that's used in a moment.

5.3.3 Parent Child

To see an example of how object types work, we'll inspect two classes. The first is ObjectParent.cs and the second is ObjectChild.cs. Both of these are in the Assets directory of the Chapter5 Unity Project and found together in the ParentChild_Scene.

Both scripts are attached to GameObjects in the ParentChild_Scene. The class declaration in the ObjectChild.cs should look like the following.

```
public class ObjectChild : ObjectParent
{

}
```

Observe that the usual `MonoBehaviour` following the colon (:) is replaced with `ObjectParent`. Now to prove that the Child inherits the functions found in its Parent, we should add a function for the Child to use. This code appears in the Parent class.

```
public void ParentAbility()
{
    Debug.Log("inheritable function.");
}
```

To see that the function can be used by Child.cs, we'll use it in the `Start()` function in the ObjectChild.cs, as follows.

```
private void Start()
{
    ParentAbility();
}
```

`ParentAbility()` is a public function found in the Parent class, not in the Child class. Running this script when it's attached to an object in the game produces the expected *inheritable function* printout in the Console panel. Remember, there's nothing inside of the Child class that has yet to have any new member functions or variables added. If we keep adding new public functions to Parent, Child will always be able to use them.

To confirm this, the ObjectChild class has the following.

```
public void ChildAbility()
{
    Debug.Log("My parent doesn't get me.");
}
```

Then, check if the Parent class can use that function. The `ChildAbility()` function in the ObjectParent's `Start()` function produces an error.

```
private void Start()
{
    ChildAbility();
}
```

As it turns out, parent's can't inherit from their children. The ChildAbility does not exist in the current context.

Even though the function is public, the parent doesn't have access to the functions that the Child class has. This is an important difference. The other main takeaway from this tutorial is to remember that Parent inherited from MonoBehaviour, as did all the other scripts we've been working with to this point.

The significance behind this discussion is that Child.cs has all of the functions found not only in Parent.cs but also in MonoBehaviour. One more thing should be noted:

```
public int ParentInt;
```

Adding a public int to the Parent class will also allow the Child class to use the ParentInt variable. This includes what is visible to the Inspector Panel in the Editor.

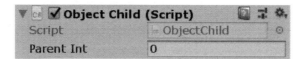

ParentInt is available as though it were declared as a part of Child, because it is. It's important to know that changing anything in the Child class will never affect the Parent class. Inheritance only works one way: The children of a parent can never change the functions in a parent. Such an occurrence rarely happens in real life as well as in C#.

5.3.4 Object

`GameObject`, is a class that inherits from `Object`. Then `GameObject` adds new functions to on top of anything that already existed in `Object`. As we have just observed from our simple inheritance example, if we find a function in `Object`, we can use it in `GameObject`.

What this means to us is that we may use any interesting functions inside of the Object in the Assembly Browser in Object as well. To view all the different classes available to you in Visual Studio, select View→Object Browser Ctrl + Alt J. Then in the Options select NameSpaces. In the left column are all sorts of items. In there is an entry for UnityEngine, expanding that opens hundreds more objects. In that list is the `Object`, or rather `UnityEngine.Object`. Selecting the `Object` found under `UnityEngine` you'll see the right panel populate with the members found in `Object`.

The members of Object are also numerous and many seem to do similar things with slight differences in how they are used. In the list is a group of `FindObjectsOfType` members.

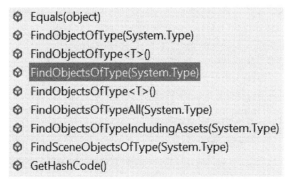

Highlighting that populates the panel below with some additional information. The text here was generated by the comments the original programmer left in their code as they wrote the function.

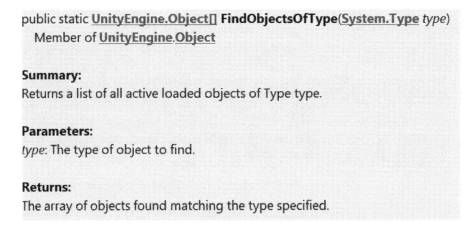

public static **UnityEngine.Object[] FindObjectsOfType**(**System.Type** *type*)
    Member of **UnityEngine.Object**

Summary:
Returns a list of all active loaded objects of Type type.

Parameters:
type: The type of object to find.

Returns:
The array of objects found matching the type specified.

It's important to get used to searching through the libraries for useful functions. Very often you'll find some solution hidden in the vast resources of Unity 3D. Many common game related tasks have code already in place waiting for you to use in your project.

Stepping through that thought process, we begin with "I'd like to find an object in the scene, but I might not know what it's called." From that, I would likely look for something called FindObjects. The objects I need to find are going to be GameObjects, so that does narrow things down a bit. Inside of `Object`, we find a function called `FindObjectsOfType()`, which is probably what we're looking for. The summary for that reads "returns a list of all active loaded object of Type." This continues with some parameters and returns.

Parameters are arguments that go into the parenthesis `()`. The returns mean the function can be assigned to a variable. We haven't covered everything necessary to completely understand what all that means yet, but we'll show how the function is used assuming you'll come up to speed soon enough.

Continuing with the ParentChild_Scene from the previous chapter, open the `ObjectFinder` script attached to the ObjectFinder GameObject in the scene. In the Start() function, we need to set up an array for every Object in the scene. Use `Object[]`; the square brackets tell the variable it's an array. We'll cover arrays in more depth in Section 5.9. Then we name it something short, like objects. Then we can have Object run its FindObjectsOfType function to fill in our array with every Object in the scene.

```
void Start ()
{
    Object[] objects = FindObjectsOfType(typeof(Object));
    foreach (Object o in objects)
    {
        Debug.Log(o);
    }
}
```

`FindObjectsOfType()` works just as `Object.FindGameObjectsOfType()`, which should be interesting. Inheritance in C# makes things complex and clever. Keep this behavior in mind in the following example. Unfortunately, System includes type `object` which is different from the UnityEngine type `Object` with an upper case O. Keyword `typeof()` informs the parameter with the type of Object, rather than Object itself. This part is a bit confusing, but we'll cover this in more detail again in Section 6.5.3.

The function assigns the objects variable an array of all the objects in the scene. The foreach. To do this, we're going to reuse the foreach loop prints out everything it finds, which is quite a lot.

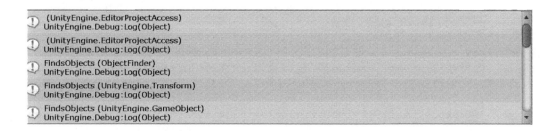

Altogether over 30 Objects have been found in the scene. This includes each component of each GameObject in the scene. The Camera, light, transform components, etc are all listed. So how do we find a specific Object like a Parent or Child?

```
ObjectParent parent = o as ObjectParent;
if (parent != null)
{
    Debug.Log("FoundParent:" + parent);
}
```

The addition to the loop will now look for all Parents in the scene. This oddly includes the ObjectChild since it inherited from ObjectParent, so it's counted as a ParentType. The first line `Object parent = o as ObjectParent;` is what is called a cast. We'll learn more about that in Section 6.5.3 again, but it's important to know how Object is the base class for all Unity Objects, and Parent is the base from which Child inherits.

> ⓘ FoundParent:ObjectParent (ObjectParent)
>   UnityEngine.Debug:Log(Object)
> ⓘ FoundParent:ObjectChild (ObjectChild)
>   UnityEngine.Debug:Log(Object)

NOTE: You could enter `Component.FindObjectsOfType()`, and this will work the same as though it were called from `Object` or `GameObject`. Inheritance is a complex topic, and right now, we're only observing how functions can be shared from the parent to children, but there's a problem when children try to share. We've used `GameObject.CreatePrimitive()` to make cubes and spheres. And we know Object has FindObjectsOfType, which both GameObject and Component can use because of inheritance. Therefore, does that mean Object.CreatePrimitive will work?

Actually, no; Object doesn't inherit functions of variables from its children. In programming, parents don't learn from their kids. Suppose `GameObject.CreatePrimitive()` is a function found in GameObject, and GameObject and Component both inherit from Object; does that mean `Component.CreatePrimitive()` will work? Again, no; in C#, children don't like to share. C# is a pretty tough family, but rules are rules.

Now we have a handle on getting an `ObjectChild` or `ObjectParent` if they're in the scene. So for instance, we could add in a `ParentObject` parent; and when we find one in the scene we assign the `Object` o to the `parent`.

5.3.4.1 A Type Is Not an Object

Type, as we've mentioned, is the name given to a class of an object. Like a vowel, or noun, type refers to the classification of a thing, not the actual thing itself. Semantics is important when dealing with programming, and it's very easy to miss the meanings behind how words are used. For instance, if we need to tell a function the type of a class, we can't simply use the class's name.

```
FindObjectsOfType(Object);
```

If the function expected the type Object and not the object of Object, you'd get an error. There's a subtle difference here. The type of an object is not the object itself. However, it's difficult to say "this is the type Child" and not the "Child" class object. The two things use the same word, so it's easy to confuse.

There is a function that will get the type of an object and satisfy functions that need types and not objects. And that's where `typeof(Object)` comes in. If we have the object Object `typeof(Object)`, we can put `Object` into the `typeof()` function and use that function as the type of an `Object` and not the class `Object`.

Give the `FindObjectsOfType()` function a `typeof(Object)` and it returns an array with every instance of Object in the scene. We can give the ObjectFinder.cs a Player to chase after. Just so we don't get confused what version of the word Player we're looking for, we should make it tremendously clear what we're looking for.

5.3.5 != null

To look for a GameObject with the ObjectChild script Add in a GameObject variable for the ObjectFinder at the class scope. The not null check is important. We'll find out why in Section 5.7.4, but for now we'll just observe how it's used.

```
GameObject foundObject;
void Update ()
{
    if (foundObject == null)
    {

    }
}
```

When the game is started `foundObject` starts off without anything assigned. Since it's not POD or Plain Old Data, the initialization of the GameObject is null. This is important since we'll check on this assignment in the Update() function in the ObjectFinder script.

```
if (foundObject == null)
{
    Object[] objects = FindObjectsOfType(typeof(GameObject));
    // a list of all game objects in the scene

    foreach (GameObject o in objects)
    {
        Debug.Log(o);
        ObjectChild child = o.GetComponent(typeof(ObjectChild)) as ObjectChild;
        if (child != null)
        {
            foundObject = o;
        }
    }
}
```

Like the previous code, we use `FindObjectsOfType`, but we use the GameObject as the type. We follow that with the same foreach, but we use `GameObject o` to list each object in the array. Then we use `ObjectChild child = o.GetComponent(typeof(ObjectChild)) as ObjectChild` to find individual components attached to the GameObject o.

Last and most important we use `if(child != null)` to assign the `foundObject` to the o in the foreach loop. The `child != null` statement is true if child is assigned. When a GameObject doesn't have a component that matches the `GetComponent` statement child is assigned null, or rather the child remains null.

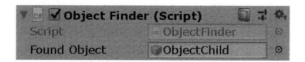

We can run the game, and check the foundObject variable. We'll see that it's ObjectChild, the gameObject in the scene Hierarchy.

The statement (thing != null) is commonly used to know when something has been found. When the something is not empty, you've found what it is you're looking for. This is a useful trick to apply for many different purposes. The statement (null != thing) can also be used. In some languages this might execute faster, but it's not as commonly used so it might look awkward.

5.3.6 What We've Learned

Using data to find data is a commonplace task in programming. With Unity 3D, we have plenty of functions available which make finding objects in a scene quite easy. When monsters go chasing after players, we need to have a simple system for allowing them to find one another.

Computers don't use senses like we do. They have another view of the game that can't be compared to how we, as players, perceive the world. By searching through data, and using algorithms, the computer-controlled characters require a different set of parameters to operate.

In one sense, the computer has complete knowledge over the game world. How that world is perceived by the computer requires our instruction. A monster's ability to understand its environment depends on our code.

5.4 Instancing

In the Instancing_Scene open the Instancing script attached to the game object of the same name. An important feature of C# and many C-like programming paradigms is the use of a class as a variable. When we use a class as a variable, it's created as a new object. Some of these classes are values, which means that the function itself can be used to assign to variables, and many classes are used as values. Using a class as an object which is itself a value is at the heart of object-oriented programming.

To make use of a class, or object, we often need to create a new instance of the class. Instancing is basically creating space in memory for a class of a more complex data type. We do this in the same way we create a variable for a simple data type. However, when assigning a value to the variable of this sort, we need to change things up a bit.

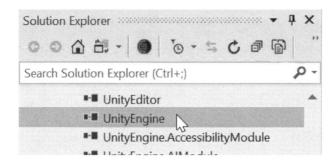

The Vector3 class is located in the guts of the UnityEngine library. Open the Object Browser. Inside there, and change the option to view namespaces and find the Vector3 object.

> ⊛ Angle(UnityEngine.Vector3, UnityEngine.Vector3)
> ⊛ AngleBetween(UnityEngine.Vector3, UnityEngine.Vector3)
> ⊛ ClampMagnitude(UnityEngine.Vector3, float)
> ⊛ Cross(UnityEngine.Vector3, UnityEngine.Vector3)
> ⊛ Distance(UnityEngine.Vector3, UnityEngine.Vector3)
> ⊛ Dot(UnityEngine.Vector3, UnityEngine.Vector3)
> ⊛ Equals(object)
> ⊛ Equals(UnityEngine.Vector3)
> ⊛ Exclude(UnityEngine.Vector3, UnityEngine.Vector3)
> ⊛ GetHashCode()
> ⊛ Lerp(UnityEngine.Vector3, UnityEngine.Vector3, float)
> ⊛ LerpUnclamped(UnityEngine.Vector3, UnityEngine.Vector3, float)

Selecting the `Vector3` object you will find that the contents are arranged alphabetically to make things easier to find.

Don't let this cacophony of information bewilder you. We only need to deal with a small portion of these objects to get started. Later, we'll be able to browse the classes in each one of these DLLs and look for classes we can include in our code.

5.4.1 Class Initialization

The reason why we don't need to create an instance for an int or a bool is that they are built-in types found in the system library. We also create our own types every time we write a new class. for our own game. Yes, we get to invent new types of data. For instance, you'll need a player type and a monster type.

For these new types, we'll want to store the status of their health and possibly their ammunition. These bits of information can be any value; however, they are usually ints or floats. Of course, to store a player's location in the world, we'll want to include a Vector3, inferring that a type can contain many other non-primitive types. Eventually, everything in the game will have a class and a type of its own.

In C#, the built-in types do not need a constructor. We'll get into constructors when we start instancing objects later in this chapter. Plain old data types (PODs) include not only the built-in types but structures and arrays as well. The term came from the C++ standards committee, and was used to describe data types that were similar between C and C++. This term can be extended to C# that shares the same POD types.

5.4.2 New

The new keyword is used to create a new instance of an object. Some data types that are assigned to a variable, do not need the new keyword. For example, when you declare an int, you simply need to set it to a number, as in `int i = 7;`. This declaration creates space in memory for an int named `i`, and then sets the value for `i` to 7. However, for more complex data types, like a Vector3, you may need to give three different float values. Unity 3D calls a 3D vector a Vector3, because there are three values stored in it: x, y, and z.

```
// creates new int i assigns 7
int i = 7;

/* creates new int j and assigns   *
 * a new int, but it's not given    *
 * any value.                       */
int j = new int();
```

The MonoBehaviour acts a bit differently. There are several constructs that are constructed with the new keyword within the MonoBehaviour, but MonoBehaviours are components that are added with a different method.

A MonoBehaviour related script is something attached to a gameObject in the scene. The Instancing. cs script attached to the gameObject in the Instancing_Scene is attached to a game object. The following attaches an example to the same game object the Instancing script is already attached to:

```
/* creates and assigns       *
 * Thing t to a new Thing    */
Thing t = new Thing();

/* creates and assigns                       *
 * Example e to new Example : MonoBejaviour  */
Example e = gameObject.AddComponent<Example>();
```

The notation seen is not regular usage of C# scripting conventions for instancing an object, but that's okay. C# allows for a lot of flexibility and the Unity conventions use this to its advantage. The explanation for the above will have to wait until a few other concepts have been discussed. It's important to understand that there's more than one system to create an instance of a class.

NOTE: Unity 3D also has a Vector2 and a Vector4 type. These are instanced in the same way as a Vector3, but have more specific uses. Vector2 only has an x and y value; Vector4 has an additional vector, w, after x, y, and z.

Normally, in 3D space, you'd need only a Vector3, but when dealing with something called quaternions, you'll need the extra fourth number in a vector; we'll get into this a bit later on.

Remember, declaring a variable starts with the type followed by the name we're assigning to the variable. Normally, you'd start with something like Vector3 SomeVector;. The difference comes in when assigning a value to the variable. To do this, we start with the new keyword, followed by the Vector3's initialization.

5.4.3 Constructors

Constructors add an extra, but necessary, step when using a variable type that's derived from an object class. With many classes, there are different ways in which they can be initialized with a constructor. Most initializations can be done without any parameters, as in the following example.

```
void Start()
{
    Vector3 vector = new Vector3();
    Debug.Log(vector);
}
```

The use of a pair of parentheses after the type refers to a constructor, or a set of parameters that can be used to build the instance when it's created. Peek at the Vector3 object and you'll see some definitions called `public Vector3(float x, float y);` and `public Vector3(float x, float y, float z);` in the opened window.

```
Vector3 vector = new Vector3(1.0f, 1.0f);
```

Constructors are named the same as the class. There's always going to be an assumed () version, with no parameters for construction. There can be any number of alternative constructors. In this case, there are two additional constructors created for Vector3().

We should also note that float is another name for single, as seen in the Assembly Browser. The word *double*, which we've mentioned in Section 4.5, has twice the amount of space in memory to store a value than a single; a single is a 32-bit floating point, and a double is a 64-bit floating point value.

We can add information, or parameters, when initializing a new Vector3 type variable. Parameters, also known as arguments, the values added to the parenthesis of a function. The different parameters are setting variables within the class we're instancing. Inside of a Vector3, there is an x, y, and z variable. Like the variables we've been using. When using parameters, we can get some guides from our integrated development environment (IDE).

Hover over the Vector3() as you type in Visual Studio you'll see the following helper dialog.

```
Vector3()
       ⬙ Vector3.Vector3() (+ 2 overloads)
```

The pop-up indicates alternative constructors for the Vector3 are available. To use the vector we created, we'll assign the object in Unity's Transform, in the Position component, to the vector variable we just assigned. This assignment will move the object to the assigned Vector3 position. We'll go into further detail on how to know what a component expects when assigning a variable when we start to explore the classes that Unity 3D has written for us.

```
Vector3 vector = new Vector3(1.0f, 2.0f, 3.0f);
transform.position = vector;
```

When this class is attached to the Main Camera in the scene and the Play-in-Editor button is pressed, we will see the following in Unity 3D. Notice entries for Position in Transform roll out in Inspector.

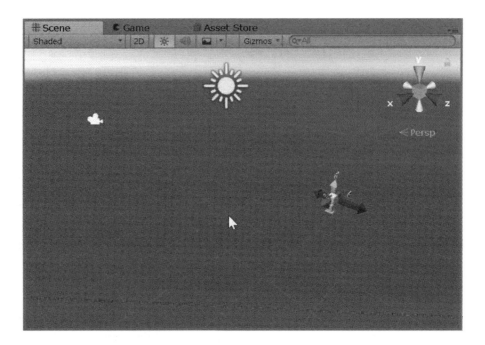

The declaration and initialization of a new vector requires an extra step. For instance, this situation can be translated into English as follows: "I'm making a new Vector3, and I'm naming it to vector. Then I'm assigning the x, y, and z to 1.0f, 2.0f, and 3.0f. Then, I'm setting the position in the Transform component to vector." Likewise, the shorter version could simply be "I'm setting the Position in the Transform component to a Vector3, with x, y, and z set to 1.0f, 2.0f, and 3.0f."

NOTE: Natural language programming, like the English translation above, has been tried before. However, the compiler's job would be to both interpret and translate English into byte code, and this has proven to be quite tricky. Interpretation of English is part intuition and part assumption. Neither of these abilities can be easily programmed into software to work consistently and perfectly predictably.

Various ways to program computers using different formatting options to make code more humanly readable have been tried many times. In the end, the formatting almost always ends up using more and more keywords, which restrains the programmer by taking away the options and freedoms that are allowed when fewer rules are applied.

You can also use an initialized vector without assigning it to a variable name first. This is perfectly valid; when Position in the object's Transform component is set, it's automatically assigned a Vector3 that's created just for the position.

```
transform.position = new Vector3(1.0f, 2.0f, 3.0f);
```

Once a new class has been initialized, you can modify the individual variables found inside of the Vector3 class. A variable found in a class is referred to as a member variable of the class. We'll go into more detail in Section 6.3.2 about what sort of variables and functions can be found in a class that Unity 3D has written for your benefit. To change one of these variables inside of a class, you simply need to assign it a value like any other variable.

```
Vector3 vector = new Vector3(1.0f, 2.0f, 3.0f);
vector.x = 3.0f;
transform.position = vector;
```

There's an interesting difference here. An f has been used: the 3.0f is assigned to the x member of vector. This informs the compiler that we're assigning a float type number to vector.x and not a double. By default, any number with a decimal with no special designation is assumed to be a double number type.

Some parameters for constructors could be expanded into their own scope. For some clarity, you're able to add a scope for the constructor of the Vector3() instantiation. In the scope live the parameter names that are used in the object being instanced.

```
Vector3 vector = new Vector3()
{
    x = 1.0f,
    y = 2.0f,
    z = 3.0f
};
transform.position = vector;
```

To tell Unity 3D we're assigning a float to the x member of vector, we need to add the suffix f after the number. This changes the number's type to float. This is related to type casting, which we will cover in Section 6.5.3. It's also worth noting that you're allowed to omit some initializations using this notation. In this form, x and y are left at 0.

```
Vector3 vector = new Vector3()
{
    z = 3.0f
};
transform.position = vector;
```

We can also assign POD as an object.

```
int i = new int();
Debug.Log("new int(): " + i); //new int(): 0
```

Adding this after the previous code block, we'll get 0 sent to the Unity 3D Console panel. We don't need to do things like this for all data types, but it's interesting to see that it's possible. Most data types can be initialized in this way. There are some tricky constructors, like string, which need some additional work for us, to understand the parameter list. The details here will have to wait till Section 6.4 in the book.

5.4.4 What We've Learned

The examples in this section created Vector3s in various ways. Setting variables in an object is controlled by how that object was written. The visibility of the variables in the Vector3 class is determined in the same fashion as we have declared variables in the objects that we have been writing. We can make changes to the x, y, and z float variables in the Vector3 class because of their public declaration.

Each nuance and use of the C# language takes some time to get used to. When certain tasks are shortened into easier-to-write code, the code ends up being harder to read. However, most of the harder tasks often have a commonly used format. These shorthand formats are sometimes called idioms.

Idioms in English do not often make the most sense when logically analyzed, but they do have specific meanings. Much like in English, programming idioms might not make sense when you look at them, but they do have a specific meaning when in use. As we make further progress, you'll be introduced to some of the more commonly used idioms in C#.

Complex objects like MonoBehaviours require several steps for the Editor and Game to come together. For this reason, MonoBehaviours do several things behind the scenes that take care of special case constructors. When you drag a script onto a game object in the scene it's not simply calling on a Constructor to attach the script. Updating the UI (user interface), creating meta files, and the like also need to take place. None of this is required of the scripts you're going to be writing, but it's important to know why we don't use new when instancing a MonoBehaviour derived class.

5.5 Static

Open the Chapter5 Unity Project's Static_Scene and open the Static script on the game object of the same name. The static keyword is a keyword that ties all instances of a class together. This allows all instances of a class to share a common variable or function. When you see static next to a function, this means you don't need to make a new instance of the class to use it. Because static functions and variables are class-wide, we access them in a slightly different way than an instance of a variable or function.

There is a static function found inside of Input called GetKey(), which we will use. The last keyword is bool, after public and static. We've seen bool before, but this is used as a return type. When we write our own functions, we'll also include our own return type, but just so you know, return types are not limited to bool. Functions can return any data type, and now we'll take a look at how this all works.

5.5.1 A Basic Example

Let's start with the Static_Scene in Chapter 5 Unity Project and open the Static script attached to the Static Game Object in the scene. The code here will send the following to the Console panel in Unity 3D.

```
void Update()
{
    bool aKey = Input.GetKey(KeyCode.A);
    if (aKey)
    {
        Debug.Log("aKey");
    }
}
```

The KeyCode object has a public variable for each key on your computer's keyboard. The Input. GetKey() function returns the bool value based on which the key is checked in the KeyCode object. We assign the bool aKey to the returned value from the Input.GetKey(KeyCode.A) function.

The statement for if (aKey) executes the Debug.Log("aKey"); which then prints out "aKey" to the Unity Console window. The GetKey() function is a member of the Input class and is accessed by using the dot operator (.). Now that we're reading libraries we need to know how to get to the members of the classes we're looking at. Peek at the definition and you'll see other static accessible members in the Input class.

```
public static bool GetKey(KeyCode key);
...public static bool GetKeyDown(KeyCode key);
...public static bool GetKeyDown(string name);
...public static bool GetKeyUp(KeyCode key);
...public static bool GetKeyUp(string name);
...public static bool GetMouseButton(int button);
...public static bool GetMouseButtonDown(int button);
...public static bool GetMouseButtonUp(int button);
...public static Touch GetTouch(int index);
...public static bool IsJoystickPreconfigured(string joystickName);
...public static void ResetInputAxes();
```

We're shown `public static bool GetKey(KeyCode key)` as the function's definition. You'll notice that we never made an instance of Input. To use the Input class, we didn't need to create an Instance of the Input object first. The static members of a class don't need to be initialized before they're used.

This process provides us with the beginnings of a player controller script. Filling in the rest of the WASD keys on the keyboard will allow us to log the rest of the most common movement keys on your keyboard. The Input class is found in UnityEngine that was included in this class with the using UnityEngine directive at the top of the class.

From previous chapter lessons, you might imagine that we'd need to create an instance of Input to make use of its member functions or fields. This might look like the following:

```
Input input = new Input();
bool aKey = input.GetKey(KeyCode.A);
```

> [●] (local variable) Input input
>
> Member 'Input.GetKey(KeyCode)' cannot be accessed with an instance reference; qualify it with a type name instead

While this syntactically makes sense, and the practice so far has been to make an instance to use its members. The `GetKey()` function is static, so we get an error when we try to use a static function. This will make more sense once we write our own static function later in this chapter.

```
Input input = new Input();
bool aKey = input.
```

> bool object.Equals(object obj)
> Note: Tab twice to insert the 'Equals' snippet.
>
> ⊘ Equals
> ⊘ GetHashCode
> ⊘ GetType
> ⊘ ToString

When we check for any functions in the input object after it's been instanced, we won't find much. The only things available are universal among all things inheriting from the object class.

The lack of functions or variables is because all the functions and variables have been marked as static, so they're inaccessible through an *instance* of Input. Statically marked functions and variables become inaccessible through an instance. This inaccessibility is related to an object's interface and encapsulation. This doesn't mean that they are completely inaccessible, however; but to see them, we'll need to write our own class with our own functions and variables.

5.5.2 Static Variables

Let's start off with a simple concept: a static variable. Using our previous analogy of toasters, each new toaster built in a factory has a unique identity. Each unit built would have a different serial number. Once in someone's house, the number of times the toasters have been used, when they are turned on and begin to toast, and their location in the world are all unique to each toaster. What they all share is the total number of toasters that exist.

The static keyword means that the function or variable is global to the class it's declared in. Let's make this clear; by declaring a variable as static, as in static `int i;`, you're indicating that you want to use the int i without needing to make an instance of the class that the variable is found in. Variables that are unique to each instance of a class are called *instance variables.* All instances of the class will share the static variable's value regardless of their instanced values.

If we create a mob of zombies, we might find it important to maintain a certain number of zombies. Too many and the computer will have problems keeping up. Too few and the player will go around with nothing to shoot at. To give ourselves an easier time, we can give each zombie a *telepathic* connection with all other zombies. A programmer would call this a *static variable* or a *static function.*

As we've seen, variables usually live a short and isolated life. For instance, the variable used in the ever-powerful for loop exists only within the for loop's code block. Once the loop is done, the variable in the for loop is no longer used and can't be accessed outside of the loop

```
for (int i = 0; i < 10; i++)
{
    Debug.Log(i); // prints 1 to 10
}
// i no longer exists.
Debug.Log(i); //i is undefined.
```

Now that we're creating objects based on classes, we need to make those classes interact with one another in a more convenient way. To keep track of the number of undead zombies in a scene, we could have the player keep track; as each zombie is created or destroyed, a message could be sent to the player.

The Player class keeping track of important zombie data is awkward. Zombie-related data should remain in the zombie class, unrelated classes should not depend on one another in this way. The more spread out your code gets, the more problems you'll have debugging the code. Creating self-contained classes is important, and prevents a web of interdependent code, sometimes referred to as spaghetti code.

Remember that when an object is created it's instanced from a single original blueprint, which can include some variables that are shared between each instance of the class. With static variables instanced cases can talk to the blueprint for a common connection between any new instances made from it.

5.5.2.1 A Basic Example

```
public class Zombie : MonoBehaviour
{
    public static int numZombies;
    void Start ()
    {
        numZombies++;
    }
}
```

Here, in a pretty simple-looking zombie class, we've got a `static` keyword placed before an `int` identified as `numZombies`. This statement turns `int numZombies`, which would normally be confined to this class alone, to an int that's shared among all zombies. As Unity 3D creates more zombies, each zombie has its `Start()` function called once the class has been instanced: `numZombies` increments by 1.

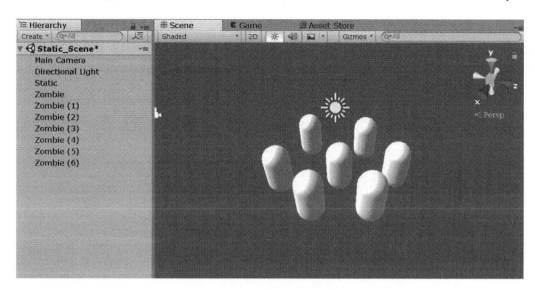

With the above code attached to a collection of different capsules, we'll be better able to see how many zombies there are in the scene through code. Just be sure that each capsule has the zombie script attached.

```
void Start ()
{
    numZombies++;
    Debug.Log(numZombies);
}
```

The `Debug.Log()` function in each Zombie's `Start()` function prints out the `numZombies` value. Each new instance of a Zombie increments the same `numZombies` variable.

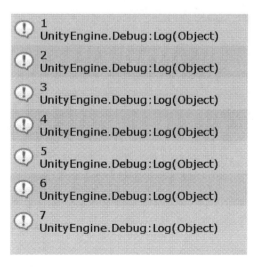

By knowing how many zombies are around, you can change a zombie's behavior, making them more aggressive, perhaps. Maybe only after five zombies have been spawned, they'll join one another and perform a dance routine. Having a shared property makes keeping track of a similar variable much easier.

When the same code is run without static before the numZombies variable, the following output is the result:

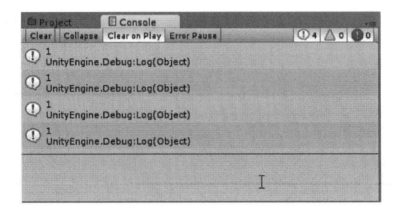

The numZombies value is independent to each instance of the zombie class. When each new Zombie instance is created it's numZombies int is initialized independently to 0. When the Start() function is called in each zombie instance the numZombies value is incremented independently from 0 to 1. Therefore when white, rob and stubbs call their own Start() function their own instance of the numZombies int is incremented, numZombies doesn't get incremented for all zombies because it's not static.

This is an interesting concept here. Up to this point, we've been thinking of classes as encapsulated independent entities. With the static keyword, there's a way to keep the separated objects connected to one another through a variable. This raises the question: Can this be done with functions?

5.5.3 Static Functions

Static functions act on behalf of all instances of the class they are a member of. They work only with static variables of the class. If we extend our zombie class with a new static function, we can use the zombie class to call a static function that can read static variables. To make the static function accessible to other classes we need to make the static function public as well.

```
public static void CountZombies()
{
    Debug.Log(numZombies);
}
```

Then we'll add a call to Zombie.CountZombies(); to find out how many zombies have been created in the Update() function of the static class, by adding it to the if (AKey) code block.

```
bool aKey = Input.GetKey(KeyCode.A);
if (aKey)
{
    Zombie.CountZombies();
}
```

Now when the A key on the keyboard is pressed, we'll get a count printed to the Console panel indicating the number of zombies in the scene along with the `Debug.Log("aKey");` Console log.

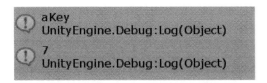

The number being printed out comes from the `public static void CountZombies();` function call being made to Zombie, not from any of the instances of the zombie class attached to the capsules in the scene.

To call static functions, you use the class name, not the name of an instanced object made from the zombie class. As you can see, there's more than one way the class identifier is used. Up to this point, we've been using the class name mostly to create an instance of that class. With a static function or variable, the class identifier is used to access that static member of the class.

5.5.4 Putting It All Together

To build a simple example with our Zombie we'll want him to chase after a player in the scene. To do that we'll open the Zombie_Scene in the Chapter5 project and add to the zombie script we've been working with. Attached to the Robo character in the scene is a Player script. To find the player we'll use the same technique as before where we use `FindObjectsOfType()`.

```
public Player player;
private void Update()
{
    if (player == null)
    {
        /* Find the player */
        player = FindObjectOfType(typeof(Player)) as Player;
    }
}
```

Once we have a handle on the script attached to the Player GameObject we can now add in a method to Move our Zombie to the player. To make use of the MoveToPlayer function we'll add the following to the `Update()`.

```
if (player != null)
{
    MoveToPlayer();
}
```

By checking that the player is not null we make sure that the reference to the player object is there and not null. And to start, our MoveToPlayer will look like the following:

```
void MoveToPlayer()
{
}
```

If you remember the system we used for the MoveToPoint script, we'll do the same again here.

```
void MoveToPlayer()
{
    Vector3 playerPos = player.gameObject.transform.position;

    Vector3 towardPlayer = playerPos - transform.position;
    transform.position = Vector3.Lerp(transform.position, playerPos, Time.deltaTime);

    Quaternion direction = Quaternion.LookRotation(towardPlayer, transform.up);
    transform.rotation = Quaternion.Slerp(transform.rotation, direction, Time.deltaTime * 5f);
}
```

At this point pressing the Play-in-Editor button should have a group of zombies marching at the player.

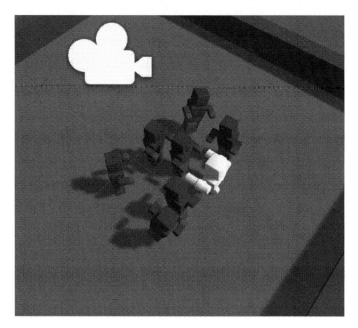

Now that the zombies are moving, it's time to get the player moving. For this we'll use a simple WASD to move the robot around.

```
public class Player : MonoBehaviour
{
    void Update()
    {
        bool w = Input.GetKey(KeyCode.W);
        bool a = Input.GetKey(KeyCode.A);
        bool s = Input.GetKey(KeyCode.S);
        bool d = Input.GetKey(KeyCode.D);
    }
}
```

Next, we a value is created for the *x* and *y* axis of input. These are used to add to the position of the character.

```
float xAxis = 0;
float yAxis = 0;
```

Next we'll use the Booleans we created for the input and use them to add or subtract from each axis.

```
if (w)
{
    yAxis += 1;
}
if (a)
{
    xAxis -= 1;
}
if (s)
{
    yAxis -= 1;
}
if (d)
{
    xAxis += 1;
}
```

Then finally we apply the new values to the direction we want to move in. The transform component has a forward value as well as a right value. Multiply these values by either +1 or −1 when a key is down. If no keys are down then we multiply the forward or right value by 0, which means we add no new value to the current direction.

```
Vector3 direction = transform.position;
direction += transform.forward * yAxis;
direction += transform.right * xAxis;
```

Once we have a vector which represents where we want to go, we can apply it to where we are.

```
transform.position = Vector3.Lerp(transform.position, direction, Time.deltaTime * 5f);
```

Next, to get the robot to rotate using Q and E:

```
bool q = Input.GetKey(KeyCode.Q);
bool e = Input.GetKey(KeyCode.E);
float rot = 0;
if (q)
{
    rot -= 10;
}
if (e)
{
    rot += 10;
}
transform.Rotate(new Vector3(0, rot, 0));
```

We handle the rotation much like we handled the positioning.

5.5.5 What We've Learned

Using static functions certainly layers a distinctive level of complexity on an already complex under-standing of what a class is. Not only do classes have functions talking to one another, they can also share information.

You should use a static variable only if all the classes of the same type need to share a common parameter. This goes the same for a static function. We'll go further into how static functions can help in Section 6.11, when we get back to some of the more complex behaviors, but for now, we'll leave off here.

Moving forward, we'll want to keep in mind that C# has static variables and functions for a specific reason. There are efficiency and optimization considerations to keep in mind as well. For instance, the player's `transform.position` is the same for each zombie. Each zombie doesn't need to have its own instance variable for the player. We could have easily converted the `Vector3 position;` in the player class to a static value.

```
public static Vector3 position;
```

The `static Vector3 position;` variable could then be used by the zombies in the following manner.

```
Vector3 direction = (Player.position - transform.position).normalized;
float distance = (Player.position - transform.position).magnitude;
```

This certainly works, and it might be considered easier to read. This would even make the `GameObject player;` obsolete since `Player.position` is a static value, and you don't need to use `GameObject. Find()` to begin with. This type of optimization should be thought of as you look at your code and dis-cover new ways to make it more efficient and easier to read.

5.6 Building A Game—Part 3

In the previous game-building chapter, we first looked at moving around a character Section 4.3. Then we looked at shooting projectiles in Section 4.10. Immobile red blocks don't stand a chance against a rapid-fire missile launcher. To add challenge, the targets should move and shoot back.

To start off we'll want a system for our bad guys to be able to find the player. We just covered static which is a great way to store a variable for anyone to access.

5.6.1 The Player

```
public class Player : MonoBehaviour
{
    public static GameObject ThePlayer;
    /*                          ↑           */
    private void Start()/*       |          */
    {   /*          ┌───────────┘           */
        /*    ↑                             */
        ThePlayer = this.gameObject;
        /*    ↑                 ↓           */
        /*    └─────────────────┘           */
        /*    assign the static             */
        /*    to this gameObject            */
    }
}
```

The static variables become accessible to any other object. This works to enable the bad guys to find the player. The `Start()` functions in the scene finishes before the first `Update()` is called by any other object in the scene.

5.6.2 The Mover

```
private GameObject _Target;
protected GameObject Target
{
    get
    {
        if (_Target == null)
        {
            // find the player, keep
            // a reference to it.
            _Target = Player.ThePlayer;
        }
        return _Target;
    }
}
```

In the `Mover.cs` script we'll use the `Player.ThePlayer` variable and keep it around as a local variable. To limit problems, an accessor is used where the `set` statement is excluded.

```
protected virtual void Update()
{
    if (Target == null)
        return;
    Vector3 TargetDirection = GetDirection(Target);
    MoveTo(TargetDirection);
    LookAt(TargetDirection);
}
```

To stop pursuing a `Target` after the player is gone, or is `null`, we stop our `Update()` with a null check. So long as the `Target` isn't null we get a `TargetDirection`, then `MoveTo()` and `LookAt()` the `TargetDirection`.

```
private Vector3 GetDirection(GameObject target)
{
    Vector3 myPosition = transform.position;
    Vector3 otherPosition = target.transform.position;
    return otherPosition - myPosition;
}
```

The `GetDirection()` function returns the `Vector3` pointing at a given `GameObject`. This value is used by the following `MoveTo()` and `LookAt()` functions. The direction is likely to change during each update, so it's refreshed at the start of the `Update()` function.

```
private void MoveTo(Vector3 targetDirection)
{
    Rigidbody rb = GetComponent<Rigidbody>();
    rb.AddForce(targetDirection, ForceMode.Force);
}
```

The MoveTo() function applies a force in the direction of the target. Get the rigid body component attached to the player and give it a push in that direction. The rigid body has a few settings to look at to make sure that this works out well.

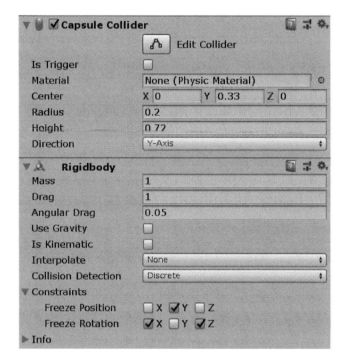

The Capsule Collider and the RigidBody work together. The collider gives the rigid body a shape, then the rigid body gives the Collider physical properties like mass and drag. Here the drag has been set to 1 to make sure that the bad guy doesn't skate around like it's on ice.

```
private void LookAt(Vector3 targetDirection)
{
    Quaternion look = Quaternion.LookRotation(targetDirection);
    transform.rotation = Quaternion.RotateTowards(transform.rotation, look, 15f);
}
```

The last thing we do is turn the bad guy around so he's looking at the player. The LookRotation() function in Quaternion gives us a rotation value. We then plug the look direction into the RotateTowards() function. The result is assigned to the bad guy's rotation value.

5.6.3 The Shooter

Inheritance means we don't need to copy too much code. Though we can see where some cross over can come into place between very similar classes. The ProjectileWeapon class isn't very complex. But we should still observe some optimizations.

```
public class Shooter : Mover
{
    public GameObject ProjectileObject;
    public GameObject ProjectileStart;
    public AudioClip BlasterShotClip;
    private float NextTime;
    public float RateOfFire;
```

The Shooter inherits from Mover. We also see a few members that look like they were copied out of the ProjectileWeapon class. That's because they were. Regardless, we inherit from Mover for a more specific reason.

```
protected override void Update()
{
    base.Update();
    ShootAt();
}
```

In Mover, the Update() function a protected virtual function. This doesn't change the fact that it's called by MonoBehaviour during the Update() cycle of the game. We take advantage of this by using the base.Update() from the Mover. Shooter inherits the MoveTo() and LookAt() functions. After the base.Update() is called we then call the ShootAt() function.

```
private void ShootAt()
{
    if (Time.time > NextTime)
    {
        NextTime = Time.time + NextShot(RateOfFire);
        Vector3 pos = ProjectileStart.transform.position;
        Quaternion rot = ProjectileStart.transform.rotation;
        Instantiate(ProjectileObject, pos, rot);
        GetComponent<AudioSource>().PlayOneShot(BlasterShotClip);
    }
}
```

A minor change here includes the ShootAt() has the same setup as the Update() loop from the ProjectileWeapon class. We exclude the critical Input.GetMouseButton() check to see if the right mouse button is being pressed.

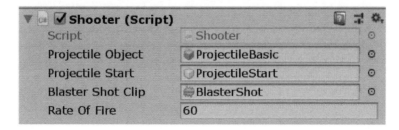

The Shooter's script component has a greatly reduced Rate Of Fire. Once there is more than one weapon in the scene the game comes to an end much faster. This is especially true if all the projectiles are aimed at the player.

5.6.4 Physics Settings

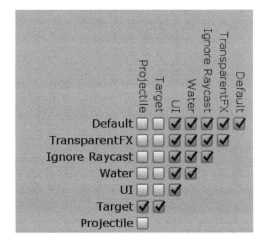

To keep things all in check on the physics, the colliders that are on both the Bad Guys and the Player are set to the Target tag. The projectiles are set to the Projectile tag. Tags allow a filter to enable the physics certain leeway to enable specific objects to pass through some colliders and hit others. In the grid above the Projectile/Target box is checked. This means that the projectiles can only contact a target. The Target/Target checkbox is also checked to prevent the characters from passing through one another.

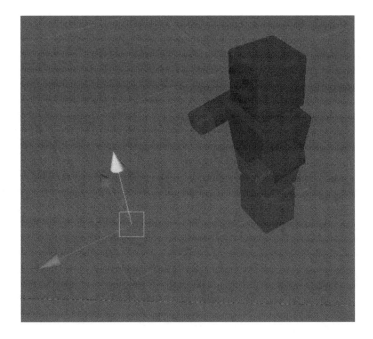

The start point is placed away from the character. This is to ensure that the projectile doesn't contact the BadGuy or the Player as the projectile is instantiated. The z axis (the blue arrow) indicates the forward direction of the starting point.

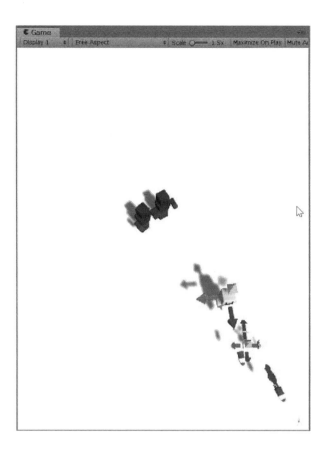

Once there are more than a few shooters in the scene we get a lot of friendly fire. We could add a few more physics filters to prevent this, but it's better to enjoy the crazy explosions for a few moments before the player is also obliterated.

5.6.5 What We've Learned

Physics layers, inheritance, and simple small classes are the key to quickly building a fun game. It may be worthwhile to make ProjectileWeapon more modular and reusable, but code is easily copied and pasted between classes anyway.

Monolithic classes which handle a multitude of responsibilities are cumbersome. Making small classes with few responsibilities allows us to attach multiple behaviors to GameObjects. Small classes make adding new layers of behavior much easier.

We saw a lot of terminology here that's yet to be covered more formally. It's important to understand how the code works in more situations than what we've seen here. This project only serves as one example of infinite possibilities.

5.7 Jump Statements and Return

Follow along with the JumpStatements_Scene Unity 3D scene in the Chapter5 Unity Project. Then open the JumpStatements script found in the scene on the JumpStatements game object. Suppose you're in the process of looking for a specific color of crayon in a large assortment of art tools. After grabbing handfuls of different pencils and pens, you find the crayon you want and stop looking through the rest of your bin. You've just used a jump statement and returned to your work with the colored crayon of your desire.

The keywords break and continue come in particularly handy when sorting through a list of objects. Like return, these keywords stop the function from further execution or they jump to a different part of the same function. return has the additional feature of coming out of a function with a value. We have looked at these keywords briefly before, but it's important to get a better understanding of break, continue, and return in use.

The keyword continue restarts a loop from the top and then continues the function again, whereas break stops the block of code it's in altogether.

5.7.1 Return

We need to love the return keyword. This keyword turns a function into data. There are a couple of conditions that need to be met before this will work. So far, we've been using the keyword void to declare the return type of a function. This looks like the following code fragment.

```csharp
void Function()
{
}
```

In this case, using return will be simple.

```csharp
void MyFunction()
{
    // code here...
    return;
}
```

This function returns void. This statement has a deeper meaning. Returning a value makes a lot more sense when a real value, something other than a void, is actually returned. Let's look at a function that has more meaning.

The keyword void at the beginning of the function declaration means that this function does not have a return type. If we change the declaration, we need to ensure that there is a returned value that matches the declaration. This can be as simple as the following code fragment.

```csharp
int MyIntFunction()
{
    //return 1.0f;
    return 1; // 1 is an int
}
```

This function returns int 1. Declaring a function with a return value requires that the return type and the declaration match. When the function is used, it should be treated like a data type that matches the function's return type.

5.7.1.1 A Basic Example

Here is a quick review class that has a function declared as `int MyNumber()` in the `Start()` function.

```
int MyNumber()
{
    return 7;
}
void Start()
{
    int a = MyNumber();
    Debug.Log(a);
}
```

When this code block is executed in the scene, 7 is printed to the Console panel. The function `MyNumber()` returned 7 when it was called. When we add some parameters to the function, we can make the return statement much more useful.

```
int MyAdd(int a, int b)
{
    return a + b;
}

void Start()
{
    int add = MyAdd(6, 7);
    Debug.Log(add);
}
```

In this fragment, we have `int MyAdd(int a, int b)`, which we then assign to int a in the `Start()` function. This prints 13 to the Console when run. We can skip a step to make the code a bit shorter.

```
Debug.Log(MyAdd(11, 12));
```

This code produces the same 13 being printed to the Console panel and should make it clear that the function can easily be used as a value.

5.7.2 Returning Objects

We can get something more interesting out of a function once it begins to return something more substantial than a simple number—this would be a more significant uses of return.

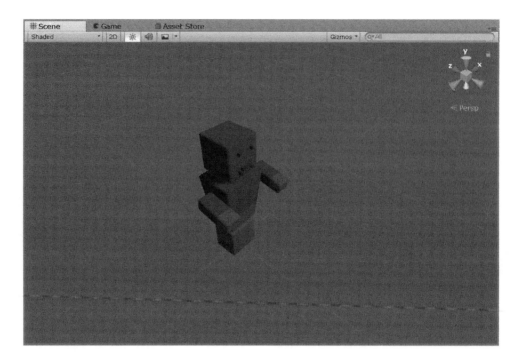

In the JumpStatements_Scene in the Chapter5 Unity Project we have a single Zombie. In the JumpStatements script on the JumpStatements game object we'll add a function that returns type `Zombie`.

```
Zombie GetZombie()
{
    return (Zombie)FindObjectOfType(typeof(Zombie));
}
```

Adding a `Debug.Log(GetZombie());` to the `Start()` function and we'll have the following text sent to the Console panel in Unity 3D.

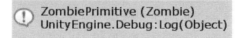

5.7.3 A Class Is a Type

Our function that returns a Zombie, is at the end of our Unity 3D C# default template. We've called our function `GetZombie()`, and we're using a simple function provided in `GameObject` called `FindObjectOfType();`, which requires a *type* to return. The different classes we create become a new type. Much as an int is a type, a `Zombie` is now a type that we created in a new class called `Zombie`. This goes the same for every class we've created, which are all types.

To inform the `FindObjectOfType()` function of the type, we use the function `typeof(Zombie)`, which tells the function that we're looking for a type `Zombie`, not an actual zombie. There's a subtle difference between telling someone we'd like a thing that is a kind of zombie, not a specific zombie. We'll get into the specifics of types in Section 6.5.3 that focuses on dealing with types, but we're more interested in return, so we'll get back to that.

```
public Zombie myZombie;
Zombie GetZombie()
{
    return (Zombie)FindObjectOfType(typeof(Zombie));
}

void Update()
{
    Debug.DrawLine(transform.position, myZombie.transform.position);
}
```

We'll leave a variable in the class for myZombie, and in the Update() we'll draw a line from the transform.position to the myZombie.transform.position. Debug.DrawLine() starts at one position and goes to another position. The second position is a function's transform.position.

```
myZombie = GetZombie();
Debug.Log(myZombie);
```

In the Start() function the GetZombie() function assigns the myZombie variable. When the scene is played in the editor look into the Scene panel, you'll see a white line being drawn between the push pin and the Zombie Primitive with the Zombie component added to it.

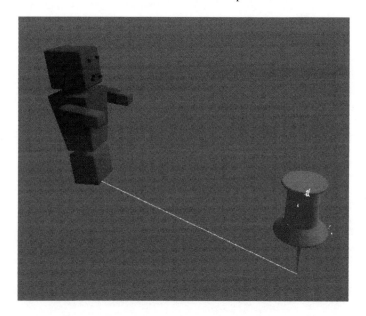

Another possible method to use would be to inquire how many zombies exist in the scene. If there are zombies then get one to draw a line. With the following method we use the static numZombies to count how many zombies are in the scene. Then we use GetZombie() as an object to draw a line to the position of the Zombie it returns.

```
if (Zombie.numZombies > 0)
{
    Debug.DrawLine(transform.position, GetZombie().transform.position);
}
```

This remarkably means that the `GetZombie().transform.position` is returning the value as though the function is the `Zombie` itself, which has some interesting consequences. Having classes, or rather objects, communicate between one another is a particularly important feature of any programming language. Accessing members of another class through a function is just one way our objects can talk to one another.

This reliance on the function breaks if there are no zombies in the scene. What would happen if we were to deactivate the Zombie by checking it off in the Inspector panel while the code is running?

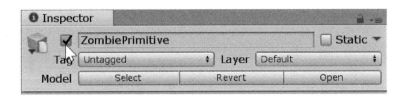

Unchecking here while the game is running will immediately bring up an error.

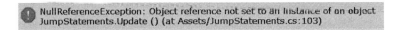

A Null Reference Exception is caused when the return type of the function has nothing to return. Errors aren't good for performance and we should handle the problem more effectively. We need to make our use of the function more robust. Likewise, if you delete the ZombiePrimitive while the game is playing we'll get this error.

> MissingReferenceException: The object of type 'Zombie' has been destroyed but you are still trying to access it. Your script should either check if it is null or you should not destroy the object.

If we need to add a check to see if Zombie is null, doing so will avoid giving the `Debug.DrawLine()` function nonexistent data. We could hold onto a Zombie variable, and check each frame if the variable is not null. Better yet, we can add the following code to the Zombie script.

```
private void OnDestroy()
{
    numZombies--;
}
```

The code above decrements the `numZombies` static value. This means that a check to see if the number of zombies is greater than 0 will be false and we'll stop drawing lines when the last zombie is gone.

5.7.4 Tuples

Various languages like Lua allowed for more than one thing to be returned from a function. For C# to return a zombie and a number you'd need to create a struct which contained a zombie and a number.

```
struct ZombieNumber
{
    public Zombie Zombie;
    public int SomeNumber;
}

ZombieNumber RetrunsZombieAndNumber()
{
    ZombieNumber zombieNumber = new ZombieNumber();
    zombieNumber.Zombie = (Zombie)FindObjectOfType(typeof(Zombie));
    zombieNumber.SomeNumber = 1;
    return zombieNumber;
}
```

To create a struct and populate it every time a variety of information was required to come from a function would be cumbersome. The eventual population of numerous structs would get messy; each struct becomes a new type. The above does return the desired result:

```
ZombieNumber zn = RetrunsZombieAndNumber();
Debug.Log("Zombie: " + zn.Zombie + " Num:" + zn.SomeNumber);
// Zombie: ZombiePrimitive (Zombie) Num:1
```

The extra structs required for returning more than one value can be avoided using a tuple or "too-ple." A tuple is a system to organize data with names much like a struct. The return value of the function changes quite a lot when returning a tuple.

```
(Zombie zombie, int number) ReturnsTuple()
{
    Zombie z = (Zombie)FindObjectOfType(typeof(Zombie));
    int n = 1;
    var zombieNumber = (zombie: z, number: n);
    return zombieNumber;
}
```

Rather than void or a type, the tuple value looks a lot like a parameter signature for the function. The syntax works the same with a type followed by an identifier. The tuple above is a (Zombie zombie, int number) which means a Zombie and an int will be returned when the function is called.

```
var zn = ReturnsTuple();
Debug.Log("Zombie:" + zn.zombie + " Num:" + zn.number);
// Zombie: ZombiePrimitive (Zombie) Num:1
```

When the function is invoked the data is stored as a var. The var type is a just-in-time type, so var can accept practically any type value. Once it's assigned, its type becomes set. In the case var zn = ReturnsTuple(); the var zn is now a type that contains the zombie and number from the ReturnsTuple() function.

```
(string outString, int outInt, float outFloat ) ReturnsStringIntFloat()
{
    return (outString: "SomeString", outInt: 1, outFloat: 1f);
}
```

Visual studio will help fill in the tuple as you type it out.

```
return (outString:inString, )
        (string outString, int outInt, float outFloat)
```

The tuple requires you to fill in the output labels with the colon. These act a bit like optional arguments, something that will be covered in a later chapter. The value stored in a tuple can be decomposed from the var, but the data contained is recognized when printed as the following:

```
Debug.Log(ReturnsStringIntFloat());
// (SomeString, 1, 1)
```

Tuples have a variety of uses by combining data into an impromptu type. The simple return value use of the tuple is just one of the several uses of a tuple. We'll have to come back to that once we get into Linq in Section 8.8 since complex tricks are involved.

5.7.5 Null Is Not Void

There is conceptual difference between void, which is *nothing,* and null, which is more like *not something.* The word *void* means there is no intention of anything to be presented, whereas *null* implies that there can be something. We may add if (target != null) and can say that target can be empty or it can be Zombie. When target isn't a zombie, target is null; when it is there, it's Zombie.

```
Zombie target = GetZombie();
if (target != null)
    Debug.Log(target);
```

We may add if(target != null)—in more readable English, "if the target is not null"—and then conditionally execute the following code block. In the case where we have a target, we can draw a line from the camera's transform.position to the target's transform.position. This code alleviates the error, and thus we don't have to worry about sending Draw.DebugLine an error-inducing null reference.

5.7.6 What We've Learned

Functions that return class objects are quite useful. The properties that are associated with the class are accessible through the function that returns it. There are various jump statements that have different results.

The return statement has a clear purpose when it comes to jumping out of a function. Not all return jump statements need to be followed by a value. If the function is declared as void MyFunction(), the return statement only needs to be return; without any value following it.

We'll cover more jump statements in a following chapter.

5.8 Arrays: A First Look

Open the ArraysAFirstLoop_Scene and open the ArraysAFirstLoop script in the scene. Arrays are nicely organized lists of data. Think of a numbered list that starts at zero and extends one line every time you add something to the list. Arrays are useful for any number of situations because they're treated as a single hunk of data.

For instance, if you wanted to store a bunch of high scores, you'd want to do that with an array. Initially, you might want to have a list of 10 items. You could in theory use the following code to store each score.

```
int score1;
int score2;
int score3;
int score4;
int score5;
int score6;
int score7;
int score8;
int score9;
int score10;
/* if you've guess there's a much better way
 * to store lots of data like that then
 * you'd be correct.
 */
```

To make matters worse, if you needed to process each value, you'd need to create a set of code that deals with each variable by name. To check if `score2` is higher than `score1`, you'd need to write a function specifically to check those two variables before switching them. Thank goodness for arrays.

5.8.1 Fixed-Sized Arrays

An array can be initialized as a fixed-sized array, or an array can be created to be a resizable; we'll get to these types of arrays in Section 5.12. A fixed-sized array is easier to create, so we'll cover that first. Dynamic arrays require a more interesting step, where an array object is instantiated before it's used.

Arrays are a fundamental part of computer programming, in general. Without arrays, computers wouldn't be able to do what they're best at: repeating a simple task quickly and consistently. We'll be covering a few different types of arrays in Sections 5.11 and 5.12, and we'll be starting with the simplest type of array: the fixed-sized array.

5.8.1.1 A Basic Example

Let's start with the Arrays project and open the scene. The concept is simple in theory, but it's so much easier to see what's going on if you use the following code and check out what's going on in the Unity 3D Inspector panel. Attach this script to the Main Camera in an empty scene, and then take a look at what shows up.

```
public class ArraysAFirstLook : MonoBehaviour
{
    public int[] scores = new int[10];
}
```

The inclusion of the square brackets tells the compiler you're creating an array of ints and naming it scores. Because we're working with a built-in type of an int, each value stored in the array is initialized to 0. A new int[] array needs to be created before it's assigned to the scores array.

The best part is that the scores array is handled as a single object; we'll get into what that means in a moment. Rather than write a function to process one number value at a time we can write a function to deal with the array and process all the number values at once. We'll look at a simple sorting method in Section 7.9.4.

Assigning scores to int[10] creates an array with 10 items. As you might imagine, you can make larger or smaller arrays by changing the number in the square brackets. There aren't any limitations to the size you can assign to an array. Some common sense should apply, however; an array with many trillions of values might not be so useful.

Each chunk of data in the array is located by what is called an *index*. The index number is an integer value since it's not useful to ask for a value between the first and second entry in the array. Arrays can be created from something other than ints as well.

```
public string[] strings = new string[10];
public float[] floats = new float[10];
```

Both these statements create valid types of arrays. You are also allowed to create new data types and make arrays of those as well. An array can be created for any type, not just numbers and strings. This isn't necessarily a requirement. We can use any valid identifier to use for an array.

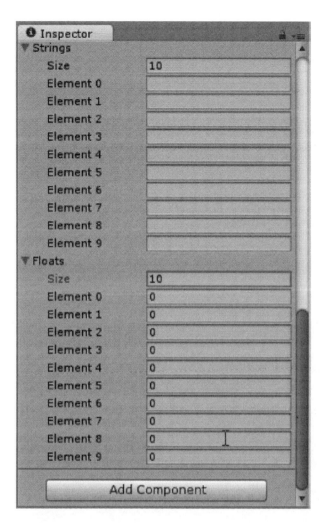

It's important to notice the difference between types. Floats, ints, and numbers in general will have 0 as the default value in the array when they are created. Strings, on the other hand, are initialized with nothing in the array; they are *null,* or, rather, they have no value assigned. You'll need to remember that an array can contain only a single type across all its entries. Therefore, an array of strings can contain only strings, an array of ints can contain only ints, and so on.

```
public string[] TopScoreList = new string[10];
```

The convention of using a plural does make for a more easily read variable name, but by no means is it necessary for identifying an array. Again, it's up to you to come up with readable variable names, and it's nice to use plurals for identifying an array.

```
public class MyClass
{
}
public MyClass[] MyClasses = new MyClass[10];
```

This creates a new class called MyClass, which for this example is a class of nothing. It's important that both sides of the MyClasses statement match. In the example above an array was created for the `MyClass` type. Unfortunately, because Unity isn't aware of what to do with MyClass, the array doesn't show up in the Inspector panel. Later, we'll figure out some ways to make this sort of information show up in Unity.

What makes an array in Unity more interesting is when we do not assign a number to set the size of the array. We can add the following statement to the list of other variables we've already added.

```
public GameObject[] GameObjects;
```

If we simply leave an array unassigned, we're free to set the size afterward. Select the Main Camera and click on the lock icon at the top right of the Inspector panel. This will prevent the Inspector from changing when you select something else in the scene. Then, select the other objects in the scene and drag them down to the `GameObjects` variable in the Inspector.

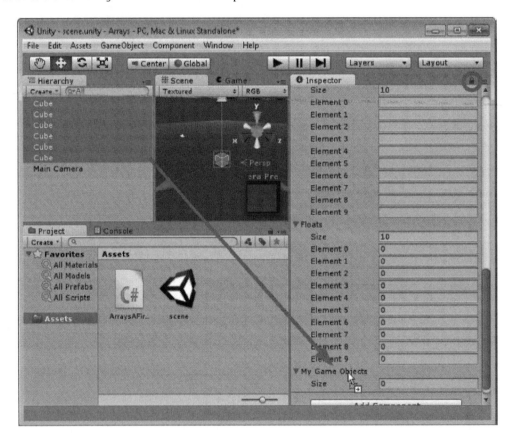

This action sets the size of the array once objects have been dragged into the array. However, this doesn't mean that the code is aware of the size of the array. The size of an array cannot easily be changed once it's been created. Therefore, how do we know how many objects are in an array? This can be accessed by the `.Length` property of the array type.

In the `Start()` function, we can use the following statement:

```
void Start()
{
    Debug.Log(GameObjects.Length);
}
```

Click the play icon and observe the Console panel. The `Debug.Log()` command will print out how many objects had been dragged into the array.

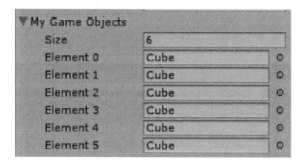

The number should reflect what is being observed in the Inspector panel, where we dragged objects into the array.

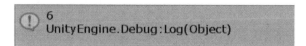

So far so good, but how do we use this? Now that we have an array of game objects from the scene, we're able to manipulate them in a for loop.

```
for (int i = 0; i < GameObjects.Length; i++)
{
    GameObjects[i].name = i.ToString();
}
```

This code changes the names of the game objects in the array to a number. The property of the array .Length returns an integer value which we can use for a few different reasons, the most practical use being to set the number of iterations in a for loop.

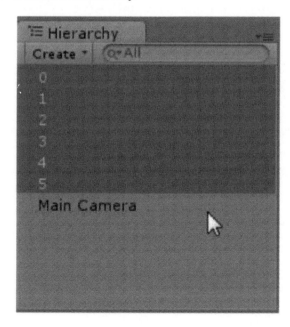

5.8.2 Foreach

This loop also happens to reflect how the objects are organized in the array. As we had experimented before with loops, we can use the array in a multitude of ways. We can also iterate over an array using the foreach loop. Once we've changed the names of each object, we can tell one from the other by its name.

5.8.2.1 A Basic Example

```
foreach (GameObject go in GameObjects)
{
    Debug.Log(go.name);
}
```

The foreach statement is dependent on the type of data found on the inside of the array. Therefore, we use GameObject go to set up a place to hold each member of the GameObjects array while in the foreach loop. If we wanted to iterate over an array of a different type, we'd have to change the parameters of the foreach loop. Therefore, to iterate over an array of ints which was declared int[] MyInts;, we'd need to use foreach(int i in MyInts) to iterate over each member of that array.

Of course, the variable's name can be anything, but it's easier to keep it short. To use foreach(int anIntegerMemberFromAnArray in MyInts), for example, would be a bit of work to key in if we wanted to do a number of operations on each int found in the array. Then again, there's nothing preventing us from spending time being verbose. We'll cover the foreach loop in more detail in Section 6.11.5.

5.8.3 Dynamic Initialization

```
float[] dynamicFloats = new float[10];
```

We can also initialize a new array in a function. This means that the array exists only while in the scope of the function and can't be accessed from outside of that function. It's important to know that the size of an array is determined ahead of its use. When the array is declared in this way, the size or rather the number of objects the array can contain is set.

Here, we split the initialization into two statements. The first line tells C# we are creating a float[] variable identified as dynamicFloats. Then, we need to populate this floats array with a new array. The array floats is then assigned a new float array of 10 indices. We cannot switch this assignment to a different type.

```
float[] dynamicFloats;
dynamicFloats = new float[10];
```

Changing the type creates an error, which we'll have to fix. There are clever ways to avoid this, but we'll get into that in Section 6.14.

We can also use a variable to set the length of the array.

```
float[] dynamicFloats;
int numFloats = 10;
dynamicFloats = new float[numFloats];
```

This code sets the length of the dynamically defined array. This can be helpful once we need to make our code more flexible to change for various game design settings. On the other hand, we can populate an array with predetermined information.

```
public int[] primes = new int[] { 1, 3, 5, 7, 11, 13, 17 };
```

The above statement declares and sets an array that has seven members and assigns each number to a low prime number value. These even show up in the Inspector panel in Unity 3D.

▼ Primes	
Size	7
Element 0	1
Element 1	3
Element 2	5
Element 3	7
Element 4	11
Element 5	13
Element 6	17

5.8.4 Using the While Loop with Arrays

Iterating through our array is pretty simple. We've covered some basic loops that handle arrays quite well. If we use a simple while loop, we can process each value stored in a fixed array.

```
int[] scores = new int[10];
int i = 0;
while (i < 10)
{
    Debug.Log(scores[i]);
    i++;
}
```

At this point, all of the values are indeed zero, so we get 10 zeros printed to our Console panel. However, there are a few interesting things to point out here. First of all, int i is initialized to 0 ahead of the while loop. We'll get into what this means later on, but remember for now that arrays start at zero. The next interesting thing is how the numbers stored in scores[] are accessed.

5.8.4.1 Setting Array Values

```
scores[0] = 10;
```

We can set the value of each index of scores to a specific value by accessing the scores by their index. When the scores array was initialized as int[10], scores now has 10 different int number spaces. To access each value, we use a number 0 through 9 in square brackets to get and set each value. The while loop starts at 0 because we started with an int i = 0; before entering the while loop.

```
int[] scores = new int[10];
int i = 0;
while (i < 10)
{
    scores[i] = UnityEngine.Random.Range(0, 100);
    Debug.Log(scores[i]);
    i++;
}
```

With this code, we're using a function called Random and using its member function Range, which we're setting to a value between 0 and 100. The index is picked by using the i that was set to 0 before the loop started. The loop starts with scores[0] being set to a random number between 0 and 100.

At the end of the while block, the i is incremented by 1 and the while loop begins again. The next time, though, we are setting scores[1] to a random number between 0 and 100.

5.8.4.2 Getting Array Values

Each time, we're getting the value from scores[i] to print. We can make this a bit more clear with the following example.

```
int[] scores = new int[10];
scores[0] = 10;
int i = 0;
while (i < 10)
{
    scores[i] = UnityEngine.Random.Range(0, 100);
    int score = scores[i];
    Debug.Log(score);
    i++;
}
```

If we add in the line int score = scores[i];, we'll get the score to the value found in scores[i]. Each value remains independent of the other values stored in the array. Because we're able to use the entirety of scores[] as a single object with index values, we're able to accomplish a great deal of work with fewer lines of code.

Arrays are simple objects with lots of uses. We'll get into a pretty interesting use in Section 5.11.3, but for now, we'll have to settle on playing with some numbers in the array.

5.8.5 What We've Learned

Arrays are useful for more than just storing scores. Arrays for every monster in the scene will make it easier to find the closest one to the player. Rather than dealing with many separate variables, it's easier to group them together. Arrays are used so often as to have special loops that make dealing with arrays very simple.

5.9 Jump Statements: Break and Continue

Open the JumpStatementsBreakAndContinue_Scene and open the corresponding script in the scene. Loops are often used to iterate through a series of matching data. In many cases, we're looking for specific patterns in the data, and we'll change what we want to do depending on the data we're sifting through. In most cases, a regular if statement is the easiest to use. When our logic gets more detailed and we need to add more complex behaviors to our code, we need to start adding in special keywords.

When we come across the one thing we're looking for, or maybe the first thing we're looking for, we might want to stop the for loop that might change our result. In this case we use the `break;` keyword.

5.9.1 A Basic Example

The following code added to the `BreakAndContinue()` function in the script demonstrates a basic effect of the break keyword.

```
for (int i = 0; i < 100; i++)
{
    Debug.Log(i);
    if (i > 10)
    {
        break;
    }
}
```

When we run this code, we'll get a printout from 1 to 11, and since 11 is greater than 10, the for loop will stop. In the for loop's second argument, we've got i < 100, because we assume that the Debug. Log(i); would work till we hit 99 before the for loop exits normally. However, since we have the if statement that breaks us out of the for loop before i reaches 100, we only get 1–11 printed to the console. Of course, there are reasons for using break other than cutting for loops short.

5.9.1.1 Continue

```
for (int i = 0; i < 100; i++)
{
    Debug.Log(i);
    if (i > 10)
    {
        Debug.Log("i is greater than 10!");
        continue;
    }
}
```

The keyword `continue` changes when a loop begins on it's next iteration. Where the `break` terminates a loop the `continue` keyword tells the loop to skip the rest of the code and continue as normal. In the loop above the Debug.Log("Got Past Continue."); only appears for the first 10 iterations of the loop. Once i is greater than 10, the continue keyword interupts the loop execution and skips the rest of the code in the for loop.

The `continue` allows the for loop to finish iterating, break escapes the for loop before it's finished iterating.

5.9.2 ZombieData

The keyword break is often used to stop a process. Often, when we go through a group of data, we might be looking for something specific; when we find it, we would need to process it. If we create an array of zombies, we'll need to assign them some specific zombie behaviors. Therefore, we might create a new ZombieData.cs class that could include some zombie information.

```
using UnityEngine;
public class Zombie : MonoBehaviour
{
    public int HitPoints;
}
```

Here's a very simple zombie class that has nothing more than some HitPoints. I'll leave the rest up to your game design to fill in. Then, in a new JumpStatementsBreakAndContinue.cs script in the UseZombieData() function, gameObjects are created and placed. Some of them have Zombie data, some don't.

```
gameObjects = new GameObject[10];
for (int i = 0; i < 10; i++)
{
    //make a game object
    GameObject go = GameObject.CreatePrimitive(PrimitiveType.Cube);

    //find a random place for it
    Vector3 position = new Vector3();
    position.x = UnityEngine.Random.Range(-10, 10);
    position.z = UnityEngine.Random.Range(-10, 10);
    go.transform.position = position;

    //name it something unique
    go.name = i.ToString();
    if (i % 2 == 0)
    {
        // pick every other one to be a zombie
        Zombie z = go.AddComponent(typeof(Zombie)) as Zombie;

        // assign a random value to the hit points
        z.hitPoints = UnityEngine.Random.Range(1, 20);
    }

    //add the game object to the array
    gameObjects[i] = go;
}
```

The for loop in Start() creates 10 new game objects temporarily stored as go. This is done with GameObject go = GameObject.CreatePrimitive(PrimitiveType.Cube); we're creating 10 cube primitives. Then, we create a new Vector3() with Vector3 position = new Vector3();. Once position is created, we give x and z a new value between –10 and 10 using Random. Range (-10, 10); and then assign the position to the new game object go with go. transform.position = position. For clarity, we give each go a new name after its iterative number from the for loop by using go.name = i.ToString();. Once the new game object go is created, we assign it to an array at the class level called gameObjects.

Then, we get to if(i % 2 == 0) {go.AddComponent(typeof(Zombie));, which assigns a new Zombie object to each go if i % 2 is 0. The i%2 is a clever way to check if a number is even or odd. Therefore, in this case, if the number is even, then we assign a new Zombie; otherwise, no Zombie is assigned. This means half of the cubes are not zombies. After creating a zombie we assign it a random value for hitPoints.

5.9.3 Foreach Again

In a normal game setting, you might have many different types of objects in a scene. Some objects might be zombies, whereas others might be innocent humans running away from the zombies. We're creating a number of game objects to simulate a more normal game setting.

```
foreach (GameObject go in gameObjects)
{
    Zombie z = (Zombie)go.GetComponent(typeof(Zombie));
    if (z == null)
    {
        /* if we don't find a zombie skip
         * the game object and move on to
         * the next one in the array.
         */
        continue;
    }

    if (z.hitPoints > 10)
    {
        Debug.Log("This has more than 10 hit points: " + z.name);
        break;
    }
}
```

Now, just for the sake of using both continue and break in some logical fashion, we use the array to check through our list of game objects using foreach (GameObject go in gameobjects). The first line, `Zombie z = (Zombie)go.GetComponent(typeof(Zombie));`, assigns a Zombie to the variable z. The next line does something interesting.

Here, null is useful; in this case, if the object in the array has no Zombie, then z will not be assigned anything. When z is not assigned anything, its data remains null. Therefore, in this case, if there's no zombie data assigned to the object in the array, we're looking at *then continue,* or in this case, *go back to the top of the loop, and move on to the next item in the array.* Continue means stay in the loop, but skip to the next item in the array.

If `Zombie z` exists, then we move to the next line down and we don't hit continue. Therefore, we can check if z.hitpoints is greater than 10; if it is, then we'll stop the loop altogether. This lets us know there's at least one Zombie that's got more than 10 hit points.

The result of this loop prints out the even-numbered named game objects and stops naming them if it comes across one that's got more than 10 hit points.

For an AI (artificial intelligence) character, it would be useful to know what objects in the scene are zombies. And your zombies should know what objects in the scenes are players. In your zombie behavior code, you might use something like the following.

```
foreach (Player p in players)
{
    if (p == null)
    {
        continue;
    }
}
```

This code is used to skip on to the next object in the scene, which might be a player. Likewise, you could do the following with null.

```
if (p != null)
{
    AttackPlayer();
}
```

This statement would be just as useful. Likewise, you can do things before using continue. If your zombie needed a list of characters in the scene, you would want to add them to an array list, which is different from an array, and you would want to add them to an array first.

```
foreach (GameObject go in gameObjects)
{
    Player player = go.GetComponent(typeof(Player)) as Player;
    if (player != null)
    {
        players.Add(player);
        continue;
    }
}
```

In the above example, we'd check the go if it's got a Player component. If it does, add it to an array list called players, and then continue; to the next object in the list.

5.9.4 What We've Learned

The previous section was a simple use of break and continue. As more complex situations arise, then using jump statements come in handy. The jump statements are often used while searching through an array of many kinds of objects.

When reading through other people's code, it's often useful to do a search for various keywords when you're interested in seeing how they are used. By searching for continue; or break;, you might find several different uses that might have not come to your mind immediately.

Discovering the different ways code can be used comes with experience, and it is something that cannot be taught in a single volume of text. The process of learning different programming features is like looking at a tool box and knowing what a screw driver looks like. It's an entirely different process to understand how it's best used.

5.10 Multidimensional Arrays

```
int[,] TwoDimensionalArray;
```

Open the MultidimensionalArrays_Scene and the corresponding MultidimensionalArrays script found in the scene. An array is a single list of objects. Each entry is identified in the array by an index. By adding an additional index, we're allowed to create an additional depth to the array. When working with a single-dimensional array, we can get several simple attributes about the contents of that array.

```
Object[] objects = new Object[10];
for (int i = 0; i < objects.Length; i++)
{
    Debug.Log(objects[i]);
}
```

With the above statement, we get 10 objects printed to the Console panel in Unity 3D. Using oneDimension.Length, we get a value representing the number of items in the array. At the moment, though, we have not added anything to the contents of each index. This situation is altered with the following change to the array's declaration.

```
Object[,] objects = new Object[2, 3];
for (int i = 0; i < objects.Length; i++)
{
    Debug.Log(i);
    /* how do we address
     * two parameters in
     * a multi dimensional
     * array?
     */
}
```

```
GameObject a = new GameObject("a");
GameObject b = new GameObject("b");
GameObject c = new GameObject("c");
GameObject d = new GameObject("d");
GameObject e = new GameObject("e");
GameObject f = new GameObject("f");
GameObject[,] twoDimensions = new GameObject[2,3] { { a, b, c }, { d, e, f } };
```

With the above statement, we get 0–5 printed to the Console panel in Unity 3D. The Array.Length parameter simply returns the total number of items in the array, but we're not able to get any specific information on how the indices are arranged. To get a better feel for the contents of the array, we might consider the TwoDimensionalArray; a grid of two columns by three rows.

5.10.1 Columns and Rows

As shown in the below image, we have a 2 by 3 grid as a representation of the GameObject[2, 3] array. Each box holds onto a GameObject. A multidimensional array has its place in programming, though it is rare, and the coding is usually better handled using a couple of single-dimensional arrays. However, it's more convenient to pass a single multidimensional array to a function than it is to pass two different single-dimensional arrays.

To utilize this array, we'll want to populate the array with some GameObjects.

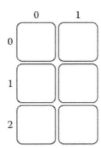

5.10.1.1 A Basic Example

Let's begin with the MultiDimensionalArray project in Unity 3D and open the scene.

```
GameObject a = new GameObject("a");
GameObject b = new GameObject("b");
GameObject c = new GameObject("c");
GameObject d = new GameObject("d");
GameObject e = new GameObject("e");
GameObject f = new GameObject("f");
GameObject[,] twoDimensions = new GameObject[2,3] { { a, b, c }, { d, e, f } };
```

Notice how the array is assigned. There are two sets of curly braces, a pair of curly braces in a set of curly braces. We group three items into two subgroups, and assign them to the 2D array. The notation {{}, {}} is used to assign a 2 by 3 array with 6 GameObjects.

Next, we'll add a function to sift through the 2D array.

```
void InspectArray(GameObject[,] gameObjects)
{
    int columns = gameObjects.GetLength(0);
    Debug.Log("columns:" + columns);
    int rows = gameObjects.GetLength(1);
    Debug.Log("rows:" + rows);
    for (int column = 0; column < columns; column++)
    {
        for (int row = 0; row < rows; row++)
        {
            Debug.Log(gameObjects[column, row].name);
        }
    }
}
```

With this code, we'll get an idea of what types of loops will work best with a 2D array. First off, we have a function with one argument. The function `InspectArray(GameObject[,] gameObjects)` takes in a 2D array of any size. Therefore, a GameObject[37,41] would fit just as well as the GameObject[2, 3] that we are using for this tutorial.

We're then using GameObjects (gos).GetLength(0); to assign our columns count. The `GetLength()` array function takes a look at the dimensions of the array. At index 0 in [2, 3], we have 2, which is assigned to columns. Next, we use GetLength(1); to get the number of rows in the 2D array.

Using two for loops, one inside of the other, we're able to iterate through each one of the objects in the 2D array in a more orderly manner. Without a system like this, we're in a more difficult situation, not knowing where in the array we are.

```
InspectArray(twoDimensions);
```

At the end of the `Start()` function, we can make use of the `InspectArray()` function and get a log of the items in each position in the 2D array.

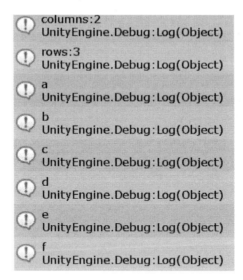

5.10.2 A Puzzle Board

In the same MultiDimensionalArrays_Scene is a Grid2D game object in the Hierarchy. Attached is the Grid2D script to follow along with. Puzzle games often require a great deal of 2D array manipulation. To start a project, we can use the Grid2D project. The code in the Grid2D.cs class will begin with the following:

```
public int Width;
public int Height;
public GameObject PuzzlePiece;
public GameObject[,] Grid;
```

A few public variables that will allow us to make changes in the editor. We can make various sizes for the grid and we'll also be able to change the puzzle piece that's used in the puzzle.

```
void Start()
{
    Grid = new GameObject[Width, Height];
    for (int x = 0; x < Width; x++)
    {
        for (int y = 0; y < Height; y++)
        {
            Vector3 position = new Vector3(x, y, 0);
            GameObject go = new GameObject("x:" + x + "y:" + y);
            go.transform.position = position;
            Grid[x, y] = go;
        }
    }
}
```

The PuzzlePiece on the script will need an object assigned to it. This means you'll have to drag the puzzle piece object in the Project under the Meshes directory to the Puzzle Piece variable in the Inspector panel.

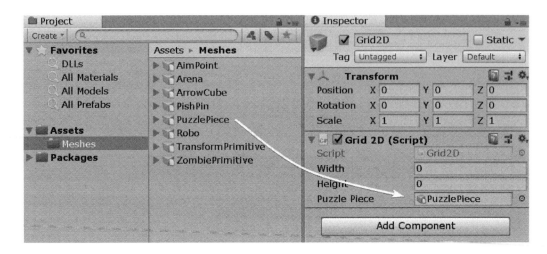

In the Grid2D.cs class, the first variables we're going to look at is the `public int Width` and `public int Height`. These two variables are made visible to the Inspector in the Unity 3D Editor. I've set both of these to 8 in the Inspector panel. This is followed by a GameObject, which we'll fill the grid with. The last variable is a 2D array, which we will fill with the GameObject PuzzlePiece.

In the Start() function, we'll add an initialization for the grid with Grid = new GameObject [Width, Height]; to set up the 2D array so we can use it. Every fixed-sized array, whether 1D, like a GameObject [], or 2D, which looks like the above GameObject [,], needs to be initialized before it's used. Before being initialized, the array is null, which means it's lacking any size or any place for us to put anything into the array.

To fill in the array, we use the following code block added to the Start() function.

```
Vector3 position = new Vector3(x, y, 0);
GameObject go = GameObject.Instantiate(PuzzlePiece) as GameObject;
go.transform.position = position;
Grid[x, y] = go;
```

This code has two functions; the first for loop iterates through each position along the x; inside of each x position, we make a column for y with another for loop. At each position, we create a new GameObject.Instantiate(PuzzlePiece) as GameObject; to assign to GameObject go. When GameObject.Instantiate() is used, an object of type object is created. To be used as a GameObject type it must be cast. Without the cast, you'll get the following warning in the Unity 3D Console panel:

Assets/Grid2D.cs(14,28): error CS0266: Cannot implicitly convert type

"UnityEngine.Object" to "UnityEngine.GameObject." An explicit conversion exists (are you missing a cast?)

This error is telling us we need to cast from Object to GameObject, quite a simple fix even if you forget to do this ahead of time.

After making a new instance, we need to use the x and y to create a new Vector3 to set the position of each puzzle piece. Use Vector3 position = new Vector3(x, y, 0); to create a new

Vector3 for each position. Once the new Vector3 position has been created and assigned, we can tell the GameObject go where it should be in the world. This is done with the statement that follows: go.transform.position = position;.

Once the GameObject has been created and positioned, we can assign it to the GameObject[,] array with Grid[x, y] = go;, where we use x and y to pick which index in the 2D array the GameObject is to be assigned to. Once this is done, we can use the Grid[x, y] to get a reference to the puzzle piece.

5.10.3 Camera and Screen Setup

To pick a puzzle piece with the mouse, we're going to need to modify the camera's settings.

Three changes are required; the first is Projection, which we'll change from Perspective to Orthographic. This will mean that lines will not converge to a point in space. *Orthographic* projection means that the line where the mouse appears over the game will be parallel with what the camera is looking at. We'll also want to resize the camera to match the grid.

```
Camera.main.orthographic = true;
Camera.main.orthographicSize = Width/2;
Camera.main.farClipPlane = 20;
```

Then the position of the camera is set to match the center of the puzzle grid. We use half the width for *x* and half the height for *y*. Then a half a unit is taken off of each to position the camera to look at the middle of a puzzle piece rather than the top right corner of a grid square.

```
float xPos = (Width * 0.5f) - 0.5f;
float yPos = (Height * 0.5f) - 0.5f;
Camera.main.transform.position = new Vector3(xPos, yPos, -5);
```

To catch the mouse pointer position in the world a collider of some kind needs to be added to the grid as well. This will allow us to find where the mouse is hovering over when the game is playing.

```
GameObject collider = GameObject.CreatePrimitive(PrimitiveType.Plane);
collider.transform.localScale = new Vector3(Width * 0.1f, 1, Height * 0.1f);
collider.transform.eulerAngles = new Vector3(-90, 0, 0);
collider.transform.position = new Vector3(xPos, yPos, 0);
```

The Plane primitive is 10 units wide and 10 units deep. To modify it to match our grid size we use `Width` and `Height` multiplied by `0.1f` to change its size. Then it's rotated up to match the grid orientation and then we move its center to match the center of the grid reusing `xPos` and `yPos`.

In the `Update()` function on the Grid2D.cs class, we can use the same ray cast to the mouse position we did in the Sample Game.

```
Ray ray = Camera.main.ScreenPointToRay(Input.mousePosition);
RaycastHit hit;
if (Physics.Raycast(ray, out hit))
{
    mousePosition = hit.point;
}
```

This gives us an *x* and *y* coordinate that will roughly match up to a puzzle piece. To get a better match, we'll need to convert the position from a float value into an int value, but we'll need to remember that values are rounded to 0 even if the value is above 0.5.

```
public int xGrid;
public int yGrid;
void PickPuzzlePiece(Vector3 position)
{
    int x = (int)(position.x + 0.5f);
    int y = (int)(position.y + 0.5f);
    if (x >= 0 && x < Width)
    {
        xGrid = x;
    }
    if (y >= 0 && y < Height)
    {
        yGrid = y;
    }
}
```

With a rough evaluation we can check that the x and y are within the bounds of the width and height values used to build the grid. To store the values an xGrid and yGrid are created to help us visualize what the values are being set to.

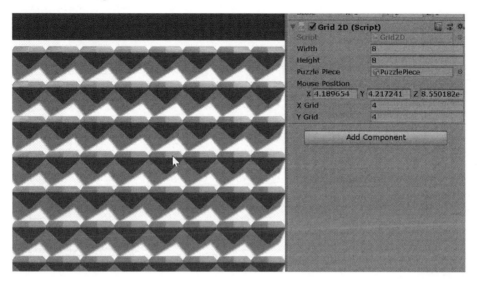

With the float value of *x* and *y* converted to an int that corresponds to a grid value, we can change the color of the puzzle piece in the grid based on where the mouse is positioned.

```
GameObject go = Grid[xGrid, yGrid];
Renderer renderer = go.GetComponent(typeof(Renderer)) as Renderer;
renderer.material.color = Color.red;
```

GameObject go = Grid[x, y]; works, but only when the cursor is over a puzzle piece. When the cursor is over a puzzle piece, we turn its material color to red. When the cursor is no longer over a puzzle piece, we get a bunch of warnings informing us we're selecting an index that is out of range.

5.10.4 Checking Range

```
IndexOutOfRangeException: Array index is out of range.
Grid2D.Update () (at Assets/Grid2D.cs:27)
```

This is true when the cursor is at −4, 7; there is no assigned object to the Grid[−4,7]; we've only assigned from 0 to 6 on the *x* and 0 to 6 on the *y*. These errors should be resolved before we move on. This can be done with an if statement or two.

```
if (x >= 0)
{
    if (x < Width)
    {
        if (y >= 0)
        {
            if (y < Height)
            {
                GameObject gameObject = Grid[x, y];
            }
        }
    }
}
```

This code checks first that x is at least 0, and then does the same for y. After that, we check that x is less than the width we chose initially, and do the same for y. However, this is a messy bit of code. It works but we can clean this up. There's nothing happening if only x < = 0; none of the if statements require any special actions to occur. They all contribute to the same assignment and color change statements at the end. That's how we know they can be reduced to one if statement.

The reduced statement looks like the following:

```
if (x >= 0 && x < Width && y >= 0 && y < Height)
{
    xGrid = x;
    yGrid = y;
}
```

However, with so many && in a single statement, the clarity of the values being checked and assigned should be separated.

```
if (x >= 0 && x < Width)
{
    xGrid = x;
}
if (y >= 0 && y < Height)
{
    yGrid = y;
}
```

Much better. Therefore, this code works to highlight every game object we touch, but the objects remain colored red. The puzzle piece should return to white when the mouse is no longer hovering over them; How would we do that? The logic isn't so simple. We could pick every other object and set it to white, but that's impractical. Strangely, the solution is to set all of the objects to white, and then color the current object red.

```
// set all of the game objects to white
for (int w = 0; w < Width; w++)
{
    for (int h = 0; h < Height; h++)
    {
        GameObject go = Grid[w, h];
        Renderer renderer = go.GetComponent(typeof(Renderer)) as Renderer;
        renderer.material.color = Color.white;
    }
}
```

Iterate through all of the game objects in a similar way to how we instantiated them. Because this code is sharing a function with x and y, where we converted the float to an int, we need to make new versions of x and y for this function; therefore, we'll use _x and _y to create a new variable for the for loops. With this, we set them all to white. After resetting all of the puzzle pieces to white, we move to the next function that sets them to red.

We're not so interested in what our scene looks like in the middle of the Update() function, just how the scene looks like at the end. None of the intermediate steps appears in the scene, until the Update() function has finished. This means we can do all sorts of unintuitive actions during the course of the Update() function, so long as the final result looks like what we need.

```
//set the one that the mouse is near to red
GameObject go = Grid[xGrid, yGrid];
Renderer renderer = go.GetComponent(typeof(Renderer)) as Renderer;
renderer.material.color = Color.red;
```

Now, we have a very simple way to detect and pick which puzzle piece is selected in a grid of objects using a 2D array and a Vector3. Of course, the strategy used here may not fit all situations. In addition, applying various offsets for changing the spacing between each object might be useful to make differently proportioned grids. Later on, you will want to add in additional systems to check for color to determine matches, but that will have to wait for Section 5.11.4.

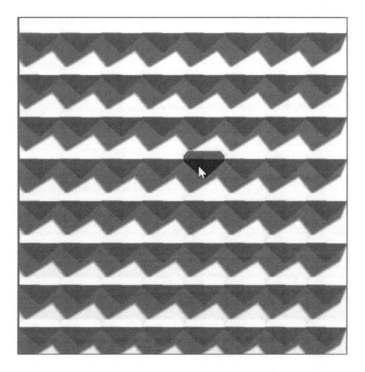

With the code moved into its own function, our Update() loop is easier to read. We're very specific about what is required to update the picked piece. We just need to remember to rename mousePosition to a position inside of the new function. We can also extend the new function to return the piece that has been picked. By breaking apart a long string of code into smaller, more simplified functions, we're able to gain more flexibility and allow for changes more easily.

5.10.5 What We've Learned

Back in the MultidimensionalArrays script arrays can be a bit of a pain to work with, but after some practice, the logic becomes more intuitive. Puzzle games that use a grid of colored objects to match up often use a 2D array to check for patterns.

We could expand the concept to more than two dimensions as well. Using the previously defined GameObjects, we could make a 3D array that looks like the following:

```
GameObject[,,] threeDimensions = new GameObject[4, 3, 2]
{
    { {a, b}, { c, d}, { e, f} },
    { {a, b}, { c, d}, { e, f} },
    { {a, b}, { c, d}, { e, f} },
    { {a, b}, { c, d}, { e, f} }
};
```

Something like this is easier to produce using code to fill in each value, but it's important to be able to visualize what a [4,3,2] array actually looks like. Though a bit impractical, these sorts of data structures are important to computing, in general. Outside of video game development, multidimensional arrays become more important to data analysis.

Large database systems often have internal functions that accelerate sorting through arrays of data in more logical ways. Of course, if you're thinking about building a complex RPG, then multidimensional arrays might play a role in how your character's items and stats are related to one another.

5.11 Array List

Fixed-sized arrays are great. When you create an array with 10 indices, adding an 11th score or more will be cause for some rethinking. You'd have to go back and fix your code to include another index. This would be very inefficient, to say the least. This is where an array list comes in handy. An ArrayList is initialized a bit differently from a more common fixed-sized array.

```
ArrayList arrayList = new ArrayList();
```

An ArrayList is a C# class that has special functions for building lists that allow for changes in the number of values stored. An ArrayList is not set to a specific size. Rather than having to pick an index to put a value into, we merely use the ArrayList function Add(); to increase the number of objects in the ArrayList. In addition, an array has a type associated with it.

An array like int[] numbers can store only a bunch of ints. An ArrayList can store any variety of object types. Another feature which we'll find out later is that an array, not an ArrayList, can have multiple dimensions, for instance, int[,] grid = new int[8,8];, which creates an 8 by 8 array. An ArrayList cannot be used like this.

The drawback with an ArrayList is the fact that we're not able to populate the list ahead of time. With the fixed-sized array we've been getting to know, we're able to assign each index a value ahead of time; for instance, consider the following:

```
int[] primeNumbers = new int[] { 1, 3, 5, 7, 11, 13, 17 };
```

We know that this statement will appear in the Inspector panel with seven numbers in a nice UI roll-out. An array list doesn't allow for this behavior, as it needs to be created and then populated after its creation. The reason why Unity 3D allows us to assign values to objects in a scene is the scene file. The scene itself has had special data or metadata added to the scene. The scene now has specific bindings created to tie the data you've created to the class attached to an object.

To simulate this in a more common Windows app, you'd have to create a secondary file that stores specific settings. When the app is started, the settings need to be read in and then assigned to the classes as they are instanced into the scene. Unity 3D has done much of the specific bindings for you, which allows your game to have scenes with arranged objects and unique settings for each object.

```
int i = 3;
arrayList.Add(i);
```

The identifier inherits the ArrayList member methods. The Add method is used to append a value to the end of the ArrayList object. The arrayList from the above code fragment is now an ArrayList type with one item. With this, we're able to use the arrayList as an object.

```
Debug.Log(arrayList[0]);
```

This statement will send 3 to the Console panel, as you might expect. In practice, the ArrayList type is often used to collect an unknown number of objects into something more manageable. Once we've gathered the objects we're looking for, it's easier to deal with the multitude of objects. Therefore, if there are between 0 and 100 zombies in a room, we can have different behaviors based on the number of zombies found. If we want to convert the ArrayList into a regular array, we'd need to do some copying from the ArrayList to the array.

In addition to allowing for any number of objects, we can also consume any variety of types in the array.

5.11.1 A Basic Example

To observe how an ArrayList is used, it's best to see it all in action; therefore, we'll start with the ArrayLists project in Unity 3D. In the scene, we can have any number of cube game objects. Should the number of objects be something that can't be predetermined, we'd want to use an ArrayList to store a list of them.

```
ArrayList arrayList = new ArrayList();
Object[] allObjects = FindObjectsOfType(typeof(Object));
foreach (Object o in allObjects)
{
    GameObject go = o as GameObject;
    if (go != null)
    {
        arrayList.Add(go);
    }
}
//initialize GameObjects Array
GameObject[] gameObjects = new GameObject[arrayList.Count];
arrayList.CopyTo(gameObjects);
foreach (GameObject go in gameObjects)
{
    Debug.Log(go.name);
}
```

The code above is attached to the ArrayLists game object. This behavior adds everything in the scene to an array. If it's an object, then we add it to the array. Afterward, we iterate through the array using foreach(Object o in AllObjects), which allows us to check if the object in the allObjects array is a GameObject. This check is done using GameObject go = o as GameObject;, and the following line checks if the cast is valid. If the cast is valid, then we add the object to our array list arrayList. This is done using the same arrayList.Add(go) function we used before.

After the iteration through the list, we end up with a final pair of steps. The first is to initialize a regular GameObject array to the size of the ArrayList. Then, we need to copy the arrayList to the freshly initialized GameObject array with arrayList.CopyTo().

The final result is an ArrayList of each game object in the scene. If we skip the cast checking of whether Object o is a GameObject, then we get an invalid cast error. This happens only when we try to copy the arrayList to the GameObject array. We can do the following in the iteration to populate the arrayList without any problems.

```
foreach (Object o in allObjects)
{
    arrayList.Add(o);
}
```

This code simply adds everything that FindObjectsOfType() finds to the arrayList. This tells us that arrayList ignores the type that it's being filled with. To see what this foreach loop is doing, we can use the following modification:

```
foreach (Object o in allObjects)
{
    Debug.Log(o);
    arrayList.Add(o);
}
```

Here, we log each o to the console. We get many more objects than you might have guessed. In the scene I've created, there are 76 different lines printed to the Console panel. The list includes the game objects as well as dozens of other objects that are added to the ArrayList; too many to spell out in this case. A regular array can accommodate only one type at a time. And a GameObject[] array can have only GameObjects assigned to each index.

Since we might not necessarily know how many GameObjects reside in the final list, we need to dynamically add each one to the ArrayList, and wait till we stop finding new GameObjects to add. Once the list is done with iteration, we can then use the final count of the arrayList, using `arrayList.Count`, to initialize the GameObject array. The ArrayList has a function called CopyTo, which is designed to copy its contents to a fixed-sized array; therefore, we use it to do just that, with the last two statements:

```
gameObjects = new GameObject[arrayList.Count];
// copy the list to the array
arrayList.CopyTo(gameObjects);
```

5.11.2 `ArrayList.Contains()`

`ArrayList.Contains()` is a static function of ArrayList. The ArrayList type has several useful functions aside from just copying to an array. Say, we add a public GameObject SpecificObject; to the ArrayLists class. Then we can drag one of the cubes in the scene to the variable in the Inspector panel.

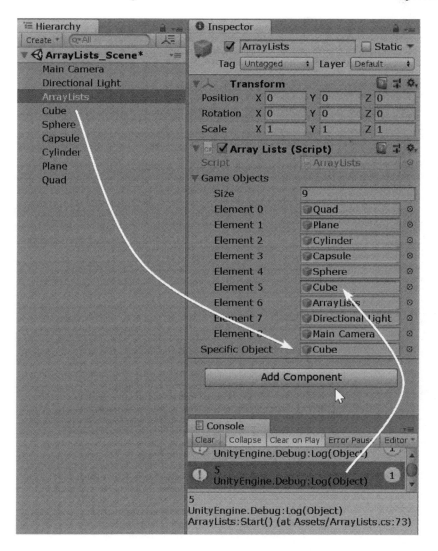

Now, we have an object and a populated array list. This allows us to search the array list for the object.

```
if (arrayList.Contains(specificObject))
{
    Debug.Log("SpecificObject:");
    Debug.Log(specificObject);
    Debug.Log("is in arrayList at index ");
    Debug.Log(arrayList.IndexOf(specificObject));
}
```

We can use two different array list functions. The first is Contains() and the second is IndexOf(). The Contains() function searches through the array list and returns true if it finds the object and false if the object isn't in the list. The IndexOf() function returns the index where the SpecificObject is found. Therefore, if the array list has the specificObject at index 5, the Debug.Log above returns 5.

5.11.3 Remove

The object that the script is a component of is found by this.gameObject, or simply, gameObject. Therefore, we may remove the object doing the searching from the list with the Remove() function. The statement that effects this behavior would look like the following:

```
if (arrayList.Contains(specificObject))
{
    arrayList.Remove(specificObject);
    //now update the list in the inspector panel
    gameObjects = new GameObject[arrayList.Count];
    arrayList.CopyTo(gameObjects);
}
```

This statement reduces the size of the array list and takes out the Main Camera, which has the array list's component attached. With the camera removed, the copied array now has only cubes in it.

If the goal is to filter the scene for specific objects, then the array list serves as a great net to fill with the types of data you need. If you don't know ahead of time how many objects you are going to find, then an array list is a useful utility class that allows for some interesting tricks. Therefore, we've looked at removing and finding an object in an array list, but we don't need to stop there.

5.11.4 Sort and Reverse

▼ Messy Ints	
Size	8
Element 0	12
Element 1	14
Element 2	6
Element 3	1
Element 4	0
Element 5	123
Element 6	92
Element 7	8

Let's add public int[] messyInts = {12,14,6,1,0,123,92,8}; to the class scope. This should appear in the Inspector panel, where we can see that messyInts is indeed a collection of messy ints. To copy the messyInts into a new ArrayList, we use AddRange();

```
ArrayList sorted = new ArrayList();
sorted.AddRange(messyInts);
sorted.Sort();
sorted.CopyTo(messyInts);
```

With the above code added to the Start() function, we get the following result once the game is run.

▼ Messy Ints	
Size	8
Element 0	0
Element 1	1
Element 2	6
Element 3	8
Element 4	12
Element 5	14
Element 6	92
Element 7	123

The elements of the array have been sorted, starting at the lowest and ending with the highest. The sort function is a nicely optimized sort function. You might expect this from the experienced computer scientists working on the C# library we've been using. If we want to reverse the order in which the numbers are sorted, then we can use the sorted Reverse(); function.

```
sorted.Reverse();
sorted.CopyTo(messyInts);
```

Having some numbers rearranged is great, but there's little inherent value to the numbers if there are no associated objects in the scene that relate to the numeric values. The Sort() function is good for simple matters where the data that's sorted has no association with anything in particular outside of the array. However, should we want to compare GameObjects in the scene, we might need to do something more useful.

5.11.5 What We've Learned

Making a custom sorting system requires some new concepts, which we have yet to get to. A specific type of class called an interface is required to create our own system of sorting. We could use this class in many different ways and take advantage of the power behind C#'s library.

A performance issue comes up with array lists. We may add objects to an ArrayList by simply using MyArrayList.Add(someObject);, which is easy. When we need to see what's in that array list, we begin to have a few problems.

As this was mentioned at the beginning of this chapter we didn't find out what happens if we use the following.

```
ArrayList arrayList = new ArrayList();
arrayList.Add(123);
arrayList.Add("strings");
```

We have an issue with the above code fragment. If we assumed the ArrayList would only contain numbers; multiplying 123 by "strings" would result in an error. Of course we can't multiply these two very different types. We'd need to do a few tricks to check if we're allowed to multiply two objects from the ArrayList. First, we'd check if both are indeed numbers, if they are then we can proceed with a multiplication statement. If not, then we'd have to find another two objects which are numbers or we'd get an error.

This process takes time, and if the array list is big, then we'd be spending a great deal of time on checking object types. If we use a regular array, we can be sure that each object in the array is the same type, or possibly null. Checking against null for each object in the list is an extra step in the process. Reducing the number of steps your function need to work will speed up your functions and code will run faster.

When dealing with arrays, we might need to stuff an array into an array. Each array inside of an array can be of a different size. Imagine array A to be 10 items long. At A[0], you can create another array B that is, for example, 3 items long. If each index of A is of a different size, you've created what is called a jagged array.

5.12 Strings

Strings are collections of letters. C# has no concept of what words are, so a string is nothing more than a collection of meaningless letters. When you use a string, it's important to remember that the data stored in it is not like words.

5.12.1 Declaring a String

Basically, strings are presented to the computer by using the " or ' operator. Strings act somewhat like an array, so we've held off until after we looked at arrays before getting to strings. Later on, strings will become a bit more useful, once we start naming GameObjects.

Strings can be used as user names and will be useful if you wanted to use them for dialog windows when talking to characters in a role-playing game. Being able to process strings is a useful skill to have for many general purpose programming tasks.

5.12.1.1 A Basic Example

Let's start with the Strings_Scene in the Chapter5 Unity Project. And open the Strings.cs script attached to the Strings game object in the scene.

```
string s = "Something in quotes.";
```

This statement creates a string with the identifier s and then assigns Something in quotes to s. Strings have several additional functions that are important. Be careful to not use smart quotes, which word processors like to use. Quotes that have directions are not the same as the quotes a compiler is expecting. Words in special quotes ("words") actually use different characters when written in a word processor.

The compiler expects a different character. The character set that most word processors use is different from what C# uses to compile. For instance, if you hold down the ALT key and enter four numbers on the number pad, you'll get a special character.

```
string s = "Something in quotes.";
Debug.Log(s);
```

Printing the s results in a predictable output to the Console panel.

> ⚠ Something in quotes.
> UnityEngine.Debug:Log(Object)

There's not a whole lot unexpected happening here. However, we can do something with strings that might unexpected.

```
s += "more words.";
```

We can add this statement just before the print (s); and get a different result. When we run the game, we get the following Console output:

> ⚠ Something in quotes.more words.
> UnityEngine.Debug:Log(Object)

We forgot to add in a space before the *more* in "more words," so it ran into the word quotes. White space is important to how we use strings. There's no logic to what's happening when we add more words to a string. To correct this, we need to add a space before *more* and we'll get a more expected result: "more words."

Strings do have some tricks that make them very useful. The string class has many member functions we can use, like Contains.

```
bool hasSomething = s.Contains("Something");
Debug.Log(hasSomething);
```

This returns `true`; the word `"Something"` is contained in the string stored in s. Use any other set of letters which doesn't appear in our string and the console will print `false`.

We can also do the following.

```
s = "First Word " + "Second Word";
Debug.Log(s);
```

The reassignment of s prints out what you might expect.

First Word Second Word
UnityEngine.Debug:Log(Object)

For argument's sake, we'll try another operator in the string declaration.

```
s = "First Word " - "Second Word";
```

Here, we're going to try to subtract "Second word" from the first. Of course, this doesn't work and we get the following error.

Assets/Strings.cs(29,17): error CS0019: Operator `-' cannot be applied to operands of type `string' and `string'

So why does the + work and not the − in our declaration? The answer is operator overloading. Operators change their meaning depending on the context in which they appear. When the + is placed between two strings, we get a different result than when we put the + between two numbers. However, strings are rather particular. It's rather difficult to say for sure what it would mean to subtract one word from another. Computers are horrible at guessing.

5.12.2 Escape Sequences

Strings in C# need to be handled very differently from a regular word processor. Formatting strings can be somewhat confusing if you treat C# like any other text format.

```
string s = "test a
    line return";
```

If you want to add in a line return, you might end up with a mess as in the above image. Sometimes called line feeds, or carriage returns, these line returns tend to break C# in unexpected ways. To add in line feeds into the string, you'll have to use a special character instead.

```
string s = "First line. \n Second Line";
Debug.Log(s);
```

Escape sequences work to convert two regular text characters into more specialized characters without needing to mess up your code's formatting. The \n creates a "new line" where it appears in the string. A \t adds a tab wherever it appears.

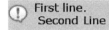

First line.
Second Line

Unity 3D diverges a bit from most C# libraries as it doesn't implement all of the different escape sequences that are generally included. For instance, \r is carriage return, as is \f that are generally included in other common .NET development environments. The \n, which creates new line sequence, is more commonly known.

In old mechanical type writers, a carriage return is a lever that would both push a roll of paper and add in a new line at the same time; hardly something you see around today, unless you're a street poet. Not all these escape characters work, but there are several others which you'll find useful.

```
Debug.Log("\"I Want Quotes!\"");
```

So, if you want quotes:

```
"I Want Quotes"
UnityEngine.Debug:Log(Object)
```

You get quotes. To get double quotes to print in your console, you'll use the \" escape sequence. Here's a list of regular escape sequences.

```
\a  (beep)
\b  Backspace
\f  Formfeed
\n  New line
\r  Carriage return
\t  Tab
\v  Vertical tab
\'  Single quote
\"  Double quote
\\  Backslash
\?  Literal question mark
```

In addition to these escape sequences, we have an additional three types that are used less often but are just as important. C# and Unity 3D will recognize some hexadecimal characters that are accessed with \x followed by two hexadecimal values. We'll find out more about these hex values and other escape sequences in a later chapter. Using hexadecimals is another way to get the more particular characters often found in other languages.

5.12.3 Verbatim Strings: @

In some cases, it's useful to use the @ operator before a string. This tells C# that we're really not interested in formatting or not being able to make modifications to our string, like string s = "This\nThat";, as opposed to the @ operator string s = @"This\nThat";

```
s = "This\nThat";
Debug.Log(s);
s = @"This\nThat";
Debug.Log(s);
```

This code produces the following:

This also means something as strange looking as:

```
            Debug.Log(s);
            s = @"this
that and
the other";
            Debug.Log(s);
```

prints to the console

```
this
that and
the other
UnityEngine.Debug:Log(Object)
Strings:Start() (at Assets/Strings.cs:57)
```

Notice that the console output includes exactly what was used in Visual Studio. If the words lined up using the indents, the white space would be included in the verbatim string. This is allowed because of the verbatim operator. When using Debug.Log(), the verbatim operator can be used to format your strings to include new lines wherever you may need them.

Strings that contain information can easily be created; it's often the case when trying to track the behavior of a creature in the scene.

5.12.4 What We've Learned

We're not going to be building any word-processing software within Unity 3D. It's not something that sounds all that fun, and there are better environments for doing that. As far as strings are concerned, we're better off using them as seldom as possible.

Very few game engines dwell on their text-editing features, Unity 3D included. If you're planning on having your player do a great deal of writing and formatting to play your game, then you might have a tough time. For most purposes, like entering character names or setting up a clan name, the string class provided will have you covered.

5.13 Combining What We've Learned

We just covered some basic uses of loops. The for and the while loop have similar uses, but the for loop has some additional parameters that can make it more versatile. We also covered some relational, unary, and conditional operators.

Together with if, else if, and else, we've got enough parts together to do some interesting logic tests. We can start to give some interesting behavior to our statements. For instance, we could build a cityscape using cubes that grows over time.

5.13.1 Timers

In the Timers_Scene project in the Chapter5 Unity Project, we'll start with the Timers.cs script attached to the Timers game object in the scene. Let's say we want to create a number of towers, but we want to create them one at a time. To do this, we should use a timer; therefore, we should start with that first.

```
void Update()
{
    Debug.Log(Time.fixedTime);
}
```

If we start with Time.fixedTime, we should see how that behaves by itself. We get a printout to the console starting with 0, which then counts up at one unit per second. Therefore, if we want some sort of action 3 seconds later, we can set a timer to 3 seconds from 0.

```
if (Time.fixedTime > 3)
{
    Debug.Log("Times Up");
}
```

If Time.fixedTime is greater than 3, "Times Up" is repeatedly printed to the console. However, we want that to print only once, since we want only one thing to happen when our if statement is executed. To do this, we should add in some way to increment the number we're comparing Time.fixedTime to.

```
if (Time.fixedTime > NextTime)
{
    NextTime = Time.fixedTime + 3;
    Debug.Log("Times Up");
}
```

With a class scoped variable called NextTime, we can store our next "Times Up" time and update it when it is reached. Running this code prints "Times Up" once the game starts. If NextTime was declared to 3, then we'd have to wait 3 seconds before the first Times Up is printed to the console.

```
public float NextTime;
public int Counter = 10;
```

Therefore, now, we have a timer. We should next add some sort of counter, so we know how many times the if statement was executed.

```
if (Counter > 0)
{
    if (Time.fixedTime > NextTime)
    {
        NextTime = Time.fixedTime + 3;
        Counter--;
        Debug.Log("Times Up");
    }
}
```

First, add in int Counter = 10 to store how many times we want to run our if statement. If the Counter is greater than 0, then we need to check our Time.fixedTime if statement. Once the timer is reset, we need to decrement our Counter by 1. Once the counter is no longer greater than 0, we stop. There's a cleaner way to do this.

```
if (Time.fixedTime > NextTime)
{
    NextTime = Time.fixedTime + 3;
    Counter--;
    Debug.Log("Times Up");
}
```

We can reduce the extra if statement checking the counter value. To merge if statements, use the && conditional operator. If either side of the && is false, then the if statement is not evaluated. Because there's no code in the if statement checking the counter, there's no reason why it can't be combined with the if statement it's containing.

Now, we have a timer and a counter. We can make this more useful by exposing some of the variables to the editor.

```
if (Counter > 0 && Time.fixedTime > NextTime)
{
    NextTime = Time.fixedTime + Delay;
    Counter--;
    Debug.Log("Times Up");
}
```

Add in public before some of the existing variables, and for good measure, let's get rid of the 3 that we're adding to Time.fixedTime and make that into a variable as well. This is common practice; use some numbers to test a feature, and then once the feature roughly works, change some of the numbers into editable parameters that may be handed off to designers.

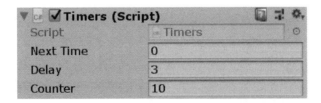

Now we can replace print ("Time Up"); with a more useful function. Once we've got the chops, we'll start replacing boxes with building pieces, but we'll leave that to the artists, the code below serves as a good example for now.

```
GameObject box = GameObject.CreatePrimitive(PrimitiveType.Cube);
box.transform.position = new Vector3(Counter * 2f, 0, 0);
NextTime = Time.fixedTime + Delay;
Counter--;
Debug.Log("Times Up");
```

This little block of code will slowly pop a new cube into existence around the scene origin. We're using Counter to multiply against 2 so each box object will appear in a different place along the *x* coordinate.

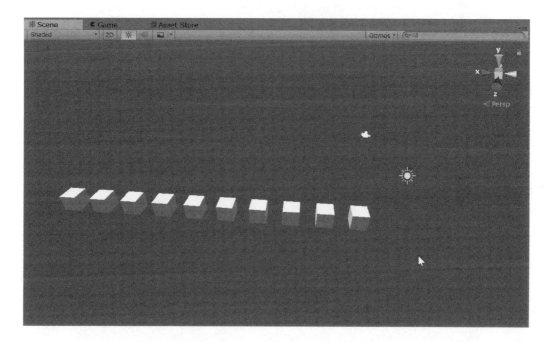

You can speed up the process by lowering the Delay value we just added. What if we wanted to have more than one box created at each counter interval? This objective can be accomplished using either a while or a for statement being run inside the if statement.

```
public float NextTime;
public float Delay = 0.5f;
public int Counter = 10;
```

Adding in the for loop is the easiest way to do this. UnityEngine.Random.Range(); is a new function that returns a number between the first argument and the second argument. We're just testing this so we can use any number to start with.

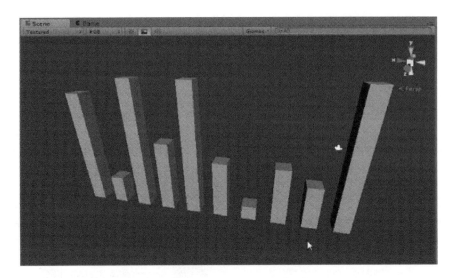

Okay, looks like everything is working as we might have expected. We should take out the numbers we're using in the Random.Range() and make them into more public parameters for use in the editor.

```
public float NextTime;
public float Delay = 0.5f;
public int Counter = 10;
public int MinimumHeight = 1;
public int MaximumHeight = 10;
public float XSpacing = 0.5f;
public float YSpacing = 0.5f;
```

Adding more variables to control spacing will also make this more interesting.

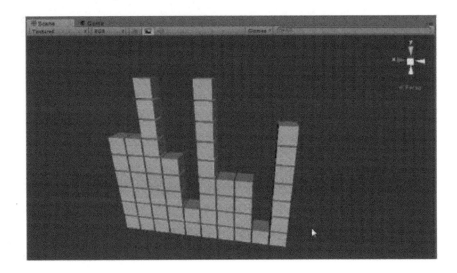

By tweaking some of the parameters, you can build something that looks like this with code alone! The reason why we should be exposing so many of these variables to the editor is to allow for creative freedom. The more parametric we make any system, the more exploration we can do with what the numbers mean.

```
if (Counter > 0 && Time.fixedTime > NextTime)
{
    int vertical = UnityEngine.Random.Range(MinimumHeight, MaximumHeight);
    for (int i = 0; i < vertical; i++)
    {
        GameObject box = GameObject.CreatePrimitive(PrimitiveType.Cube);
        box.transform.position = new Vector3(Counter * XSpacing, i * YSpacing, 0);
    }
    NextTime = Time.fixedTime + Delay;
    Counter--;
    Debug.Log("Times Up");
}
```

If you feel adventurous, then you can add in a second dimension to the stack of cubes.

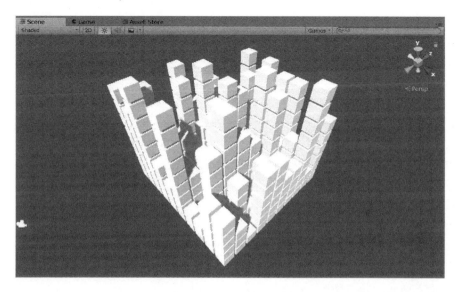

Look at that. What started off as some cube-generating system turned into some 3D pixel art city generator.

```
if (Counter > 0 && Time.fixedTime > NextTime)
{
    for (int i = 0; i < 10 ; i++)
    {
        int vertical = UnityEngine.Random.Range(MinimumHeight, MaximumHeight);
        for (int j = 0; j < vertical; j++)
        {
            GameObject box = GameObject.CreatePrimitive(PrimitiveType.Cube);
            Vector3 position = new Vector3()
            {
                x = Counter * XSpacing,
                y = j * YSpacing,
                z = i * ZSpacing
            };
            box.transform.position = position;
        }
    }
    NextTime = Time.fixedTime + Delay;
    Counter--;
    Debug.Log("Times Up");
}
```

If we spend more time on this, then we can even start to add little cubes onto the big cubes by setting scale and position around each of the cubes as they are generated. We won't go into that right now; I'll leave that on to you to play with.

5.13.2 What We've Learned

We're starting to build more complex systems. Adding functions to classes and using them in for loops is a fairly flexible and reusable setup. What's important here is to understand a bit of the thought process of writing a complex system. We started off with one line, made sure that the line of code worked, then added another line or two. After several iterations we went from a simple timer to a small cube shaped pixel like city scape.

We should be a bit more comfortable reading complex algorithms in the functions we read on forums and in downloaded assets. If we come across something new, then we should be able to come up with some search terms to find out what we're looking at.

5.14 Leveling Up: On to the Cool Stuff

We've come further along than most people who set out to learn how to program. By now, you should be able to read through some code and get some idea of how it's working. We've gotten through some of the tough beginnings of learning how to write in C#, but things are just about to get more interesting.

The clever tricks that programmers use to save time are about to start to come into play. If you take the time, you should review Chapters 1 through 4 to strengthen your grasp of the core concepts we've been studying.

There's an interesting topic that hasn't found a place in any chapters yet. If you open the MagicComponent project in Unity 3D, you'll be able to see some interesting behavior. Say we have an object in the scene with a component attached. We'll look at something called FirstComponent.cs attached to a cube.

If the Main Camera has a component attached that has a couple of variables that are set for FirstComponent and SecondComponent, how do we add the GameObject's component to that slot in the Inspector panel? We drag it, of course!

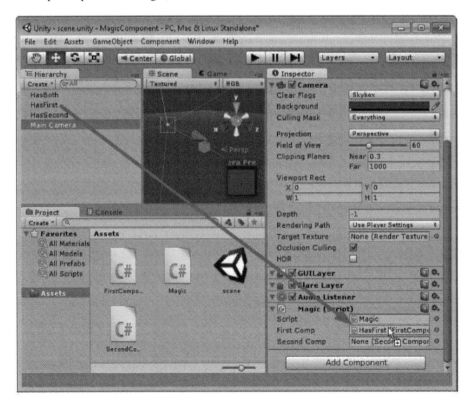

Therefore, even though the variable isn't GameObject, you can still drag the object from the scene into the Inspector panel. Unity 3D is clever enough to find a component of the same type as the slot in the Inspector.

This feature also means that any variable changed on the object in the scene will have a direct connection to the Magic.cs class that is holding onto the variable. This means a couple of strange things. First, the objects in the scene are instances, but they are acting in a rather weird limbo. Second, the connection between variables is stored in some magic data stored in the scene file.

The weird limbo infers that when you drag a class onto an object in the editor, it is immediately instanced. This behavior is unusual in that this only happens in the Unity 3D Editor, your player and the finished game never has any behavior like this. The class instances an object and attaches it to the `GameObject` in the scene, as though you used `GameObject.Instance()` or even new `FirstComponent();`, or perhaps `Component.Add();`, and added it to the `GameObject` in the scene.

The fact that the `Start()` and `Update()` functions aren't called means that the game isn't running. However, the class is still an instanced object created by the .cs file in the Assets directory. There are editor scripts that do run while the game might not be playing. Editor scripts are often used to help game designers.

Editor scripts can be used to create tools and other fun interfaces specifically for the Unity 3D Editor. These are often not running while the game is playing. We shouldn't venture too far into Unity 3D-specific tricks as this distracts us from learning more about C#, but it's fun to know what to look for if we want to build our own C# tools for Unity 3D.

The strange fact that the variable in Magic.cs has a handle on an object in the scene without having to run `GameObject.Find();` or `Transform.Find();` means that there's a lot going on in the scene file. All of this is actually stored in the meta files that seem to be appearing as you work with others on Unity 3D projects.

These meta files are required for these magic data connections between objects in a Unity 3D Scene file. Of course, other file settings and project settings are also stored in these meta files. If you open one, you'll find many things called GUIDs, which stands for globally unique identifiers, and they're used in meta files to find a specific object in the scene and apply settings to them.

It wasn't long ago when game engines referenced everything in the scene by their GUID alone. Today, they're at least hidden from view, but they still affect our lives as game programmers. We can't reference a specific object by name alone. If you've got several objects named GameObject, then you're going to have a rough time remembering which one actually has the data you're looking for. Because of this, everything is assigned a GUID and that's just the way it's gotta be.

6

Intermediate: The Tricks of the Trade

The coming chapters are big, dense, and exciting. Getting into a programming language means discovering many cool tricks. The basics of most programming languages have already been covered.

From here on out, you'll be learning some of the more clever systems that make the C# language elegant and concise. Rather than having long chains of if-else statements, you can use a switch statement. Rather than having a large uncontrolled nest of different variables, you can group them together in a struct.

Don't worry about not making rapid progress; learning is more about the journey than it is about the goal. Of course, if you do have a goal of making a featured mobile game, then by all means, speed forth toward your goal. Just try not to skip around too much; there's much stuff that is explained for a reason.

6.1 What Will Be Covered in This Chapter

The long journey begins. We're going to cover some important concepts here, including the following:

- Classes as objects
- Class constructors
- Arrays
- Enums
- Switch statement
- Structures
- Namespaces
- More on functions
- More on inheritance
- More on type casting
- Some work on vectors
- Goto
- Out parameter
- Ref parameter
- Operator overloading

This chapter discusses a few concepts more than once, or rather, we look at different aspects of type casting, for instance, but we divide the concept over more than one chapter. In between the chapters, we cover a few other concepts that do relate back to the topic. Learning a single concept can mean taking in a few separate concepts before coming back to the original topic.

6.2 Review

By now you've been equipped with quite a vocabulary of terms and a useful set of tools to take care of nearly any basic task. Moving forward, you'll only extend your ability and come to grips that you've still got a long way to go. Even after years of engineering software, there's always more to learn. Even once you think you've covered a programming language, a new version is released then you need to learn more features.

Aside from learning one language, most companies will eventually toss in a task that involves learning another programming language. In a modern setting, it's likely you'll need to learn some of the programming languages while on the job. This might involve knowing something like Scala or PHP, yet another programming language you'll have to learn.

Learning additional programming languages isn't as daunting as you might think. Once you know one language, it's far easier to learn another. The keyword var is used in many other programming languages in the exact same context. It's a keyword used to store a variable. In C#, we see `var v = "things";`, which is similar to JavaScript where `var v = "things";`.

So far, the principles that have been covered in this book are general enough such that almost every other programming language has similar concepts. Nearly all languages have conditions and operators. Most languages use tokens and white space in the same way as well.

6.2.1 Class Members

Classes provided by Unity 3D become accessible when you add using UnityEngine at the top of your C# code. All the classes found inside of that library have names which you can use directly in your own code. This includes Input, and all the members of Input are imported into your code.

6.2.1.1 A Basic Example

Follow along with the ClassMembers_Scene and the ClassMembers script found in the Chapter 6 Unity 3D project. Let's start off with a new class that will have some functions in it. We've done this before by creating a new C# class in the Project panel.

```
public class Members
{
    public void FirstFunction()
    {
        Debug.Log("FirstFunction");
    }
}
```

Create a new class called Members.cs because we're going to use members of the Members class. Then we'll add public `void FirstFunction()` with `Debug.Log("First Function");` to print to the Console panel when it's invoked.

There are two classifications for the stuff that classes are made of: data members and function members. As you might imagine, function members are the lines of code that execute and run logic on data. Data members are the variables that are accessible within the class.

In our Example class we've been abusing a lot, we'll add in the following line to the `Start()` function:

```
void Start()
{
    Members m = new Members();
}
```

This creates what's called an instance. We're assigning the identifier m to being a new copy or instance of the Members class. The keyword new is used to create new instances. `Members();` is used to tell the new keyword what class we're using. It seems like we're using the class as a function, and to a limited extent we are, but we'll have to leave those details for Section 6.3.3.1.

The m variable that is an instance of the Members class is now a thing we can use in the function. When we use m, we can access its members.

```
28          void Start()
29          {
30              Members m = new Members();
31              m.
32          }
            Equals
void Members.FirstFunction()   FirstFunction
34              GetHashCode
35              GetType
                ToString
```

Type "m." and a new pop-up will appear in Visual Studio showing a list of things that m can do. FirstFunction, as well as a few other items, is in the list. These other items were things that Object was able to do. Accessing the different functions within a class is a simple matter of using the dot operator.

```
void Start()
{
    Members m = new Members();
    m.FirstFunction();
}
```

Finish off the m. by adding `FirstFunction();`. Running the script when it's attached to a cube or something in the scene will produce the following Console output. Objects and its members have many uses; though, this might not be clear from this one example.

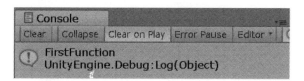

6.2.1.2 Thinking Like a Programmer

A peek into a programmer's thinking process reveals a step-by-step process of evaluating a situation and finding a solution for each step. The plan begins with an overall goal but finding the small incremental steps to reach the goal are just as important.

Gathering data and then doing something with the data follows. Then logic takes the front seat in this case, as the programmer needs to not only investigate each function, he or she must use but also clean up the thinking process as he or she writes code.

Intuition and deduction are a huge part of programming. The programmer needs to guess what sort of functions he or she should be looking for. With each new development environment, the programmer needs to learn the software's application programming interface, the interface between you (the programmer) and the application you're working with, in this case, Unity 3D.

At this point, we have some basic tools to do something interesting with our game scene. However, to make a game, we're going to read input from the keyboard, mouse, and any other input device that the player might want to use. An appropriate place to start would be looking up the word "input" in the Solution Explorer in Visual Studio.

Dig into the UnityEngine.dll and expand the UnityEngine library. You should find an Input class that looks very promising. From here, we can start hunting for a function inside of input that might be useful for us. At this point, I should mention that programmers all seem to use a unique vocabulary.

The words "Get," and "Set" are often used by programmers for getting and setting values. For getting a keyboard command, we should look for a function that gets things for us. We can find "GetKey" in the numerous functions found in Input.

```
public static bool GetKey (string name)...
public static bool GetKey (KeyCode key)...
public static bool GetKeyDown (string name)...
public static bool GetKeyDown (KeyCode key)...
public static bool GetKeyUp (string name)...
public static bool GetKeyUp (KeyCode key)...
```

There seems to be a string name and KeyCode key for each one of the functions. We did mention that reusing names for things means erasing a previously used name. However, this doesn't always hold true. In the case of functions, when you duplicate a name, you're allowed to share the name, as long as you do something different with the arguments found in parentheses. This is called overriding, and we'll learn more about that in Section 6.13.1. It's just good to know what you're looking at so you don't get too lost.

So now that we've found something that looks useful, how do we use it? The "GetKey" function looks like its public function, which is good. Functions with the keyword public are functions that we're allowed to use.

The context when using the dot operator in numbers changes an int to a double or float if you add in an f at the end of the number. When you add the dot operator after the name of a class found in UnityEngine, you're asking to gain access to a class member. In this case, we found GetKey inside of Input, so to talk to that function we use the dot operator after Input to get to that function.

There were two GetKey functions: The first had "KeyCode key" and the second had "string name" written in the arguments for the function. This means we have two options we can use.

When you add the first parenthesis, MonoDevelop pops up some helpers.

These help you fill in the blanks. There are many KeyCode options to choose from. You can see them all by scrolling through the pop-up. I picked the KeyCode.A to test this out. I'm guessing that pressing the A key on the keyboard is going to change something. In the Example.cs file, add in the following:

```
bool AKey = Input.GetKey(KeyCode.A);
Debug.Log(AKey);
```

We're setting the bool AKey to this function; why a bool and why even do this? Remember that the function was designated as a public static bool. The last word is the reason why we're using a bool AKey. The variable type we're setting matches the return type of the function.

Finally, we're printing out the value of AKey. Run the game and press the A key on your keyboard and read the Console output from Unity 3D.

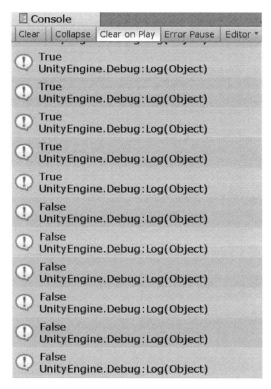

When the A key is down, we get True; when it's not down, we get False. It looks like our hunch was correct. Our AKey bool is now being controlled by the Input class' member function GetKey. We know the return type of GetKey because of the bool that was written just before the name of the function. We also know how to access the function inside of Input through the dot operator.

Let's keep this going. Make a bool for WKey, SKey, and DKey. This will allow us to use the classic WASD keyboard input found in many different games. Then we'll make them set to the different GetKeys that we're going to use from Input.

Now we're going to make our cube move around, so we're going to look at the Transform class. To move our cube around, we're going to keep track of our current position. To do this, we're going to make a Vector 3 called pos as a class scoped variable.

```
position = transform.position;
```

The first thing we want to do is set the pos to the object's current position when the game starts. This means we can place the cube anywhere in the scene at the beginning of the game and the pos will know where we're starting.

```
bool AKey = Input.GetKey(KeyCode.A);
bool WKey = Input.GetKey(KeyCode.W);
bool SKey = Input.GetKey(KeyCode.S);
bool DKey = Input.GetKey(KeyCode.D);
```

In the function named Update(), we're going to set the transform.position of the cube to pos in each frame. This means that if we change the x, y, or z of the pos Vector3 variable, the cube will go to that Vector3. Now all we need to do is change the position.x and position.z when we press one of the keys.

```
if (AKey)
{
    position.x = position.x - 0.1f;
}
if (DKey)
{
    position.x = position.x + 0.1f;
}
if (WKey)
{
    position.z = position.z + 0.1f;
}
if (SKey)
{
    position.z = position.z - 0.1f;
}
transform.position = position;
```

I've added an if statement controlled by each bool we created at the beginning of the Update() function. Then we changed the position.x and position.z according to the direction I wanted the cube to move in by adding or subtracting a small value. Try this out and experiment with some different values.

This is not the only solution, nor is it the best. This is a simple solution and rather restricted. The speed is constant, and the rotation of the cube is also fixed. If we want to improve on this solution, we're going to need a better way to deal with many variables.

A big part of programming is starting with something basic and then refining it later. You start with the things you know and add to it stuff you figure out. Once you learn more, you go back and make changes. It's a process that never ends. As programmers learn more and figure out more clever tricks, their new code gets written with more clever tricks.

6.2.2 Return

The return keyword is powerful and it's a very clever trick. It's used in a couple of different ways, but certainly the most useful is turning a function into data. If a function doesn't give out data, it's given the return type void. For instance, we've been using void Start() and void Update().

void indicates that the function doesn't need to return any data; using the keyword return in a function like this returns a void or a nothing. Any keywords that precede the return type modify how the function operates; for instance, if we wanted to make a function available to other classes, we need to precede the return type with the keyword public.

6.2.2.1 A Basic Example

Using the return keyword gives a function a value. You're allowed to use the function name as though it were the function's return value.

```
int ImANumber()
{
    return 3;
}
```

In the `Start()` function the following sends 3 to the console.

```
Debug.Log(ImANumber());
```

When you run this basic example, you'll see a 3 printed out in the Console panel. To prove that `ImANumber()` is just a 3, you can even perform math with the function. In the following example, you'll get many 6 s being printed out to the Console panel.

```
Debug.Log(ImANumber() + ImANumber());
```

Most often when we want to reduce complexity within a single function, we need to separate our code into other smaller functions. Doing so makes our work less cluttered and easier to manage. Once the code has been separated into different smaller functions, they become individual commands that can contain their own complexity.

We're going to reduce the number of lines required in the Update loop. To do this, we'll write our own function with a return type Vector3. Reducing the number of lines of code you have to muddle through is sometimes the goal of clean code.

`ImANumber()` isn't a variable; it's a function; more so, it's a function that returns a value. In other words, you will not be able to assign something to `ImANumber()` as in the following example:

```
ImANumber() = 7;
```

There are ways to do something like this. We'll need to use the contents in parentheses to assign `ImANumber()` a value for it to return.

6.2.3 Arguments aka "Args" (Not Related to Pirates)

We've seen the use of arguments (also known as args) earlier when we initialized a "Vector3 (x, y, z);" with three parameters. Review with a function that's very simple and takes one arg.

6.2.3.1 The Basic Example

This function takes a number and returns it.

```
int INeedANumber(int number)
{
    return number;
}
```

The function `int INeedANumber (int number)` is used in our `Start()` function. The argument field is populated with `int number`, indicating two things. First is the type that we expect to be in our function's argument list as well as a name or an identifier for the int argument. The identifier number from the argument list exists throughout the scope of the function.

```
Debug.Log(INeedANumber(1));
```

```
int val = INeedANumber(3) + INeedANumber(7);
Debug.Log(val);
```

In this second example, we use the INeedANumber() function as a number. It just so happens to be the same number we're using in its argument list. When we print out val from this, we get 10 printed to the Console panel. However, this doesn't have to be the case.

```
Debug.Log(INeedANumber(1));
```

```
int val = INeedANumber(3) + INeedANumber(7);
Debug.Log(val);
```

If we were to modify the return value to number +1 and run the previous example, we'd have 12 printed out to the Console panel. This would be the same as adding 4 and 8, or what is happening inside of the function 3 + 1 and 7 + 1.

6.2.3.2 Multiple Args

When you see functions without anything in parentheses, programmers say that the function takes no args. Or rather, the function doesn't need any arguments to do its work. We can expand upon this by adding another argument to our function. To tell C# what your two arguments are, you separate them with a comma and follow the same convention of type followed by identifier.

```
int INeedTwoNumbers(int a, int b)
{
    return a + b;
}
```

This is used in the Start() function which looks like the following:

```
Debug.Log(INeedTwoNumbers(7, 10));
```

The function takes two arguments, adds them together, and then prints out the result to the Unity 3D's Console panel. Just for the sake of clarity, you're allowed to use any variety of types for your args. The only condition is that the final result needs to match the same type as the return value. In more simple terms, when the function is declared, its return type is set by the keyword used when it's declared.

This also includes data types which you've written. We'll take a look at that in a bit, but for now we'll use some data types we've already seen.

```
int INeedTwoNumbersOfDifferentTypes(int a, float b)
{
    return a + (int)b;
}
```

Mixing different types together can create some interesting effects, some of which might not be expected. We'll study the consequences of mixing types later on as we start to learn about type casting, but for now just observe how this behaves on your own and take some notes. To convert a float value to an int value, you precede the float with the number type you want to convert it to with (ToType) DifferentType, but we'll get into type conversions again later.

So far we've been returning the same data types going into the function; this doesn't have to be the case. A function that returns a boolean value doesn't need to accept booleans in its argument list.

```
bool NumbersAreTheSame(int a, int b)
{
    bool returnValue;
    if (a == b)
    {
        returnValue = true;
    }
    else
    {
        returnValue = false;
    }
    return returnValue;
}
```

In this case, if both a and b are the same number, then the function returns true. If the two numbers are different, then the function returns false. This works well, but we can also shorten this code by a couple of lines if we use more than one return.

```
bool NumbersAreTheSameSimple(int a, int b)
{
    if (a == b)
    {
        return true;
    }
    else
    {
        return false;
    }
}
```

The return keyword can appear in more than one place. However, this can cause some problems. If we return a value based on only a limited case, then the compiler will catch this problem.

```
bool NumbersAreTheSameSimple(int a, int b)
{
    if (a == b)
    {
        return true;
    }
    // else
    // {
    //      return false;
    // }
}
```

This example will cause an error stating the following:

```
Assets/Example.cs(16,6): error CS0161: "Example. NumbersAreTheSame(int,
int)": not all code paths return a value
```

The most simple form of the above returns on a single line.

```csharp
bool NumbersAreTheSameMostSimple(int a, int b)
{
    return a == b;
}
```

The rest of the possibilities need to have a return value. In terms of what Unity 3D expects, all paths of the code need to return a valid bool. The return value always needs to be fulfilled, otherwise the code will not compile.

6.2.3.3 Using Args

Doing these little changes repeatedly becomes troublesome, so they leave some things up to other people to change until they like the results. Each function in the Input class returns a unique value. We can observe these by looking at the results of Input.GetKey().

```csharp
Debug.Log(Input.GetKey(KeyCode.A));
```

Once you type in Input, a pop-up with the members of the Input class is shown. Among them is GetKey. Once you enter GetKey and add in the first parenthesis, another pop-up with a list of various inputs is shown. Choose the KeyCode.A. Many other input options are available, so feel free to experiment with them on your own.

To test this code out, run the game and watch the output in the Console panel. Hold down the "a" key on the keyboard and watch the false printout replaced with true when the key is down. Using the print() function to test things out one at a time is a simple way to check out what various functions do. Test out the various other keys found in the Input.GetKey() function.

```csharp
Vector3 Movement(float dist)
{
    Vector3 vector = Vector3.zero;
    if (Input.GetKey(KeyCode.A))
    {
        vector.x -= dist;
    }
    if (Input.GetKey(KeyCode.D))
    {
        vector.x += dist;
    }
    if (Input.GetKey(KeyCode.W))
    {
        vector.z += dist;
    }
    if (Input.GetKey(KeyCode.S))
    {
        vector.z -= dist;
    }
    return vector;
}
```

We should add an argument to the Movement() function. With this we'll add in a simple way to change a variable inside of the Movement() function and maintain the function's portability. Replace the 0.1f value with the name of the argument. This means that anything put into the function's argument list will be duplicated across each statement that uses it.

This means we need to pass in a parameter to the argument list in the Movement() function. We can test by entering a simple float, which is what the Movement() argument list expects.

```
transform.position += Movement(0.2f);
```

This means we're just reducing the number of places a number is being typed. We want to make this number easier to edit and something that can be modified in the editor.

public float Speed;

Add in a public float so that the Inspector panel can see it. Then add the variable to the Movement()'s parameter list.

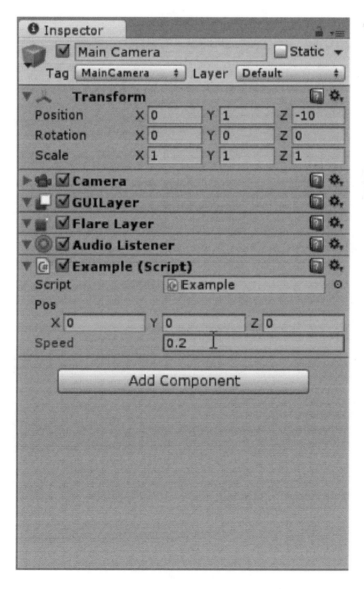

Change the value for Delta in the Inspector panel and run the game. Now the WASD keys will move the cube around at a different speed, thanks to the use of a public variable. There are a few different ways to do the same thing. For instance, we could have ignored using the arguments and used Delta in place of Dist. However, this means that the function would rely on a line of code outside of the function to work. Everywhere you want to use the function, you'd have to write in a public float Delta statement at the class level.

6.2.4 Assignment Operators

Operators that fill variables with data are called assignment operators. We've been using = to assign a variable a value in the previous chapters. There are different types of assignment operators that have added functionality.

```
void UpdateAssignmentOperators()
{
    transform.position += new Vector3(0.1f, 0, 0);
}
```

Introduce the += operator to the Vector3. When operators are used in pairs there are no spaces between them. The + operator adds two values together. The = operator assigns a value to a variable. If there was white space between the + and the =, this would raise a syntax error. The += operator allows you to add two vectors together without having to use the original variable name again. This also works with single numbers. An int MyInt += 1; works just as well. Rather than having to use position.z = position.z + 0.1f, you can use position.z += 0.1f, which is less typing. If you run the code up above, then you'll see your cube scooting off in the positive *x* direction.

6.2.4.1 A Basic Example

The example uses a function called in the Update() function in the ClassMembers script. As we have seen with the ++ and the -- unary operators, the += operator and its negative version, the -=, work in a similar way. One important and easy-to-forget difference is the fact that the ++ and -- works only on integer data types. The += and -= work on both integer and floating point data types.

```
float f = 0;
void UpdateAssignmentOperators()
{
    f += 0.25f;
    Debug.Log(f);
}
```

In this example, the f variable will be incremented 0.25f with each update call. In the code fragment above, this increase is something that cannot be done with an integer. This is like using f = f + 0.25f; though the += is a bit cleaner looking, or "less verbose" as a programmer might say. The change is primarily aesthetic, and programmers are a fussy bunch, so the += is the preferred method to increment values.

A part of learning how to program is by decoding the meaning behind cryptic operators, and this is just one example. We're sure to come across more mysterious operators, but if you take them in slowly and practice using them, you'll learn them quickly.

```
transform.position += Movement(Speed);
```

Rather than using a new Vector3 to add to the transform.position, we want to use a function. To make this work, the function has to have a Vector3 return type. For a function to return the type, we need to include the keyword return in the function.

```
void UpdateAssignmentOperators()
{
    transform.position += Offset();
}

Vector3 Offset()
{
    return new Vector3(0.1f, 0.2f, 0.3f);
}
```

This function is now a Vector3 value. Based on any external changes, the value returned can also change. This makes our function very flexible and much more practical. Again, the cube will scoot off to the *x* if you run this code. This and the previous examples are doing the exact same thing. Don't forget that C# is case sensitive, so make sure the vector is named the same throughout the function.

```
Vector3 vector = Vector3.zero;
if (Input.GetKey(KeyCode.A))
{
    vector.x -= dist;
}
if (Input.GetKey(KeyCode.D))
{
    vector.x += dist;
}
if (Input.GetKey(KeyCode.W))
{
    vector.z += dist;
}
if (Input.GetKey(KeyCode.S))
{
    vector.z -= dist;
}
return vector;
```

If += works to add a number to a value, then -= subtracts a value from the number. There are some more variations on this, but they're going to have to wait for Section 8.9.

The Movement() function is portable. If you copy the function into another class, you have made reusable code. As any programmer will tell you, you should always write reusable code. The function operates mostly on its own. It relies on very few lines of code outside of the function. There are no class scoped variables it's depending on, so you need to only copy the lines of code existing in the function.

This function is not completely without any external dependencies. The Input.GetKey function does rely on the UnityEngine library, but there are ways to reduce this even further. To figure out other ways to reduce complexity and dependencies, we need to learn more tricks.

Wherever you need to read input and return a Vector3 to move something, you can use this function. Copy and paste the function in any class, and then add the transform.position += Movement (); into the Update() function of that object, and it will move when you press the WASD keys.

6.2.5 What We've Learned

The earlier discussion was an introduction to arguments and return values. We started to learn a bit about how to use members of classes and how to find them. There's still a lot more to learn, but I think we have a pretty good start and enough of a foundation to build on by playing with things in the game engine.

It's time to start having functions talk to other functions, and to do this, we're going to start writing some more classes that can talk to one another. Accessing other classes is going to require some more interesting tricks, and with everything we learn, we expand the tools that we can build with.

6.3 Building a Game—Part 4

What the player sees while playing is an important part of how the game is played. Camera control is just as important as Player control. We created a simple input system to move and shoot for the player. Adding some basic camera behavior should follow.

6.3.1 ChaseCamera

If the goal is to simply have the camera follow the player we can do this with a simple script that uses the player's x and z coordinates and adds that to the camera. There are a few tricks that we need to look at to get something that works as we expect. To start we'll begin with a script that looks like the Mover script from Chapter 5.

```
public class ChaseCamera : MonoBehaviour
{
    private GameObject _Target;
    private GameObject Target...

    private void Update()
    {
        if (Target == null)
            return;
    }
}
```

A camera that follows the player should keep its relative position away from the Player. The difference between the target position between frames can be used to move the camera.

```
private Vector3 Offset;
private void Update()
{
    if (Target == null)
        return;
    // Calculate the difference between previous position
    // and the new position.
    Vector3 diff = Target.transform.position - Offset;
    // Move the camera that difference.
    transform.position += diff;
    // update the Offset value.
    Offset = Target.transform.position;
}
```

As the player moves and updates are called, we calculate that movement by maintaining a Vector3 Offset. As the Player object moves around the Target.transform.position changes. We track that difference as the player's position - Offset. Once calculated we add that to the camera's position. After the camera's position is updated, the Offset is updated with the current position of the Target.

6.3.2 Tile Floor Generator

So that was a simple example of a camera following system. But what about the environment? Running around on a plain white floor isn't exciting. A procedurally generated floor plane might be more interesting.

```
[ExecuteInEditMode]
public class FloorGenerator : MonoBehaviour
{
    // Trigger in the Inspector Panel to
    // generate tiles
    public bool GenerateTiles;
    // Original prefab objects to make
    // a tile floor from
    public GameObject[] TileOriginals;
    // a List of tiles to store if
    // we want to make new tiles
    public GameObject[,] TileObjects;
    // How many tiles to make
    public int Width;
    public int Depth;
    private List<GameObject> TileObjectList;
```

Various systems in the script can be updated in the Editor before the game begins. These are added with what is called an Attribute. The Attribute called [ExecuteInEditMode] can be added to a script to enable it's execution before the game has started. We'll cover this in more detail in Section 8.10. The short story is that this specific Attribute allows the Update() to be computed while we are setting up the Scene.

```
if (GenerateTiles)
{
    GenerateTiles = false;
```

To control how often we generate the tiles we use a bool `GenerateTiles`. This keeps the `Update()` from generating new tiles every frame. An array is used to keep a reference to a couple of prefabs that we'll use to generate the tile floor from. In this case we have a light and a dark tile. A `List<GameObject>` named `TileObjectList` is used to store the generated tiles. With this we can store the tiles that are generated. This is used to remember the generated tiles, so we can clear them before generating new ones. The list is used to iterate through all the generated tile objects.

```
//clear any tiles that might already be there
foreach (GameObject tile in TileObjectList)
{
    DestroyImmediate(tile);
}
TileObjectList = new List<GameObject>();
```

`Width` and `Depth` parameters are used to store the `TileObjects` in a 2D array. A simple system to alternate through the different tiles is used to pick which original tile to make an instance of.

```
TileObjects = new GameObject[Width, Depth];
for (int x = 0; x < Width; x++)
{
    for (int z = 0; z < Depth; z++)
    {
        int o = (z + x) % TileOriginals.Length;
        TileObjects[x, z] = GameObject.Instantiate(TileOriginals[o], transform);
        TileObjects[x, z].transform.position = new Vector3()
        {
            x = x - (Width / 2),
            z = z - (Depth / 2)
        };
        // keep track of what to delete when we
        // need to make a new set of tiles.
        TileObjectList.Add(TileObjects[x, z]);
    }
}
```

The value `int o = (z + x) % TileOriginals.Length;` will increment with each object. This then returns a value that's incremented up through each tile. The value is limited to the number of tiles in the originals list. The position of each tile instance is then positioned with x −(Width/2) and z − (Depth/2). This makes the tiles generated around the origin. Without this, the tiles begin at the origin but only expand in the positive quadrant away from the origin. As the tiles are created they're added to the List to easily delete them when the size is changed and a new set of tiles is created.

Once the tiles are generated, a list copies them to the `TileObjects` array so we can delete them before making a new set.

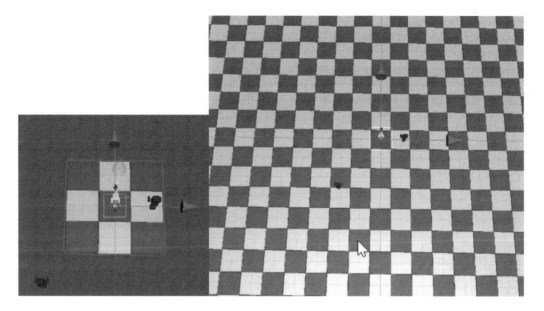

Now a small array or a large array of tiles can be generated. Change the `Width` and `Depth` parameters and click on the `GenerateTiles` bool check box to change the size of the grid.

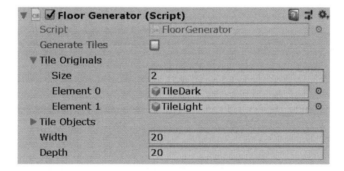

Using a script to generate results in the editing of a Scene is useful. When the generated data is saved in the scene it's not generated again unless the editor is run. Manually duplicating and placing tiles would be tedius. It's better to spend time coming up with new game play elements rather than placing tiles.

There are some considerations when it comes to using a system to generate tiles. The first is that we need to keep a list of things that were created. When a checkbox triggers the creation of many objects, we should delete the ones that are already in the scene.

6.3.3 What We've Learned

Plenty of new syntax was seen in this chapter. Your familiarity with how the keywords and variable types are created and used will catch up to what was just seen in the coming chapters. This project should serve as a starting point to dismantle and experiment with.

The code here is purposely written in small easily digested chunks. Each class has a clear and focused purpose. In practice, code should be written in small easily separated components. This makes editing and changing how each component works easier. Keep that in mind when you begin work on your own project.

6.4 Class Constructors

Follow along with the ClassConstructors script found in the ClassConstructors_Scene on the ClassConstructors object in the Chapter6 Unity 3D project. In the script is written the following example:

```
class Zombie
{
}
```

We start off with very little information. As we assign member fields and member functions, we create places for the class to store data and provide the class with capability.

```
class Zombie
{
    public string Name;
    public int BrainsEaten;
    public int HitPoints;
}
```

The use of these parameters is inferred by their name and use. When we create a new Zombie() in the game, we could spend the next few lines initializing his parameters. Of course, we can add as many parameters as needed, but for this example, we're going to limit ourselves to just a few different objects.

```
void Start()
{
    Zombie rob = new Zombie();
    rob.Name = "Zombie";
    rob.HitPoints = 10;
    rob.BrainsEaten = 0;
}
```

One simple method provided in C# is to add the parameters of the classes in a set of curly braces. Each field in Zombie is accessible through this method. Each one is separated by a comma, not a semicolon.

```
Zombie rob = new Zombie()
{
    Name = "Zombie",
    HitPoints = 10,
    BrainsEaten = 0
};
```

Note the trailing ";" after the closing curly brace. This system doesn't do much to shorten the amount of work involved. With each public data field provided in the Zombie class, we need to use the name of the field and assign it. Doing this for every new zombie might seem like a bit of extra work.

While building prototypes and quickly jamming code together, shortcuts like these can inform how we intend to use the class object. Rather than coming up with all possibilities and attempting to predict how a class is going to be used, it's usually better to use a class, try things out, and then make changes later.

6.4.1 A Basic Example

A class constructor would save a bit of extra work. You might have noticed that the statement `Zombie rob = new Zombie()` has a pair of parentheses after the class it's instancing. When a class `Zombie()` is instanced, we could provide additional information to this line. To enable this, we need to add in a constructor to the `Zombie()`'s class. This looks like the following:

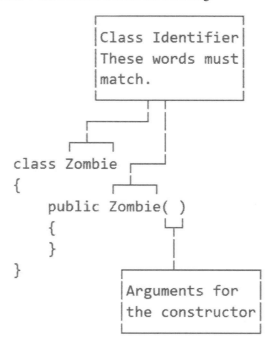

To give this example more meaning, we'll use the following code:

```
class Zombie
{
    public string Name;
    public int BrainsEaten;
    public int HitPoints;
    /*  ...
    public Zombie()
    {
        Name = "Zombie";
        BrainsEaten = 0;
        HitPoints = 10;
    }
}
```

After the data fields, we create a new function named after the class. This function is called a class constructor. The function public `Zombie()` contains assignment statements that do the same thing as the previous class instantiation code we were using.

```
Zombie rob = new Zombie();
```

This statement `Zombie rob = new Zombie();` invokes the `Zombie()` constructor function in the Zombie class. When the Constructor function is called, `Name`, `BrainsEaten`, and `HitPoints` are all assigned at the same time. However, this will assume that every zombie is named "Zombie," has eaten no brains, and has 10 `HitPoints`. This is not likely the case with all zombies. Therefore, we'd want to provide some parameters to the class constructor function.

```
public Zombie(string name, int hitPoints)
{
    Name = name;
    BrainsEaten = 0;
    HitPoints = hitPoints;
}
```

By adding in a few parameters to the interface, we're allowed to take in some data as the class is instanced.

```
Zombie rob = new Zombie("Rob", 10);
```

When we create a new zombie, we're allowed to name it and assign its hit points at the same time without needing to remember the identifiers of the data fields of the classes. When the constructor is invoked, the first field corresponds to a `string name`, which is then assigned to `Name` with the `Name = name;` statement.

Assume a new zombie has not had a chance to eat any brains just yet, so we can assign it to 0 when it's instanced. Finally, we can use the second argument `int hitPoints` and use that to assign to the instance's `HitPoints` with the `HitPoints = hitPoints;` statement in the constructor.

Class constructors allow us to instantiate classes with unique data every time a new class is instanced. Putting this into use involves a few extra steps.

```
float height;
GameObject gameObject;
public Zombie(string name, int hitPoints, Vector3 startPosition)
{
    Name = name;
    BrainsEaten = 0;
    HitPoints = hitPoints;

    // find the zombie from the Resources folder.
    gameObject = Resources.Load("ZombiePrimitive") as GameObject;
    // add the resource to the scene.
    Instantiate(gameObject);

    gameObject.name = Name;
    gameObject.transform.position = startPosition;
    height = Random.Range(1f, 3f);
    gameObject.transform.localScale = new Vector3()
    {
        x = 1,
        y = height, // give him a random height
        z = 1
    };
}
```

By adding a mesh to each zombie, we can more directly observe the instantiation of a new zombie in a scene. To make this more clear, we create a vector with a random *x* and a random *z* position so that they can appear in different places.

```
string[] names = new string[] { "Stubbs", "Rob", "White" };
for (int i = 0; i < names.Length; i++)
{
    Vector3 startPosition = new Vector3(i, 0, 0);
    Zombie z = new Zombie(names[i], Random.Range(5, 10), startPosition);
}
```

To make use of the different parameters, we create a new list of zombie names. Then in a for loop, we create a new zombie for each name in the list. For good measure, we assign a random number of hit points for each one with `Random.Range(10,  15)` which assigns a random number to each zombie between 10 and 15.

6.4.2 What We've Learned

A class constructor is very useful and should almost always be created when you create a new class. We are also allowed to create multiple systems to use a constructor. We'll get around to covering that in Section 6.13.1 on function overrides, but we'll have to leave off here for now.

When building a class, it's important to think in terms of what might change between each object. This turns into options that can be built into the constructor. Giving each object the ability to be created with different options allows for more variations in game play and appearance. Setting initial colors, behaviors, and starting variables is easier with a constructor. The alternative would be to create the new object and then change its values after the object is already in the scene.

6.5 Arrays Revisited

By now, we're familiar with the bits of knowledge that we'll need to start writing code. In Chapter 7, we'll become more familiar with the integrated development environment known as Visual Studio, and we'll go deeper into variables and functions.

Let's start off with a task. Programmers usually need something specific to do, so to stretch our knowledge and to force ourselves to learn more, we're going to do something simple that requires some new tricks to accomplish. If we're going to make a game with a bunch of characters, we're going to make and keep track of many different bits of information such as location, size, and type.

6.5.1 Using Arrays in Unity 3D

To follow along open the Chapter 6 Unity Project and open the ArraysRevisited_Scene and open the ArraysRevisited script attached to the game object of the same name.

So far, we've dealt with variables that hold a single value. For instance, int i = 0; in which the variable i holds only a single value. This works out fine when dealing with one thing at a time. However, if we want a whole number of objects to work together, we're going to have them grouped together in memory.

If we needed to, we could have a single variable for each box GameObject that would look like the following:

```
public GameObject box1;
public GameObject box2;
public GameObject box3;
public GameObject box4;
public GameObject box5;
public GameObject box6;
public GameObject box7;
public GameObject box8;
public GameObject box9;
public GameObject box10;
```

While this does work, this will give a programmer a headache in about 3 seconds, not to mention if you want to do something to one box, you'd have to repeat your code for every other box. This is horrible, and programming is supposed to make things easier, not harder on you. This is where arrays come to the rescue.

```
public GameObject[] boxes;
```

Ah yes, much better, 10 lines turn into one. There's one very important difference here. There's a pair of square brackets after the GameObject to indicate that we're making an array of game objects. Square brackets are used to tell a variable that we're making the singular form of a variable into a plural form of the variable. This works the same for any other type of data.

```
//a single int
int MyInt;
// an array of ints
int[] MyInts;
// a single object
object MyObject;
//an array of objects
object[] MyObjects;
```

To tell the boxes variable how many it's going to be holding, we need to initialize the array with its size before we start stuffing it full of data. This will look a bit like the Vector 3 we initialized in Section 3.10.2. We have a couple of options. We can right out tell the boxes how many it's going to be holding.

```
public GameObject[] TenGameObjects = new GameObject[10];
```

Or we can initialize the number of boxes using the Start() function and a public int variable.

```
public int numBoxes = 10;
public GameObject[] SomeBoxes;
private void Start()
{
    SomeBoxes = new GameObject[numBoxes];
}
```

In the above code, we're going to add a numBoxes variable and then move the initialization of the boxes variable to the Start() function using the numBoxes to satisfy the array size. In the Unity Inspector panel you'll see a field "Num Boxes" appear rather than numBoxes. Unity automatically changes variable names to be more human readable, but it's the same variable.

In the editor, we can pick any number of boxes we need without needing to change any code. Game designers like this sort of stuff. Once you run the game, the boxes array is initialized. To see what is contained in the array, you can expand the boxes variable in the Inspector panel and get the following:

▼ ⓖ ☑ **Example (Script)**	🗀 ⚙,
Script	ⓖ Example ⊙
▼ Boxes	
Size	10
Element 0	None (Game Object) ⊙
Element 1	None (Game Object) ⊙
Element 2	None (Game Object) ⊙
Element 3	None (Game Object) ⊙
Element 4	None (Game Object) ⊙
Element 5	None (Game Object) ⊙
Element 6	None (Game Object) ⊙
Element 7	None (Game Object) ⊙
Element 8	None (Game Object) ⊙
Element 9	None (Game Object) ⊙
Num Boxes	10

We've got an array filled with a great deal of nothing, sure. However, it's the right number of nothing. Since we haven't put anything into the array of GameObjects we shouldn't be surprised. So far everything is going as planned. Testing as we write is important. With nearly every statement we write, we should confirm that it's doing what we think it should be doing. Next, we should put a new cube primitive into each one of the parts of this array.

6.5.1.1 Starting with 0

Zeroth. Some older programming languages start with 1. This is a carryover from FORTRAN that was created in 1957. Some programming languages mimic this behavior. Lua, for example, is a more modern programming language that starts with 1. C# is not like these older languages. Here we start with 0 and then count to 1; we do not start at 1. Thus, an array of 10 items is numbered 0 through 9.

Now we have an empty array, and we know how many things need to be in it. This is perfect for using a for loop. Numbering in C# may seem a bit strange, but a part of numbering in programming is the fact that 0 is usually the first number when counting.

We get accustomed to counting starting at 1, but in many programming paradigms, counting starts with the first number, 0. You might just consider the fact that 0 was there before you even started counting. Therefore, the first item in the boxes array is the 0th or *zeroth* item, not the first. It's important to notice that when dealing with arrays, you use square brackets.

```
SomeBoxes = new GameObject[numBoxes];
for (int i = 0; i < numBoxes; i++)
{
}
```

Right after we initialize the boxes array, we should write the for loop. Then we'll create a new box game object and assign it to the boxes.

```
SomeBoxes = new GameObject[numBoxes];
for (int i = 0; i < numBoxes; i++)
{
    GameObject box = GameObject.CreatePrimitive(PrimitiveType.Cube);
    SomeBoxes[i] = box;
}
```

Notice the notation being used for boxes. The SomeBoxes[i] indicates the slot in the array we're assigning the box we just made. When the i = 0, we're putting a box into SomeBoxes[0]; when i = 1, we're assigning the box to SomeBoxes[1] and so on.

Items in the array are accessed by using an int value in the square brackets. To check that we're doing everything right, let's run the code and check if the array is populated with a bunch of cube primitives just as we asked. Therefore, if you want to get some information on the fourth cube, you should use SomeBoxes[3]; again the 0th, pronounced "zeroth," item makes it easy to forget the index in the array we're referring to.

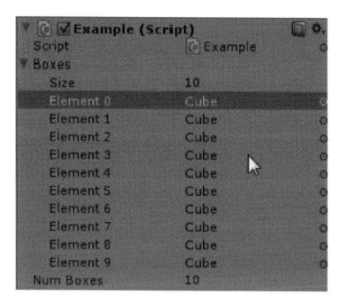

So far this is promising. We created an array called boxes with 10 items. Then we wrote a for loop that creates a box on every iteration and then adds that box into a numbered slot in the boxes array. This is working well. Arrays lend themselves very well for iterating through.

We need to match the variable type with the type that's inside of the array. Because the array boxes[] is filled with type GameObject, we need to use GameObject on the left of the in keyword. To the right of the in keyword is the array we're going to iterate through.

We're accessing all of the array, not just a single item in it, so we don't need to use something like foreach(GameObject g in boxes[0]) which would infer that at index 0 of boxes, there's an array for us to iterate through. Though arrays of arrays are possible, it's not our goal here.

Iterating through arrays with the foreach doesn't give us the benefit of a counter like in the for loop, so we need to do the same thing as if we were using a while loop or a heavily rearranged for loop by setting up a counter ahead of time.

Let's check our Console panel in the editor to make sure that this is working. It looks like the loop is repeating like one would expect. At the beginning of the Update() function, int i is set to 0; then while the foreach loop is iterating, it's incrementing the value up by 1 until each item in boxes has been iterated through.

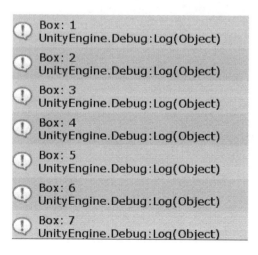

Put the i to some use within the foreach() loop statement by multiplying the x of the vector by i * 1.0f to move each cube to a different x location. Note that multiplying any number against 1 is all that interesting, but this is just a simple part of this demonstration. Again, check in the editor to make sure that each cube is getting put in a different x location by running the game.

```
int i = 0;
foreach (GameObject go in SomeBoxes)
{
    go.transform.position = new Vector3(i * 1.0f, 0, 0);
    i++;
    Debug.Log("Box: " + i);
}
```

So far everything should be working well. You can change the offset by changing the value that the i is being multiplied by. Or, better yet, we should create a public variable to multiply the i variable by.

```
public float Spacing;
```

If you create a new public float spacing in the class scope, you can use it in your foreach loop.

```
go.transform.position = new Vector3(i * Spacing, 0, 0);
```

By adding this here, you can now edit spacing and watch the cubes spread apart in real time. This is starting to get more interesting! Next let's play with some math, or more specifically Mathf.

6.5.1.2 Mathf

The Mathf class is filled with many commonly used math helpers. Mathf contains many functions such as abs for absolute value, and Sin and Cos for sine and cosine. To start with, we're going to create a float called wave and we'll assign that to Mathf.Sin(i); which produces a sine wave when we put wave in place of y in the Vector3.

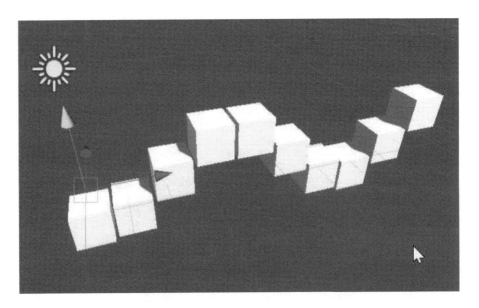

To make this animated, we can use another useful trick from the `Time` class. Let's take a moment to thank all the busy programmers who know how to implement the math functions we're using here. There's more to these functions than just knowing the mathematics behind the simple concept of something like `Sin`. There's also a great deal of optimization that went into making the function work. This sort of optimization comes only from years of computer science experience and lots of know-how and practice. The mechanics behind this stuff is far beyond the scope of this book, so we'll just take advantage of their knowledge by using `Mathf`.

```
int i = 0;
foreach (GameObject go in SomeBoxes)
{
    float wave = Mathf.Sin(Time.fixedTime + i);
    go.transform.position = new Vector3(i * Spacing, wave, 0);
    i++;
}
```

6.5.1.3 Time

`Time.fixedTime` is a clock that starts running at the beginning of the game. All it's doing is counting up. Check what it's doing by printing it out using `Debug.Log(Time.fixedTime);` and you'll just see a timer counting seconds. The seconds will be the same for all of the cubes, but by adding int `i` to each cube's version of wave, each one will have a different value for the wave.

We could have had a public double `1.0` and incremented this with a small value, 0.01, for instance. This will have a similar effect to Time.fixedTime. The difference here is that `fixedTime` is tied to the computer's clock. Any slowdowns or frame rate issues will result in your Sin function slowing down as well.

What you should have is a slowly undulating row of cubes. This is also a pretty cool example of some basic math principles in action. We could continue to add more and more behaviors to each cube in the array using this method of extending the foreach statement, but this will only get us so far.

Once we want each cube to have its own individual sets of logic to control itself, it's time to start a new class. With the new class, it's important that we can communicate with it properly. Eventually, these other cubes will end up being zombies attacking the player, so we're on the right track.

6.5.2 Instancing with `AddComponent();`

The project contains a script named `Monster` which is added to the array using the `AddComponent()` function found in the `GameObject` class. The `GameObject` is a class written to handle everything related to how Unity 3D manages characters, items, and environments in a scene. Should you leave this comfortable game development tool and move on to some other application development, you will have to most likely use a different function to perform a similar task.

When you have a `GameObject` selected in the game editor, you have an option to add component near the bottom of the Inspector panel. We used this to add the ArraysRevisited script to our first cube. This should lead you to thinking that you can also add component with code. Looking into `GameObject`, you can find an `AddComponent()` function with a few different options.

```
MonsterBoxes = new GameObject[numBoxes];
for (int i = 0; i < numBoxes; i++)
{
    GameObject box = GameObject.CreatePrimitive(PrimitiveType.Cube);
    box.AddComponent(typeof(Monster));
    MonsterBoxes[i] = box;
}
```

You can use box.AddComponent(typeof(Monster)); to tell the box to add in the script of the same name. If there wasn't a Monster script you get an error but Visual Studio can fix the problem by generating a class.

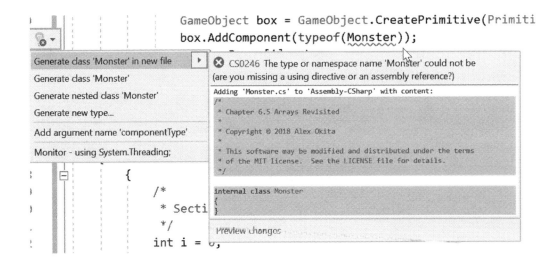

After generating a class add using UnityEngine and : MonoBehaviour; change internal to public and you've converted the generic class to a Unity 3D component for use in the scene.

```
using UnityEngine;
public class Monster : MonoBehaviour
{

}
```

To prove that the script is behaving correctly, add in a print function to the Start() function of the Monster.cs file.

```
void Start()
{
    Debug.Log("Im Alive!");
}
```

When the game starts, the ArraysRevisited.cs will create a bunch of new instances of the Monster.cs attached to each cube. When the script is instanced, ArraysRevisited executes the Start() function. The Console should reflect the fact that the Start() function was called when the Monster script was instanced.

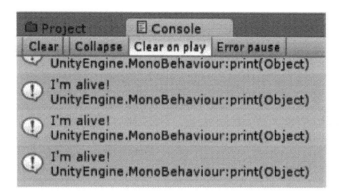

This reduces the amount of work a single script needs to do. Each object should manage its own movement. To do this, each object will need its own script. In the Monster.cs file, we need to replicate some of the variables that we created in the ArraysRevisited.cs file.

```
public int ID;
public float Spacing = 1.1f;
```

Remember that we need to make these public, otherwise another script cannot find them. MonoDevelop is already aware of these variables.

After the box is created, we need to add in the "Monster" class to it. However, that's just half of the task necessary to get our script up and running. We added an ID and a spacing value to Monster.cs, but we have yet to initialize them. We need to get a connection to the component we just added to the box object. To do this, we need to use GetComponent(), but there's a bit more than just that.

6.5.3 Type Casting Unity 3D Objects

GetComponent() returns a component type, but it's unaware of the specific type we're looking for. We use some type casting to convert one type to another. Remember from before, we can turn an int 1 to a float 1.0f through type casting.

When type casting between objects or reference types, things get tricky. A component is about as general as Unity 3D will get. However, we want a type Monster when we get that component back. Therefore, we need to say, "I want this component from the box as a type monster." To do this, C# has the keyword as for some basic type casting.

```
MonsterBoxes = new GameObject[numBoxes];
for (int i = 0; i < numBoxes; i++)
{
    GameObject box = GameObject.CreatePrimitive(PrimitiveType.Cube);
    box.AddComponent(typeof(Monster));
    Monster m = box.GetComponent(typeof(Monster)) as Monster;
    MonsterBoxes[i] = box;
}
```

After adding the component, we need to get access to it. Therefore, we create a Monster variable named m. Then we use the GetComponent(); function to get a type of Monster, and we ask that we get it as a type Monster by adding as Monster after we ask for it.

This cast is necessary because GetComponent() doesn't necessarily know what it's getting; other than it's some component type, you have to tell it what it's getting. Monster and typeof Monster appear in different places. This is the difference between the word "Monster" and the actual class object called Monster. The object is what is used after the as keyword because we're referring to the type, not what it's called. This might be a little bit confusing, but GetComponent() is expecting a type and not an object for an argument.

When you enter the m., a dialog box pops up in Visual Studio. This is a handy helper that shows you all members in the object. This also shows you any of the public variables you may have added to the class. Now that we have a connection to the Monster script that's attached to the box, we can set a couple of parameters.

```
Monster m = box.GetComponent(typeof(Monster)) as Monster;
m.ID = i;
```

We use the dot notation to access the members of the Monster class found in m. Therefore, m.ID is i that increments with each new box made. Then the spacing will be the spacing we set in the Example. cs file.

```
13      // Update is called once per frame
14      void Update () {
15          float wave = Mathf.Sin( Time.fixedTime + ID);
16          transform.position = new Vector3(ID * spacing, wave, 0.0f);
17      }
```

Add a very similar line of code to the Update() in the Monster.cs file and then remove it from the Update() in the ArraysRevisited.cs file. The spacing was only set once when the object was created, which you can't update it by sliding on the ArraysRevisited.cs file. However, each object is acting on its own, running its own script.

There are a few different ways to use GetComponent(), but we'll look at those in Section 6.14 when we need to do more type casting. Not all casting operations work the same. We're going to change a few other things we're doing to make the movement behavior more interesting as well, but we will need to learn a few more tricks before we get to that.

Alternatively, we can assign and get the `Monster` m variable at the same time with the following notation:

```
Monster m = box.AddComponent(typeof(Monster)) as Monster;
```

This automatically assigns m as it's assigned to the box component. The component assignment and the variable assignment save a step.

6.5.4 What We've Learned

This was a pretty heavy chapter. The new array type was used to store a bunch of game objects, but it could have easily been used to store a bunch of numbers, or anything for that matter. We learned about a foreach loop that is handy for dealing with arrays.

In this chapter, we also made use of some math and found a nice timer function in the `Time` class. Afterthat, we figured out how to attach script components through code, and then we were able to gain access to that component by `GetComponent()` and a type cast to make sure it wasn't just a generic component.

There are still a few different data types we need to study. Now that we're dealing with so many types, we're going to learn more about type casting as well.

6.6 Enums

Start with the Chapter6 Unity Project's Enum_Scene and open the Enum script on the object of the same name. We've got two classes, an Example.cs and a Monster.cs, we've got the Example.cs creating and assigning objects, effectively spawning a Monster. We could take the older version of the Example.cs we wrote and turn it into Player.cs, which would give us a total of three objects.

```csharp
public class Player : MonoBehaviour
{
    public float Speed = 1;

    // Update is called once per frame
    void Update()
    {
        gameObject.transform.position += Movement(Speed);
    }

    Vector3 Movement(float dist)
    {
        Vector3 vec = Vector3.zero;
        if (Input.GetKey(KeyCode.A))
        {
            vec.x -= dist;
        }
        if (Input.GetKey(KeyCode.D))
        {
            vec.x += dist;
        }
        if (Input.GetKey(KeyCode.W))
        {
            vec.z += dist;
        }
        if (Input.GetKey(KeyCode.S))
        {
            vec.z -= dist;
        }
        return vec;
    }
}
```

Therefore, here's the Player.cs I'm using for this chapter; we're going to use this to move the little box around in the scene. We'll pretend that the box is a pretty cool-looking monster hunter armed with a sword, shotgun, or double-barreled shotgun.

We may want to rename the Example.cs to something like MonsterSpawner.cs or MonsterGenerator.cs, but I'll leave that up to you. Just remember to rename the class declaration to match the file name. This will spill out monsters to chase the player around. Then the Monster.cs attached to each of the objects that the MonsterSpawner creates will then seek out the player and chase him around. At least that's the plan.

NOTE: Prototyping game play using primitive shapes is a regular part of game development. This is somewhat related to what has become to be known as "programmer art." Changes to code often mean changes to art. It's difficult to build a game keeping art and code parallel. Often a simple change in code means days of changes to art. It's quite often easier to prototype a game making no requests of an artist. Most of the time, the programmer doesn't even know himself what to ask of an artist.

6.6.1 Using Enums

The keyword "enum" is short for enumeration. A programmer might say that an enum is a list of named constants. The meaning may seem obtuse. Translated, an enumeration is a list of words that you pick. For our Monster to have a better set of functions for its behavior, we're going to create a new enum type called MonsterState.

We've already interacted with the PrimitiveType enum.

```
namespace UnityEngine
{
        public enum PrimitiveType
        {
                Sphere = 0,
                Capsule = 1,
                Cylinder = 2,
                Cube = 3,
                Plane = 4,
                Quad = 5
        }
}
```

An enum replaces an ambiguous value with a human readable value. You technically don't need to use an enum to compare values to control logical statements.

```
enum YesOrNo
{
    yes,
    no
};
YesOrNo yesOrNoEnum;
```

An enum with two values is not necessarily more clear than `bool yesNoBool` since both only have two values. In practice you'd look at something like

```
if (yesOrNoEnum == YesOrNo.yes)
{
    Debug.Log("yes");
}

bool yesOrNoBool = true;
if (yesOrNoBool == true)
{
    Debug.Log("yes");
}
```

And if you saw `if(primitiveInt == 0){Debug.Log("Sphere");}` you'd be able to react in a similar way only using integer values, but you'd have to remember what each value was supposed to represent. This ends up being prone to error if you thought `primitiveInt == 2` might be Capsule.

```
int primitiveInt = 0;
/* 0 = Sphere,    *
 * 1 = Capsule,   *
 * 2 = Cylinder,  *
 * 3 = Cube,      *
 * 4 = Plane,     *
 * 5 = Quad       */

if (primitiveInt == 0)
{
    Debug.Log("Sphere");
}
```

Conversely an enum with many hundreds of values is also not necessarily clearer than something more usable like a string as a name. Though we have seen that enums can store many different names. For instance, the InputType enum had a different enumeration for every key on the keyboard and each input for your mouse or trackpad and controller.

Enumerating through a long list of defined objects is to help name every possibility with something more useful than a simple numeric index. It's important to remember that enumerations don't need to follow any pattern. It's up to you to decide on any organization to keep your enums organized.

At the top of the Enums class there's a `public PrimitiveType MyPrimitiveType;`

```
public PrimitiveType MyPrimitiveType;
/* Right Click on PrimitiveType to go to the    *
 * definition and see what the enum looks like. */
```

In the editor, you'll see the availability of a new pop-up of the different PrimitiveTypes. In the `Start()` function, we use the CreatePrimitive member function in GameObject to create a new object of the selected type.

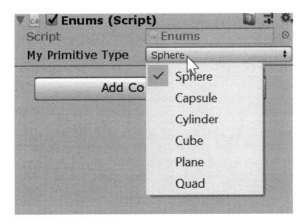

We can extend this more to get a better feel of how enums work for us by creating our own enums. A new enum is a new type of data. New data types are easy to create, especially for enums.

```
public enum MyColors
{
    red,
    blue,
    green
};
```

In this case, we use the `public` keyword followed by `enum` to tell the compiler we're creating a new enum which can be made accessible to other classes. We follow the declaration with a name. In this case, `MyColors` is the name of our new enum. Following the name of the enum, we need to start a new code block with any number of words separated by commas. Just don't add a comma after the last word in the list.

```
/* also valid                                   *
 * public enum MyColors {red, blue, green };   */
public MyColors MyColor;
```

To be clear, declaring an enum doesn't require the line breaks between each word. White space has no effect on how an enum, or practically any variable for that matter, is declared. After the new data type is created, we need to create a variable that uses that data type.

A `public MyColors` with the name `MyColor` follows the declaration of the enum. In the editor, we'll be able to pick the enum we want from our new list of words we added to the enum `MyColors`.

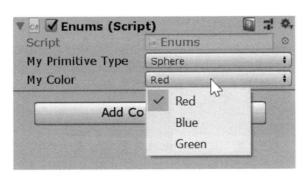

To make use of the enum, we can use several different methods. The system we might already be familiar with is using a bunch of different if statements.

```
gameObject = GameObject.CreatePrimitive(MyPrimitiveType);
MeshRenderer meshRenderer = gameObject.GetComponent(typeof(MeshRenderer)) as MeshRenderer;
Material material = meshRenderer.material;
if (MyColor == MyColors.red)
{
    material.color = Color.red;
}
if (MyColor == MyColors.blue)
{
    material.color = Color.blue;
}
if (MyColor == MyColors.green)
{
    material.color = Color.green;
}
```

This setup is clumsy; after the object is created, we check for what word `MyColor` is set to. Compare it against the MyColors's options and act when you've got a match. A slightly cleaner solution is to use a `switch()` statement.

Just as a note, if you look at the scene and all you see is a black sphere, you might need to add in a directional light. Without any lights, every object in the scene will appear dark since there's no light to illuminate them. You can add in a light by selecting GameObject → Create Other → Directional Light. This will drop in a light that will lighten up any objects in your scene.

6.6.2 Combining What We've Learned

We've been using `PrimitiveType.Cube` to generate our example monsters. We could just as easily change that to a sphere or anything else in the PrimitiveType enum. As we've seen, the PrimitiveType has some words that reflect what type of Primitive we can choose from. Likewise, we're going to make a list of states for the monster to pick.

```
public enum MonsterStates
{
    standing,
    wandering,
    chasing,
    attacking
}
public MonsterStates MonsterState;
```

Enums are declared at the class scope level of visibility. `MonsterState` is now another new data type. When setting up enum names, it's really important to come up with a convention that's easy to remember.

If you make both the enum MonsterState and mState public, you'll be able to pick the state using a menu in the Unity's Inspector panel. You should consider using enums for setting various things such as weapon pickup types or selecting types of traps.

Then, just as we define any other variable, we declare a variable type and give type a name. This is done with the line `MonsterState mState;` which gives us mState to use throughout the rest of the `Monster` class. mState is a variable with type MonsterState. In some instances, we may need to ignore what was set in the editor. To set an enum in code rather than a pop-up, we can use the following code. To use the mState, we need to set it when the Monster.cs is started.

```
void Start()
{
    Debug.Log("Im Alive!");
    MonsterState = MonsterStates.standing;
}
```

mState is set to `MonsterStates.standing;` this allows us to use mState in the `Update()` function to determine what actions we should take. Like before, we could use a series of `if` statements to pick the actions we could take. For instance, we could execute the following code:

```
if (MonsterState == MonsterStates.standing)
{
    Debug.Log("Standing monster is standing...");
}
if (MonsterState == MonsterStates.wandering)
{
    Debug.Log("Wandering monster is wandering...");
}
if (MonsterState == MonsterStates.chasing)
{
    Debug.Log("Chasing monster is chasing...");
}
if (MonsterState == MonsterStates.attacking)
{
    Debug.Log("Attacking monster is attacking...");
}
```

This will work just fine, but it's rather messy. If we add more enums to the MonsterState, we will need more `if` statements. However, there's an easier way to deal with an enum, so it's time to learn a new trick.

6.6.3 What We've Learned

So far enums have been made to make a list of options. Normally, enumerations are limited to a single option, but this doesn't always have to be the case. Enums are capable of multiple options, which has been discussed throughout this section.

Using an enum means to take action based on a selection. An enum is actually based on a number. You can cast from an enum to an `int` and get a usable value. When this is done, the first name in an enum is 0 and anything following is an increment up in value based on its position in the list of enumerations.

Therefore, based on the following code, the logged value is 3 since the first state is 0 and the fourth state is 3.

```
int number = (int)MonsterState;
Debug.Log(number);
```

There are other ways in which the enum can be manipulated, but to understand how and why this works, we'll want to cover a few other topics before getting to that.

6.7 Switch

To follow along open the Switch_Scene and begin with the Switch script attached to the switch game object. The switch comes into play often once we have reached more than one condition at a time. For instance, we could come across a situation where we are looking at a lengthy ladder of `if-else` statements.

```
public int intValue;
void IfElseLadder()
{
    if (intValue == 0)
    {
        Debug.Log("int is Zero");
    }
    else if (intValue == 1)
    {
        Debug.Log("int is One");
    }
    else if (intValue == 2)
    {
        Debug.Log("int is Two");
    }
    else if (intValue == 3)
    {
        Debug.Log("int is Three");
    }
    else if (intValue == 4)
    {
        Debug.Log("int is Four");
    }
    else
    {
        Debug.Log("int is greater than 4 or less than 0");
    }
}
```

There should be something awkward about this block of code. There is in fact a system in place called a switch statement that was made to alleviate the awkwardness of this long chain of if-else statements. The switch starts with the keyword switch followed by a parameter () that controls a block of code encapsulated by a pair of curly braces {}.

```
void SwitchStructure()
{
    switch (someVariable)
    {
    }
}
```

The contents of the switch statement use the keyword case. Each case is fulfilled by an expected option that matches the argument in the switch parameter.

6.7.1 A Basic Example

A switch can be used with any number of types in the parameter. The awkward if-else ladder we saw just before can be replaced with a much more simple switch() statement.

```
void SwitchStatement()
{
    switch (intValue)
    {
        case 0:
            Debug.Log("int is Zero");
            break;
        case 1:
            Debug.Log("int is One");
            break;
        case 2:
            Debug.Log("int is Two");
            break;
        case 3:
            Debug.Log("int is Three");
            break;
        case 4:
            Debug.Log("int is Four");
            break;
        default:
            Debug.Log("int is greater than 4 or less than 0");
            break;
    }
}
```

This is a basic switch with a case. The case is followed by 1 or 2 ending with a colon. Before another case, there's a couple of statements, with the last statement being break; that ends the case: statement. The first case 1: is executed because i == 1; or in more plain English, i *is* 1 that fulfills the condition to execute the code following the case. The break; following the statements jumps the computer out of the switch statement and stops any further execution from happening inside of the switch statement.

```
switch (intValue)
{
    case 0: Debug.Log("int is Zero"); break;
    case 1: Debug.Log("int is One"); break;
}
```

When you deal with short case statements, it's sometimes easier to remove the extra white space and use something a bit more compact. Each case is called a *label*; we can use labels outside of a switch statement, but we will have to find out more about that in Section 6.7.5.

The switch statement is a much better way to manage a set of different situations. Upon looking at the switch statement for the first time, it might be a bit confusing. There are a few new things going on here. The general case of the switch is basically taking in a variable, pretty much of any type of POD (Plain Old Data). The code then picks the case statement to start. The main condition is that all of the cases must use the type that is used in the switch() argument. For instance, if the switch statement sees an enum argument, you can't use a case where the enum is compared to an int.

The advantage of switch may not be obvious when looking at the block of code that was written here. The important reason why switch is useful is speed. To step through many different if statements, the contents of each argument needs to be computed.

Having a dozen "if" statements means that each one needs to be tested even though the contents of the statement are to be skipped. When using a switch, the statement needs to have only one test before evaluating the contents of the case.

The switch statement can use a few different data types, specifically integral types. Integral types, or data that can be converted into an integer, include booleans or bools, chars, strings, and enums. In a simple boolean example, we can use the following:

```
bool someBool = true;
switch (someBool)
{
    case true: Debug.Log("true"); break;
    case false: Debug.Log("false"); break;
}
```

With integers where int i = 1; switch(i) {} is used to pick the case which will be used. Using integers allows for a long list of cases when using a switch statement.

With a switch statement, if the argument matches the case then code is executed until break; jumps out of the switch. Each appearance of the keyword case is called a case label. Cases are built by using the keyword case followed by the value we are looking for from the variable used in the switch. After the case label is declared, any number of statements can be added. The code following the colon after the case statement is evaluated until the break; statement that stops the switch. The break statement must appear before another case label is added.

6.7.2 Default

What if there's a case that's not included in the switch statement? It would be difficult to cover every case for an integer. You'd have to write a case for every and any number. That's where the default: case comes in. When dealing with any of the switch statements, a default condition can be added when a case appears that isn't handled.

```
int i = 3;
switch (i)
{
    case 0:
        Debug.Log("i is Zero");
        break;
    case 1:
        Debug.Log("i is One");
        break;
    case 2:
        Debug.Log("i is Two");
        break;
    default:
        Debug.Log("Every other number");
        break;
}
```

With the default added, any conditions that aren't taken care of can be handled. If the default isn't added, then any unhandled case will be ignored and the switch will skip any code from any of the cases. The default case is an optional condition when working with the switch statement.

```
public enum Cases
{
    First,
    Second,
    Third,
    Fourth,
    Fifth,
    Sixth,
    Seventh
}
public Cases MyCase;
```

Of course, a switch statement seems to be most at home when in use with an enum. A slightly different variation on the appearance of the enum itself is that we need to use the dot operator to compare the incoming value against one of the enum values.

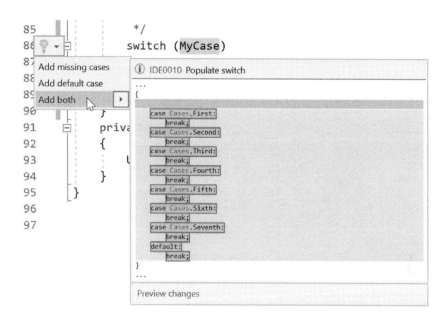

Here we have an elaborate array of cases, each one falling in order based on the enum values for Cases. Writing all of the cases might feel tedius, so Visual Studio has some short cuts for you. Highlight the `MyCase` in the switch statement and click on the lightbulb waiting in the left margin. From here you can select adding just the missing cases, a default case or both.

```
switch (MyCase)
{
    case Cases.First:
        break;
    case Cases.Second:
        break;
    case Cases.Third:
        break;
    case Cases.Fourth:
        break;
    case Cases.Fifth:
        break;
    case Cases.Sixth:
        break;
    case Cases.Seventh:
        break;
    default:
        break;
}
```

Select the "Add both" option from the popup to fill in the switch case cases with all possible case labels for the enum automatically. From here it's just a matter of filling in what happens in each case. Inside of the Unity 3D Editor, the C# class provides a useful roll-out in the Inspector panel when assigned to a GameObject.

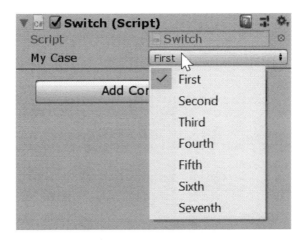

This conveniently gives us the opportunity to pick an enum and watch the Debug.Log() send different strings to the Console panel. It's important that you note what variable is being used in the switch statement's argument. It's often mistaken to use switch(Cases) with the type in the argument. This of course doesn't work as expected. Here we get the following error:

Assets/SwitchStatements.cs(21,25): error CS0119: Expression denotes a "type," where a "variable," "value" or "method group" was expected

Each case statement must have a break; statement before the next case appears. You can have any number of statements between case and break, but you must break at the end. This prevents each case from flowing into one another. If you forget to add break after the first case statement, then you get the following warning:

Assets/SwitchStatements.cs(21,17): error CS0163: Control cannot fall through from one case label to another

It's easy to forget to add these breaks, but at least we are informed that we're missing one. However, we're directed to the beginning of the switch statement. It's up to you to make sure that there's a break statement at the end of each case. It's also required after the default case.

Normally, the default label is the last case at the end of the series of case labels. However, this isn't a requirement. You can write the default label anywhere in the switch statement. Style guides usually require that you put the default at the very end of the switch. Not doing so might invoke some harsh words from a fellow programmer if he or she finds a misplaced default label.

As a convenience, C# can decode each case as a string. This may seem like an obvious feature, but it's something that has yet to come to older more established languages like C++.

```
case Cases.First:
    Debug.Log(MyCase);
    break;
```

The case above will simply print the following to the Console window:

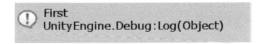

6.7.3 More On Cases

Switch statements are a common combination. Each label is clear and the parameter for the switch is also quite clear. We know what we're expecting and its obvious what conditions each case needs to be written for.

```
enum MoreCases
{
    FirstCase,
    SecondCase,
    ThirdCase
}
```

The above enum might be quite contrived, but we know how many labels we need if we use this case in a switch. It should be obvious that our first case label should look like case `cases.firstCase:` and we should fill in the rest of the case statements in order.

switch statements are limited to a select different types of data.

```
float f = 2.0f;
switch (f)
{
    case f < 1.0f:
        Debug.Log("less than 1");
        break;
}
```

The above code might look valid, but we'll get the following error:

```
Assets/Test.cs(15,1): error CS0151: A switch expression of type "float"
cannot be converted to an integral type, bool, char, string, enum or nullable
type
```

A switch is only allowed "`integral, bool, char, string, enum, or nullable`" types of data. We have yet to cover some of these different data types, but at least we know what a data type is. We do know that we can use `ints` and `enums`. In most cases, this should be enough. Switch statements should be used when one and only one thing needs to happen based on a single parameter.

```
int a = 0;
int b = 1;
switch (a)
{
    case 0:
        switch (b)
        {
            case 1:
                Debug.Log("might be more confusing...");
                break;
        }
    break;
}
```

Having a switch statement nested in one of the cases of another switch statement isn't common. There's nothing really stopping you from being able to do this, but it's probably better to look for a more elegant solution.

```csharp
int c = 0;
switch (c)
{
    case 0:
        ZerothFunction();
        break;
    case 1:
        FirstFunction();
        break;
}
```

Each case can simply call on a more complex function.

```csharp
void FirstFunction()
{
    Debug.Log("First Case");
}

void ZerothFunction()
{
    Debug.Log("ZerothCase");
}
```

Using a function in each case is a simple way to keep things tidy, though it's not always clear what's going on. Anyone reading the code will be forced to jump back and forth between the switch and the different functions. However, this does mean that you might be able to make more switch cases within each function in the switch statement.

```csharp
int a = 0;
switch (a)
{
    case 0:
        a = 1;
        FirstFunction(a);
        break;
    case 1:
        Secondfunction();
        break;
}
```

Once a case is entered, the `switch()` statement is finished. The parameter in the case of the switch statement is no longer evaluated once in a case. This also means that the parameter can be manipulated before it's used in the case.

```
                          ┌─────────────────────────┐
                        ┌─│ ① variable set to 0     │
int a = 0;──────────────┘ ├─────────────────────────┤
switch(a)─────────────────│ ② value 0 enters switch │
{                         └─────────────────────────┘
    case 0:───────────────┬──│ ③ case 0: is evalueated
        a = 1;────────────│  │ ④ variable a is assigned a new value
        FirstFunction(a);─│  │ ⑤ new value 1 is entered into FirstFunction
        break;────────────│  │ ⑥ case closed.
    case 1:
        SecondFunction();
        break;
}

┌──────────────────────────────────────────────────┐
│ ⑦ After the break; we start again down here.      │
└──────────────────────────────────────────────────┘
```

When we enter the case 0: we set the value that entered into the case to 1. This means that the data going into the function after that change gets a new value for a.

```
void FirstFunction(int i)
{
    switch (i)
    {
        case 0:
            Debug.Log("I won't get called.");
            break;
        case 1:
            Debug.Log("incoming case is 1");
            break;
    }
}
```

Because a = 1; appears after we've entered the case and is followed by a break;, case 1: is not triggered, and we don't skip to the second case. The logic might seem cloudy, but it's important that we really understand what's going on here.

Inside of the switch statement, the switch cannot change our destination once we've arrived at a label. After we've got to the label, we can change the data that got us there. Once we get to the break; at the end of the case, we leave the switch and move to any statements that follow the switch statement code block.

```
switch (a)
{
    case 0:
        FirstFunction(a);
        continue;
}
        No enclosing loop out of which to break or continue
```

A switch is not a loop, so we can't go back to the beginning of the switch by using continue; actually this is just an error telling you that there's no loop to continue to. A switch statement isn't meant to be looped; there are systems that allow this, but in general, these sorts of statements are one-way logic controls. A switch can work only with a single argument.

Something like switch (a, b) could make sense, but this isn't the case. Keeping things simple is not only your goal, but you're also limited by what is allowed. In some cases, the language can force simplicity. In practice, it's best to keep things as simple as possible if only for the sake of anyone else having to understand your work.

6.7.4 Fall Through

Using the break; statement jumps us out of the switch. Therefore, something like the following will execute one or the other statements after the condition and jump out of the switch.

```
switch(condition)
{
    case firstCondition:
        //Do things
        break;
    case secondCondition:
        //Do something else
        break;
}
```

If we want to, a case can be left empty, and without a break; included, anything in the case will "fall through" to the next case until the code is executed and a break; statement is found.

```
switch(condition)
{
    case firstCondition:
    case secondCondition:
        //Do something else
        break;
}
```

In the above example, if we get to case first condition:, we'll simply find the next case afterward and run the code there until we hit the next break; statement. It's rare to use this in practice as the conditions included act the same; in this case, both the first and second conditions do the same thing. However, things get a bit more awkward if we need to do something like the following:

```
switch(condition)
{
    case firstCondition:
    case secondCondition:
        //Do something else
        break;
    case thirdCondition:
    case fourthCondition:
    case fifthCondition:
        //Do another thing
        break;
}
```

Here we have two different behaviors based on five different conditions. The first two and the next three cases can result in two different behaviors. Although you might not use this behavior immediately, it's important to know what you're looking at if you see it. There are some catches to how this can be used.

```
switch(condition)
{
    case firstCondition:
        //Do Something ─────── not allowed without
    case secondCondition:      break; after.
        //Do something else
        break;
    case thirdCondition:
        //Do another thing
        break;
}
```

In the above example, our first condition might have some added code before the second condition. This might visually make sense; go to the first condition, execute some instructions, fall through to the next case, do more instructions, and break. However, this behavior isn't allowed in C#.

In order to accomplish what was described, we need to be more explicit.

6.7.5 goto Case

```
Cases someCases = Cases.First;
switch (someCases)
{
    case Cases.First:
        FirstFunction();
        goto case Cases.Second; // Jumps to next case
    case Cases.Second:
        SecondFunction();
        break;
}
```

Using the goto keyword allows us to hop from one case in the switch statement to another. This allows for an expected fall through-like behavior, but also gives us an added functionality of going to any other case once inside of the switch statement.

```
switch (someCases)
{
    case Cases.First:
        FirstFunction();
        goto case Cases.Third;
    case Cases.Second:
        SecondFunction();
        break;
    case Cases.Third:
        ThirdFunction();
        goto case Cases.Second;
}
```

The utility of the above statement is questionable. Although the statement is valid, it's hardly something that any programmer would want to read. Bad habits aside, should you see this in someone else's code, it's most likely written as a work-around by someone unfamiliar with the original case.

Aside from being awkward and strange looking, it's important that the switch case finally lead to a break, otherwise we're caught in the switch statement indefinitely. Debugging a situation like this is difficult, so it's best to avoid getting caught in a switch statement longer than necessary.

Strange and unusual code practices when working inside of a switch statement aren't common, as the regular use of a switch statement is quite simple. If you need to do something more clever, it's better to have a switch statement that points toward a function with additional logic to handle a more specific set of conditions.

6.7.6 Finite State Machine

A finite state machine is a system used to control the flow of processes in a complex system. In some ways, Unity has provided us with various ways to control when and how objects are started and updated with the `Start()` and `Update()` methods in MonoBehaviour. Enums will help keep track of specific character update states "Updateing Idle" "Updating walk" etc. A lot of this might sounds familiar if you've used Unity 3D's animation system.

A simple system to manage transitions between states is the FiniteStateMachine script attached to the object of the same name in the Switch_Scene. Each step of a process, or state of mind for a character, can be represented as a "state" to enter and exit. The character or object can only be in one state at a time. This is where finite state comes from. The machine infers there's some mechanism that's controlling the state transitions.

For our cylinder the finite states are waiting, changing colors, picking colors, and color changed. These are represented in an enum:

```csharp
public enum ChangingStates
{
    Waiting,
    PickingColor,
    ChangingColor,
    ColorChanged
}
public ChangingStates MyState;
```

The variable is stored as `MyState` which is public so it's visible in the Inspector panel in the editor. We also have setup some additional variables to store colors and time.

```csharp
private float ColorTime;
private Color MyColor, NextColor;
private Material MyMaterial;

// Start is called before the first frame update
void Start()
{
    MyMaterial = GetComponent<MeshRenderer>().material;
    ColorTime = Time.time + 1;
}
```

These are setup at and used while the states are updated. To change color we set the `NextColor` by picking random values for a color to transition to. The `PickColor()` function creates a new color and stores the value in the `NextColor` variable.

```
private void PickColor()
{
    float r = Random.Range(0f, 1f);
    float b = Random.Range(0f, 1f);
    float g = Random.Range(0f, 1f);
    NextColor = new Color(r, g, b);
    ColorTime = Time.time + 3;
}
```

This is called once the state decides it's time to pick a color, then the finite state changes to a color changing state where we use a `ChangeColor()` function to smoothly change from the previous color to the next color:

```
private void ChangeColor()
{
    MyColor = Color.Lerp(MyColor, NextColor, Time.deltaTime);
    MyMaterial.color = MyColor;
}
```

After the color blend has finished we set a moment of time to admire the selected color in an idle state called Waiting:

```
private void ColorChanged()
{
    ColorTime = Time.time + 1;
}
```

The states can be seen updated in the `Update()` function with a switch statement:

```
switch (MyState)
{
    // Hold onto color here for a second
    // then pick a color
    case ChangingStates.Waiting:
        WaitForColor();
        if (Time.time > ColorTime)
        {
            Debug.Log("Finished Waiting...");
            MyState = ChangingStates.PickingColor;
        }
        break;
    // pick a random color, then go to changing color.
    case ChangingStates.PickingColor:
        PickColor();
        Debug.Log("Color Picked...");
        MyState = ChangingStates.ChangingColor;
        break;
    // allow some time to lerp between colors
    case ChangingStates.ChangingColor:
        ChangeColor();
        if (Time.time > ColorTime)
        {
            Debug.Log("Color Changed...");
            MyState = ChangingStates.ColorChanged;
        }
        break;
    // finish color change
    case ChangingStates.ColorChanged:
        ColorChanged();
        Debug.Log("Finished Color Change.");
        MyState = ChangingStates.Waiting;
        break;
    default:
        break;
}
```

The different states `Waiting`, `PickingColor`, `ChangingColor` and `ColorChanged` are called sequentially. When the switch statement enters a case, settings are updated, and the `MyState` is set to the next state to enter. This pattern works for many different situations. Characters talking, walking, stopping and running can all have similar finite states to enter and leave.

This is a simple form of a finite state machine and works linearly. A common variation is to store a "previous" state. This allows us to react to the state we're entering knowing what state we left. For characters to enter an Idle state from a hit reaction means we can pick a different animation to blend between the two states. A simple but powerful design pattern.

6.7.7 What We've Learned

The switch statement is powerful and flexible. Using special case conditions where we use either the fall-through behavior or goto case statement, we're able to find additional utility within the switch statement.

Just because we can doesn't mean we should use fall-through or goto case. Often, this leads to confusing and difficult-to-read code. The bizarre and incomprehensible fall-through or goto case should be reserved for only the most bizarre and incomprehensible conditions. To avoid bad habits from forming, it might be better to forget that you even saw the goto case statement.

Now that warnings have been issued, experimenting and playing with code is still fun. Finding and solving problems with unique parameters is a part of the skill of programming. Using weird and strange-looking structures helps in many ways. If we're able to comprehend a strange set of code, we're better equipped to deal with more regular syntax.

switch statements can be used with any number of different parameters. Strings, ints, and other types are easily used in a switch statement.

```
string s = "Some Condition";
switch (s)
{
    case "Some Condition":
        // Do things
        break;
    case "Other Condition":
        // Do something else
        break;
}
```

6.8 Structs

Data structures specific and concise organization of information. By themselves floats, ints, and Vector3 are useful. However, copying and moving around each variable individually can look rather ugly. This lack of organization leaves more opportunity for errors.

```
float X;
float Y;
float Z;
void SetX(float x)
{
    X = x;
}
void SetY(float y)
{
    Y = y;
}
void SetZ(float z)
{
    Z = z;
}

void SetValues()
{
    SetX(1.0f);
    SetY(1.0f);
    SetZ(1.0f);
}
```

When having to deal with a complex character or monster type, collections of data should be organized together. The best way to do this is by using a struct, or structure. A Vector3 is a basic collection of three similar data types: a float for X, Y, and Z. This is by no means the limitation of what a structure can do.

```
Vector3 Vector;
void SetVector()
{
    Vector = new Vector3(1, 1, 1);
}
```

6.8.1 Building a Struct

Begin with the Structs_Scene in the Chapter6 Unity Project. In the scene open, the Structs script on the Structs game object in the scene. Structures for a player character could include the location, health points, ammunition, weapon in hand, and weapons in inventory and armor, and other related things that should be included in the player.cs, not excluded. To build a struct, you use the keyword struct followed by an identifier. This is very similar to how an enum is declared. What makes a structure different is that we can declare each variable in the struct to different data types.

After a structure is built to access any of the public components of the structure, you use dot notation. For example, `playerDataStruct.HitPoints` allows you to access the int value stored in the structure for `HitPoints`. PlayerData now contains the vital values that relate to the player.

```
public struct PlayerDataStruct
{
    public Vector3 Position;
    public int HitPoints;
    public int Ammunition;
    public float RunSpeed;
    public float WalkSpeed;
}
PlayerDataStruct playerDataStruct;
```

When you first look at declaring and using a struct, there might seem a few redundant items. First, there's a public struct PlayerData, then declare a PlayerData to be called playerData, and notice the lowercase lettering on the identifier versus the type. The first time PlayerData appears, you're creating a new type of data and writing its description.

6.8.2 Struct versus Class

At the same time, the struct may look a lot like a class and in many ways it is. The principal differences between the struct and the class is where in the computer's memory they live and how they are created. We'll discuss more on this in a moment.

You fill in some variables inside of the new data type and name the data inside of the new type. This new data type needs to have a name assigned so we know how to recognize the new form of packaged data. Therefore, `PlayerDataStruct` is the name we've given to this new form of data. This is the same as with a class.

The second appearance of the word `PlayerDataStruct` is required if we want to use our newly written form of data. To use the data, we write a statement for a variable like any other variable statement. Start with the data type—in this case, `PlayerDataStruct` is our type—then give a name, or identifier, to call a variable of the stated type. In this case, we're using `playerDataStruct` with a lowercase p to hold a variable of type `PlayerDataStruct`.

A struct is a data type with various types of data within it. It's convenient to packaging up all kinds of information into a single object. This means that when using the struct, you're able to pass along and get a breadth of information with a single parameter. This matters most when having to pass this information around.

This system of using a struct as data means that a struct is a value type, whereas a class is a reference type. You might ask what the difference between a value type and a reference type is. In short, when you create a struct and assign a value to it, a new copy is made of that struct. For instance, consider the following:

```
PlayerDataStruct otherPlayerStruct = playerStruct;
```

In this case, `otherPlayerStruct` is a new struct, where we make another version of `playerStruct` and copy the contents into `otherPlayerStruct`. Therefore, if we make `PlayerDataStruct pd2` and assign `playerStruct` to it, or even `otherPlayerStruct`, we'll have yet another copy of that same data in a new variable. Each variable `otherPlayerStruct`, `pd2`, and `playerDataStruct` now all have unique versions of the data.

However, should we change struct to class, we'd have a different arrangement.

```
public class PlayerDataClass
{
    public Vector3 Position;
    public int HitPoints;
    public int Ammunition;
    public float RunSpeed;
    public float WalkSpeed;
}
PlayerDataClass playerDataClass;
```

The only change to the above code is changing struct to class. This is still a perfectly valid C# class and appears to be the same as a struct, but the similarities cease once a variable is assigned. The differences can be seen in the following simple example.

```
void Start()
{
    PlayerDataStruct playerStruct = new PlayerDataStruct();
    PlayerDataClass playerClass = new PlayerDataClass();
    playerStruct.HitPoints = 1;
    playerClass.HitPoints = 1;

    PlayerDataStruct otherPlayerStruct = playerStruct;
    otherPlayerStruct.HitPoints = 3;
    Debug.Log(playerStruct.HitPoints + " and " + otherPlayerStruct.HitPoints);
    // 1 and 3
    PlayerDataClass otherPlayerClass = playerClass;
    otherPlayerClass.HitPoints = 3;
    Debug.Log(playerClass.HitPoints + " and " + otherPlayerClass.HitPoints);
    // 3 and 3
}
```

In the above code, we use both the PlayerDataStruct and PlayerDataClass. Both have a public field called int HitPoints; once in the Start() function a new PlayerDataStruct() and a new PlayerDataClass() are created. As soon as these classes are created, we assign 1 to the .HitPoints fields in both the struct and the class.

After this, we have an interesting change. Using the PlayerDataStruct otherPlayer-Struct = playerStruct, we create a copy of the PlayerDataStruct from playerStruct and assign that copy to otherPlayerStruct. Doing the same thing to PlayerDataClass otherPlayerClass, we assign playerClass to otherPlayerClass. If we check the value of playerClass.HitPoints and otherPlayerClass.HitPoints, we get 1 and 3, respectively.

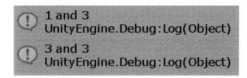

Doing the same thing to `playerClass.HitPoints` and `otherPlayerClass.HitPoints`, we get 3 and 3, respectively. How did this happen and why is mc.a changing the value of mClass.a? When a class is assigned to a variable, only a *reference* to the class is assigned. A new copy is not made and assigned to the variable mc.

In the statement `PlayerDataClass otherPlayerClass = playerClass;`, we assign other-`PlayerClass` a reference to `playerClass`. This contrasts to `PlayerDataStruct otherPlay-erStruct = playerStruct`, where ms gets a copy of the value stored in `playerStruct`. After a struct is assigned, it becomes an independent copy of the struct that was assigned to it. To break the reference, we cannot use mc = mClass, otherwise a reference will be created.

```
PlayerDataClass anotherPlayerClass = new PlayerDataClass();
anotherPlayerClass.HitPoints = playerClass.HitPoints;
anotherPlayerClass.HitPoints = 7;
Debug.Log(playerClass.HitPoints + ":" +
        otherPlayerClass.HitPoints + ":" +
        anotherPlayerClass.HitPoints);
// 3:3:7
```

By making a new instance of `PlayerDataClass` called anotherPlayerClass, we can assign the value from `playerClass.HitPoints` to `anotherPlayerClass.HitPoints`, which will avoid a reference from being created between anotherPlayerClass and playerClass. The above code prints out the following output:

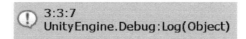

Even though we assigned the `.HitPoints` field of anotherPlayerClass to playerClass. `HitPoints`, we lose the reference between anotherPlayerClass and playerClass. When we change `anotherPlayerClass.HitPoints` to 7, it has no effect on `otherPlayerClass.` `HitPoints` and `playerClass.HitPoints`. The differences between the struct and the class is subtle but distinct.

The values of structs are copied when assigned in the `otherPlayerStruct = playerStruct` fashion. To accomplish the same behavior with a class, we need to assign each field separately with `anotherPlayerClass.HitPoints = playerClass.HitPoints;`. Only in this fashion can we actually a copy of the value to `anotherPlayerClass.HitPoints` from `playerClass.HitPoints`, not a reference.

6.8.3 Without Structs

The alternative to the struct is to use another form of data containment like the array. Each object in the array can hold a different data type, but it must be addressed by its index number in the array. It would be up to you to remember if the walk speed was at index 4 or 3 in the array. Organizational issues make this far too easy to mess up and forget which index holds what data.

Once you start adding new types of data to this method of record keeping, chances are you'll forget something and your code will break. There are languages out there that don't have structs, and this is the only way to manage a collection of data types. Be thankful for structs.

```
object[] playerDataArray = new object[5]
{
    new Vector3(),   // Position
    10,              // HitPoints
    13,              // Ammunition
    6.5f,            // Run Speed
    1.2f             // Walk Speed
};
object[] copyOfPlayerDataArray = playerDataArray;
Debug.Log(playerDataArray[1]);
// 10
copyOfPlayerDataArray[1] = 1;
Debug.Log(playerDataArray[1] + ":" + copyOfPlayerDataArray[1]);
// 1:1
```

An array of objects allows for different types of data to be mixed together. In the case where we copy one array into another, we get a reference. So in the above we check playerDataArray[1] and get 10 reflecting how the array was initialized. When we make a new array and set copyOfPlayerDataArray to playerDataArray and change the copy's second value to 1, this changes the original as well.

When another creature contacts the player, it should be given a copy of the entire PlayerData stored. This confines all the data into a single object and reduces the need for making separate operations to carry over different data. To do the same to a class, we'd have to use the same idea of copying each parameter one at a time because of the earlier mentioned behavior between a class and struct assignment.

6.8.4 Handling Structs

Structs are best used to contain a collection of data for an object. If we wanted to make a simple set of parameters for a box, we might use the following struct:

```
struct BoxParams
{
    public float width;
    public float height;
    public float depth;
    public Color color;
}
```

With this added to a new class attached to a box in the scene in Unity 3D, we have a system of storing and moving a collection of data using a single object. Within this object, we've assigned public variables for width, height, depth, and color.

To make use of this, we can adjust each one of the parameters individually within the structure using the dot operator.

```
BoxParams box = new BoxParams();
box.width = 2;
box.height = 3;
box.depth = 4;
box.color = Color.red;
```

We can access the box variables and assign them values. Once usable values are assigned to the BoxParams box, we can use them as a variable passed to a function.

```
void CreateCube(BoxParams b)
{
    GameObject go = GameObject.CreatePrimitive(PrimitiveType.Cube);
    go.transform.localScale = new Vector3(b.width, b.height, b.depth);
    go.GetComponent<MeshRenderer>().material.color = b.color;
}
```

The function can access the BoxParams passed to it using the same dot accessor and expose values that were assigned to it; the dot is an operator, and not exclusive to just accessors, but properties, functions, and all struct and class members. The first statement creates a new Vector 3 size. The size is then assigned a new Vector3(), where we extract the width, height, and depth and assign those values to the Vector3's x, y, and z parameters.

Once the Vector3() is created, we assign the values to the gameObject.transform.localScale. After this, we're also able to change the gameObject material's color by assigning the renderer.material.color to the b.color from the BoxParams values.

6.8.5 Accessing Structs

If a structure is limited to the class where it was created, then it becomes less useful to other classes that might need to see it. By creating another class to control the camera, we can better understand why other classes need access to the cube's BoxParams.

```
public class OtherClass
{
    //BoxParams Not accesible
}
```

By moving the struct outside of the class, we break out of the encapsulation of the classes.

```
// not inside of the Structs script
public struct PublicBoxParams
{
    public float width;
    public float height;
    public float depth;
    public Color color;
}
public class OtherClass
{
    //BoxParams Not accesible
    PublicBoxParams box;
    //Public Box Params is visible!
}
```

A new struct called `PublicBoxParams` lives outside of the Structs class scope. This changes the `PublicBoxParams` into a globally accessible struct.

When a class is made, its contents are encapsulated within curly braces. The variables or functions created inside of the class contents are members of that class. Should any new enum or struct be moved outside of that class, it becomes a globally declared object.

6.8.6 Global Access

In practice, it's a good idea to have a more central location for your globally accessible structs and enums. The term global just means to be accessible to the entire project. An additional class in the project called Globals.cs can contain the following code:

```
using System.Collections;
using System.Collections.Generic;
using UnityEngine;
/*   ...

public struct BoxParameters
{
    public float width;
    public float height;
    public float depth;
    public Color color;
}
```

With something as simple as this, we're able to create a central location for all globally accessible information. Starting with simple things such as public struct `BoxParameters`, we can then continually add more and more useful information to our globally accessible data. Each C# script file need not declare a class. Although it's common, it's not restrictively enforced that a C# script file contains a class. Utility files like a Globals.cs are handy and can provide a clean system in which each programmer on a team can find handy structures that can be shared between different objects in the scene.

6.8.7 What We've Learned

In Section 6.8.6, we talked about global access. This concept is not that new. When you write a class, in this case Structs, it's accessible by any other class. Therefore, when we assigned Structs to the Struct game object in the scene, it's able to use the global version of `BoxParameters`.

```
public class OtherClass
{
    //BoxParams Not accesible
    PublicBoxParams box;
    //Public Box Params is visible!

    BoxParameters globalBox;
    // Found in Global.cs
}
```

6.9 Class Data

Open the ClassData_Scene find the ClassData script in the hierarchy attached to the ClassData game object to follow along. Using a struct is preferred over a class due to how the computer manages memory. Without going into detail, one type of memory is called the heap and the other is the stack. In general, the stack is a smaller, more organized, faster part of the memory allocated to your game. The heap is usually larger and can take longer to access than the stack.

Values can be allocated to the stack, and a struct is a value type; thus, a stack can be accessed faster than a class. Though often structs and other value types are used in ways that disallow their allocation to the stack, they go into the heap instead. Classes and other reference data types end up in the heap regardless.

In a simple function call, the variables that appear in it are all pushed into the stack. As soon as the function is complete, any of the temporary values created and used inside of the function are immediately destroyed once the function is done executing.

```
void DoThings()
{
    int[] arrayOfInts = new int[100];
    for (int i = 0; i < 100; i++)
    {
        arrayOfInts[i] = i;
    }
}
```

The DoThings() function does pretty much nothing, but makes an array of ints that are added to the stack. As soon as this function is done, the array of ints is cleared out. In general, the stack grows and shrinks very fast. The second object that's added to the stack is the int i, which is being used inside the for loop.

The primary advantage a class has over a struct is the addition of a constructor and class inheritance. Aside from that, you're able to add assignments to each variable in a class as it's created.

```
struct MyStruct
{
    public int a = 0;
    public MyStruct()
    {
    }
}
```

MyStruct.MyStruct()

Structs cannot contain explicit parameterless constructors

A struct cannot have a parameterless constructor. Also, a struct cannot have variables initialized as they are declared.

```
struct MyStruct
{
    public int a = 0;
}
```

(field) int MyStruct.a

'MyStruct': cannot have instance property or field initializers in structs

On the other hand, as we've seen before, a class does allow this.

```
class MyClass
{
    public int a = 0;
    public MyClass()
    {
    }
}
```

In a struct, you're not allowed to assign values to the fields. Therefore, `public a = 0;` is allowed only in a class. Default values are allowed only in classes. Likewise, the constructor `public MyStruct()` isn't allowed, but it is in a class. In addition we're structs cannot inherit properties from another struct.

```
struct AddingToMyStruct : MyStruct
{
}
```

struct MyStruct

Type 'MyStruct' in interface list is not an interface

We could easily declare a class that has nothing more than data in it; this will look much like any struct.

```
class PlayerData
{
    public Vector3 Position;
    public int HitPoints;
    public int Ammo;
    public float RunSpeed;
    public float WalkSpeed;
}
```

This would do the same things as a struct of the same complexity is concerned. However, a struct has the chance to be a bit faster than a class to access. A struct is also a step up from an enum. The declaration might look somewhat similar, but an enum doesn't allow any values to be assigned to its constituent declarations.

6.9.1 Character Base Class

For all the monsters and players to have an equal understanding of one another, they need to share a common base class. This means that simply they all need to share the same parent class that holds data structures, which all of them are aware of. This concept is called inheritance, and it's something that only a class can do.

```
public class BaseMonster
{
}

public class Zombie : BaseMonster
{
}
```

The Zombie uses the `: BaseMonster` statement to tell C# that the Zombie is inheriting from BaseMonster. We will go into this again in Sections 6.13 and 6.23, but it's important that we're used to seeing this notation and what it's for.

Once each type of character shares the same parent class, it can use the same data. This is important so that zombies can understand what data makes up a human, and vampires can know to avoid zombie blood. To do this, the zombies need to know how to deal with the player's data structure and the player needs to know how to deal with zombies and vampires.

When we start our game, we're going to have a starting point for the player and for each monster. Classes are a clean way to store data when a game is started. Starting data can include basic chunks of information that don't change, such as minimum and maximum values.

Structs don't allow you to declare values for variables when they are created. Classes, on the other hand, do allow you to assign values. More important, we can make them unchangeable.

6.9.2 Const

The const keyword is used to tell anyone reading the class that the value assigned cannot change during the game. The keyword is short for constant, and it means that you shouldn't try to change it either. There are a few different ways which you can assign a value to behave the same as a const, but just by looking at the code, you should know that the following code has a value that shouldn't be changed while playing.

```
public class BaseMonster
{
    /*  ...
    const int MaxHitPoints = 10;
}
```

If a value is declared to be `const`, then you should keep in mind how it's used. These are good for comparisons, if a value is greater than `MaxHitPoints`, then you have a very clear reason for why this value is set.

When you've declared a class and set several `const` values, this gives the class purposeful location to store all kinds of "set in stone" numbers. One problem with giving a class const values is that they cannot be changed after they have been set. So make sure that these values shouldn't need to change once the game is running.

This allows you to create a constant value for the class. To make the value accessible, we need to change the declaration. In addition, a const value must be initialized. This means const int `MaxHitPoints;` isn't valid. Visual Studio will warn:

```
public const int MaxHitPoints;// = 10;
```

> ▣ (constant) int BaseMonster.MaxHitPoints
>
> A const field requires a value to be provided

The proper declaration will look like the following:

```
public const int MaxHitPoints = 10;
```

> ▣ (constant) int BaseMonster.MaxHitPoints = 10

The accessor must come before the readability of the variable. Likewise, this can also be made `private const int MaxHitPoints =10;`. This allows you to set the value when writing the code for the classes. However, if you want to make a variable have a limited availability to set, then we can use a different declaration.

6.9.3 Readonly

The readonly declaration allows you to change the variable only when a class is declared or as it's written when it was initialized.

```
public readonly int MaxMagicPoints = 10;
public void SetMaxMagicPoints(int mp)
{
    MaxMagicPoints = mp;
}
```

> ● (field) int BaseMonster.MaxMagicPoints
>
> A readonly field cannot be assigned to (except in a constructor or a variable initializer)

This means that a readonly variable can only be set in a variable, an initializer, or a constructor. This means that the only way to set `MaxHitPoints` can be with the following code:

```
public BaseMonster(int maxMP)
{
    MaxMagicPoints = maxMP;
    // this is valid
}
```

By using a constructor, we can set the `MaxMagicPoints` once, or we can use the value when the variable is declared. Therefore, the first way `MaxMagicPoints` can be set is when we use the initialization line public `readonly int MaxMagicPoints = 10;` where we set `MaxMagicPoints` to 10, or in the constructor where we set the value to the `(int maxMP)` in the argument list. This differs from the const keyword, where we can use the initializer only to set the value of the variable `MaxMagicPoints`.

When you add in constructors to a base class, or a class that you're expecting other classes to inherit from, it's important to remember that each child class needs to build corresponding inheriting functions.

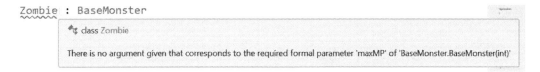

A quick fix for this is to allow Visual Studio to write the required functions for you.

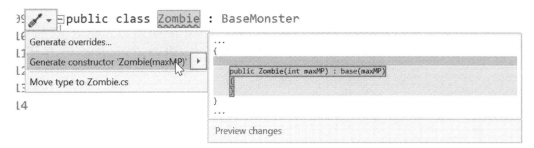

You'll notive a very similar use of: `base(maxMP)` following the `Zombie()` constructor.

```
public class Zombie : BaseMonster
{
    public Zombie(int maxMP) : base(maxMP)
    {
    }
}
```

There are other consequences to the inheriting from different classes. There will be more in-depth study of these effects in a later chapter when we look at functions again in Section 6.11.

These are only simple uses of the const and readonly variable declarators. Once you begin reading other programmer's code you've downloaded online or observed from team members, you'll get a better idea of the various reasons for using these keywords. It's impossible to cover every context in a single chapter.

The primary reason for these keywords is to prevent misunderstanding between engineers. If you have a good reason for setting a value that should never change then you'll use const. If you have a reason to make a value only change when an object is first created, then you'll use readonly. If you write code that depends on the value and assumes it's never going to change then it's good to prevent anyone from changing it.

6.9.4 What We've Learned

Using these keywords is quite simple, and it makes quite clear what you're allowed to do with them. Understanding what keywords mean to the accessibility of the variable, you'll gain insight into how the value is intended to be used.

Keywords const and readonly mean that the variable cannot be changed either outside of an initial declaration or as the code is written. This means that the value needs to remain unchanged for a reason. Of course, knowing that reason requires a great deal of context, so it's impossible to lay out every reason here. However, it's safe to assume someone added the declaratory keyword for a reason.

6.10 Namespaces

Follow along with the Namespaces_Scene and open the NameSpaces script on the game object of the same name. Classes are organized by their namespace. A namespace is a system used to sort classes and their contained functions into named groups. This helps isolate classes with the same name which would conflict without a namespace.

```
/* Section namespaces protect the contents of this section       *
 * from interfering with the contents of another section         */
namespace Chapter6_10_1
{
```

It will be problematic if programmers in the world come up with unique names for their classes and functions. Namespaces are used to control scope. By encapsulating functions and variables within a namespace, you're allowed to use names within the namespace that might already be in use in other namespaces.

6.10.1 A Basic Example

A namespace is basically an identifier for a group of classes and everything contained in the classes. The same rules as variable naming applies to namespace identifiers. Within that namespace, we can declare any number of classes. Starting in the Chapter6 Unity Project, we'll look at the NameSpaces_Scene and the NameSpaces.cs class in the scene on the object of the same name.

```
namespace MyNamespace
{
}
```

A namespace is declared as seen above. This assigns the identifier following the keyword to a new namespace. A namespace gives us a way to group objects under a unique identifier. In this case, MyNamespace.

A namespace doesn't collide with another namespace in the same scope. Instead, the contents of a namespace can collide with one another. A namespace only expands the scope of an exsisting namespace. Inside of a second MyNamespace, we can add in a new class with its own functions. However, to make the class available to anyone who wants to use the class in the namespace, we need to make it public.

```
namespace MyNamespace
{
    public class SomeClass
    {
    }
}
```

The using directives haven't been added to any of the namespaces in the file. In the above MyNamespace SomeClass exists without access to UnityEngine functions like Debug.Log(). To enable this a directive needs to be added to the namespace.

```
namespace MyNamespace
{
    /* Adds the UnityEngine library   *
     * to this scope of MyNamespace   */
    using UnityEngine;
    public class MyClass
    {
        public void MyFunction()
        {
            //Debug.Log() comes from UnityEngine
            Debug.Log("MyClass says Hello from MyNamespace");
        }
    }
}
```

The directives can exist at the beginning of any namespace. The scope of each directive added to a namespace is limited to the scope where it was declared. In this case, MyClass has access to Debug.Log where as the previous SomeClass does not.

As was said in an earlier chapter, we can slightly bend the rules for directives always appearing at the top of a file. The objects written in a file exists in a global unnamed namespace. The class and directives appear in the unnamed namespace and can be access globally without a directive.

```
namespace MyNamespace
{
    public class AnotherClass
    {
        void SomeFunction()
        {
            global::UnityEngine.Debug.Log("Using Global");
        }
    }
}
```

NOTE: Not that this is commonly used, but `global::` can be prefixed ahead of a function or type in a declaration. This only really matters if you want to use a namespace that's already in use in a library like System, for instance. This means that if you create your own namespace System, to use libraries in the .NET system then you'd need to prefix `global::` to access them.

6.10.2 Directives in Namespaces

As a namespace is created the contents become accessible through directives. The previous chapter created a namespace called `MyNamespace` inside of a `Chapter6_10_1` namespace. To access the objects in that namespace the using `MyNamespace` can be added to any other namespace like adding using `UnityEngine`.

```
namespace SecondNamespace
{
    using UnityEngine;
    using Chapter6_10_1.MyNamespace;
    public class UniqueClass
    {
        private Chapter6_10_1.MyNamespace.MyClass myClass;
        public void UseOtherNamespace()
        {
            myClass = new MyClass();
            myClass.MyFunction();
        }
    }
}
```

In the `Chapter6_10_2` namespace we use a `SecondNamespace` to declare a new scope. This allows `UniqueClass` to access the directives present in the `SecondNamespace`. Here, both `UnityEngine` and the previous chapter's `MyNamespace` are accessible.

The `UseOtherNamespace()` function in `UniqueClass` is allowed to instantiate a new MyClass from the `Chapter6_10_1.MyNamespace` scope. It should also be noted that the lighter shading of some of the directives indicate that they are not necessary. Visual Studio knows where MyClass comes from and indicates the use of unnecessary keywords by shading them lighter.

```
namespace SecondNamespace
{
    using UnityEngine;
    /* Unity finds the only MonoBehaviour that matches the file name   *
     * and uses this as the component to attach to the gameObject      *
     * in the scene.                                                   */
    public class NameSpaces : MonoBehaviour
    {
        private void Start()
        {
            UniqueClass uniqueClass = new UniqueClass();
            uniqueClass.UseOtherNamespace();
        }
    }
}
```

By wrapping the `NameSpaces: MonoBehaviour` in the `SecondNamespace` the `UniqueClass()` is accessible without adding a directive. Within a namespace the objects are accessible without adding any directives.

This shows where the function was called and what namespace the function originated in. In most cases, you'll create a new namespace for the classes in your new game. This becomes particularly important when you need to use third-party libraries. You might have a function called `Random()`, but another library might also have a function with the same name.

6.10.3 Ambiguous References

Coming up with unique names for every variable, class, or function can be difficult. Another class might already use commonly used words like speed, radius, or vector. Namespaces offer a system to help separate your class member names from another class that might already be using the same names. In the same Namespaces_Scene open the AmbiguousNamespaces.cs script on the NameSpaces game object.

```
using UnityEngine;
using Chapter6_10_2.SecondNamespace; // has UniqueClass
using AnotherNamespace;              // has UniqueClass
```

This will involve duplicates for the UniqueClass, which is cause for some problems. Then Unity 3D will show you the following error:

```
// which UniqueClass to use?
UniqueClass uniqueClass = new AnotherNamespace.UniqueClass();
```

```
class Chapter6_10_3.AnotherNamespace.UniqueClass

'UniqueClass' is an ambiguous reference between 'Chapter6_10_3.AnotherNamespace.UniqueClass' and 'Chapter6_10_2.SecondNamespace.UniqueClass'

Show potential fixes (Alt+Enter or Ctrl+.)
```

Ambiguous references become a common problem when we include many different namespaces. We could possibly fix this by changing the name of the classes in one of the functions, but that wouldn't be possible if the reference came from a dynamic linking library (DLL) or another author's code. We could also change namespaces which we're using, but again, that would be a work around and not a solution.

If we hover over the class with the cursor in Visual Studio, we'll get a pop-up telling us which version is currently being used. Of course, this is just a guess, and a bad one at that. This can be resolved by expanding the declaration using the Namespace dot operator and picking the to uniquely identify the `UniqueClass` we want from the other namespace.

```
/* this is more specific */
AnotherNamespace.UniqueClass uniqueClass = new AnotherNamespace.UniqueClass();
Chapter6_10_2.SecondNamespace.UniqueClass secondUniqueClass = new Chapter6_10_2.SecondNamespace.UniqueClass();
```

Of course, it's not the most pretty, but this is the most correct method to fix the namespace we're requesting a `UniqueClass()` object from. Things can get too long if we need to nest more namespaces inside of a namespace.

Long namespaces represent a little bit of a style problem. It's cleaner to use short statements. So how would we avoid needing to use dot operators to access directives with shorter names?

6.10.4 Alias Directives

Attached to the same NameSpaces game object is also a script called `UsingAliasDirectives`. Open this to follow along. Sometimes namespaces can get quite long. Often when you need to refer to a namespace directly you may want to shorten the name into something easier to type. Alias directives make this easier.

```
using UnityEngine;
/* This allows you to shorten the name of a      *
 * namespace to something easier to use.          */
using Sub = Chapter6_10_3.AnotherNamespace.SubSpace;
```

A directive is aliased using the syntax `using x = UnityEngine;` for instance. When we have a namespace nested in another namespace, we can assign that to an identifier as well. To shorten `AnotherNamespace.SubSpace` to `Sub`, we use a statement that looks like `using Sub = AnotherNamespace.SubSpace;` to reduce how much typing we need to use to express which namespace we're using.

```
/* uses Sub rather than                          *
 * Chapter6_10_3.AnotherNamespace.SubSpace       */
Sub.SubSpaceClass subClass = new Sub.SubSpaceClass();
subClass.UseSubSpaceFunction();
```

Now we can reduce the declaration to a shorter statement. Of course, unless we have an ambiguous name to worry about, there's no need for being so explicit with the function we're specifically trying to call. With descriptive function and variable names, we can avoid directive aliases.

6.10.5 What We've Learned

This is a simple way to allow multiple classes to work together by sharing a class through a namespace. Decisions around how you organize the code for your game should include how to separate classes by namespace. In a practical sense, namespaces follow function. A Utilities namespace would include classes you use as tools for your game. A game title is a good root namespace.

A Utilities namespace for your game would be a member of the game namespace. The namespace should also contain common structs that every class will need to make use of. So a `game.dataTypes` namespace would help organize where those are stored. These are just some example of the sorts of namespaces that would be useful to help organize your game.

6.11 Functions Again

So far, we've been working in either the `Start()` function or the `Update()` function because they are entry points. Because of this, they are automatically called by the engine. In a non-Unity 3D Engine program, the default entry point would be something like `public static void Main()`.

6.11.1 Parameter Lists

When a function is called, its identifier followed by its parameter list is added to code. Parameters are like little mail slots on the front door of a house. There might be a slot for integers, floats, and arrays. Each slot on the door, or argument in the parameter list, is a type followed by an identifier.

If we look at a basic example, we'll see how all this works.

```
public class FunctionsAgain : MonoBehaviour
{
    int a = 0;
    void SetA(int i)
    {
        a = i;
    }
}
```

The function declaration `void SetA (int i)` takes in one parameter of type `int`. This is a simple example of a value parameter; there are other types of parameters which we'll go into next. The value parameter declares the type and an identifier whose scope is limited to the contents of the function it's declared with.

```
void Start()
{
    Debug.Log("a:" + a); //0
    SetA(3);
    Debug.Log("a:" + a); //3
}
```

To use our function, add in the preceding lines of code to the `Start()` function in Unity 3D. When you start the game, you'll see a 0 followed by a 3. We can do this any number of times, and each time we're allowed to change what value we set A to. Of course, it's easier to use a = 3 in the `Start()` function, but then we wouldn't be learning anything.

6.11.2 Side Effects

When a function directly sets a variable in the class the function lives in, programmers like to call this a side effect. Side effects are usually things that programmers try to avoid, but it's not always practical. Writing functions with side effects tend to prevent the function from being useful in other classes. We'll find other systems that allow us to avoid using side effects, but in some cases, it's necessary.

```
int b;
void SetBtoFive()
{
    b = 5;
}
```

The above `SetBtoFive()` function sets `int b` to 5. The `SetBtoFive()` function does have a clear purpose, setting b to 5, but there's nothing in the function that indicates where the variable it's setting lives. If the variable lived in another class which `FunctionsAgain` inherited from, then you wouldn't even see the variable in this class.

Once the complexity in a class grows, where and when a variable gets changed or read becomes more obscure. If a function remains self-contained, testing and fixing that function becomes far easier. Reading what a function does should not involve jumping around to find what variable it's making changes to. This brings us back to the topic of scope. Limiting the scope or reach of a function helps limit the number of places where things can go wrong.

```
int b;
void SetBtoFive()
{
    b = 5;
}
public void SetBAgain()
{
    b = new int();
}
```

The more functions that have a side effect, the more strange behaviors might occur. If an `Update()` function is expecting one value but gets something else entirely, you can start to get unexpected behaviors. Worse yet, if `SetBAgain()` is called from another class and you were expecting a to be 5, you're going to run into more strange behaviors.

6.11.3 Multiple Arguments

There aren't any limits to the number of parameters that a function can accept. Some languages limit you to no more than 16 arguments, which seems acceptable. If your logic requires more than 16 parameters, it's probably going to be easier to separate your function into different parts. However, if we're going to be doing something simple, we might want to use more than one parameter anyway.

```
int c = 0;
void SetCtoLeftPlusRight(int left, int right)
{
    c = left + right;
}
```

We can add a second parameter to `SetCtoLeftPlusRight()`. A comma token tells the function to accept another variable in the parameter list, For this example, we're using two ints to add to one another and assign a value to c. There isn't anything limiting the types we're allowed to use in the parameter list.

```
void SetAtoLeftBtoRight(int left, int right)
{
    a = left;
    b = right;
}
```

The function with multiple parameters can do more. Value parameters are helpful ways to get data into a function to accomplish some sort of simple task. We'll elaborate more on this by creating something useful in Unity 3D.

6.11.4 Useful Parameters

Often, we need to test things out before using them. Let's say we want to create a new primitive cube in the scene, give it a useful name, and then set its position. This is a simple task, and our code might look like the following:

```
GameObject go = GameObject.CreatePrimitive(PrimitiveType.Cube);
go.name = "MrCube";
go.transform.position = new Vector3(0, 1, 0);
```

Our cube is given a name, and it's assigned a place in the world. Next, let's say we want to make a bunch of different cubes in the same way. We could do something like the following:

```
GameObject go = GameObject.CreatePrimitive(PrimitiveType.Cube);
go.name = "MrCube";
go.transform.position = new Vector3(0, 1, 0);
GameObject go1 = GameObject.CreatePrimitive(PrimitiveType.Cube);
go.name = "MrsCube";
go.transform.position = new Vector3(0, 2, 0);
GameObject go2 = GameObject.CreatePrimitive(PrimitiveType.Cube);
go.name = "MissCube";
go.transform.position = new Vector3(0, 3, 0);
GameObject go3 = GameObject.CreatePrimitive(PrimitiveType.Cube);
go.name = "CubeJr";
go.transform.position = new Vector3(0, 4, 0);
```

If this code looks horrible, then you're learning. It's accomplishing a task properly, but in terms of programming, it's horrible. When you intend to do a simple task more than a few times, it's a good idea to turn it into a function. This is sometimes referred to as the "Rule of Three," a term coined in an early programming book on refactoring code.

6.11.4.1 The Rule of Three

The Rule of Three is a simple idea that any time you need to do any given task more than three times manually, it would be better served by creating a new single procedure to accomplish the task. This reduces the chance of error in writing the same code more than three times. This also means that changing the procedure can be done in one place.

```
void CreateANamedObject(PrimitiveType pType, string name, Vector3 pos)
{
    GameObject go = GameObject.CreatePrimitive(pType);
    go.name = name;
    go.transform.position = pos;
}
```

We take the code that's repeated and move it into a function. We then take the values that change between each iteration and change it into a parameter. In general, it's best to put the parameters in the same order in which they're used. This isn't required, but it looks more acceptable to a programmer's eyes.

```
CreateANamedObject(PrimitiveType.Cube, "MrCube", new Vector3(0, 1, 0));
```

We then test the function at least once before writing any more code than we need to. If this works out, then we're free to duplicate the line of code to accomplish what we started off doing.

```
CreateANamedObject(PrimitiveType.Cube, "MrCube", new Vector3(0, 1, 0));
CreateANamedObject(PrimitiveType.Cube, "MrsCube", new Vector3(0, 2, 0));
CreateANamedObject(PrimitiveType.Cube, "MissCube", new Vector3(0, 3, 0));
CreateANamedObject(PrimitiveType.Cube, "CubeJr", new Vector3(0, 4, 0));
```

Again, though, we're seeing a great deal of duplicated work. We've used arrays earlier, and this is as good a time as any to use them. By observation, the main thing that is changing here is the name. Therefore, we'll need to add each name to an array.

```
string[] names = new string[]
{
    "MrCube",
    "MrsCube",
    "MissCube",
    "CubeJr"
};
```

The variable declaration needs to change a little bit for an array. First of all, rather than using type identifier;, a pair of square brackets are used after the type. The statement starts with `string[]` rather than string. This is followed by the usual identifier we're going to use to store the array of strings.

Unlike an integer type, there's no default value that can be added in for this array of strings. To complete the statement, we need to add in the data before the end of the statement. The new keyword is used to indicate that a new array is going to be used. The array is a special class that's built into C#. Therefore, it has some special abilities that we'll get into later.

Now that we've declared an array of names, we'll need to use them.

6.11.5 Foreach versus For

The foreach loop is often our goto loop for iterating through any number of objects.

```
foreach (string s in names)
{
    Debug.Log(s);
}
```

The parameters for the foreach also introduce the keyword in that tells the foreach iterator what array to look into. The first parameter before the in keyword indicates what we're expecting to find inside of the array. Therefore, for this use of the foreach iterator, we get the output in the following page.

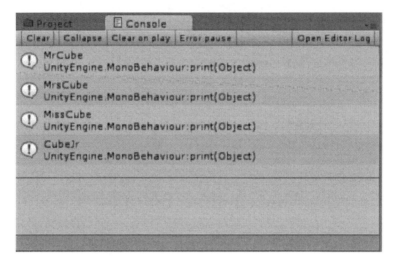

As expected, we get a list of the names found in the array we added. As we add in new functions and variables, it's important to test them out one at a time. This helps make sure that you're headed in the right direction one step at a time. Now we can switch out the print function for the clever function we wrote now.

```
foreach (string s in names)
{
    CreateANamedObject(PrimitiveType.Cube, s, new Vector3(0, 1, 0));
}
```

The foreach loop in some respects operates in the same way as a while loop.

```
float y = 1.0f;
foreach (string s in names)
{
    CreateANamedObject(PrimitiveType.Cube, s, new Vector3(0, y, 0));
    y += 1.0f;
}
```

It's simple to add in a variable outside of the loop that can be incremented within the loop.

It's time to admire our clever function. The foreach means we can add in any number of names to the array and the tower of cubes will get taller with named boxes.

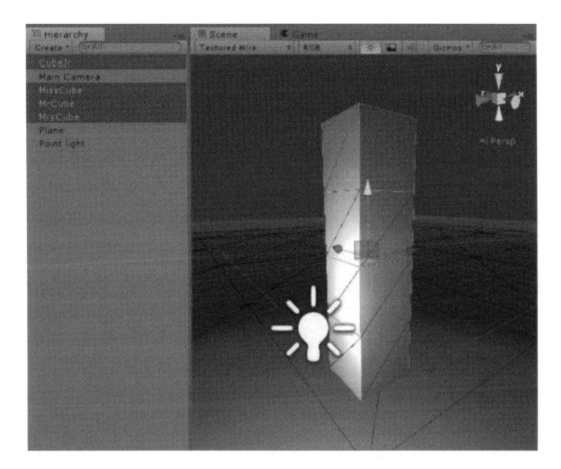

6.11.6 What We've Learned

The foreach loop is useful in many ways, but it's also somewhat limited. If we had more than one array to iterate through at the same time, we'd have some difficulties. In some cases, it's easier to use a regular for loop. Arrays are lists of objects, but they're also numbered.

Arrays are used everywhere. On your own, experiment by adding more parameters to the function and more names to the list. We'll look at how to use other loops with multidimensional arrays and even jagged arrays in Chapter 7.

6.12 Unity 3D Execution Order

C# is an imperative language, which means that operations are executed in order, first one thing and then another. When Unity 3D makes an instance of a new gameObject with MonoBehaviour components, each component will have at least five functions called on it before the end of the frame where it was created. Additional rendering calls can be called as well.

Specifically, the `Start()` and `Update()` functions in Unity 3D are called in each MonoBehaviour in a specific order. Several other functions are also used by Unity 3D, and they each have specific moments when they are called. In Visual Studio the key-combo: CTRL+Shift+M will open the Implement Unity Messages dialog box:

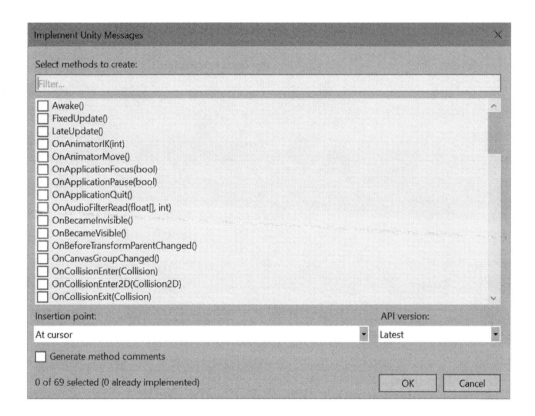

Of the 69 messages that all MonoBehaviours will receive in game, here are 8 used most often:

```
Awake()
OnEnable()
Start()
FixedUpdate()
Update()
LateUpdate()
OnDisable()
OnDestroy()
```

The order of this should make sense, considering that C# will execute statements in order. However, what happens when another class is instanced in the `Awake()` function and it too will have its own `Awake()`, `OnEnable()`, and `Start()` functions?

6.12.1 A Basic Example

Begin by examining the ExecutionOrder project; the ExecutionOrderFirst.cs class will look a bit like the following:

```
public class ExecutionOrderFirst : MonoBehaviour
{

    void Awake()
    {
        Debug.Log("First Awake");
    }

    void OnEnable()
    {
        Debug.Log("First OnEnable");
    }

    void Start()
    {
        Debug.Log("First Start");
    }

    void FixedUpdate()
    {
        Debug.Log("First FixedUpdate");
    }

    void Update()
    {
        Debug.Log("First Update");
    }

    private void LateUpdate()
    {
        Debug.Log("First LateUpdate");
        Destroy(this);
    }

    private void OnDisable()
    {
        Debug.Log("First OnDisable");
    }

    private void OnDestroy()
    {
        Debug.Log("First OnDistroy");
    }
}
```

This prints out the following:

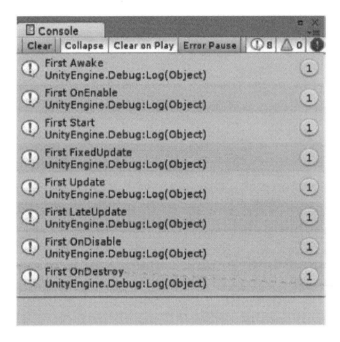

The Console shows that the code is executed in the same order in which we laid them out in the class. When the LateUpdate() function is called, we use Destroy(this); to begin deleting the class from the scene. When the class begins to delete itself, it's first disabled and then deleted.

When a new instance of a MonoBehaviour is created, it will also call its Awake(), OnEnabled(), and Start() functions. Intuitively, it would make sense if you create an object in the Awake() function; the new object might wait till the end of Awake() before it begins its Awake() function. However, this isn't always the case.

```
void Awake()
{
    Debug.Log("Awake Start");
    this.gameObject.AddComponent(typeof(Second));
    Debug.Log("Awake Done");
}
```

Say we create a new class called Second.cs and have it log its Awake() and Start() functions as well. Then, in the Second.cs class we have the following code:

```
void Awake()
{
    Debug.Log("Second Awake");
}


void OnEnable()
{
    Debug.Log("Second OnEnable");
}
```

This produces the following output:

Before the First class was created, the Second was able to get its Awake() done and move on to OnEnable() without interruption. First waited for Second to finish its Awake() and OnEnable() functions before First finished its own Awake() function. Afterward, OnEnable() of the First was finally called, even if Second took its own time to finish its Awake() function.

```
Debug.Log("Second Awake Start");
for(int i = 0; i < 1000; i++)
{
    Debug.Log("Wait!");
}
Debug.Log("Second Awake Done.");
```

The ExecutionOrderFirst.cs class finishes its `Awake()` function, then the ExecutionOrderSecond.cs class finishes its `Awake()` function and starts its `OnEnable()`. After, ExecutionOrderFirst finishes its `Awake()` and starts its `OnEnable()` function. The First and Second being their Start() function. Notice that "First Awake Done" doesn't appear until after "Second OnEnable." The "Second OnEnable" is only printed once the "Second Awake Done" is printed, indicating that the for loop was able to finish.

When more objects are being created, the order in which these functions are called becomes more difficult to sort out. If you created several different objects, some of them might take even longer or shorter to finish their `Awake()`, `OnEnable()`, and `Start()` functions. Figuring all of this out takes a bit of thinking things through.

6.12.2 Component Execution Order

The execution of classes becomes a bit more confusing when they're attached to a gameObject as a prefab. In the scene, adding Second and Third classes to the Main Camera will show us some unexpected results.

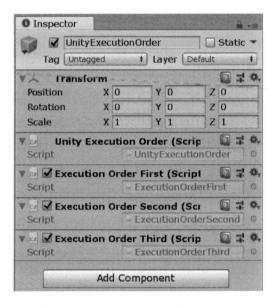

Once all three MonoBehaviours have been attached to the Main Camera, we can observe the execution order of the functions found in each class.

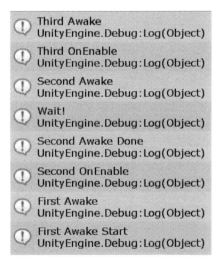

The `Third Awake()` and `OnEnable()` are called before the Second and the First even though the components look like they've been reordered in the opposite order on the game object they are attached to. However, this isn't always the case.

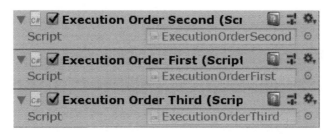

In the above screenshot, we swapped the First component with the Second. Even after changing the order in which they appear in the components list, we get no change in the Console's log output. This tells us that there's no specific order in which the objects are created and how they are ordered in the gameObject's components list. However, there is a simple system in which we can change the execution order manually.

Select the ExecutionOrderFirst.cs file in the Project Assets directory. To the top right is a button labeled Execution Order…

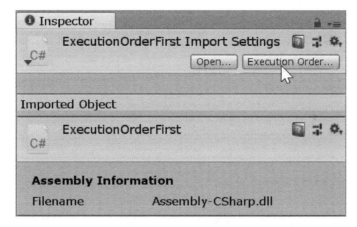

After your classes have been added to the list, you can make any changes by altering the number in the box to the right. Clicking on the—icon removes them from the list. Press Apply once you've added all your classes to the list.

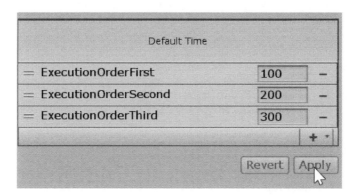

Once the scripts have been added to this list, they are guaranteed to be called in this order, ignoring how they are ordered in the components list on the gameObject they've been added to. Playing the scene with the components attached to the Main Camera in any order will always result in the following output:

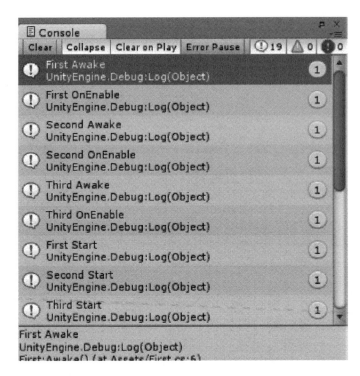

After the scripts order is set, the Console panel shows us a more expected result. You could use a single GameController.cs class that operates as a central dispatch of updates. This would be a monolithic update system which every other class waits for an update from.

For now it's important that we observe how the functions operate and how to best use these behaviors to our advantage. From observation, we know that we can maintain when each function is called.

6.12.3 What We've Learned

In this chapter, we looked at how to manage execution order between multiple classes. For simple projects, this execution ordering system should suffice. However, when you're not inheriting from MonoBehaviour, this management system will no longer work.

Once we get into more complex systems that do not inherit from MonoBehaviour, we'll build our own system for managing the execution order. There are systems that allow you to better control what functions are called and when, but we'll have to learn a few other things before getting to that.

Unity 3D expects many different things of your classes when you inherit from MonoBehaviour. If you include an Update() function, it will automatically be called on every frame. However, when there are too many Update() functions on too many classes running in a scene, Unity's frame rate can suffer.

Once a game gets moving along and creatures and characters are spawning and dying, it's impossible to know when and in what order each function is executed. Each object in the scene should be able to operate on its own. If an object depends on a variable, the value of which needs to be updated before it's used, then you may run into problems reading stale data.

6.13 Inheritance Again

Inheriting members of a parent class is only one facet of what inheritance does for your code. The behaviors of the functions also carry on in the child classes. If the parent has functions that it uses to find objects in the world, then so do the children. If the parent can change its behavior based on its proximity to other objects, then so do the children.

The key difference is that the children can decide what happens based on those behaviors. The data that is collected can be used in any way. A child class inherits the functions of its parent class. When the child's function is executed, it operates the same way as its parent. It can be more interesting to have the child's function behave differently from the inherited version of the function.

6.13.1 Function Overrides

The override keyword following the public keyword in a function declaration tells the child version of the function to clear out the old behavior and implement a new version. We've seen how member functions work when they're used by another class. Now we're going to see how to effect the operation of inherited functions.

6.13.1.1 A Basic Example

Revisiting the Parent–Child relation again in the Chapter 6 Unity Project in the InheritanceAgain_Scene. We find the following code to the ParentClass:

```
public class ParentClass
{
    public void ParentFunction()
    {
        Debug.Log("Parent Says Hello.");
        FunctionA();
        FunctionB();        .
    }

    public void FunctionA()
    {
        Debug.Log("Parent Function A Says Hello.");
    }

    public void FunctionB()
    {
        Debug.Log("Parent Function B Says Hello.");
    }
}
```

When the `ParentFunction()` is called in the `Start()` function of the InheritanceAgain script in the InheritanceAgain_Scene, this will produce the expected "Parent says Hello." followed by "Parent Function A says Hello." and then "Parent Function B says Hello." in the Console panel.

ChildClass is based on ParentClass, and we have an opportunity to make modifications by adding layers of code. To make see this modification, we need to reuse the code from the ParentClass class in the ChildClass. The ParentFunction() is called from the ChildFunction() of the Child class.

```
public class ChildClass : ParentClass
{
    public void ChildFunction()
    {
        ParentFunction();
    }
}
```

Running this will produce the same output to the Console panel as the Parent class. Right now, there is no function overriding going on. If we intend to inherit a function and add modifications to it, we should make the Parent class allow for functions to be overridden by adding the virtual keyword to the function we plan to override.

```
public virtual void FunctionA()
{
    Debug.Log("Parent Function A Says Hello.");
}
```

Adding the `virtual` keyword after the `public` declaration and before the return data type, we can tell the function it's allowed to be overridden by any class inheriting its functions. Back in the ChildClass, we have the option to override the virtual function.

```
public override void FunctionA()
{
    base.FunctionA();
    Debug.Log("Child's Addition to Function A.");
}
```

This has an added instruction for `FunctionA()`. As you might expect, the output to the Console panel has a new addition. The Child class will send new data to the Console that should read:

Without the keywords override and virtual, we get the following warning:

We can see this in the `ChildClass` `FunctionB()` and watch the resulting output. In the `ChildClass`, we'll add in the new keyword. However, the output will remain the same as though the Parent class' version of `FunctionB()` was being used. This is because the `FunctionB()` living in the `ChildClass` is a new one, and not the one being used by the `ParentFunction()`.

```
public new void FunctionB()
{
    Debug.Log("Child's New FunctionB? I'm too new and not called from anywhere.");
}
```

To explain a bit more about what happened when `ParentFunction()` is called.

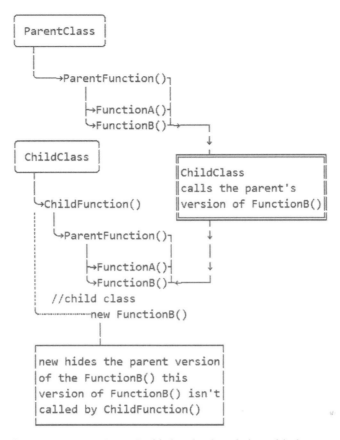

The ChildClass has a new FunctionB() this breaks the relation with the ParentClass version of FunctionB(). So when ParentFunction is called, the Parent's version of FunctionA and FunctionB are called. By using the override on a virtual function we add new behaviors to the FunctionA that's called in the ParentClass.

however when we use override the following happens.

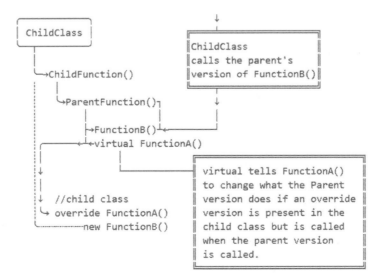

So when `ChildFunction()` is calling on `ParentFunction()` to run `FunctionA()` we get the added behavior that was created in the `ChildClass` version of `FunctionA()`. The difference between `override` and `new` when inheriting a function or variable from a parent create very different behaviors.

6.13.1.1.1 Base

The Child class' version of the `FunctionB` hides the inherited member from its `ParentClass`. Hiding means that the parent version of `FunctionB` cannot be directly called by the `ChildClass`. When the child calls the new `FunctionB()`, only the `ChildClass` version is visible.

On the other hand, we have overridden `FunctionA()` from the `ParentClass`. To use the original version, we can add the keyword `base` version in `FunctionA` which was overridden.

```
public override void FunctionA()
{
    base.FunctionA();
    //"Parent Function A Says Hello."
}
```

This produces the expected "`Parent Says Hello.`" to be printed out in the Console panel. For the `ChildClass` to take over the `FunctionA()` and create its own version of the function, omit the base `FunctionA()` and the contents of the parent version of `FunctionA()` will be skipped.

Therefore, when the InheritanceAgain script `Start()` function calls on the ParentClasses `ParentFunction()`, the ParentClass version of `FunctionA()` is called printing "`Parent Function A Says Hello.`" When the ChildClasses `ChildFunction()` calls on `ParentFunction()` the overridden `FunctionA()` is called, but the new `FunctionB()` isn't called.

6.13.2 Class Inheritance

We've seen a bit about how a function can inherit some members from a parent version of a class. To see how this works lets investigate some nested classes for some new Monsters.

```
class BaseMonsterClass
{
    public int HitPoints;
}
class ZombieClass : BaseMonsterClass
{
    public int BrainsEaten;
}
class VampireClass : BaseMonsterClass
{
    public int BloodSucked;
}
```

In the InheritanceAgain script, we've added `BaseMonsterClass` and `ZombieClass` as well as `VampireClass`. Both `ZombieClass` and `VampireClass` are followed with: `BaseMonsterClass` to indicate that they are both inheriting functions and fields from `BaseMonsterClass`.

6.13.2.1 Sharing Common Attributes

The whole point of inheritance is the ability to create a general class of object from which child objects can inherit the same properties. If all the characters in a game are going to share a system for taking damage, then they should all use the same system. Games use "mechanics" as a generalized term for game rules. Often used like "this game's mechanics are fun." Recovering health, taking damage, and interacting with objects should all be added to what is called a *base class*.

Consider building base classes for things such as destructible objects and monsters. Base classes allow for the multitude of objects in your game to have a shared attribute for something obvious like hitpoints and share the ability of the player to interact with them. Breaking down a door and basting away a zombie shouldn't require a different set of code to accomplish the same thing.

By adding public int HitPoints to BaseMonsterClass, we've given both Zombie and Vampire a HitPoints variable. This is a main strength of why we need to use inheritance. Objects that share common attributes should be able to share that data. We need to make this public so that when the class is used, you can access the HitPoints variable from outside of the class. To demonstrate, we'll need to make some instances of both the zombie and the vampire.

```
ZombieClass zombie = new ZombieClass();
VampireClass vampire = new VampireClass();
zombie.HitPoints = 10;
vampire.HitPoints = 10;
/* Assignment of HitPoints = 10
 * every time might be redundant.
 */
```

Now Vampires and Zombies have HitPoints. In the Start() function, we'll create a new Zombie and a new Vampire. Then we'll give them some starting HitPoints by using the identifier and adding .HitPoints = 10; to make the assignment.

However, if we add in a constructor, we can put the HitPoints = 10; into the constructor for the Monster instead! While we're at it, extend the Monster by adding a capsule to its presence. We'll also make him announce himself when he's created.

```
public int HitPoints;
public GameObject gameObject;
public BaseMonsterClass()
{
    HitPoints = 10;
    gameObject = GameObject.CreatePrimitive(PrimitiveType.Capsule);
    Debug.Log("A New Monster Rises!");
}
```

To make use of the HitPoints variable, we will create a function that will deal with damage done to the Monster. Adding in a new public function that returns an int called TakeDamage will be a good start.

```
public virtual int TakeDamage(int damage)
{
    return HitPoints - damage;
}
```

In the TakeDamage() argument list is (int damage) that will return the HitPoints - damage to let us know how many HitPoints the monster has after taking damage. Now both the Zombie and the Vampire can take damage. To allow the Zombie and Vampire to reuse the function and override its behavior, we add in virtual after the public keyword.

```
class VampireClass : BaseMonsterClass
{
    public int BloodSucked;
    public override int TakeDamage(int damage)
    {
        return HitPoints - (damage / 2);
    }
}
```

Perhaps we've decided vampires are more durable than zombies, we'll make the vampire take half the damage that is dealt to him. Using public override tells the function to take over the original use of the Monster.TakeDamage() function. This allows us to reuse the same function call on both zombies and vampires. For the Zombie, we'll return the default result of the Monster.TakeDamage() function by using return base. TakeDamage(damage);. Remember, the keyword base allows us to refer the original implementation of the code. The following appears in the Zombie:

```
public override int TakeDamage(int damage)
{
    return base.TakeDamage(damage);
}
```

In the Start() function, we'll make the following uses of zombie and vampire. The following code produces 5 and 8:

```
Debug.Log(zombie.TakeDamage(5));
Debug.Log(vampire.TakeDamage(5));
```

This looks useful, though remember that we're dealing with int values and not float. When we divide int 5 by int 2, we get 3, not 2.5. When building new objects, the goal is to reuse as much code as possible. Likewise, we can leave the TakeDamage() out of the zombie altogether if we don't need to make any changes.

However, it's sometimes unclear what's going on and might end up being less obvious when damage is dealt to the two monsters. In the end though, it's up to you to choose how to set up any functions that are inherited from your base monster class.

This should serve as a fair example as to what objects and classes are created in the way they are. When functions and variables are separated in classes, they allow you to compartmentalize for very specific purposes. When you design your classes, it's important to keep object-oriented concepts in mind.

6.13.3 Object

Changing behaviors of previously implemented functions is fundamental to object-oriented programming (OOP). The base class from which all classes in Unity 3D inherit is object. The .Net Framework provides object as a foundation for any other class being created. This allows every new object a common ground to communicate between one another.

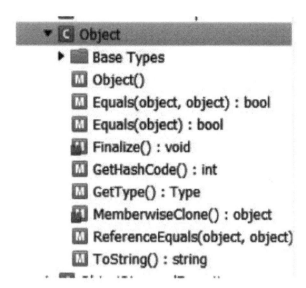

In Visual Studio the Solution Explorer panel is a regular fixture in the default layout. From here the a class diagram can be created from a each file in the solution. Selecting View Class Diagram shows a view which allows you to further edit your work in a more visual manner.

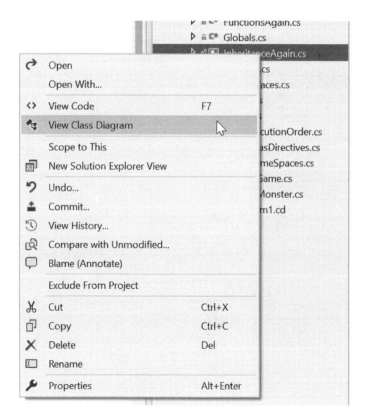

There have been many attempts to make a more visual system to build code. Viewing the class diagram for the InheritanceAgain.cs class you get a view similar to the following: Clicking on the icon on the top right of each box expands the object showing its contents. Using this view you're able to add new functions, aka methods, properties, fields, events, constructors, destructors, and constants. Further in the Class Details panel you're able to add type, parameters, and more to each added feature. It's a fun feature, and something which might help quickly build a useful start for your next game object.

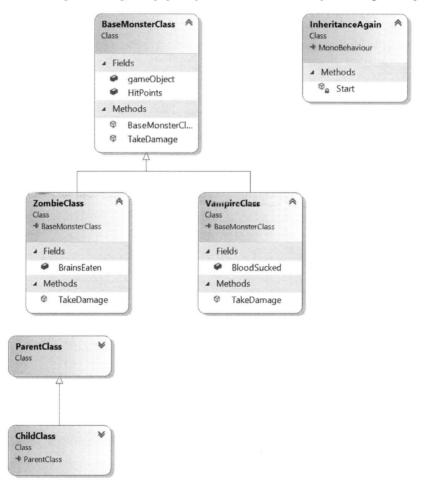

In addition to this view you'll also want to concern yourself with the Class View found in the View→Class View CTRL+Shift+C. This will allow you to expand each class to view the base types an object is inheriting from.

From here you can double click on the lowest class which InheritanceAgain is based on. The following Object Browser view is opened to reveal `public class Object Member of System`.

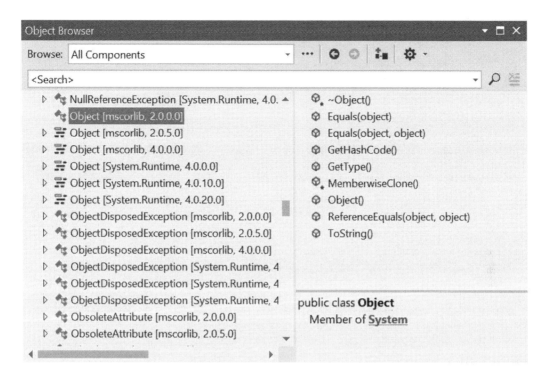

Object reveals several functions available to every class inheriting from it. The function `ToString()` is used every time we use values which are not strings in the `Debug.Log()` function in Unity 3D. In the ZombieClass we could add an override for `ToString()` with a custom value.

```
public override string ToString()
{
    return "I'm a Zombie!";
}
```

Using the override we get to see the following printed out to the Unity Editor's console panel:

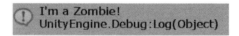

In your own project you may want to add more useful information to the `ToString()` override, but this should work as a starting point.

It's useful to find functions that are already in use and update them to fit our current class. The object class was created with `ToString()`, which provides every object in C# to have some sort of `ToString()` behavior. This also means that we can override `ToString()` with pretty much any class we create.

6.13.4 What We've Learned

At this point, we've got a great deal of the basics down. We can write classes and we know how the basics of inheritance work. This is important, as we proceed to use inheriting properties and methods more and more. We've studied a bit of flow control systems using if and switch, which are indispensable statements.

We've created several classes already, but we've yet to really use classes as objects. In Chapters 7 and 8, we're going to learn the core of what OOP is all about.

6.14　Type Casting Again

Type casting is the process of converting one data type into another. To follow along open the Chapter 6 Unity Project's CastingAgain_Scene and open the CastingAgain script on the CastingAgain game object in the scene. When programmers use the word *integral type*, they mean things that can be numbered.

```csharp
enum SimpleEnums
{
    FirstValue,
    SecondValue,
    ThirdValue
}

void Start()
{
    SimpleEnums simpleEnum = SimpleEnums.SecondValue;
    int convertedEnum = simpleEnum as int;
}
```

As we can see, we've written an enum with three options. With simpleEnums.SecondValue we try to change it into an int.

As we try to cast `simpleEnum as int;` we get an error!

> Assets/CastingAgain.cs(26,40): error CS0077: The `as` operator cannot be used with a non-nullable value type `int`

The as operator can't be used for this because an int is not actually an enum. Therefore, we get a conflict here. We're trying to use the enum as though it were already an int, which it's not. There is a way to convert different types from one to another.

```csharp
void Start()
{
    SimpleEnums simpleEnum = SimpleEnums.SecondValue;
    int convertedEnum = (int)simpleEnum;
    Debug.Log("convertedEnum: " + convertedEnum);
    // convertedEnum: 1
}
```

The line `int convertedEnum = (int)simpleEnum;` uses the explicit cast (int) to convert the SimpleEnums value into an int value. This isn't always possible, but in some cases, this will work when an explicit cast has been defined. Explicit casting requires the type's destination to have been expected. When the programmer creates a new data type, they may expect a conversion to another type. In this case, enum to int, the C# developers created a definition to enable that type conversion explicitly. Thus the naming: explicit type cast operator.

So why is "convertedEnum: 1" in the Console when we run the game? Remember that numbering lists in C# starts at 0, so the second item in a list will be indexed at 1. Of course, not all explicit conversions work. For instance, you can't turn a Monster GameObject into a float value. Zombies aren't just numbers!

6.14.1　(<Type>) versus "as"

We're starting to see the difference in type casting methods. The difference between (<Type>) cast and the as cast can come up during an interview process if you're trying to get a job as a programmer.

We should also note that some casting is also going on when we use float f = 1; where 1 is an int value, but it's accepted into a float f without any question. This is an implicit cast, or rather this is a cast that is accepted without any explicit cast operation. This also works for a double d = 1.0f; where 1.0f is a float value and d is a double.

The two different methods we can use are called *prefix casting* and *as casting*. Prefix casting is what the (int) syntax is called; this is also referred to as an explicit cast operator. The as operator works a bit differently than the explicit cast operator.

```
class Humanoid
{
}

class Zombie : Humanoid
{
}

class Person : Humanoid
{
}
```

Here we have three classes: Humanoid, Zombie, and Person. The Zombie and Person inherit from the Humanoid class. Discovering the differences with as and (Type) is significant only once we start getting into the nitty-gritty of doing something with the results of the type casting.

```
void CastingHumanoids()
{
    Humanoid h = new Humanoid();
    Zombie z = h as Zombie;
    Debug.Log(z);
    //"Null"
}
```

In the CastingAgain script the Start() function calls CastngHumanoids() where we perform the cast as seen above using the as-casting method. A new Humanoid h, instantiates a new Humanoid type object identified as h. Then a Zombie identified as z is assigned h as Zombie. This assumes that the Humanoid is a Zombie type convertable. When we use Debug.Log(z), we get Null.

> ⊘ Null
> UnityEngine.Debug:Log(Object)

Compare this result to the following explicit cast operator. If we use the prefix system as in the following example code:

```
Zombie x = (Zombie)h;
Debug.Log(x);
```

We get a different result, this time an error:

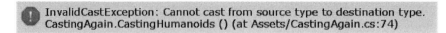

> InvalidCastException: Cannot cast from source type to destination type.
> CastingAgain.CastingHumanoids () (at Assets/CastingAgain.cs:74)

This tells us that a type Humanoid cannot be converted to a type Zombie. This doesn't change when converting between a Person and a Zombie. To create an explicit cast, we need to implement a function to allow the cast to work.

```
Person p = new Person();
Zombie zombieFromPerson = p as Zombie;
```

As before, we get a similar error.

> Assets/CastingAgain.cs(79,23): error CS0039: Cannot convert type 'CastingAgain.Person' to 'CastingAgain.Zombie' via a built-in conversion

The last part of the error indicates some built-in conversion. We need to add some lines of code to allow us to build in a cast between Zombie and Person.

You can imagine that this would happen quite a lot when playing a zombie game. C# is trying to make changes to the data to conform it so that it matches the type we're asking for it to be converted to. In some cases, the as operator is more appropriate than the prefix operator. A Null is much easier to deal with than an error. This conversion makes sense only when the types are incompatible if there is no conversion possible.

We can cast between ints and floats, no problem aside from losing numbers after a decimal. There are conversions available through C#, but no effort has been made to convert a Humanoid to a Zombie. A method should be made available to do so. The conversion work has been written for the built-in data types. The work has not yet been done to convert between a Person and a Zombie, so we shall do this.

6.14.2 User-Defined Type Conversion

Continuing, observe the code for the CastableHumanoid, which has some HitPoints.

```
class CastableHumanoid
{
    public int HitPoints;
}
```

This way we can have some significant meaning for converting between a Person and a Zombie. For this example, assume zombies use negative hitpoints and a person has a positive number for hitpoints. Thanks to inheritance, we can safely assume that both the Person and the Zombie will have a HitPoints property when they derive from the CastableHumanoid class.

Now we'll create a new function in the CastablePerson, so we can convert him into a CastableZombie.

```
class CastablePerson : CastableHumanoid
{
    static public implicit operator CastableZombie(CastablePerson person)
    {
        CastableZombie castable = new CastableZombie();
        castable.HitPoints = person.HitPoints * -1;
        return castable;
    }
}
```

With this we can see that we'll need to add a few new keywords. The keywords implicit and operator work together to allow us to use the CastableZombie cast when working with a CastablePerson type object. Now we can check what the hitpoints of a Person is if it was to be treated as a Zombie type object.

```
void CastingCastableHumanoids()
{
    CastablePerson p = new CastablePerson();
    p.HitPoints = 10;
    CastableZombie z = p as CastablePerson;
    Debug.Log("Cast Zombie: " + z.HitPoints);
    //"Cast Zombie: -10"
}
```

Through the implicit keyword, we can quite nicely assign the Zombie z to the Person type. We're also allowed to do something very simple like the following code sample:

```
CastableZombie personZombie = new CastablePerson();
Debug.Log(personZombie);
```

This automatically assigns personZombie a new CastablePerson() that is then implicitly converted to a CastableZombie upon assignment. Likewise, we can use a prefix conversion and get the same result by using an as operator.

```
CastablePerson p = new CastablePerson();
p.HitPoints = 10;
CastableZombie z = (CastableZombie)p;
Debug.Log(z + " " + z.HitPoints);
// CastableAgain+CastableZombie -10
```

Should you want to get the average health in a scene—zombies, vampires, mummies, and humans together—you'd want to iterate through a single data type. Get all gameObjects in the scene, then cast every component to humanoid. You'll have a humanoid for every zombie, vampire, mummy, and human in the scene. If you can't cast it to a humanoid, you'll get a null object. Null objects can be ignored and skipped. All that's left to do is calculate the average health.

6.14.3 Implicit versus Explicit Type Conversion

Explicit casts are used if there is a conversion that might end with some loss of data. Implicit casts assume that no data is lost while converting from one type to another. Explicit implies you understand that the conversion isn't going to be perfect.

For instance, if a zombie has a regeneration ability, the functions for that will be lost when you've cast a zombie to humanoid through the explicit type cast. You can cast a humanoid to as a zombie since it's assumed all attributes of a humanoid are still present in the zombie. Consider the following:

```
CastableHumanoid[] humanoids = new CastableHumanoid[]
{
    new CastableZombie(),
    new CastablePerson(),
    new CastableHumanoid(),
    new CastableZombie(),
    new CastablePerson()
};

foreach (CastableHumanoid humanoid in humanoids)
{
    Debug.Log(humanoid + " is a humanoid");
}
```

An array of humanoids is populated with zombies humanoids and persons. Each one of these is indeed a type of CastableHumanoid. They all share the same attributes as a CastableHumanoid. Adding a public bool isZombie; to the zombie makes the CastableZombie unique from the CastablePerson.

```
class CastableZombie : CastableHumanoid
{
    public bool isZombie;
    static public implicit operator CastablePerson(CastableZombie zombie)
    {
        CastablePerson castable = new CastablePerson();
        castable.HitPoints = 1;
        // imply you've revived someone
        // and they're barely alive.
        return castable;
    }
}
```

A variable which appears in a derived class but not in its base class is new data. This addition isn't something that the CastableHumanoid has available. Thus if you were to try to access the CastableZombie's isZombie bool from the CastableHumanoid type you'll get an error:

```
foreach (CastableHumanoid humanoid in humanoids)
{
    Debug.Log(humanoid + " is a humanoid");
    Debug.Log("humanoid has: " + humanoid.HitPoints + "HP");

    if (humanoid.isZombie)//variable could not be found!
    {
        Debug.Log("humanoid is a zombie?");
    }
}
```

The variable isZombie could not be found in CastableHumanoid. The process of going up and down in the relationship between base classes and derived classes is called Upcasting and Downcasting. The fancy view class diagram could reveal that both CastablePerson and CastableZombie can be "Upcast" to a CastableHuman and a CastableHuman can be "Downcast" to either a CastablePerson or a CastableZombie.

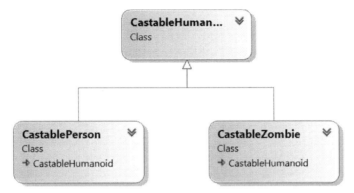

This upcasting and downcasting can also be seen when casting an int to a float. The int value 1 is the same as a float value 1.0, an implicit cast infers that nothing is lost. In some edge cases, there can be data lost, so implicit casts are not perfect, though they are generally reliable.

It also just so happens that all of this is the effect of what is called "Polymorphism"; a programming term that covers the topic of casting between types and type conversion. The roots of the word "Poly" is Greek for "many"; the second root is "morph" or "shape."

6.14.4 What We've Learned

Using the explicit and implicit type casts requires a bit of thought. When dealing with a large number of different types, we need to keep in mind what we're trying to accomplish by casting between types. In many cases, we should avoid unnecessary cast operations.

If data needs to be shared between different classes, it's better to create a parent class, or base class from which child classes inherit. Rather than requiring specific casts between people and zombies, a new version should be instanced between the two without using a cast.

Most casts should only be between specific data types. It should also be noted that casting is allowed between structs.

```
struct A
{
    public static explicit operator B(A a)
    {
        return new B();
    }
}


struct B
{
    static public explicit operator A(B b)
    {
        return new A();
    }
}
```

Here we can make an explicit cast from a to b and back again. Though there's nothing really going on here, a struct is somewhat different from a class, but offers many of the same functionality. Defining explicit cast operators is one of the shared abilities between a class and a struct.

6.15 Working with Vectors

Vector math is something that was taught in some high school math classes. Don't worry, you're not expected to remember much of that. Vector math is easily calculated in C# using the Unity 3D libraries, as vector math is often used in video games to move objects around.

Adding, subtracting, and multiplying vectors is easy in Unity 3D. We'll look at how simple vector math is in Unity 3D in this section using the Vector3() object.

There are also many tools added into the MonoBehaviour class we've been inheriting for most of the classes we've been writing. Only Start() and Update() have been added to our prebuilt class we've been starting with, but there are many others which we haven't seen yet.

6.15.1 Vectors Are Objects

Start with the WorkingWithVectors script attached to the game object of the same name in the WorkingWithVectors_Scene in the Chapter6 Unity Project. From this same Chapter 6 project in Section 6.5 Arrays Revisited, we worked on a Monster: MonoBehaviour where we made some simple floating cubes.

```
public int numMonsters;
//Use this for initialization
void Start()
{
    for (int i = 0; i < numMonsters; i++)
    {
        GameObject sphere = GameObject.CreatePrimitive(PrimitiveType.Sphere);
        sphere.AddComponent<Monster>();
        Vector3 pos = new Vector3()
        {
            x = Random.Range(-10, 10),
            z = Random.Range(-10, 10)
        };
        sphere.transform.position = pos;
    }
}
```

Random.Range(); is a new function. Random is an class located in the UnityEngine namespace. We use this to give us a number between -10 and 10. The two arguments are separated by a comma. The first argument is the minimum value and the second number is the maximum value we want. Then Random sets the x and z to a number between these two values.

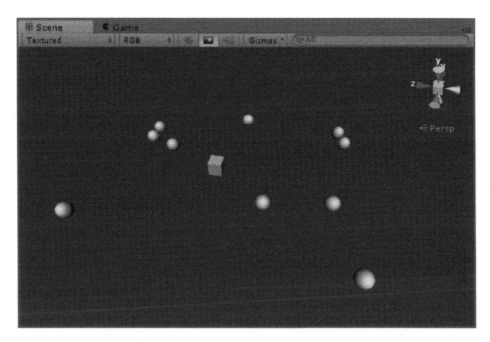

Assuming that NumMonsters is set to 10 or so, play the game and `MonsterGenerator` creates a field of sphere monsters placed randomly in the x and z directions. As an alternative, we could have put the positioning information inside of the monster himself using the `Start()` function.

6.15.2 Stepping through MonsterGenerator

We introduced breakpoints in Section 4.12.9, but this is a good point to come back to how breakpoints are used to see how your code is working. Why does each monster appear at a different place? Let's add in a breakpoint near the first line within the "for" statement.

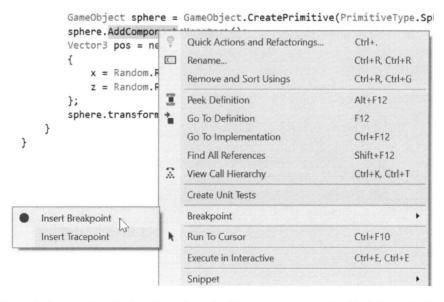

Here, I have the breakpoint added on line where the Monster component is added. Press the Run button and attach Visual Studio to Unity 3D.

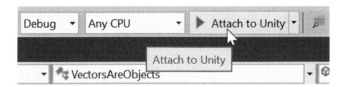

In MonoDevelop, select Run → Start Debugging and then select Unity 3D in the following pop-up panel. Go back to the Unity 3D editor and press the Play button. You may notice not much happening in Unity 3D, which means that MonoDevelop grabbed Unity 3D's thread and is holding it at the breakpoint.

Start stepping through the code. Pressing the F10 key on the keyboard will push the arrow one line at a time through the "for" statement. After pressing it once, you'll notice that the highlighted line will begin to move over your code. Also notice the data populating the Callstack and the Locals windows that open below the code.

Click on the word "sphere." Each instance of the word will highlight and a new dialog box will open up with specifics on the new sphere object. Hover the cursor over "sphere" to invoke a pop-up with information on the sphere object.

```csharp
for (int i = 0; i < numMonsters; i++)
{
    GameObject sphere = GameObject.CreatePrimitive(PrimitiveType.Sphere);
 ▶| sphere.AddComponent<Monster>();
    Vecto ▶ ● sphere  "Sphere (UnityEngine.GameObject)"  ⇥
    {|
        x = Random.Range(-10, 10),
        z = Random.Range(-10, 10)
    };
    sphere.transform.position = pos;
```

Step again and we'll get details on the new `Vector3` called `pos`, which I'm using as an abbreviation of "position." Press F10 to *step over* once to move to the next line.

```csharp
sphere.AddComponent<Monster>();
 ▶| Vector3 pos = new Vector3()
    {                  ▶ ● pos  "(0.0, 0.0, 0.0)"  ⇥
        x = Random.Range(-10, 10),
        z = Random.Range(-10, 10)
    };
    sphere.transform.position = pos;
```

It's important to understand that data isn't fulfilled on the line it's created on. Only after stepping one more line with F10 does the data become fulfilled.

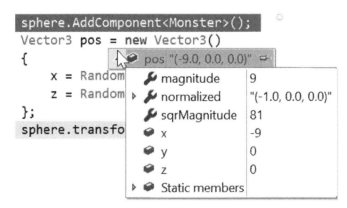

Step through a few more times, and allow a few monsters to be created. With each iteration the values for pos will have changed to different values.

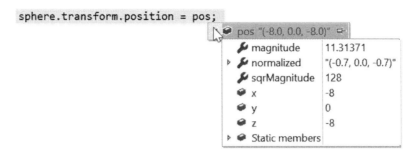

Keep on pressing F10 and you'll be able to follow the flow of the code as each line highlights again. Each time the line is executed, the values coming from the `Random.Range()` function will be different. Therefore, the code will scatter the monsters around the `MonsterGenerator`.

Unity and Visual Studio are rather locked together. Unity is stuck in debug mode and Visual Studio is holding onto Unity's activity. To release Unity from Visual Studio's hold, press the "stop debugging" button.

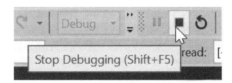

This releases Unity from Visual Studio's debugger and the two apps will act independently again. Connecting Visual Studio to Unity allows you to thoroughly inspect how your code is updated as the game is played, a powerful tool for finding bugs and figuring out where they originate from.

The option of where to set the initial position of an object is up to the programmer. It's up to you to decide who and where the position of a new object is set. This flexibility allows you to decide how and when code is executed.

6.15.3 Gizmos

While stepping through code helps a great deal with understanding how our code is being executed, visualizing things as they move can be more helpful. That's where Unity 3D has provided us with a great deal of tools for doing just that.

Unity 3D calls its helper objects "Gizmos." Visualizing data is carried out by using Gizmos to draw lines and shapes in the scene. In other game engines, this may be called DrawDebugLine or DrawDebugBox. In Unity 3D, the engineers added the Gizmos class. The members of this class include DrawLine and DrawBox.

Colored lines, boxes, spheres, and other things can be constructed from the code. If we want to draw a line from the monster to a target, we might use a line between the two, so we know that the monster can "see" its next meal. It's difficult to mentally visualize what the vectors are doing. Having Unity 3D display them in the scene makes the vector math easier to understand.

6.15.3.1 A Basic Example

Open the Gizmo script attached to the game object of the same name in the in the Working With Vectors_Scene. project is the `DrawLine()`; function that requires two arguments or parameters. The first argument is a start vector followed by an end vector. In the Gizmo script is the `OnDrawGizmos()` after the `Start()` and `Update()` functions. The `OnDrawGizmos()` can be placed before or after the `Start()` or `Update()` function, but to keep organized we'll add it after the preconstructed functions.

```csharp
public class Gizmos : MonoBehaviour
{
    // Start is called before the first frame update
    void Start()
    {

    }

    // Update is called once per frame
    void Update()
    {

    }

    private void OnDrawGizmos()
    {
        |
    }
}
```

To see what's going on, create a new Sphere GameObject Object using the GameObject → Create Other → Sphere menu, and then add the Gizmos.cs component in the Inspector panel.

To draw a Gizmo, we'll need to pick the Gizmo we want to use.

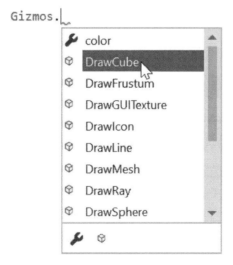

When we start with "Gizmos." we are presented with quite a list of things we can try out. Thanks to MonoDevelop, it's quite easy to figure out how these are used. Each function has some pretty clear clues as to what data types are used and what they are for.

```
Gizmos.DrawCube()
```
void Gizmos.DrawCube(**Vector3 center**, Vector3 size)
Draw a solid box with center and size.

Starting with "DrawCube," we'll be prompted with a Vector3 for the cube's center and another Vector3 for the cube's size. To fulfill the DrawCube member function in Gizmos, enter the following arguments:

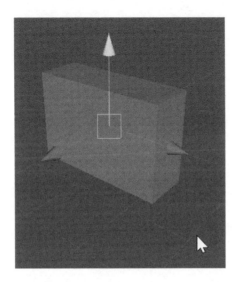

The Gizmo will be drawn with the center point at Vector3.zero which is the scene's origin, and the size will be Vector3 (1, 2, 3), making the object 1 unit wide, 2 units tall, and 3 units deep. Gizmos are interesting as they represent some very useful debugging tools. Gizmos do not draw in the game, they're only visible in the Scene view in the editor.

6.15.3.2 DrawRay

Some of the other Gizmo functions require data types we haven't encountered yet, such as rectangles and rays. With a little bit of detection, we can figure out how these work. Let's start off with a DrawRay we're presented with (Ray r) as its argument. We can start with a new Ray (and we'll be given a (Vector3 origin, Vector3 direction)).

We can fulfill this with Gizmos.DrawRay(new Ray(new Vector3 (0, 0, 0), new Vector3 (0, 1, 0)));. This might seem like a bit of a convoluted line to read, so we can make this more easy to read by breaking out one of the arguments.

```
Ray ray = new Ray();
ray.origin = Vector3.zero;
ray.direction = Vector3.up;
Gizmos.DrawRay(ray);
```

This code will produce a simple white line that starts at the origin and points up in the *y*-axis 1 unit. Rays are useful tools that show an object's direction or angle of movement. We'll take a closer look once we get more used to how Gizmos are used. Assuming the object with the script applied is a cube at the origin of the scene, you'll have a similar effect to the following figure:

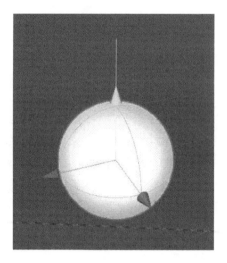

6.15.4 Using Gizmos

```
Gizmos.DrawLine(transform.position, Vector3.zero);
```

The `Gizmos DrawLine()` from `transform.position` to `Vector3.zero` traces a line from the object's center to the scene origin. The appearance of the `Gizmos` class cannot function outside of the `OnDrawGizmos()` function. Using the `Gizmos` class in an `Update()` function will not produce any results.

Now we're drawing a bunch of white lines from the center of the Gizmo game objects to the center of the world. To make use of this we can attach a Player class to an object in the scene and have the spheres draw a line to it

Gizmos are intended to help debug a scene and provide various visual aids to the game designer to help setup a scene.

6.15.5 What We've Learned

Unity 3D has many tools built in for doing vector math functions. It's a good idea to figure out how they're used. We'll explore as many different uses of these tools as we can, but we're going to be hard pressed to see all of them.

A Gizmo is a handy tool to help see what your code is trying to do. Gizmos draw lines, boxes, and other shapes. You can even have text printed into your 3D scene for debugging purposes. Again, we'll try to use as many of the different Gizmos as we can.

The sort of optimization we did here is in the reduction of lines of code only. There was no actual change to the speed at which the code here was executed. There are some cases in which a line or two should be added to speed things up.

For now, we're going to focus on keeping our code clear and readable. Later, we'll learn some basic programming idioms. Programming idioms are little tricks that programmers often use to reduce complex tasks to just a line or two. They're sometimes rather cryptic, but once you understand them, they're quite useful.

6.16 goto Labels

We've gone through several of the usually employed logical controls in Section 4.11.3. This time we have the goto keyword. It is a commonly misused control statement, and it's about time we learned about how it's used.

The goto keyword allows you to jump around in a statement. The non-linear behavior is one of the reasons why most programmers would tell you to avoid using goto if it's unnecessary. When using many goto statements, you end up making your code difficult to read as you need to jump around to follow the flow. It's still important to understand how goto works if you come across it so lets go ahead and learn how goto works.

A goto statement is the keyword `goto` followed by an identifier, which is referred to as a *label*. This looks like `goto MyLabel;` which tells C# which label to go to, in this case as `MyLabel;` which is the identifier followed by a colon.

To follow along, open the GotoLabels_Scene in the Chapter6 Unity Project, then open the GotoLabels script found on the GotoLabels game object in the scene. A goto statement should be encapsulated by some sort of logical statement. It's very easy to get caught in a loop with a goto statement. This has a similar behavior to `for(;;)` and `while (true)` which will hold Unity 3D in an endless loop forcing you to kill the process from the Task Manager.

```
StartOver:
goto StartOver;
```

Using a label and a goto in this way will create an infinite loop that will require you to kill Unity 3D from the Task Manager.

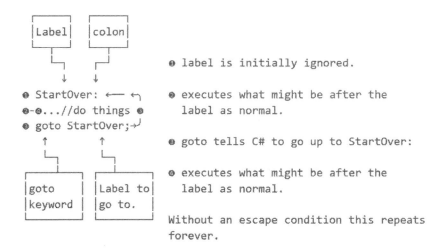

● label is initially ignored.

● executes what might be after the
  label as normal.

● goto tells C# to go up to StartOver:

● executes what might be after the
  label as normal.

Without an escape condition this repeats
forever.

The statement StartOver: acts as bookmark. Initially the bookmark has no effect on how code is executed. Anything after the identified label is executed as normal. When the goto is reached execution jumps to the bookmark and continues executing code from that point on. There's nothing wrong with the above statemen syntactically, and it's just not very useful. The flow of execution can be controlled by other means between the label and the goto statement.

```
int num = 0;

StartOver:

num++;
if (num > 3)
{
    goto Stop;
}

Debug.Log("Looping: " + num + " times.");
goto StartOver;

Stop:

Debug.Log("Stopped.");
```

This code runs until num has incremented to more than 3. Then the goto Stop: is reached and we skip over the Debug.Log(); and goto StartOver; statements and continue after the Stop: label. The console in Unity 3D has the following output. In this case the goto Stop; acts as our escape from the repeating loop.

This is the same as `for(int i = 0; i < 3; i++);` only some might find it a bit harder to read. Of course, it's up to you to choose when to use a goto statement, but there are some useful cases. Finding a good reason to use the goto statement comes with experience in spotting when it might be useful. Because they're tricky to use and to read, most programmers shy away from using them at all. We're learning as much as we can in this book, so we may also learn how it's used.

6.16.1 Skipping Down

In a very simple form a goto label can be used to skip code based on a condition.

```
int num = 0;/*  setting this to 1          */
if (num > 0)/*  will jump our code         */
{                        /*                 */
    goto FirstLabel;   /* from here→¬       */
}                               /*  ↓       */
Debug.Log("Before FirstLabel:"); /*  | skipped */
FirstLabel:                     /*  ↓       */
Debug.Log("After FirstLabel:");  /*←┘ to here */
```

By adding in a public int num to the class, we're able to pick the goto label we're using. If we set num to 0, then both print statements will be executed. If the number is greater than 0, then only the second "After FirstLabel:" print function will be executed.

When we started off with the switch statement, we looked at the keyword case. The case keyword set up conditions which the statement would skip through till a case fits the statement. It then executed the code that followed the case.

switch and goto statements share the colon (:) notation for labels. However, goto lets you set up labels anywhere in a code block, whereas the switch statement allows labels only within the switch statement. When goto is used, it sends the software to the line following the label it was told to jump to.

6.16.2 Zombie State Machine

In the GoToLabels_Scene are some ZombieWithStates game objects. On these is a ZombieWithStates script. The script has an enum MovementStates where we've defined an Idleing, Wandering, Looking, Chasing, and Feeding.

For this project we'll create a zombie which stands around for a moment. After some time, the zombie may decide to look for a meal or just wander before standing around again. If the zombie encounters a meal they'll pursue for a moment, then eat or give up and go back to standing around.

```
public enum MovementStates
{
    Idleing,
    Wandering,
    Looking,
    Chasing,
    Feeding
}
public MovementStates MovementState;
public float StateTimer;
```

Labels can allow us to group statements together in a single function. The intent would be to allow us to quickly prototype different behaviors. After a state change check we use a switch statement to jump our execution to different labels later in the same function. This acts as a hub to determine where in the function to go to.

```
switch (MovementState)
{
    case MovementStates.Idleing: goto Idle;
    case MovementStates.Wandering: goto Wander;
    case MovementStates.Looking: goto Look;
    case MovementStates.Chasing: goto Chase;
    case MovementStates.Feeding: goto Feed;
}
```

The labels live at the bottom of the `Update()` function waiting to be filled in with their behaviors. For now, we've just added a `Debug.Log()` in place to update which state the Zombie is in.

```
Idle:
Debug.Log("Idle");
goto UpdateTimer;

Look:
Debug.Log("Look");
...
goto UpdateTimer;

Wander:
Debug.Log("Wander");
...
goto Look;

Chase:
Debug.Log("Chase");
...
goto UpdateTimer;

Feed:
Debug.Log("Feed");
...
goto UpdateTimer;
```

After spending time in each mode, the statement jumps to an `UpdateTimer:` label. Under the `UpdateTimer` label of the same function we're checking the `StateTimer`. Once the game time has past the `StateTimer`, we pick a new length of time for the `StateTimer` and pick a new `MovementState`.

```
UpdateTimer:
if (Time.time > StateTimer)
{
    StateTimer = Time.time + Random.Range(3.0f, 7.0f);
    switch (MovementState)
    {
        case MovementStates.Idleing:
            switch (Random.Range(0, 3))
            {
                case 0:
                    MovementState = MovementStates.Idleing;
                    break;
                case 1:
                    MovementState = MovementStates.Looking;
                    break;
                case 2:
                    MovementState = MovementStates.Wandering;
                    break;
            }
            break;
        case MovementStates.Wandering:
        case MovementStates.Looking:
        case MovementStates.Chasing:
        case MovementStates.Feeding:
            MovementState = MovementStates.Idleing;
            break;
    }
}
// escape from Update()
return;
```

In the `UpdateTimer:` label we decide that if zombie is in Idle, then we're able to pick a different state, either continue to `Idle`, change to `Looking`, or change to `Wandering`. This provides us with some opportunity for variations in behavior.

After the game time has run past the `StateTimer` we return to `Idle`. The first label to inspect is the `Look:` label. This is a basic function that we'll want to use to update what direction the zombie is facing.

```
// update rotation
transform.rotation = Quaternion.RotateTowards(transform.rotation, targetRotation, 5f);
```

To rotate the character, we create a targetRotation value. The direction of we want to face the character. To smoothly rotate the character toward the targetRotation we call `RotateTowards()`.

To check when `RotateTowards()` is finished rotating the character, we check the angle between the character's current facing and the target using `Quaternion.Angle()`. Once the angle is less than a fraction of a degree we pick a new targetRotation value.

```
// checking if we're facing our target direction
float angle = Quaternion.Angle(transform.rotation, targetRotation);
if (angle < 0.1f || angle == 180)
{
    Vector3 dir = new Vector3()
    {
        x = Random.Range(-1f, 1f),
        y = 0,
        z = Random.Range(-1f, 1f)
    };
    targetRotation = Quaternion.LookRotation(dir, transform.up);
}
```

If we then look at the Wander: label we see the Zombie move in its forward direction. Then the code jumps back to the Look: label to continue picking new directions to look in.

```
Wander:
transform.position += transform.forward * 0.01f;
goto Look;
```

By adding a single line of code and jumping back into the Look: label we're able to add a new layer of behavior quickly and easily. Without too much effort we're able to add additional layers of behavior with simple jump statements using goto. The jump statements can also be used within loops.

If we come across a human, the zombie should chase after him. To accomplish this there are HumanWithStates scripts attached to the Human objects in the scene. The HumanWithStates script is based on the ZombieWithStates class. This means that it will inherit the Update() function with the chase and feed behaviors as well.

6.16.3 This as a Reference to Yourself

This can be skipped by checking if the class is a HumanWithStates, jumping out of the update look, and going to the UpdateTimer label early.

```
if (this.GetType() == typeof(HumanWithStates))
    goto UpdateTimer;
```

The above does two things. The first part of the statement is this. GetType() the type of data were it to be a ZombieWithStates would return the type ZombieWithStates. Then it compares it to a typeof(HumanWithStates). The inherited version of the script is HumanWithStates and the if statement returns true, the zombie does not.

When true, the goto jumps the execution of the script to the UpdateTimer label. The zombie will continue to execute past the jump statement and continue to update its behavior for seeking out humans to prey on.

The this keyword behaves as though it's the class it's in. In many ways the keyword is redundant, but it does serve as a visual reminder to the programmer as to what we're checking on. The statement could have easily been GetType() == typeof(HumanWithStates). By using the this keyword ahead of GetType() we make it more clear as to what object we're getting the type of.

6.16.4 Just for Zombies

With a type check we can block the human from accessing Zombie actions. For the zombie to do zombie like things we should sort through the scene, find humans, and chase after the closest one in range.

```
HumanWithStates closestHuman = null;
GameObject[] allGameObjects = GameObject.FindObjectsOfType<GameObject>();
float closest = Mathf.Infinity;
Vector3 direction = Vector3.zero;
foreach (GameObject go in allGameObjects)
{
    HumanWithStates human = go.GetComponent<HumanWithStates>();
    if (human != null)
    {
        float distance = (go.transform.position - transform.position).magnitude;
        //check if it's a zombie
        if (distance < closest)
        {
            closestHuman = human;
            direction = go.transform.position - transform.position;
            closest = distance;
        }
    }
}
```

At the first block of code at the start of each Update() loop, we populate a list with all-GameObjects. To check only humans in the scene we use GetComponent<HumansWithS tates>() to check if the object has a human script attached. If the object is a human, then we calculate the distance to it.

By storing the closest distance, we can check if there's a closer human than the previous human checked. As we update the values we keep a record of the shortest distance the closest human, and the direction that human is in.

```
if (closest < 5)
{
    targetRotation = Quaternion.LookRotation(direction, transform.up);
    transform.rotation = Quaternion.RotateTowards(transform.rotation, targetRotation, 5f);
    MovementState = MovementStates.Chasing;
}
```

In the section of the code the Zombie is allowed access, we check if any humans are within 5 units away. If there are then we use the stored direction and update the targetRotation toward the human. Once we've taken aim at a human, we change to MovementState.Chasing.

Once we jump down to the Chase: label we check if the closest human is within feeding range. If not, we continue to move toward the target.

```
if (closest < 0.25f)
{
    MovementState = MovementStates.Feeding;
}
transform.position += transform.forward * 0.01f;
```

Once we're in range to feed we take care that there's a human to eat with a null check. Finally, we swap in a ZombieWithStates component as well as the character mesh.

```
if (closestHuman != null && closest < 0.25f)
{
    // convert human to zombie
    Transform zombiePrimitive = transform.Find("ZombiePrimitive");
    if (zombiePrimitive == null)
        return;
    Destroy(closestHuman.transform.Find("HumanPrimitive").gameObject);
    GameObject newZombie = GameObject.Instantiate(zombiePrimitive.gameObject);
    newZombie.transform.parent = closestHuman.gameObject.transform;
    newZombie.transform.localPosition = Vector3.zero;
    newZombie.transform.localRotation = Quaternion.identity;
    closestHuman.gameObject.AddComponent<ZombieWithStates>();
    Destroy(closestHuman);
    return;
}
```

6.16.5 What We've Learned

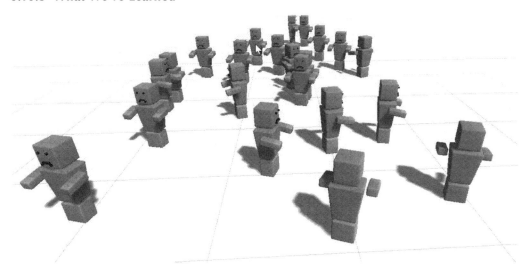

Goto labels don't have to be cumbersome to be useful. As a simple divider to a long Update() function, they can work for you and remain clear so long as the mechanism that switches between labels is clear and contained in one place such as a switch statement.

You can easily make an argument to leave all the logic within the switch statement and avoid the labels altogether, but this can easily make the switch statement larger and bulkier than necessary as well. In the end, the only difference is readability. If by using labels you make your code easier to follow, then using labels is fine. If your switch statement begins to overflow with different cases, then you might want to try another system outside of the switch, and labels might be a nice option.

On your own it's a good idea to see what this code would look like by adding different states. Perhaps when a zombie gets close enough to a human, that human could turn into a zombie. When a pair of humans gets close to a zombie, then the zombie might turn into a human. Simple mechanics like this can quickly add a very unpredictable level of behavior and emerge into a game mechanic simply through experimentation with the code itself.

6.17 More on Arrays

In the previous chapter we generated an array by using the FindAllObjectsOfType() function. This returned an array filled with everything in the scene, cameras and lights included. To iterate through the array we used the foreach() function and searched every game object for a human component. Using that array we were also able to find the closest human to the zombie.

Arrays have a few different descriptions. Your standard array is called a single-dimensional array. The Array of game objects from the previous example is a single dimensional array. Other array types include multidimensional and jagged. Arrays can store any data type; this includes other arrays.

6.17.1 Length and Count

Declaring an array is simple and uses a different operator than a class or function to contain its data. The square brackets [and] are used to tell the compiler that your identifier is going to be used for an array. The following statement declares an array of integers:

```
int i;
/* a single int value */
int[] ints;
/* array of ints without any values */
Debug.Log(i + ints[0]);
/* Cannot use i or ints without values */
```

We can dynamically declare an array of ints using the following notation. Use curly braces { } to contain the contents of the array assigned to primes.

```
int[] primes = new int[] { 1, 3, 5, 7, 11, 13, 17, 23, 27, 31 };
/*  ↑                ↑              */
/*  ┌────────────────┴──────────┐  */
/*  │ brackets tell lexer to    │  */
/*  │ create array for given type│ */
/*  └───────────────────────────┘  */
```

Arrays have several functions associated with them, which we can use with different loops. To get the number of items in an array, we use the Length property of the array.

6.17.1.1 A Basic Example

In the MoreOnArrays scene start with the MoreOnArrays.cs script attached to the MoreOnArrays game object in the scene.

```
int[] primes = new int[] { 1, 3, 5, 7, 11, 13, 17, 23, 27, 31};
int primeLength = primes.Length;
```

In this example, we assign primeLength to the Length of the primes array. We'll see why this is more useful than creating an array of a set length ahead of time in a moment. To use this in a for loop, we use the following syntax shown in the following code fragment added to the Start() function:

```
for (int i = 0; i < primesLength; i++)
{
    Debug.Log(primes[i]);
}
```

This code prints out a new line for each number stored in the array. Each time the for loop iterates, the int i moves to the next item in the array starting with the zeroth index. Once the end of the list is reached, the for loop exits. We could also use a while loop to do the same thing.

```
int j = 0;
while (j < primesLength)
{
    Debug.Log(primes[j++]);
}
```

This produces the same output with the brevity of the while syntax, but the counter j required for the while loop needs to live outside of the while statement's code block. Something to consider for why we'd store the Length property is performance.

Consider the Length property of an array needs to be looked up may take several nano seconds. Each iteration of a for loop and a while loop would need ask the array for the Length property. By storing an arrayLength by request the Length property once you've shaved off a few nano seconds of compute time.

```
/*                    ┌──────────────────────┐      */
/*                    │  Length needs to be  │      */
/*                    │  requested every loop │      */
/*                    └──────────┬───────────┘      */
/*                               ↓                   */
for (int i = 0; i < primes.Length; i++)
{
    Debug.Log(primes[i]);
}
```

Yet another option, and one that's slightly tailored for an array, is foreach.

6.17.2 Foreach: A Reminder

With an array of ints in our primes variable, we can use the following syntax to print out each item in the array:

```
int[] primes = new int[] { 1, 3, 5, 7, 11, 13, 17, 23, 27, 31 };
foreach (int p in primes)
{
    Debug.Log(p);
}
```

This syntax is quite short, simple, and easy to use. The keyword in assigns the int p variable to each element in the primes array it's given. Using a foreach loop we lose a counter to keep track of the number of iterations we've looped through the statement.

Which form you use is up to you, but it's important to know that you have more than one option. Of course, you can use any identifier for counting indexes; int j could just as easily be int index or anything else that makes sense. Though the common convention is to use the for (int i = 0; i < items; i++) form for iterating through an array, the int i variable initialized in the parameter list of the for loop can be used for various things related to the element we're stepping through in the array. We often need to know where we are in the array. If this information isn't necessary, then it's easier to stick to the foreach iterator when using an array.

We can declare arrays of different lengths by using different bits of data. Each one is of a different length. Using the Length property of each array, it's easier for us to print out each array without knowing how many items are stored in each one.

```
int[] primes = { 1, 3, 5, 7, 11, 13, 17, 23, 27, 31 };
int[] fibonacci = { 0, 1, 1, 2, 3, 5, 8, 13, 21, 34, 55, 89, 144 };
int[] powersOfTwo = { 1, 2, 4, 8, 16, 32, 64, 128, 255, 512, 1024 };
```

Of course, these aren't complete sets of numbers, but that's not the point. They are different lengths, and we don't need to keep track of how many items are stored in each array to print out their contents.

```
int[] primes = { 1, 3, 5, 7, 11, 13, 17, 23, 27, 31 };
int[] fibonacci = { 0, 1, 1, 2, 3, 5, 8, 13, 21, 34, 55, 89, 144 };
int[] powersOfTwo = { 1, 2, 4, 8, 16, 32, 64, 128, 255, 512, 1024 };
ArrayList numbers = new ArrayList{ primes, fibonacci, powersOfTwo};
int numArrays = numbers.Count; /* ArrayList uses .Count, not .Length */
for (int i = 0; i < numArrays; i++)
{
    int[] nums = numbers[i] as int[];
    int items = nums.Length;
    for (int j = 0; j < items; j++)
    {
        Debug.Log(nums[j]);
    }
}
```

In the above code fragment, we've added in three different arrays of integers. After that we declare a new `ArrayList` called numbers fulfilled with a new `ArrayList` {primes, fibonacci, powersOfTwo};. This fills the new `ArrayList` with the three different `int[]` arrays, where each `int[]` has a different `Length` property.

ArrayLists differ from a regular array in that its `Length` property is called `Count`. Therefore, to get the number of items stored in the `ArrayList`, we use `numbers.Count` rather than `Length`. This is assigned to an int numArrays for use in a for loop.

To learn about the difference, we could post on a forum, "How do I get the size of an ArrayList?" Alternatively, we could right click on the `ArrayList` type and select Go To Definition F12 from the following pop-up:

This brings us to the declaration of classes and all of the things that the `ArrayList` allows us to do.
Scroll through the options till we find something we can use.

```
public virtual int Count
{
    get;
}
```

In the Assembly Browser, we'll find a Count property that sounds reasonably usable. It's possible to do many different things with the other options found in the ArrayList class, so we'll experiment with them next.

It's important to remember the Go To Definition function in Visual Studio to be a self-sufficient programmer. If it's late at night and you have a final or dead-line due in the morning, you may not have enough time to wait for an answer on a forum.

Unfortunately, there aren't so many options with the int[] as this brings you to only what an int32 is defined as. Luckily, most of the questions have been asked about how to deal with an array in C#. There is, however, a class definition for Array. This can be found by using the Search field in the Assembly Browser.

From here, you can find all the functions and properties available to use with the Array type. The ArrayList's count can be used as a condition to stop the for loop. Once we have the ArrayList's count, it's used in the following for loop as the condition to stop the loop.

```
int numArrays = numbers.Count;
for (int i = 0; i < numArrays; i++)
{
}
```

This code will allow us to iterate through each array stored in the numbers array list. Next, we need to get the int[] array stored at the current index of the array list. This is done by using the for loop's initializer's int i variable and a cast. ArrayList stores each item as a generic object type. This means that the item at numbers[i] is an undeclared type of object. In this case, the object stored at the index is an int[] type.

```
int[] nums = numbers[i] as int[];
```

Casting the object to an int[] is as simple as numbers[i] as int[];. Without this cast, we get the following error:

❌ CS0266   Cannot implicitly convert type 'object' to 'int[]'. An explicit conversion exists (are you missing   Assembly-CSharp   MoreOnArrays.cs   97   Active
a cast?)

This assumes that an object is trying to be used as an int[], as indicated by the declaration int[] nums, and to do so, we need to use the as int[] cast. Once nums is an int[] array, we can use it as a regular array. This means we can get the nums.Length to start another for loop.

```
/*  ❶ nums assumes the type array of ints              */
/*   ┌─────────────────────────────┐  ┌──────────────┐ */
/*   ↓                             │  │ ❷ this allows │*/
int[] nums = numbers[i] as int[];/*  ├─┤   the use of │*/
int items = nums.Length;/*  ←───────┘  │   .Length    │*/
                    /*                  └──────────────┘*/
```

This loop will begin the next loop printing out each item stored in the nums integer array. As we did earlier, we use the following fragment:

```
for (int j = 0; j < items; j++)
{
    Debug.Log(nums[j]);
}
```

This fragment is inside of the first for loop. Using this, we'll get each item of each array stored at each index of the numbers array list. This seems like a great deal of work, but in truth it's all necessary and this will become second nature once you're used to the steps involved in dealing with arrays.

`ArrayLists` allow you to store any variety of object. To store an array of arrays, you need to use an `ArrayList`. What might seem correct to start off with might be something like the following:

```
int notAvailable = numbers.Length;
```

In fact, this is syntactically correct, and intuition might tell you that there's no problem with this. However, the Array type isn't defined as it is without any type assigned to it. However, we can use the following:

```
object[] obj_numbers = { primes, fibonacci, powersOfTwo };
```

This turns each `int[]` into an object, and numbers is now an array of objects. To an effect we've created the same thing as before with the `ArrayList`; only we've defined the length of the Numbers array by entering three elements between the curly braces.

For clarification, we can use the foreach iterator with both the `ArrayList` and the `int []` array.

```
object[] obj_numbers = { primes, fibonacci, powersOfTwo };
foreach (int[] nums in obj_numbers)
{
    foreach (int n in nums)
    {
        Debug.Log(n);
    }
}
```

This produces the same output to the Console panel in Unity 3D as the previous version; only it's a lot shorter. It's important to recognize the first foreach statement contains `int [] nums in obj_numbers` as each element in the `obj_numbers` array is an `int []` array type.

6.17.3 Discovery

Learning what a class has to offer involves a great deal testing. For instance, we saw many other functions in `ArrayList` which we didn't use. We saw Count that returned an integer value. This was indicated when the listing showed us Count: int in the Assembly Browser.

However, it's good to learn about the other functions found in `ArrayList`. Let's pick the `ToArray()`: `object[]` function; this sounds useful, but what does it do? More important, how do we find out? The steps here begin with testing various features one at a time.

The return type indicates that it's giving us an object, so let's start there.

```
ArrayList numbers = new ArrayList { primes, fibonacci, powersOfTwo };
object thing = numbers.ToArray();
Debug.Log("thing is: " + thing);
```

This sends the following output to the Console panel:

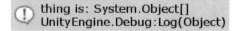

thing is: System.Object[]
UnityEngine.Debug:Log(Object)

The `thing` is apparently a `System.object[]` that was sent to the Console output panel. From this, we learned that thing is, indeed, an `object[]`, or rather it's an array of objects. What can we do with this? Let's change this to match what we've observed.

```
object[] anotherThing = numbers.ToArray() as object[];
Debug.Log("anotherThing Length: " + anotherThing.Length);
```

Now that we know it's an array, let's cast it to being a proper array by adding in a cast. Now the thing returns a length. We get 3 sent to the Console panel of Unity 3D when we press the Play game button. But what's going on here? Remember that earlier we had to use `numbers.Count` to get the size of the ArrayList. Now we're dealing with a regular Array, not an ArrayList. Therefore, should we need to use an Array and not an ArrayList, this function could come in handy! Good to know.

This little exercise is important; a part of learning any new language is testing the code that you discover when browsing through a class' functions. Anything listed in the Assembly Browser is there for a reason. At some point, somebody thought the function was necessary, so he or she added it.

6.17.4 Putting It Together

Arrays are used for storing many objects and commanding them in a coordinated manner. We did this earlier by making a line of undulating cubes. However, what if we want to keep track of a multitude of monsters approaching the player?

You're likely to have a situation where a designer makes a feature request: A weapon to shoot the zombies with; a self-operated gun turret. The turret has two features. First it should only shoot at the nearest zombie. Second, it will only shoot zombies not near any humans as to not accidentally hit the human with a projectile.

This project begins in the `MoreOnArrays _ Continued _ Scene` in the Chapter6 Unity Projects. In this scene is a new GunTurret game object. On this is a GunTurretController and a GunTurretLogic script. The logic used to pick targets is what we're going to focus on, so we'll open the GunTurretLogic script and see how arrays are used there.

The first thing we'd need to do is figure out how to find the zombies and humans. We'll start with a couple of arrays.

```
GameObject[] allObjects = FindObjectsOfType<GameObject>();
ArrayList zombies = new ArrayList();
ArrayList humans = new ArrayList();
```

These three arrays are arranged so we have `allObjects` which finds all `GameObjects` in the scene. After this we have an empty `ArrayList` setup for zombies and another for humans. As you might expect we will need to search through the `allObjects` array to find humans and zombies.

```
foreach (GameObject go in allObjects)
{
    HumanWithStates aHuman = go.GetComponent<HumanWithStates>();
    ZombieWithStates aZombie = go.GetComponent<ZombieWithStates>();
    bool isHuman = aHuman != null;
    bool isZombie = aZombie != null;
    {
        if (isHuman)
        {
            humans.Add(go);
        }
        if (isZombie)
        {
            zombies.Add(go);
        }
    }
}
```

With our first block of code we'll use a check to see if there is a human or a zombie component attached to the game object in the allObjects array. To confirm the component, use a null check for isHuman and isZombie. We've used this method to find specific game objects before where we had zombies searching for humans. However, we have to check how they are different, yet actually quite similar.

6.17.4.1 Breakpoint, Observing Inheritance

To observe how class inheritance and casting behaves add a breakpoint. To look at what was added to the zombies ArrayList we'll have to add a break point to the point after it's been filled. The importance of learning how to use breakpoints to debug code is difficult to fully express. Hours can be wasted searching for a bug that could easily be found by stepping through code.

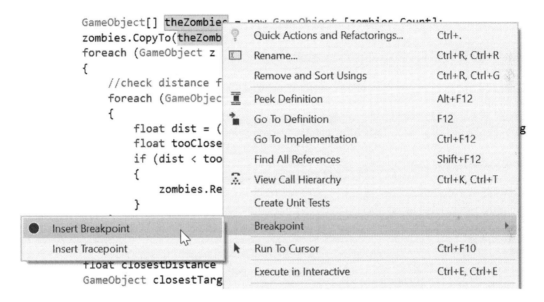

To observe something easily overlooked, we'll add the breakpoint to where zombie array list is used. For the debugger in Visual Studio to work, have Unity up and running in the background where Scene has the script with the added breakpoint.

Click the Attach to Unity button and wait for Visual Studio to make the connection to Unity. After a moment, Visual Studio will build the source code and indicate it's ready for the Scene to start playing in editor. In the Unity Editor, press the Pause button before pressing the Play button. Starting the game paused will ensure that we catch the first update loop of the scene. If we haven't hit the breakpoint, then Unity will wait for the step button to be pressed.

The third button will step Unity a single update cycle at a time. Visual Studio's debugger should catch the update of the zombie ArrayList.

```
                                    GunTurretLogic                                    Upd
        if (isHuman)
        {                                          [0]   "ZombieWithStates (10) (UnityEngine.GameObject)"
            humans.Add(go);                        [1]   "ZombieWithStates (3) (UnityEngine.GameObject)"
        }                                          [2]   "ZombieWithStates (UnityEngine.GameObject)"
        if (isZombie)                              [3]   "ZombieWithStates (4) (UnityEngine.GameObject)"
        {                                          [4]   "HumanWithStates (8) (UnityEngine.GameObject)"
            zombies.Add(go);                       [5]   "ZombieWithStates (8) (UnityEngine.GameObject)"
        }                                          [6]   "ZombieWithStates (6) (UnityEngine.GameObject)"
    }                                              [7]   "HumanWithStates (1) (UnityEngine.GameObject)"
}                                                  [8]   "ZombieWithStates (1) (UnityEngine.GameObject)"
                                                   [9]   "ZombieWithStates (9) (UnityEngine.GameObject)"
GameObject[] theZombies = new GameObject [zombies. [10]  "HumanWithStates (3) (UnityEngine.GameObject)"
zombies.CopyTo(theZombies);                        [11]  "ZombieWithStates (2) (UnityEngine.GameObject)"
foreach (GameObject z in theZombies)               [12]  "ZombieWithStates (5) (UnityEngine.GameObject)"
{                                                  [13]  "HumanWithStates (10) (UnityEngine.GameObject)"
    //check distance from zombie to all humans     [14]  "HumanWithStates (7) (UnityEngine.GameObject)"
    foreach (GameObject h in humans)
    {
```

In the array list you'll notice `Humans` were added. The gate catching `isZombie` must be true for the humans to be added to the zombie list. The `HumansWithStates` class inherited from `ZombieWithStates`, so in a sense, they are zombies with added or modified features. In the statements where humans and zombies get their components from the game object both prove true with humans. A cast from zombie to human gets inferred so `isZombie` is always true.

The `isHuman` is only true when the component is a Human since it's an evolution of the Zombie. If you were to use object instead of `ZombieWithStates` then you'd add every type of component and object in the scene, transforms, lights, cameras, etc. The object class is the base class of every construct in the scene. The `HumanWithStates` class is based on `ZombieWithStates` so the `isZombie` gate adds humans to the zombies `ArrayList`. So, after the first update, you get an array of 22 objects on the first Update with both humans and zombies.

```
if (isHuman)
{
    humans.Add(go);
    continue; // added to skip the zombies.Add(go); statement.
}
```

To avoid that you can add a continue; jump statement to finish the loop early and skip any following statements in the foreach loop. As an alternative you could also use the following condition to add the game object to the zombies ArrayList.

```
if (!isHuman && isZombie)
{
    zombies.Add(go);
}
```

The statement can be read as: if value `isHuman` is false and value `isZombie` is true; add go to the zombies list. Running the code again in the debugger will need a re-build of the code.

Press Stop Debugging (Shift+F5) to release the breakpoint. Make your code changes, press Attach to Unity again to check your changes press Play in Unity. This time around rather than all humans and zombies, the zombies ArrayList should only contain 11 objects exclusively of zombies. The Autos view in Visual Studio will also show you the variables involved with BreakPoint.

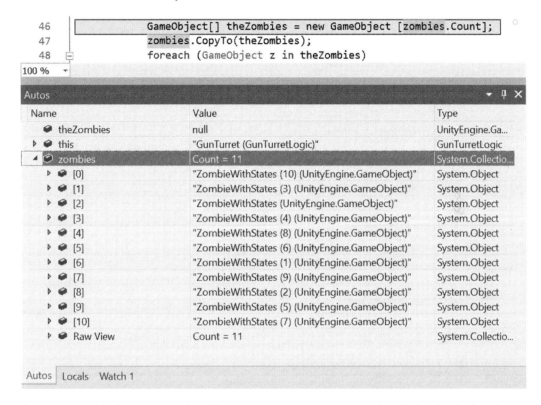

Once you're satisfied with the results of the debugging session, you can delete the breakpoint by selecting the highlighted line and from the right-click menu select Delete Breakpoint.

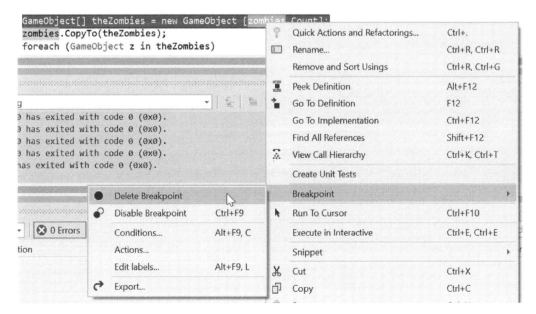

Now that we have a clean list of zombies, we're able to parse through them and check each zombie's proximity to the humans.

```
GameObject[] theZombies = new GameObject [zombies.Count];
zombies.CopyTo(theZombies);
foreach (GameObject z in theZombies)
{
    //check distance from zombie to all humans
    foreach (GameObject h in humans)
    {
        float dist = (z.transform.position - h.transform.position).magnitude;
        float tooCloseToZombie = 1.0f;
        if (dist < tooCloseToZombie)
        {
            zombies.Remove(z);
        }
    }
}
```

To start, we've decided arbitrarily that 1.0f units is what we'll consider too close for a human to be near a zombie to be considered a valid target for the turret to aim at. The statement `dist < tooCloseToZombie` will remove the zombie game object from the ArrayList of zombies. With the reduced list we then search through them for the closest remaining zombie to the turret.

The use of the ArrayList affords the Remove() object function. With a fixed sized array like GameObject[] theZombies, there is no Remove feature. You can take an object out of a fixes sized array, but the empty spot would still exist as a null. Finally with the reduced ArrayList we're able to search for the closest zombie to the turret.

```
float closestDistance = Mathf.Infinity;
GameObject closestTarget = null;
foreach (GameObject zombie in zombies)
{
    float dist = (zombie.transform.position - transform.position).magnitude;
    if (dist < closestDistance)
    {
        closestDistance = dist;
        closestTarget = zombie;
    }
}
```

Once we're done finding the closest one, we assign it to the GameObject `closestTarget`. And hand that off to the `GunTurretController`.

```
if (closestTarget != null)
{
    GunTurretController controller = GetComponent<GunTurretController>();
    controller.ShootAtTarget(closestTarget);
    Debug.DrawLine(closestTarget.transform.position, transform.position, Color.red);
}
```

The controller object here has a ShootAtTarget(GameObject target) function that performs the actions necessary to aim the turret at the target and launch a projectile.

After completing the features requested by the designer it may seem unfortunate that the zombies standing next to humans are not targeted. Perhaps this is something that should be brought to the attention of the designer.

6.17.5 What We've Learned

We'll leave off here for now and move on to a different topic next. Arrays are a fundamental part of programming in general. A database is not much more than a complex array of different types of data. The principal difference is that a database has some relational connections between one element and another. Arrays without this relational data mean you'll have to keep track of the different relations.

Sorting through objects is an important part of general computing that many algorithms do nothing more than sort and organize values. Computer scientists spend years trying to speed up these sorting processes. We can't necessarily spend too much time on comparing these different methods of sorting in this book, as the field of study has filled countless volumes of text. If it were not for this importance, companies wouldn't base their entire business on storing, sorting, and organizing data.

You could imagine dealing with a few dozen monster types; each one with different sets of data, stats, and members can quickly become cumbersome to deal with. There are ways to maintain some control; that's where data structures come into play.

6.18 Out Parameter

We have been thinking that functions return a single value. Another method to get more than one value from a function is to use the `out` keyword in the parameters. The `out` keyword is usable in most situations even if you need only one return value though its use is different from how return is used.

```
int GetSeven()
{
    return 7;
}
```

The above is a function that simply returns 7. In use, you might see something like the following code fragment:

```
void GettingSeven()
{
    int Seven = GetSeven();
}
```

What limits us is the ability to return multiple values. What we'd like to be able to do is something like Lua that looks like the following:

```
function ReturnsSevenAndEleven()
    return 7, 11
end
local seven, eleven = ReturnsSevenAndEleven()
```

Lua has some clever tricks like returning multiple values. With some extra work in C# we can simulate various work arounds, or a tuple as we have seen in Section 5.7.4. This is not elegant to say the least, and this does not mention the performance issues that will creep up if something like this is used too often.

```
ArrayList GetSevenEleven()
{
    ArrayList list = new ArrayList();
    list.Add(7);
    list.Add(11);
    list.Add("Eleven");//not an int?
    return list;
}
```

```
void GettingSevenEleven()
{
    ArrayList list = GetSevenEleven();
    int seven = (int)list[0];
    int eleven = (int)list[1];
}
```

From the above example, we created a function called `GetSevenEleven()` that returned a 7. return which is used to provide a system to turn the function into some sort of value, which can be an array, but then we start to lose what sort of data is inside of the array. Because of this, we will run into type safety issues. For instance, we could modify the statement in `sevenEleven()` to look like the following:

```
ArrayList GetSevenEleven()
{
    ArrayList list = new ArrayList();
    list.Add(7);
    list.Add("Eleven");//not an int?
    return list;
}
```

The parser will not catch the error, until the game starts running and the GetSevenEleven() function is called and the int eleven tries to get data from the array. You will get this printed out to the Console panel.

> **InvalidCastException: Specified cast is not valid.**
> **OutParameter.GettingSevenEleven () (at Assets/OutParameter.cs:36)**

This type of error is not something we'd like to track down when you're using an array for use with numbers. Vague errors are rarely fun to figure out. It's best to avoid using anything like the code mentioned above.

The advantage of the tuple is knowing the parameters that went into the return value. However, tuples can often add to the complexity of a function's signature. Ultimately, the reason for using any one system over another is readability. The out parameter flows nicely, the value goes into the function and can be used immediately. Tuples need to get assigned to a var and then the var's members can be used after.

6.18.1 A Basic Example

In the OutParameter script, The parameter seven is defined in the argument in the GetSevenOut() function. In the body of the function the int 7 is assigned to the seven parameter which is then sent to the out parameter. Values used for the out parameter need to be created in the body of the function. Incoming values are ignored and new values are assigned to the variable. The out parameter works in one direction—out.

```
void GetSevenOut(out int seven)
{/*                         ↑            */
    seven = 7; /*           |            */
}/*    └──●───────────────→ ┘            */
 /* ● variable given to seven            */
 /*   gets assigned 7                    */
```

When the function is used you'll see something like the following:

```
int i = 0;/* int i goes in as 0     */
/*    └──●─────────┐  i = 0          */
GetSevenOut(out i);
/*          ┌──●───┘   i = 7         */
Debug.Log(i);/* comes out as 7       */
```

You need to do a couple of things before the out keyword is used. First, you need to create a new variable to assign to the function. Then to use the function, you need to put that variable into the parameters list preceded by the same out keyword. When the function is executed, it looks at the variable's value inside of it and sends it back up to the parameters list with its new value. Of course, we can add more than one out value.

```
void GetThreeValuesOut(out int first, out int second, out int third)
{/*                              ↑             ↑              ↑   */
    first = 1;/* assigned 1      |             |              |   */
 /*    └──●────────────────────→ ┘             |              |   */
 /*                                            |              |   */
    second = 2;/* assigned 2                   |              |   */
 /*    └──●────────────────────────────────→ ┘               |   */
 /*                                                           |   */
    third = 3;/*   assigned 3                                 |   */
 /*    └──●───────────────────────────────────────────────→ ┘   */
}
```

Using more than one out parameter allows you to create multiple values.

```
/* this works with multiple values                  */
int i, j, k;
/*      |    |    └●→────────────────────────────┐   */
/*      |    └●→───────────────────────────┐     |   */
/*      └●→──────────────────┐i = 0 |j = 0 |k = 0   */
GetThreeValuesOut(out i, out j, out k);
/*                    ┌────┘i = 1 |j = 2 |k = 3      */
/*                    |          └──┐    └────┐      */
/*                    ●             ●         ●      */
/*                    ↓             ↓         ↓      */
Debug.Log("i: " + i + " j: " + j + " k: " + k);
```

The above code produces the following in the Console:

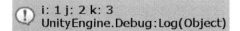

i: 1 j: 2 k: 3
UnityEngine.Debug:Log(Object)

Using the function in this way allows you to produce many useful operations on incoming values as well. The additional benefit is the fact that the function can act as a pure function. This means that as long as none of the variables inside of the function rely on anything at the class level, the code can be copied and pasted or moved to any other class quite easily.

```
void GoingInAndOut(int inValue, out int outValue)
{/*                     ┌←●────────┘            ↑    */
    outValue = inValue * 2;/*                   |    */
 /*       └●→────────────────────────────────┘   */
}/*  outValue is set to inValue multiplied by 2 */
```

The outValue can be based on incoming parameters.

```
int i = 0;
/*    └●→────────────────┐   i = 0             */
GoingInAndOut(6, out i);
/*              ┌←●────────┘   i = 12          */
Debug.Log(i);/* comes out as 12               */
```

This example shows an incoming parameter that is multiplied by 2 before it's assigned to the outValue parameter. The out keyword is handy and allows for more tidy functions. A simple function in Unity is called the Physics.Raycast(); function.

```
Ray ray = new Ray(transform.position, transform.forward);
RaycastHit raycastHit;
/*          └●→────────────────┐                                    */
if(Physics.Raycast( ray, out raycastHit))
{/*      ↓              |   hit value has a point                   */
 /* conditional statement |   in the world where it hit something...    */
 /* if there's anything   |          ●              ●  and orientation of */
 /* actually hit by the ray └────────────────────────┐ the surface it hit */
    AimPoint.transform.position = raycastHit.point;/*      ↓ */
    Quaternion normal = Quaternion.LookRotation(raycastHit.normal, AimPoint.transform.up);
    AimPoint.transform.rotation = normal;
}
```

The function returns a bool, true if the raycast hits something, and false if it doesn't. In the scene, the OutParameters object is aimed at a lower area of a sphere.

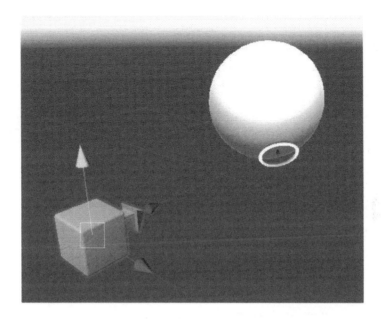

When we play the scene the AimPoint object jumps to the point on the sphere where the ray intersects with a physics object.

Compare the out parameter with how a tuple works. The readability doesn't indicate what values are contained in `var  abc`. The values are masked, and you'd need to have the function close by to read what's hidden in the `abc` variable before it's assigned.

```
(int a, int b, int c) GetThreeValuesOut()
{
    return (a: 1, b: 2, c: 3);
}
/*                                                */
/*    ┌─●──┐  a var gets assigned the tuple       */
var abc = GetThreeValuesOut();
/*    │          one value contains all three members */
/*    └─●──────────┬──────────┬──────────┐        */
/*                 ↓          ↓          ↓         */
Debug.Log("a: " + abc.a + " b: " + abc.b + " c: " + abc.c);
```

This shouldn't diminish the usability of a tuple by any means, it's just something to keep in mind when choosing between out parameters or a tuple return value. The tuple requires unboxing from a var, out is explicit.

6.18.2 Simple Sort (Bubble Sort)

In the scene are plenty more Spheres to deal with. Lists of monsters and values make for an important part of any list of data when making decisions on what to do in an environment.

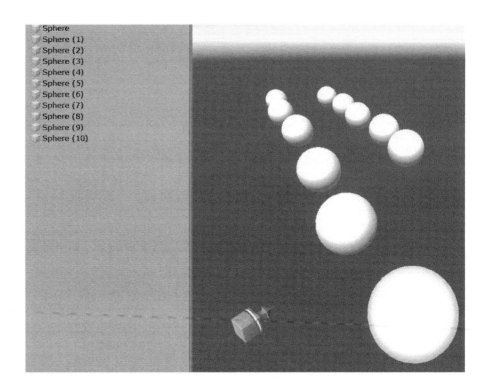

Around our OutParameter object we have several other game objects duplicated from the sphere where we cast a ray. We're going to create a simple ArrayList that will have all the objects in the scene added to it. Then we're going to create a new `GameObject[]` array that will be sorted based on the distance to the capsule.

Sorting algorithms have a long history in computer programming. Many thesis papers have been written on the topic. However, we're going to make use of a simple sort algorithm to order an array of game objects from the shortest distance to the longest distance.

We'll start with a simple system to get an ArrayList of objects in the scene.

```
GameObject[] allObjects = FindObjectsOfType<GameObject>();
ArrayList sphereList = new ArrayList();
foreach(GameObject go in allObjects)
{
    bool isSphere = go.name.Contains("Sphere");
    if(isSphere)
    {
        sphereList.Add(go);
    }
}
```

The `allObjects` `GameObject[]` array gathers all of the GameObjects in the scene. Then an ArrayList called sphereList is created to store any object with "sphere" in its name.

After the sphereList is populated, a new `GameObject[]` array is created to store the unsorted `sphereList`.

```
/* now we have some objects to sort*/
GameObject[] spheres = new GameObject[sphereList.Count];
/* copy the list to the array */
sphereList.CopyTo(spheres);
```

Now we're ready to sort through the sphereList based on distance by plugging in the target gameObject, the unsorted array and the sorted array into the SortDistanceFromObject function.

```
bool SortDistanceFromObject(GameObject target, GameObject[] unsorted, out GameObject[] sorted)
{
    int len = unsorted.Length;
    for (int i = 0; i < len; i++)
    {
        /* start at the beginning of the array */
        for (int j = 0; j < len - i - 1; j++)
        {
            /* then compare everyone against every other one */
            /* get positions of an object in the array  */
            /* and the following one.                   */
            Vector3 posA = unsorted[j].transform.position;
            Vector3 posB = unsorted[j + 1].transform.position;

            /* get the distance of each object from the target */
            float distA = (posA - target.transform.position).magnitude;
            float distB = (posB - target.transform.position).magnitude;

            /* compare distances */
            if(distA > distB)
            {
                /* if B is further than A then swap them */
                GameObject temp = unsorted[j];
                unsorted[j] = unsorted[j + 1];
                unsorted[j + 1] = temp;
            }
        }
    }
    sorted = unsorted;
    return sorted.Length > 0;
}
```

The first outer loop for(int i = 0; i < len; i++) starts with the first object in the unsorted list. The inner loop for(int j = 0; j < len – i – 1; j++) iterates through the rest of the array.

To clarify, assume we might have an array with 4 items. The outer loop starts with item 1, then the inner loop compares the first item against the second. The second to the third, and the third item to the fourth. The outer loop counts up 1, then the inner loop compares first to second, and second to third. Then the last iteration compares the first and second again. Each time swapping the lower value toward the first value in the array.

The unsorted array is now sorted so we can assign the array to the out parameter's sorted GameObject[] array.

```
sorted = unsorted;
return sorted.Length > 0;
```

6.18.3 Simple Sort Proof

To test our sort, we'll use a for loop. Each higher value in the array will hold onto a different model. The furthest model will be the last in the array and thus have the highest index in the array. The closest object will be at GameObjectArray[0], and the furthest one will be at the end of the array. Therefore, if there are 10 objects in the scene, the furthest object will be at GameObjectArray[9]. Remember that arrays start at 0, not 1.

```
/* now send the unsorted array to the function, then get a sorted array out */
if(SortDistanceFromObject(gameObject, spheres, out spheres))
{
    int lineHeight = 1;
    foreach(GameObject go in spheres)
    {
        Vector3 up = new Vector3(){ y = lineHeight++ * 0.5f};
        Debug.DrawRay(go.transform.position, up, Color.red);
    }
}
```

To help visualize how the objects are arranged in the array we'll draw a longer line based on the position the object is in the array. The first item will have a short red line, and the last item will have the longest line drawn up from the game object.

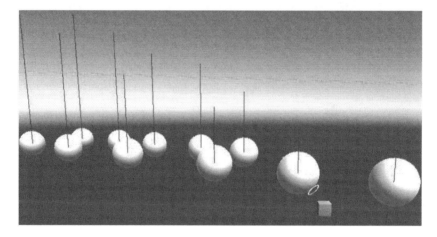

As you move the OutParameter game object around in the scene, you'll notice the length of the lines changing based on the distance away from the capsule. This means that you can use this sort algorithm to place a priority on which object is closest and which is the furthest away based on its index in the array.

6.18.4 What We've Learned

We should leave off here for now; sorting is a very deep topic that leads into the very messy guts of computer science. The algorithm isn't complete and lacks any efficiency. It's effective, but only superficially. The only reason why this works at all is the fact that Update() is called many times per second.

Bubble sorting is slow. For just the hand full of items we have in the scene, it's performance will not hinder your computers frame rate. However with many more objects the performance will get worse.

Most of the commonly used sorting algorithms have names such as bubble sort, heap sort, or quick sort. This means we looked at the first two elements in the array, and if one had some greater value than the other, we swap them.

For games such as tower defense, or anything where a character needs to shoot at the closest target and then move on to the next closest, we can use sorting to help provide the character with some more interesting behaviors. Perhaps he can target more than one object with different weapons at the same time. Maybe the character can simply shoot at the closest three objects. The great thing about writing your own game is that you can explore behaviors like this freely, but only once you understand how to use the code you're writing.

In the end, we're required to keep our code as simple as possible. The out keyword is best used when we can't return a single value. In the case with a single return value, the later version of sortObjects where we simply return the sorted array is more readable.

6.19 Ref Parameter

The `ref` keyword, which is short for *reference,* works with variables in a slightly less intuitive way than we have experienced to this point. This is related to how we've been thinking about variables. In the usual case, we use the statement `int x = 1;`, and now when we use x, we can assume we're dealing with the value it's storing.

The difference with `ref` enters when we start to manipulate the data stored under an identifier. If we use a statement like `x = 1; y = x;`, we aren't actually taking x and putting it into y. What's really going on is that y is looking at the value that x is holding onto and changes its own value to match what x is storing.

```
int x = 1; /* Initial assignment of the value 1 is put into x   */
/*      └1→┐     the value of x is 1                              */
int y = x; /* the value 1 in x is copied into y                  */
/*      └←1─┘     y is assigned 1, the value from x               */
/* no link to x has been made.                                   */
     y = 3; /* y is assigned 3, x is still 1                      */
/*      └←3─┘                                                     */
Debug.Log("x: " + x); // "x: 1"
Debug.Log("y: " + y); // "y: 3"
```

In memory, y is storing a 1 and x is storing a different 1. However, functions can use the `ref` in its parameter list. This maintains a link to the original variable.

This may seem hard to understand, and to be honest, it is. This concept is one that takes a while to get used to and that is why some programming languages are more difficult to learn than others. However, the concept becomes more apparent when we see the code in action.

6.19.1 A Basic Example

The `ref` keyword acts somewhat like the `out` keyword. In practice we'll see how they differ with the following example code fragment.

```
void UseRefManipulateValue()
{
    int x = 3;/* ────────────────┐              */
    int y = 3;/*                  ║              */
            /*                    ║              */
    RefManipulateValue(ref x, y);                */
            /*          └──────────────────┐     */
    Debug.Log("UsingRefManipulation: x:" + x + " y:" + y);
    /* "UsingRefManipulation: x: 4 y: 3          */
}
void RefManipulateValue(ref int refValue, int notRefValue)
{                /* linked to x   ║            |    */
    refValue++;/*↩ ═══════════════╝  just value |   */
    notRefValue++;/*← ───────────────────────────┘  */
}
```

The code above takes in the ref of x which is assigned in by the parameters of the function. The in argument now has a direct connection to the contents of x. When `refValue++;` is executed, the value that x was holding is incremented. A link to the original value is maintained. After the function is completed, the value of the original x has been modified.

The y value on the other hand, is handled like a regular variable in the `RefManipulateValue()` function. The `notRefValue++;` is run, but the increment doesn't change the value stored in y. Without the `ref` keyword, the link to the original variable isn't maintained.

The difference between ref and out can become obvious when you see them together. When using ref you can assume that the value is already initialized before being used in the function. Using the out keyword, it's necessary to initialize a value within the body of the function before assigning the value for the out parameter.

```
void UseRefAndOut()
{
    int x = 3;
    int y = 3;
    RefAndOut(ref x, out y);
    Debug.Log("UsingRefAndOut: x:" + x + " y:" + y);
    /* "UsingRefAndOut: x: 4 y: 1                    */

}
void RefAndOut(ref int refValue, out int outValue)
{/*                              ↓ ↑              ↑    */
 /*      ┌──────────────────────────┘ │          │    */
 /*  ↓                                 │          │    */
    refValue++;/*                      │          │    */
 /*  ↓                                 │          │    */
 /*  └──────────────────────────────┘ │          │    */
    outValue = 0;/* new value created   │          */
    outValue++;   /*─────────────────────┘          */
}
```

To get a similar effect with ref using out you'd need to provide an in as well. The following example shows the first `refValue` incremented, the second `value` is then manipulated in the body of the function before being assigned to the `outValue`.

```
void UseRefAndInAndOut()
{
    int x = 1;
    int y = 1;
    int z = 1;
    RefAndInAndOut(ref x, y, out z);
    Debug.Log("UsingRefAndInAndOut: x:" + x + " y:" + y + " z:" + z );
    /*"UsingRefAndInAndOut x: 2 y: 1 z: 2"                    */
}
void RefAndInAndOut(ref int refValue, int value, out int outValue)
{/*                          ↕            ↓            ↑ */
 /*      ┌───────────────────────┘        │            │ */
    refValue++;/*                          │            │ */
 /*      ┌───────────────┘                 │            │ */
    outValue = value + 1;/*                 │            │ */
}/*      └──────────────────────────────────────────────┘ */
```

6.19.2 Code Portability Side Effects

A side effect is the result of a function manipulating values that are not directly within the scope of the function.

```
public int publicX;/*←┐                              */
void IncrementX()  /* | directly manipulate        */
{                  /* | class wide variable.        */
    publicX += 1;  /*←┘                             */
}
```

When the `IncrementX()` function is used, the `publicX` variable in the class scope is incremented.

```
Debug.Log(publicX); // "0"
IncrementX();
Debug.Log(publicX); // "1"
```

There is no problem with using a function like this. The fact that the Increment function works only on the `publicX` variable means that you know exactly what it's allowed to do, and what it's limited to.

Reusing code can help speed along your own development. Often, you'll find simple tricks that help with various tasks. When we talk of reusing code, we need to think about how a function interacts with its input and output to consider portability. If a function relies on the class it was written in, then it becomes less portable. When a function can operate on its own, it becomes more utilitarian and more portable.

Consider the `SortDistanceFromObject` code from the previous chapter. We replaced the in and out parameters with ref. This reduces the amount of work going into the parameters.

```
bool SortDistanceFromObject(GameObject target, ref GameObject[] sortableObjects)
{
    int len = sortableObjects.Length;
    for (int i = 0; i < len; i++)
    {
        int restLen = len - i - 1;
        /* start at the beginning of the array */
        for (int j = 0; j < restLen; j++)
        {
            /* then compare everyone against every other one */
            /* get positions of an object in the array   */
            /* and the following one.                     */
            Vector3 posA = sortableObjects[j].transform.position;
            Vector3 posB = sortableObjects[j + 1].transform.position;

            /* get the distance of each object from the target */
            float distA = (posA - target.transform.position).magnitude;
            float distB = (posB - target.transform.position).magnitude;

            /* compare distances */
            if(distA > distB)
            {
                /* if B is further than A then swap them */
                GameObject temp = sortableObjects[j];
                sortableObjects[j] = sortableObjects[j + 1];
                sortableObjects[j + 1] = temp;
            }
        }
    }
    return sortableObjects.Length > 0;
}
```

This version is considerably more portable; you only need to give it a gameObject to sort distances from and an array of game objects to sort. To copy and paste code from place to place is much easier than re-typing. Most programming tools even come with built-in code snippet management tools. Visual Studio has it's code snippets manager under Tools→Code Snippets Manager…

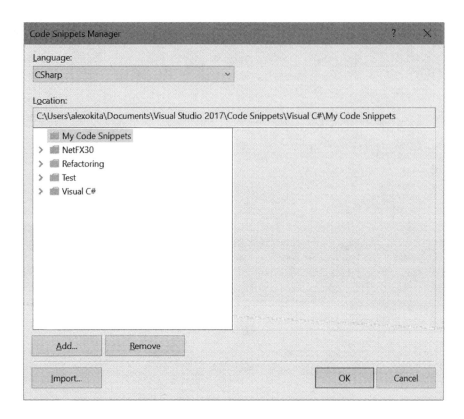

6.19.3 What We've Learned

In Section 6.18, we covered the out keyword, and here we learned the ref keyword. Values coming in to a parameter using the out keyword are not initialized with any value.

```
void OutFunction(out int outValue)
{
    outValue++;
    /* the above doesn't work since */
    /* it assumes outValue already  */
    /* has a value.                 */
}
```

In much the same way you're not able to increment an int that has no assigned value.

```
int noValue;
noValue++;
/* works the same way, you can't    */
/* increment an int that has no value */
/* assigned yet.                    */
/*                                  */
```

With no value to increment in the int, you're not able to add 1 to nothing. That being the case though you're able to assign a value to the outValue and pass that along to the variable given to that parameter. Assuming of course that the types match.

```
void OutFunction(out int outValue)
{
    outValue = 7;
}
void UsingOutFunction()
{
    int localInt;
    /*       └─────────────┐            */
    /*                     ↓ unassigned int */
    OutFunction(out localInt);
    /*                   └───────┐        */
    /*          assigned value 7 ↓        */
    Debug.Log("localInt: " + localInt);
}
```

The ref keyword on the other hand assumes that the incoming data has already been initialized.

```
void RefFunction(ref int refValue)
{
    refValue++;
}
void UsingRefFunction()
{
    int localInt;
    RefFunction(ref localInt);
    Debug.Log("UsingRefFunction: " + localInt);
}
```

If the variable given to a ref has no value, then you'll get the same error of using an unassigned local variable. The difference here is that the error occurs before getting to the body of the RefFunction(). To allow either of these to work, the variable in use needs to have a value before it's used.

```
int localInt = 0;
RefFunction(ref localInt);
Debug.Log("UsingRefFunction: " + localInt);
```

There are plenty of options and each has a purpose. It's important to know how to accomplish a task using different methods. Readable, easy to understand code should always be the goal.

Ultimately, your skill dictates how complex your own code will be. Your ability to read your own code may even help others who encounter your work. You express your ideas and methods through code. Different programming languages have different levels of expressiveness or expressivity. Basically, some languages are stricter, while others allow for more than one way to carry out any given task.

The expressivity of C# is high, allowing you to try out many different methods to do the same thing. There are more commonly used systems, but by no means should you feel limited to a commonly used syntax. If you feel that a less commonly used syntax is more helpful, use it.

6.20 Type Casting Numbers

We need to know more about a variety of different data types and how they're used before we can begin to understand how and why type casting is important. At this point, we need more casting from one type of data into another. Now that we've had a chance to use a wide variety of different data types, it's time we started learning why converting from one type to another is necessary.

From the array exercises we used cast from object to float, but why is this required? C# is a *type-safe* programming language. What this means is that your code is checked for mixed types before it's compiled into machine-readable code. This is done to prevent any errors that show up while the code is running. When converting between types that are similar, we don't usually see too many errors. In the following code sample, we demonstrate why we don't want to use an integer for setting an object's position or rotation.

```
FloatRotationY += Time.deltaTime;
/*    ↑                        ↓ The amount of time that's passed between Updates */
/*    └───────────────────┘ slowly increases FloatRotationY                      */
/*            ┌──────────┐           */
/*            │cast to int│          */
/*            └────┬─────┘           */
/*                 ↓                 */
IntRotationY = (int)FloatRotationY;
/*    ↑                        ↓ only the whole digit of float gets carried through */
/*    └─( X.000...000)──┘ the cast from float to int                                */
/*         ↑                         */
/*  only numbers past the decimal    */
/*  are carried over                 */
```

```
IntPointer.transform.localEulerAngles = new Vector3(0, IntRotationY, 0);
FloatPointer.transform.localEulerAngles = new Vector3(0, FloatRotationY, 0);
```

In the TypeCastingNumbers_Scene is a rotation indication game object. The script in control is attached to the TypeCastingNumbers game object. The white pointer has its rotation controlled with a float value that's incremented with Time.deltaTime. The red pointer is controlled with an int value that's cast from the value driving the white pointer.

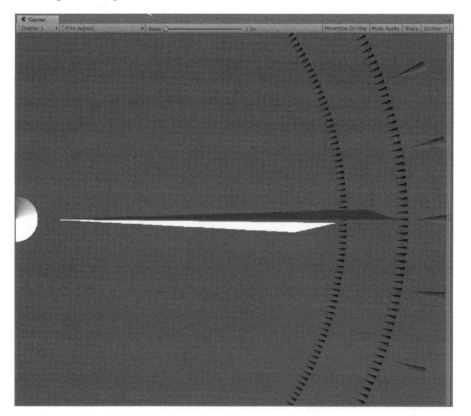

As time passes, the white pointer smoothly rotates, the red pointer ticks, skipping directly to the next degree marker on the rotation indicator.

Simply put, an integer is a whole number such as 1, 2, and 3. A fraction can have a value between 1 and 2, for example, 1.5625. Therefore, if we change from an int to a float, we'll get a smooth movement. This becomes more apparent when we look at the values in the Inspector panel in the editor.

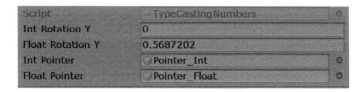

Going in the other direction, from int to float, we don't need to use a cast operator. This is because there are no values being lost.

```
float FloatFromInt = IntRotationY;
/*            ↑                ↓ going from int to float doesn't require a cast */
/*          └─( X.??? )────┘ since we don't lose any values in the cast     */
```

A cast from int to float is still being done, it's just an implicit cast operation.

6.20.1 Number Types

This leads us to numbers having a size. In fact, so far we've used int and float, and there was even mention of a double. However, why do these have a size related to them and how is an int smaller than a float? This is a computer science question, and to explain this, we need to remember how computers count.

In the old days, when computers had moving parts, instructions were fed to them using a flat piece of physical media with holes punched into it. Each hole in the media represented either a 0 or a 1, which was then converted back into decimal numbers which we use in our everyday life. The primary limitation in these old computers was size, and to hold big numbers, computers needed to be physically bigger.

Each number was stored in a series of switches. In 1946, the Electronic Numerical Integrator and Computer (ENIAC) used flip-flop switches to store a number; imagine a light switch, with *on* being a 1 and *off* being a 0. Each group of switches was called an accumulator and it could store a single 10-digit number for use in a calculation. Altogether with 18,000 vacuum tubes and weighing over 25 tons, the ENIAC could store a maximum of 20 numbers at a time.

Because programming languages have such a deep-rooted history with limited data space, numbers today still have similar limitations. On your PC, you might have the memory to store many hundreds of billions of numbers, but this doesn't hold true for every device. Every year new smaller, more portable devices show up on the market, so it's good to be aware that forming bad habits of wasting data space will limit the platforms you can write software for.

6.20.2 Integers

It's important to know how computers convert 1s and 0s into decimal numbers. To explain, let's start with a 4-bit number. This would be a series of four 1s or 0s. A zero would be as simple as 0000. Each place in the number is a different value. The first place is either a 1 or a 0, the second 2 or 0, the third 4 or 0, and the fourth 8 or 0. Each whole number between 0 and 15 can be represented with these 4 bits.

To demonstrate 0101 means 2 + 8 or 10. An interesting change is to shift both 1s to the left to get 1010 that translates to 1 + 4 or 5. This is called a bit shift, or in this case a shift left. The number 15 looks like 1111. It just so happens that a 4-bit number is called a *nibble*. A nibble also happens to easily represent a single hex number.

Hex numbers are used often when dealing with assigning colors on a web page. Hex numbers range from 0 to 9 and include an additional A through F to fill in the last six digits. A color is denoted by three

8-bit numbers for red, blue, and green. An 8-bit number is called a *byte*. Each color gets a range from 0 to 255. This turns into a two-digit hex number. Therefore, 0 is 00 and 255 is FF in hex.

6.20.2.1 Signed Numbers

Today C# uses numbers starting with the *sbyte* up to the decimal. The sbyte is a number from –127 to 127, and the byte is a number from 0 to 255. The s in the sbyte is an abbreviation of the word *signed*. Therefore, you can actually call an sbyte a *signed byte*.

This is an important difference: Signing a number means it can be either positive or negative. However, you lose half the maximum range of the number since one of the 1s and 0s is used to tell the computer if the number is positive or negative. If we use the first bit to represent the signedness of a number in terms of our nibble, this turns 0100 into positive 1, while 1100 turns into negative 1. Negative 3 is 1110 and negative 7 is 1111, or "negative + 1 + 2 + 4."

sbyte	8 bits	−128 ↔ 127
Byte	8 bits	0 ↔ 255
Short	16 bits	−32,768 ↔ 32,767
Unsigned short	16 bits	0 ↔ 65,535
Int	32 bits	−2,147,483,648 ↔ 2,147,483,647
Unsigned int	32 bits	0 ↔ 4,294,967,295
Long	64 bits	−9,223,372,036,854,775,808 ↔ 9,223,372,036,854,775,807
Unsigned long	64 bits	0 ↔ 18,446,744,073,709,551,615

The above table represents most of the useful varieties of integer numbers. None of these have a decimal point in them to represent a fraction. Numbers that do have a decimal are called floating point numbers. We've used float and double as well; only that it hasn't been so obvious.

6.20.3 Floating Point

Floating point numbers have been a focus of computers for many years. Gaining floating point accuracy was the goal of many early computer scientists. Because there are an infinite possibilities of how many numbers can follow a decimal point, it's impossible to truly represent any fraction completely using binary computing.

A common example is π, which we call pi. It's assumed that there are an endless number of digits following 3.14. Even today computers are set loose to calculate the hundreds of billions of digits beyond the decimal point. Computers set aside some of the bits of a floating point number aside to represent where the decimal appears in the number, but even this is limited.

The first bit is usually the sign bit, setting the negative or positive range of the number. The following 8 bits is the exponent for the number called a mantissa. The remaining bits are the rest of the number appearing around the decimal point. A float value can move the decimal 38 digits in either direction, but it's limited to the values it's able to store.

We will go further into how numbers are actually stored in terms of 1s and 0s in Section 8.9. For now just understand that numbers can represent only a limited number of digits. Without special considerations, computers are not able to handle arbitrarily large numbers.

To cast a float into an int, you need to be more explicit. That's why C# requires you to use the cast and you need to add the (int) in int IntYRotation = (int)FloatYRotation;. The (int) is a cast operator; or rather (type) acts as a converter from the type on the right to the type needed on the left.

6.20.4 What We've Learned

There's still a bit left to go over with numbers, but we'll leave off here for now. A CPU is a collection of transistors. The computer interprets the signal coming from each transistor as a switch which is either on or off.

Computers collect these transistors into groups to accomplish common tasks. A floating point unit (FPU) is a collection of transistors grouped together to assist in floating point number processing. A graphics processing unit (GPU) is a variety of different groups of transistors specifically used to compute computer graphics.

These groups of transistors are built with highly complex designs. Their organization was designed by software to accomplish their task quickly. Software was used to build the hardware designed to run more software. It all sounds a bit of catch-22, but at least we have some historic reference where all of this comes from.

6.21 Types and Operators

Most of the operators we've been using compare equally. This works just fine when dealing with numbers. However, we can use operators on types that are not numbers, but which comparative operators can we use?

For number types, we can use relational operators. This affords us the ability to set booleans by using greater than >, less than <, greater than or equal to ≥, and less than or equal to ≤. All of these operators produce a boolean result.

```
float a = 1.0f;
float b = 3.0f;
bool c = a > b;// false
bool d = a < b;// true


Debug.Log("c:" + c + " d:" + d);
```

As you might imagine, math operators such as add +, subtract −, multiply X, divide /, and modulo % work on any number type data. However, we can also use the + on the string type.

```
string a = "hello, ";
string b = "world.";
string c = a + b;


Debug.Log("c: " + c);
```

In the fragment shown string c is assigned a + b. When sent to the Unity console we get "hello, world." Printed from the Debug.Log() function. Some other things we can do with strings are comparisons.

```
string a = "hello, ";
string b = "world.";
bool c = a == b; // false
bool d = a == "world."; // true
bool e = a == "hello, "; // false
bool f = a != b; // true
string g = a + b; // hello, world.
```

where c is assigned (a == b), we get false. Likewise, we can use numbers and compare their values as well. We can also use the not equal != operator on strings in the assignment for f. The comparative operator !=, or not equal operator, works on strings as well as numbers. Knowing which operators takes a bit of intuition, but it's important to experiment and learn how types interact with one another.

Another system in which a string could be used is in a switch statement.

```
string a = "hello";
switch (a)
{
    case "hello":
        Debug.Log("a was hello");
        break;
    case "world":
        Debug.Log("a was world");
        break;
    default:
        break;
}
```

In a switch statement the input value is compared against each case. In the code fragment before we used d = a == "hello,"; where d was assigned true. In a switch statement the value that proves true will get executed. In the switch statement here we'll get Debug.Log("a was hello"); to execute.

6.21.1 GetType()

We can also compare data types. This becomes more important later when we start creating our own data types. To know how this works, we can use the data types that are already available in C#.

```
int a = 7;
string b = "hello";
bool c = a.GetType() == b.GetType();
Debug.Log("a and b are the same type? " + c);
// "a and b are the same type? False"
```

The built-in types in C# have a function called GetType() which allows us to check against what type of data each variable is. In this case, int a is a System.Int32 which is not the same as a System.String.

```
int a = 7;
string b = "7";
bool c = a.ToString() == b;
Debug.Log("a as a string is the same as b? " + c);
// "a as a string is the same as b? True"
```

Even though we have two different types here, we can convert an int to a string by using the ToString() function in the Int32 data class. Here we've got an int 7 and we're comparing it to the string "7"; when the int is converted to a string, the comparison results in True.

```
int a = 7;
float b = 7.0f;
bool c = a == b;
Debug.Log("int a == float b? " + c);
// "int a == float b? True"
```

Dissimilar numeric values can also be compared so long as there's no imprecision of the value with a decimal point. An `int` 7 and a `float` 7.0f are still equal.

6.21.2 More Type Casting

We can compare ints and floats without conversion. This works because C# will convert the int to a float implicitly before the comparison is made. However, C# does know that they are different types.

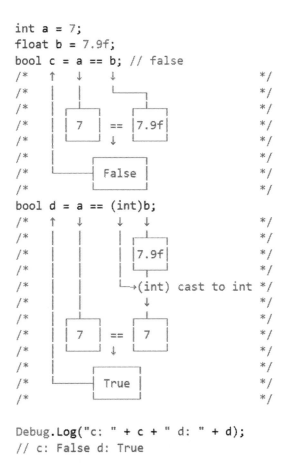

```
Debug.Log("c: " + c + " d: " + d);
// c: False d: True
```

We can force the cast using the `(int)` on b that was assigned 7.9f, which we know is clearly greater than 7. However, when we cast `float` 7.9f to an int, we lose the numbers following the decimal. This makes the cast version of the comparison true.

Can we cast a string to a number data type?

```
int a = 7;
string b = "7";
bool c = a == (int)b;
// Cannot convert type 'string' to 'int'
```

No, there's no built-in method to allow us to change a string data type into an int or any other number type. Therefore, type conversion has limitations. However, don't let this get in your way. Comparing values should used with like types to begin with. What else can we compare?

```
GameObject a = GameObject.CreatePrimitive(PrimitiveType.Capsule);
GameObject b = GameObject.CreatePrimitive(PrimitiveType.Capsule);
bool c = a == b;
Debug.Log("GameObjects a == b? " + c);
// GameObjects a == b? False
```

What is being compared here? Well, these are two different objects in the scene. Even though they share a good number of attributes, they are not the same object. A clear way to compare two instances of a game object is to use the following fragment:

```
int a_InstanceID = a.GetInstanceID();
int b_InstanceID = b.GetInstanceID();
Debug.Log("a_InstanceID: " + a_InstanceID);
// a_InstanceID: -2500
// though the number itself will change every time you run the game
Debug.Log("b_InstanceID: " + b_InstanceID);
// b_InstanceID: -2510
// though the number itself will change every time you run the game
Debug.Log("GameObjects a_InstanceID == b_InstanceID? " + c);
// GameObjects a_InstanceID == b_InstanceID? False
```

Here we're being more specific as to what we're comparing. If every object in the scene has a unique instance ID, then we're going to more clearly debug and test what's being compared when we need to check objects in the scene for matches. When we compare objects in the scene, which don't have a clear comparison, there's usually a method to allow us to make a more readable difference between objects.

```
GameObject a = GameObject.CreatePrimitive(PrimitiveType.Capsule);
GameObject b;
b = a;
bool c = a == b;
Debug.Log("GameObject a == b? " + c);
// GameObject a == b? True
```

In this case, yes, they are the same object, so the behavior is correct. However, again we should do the following to ensure that we're comparing something more easily debugged.

```
GameObject gameObject = GameObject.CreatePrimitive(PrimitiveType.Capsule);
int a = gameObject.GetInstanceID();
int b;
b = a;
bool c = a == b;
Debug.Log("InstanceIDs a == b? " + c);
// InstanceIDs a == b? True
```

It's always important to understand what our code is doing. Comparing types between one another is useful for a multitude of situations. Checking for projectile types on targets, puzzle pieces types, or specific environment props.

In the case where we are looking to see if they are GameObjects, we'd need to check for type. This means that we can make sure that we're looking for GameObjects. To do this, we need to check if one object's type matches another object's type.

```
GameObject a = GameObject.CreatePrimitive(PrimitiveType.Capsule);
GameObject b = GameObject.CreatePrimitive(PrimitiveType.Capsule);
Type aType = a.GetType();
Type bType = b.GetType();
bool c = aType == bType;
Debug.Log("aType: " + aType + " bType: " + bType + " aType == bType? " + c);
// aType: UnityEngine.GameObject bType: UnityEngine.GameObject aType == bType? True
```

There is a very important difference here. We're starting with two GameObjects. This allows us many more options than an int type. GameObjects may have many components or scripts attached for more specific comparisons.

```
GameObject a = GameObject.CreatePrimitive(PrimitiveType.Capsule);
a.AddComponent<ZombieComponent>();
// check if the GameObject a is a zombie by looking for the attached zombie component
ZombieComponent component = a.GetComponent<ZombieComponent>();
Type b = component.GetType();
Type c = typeof(ZombieComponent);
bool d = b == c;
Debug.Log("b type: " + b + "c type: " + c + "b == c?" + d);
```

Using `AddComponent()` we attach a `ZombieComponent: Monobehaviour` to the instance of a GameObject when the game is started. To follow up we then ask the GameObject if it has a ZombieComponent attached using the `GetComponent()` function. Then we check the type of the component and compare it to the `typeof(ZombieComponent)` and we get `True`.

In Unity 3D when collisions occur between game objects that have physics components attached, the `OnCollisionEnter()` event will provide the GameObjects that are involved in the collision. To discover what hit the GameObject you use the same `GetComponent()` and take action based on the presence of specific attached scripts. The significant take-away here is the fact that the type of data in memory has a type, rather, a form or shape that each data has in the computer's memory.

We've come to expect the names of some objects are what we have written them as. When we write the type of an int to the console with `Debug`.

```
System.Int32 a = 1;
int b = 3;
bool c = a.GetType() == b.GetType();
Debug.Log("a == b? " + c);
// "a == b? True


System.Single d = 1.0f;
float e = 3.0f;
bool f = d.GetType() == e.GetType();
Debug.Log("d == e? " + f);
// "d == e? True
```

The fragment is showing that the `System.Int32` and `int` are equivalent types. So too are the `System.Single` and the float. These certainly act the same, but how are they being created with different names to define the same type?

6.21.3 Type Aliasing

We could use the above code in place of float, but float is the naming convention that started with C#. Therefore, we'll give in to convention and use float rather than System.Single, even though both are acceptable by C#. The word float came from someone early on in C# who decided to add a type alias. We can add our own type aliases with a using statement.

```
using MyOwnType = System.Int16;
/*    new name for an old type */
```

Along with the directives at the top of the TypesAndOperatives.cs file, we can add in another using directive. Adding using MyOwnType, we can assign it to System.Int16; which turns our identifier MyOwnType into a System.Int16.

```
MyOwnType a = 1;
Debug.Log("a is a: " + a.GetType());
// "a is a: System.Int16"
```

Using the above fragment tells us that the type of a is a System.Int16.

Therefore, the float was assigned to System.Single somewhere in the depths of Unity 3D. It's unlikely that we're going to find out where the convention of using float is a Single, but it's important to know how the keyword was assigned. The fact is that the float keyword, even though it has become superfluous in programming, is still just the alias given to a System.Single.

Likewise, int or double, and some other keywords we commonly use are just aliases to simplify our code. Other systems have aliased the system types with words such as bigint, smallint, and tinyint as mappings to different numbers of bytes held for the integer value.

Therefore, now that we know a bit where types come from and how to convert one type into another, it's time to put this to some use.

6.21.4 Boxing and Unboxing

Boxing is the term that programmers use when a generic container is used to assign a multitude of types. Once it's discovered what has been "put in a box," we can decide what to do next. When the data is pulled from the variable, you "unbox" the data once you know what it is and what to do with it.

Back when we created the HumanWithStates we had it inherit from the ZombieWithStates. It's possible to describe the HumanWithStates as a ZombieWithStates with new features. Because of this we can assign any child of a type to its parent.

```
GameObject a = GameObject.CreatePrimitive(PrimitiveType.Capsule);
// remember, HumanWithStates : ZombieWithStates?
ZombieWithStates b = a.AddComponent<HumanWithStates>();
/*        ↑                          ↑        */
/*        └──────────────┬───────────┘        */
/*                       │                     */
/*              ┌────────┴────────┐            */
/*              │types don't match│            */
/*              │but HumanWithStates│          */
/*              │inherits from    │            */
/*              │ZombieWithStates │            */
/*              └─────────────────┘            */
```

Like the `HumanWithStates` inherited from `ZombieWithStates`, the `ZombieWithStates` inherited from `MonoBehaviour`. And so, a `ZombieWithStates` can be assigned to a `MonoBehaviour` type object.

```
GameObject c = GameObject.CreatePrimitive(PrimitiveType.Capsule);
MonoBehaviour d = c.AddComponent<ZombieWithStates>();
/*         ↑                                    ↑        */
/*         └──────────────────────────────────┘        */
/*                     │                                 */
/*         ┌───────────┴───────┐                         */
/*         │types don't match  │                         */
/*         │either but         │                         */
/*         │ZombieWithStates   │                         */
/*         │inherits from      │                         */
/*         │MonoBehaviour      │                         */
/*         └───────────────────┘                         */
```

This also means that since everything we've been seeing so far inherit from object, we can assign anything to an object.

```
object e = GameObject.CreatePrimitive(PrimitiveType.Capsule);
/* ↑              ↑                                    */
/* └──────────────┘                                    */
/*         │                                           */
/* ┌───────┴──────────┐                                */
/* │GameObject inherits│                               */
/* │from object        │                               */
/* │but every class in │                               */
/* │C# inherits from   │                               */
/* │object!            │                               */
/* └───────────────────┘                               */
object f = 1;
object g = 1.0f;
object h = new object[] {1, 1.0f, e, d, c, b, a};
```

In this case we have `e` `d` `c` `b` and a being the objects we've been using in the previous two code fragments as well as an int `1` and a float `1.0f`. Notice the last line. We've assigned object h to an array `object[]`. If we think carefully about what's going on here `object[]` and object should be different types.

```
object h = new object[] {1, 1.0f, e, d, c, b, a};
Debug.Log("what is h really? " + h);
// what is h really? System.Object[]
```

The `Debug.Log` tells us that object h is actually a `System.Object[]`, so it is indeed an array "boxed" in object. To unbox the array from object we use the as `object[]` operator.

```
object[] objArray = h as object[];
foreach(object o in objArray)
{
    Debug.Log("got object from objArray: " + o);
}
```

To discover the type hidden in the box we need to check the type assigned as an object.

```
foreach(object o in objArray)
{
    if(o is GameObject)
    {
        Debug.Log("got a GameObject!");
    }
}
// got a GameObject!
// got a GameObject!
// got a GameObject!
```

The use of the `is` operator can be used to compare the type of object. In the case here we check if object o in the objArray `is` GameObject. If the statement is true then we print "got a GameObject!" and we get that printed to the console three times. Since e c and a are GameObjects, this is correct. Something that might surprise you are the things in the Scene you might not know about.

```
UnityEngine.Object[] allObjectsInTheScene = FindObjectsOfType<UnityEngine.Object>();
foreach(UnityEngine.Object o in allObjectsInTheScene)
{
    Debug.Log("Object: " + o);
}
```

The fragment above exposes the hidden objects lurking in the scene. Objects like the NavMeshSettings, LightMapSettings, RenderSettings, StreamingManager, and ResourceManagers are all working in the shadows of your scene. It's also important to note that object and Object are not the same thing. `System.object` and `UnityEngine.Object` do conflict on some level. The UnityEngine version has more to do with the actual game engine itself.

The system version has more to do with data types that even `UnityEngine.Object` inherit from. Unfortunately, the function `FindObjectsOfType()` comes from the UnityEngine. Because of this it's a feature that doesn't exist in `System.object`. The features you're allowed to do with boxing are limited to the eldest parent.

6.22 Operator Overloading

With all of the work we did discovering types and seeing how they can be interchanged it's important to see how they can be used a bit more definitively. In cases like ints floats and the like, we can apply math operators. Both int and float are types that inherit from object.

What happens if you'd like to do something specific when you add one zombie to another? Operators, like anything else it seems in C#, can have additional functionality added to them. When it comes to dealing with new classes, we need to manage data using methods which we feel fit. In most cases, operator overloading should be considered a bit like voodoo.

```
Zombie a = new Zombie();
Zombie b = new Zombie();
Zombie c = a + b;
// Operator + cannot be applied to operands of type 'Zombie' and 'Zombie'
```

In a more practical sense, a puzzle game could have a special class used to handle each puzzle piece. To facilitate how the puzzle combines points and position, the class could store an x and y position as well as a point value.

```
public class Puzzle
{
    public int x;
    public int y;
    public int points;
}
```

Operator overloading of a non-numerical value can result in a loss of readability. For purposes of learning how to do this, we'll ignore this. In most cases math operations should be deployed on the number values in a class. When it makes sense, math operations can be used on a new class with a reasonable outcome.

6.22.1 A Basic Example

With the Operator Over loading script in the Operator Over loading_Scene from the Operator Over loading Game Object, lets skip down to the public class Puzzle. In the class we have a new function signature.

```
/*                                                                          */
/* |Accessibility|static means    |return type  |indicates we |the operator|*/
/* └────────────┐the function is  |the addition |will override|to be       |*/
/*              |available to all |of a puzzle  |an operator  |over-ridden |*/
/*              |objects of this  |to a puzzle  |             |            |*/
/*              |type             |is another   |             |            |*/
/*              |                 |puzzle       |             |            |*/
/*              |                 |             |             |            |*/
/*              |                 |             |             |            |*/
/*              |                 |             |             |            |*/
/*              |                 |             |             |            |*/
/*              ↓        ↓         ↓        ↓    ↓                          */
        public static Puzzle operator + (Puzzle a, Puzzle b)
        {
            Puzzle p = new Puzzle()
            {
                x = a.x + b.x,
                y = a.y + b.y,
                points = a.points + b.points
            };
            return p;
        }
```

In the class structure, a new function to add Puzzle pieces together requires a new syntax. The important new parts is the operator + section of the function. The function parameters are the operands to be added. The keywords public and static relate to the accessibility of the function and the Puzzle keyword indicates the return type of the function.

To create a Puzzle object to return we add the members of each parameter argument together to create the new Puzzle object.

```
Puzzle a = new Puzzle()
{
    x = 1,
    y = 2,
    points = 1
};
Puzzle b = new Puzzle()
{
    x = 0,
    y = 1,
    points = 3
};
Puzzle c = a + b;
Debug.Log("c.x: " + c.x + " c.y: " + c.y + " c.points: " + c.points);
// c.x: 1 c.y: 3 c.points: 4
```

When we add `Puzzle` a to `Puzzle` b we get `Puzzle` c, the result as indicated by the operation when `Puzzle` p was created in the operator override function. Conceptually there are now three Puzzle objects in existence, one for each operand, a and b, and one for the result of the addition, c. After they're used and the addition is finished, unless you store the result, all three are deleted once the function they are used in is complete.

By including a + override we should also include the − override as well. Just because a + was created for the class doesn't necessarily dictate that a − override should exist. The string class has a + but no − because it's not as obvious as what to do when you subtract a string from another string.

```
public static Puzzle operator -(Puzzle a, Puzzle b)
{
    Puzzle p = new Puzzle()
    {
        x = a.x - b.x,
        y = a.y - b.y,
        points = a.points - b.points
    };
    return p;
}
```

6.22.2 Overloading*

We're not restricted to overloading a class by a class. We can overload our `Puzzle operator` * with a number. To double a Puzzle piece we could conceptually use the following:

```
public static Puzzle operator *(Puzzle a, int b)
{
    Puzzle p = new Puzzle()
    {
        x = a.x * b,
        y = a.y * b,
        points = a.points * b
    };
    return p;
}
```

In the above example, we take `Puzzle` a and multiply it by `int` b. To make use of the new operator, our code would have to look something like the following:

```
Puzzle a = new Puzzle() { x = 1, y = 2, points = 3 };
int b = 3;
Puzzle c = a * b;
Debug.Log("c.x: " + c.x + " c.y: " + c.y + " c.points: " + c.points);
// c.x: 3 c.y: 6 c.points: 9
```

In this case, `c = a * b;` takes the original and then multiplies it by 3 and assigns the new value to c. Another effect of using the * with an int in the override is the ability to use the *= operator.

```
c *= 3;
Debug.Log("c.x: " + c.x + " c.y: " + c.y + " c.points: " + c.points);
// c.x: 9 c.y: 18 c.points: 27
```

This might bring up the question, can we use += as well?

```
public static Puzzle operator +(Puzzle a, int b)
{
    Puzzle p = new Puzzle()
    {
        x = a.x + b,
        y = a.y + b,
        points = a.points + b
    };
    return p;
}
```

Using a different set of parameters we can add the ability to add an int to the values of the `Puzzle`.

```
c += 1;
Debug.Log("c.x: " + c.x + " c.y: " + c.y + " c.points: " + c.points);
// c.x: 10 c.y: 19 c.points: 28
```

The result of adding 1 to all the values in the Puzzle has the effect you might guess when used. The utility of adding 1 to all three members of Puzzle might be questionable, but certainly it could be used for only the points. The problem with this becomes more apparent once we start using them. If we assumed `c += 1` was only to be used to add value to the points we could do such a thing. We could also assume that adding puzzle c += a Vector2Int could just modify two of the parameters in the Puzzle object.

```
public static Puzzle operator +(Puzzle a, Vector2Int b)
{
    Puzzle p = new Puzzle()
    {
        x = a.x + b.x,
        y = a.y + b.y,
        points = a.points
    };
    return p;
}
```

We can omit adding a value to a.points, but we do need to include a.points in new Puzzle p before returning it. Otherwise the new value after the + operation will have 0 points. A revised version of the + overload should look like the following as well.

```
public static Puzzle operator +(Puzzle a, int b)
{
    Puzzle p = new Puzzle()
    {
        //x = a.x + b,
        //y = a.y + b,
        x = a.x,
        y = a.y,
        points = a.points + b
    };
    return p;
}
```

With the modifications to the code, we're now able to move puzzle objects around with a Vector2Int and adjust the values with a single int. Conceptually keeping track of what's going on can be difficult. Adding, multiplying, and incrementing in different ways with different values is confusing. This means that we've lost some readability; not always the best option. However, in light of this, does this mean we should never use operator overloading? The readability of the code is the only thing we need to question.

Up until recently there wasn't a Vector2Int object available in Unity 3D, there was only Vector2 which uses float values for x and y. Puzzle game authors often created their own version of Vector2Int to help facilitate keeping objects in a grid. This meant replicating the available operator overrides in Vector2 for their own integer version of the same function. Perhaps if you were to require a specific type for your own game it's important to understand how to write operator overrides.

In addition to the previous examples using + and *, we can also overload the true and false keywords. For operators such as > and <, we can test if one puzzle object is more valuable than another.

6.22.3 Overloading < and >

Rather than returning a new Puzzle, operators return a bool value. The operators < and > can be overridden to return a true or false value. The code fragment that accomplishes this is as follows:

```
public static bool operator <(Puzzle a, Puzzle b)
{
    return a.points < b.points;
}
```

Before we can use this, Unity 3D will likely remind us that we're forgetting something with the following error message: "The operator 'OperatorOverloading.Puzzle.operator <(OperatorOverloading.Puzzle, OperatorOverloading.Puzzle)' requires a matching operator '>' to also be defined."

```
public static bool operator >(Puzzle a, Puzzle b)
{
    return a.points > b.points;
}
```

To comply, we'll add in the opposite version of the less than < operator overload. A quick copy/paste and a replacement of less than < to greater than > is all it takes to allow us to use the less than < and greater than > overload.

To continue with our example, we can use the following few statements to check if our overload is working.

```
Puzzle a = new Puzzle() { points = 1 };
Puzzle b = new Puzzle() { points = 7 };
bool c = a > b;
Debug.Log("a > b? " + c);
// a > b? False

bool d = a < b;
Debug.Log("a < b? " + d);
// a < b? True
```

The initialization of the Puzzle sets points for a to 1 and b to 7. Then Puzzle object a does indeed have fewer points than `Puzzle` b. In this if statement, we do get a is not greater than b, and a is less than b.

However, you decide to use overloaded operators is left to how you've decided to work with your classes. In many cases, if you find yourself comparing a few variables between two objects of the same class to execute some block of code, then you should consider using an operator overload. Likewise, if you find yourself adding multiple things together using the + for multiple attributes, then that's another candidate for an overload.

6.22.4 What We've Learned

With all of what we just learned, you should be able to see how overriding less than < and greater than > can be useful in terms of sorting. You'd be able to make a sort based on specific properties between classes. Comparing distances and threat levels can be a very interesting behavior.

Some of what we're doing here is a bit awkward and mostly contrived. In general, greater than > and less than < should be used to compare more numeric values. In the above code, comparing two zombies directly is misleading. Are we comparing size, armor, and number of brains eaten? It's impossible to know with the operator alone. In this case, a.armor > b.armor would make far more sense.

It's important to always leave the code in a readable state. Simply comparing two classes against one another makes it impossible to know exactly what it is we're comparing. This also goes for any other math operator. In general, math operations are best suited for numbers, not zombies.

6.23 Controlling Inheritance

Understanding the details of inheritance is key to using any object-oriented programming (OOP). Polymorphism, specialization, and encapsulation are considered the three pillars of OOP. Polymorphism is related to how classes inherit traits from one another. To be fair, some consider inheritance as a pillar on its own.

If someone needs to add behaviors to a class, but you require something like movement to remain consistent between all characters in your game, then you'll have to implement various systems to keep people from breaking your code. A sealed class, often referred to as a final class, cannot be inherited from. This sort of data ends the line as far as inheritance is concerned. This class is used when you want to finalize a class and prevent any further inheritance.

The common metaphor used to describe inheritance is a family tree; however, what more closely describes class inheritance is biological classification or scientific taxonomy. This is a system to organize and categorize organisms into groups such as species, family, and class. Each category is a taxonomic rank.

To biologists the species *Agaricus bisporus,* the average button mushroom, belongs to the genus *Agaricus* of the family Agaricaceae of the order Agaricales in the phylum Basidiomycota in the kingdom Fungi. That's quite a mouthful, even if you don't like them on pizza.

In a very similar way, when you create a Zombie: MonoBehaviour, you are creating a class Zombie based on MonoBehaviour, Behaviour, Component, Object, and object. Notice that Object with an uppercase O is based on object with a lowercase o.

In this ranking and categorizing of mushrooms and zombies, the hierarchy that is formed means there are common traits shared among objects. A death cap mushroom is a fungus like a button mushroom. Both share common traits, reproduce by spreading spores, and have similar structures made of chitin. One of these makes pizza deadly, and the other just makes pizza yummy.

In a similar way, all of the classes we've written based on MonoBehaviour share common features, for example, Start() and Update(). From Behavior, they are inherit enabled. From Component, they inherit various messaging and component properties. UnityEngine.Object gives them the ability to instantiate or destroy themselves and find one another. Finally, System.object gives them all ToString().

Nature might take eons to create a new class of life. For a programmer, a new class in Unity 3D just takes a few mouse clicks. Programmers also have the ability to override how inherited functions behave. However, unexpected behaviors usually result in bugs. To control this, it's best to put preventative measures around inherited functions through encapsulation and special controls.

6.23.1 Sealed

The sealed prefix to a function is one of the systems that allows you to control how a function is inherited. Once you've written a well-constructed class, it's a good idea to go back and prevent anyone from breaking it. The sealed keyword prevents a class member from being misused by a child inheriting the member.

One commonly written class is a timer. The timer should have some features such as setting the length of time for the timer, asking for how much time is left, pausing and restarting the timer, and events for when the timer ends and starts.

If you want all of the timers to behave exactly the same, then you'll have to prevent anyone from making any unnecessary modifications to the timer class. This is why they need to be sealed. A sealed class is meant to prevent any further modifications from the point where it has been sealed.

6.23.1.1 A Basic Example

Adding in the sealed keyword before the class keyword does the trick. Once this is added, no class can inherit from the class. In the ControllingInheritance_Scene open the ControllingInheritance script on the appropriately named game object.

```
sealed class FinalizedObject
{
}

class InheritFromSealed : FinalizedObject
{
}
/* cannot derive from sealed type 'ControllingInheritance.FinalizedObject' */
```

Once in place, you can create another class in an attempt to inherit from it. The following class tries to inherit from the sealed class. It would be easy to remove the sealed keyword from the class and open it up for basing more classes on it. However, this does inform you that you are indeed making a change that isn't intended. This behavior is meant to limit the amount of tampering of a class written to do something specific. Usually, classes written with sealed are for very basic and very widely available functions that shouldn't require any other class to inherit from it.

We do have one option open to us in order to add additional functionality to a sealed class.

6.23.2 Extension Functions

An Extension is a secondary class that contains a function that we intend to use to add to a sealed class.

```
static class FinalizedObjectExtension
{
    public static void ExtensionFunction(this FinalizedObject finalObj)
    {
        Debug.Log("Extending the finalizedObject.");
    }
}
```

A static class means that the class members are available globally. This is required such that the ExtensionFunction is available to any FinalizedObject. The first argument to the ExtensionFunction is this FinalizedObject finalObj where this indicates that the function relates to the FinalizedObject identified as finalObj. To use the ExtensionFunction as a member of the sealed class use the regular dot operator as though it were a member of the FinalizedObject.

```
void UsingControllingInheritance()
{
    FinalizedObject finalizedObject = new FinalizedObject();
                                      /*              |            */
    finalizedObject.ExtensionFunction();/*←──────────┘            */
    /*                          ↑                                 */
}   /*                          |                                 */
    /*         ┌─────────────────────────────────────┐           */
    /*         │function not actually written in│              */
    /*         │the FinalizedObject class.       │              */
    /*         └─────────────────────────────────────┘           */
```

The instance of the FinalizedObject identified as finalizedObject has access to the new ExtensionFunction() which was written in the static class FinalizedObjectExtension. To add parameters to the function you'd add them after the first argument.

```
public static void AnotherExtension(this FinalizedObject finalObj, int someArg)
{
    Debug.Log("AnotherExtension: " + someArg);
}
```

In the above, someArg takes an int and adds it to the end of the Debug.Log output. To make things more interesting, it's possible to add extensions to other classes in the same FinalizedObjectExtension static class.

```
sealed class AnotherSealedClass
{
    public void SealedFunction(int sealedArg)
    {
        Debug.Log("SealedFunctions's sealedArg:" + sealedArg);
    }
}
```

With the addition of AnotherSealedClass, we've also added a function which prints out an input argument. An extension can access the members of the class in the body of the extended function.

```
public static void AnotherExtension(this FinalizedObject finalObj, int someArg)
{
    Debug.Log("AnotherExtension: " + someArg);
}

public static void AnotherExtension(this AnotherSealedClass anotherClass, int anotherArg)
{
    anotherClass.SealedFunction(anotherArg);
}
```

The second version of AnotherExtension just changes the type for the first argument. In technical terms it's the same function with a different signature, this is allowed since it's now a regular function override.

```
finalizedObject.AnotherExtension(7);
// AnotherExtension: 7

AnotherSealedClass another = new AnotherSealedClass();
another.AnotherExtension(3);
//SealedFunctions's sealedArg:3
```

In the same FinalizedObjectExtension static class the ExtendingAnotherSealedClass function uses a different signature. This allows for both the first example of the finalized object and the anotherSealedClass to have access to a similarly named AnotherExtension() extension function.

The key notion is that a class that is widely available should be stable and unchanging. Reliability is key for preventing too many bugs from creeping into your code. The different accessibility modifications such as sealed are intended to help prevent unexpected behavior. Of course, this doesn't by any stretch of the imagination mean that it prevents bugs completely.

6.23.3 Abstract

If a sealed class means it's not intended to be extended upon, an abstract is the opposite. An abstract is a class which is required to be extended. The abstract keyword is used to tell inheriting classes that there's a function they need to implement. If you forget to implement a function that was marked as abstract, Unity 3D will remind you and throw an error.

6.23.3.1 A Basic Example

To inform another programmer or yourself that you need to implement a specific function, the abstract keyword is used. Setting up a class to inherit from helps you plan your classes and how the classes are intended to be used.

```
abstract class BaseCounter
{/*    ↑                            ┌─────────────┐    */
  /*   └──────────────────────┐     │abstract     │    */
     public int Counter;/* ├─┤declaration│    */
     /*              ┌──────────┘     └─────────────┘    */
     /*              ↓                                    */
     public abstract void IncrementCounter();
}
```

An `abstract` `BaseCounter` class has a defined abstract `void` `IncrementCounter();` created. As a class implements the `BaseCoutner`, Visual Studio immediately warns you to Implement Abstract Class.

```
class ImplementsCounter : BaseCounter
{

}
```

Implement Abstract Class ▶   ❌ CS0534 'ControllingInheritance.ImplementsCounter' does not
Add accessibility modifiers   implement inherited abstract member
                                     'ControllingInheritance.BaseCounter.IncrementCounter()'

```
...
{
    public override void IncrementCounter()
    {
        throw new System.NotImplementedException();
    }
}
...
```

Preview changes

Fix all occurrences in: Document | Project | Solution

The implementation uses override to indicate it's implementing the abstract function. If you add a body to the abstract function another error comes up to tell you a body for an abstract function is not allowed.

```
public abstract void IncrementCounter()
{
}
```

⊘ void BaseCounter.IncrementCounter()

'ControllingInheritance.BaseCounter.IncrementCounter()' cannot declare a body because it is marked abstract

The `abstract` keyword implies that the function declared is to be implemented by its inheriting class. The programmer implementing from the `BaseClass` there are important functions which must be filled in. The implementation, however, is left up to the author of the inheriting class.

This only means to inform you that you cannot implement an abstract function. You must rely on a child class making the implementation. The intent here is to provide a clear and specific structure for all classes inheriting from the `BaseClass`. This assumes there is a common structure between all the classes using the abstract class.

To continue, we should make a sibling class similar to ChildClass with a different implementation of the `IncrementCounter()` call.

```
public override void IncrementCounter()
{
    Counter++;
    Debug.Log("Counter: " + Counter);
}
```

With this we increment `Counter` by 1 each time the function is called. The `UseCounter()` function is called in `Start()`, and we get some numbers going up.

```
void UseCounter()
{
    ImplementsCounter counter = new ImplementsCounter();
    counter.IncrementCounter();
    counter.IncrementCounter();
    counter.IncrementCounter();
    counter.IncrementCounter();
    counter.IncrementCounter();
}
```

This results in the following Console output:

If the classes are considered final, they can be sealed.

```
sealed class ImplementsCounter : BaseCounter
{
    public override void IncrementCounter()
    {
        Counter++;
        Debug.Log("Counter: " + Counter);
    }
}
```

This means that the IncrementsCounter can no longer be derived from. However, this doesn't apply any sibling that hasn't been sealed. A sibling is considered a branch from BaseClass. C# is informing us that it cannot create an instance of the abstract class or interface BaseClass. An interface works in a similar way to an abstract class, but with a few more restrictions. All these mechanisms are there to prevent problematic issues that have come up with different languages. We'll get into the hows and whys of the interface in Section 7.6.4.

6.23.4 Abstract: Abstract

The Abstract topic should be expanded to look at additional abstract classes inheriting from abstract classes. These can be used to add more diversity to a simple base class. By creating a branch that is also abstract, you can add more data fields and functions to provide a variation on the first idea.

```csharp
abstract class BaseLimitCounter : BaseCounter
{
    public int Limit;
    public abstract bool AtLimit();
    public abstract void SetLimit(int l);
    public override void IncrementCounter()
    {
        Counter++;
        Debug.Log("Counter: " + Counter);
    }
}
class LimitCounter : BaseLimitCounter
{
    public override bool AtLimit()
    {
        return Counter >= Limit;
    }

    public override void SetLimit(int l)
    {
        Limit = l;
    }
}
```

The key function behind using abstract classes is to create a commonality between all the deriving classes. They'll all use the same `IncrementCounter()` function. `BaseLimitCounter` implements the `IncrementCounter()` function the same as any other class based on the `BaseCounter` abstract class.

Organizationally, `LimitCounter` only has two new functions. A check to see if we're at the limit and a function to set the limit. By breaking up the classes into separate files we've kept the amount of code contained in each class to a minimum. This prevents a single class from becoming overly complex and allows for focus of purpose. In a team of programmers, separating files also provides a means of isolating work. When multiple people are working on a single file work changes can collide, and work can be lost.

Additional fields and functions are added in the abstract class BaseLimitCounter that is based on the abstract class `BaseCounter`. This avoids making modifications to the BaseCounter, as there might be other classes relying on its stability. Keeping code in use intact is necessary to avoid conflict. Modifications to a base could cause problems to ripple through the rest of the project.

The implementation the abstract member `AtLimit();` and `SetLimit(int)` means that we get to keep our current implementation of `IncrementCounter()` and we need to add only the missing functions.

```csharp
void UseLimitCounter()
{
    LimitCounter limitCounter = new LimitCounter();
    limitCounter.SetLimit(3);
    Debug.Log("at limit: " + limitCounter.AtLimit());
    // "at limit: False"
    limitCounter.IncrementCounter();//already implemented in BaseLimitCounter
    // "Counter: 1"
    limitCounter.IncrementCounter();
    // "Counter: 2"
    limitCounter.IncrementCounter();
    // "Counter: 3"
    Debug.Log("at limit: " + limitCounter.AtLimit());
    // "at limit: True"
}
```

6.23.5 Putting This to Use

We'll start with a construct that's used often for many different game systems.

```
abstract class BaseTimer
{
    public float EndTime;
    public float Timer;
    public abstract void SetTime(float time);
    public abstract void BeginTimer();
    public abstract bool Ended();
}
```

An `abstract BaseTimer` gives us a few abstract members to work with. The three functions will set when the timer will end, when it begins and whether or not it's ended. Also in the `BaseTimer` class is a float variable for the `Timer` and the `EndTime` values.

The implementation of this abstract class is called `GameTimer`, in which we can set a number of seconds and check for the `Ended()` boolean to become true.

```
class GameTimer : BaseTimer
{
    public override void SetTime(float time)
    {
        throw new System.NotImplementedException();
    }

    public override void BeginTimer()
    {
        throw new System.NotImplementedException();
    }

    public override bool Ended()
    {
        throw new System.NotImplementedException();
    }
}
```

The `GameTimer` can make use of Visual Studio's handy auto complete tools which create the appropriate overrides.

```
class GameTimer : BaseTimer
{
    public override void SetTime(float time)
    {
        Timer = time;
        Debug.Log("GameTimer set for: " + Timer + " seconds.");
    }

    public override void BeginTimer()
    {
        EndTime = Time.fixedTime + Timer;
        Debug.Log("GameTimer EndTime: " + EndTime);
    }

    public override bool Ended()
    {
        return Time.fixedTime >= EndTime;
    }
}
```

Each function requires thought as to how best implement each function. The intent of each function can be interpreted by the engineer. What's important is that the class works as expected, not necessarily how it works.

The `SetTime` assigns the argument `time` to the `Timer` value. This value doesn't change unless `SetTime` is used again to change the `Timer`'s value. The `BeginTimer` function sets the `EndTime` to the current time with the addition of the `Timer`'s value. So if the `Timer` was set to 3 seconds the `EndTime` becomes now + three seconds, or Three seconds from now. Finally the `Ended()` function checks if the current time is equal or exceeded the `EndTime` value. The function returns false so long as the current time is less than the `EndTime` value.

To use the new class it's instanced when the game begins using a `Start()` in a MonoBehaviour script in the scene. A `gameTimer` object is stored in the script and is assigned a new instance of the `GameTimer` class.

```
GameTimer gameTimer;
void UseGameTimer()
{
    gameTimer = new GameTimer();
    gameTimer.SetTime(3);
    gameTimer.BeginTimer();
}
```

The `Update()` then checks on every frame for the timer's `Ended()` function. By opting to not inherit from MonoBehaviour, `GameTimer` class doesn't need to rely on its own `Update()` function. As the class it's used in checks with an `Update()` the GameTimer ultimately gets updated every frame.

```
void Update()
{
    if (gameTimer.Ended())
    {
        Debug.Log("GameTimer Ended.");
    }
}
```

Once the `gameTime.Ended()` returns true we log "GameTimer Ended." Running the scene will instance the GameTimer as soon as the scene starts. Three seconds later the GameTimer Ended will repeat in the Console window.

6.23.6 What We've Learned

We can continue to make variations on the `BaseTimer` class easily. We could make an implementation which returns true until the timer has ended. All we'd have to do is switch one operator in the `Ended()`.

```
class NotGameTimer : GameTimer
{
    public override bool Ended()
    {
        return !(Time.fixedTime >= EndTime);
    }
}
```

The only function that we need to override in NotGameTimer is the Ended() function. When NotGameTimer inherits from GameTimer, both the BeginTimer and SetTime functions are already in place.

```
notGameTimer = new NotGameTimer();
notGameTimer.SetTime(3);
notGameTimer.BeginTimer();
```

The Update() function in the script in use in the scene checks with a very similar if statement.

```
if (notGameTimer.Ended())
{
    Debug.Log("NotGameTimer has not Ended");
}
```

As soon as the BeginTimer() function is called, the notGameTimer.Ended() is true until the time ends. Making minor changes to a class built around inheriting functions makes testing and creating new behaviors much easier. Any individual change on a base can have wide-reaching problems if unchecked. C# in general is built to allow for these sorts of behaviors, for better or worse.

6.24 Building A Game—Part 5

As we layer more and more behaviors onto the environment or characters in the scene we can begin to see a game take shape. Adding the Damage System to a wall tile makes for instant doors. Monsters can still get in, but it takes longer. Finding what makes a game fun is in part the job of the designer. As a programmer you're integral to finding something interesting and making it into something fun.

6.24.1 Generating Rooms

After building a system to generate a floor it's time to setup a system to build rooms with walls. The floor tile 2D array gives us a grid in which we can cut out rooms. Various systems to build a dungeon level exist, and many examples are available in C#. As a starting point we'll go into some of the basic steps to build a set of room walls.

```
[ExecuteInEditMode]
public class RoomGenerator : MonoBehaviour
{
    public bool GenerateRooms;
    public GameObject WallObject;
    public int RoomCount = 5;
    // minimum is 5.
    public int MaxRoomWidth = 7;
    public int MaxRoomDepth = 7;
    private List<GameObject> WallObjectList;
```

We start with the [ExecuteInEditMode] tag. This allows us to build the rooms and save them in the scene. Tags like this will enable faster testing of the code as well, since we don't need to wait for the game to play to test out the code. Having the editor open while we edit code narrows the iteration time.

```
// Update is called once per frame
void Update()
{
    if (GenerateRooms)
    {
        GenerateRooms = false;

        // clear any walls
        if (WallObjectList != null)
        {
            foreach (GameObject wall in WallObjectList)
            {
                DestroyImmediate(wall);
            }
        }
        // create list to remember objects to clear
        WallObjectList = new List<GameObject>();
```

In the Update() loop a similar bool is used to prevent continuous iterations. We're also creating a list of wall objects that need to be cleared when the generation is redone. DestroyImmediate() is a editor specific function that's used outside of the game play cycle. This skips over the objects OnDestroy() function that might play a particle effect when the object is destroyed. After the objects are cleared, we create a fresh list to populate later in the function.

```
/*          14-6 = 8                                      */
/*                                                        */
/*        x ┌──────────┐ x x x x x                        */
/*          12345678901234                                */
/*      x1 ┌────────────────┐  Width  = 14                */
/*      ┌2 ║①──────┐ ■ ■ □ □ □ □║  Height = 13            */
/*      │3 ║│ ○ ○ │ ■ ■ ■ □ □ □ □║  ① is the first valid point */
/*      │4 ║│ ○ ○ │ ■ ■ ■ □ □ □ □║     to start a room.   */
/* 13 │5 ║│ ○ ○ │ ■ ■ ■ □ □ □ □║                          */
/* -6 │6 ║└──────┘ ■ ■ ■ □ □ □ □║                          */
/* ──│7 ║ ■ ■ ■ ■ ■ ■ ■ □ □ □ □║  if MaxRoomWidth/Depth = 5 */
/*  7 └8 ║ ■ ■ ■ ■ ■ ■ ■②──────┐║  ② Last point in the area that */
/*      x9 ║ □ □ □ □ □ □ □ │ ○ ○ ○ │║    can fit a 5x5 room */
/*      x0 ║ □ □ □ □ □ □ □ │ ○ ○ ○ │║                      */
/*      x1 ║ □ □ □ □ □ □ □ │ ○ ○ ○ │║                      */
/*      x2 ║ □ □ □ □ □ □ □ └──────┘║                        */
/*      x3 ╚════════════════╝                              */
/*                                                        */
/* if a room is going to be a                              */
/* maximum size of 5x5 then the                            */
/* last point we can select in                             */
/* each row is 5 away from the                             */
/* edge.                                                   */
```

A bit of the logic to picking where to create rooms is diagrammed in the code in the form of a comment. We want to have a max width provided for the room so Something like 7×7 is easy to work with. Next, we'll want to know that each room is started at the same corner. In the diagram it's the top left. This means that we'll want to acknowledge that there's a safe space in which we can create a room.

```
// get some data for floor size
FloorGenerator generator = GetComponent<FloorGenerator>();
// get safe area
int maxW = 1 + generator.Width - MaxRoomWidth;
int maxD = 1 + generator.Depth - MaxRoomDepth;
```

Collect the data required to calculate the safe area. The generator object is the FloorGenerator used in the last chapter to create the floor tiles. This provides us with our maximum size minus the maximum size for a room.

```
for (int i = 0; i < RoomCount; i++)
{
    // a point somewhere in the safe zone
    int x = Random.Range(1, maxW);
    int z = Random.Range(1, maxD);
    MakeRoom(x, z, generator);
}
```

Using the maximum sizes we can populate the scene with the number of rooms requested. The function MakeRoom takes a random position in the safe area and creates a random position in the safe area.

```
void MakeRoom(int x, int z, FloorGenerator generator)
{
    // make a room size startPoint + width/height
    int sizeX = x + Random.Range(5, MaxRoomWidth);
    int sizeZ = z + Random.Range(5, MaxRoomDepth);
```

The MakeRoom function takes the starting point and generates a randomly sized room with a minimum of 5 to the maximum specified in the editor. The size value is then used in an imbedded for loop. The logic starts with the following:

```
// generate walls for the room
for (int sX = x; sX < sizeX; sX++)
{
    for (int sZ = z; sZ < sizeZ; sZ++)
    {
```

A for loop to iterate across and for each step across we step down the Z axis. A check for either the north south edge or the east west edge is made to generate a wall.

```
bool isEdge = sX == x || sX == sizeX - 1 || sZ == z || sZ == sizeZ - 1;
if (isEdge)
{
    GameObject wall = Instantiate(WallObject, transform);
    WallObjectList.Add(wall);
    wall.transform.position = new Vector3()
    {
        x = sX - (generator.Width / 2),
        z = sZ - (generator.Depth / 2)
    };
}
```

The logic for this appears in a long chain of || statements. We check if x is the starting edge or the ending edge. This can also be read as "is left or is top or is bottom or is right"; create wall.

Clicking on the GenerateRooms check box a few times will create overlapping rooms. Fairly often though a random set of rooms that aren't touching can be generated.

More sophisticated systems that do this overlap check can also be created. A system can look at each corner and compare them to other corners to check that the rooms aren't covering the same space. I'll leave that up to you to experiment with.

6.24.2 What We've Learned

Rogue like dungeon generators have plenty of code resources available. Generating rooms with walls is one of the first steps toward a complete dungeon. Next comes adding hallways and doors. Starting with a center point of each room then drawing a line from room to room creates an array for a hallway to be generated from.

The logic required for figure out where to place the walls can be worked out on paper first. The diagrams here are intended to help visualize what the code is going to do. Truth be told, the code here started off as a diagram as what needed to be done before the logic was created to carry out the steps necessary to create the rooms.

6.25 Leveling Up

Building up some skills. We're getting deep into C#. This section contains a great deal of the things that make C# powerful and flexible. A great deal of the code we've learned up to this point allow us to get functional and get some basic work done. Even some of the more complex tasks can be completed with what we already know.

We had a short introduction to the more interesting constructs that make up C#. It's about time we had a short review of constructors, namespaces, and inheritance. We'll also look at more uses of arrays, enums, and goto labels. All these systems make up a part of the skills that every C# programmer uses.

7

Advanced

Chapter 6 was complex and covered many interesting topics. No doubt if you've gotten this far you're willing to find out more about what C# can do. With the content of Chapters 1 through 5, you would be capable of quite a lot. Continue to learn more clever tricks.

Most game logic and control systems need only the fundamentals that have been provided in Chapters 3 through 6. Once the behaviors need more coordinated events and simultaneous actions, you'll need to learn a few more tricks.

To make your work more predictable and to prevent bugs, you'll need practice; there are also some features that make C# more precise. This is to say that you would be able to enforce your own structure to how you allow others to work with your code in the ways you intended.

Since programming is just reading and writing text, there are many things that can go wrong. A simple misspelling or misplaced dot operator can break everything. There are many systems which you can use to help your fellow programmers follow your instructions through how they interact with what you've written.

7.1 What Will Be Covered in This Chapter

Many layers of simple code with layers of basic logic create a complex behavior. C# allows for different ways to keep your code contained in simple classes and functions. Simple classes and functions are easier to write and debug. Complex behaviors required for game interactions come about when you combine many simple behaviors with interesting logic.

We'll look at the following features in this chapter:

- Visual Studio's user interface (UI) and navigation of some of their interface widgets
- Further exploration into comments
- More function overloading
- More on base classes
- Optional parameters in functions' argument lists
- Delegate functions and events
- Class interfaces
- Class constructors again
- Basic preprocessor directives
- Exceptions
- Generics
- Events
- Unity 3D-friendly classes
- Destructors
- Concurrency and coroutines and even threads!
- Dictionary, stack, and queue types
- Callbacks
- Lambda expressions
- Accessors or properties

7.2 Review

In the previous chapter, we looked at some interesting material. We were able to overload the regular + and – with some new functionality. We looked at a few new ways to use the argument list in a function and write a loop.

There are some additional concepts worth mentioning. There are several online articles on the allocation of objects to either the stack or the heap. The heap is built up in order, but isn't rearranged too often.

When objects are added to the heap, the size of the heap grows. When objects are destroyed, they leave holes in the heap. This leaves gaps between the objects that were not deleted. Suppose we have 100 spaces in memory and object A takes up addresses from 1 to 20, B takes up from 21 to 40, and C takes up from 40 to 60. When object B is removed, spaces 21 to 40 are empty, between A and C. If a new object D is only a bit bigger than 20 spaces, say 22, it needs to find the next biggest place at the end, so D uses 61 to 82. If another object D is created, we're out of luck and the game stops running due to lack of memory.

The stack, however, is more organized based on how your code is executed. When a for loop is started, the int i = 0; parameter is always tossed into the top of the stack; as soon as it's no longer needed, it's chopped off, leaving room for the next object to be added to the stack.

In the end, memory management is a result of how you've arranged your data. So long as you use structs to move around large amounts of complex data, you'll most likely be allocating them to the stack. By instancing too many classes, you're leaving yourself to the heap that can eventually lead to memory problems. There is a problem if a stack is passed around in a class, in which case you're still working in the heap.

7.2.1 Moving Forward

We don't want to limit our experiences to the lessons we've just managed to get through. There's still plenty left to learn when it comes to the interesting parts of C#. In this chapter, we'll learn how to make C# bend to our will. Or at the very least, we'll come to understand what some of the more complex concepts look like.

We'll find out more about how functions can have different numbers of arguments. We'll even learn how a variable can be a function. Interfaces are special chunks of classes that serve as a template for other classes to follow. Then we'll look at some more interesting uses of those interfaces.

Later, we'll explore some more possibilities of how arrays can be handled and some simple tricks to make those arrays more manageable. Interfaces come into play again when dealing with arrays. After all, much of what computers are good at is iterating through long lists of data.

Speaking of data, because not all data is the same, we'll need to learn how to make functions more accepting of different types of data and still do what we expect them to. We can generalize functions to operate on practically any type of data.

After this, we'll finish some of the functionality of how C# works and then move on to how to use C# to its fullest. Many of the lessons in the following chapters are transferable to other languages. Modern features such as delegates and lambda functions are common among many other languages. Learning the principles of how modern programming features work in C# is useful in any other modern programming language.

Programming languages are as much about communicating to the computer as they are about conveying your thought process to another programmer reading your code.

7.3 Visual Studio

Visual Studio Community is a free version of the Visual Studio Software which has been in development by Microsoft for a few decades. Previous versions of Unity 3D were bundled with MonoDevelop, which is still an option if you'd like to try it out.

The Visual Studio the Installation app helps install plugins and components. One of the components is the Game development with Unity add-on. In addition to Unity, plenty of other add-ons are available.

Individual components enable development with C++, Python, and F#. This enables web, machine learning, and database software development as well.

Visual Studio has the advantage of being a wide audience and allows you to create software for much more than Unity 3D. Another option is Visual Studio Code, a light weight version of Visual Studio intended initially for Web Development. It's possible to have several integrated development environments (IDEs) installed side-by-side on your computer. To select which IDE is launched from Unity open the Preferences panel:

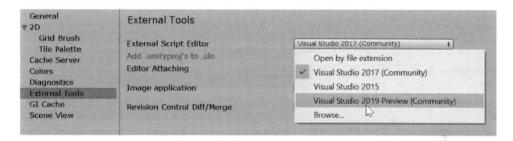

From here select the editor installed, if it's not in the list then you'll need to Select Browse and find the app you intend on using for editing scripts.

The main advantage of using an IDE software like Visual Studio over a plain text editor is a feature called the debugger. Aside from that are other features like syntax highlighting, auto completion, and syntax error checking. The debugger allows you to watch variables update with live values from the game and walk, line at a time, through your code to watch for errors as they happen.

In the coming chapters we'll cover some of the more useful features of your IDE as it's an important part of becoming a skilled game developer. The debugger is also very helpful to learn what your code is doing in a more visual manner.

7.3.1 The Debugger

When your code compiles, your game runs in the editor and you still get unexpected results; what are you to do? The debugger is there to let you see your code in action. Visual Studio has the ability to connect directly to the Unity 3D Editor while your game is running and pause your game as it executes each line of code you've written.

Let's look at how this works.

7.3.2 Mono History

Mono is open-source, free-to-use software. Mono is an implementation of the .NET Framework. Microsoft based their .NET Framework for C# language on the European Association for Standardizing Information and Communication Systems (ECMA). Like many European acronyms, because of language translation, the letters are unrelated to the words in the acronym.

The parts that come together to help build games in Unity are the C# language version and the .NET run time version. Both the language and .NET have different update schedules and version numbers. As of October 2018, .NET was up to version 4.7.2, thus Unity supports version 4.x keeping up with the latest features. C# at the same time saw a release on May 2018, bringing it up to version 7.3 to match features supported in the latest .NET.

As confusing as this might seem, the engineers at Unity are now trying to keep their version of the Unity.NET run-time up to date. Before 2017, this wasn't the case. Unity was using the Mono Runtime, which was behind the official standard, so for several years Unity was stuck on .NET version 2 and many features of the programming language were left out. Thankfully, this is no longer the case.

The Mono compiler was first developed by Miguel de Icaza, Ravi Pratap, Martin Baulig, and Raja Harinath. The compiler had many other contributors that helped improve and standardize how the internals work. Many improvements are continuously added every year.

Unity uses its own .NET run time. The latest version of Unity is compatible with the latest features of the C# language. There are a few things to keep in mind when looking at compatibility across different platforms. Now that you're learning C#, you'll be able to use your new language skills to build apps for practically every modern platform, with caviots.

In an effort to maintain cross-platform compatibility, Unity 3D utilizes Mono 4.x, though this is a recent addition. It's this broad platform compatibility that enables Unity 3D to support practically every form of distribution, including browsers, phones, and the most common PC operating systems.

Another commonly used framework is Oracle Systems' Java. Java has taken on many different forms and supports many different devices, including Blue-ray players and other more specific embedded systems. Because of Apple's strict platform requirements, Java has been greatly barred from iOS. Because of this restriction, C# is a better choice for developing mobile games. If you intend to write programs specifically for iOS, you would need to learn Objective-C or Swift. These languages are exclusive to Apple products.

After you write code, a compiler interprets the code and converts it into machine-readable language. The compiler first parses or converts your human-readable code into a computer-readable format called an intermediate language.

When your code is parsed, it's scanned for errors and syntax. Once this passes, various optimizations are applied. Extraneous comments, unreachable code, and unused variables are omitted during this conversion. Finally, the intermediate language is generated, which is then converted into machine code specific to the central processing unit (CPU) and operating system.

In the case with Unity 3D, the C# compiler eventually builds a file that is compiled just before the game begins. This library works similar to the libraries that you include in your own C# code. Because the code written for Unity 3D is based on MonoBehaviour, Unity 3D is able to make its connections into your code.

You may have become used to the fact that one operating system cannot normally run an application built for another operating system. For instance, you can't natively run an application built for Android on your PC. Even more difficult is emulating another CPU architecture altogether. This is because the binary executable that is produced by a compiler needs to know what to convert your language into ahead of time.

7.4 Function Overloading

Overloading, in the programming sense, means use of the same function name with different parameter values. Functions, so far, have had a single purpose once they're written. This most directly relates to the parameters which we give them. For example, consider the following.

7.4.1 A Closer Look at Functions

Open the FunctionOverloading_Scene and find the script attached to the FunctionOverloading Game Object. If we consider the following code for a moment, it looks like we're trying to write a function that returns half the value of a number fed into the parameter.

```
void UseDifferentFunctions()
{
    int a = 8;
    float b = 7f;
    int halfA = HalfInt(a);
    float halfB = HalfFloat(b);
    Debug.Log("halfA: " + halfA + " halfB: " + halfB);
    // halfA: 4 halfB: 3.5
}

int HalfInt(int a)
{
    return a / 2;
}

float HalfFloat(float a)
{
    return a / 2;
}
```

The function HalfInt() accepts an int and returns that int value divided by 2. HalfFloat() accepts a float value and returns a float that's half the value fed into its parameter.

What if we wanted to use the same function name for both? This would certainly make remembering the function's name a lot easier. The function name HalfValue() would be a lot easier than remembering HalfInt(), HalfFloat(), HalfDouble(), and anything else we might want to divide into two. We're actually allowed to do this quite easily using function overloading.

7.4.1.1 A Basic Example

```
void UseFunctionOverloading()
{
    int a = 8;
    float b = 7f;
    int halfA = HalfValue(a);/* ──────────────────────┐    */
    float halfB = HalfValue(b);/* ──────────────────┐ │    */
    Debug.Log("halfA: " + halfA + " halfB: " + halfB);/*│ │    */
    // halfA: 4 halfB: 3.5                             │ │
}/*                                               ┌───┘ │    */
 /*              ↓ a is an int so it uses this version │    */
int HalfValue(int i)//                                 │    */
{           //                                         │    */
    return i / 2;   //                                 │    */
}/*                                               ┌────┘    */
 /*              ↓ b is a float, so it uses this version    */
float HalfValue(float f)
{
    return f / 2f;
}
```

This code might seem a bit awkward, given in our learning that once an identifier has been used, it can't be used again for a different purpose. In C# we're allowed to do this with functions. This is one of the few places this is allowed. In many cases the return value would be the same as to avoid unexpected return types from a similarly named function.

```
/* Both return int, but use different parameters  */
/*           uses a float                         */
/*               ↓                                */
int HalfToInt(float f)
{
    return (int)f / 2;
}
/*           uses an int                          */
/*               ↓                                */
int HalfToInt(int i)
{
    return i / 2;
}
```

In this case the two functions match both input parameters and return values. The only difference is how the value is calculated. In this case, C# will complain that there is no difference between the two functions.

```
int HalfFull(int i)
{
    return i / 2;
}

int HalfFull(int i)
{
    return i * 0.5f;
}
```

7.4.2 Function Signature

Here, we have the same function written twice, but we get an error this time that the function is already defined! And, as a matter of fact, yes, it has already been defined once before. A function is defined by not only its identifier but also its parameters. The function name and its parameter list together are called a *signature*.

The return type is not a part of a function's signature. What this means is best illustrated by the following code fragment.

```
int ReturnValue()
{
    return 1;
}
// return value doesn't count
// as a part of the signature
float ReturnValue()
{
    return 1f;
}
```

Unfortunately, C# isn't smart enough to understand that we're asking for one of two different functions here. Because the return type is not included when looking at a function signature, the two functions look the same to C#. The code fragment above results in an error.

7.4.3 Different Signatures

So far, we've used a single parameter for the above examples. This doesn't need to be the case. We're allowed to use as many different parameters as we require.

```
public static int Overloaded()
{
    return 1;
}
public static int Overloaded(int a)
{
    return a + 1;
}
public static float Overloaded(int a, float b)
{
    return a / b;
}
public void UseOverloads()
{
    int a = Overloaded();
    int b = Overloaded(1);
    float c = Overloaded(1, 3f);
    Debug.Log("a: " + a + " b: " + b + " c: " + c);
}
```

The above code uses no parameters in the first version of the function `Overloaded()`; this is followed by a single `int`, and then we're using an `int` and a `float`. However, all three of these have return values. Can we do the same with the ref and out as well? Let's add the following code to the versions of the above-mentioned functions and see what happens next.

```
public static void Overloaded(int a, ref float b)
{
    b = (float)a / 3;
}
```

It's important to remember that there are two Overloaded functions that start with int and use a float.

```
float d = 7;             /* initialized to 7                              */
Overloaded(3, d);        /* doesn't use ref in signature                  */
Debug.Log("d: " + d);    /* doesn't change from initialized version       */
// d: 7                  /* prints 7 since it didn't get changed          */
Overloaded(3, ref d);    /* this one uses ref which is a different signature */
Debug.Log("d: " + d);    /* d has been modified by ref                    */
// d: 1                  /* prints 1 since it's been modified 3/3          */
```

An int followed by a float will use a different version of the Overloaded function than an int and a ref float.

```
public static double staticDouble;
public static void Overloaded(double d)
{
    staticDouble = d;
}
```

Again, it's important to remember that the use of a 9.0 without the f means a double 9.0 not float 9.0f. So when you use the following:

```
Debug.Log("staticDouble: " + staticDouble);
// staticDouble: 0
Overloaded(9.0);
Debug.Log("staticDouble: " + staticDouble);
// staticDouble: 9
```

We get an expected result of a function that's overloaded to use a double and not a float. A function's signature is a function name and a list of parameters. For a function overload to work, we can use the same function name, but overloads require that each function have the same name but a different parameter list.

Why is this so important; wouldn't using the same name with different results end up being confusing? If the intent remains the same, this is easy to reconcile; we'll see how this works before the end of the chapter.

7.4.4 Putting It Together

By creating functions with overloads, we're allowed to give ourselves some options when using the same function name. Making our code more flexible without adding complexity is possible with very few changes to the function.

```
GameObject CreateObject()
{
    GameObject g = GameObject.CreatePrimitive(PrimitiveType.Cube);
    return g;
}
GameObject CreateObject(PrimitiveType primitive)
{
    GameObject g = GameObject.CreatePrimitive(primitive);
    return g;
}
GameObject CreateObject(PrimitiveType primitive, Vector3 position)
{
    GameObject g = GameObject.CreatePrimitive(primitive);
    g.transform.position = position;
    return g;
}
void UseCreateObject()
{
    GameObject a = CreateObject();
    // makes a cube
    GameObject b = CreateObject(PrimitiveType.Capsule);
    // makes a capsule
    Vector3 position = new Vector3(0, 0, 1f);
    GameObject c = CreateObject(PrimitiveType.Sphere, position);
    // makes a sphere at x:0, y:0, z:1
}
```

This code sample was created for an Example.cs assigned to an object in the scene. I assigned it to the Main Camera in an empty new scene in the Unity 3D editor. There are three versions of CreateObject(), each one having a different signature. In the UseCreateObject() function, each version is used to demonstrate going from no parameters to two parameters. Of course, you can add as many parameters as you think are manageable.

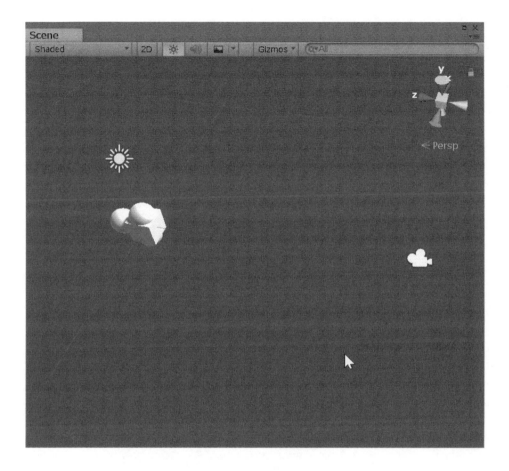

The objects in the image above would be made in the scene based on the three functions we just wrote. We have access to the three objects assigned as a, b, and c in the Start() function, so we can make additional changes to them in the Start() function.

7.4.5 Not Quite Recursion

Where function overloading becomes interesting is when a function refers to an overloaded version of itself. The logic here is that a function can be accessed in one of two different forms without needing to write another function. The scenario arises when you have a simple function, say, drawing a word to the screen with some debug lines.

The task starts off with drawing a letter, so first we'll want to build a system for storing letters. We'll also want to create some system to give the collection of array points of a letter to whoever is asking for it. We'll start off with two letters; I'll let you figure out the rest on your own.

7.4.6 DrawWords

This DrawWord project example is available with the full alphabet available in the Unity 3D projects downloaded from GitHub along with the rest of the content for this book, but here we'll look at a shorter fragments of the code taken from the DrawWords C# class.

```csharp
public static Vector3[] A = new[]
{
    new Vector3(-1, -1, 0),
    new Vector3(-1, 0, 0),
    new Vector3(0, 1, 0),
    new Vector3(1, 0, 0),
    new Vector3(-1, 0, 0),
    new Vector3(1, 0, 0),
    new Vector3(1, -1, 0)
};

public static Vector3[] B = new[]
{
    new Vector3(-1, -1, 0),
    new Vector3(-1, 1, 0),
    new Vector3(0, 1, 0),
    new Vector3(1, 0, 0),
    new Vector3(-1, 0, 0),
    new Vector3(1, 0, 0),
    new Vector3(1, -1, 0),
    new Vector3(-1, -1, 0)
};
```

Here, we are looking at two letters A and B stored in the form of 3D points in space. The Vector3[] is an array of Vector3s and the A or B identifies the array. They are rather boxy since they're made of only a few points each.

```csharp
public static Vector3[] ToVectorArray(char c)
{
    switch (c)
    {
        case 'A':
            return A;
        case 'B':
            return B;
        OtherLetters
    }
}
```

In the same class is the ToVectorArray returns which set of points based on an incoming type char. We'll look at what a char is in a moment.

```
public static void DrawWord(char c, float scale, Vector3 position, Color color)
{
    Vector3[] lines = ToVectorArray(c);
    for (int i = 1; i < lines.Length; i++)
    {
        Vector3 start = (lines[i - 1] * scale);
        start.x *= spacing;
        Vector3 end = (lines[i] * scale);
        end.x *= spacing;
        Debug.DrawLine(start + position, end + position, color);
    }
}
```

In the above code, the function DrawWord() accepts a char c, as well as a scale, position, and color. This then asks for the lines to draw using the ToVectorArray function. Once the vectors are assigned to the array called lines, the for() loop iterates through each line segment.

The char type is short for character. A char is a single character in a string. Rather, a string is an array of chars. Chars can be only letters, numbers, or symbols; when we use "hello," we are assembling chars to make a word.

For readability, we create a start and an end Vector3 in the for loop. This takes the previous Vector3 and assigns that to start. An important, yet somewhat not-so-obvious, step here is to start the for loop with int i = 1; rather than 0. The start of the line begins with lines [i–1] that means that if the loop begins with i = 0;, the first line point will be lines [–1] that would give us an index out of range error. Remember that an array always starts at 0.

This function isn't only meant to draw a single letter. Instead, we'll write another version of the exact same function with the following code:

```
public static void DrawWord(string word, float scale, Vector3 position, Color color)
{
    //convert to uppercase first
    string uLetters = word.ToUpper();
    char[] letters = uLetters.ToCharArray();
    if (letters.Length > 0)
    {
        for (int i = 0; i < letters.Length; i++)
        {
            float offset = (i * scale);
            Vector3 offsetPosition = new Vector3()
            {
                x = position.x + offset,
                y = position.y,
                z = position.z
            };

            DrawWord(letters[i], scale, offsetPosition, color);
        }
    }
}
```

This version of the same function does a couple of things. First, we change the function's signature, which means that rather than char c as the first parameter, we use string word instead. This changes the signature in such a way that this DrawWord() function is now an overloaded version of the first DrawWord() function. We should convert string word into upper case. This conversion to upper case is necessary to convert any lower case letters to allow the `ToVectorArray()` function to convert each letter to an array of vectors. Once we have the string converted from something like "abba" to "ABBA" by using string `uLetters = word.ToUpper();`, we're ready for the next step.

To convert this string to an array of chars, we use the statement `char[] letters = uLetters.ToCharArray();`, where the `ToCharArray()` function in string returns an array of uppercase chars. So long as the array comes back with at least one result, we continue to the next for loop.

In this for loop, we start at the beginning of the char array. To keep the letters from piling up on top of one another, we create an offset, so each letter can start at a new location. This is done with `float offset = (i * scale);`, which we then use to create a new `offsetPosition` Vector3. The x of the `offsetPosition` is the only place where we need this `offset + position.x;` the y and z will just use the parameter at the beginning of the function.

When we use the overloaded version of the function in the function, we use the char parameter `DrawWord(letters [i], scale, offsetPosition, color);`, where letters [i] is passing a char to the function rather than a string. The overloaded version is automatically used.

To see our code in action, add the DrawWords.cs class as a component to the Main Camera in a new scene in the Unity Editor.

```
void UseDrawWords()
{
    DrawWords.DrawWord("Words Are Being Drawn", 1, Vector3.zero, Color.red);
}

private void Update()
{
    UseDrawWords();
}
```

In the `Update()` function we call `UseDrawWords()`. In that function we call `DrawWord()` word at the origin by using `Vector3.zero`, with scale of 1, `Color.red;`, so they're easier to see.

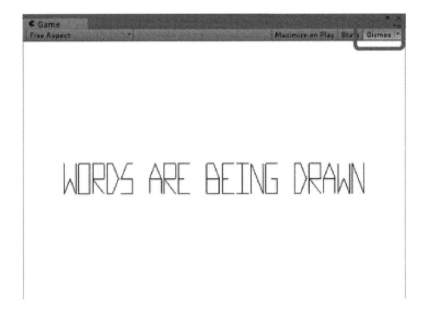

The `Letters` class is added after the `DrawWords` class in the same file. Make sure that the Gizmos button on the top right of the Game view port is turned on; otherwise, the `Debug.DrawLines()` function will not be visible in the `Game` view panel.

7.4.7 What We've Learned

The above discussion also works as an interesting example of code portability. The `Letters` class is self-contained and doesn't depend on anything other than `UnityEngine` for the `Vector3` data type and the `Debug.DrawLine()` function. Overloading a function should come naturally when you want to use the same function in different ways. This also means that you can simply use `DrawWord('A', 1.0f, new Vector3.zero, Color.red);` to draw a single character.

7.5 Accessors (or Properties)

Encapsulation is an important property of any class. Keeping a class protected from misuse is critical if you want to keep your sanity when the time to debug anything comes. Consider the following class:

```
class MyNumberProperty
{
    public int PositiveNumbersOnly;
}
```

The `public int PositiveNumbersOnly` is open to anyone who wants to make changes. For the most part, this is just fine. Any objects can go in and make changes to the `PositiveNumbersOnly` value stored in the `MyNumberProperty` class anytime. This includes changing the positive number to a negative one. If having a positive number is critical for any of MyNumberProperty's functions, we might start to run into problems. To protect this number, you could have the access to the following:

```
class MyReadOnlyProperty
{
    public readonly int PositiveNumbersOnly;
}
```

This statement changes the read/write ability of `PositiveNumbersOnly` to read only. This also means that the class where the value lives in cannot freely change that value. Changing the value isn't allowed from outside of the class either. The only time this value can be set is on creation in the constructor.

```
class MySetOnceNumbers
{
    public readonly int ReadOnlyOne = 1;//set on initialization
    public readonly int SetByParamOnCreation;
    public readonly int SetOnCreation;

    /* Constructor */
    MySetOnceNumbers(int numberParameter)
    {
        /* Set once by parameter */
        SetByParamOnCreation = numberParameter;
        /* Set by assignment in constructor */
        SetOnCreation = 7;
    }
}
```

This example shows the three ways in which a `readonly` value can be set. The first is ReadOnlyOne which is assigned in its initialization. This becomes a hardcoded value, something that's not allowed to change after it's written in code. The second value SetByParamOnCreation is set by a value in the parameter when you instance the class. Once the class is instanced, that value cannot be changed. The last is SetOnCreation, which is assigned in the constructor as a hardcoded value. This cannot be changed again once it's assigned.

Should we want to protect a value internally, we should make it private, and then make a publiclly available version which has some checks to block values we don't want.

```
class MyPositiveAccessor
{
    /* ┌───────────────────────┐ */
    /* │ This value isn't visible │ */
    /* │ outside of this class    │ */
    /* │ this is internal to this │ */
    /* │ class alone.             │ */
    /* └───────────┬───────────┘ */
    /*             ↓               */
    private int privatePositiveNumber;

    /* ┌───────────────────────┐ */
    /* │ This value is visible    │ */
    /* │ outside of the class.    │ */
    /* └───────────┬───────────┘ */
    /*             ↓               */
    public int publicPositiveNumber
    {
        get
        {
            return privatePositiveNumber;
        }
        set
        {
            if (value >= 0)
            {
                privatePositiveNumber = value;
            }
            else
            {
                privatePositiveNumber = 0;
            }
        }
    }
}
```

Here we have a private value called privatePositiveNumber and a public value called public-PositiveNumber. We'll plan on using one of them inside of the class, whereas we'll make the other publiclly available. Presume the value for a positive number should never be negative. To prevent the privatePositiveNumber from ever getting incorrectly set to a negative number, accessors allow logic in the set parameter for publicPositiveNumber to keep valid values.

7.5.1 Value

The placement of privatePositiveNumber = value; in our code is important. The value keyword is the input where privatePositiveNumber gets assigned. Where we use the get{} set{} notation, value is a catcher's mitt to snag incoming data. This accounts for any value entering the variable. This could be a struct, a string, or anything at all, so long as the type matches up.

7.5.1.1 A Basic Example

In its most simple form, the `get;set;` notation can be as simple as follows:

```
class GetSet
{
    public int MyInt{get;set;}
}

void UseGetSet()
{
    GetSet getset = new GetSet();
    getset.MyInt = 10;
    Debug.Log("getset.MyInt: " + getset.MyInt);
    // "getset.MyInt: 10"
}
```

At this point, there's no difference between `public in myInt;` and `public int myInt{get;set;};` the two operate essentially the same. What we're starting to produce here is a simple system where we're allowed to add in some logic to how a value is assigned.

To make full use of the accessor, we need to have two versions of a variable: the public accessor and a value that remains private within the confines of the class. This ensures a certain level of encapsulation that defines what object-oriented programming is all about.

```
class GetSetWithValues
{
    private int privateInt;
    public int publicInt
    {
        get
        {
            return privateInt;
        }
        set
        {
            privateInt = value;
        }
    }
}
```

The above code has a `private int privateInt` and `public int publicInt` with an accessor. This is a standard notation that should be used to define a variable for a cleanly encapsulated class. This too operates the same as the previous {`get;set;`}, only with the idea that it's redirecting an incoming data `value` from a public variable to a private variable hidden inside of the class.

7.5.2 Set Event

One of the advantages of an accessor is the ability to add logic to how a number is set. In addition to logic is the ability to raise an event. As in Section 7.5.1 from before, we'll want to add the delegate and the event to the GetSet class. Inside of the set element of the accessor, we'll make a check to see if there are functions delegated to the handler and then raise an event.

```csharp
class GetSetWithEvent
{
    private int privateInt;
    public int publicInt
    {
        get
        {
            return privateInt;
        }
        set
        {
            if (value <= 0)
            {
                privateInt = 0;
            }
            else
            {
                privateInt = value;
            }
            if (IntSetEvent != null)
            {
                IntSetEvent(privateInt);
            }
        }
    }
    public delegate void SetIntEventHandler(int i);
    public event SetIntEventHandler IntSetEvent;
}

void UseGetSetWithEvent()
{
    GetSetWithEvent getset = new GetSetWithEvent();
    getset.IntSetEvent += OnIntSet;
    getset.publicInt = 7;
    getset.publicInt = -13;
}

void OnIntSet(int i)
{
    Debug.Log("OnIntSet Called: " + i);
}
```

The above code instances the new class and then adds the OnIntSet() function to the getset. IntSetEvent inside of the GetSetWithEvent class. Once the value is set on the following line, we get the following output from the Console:

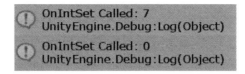

This is a very useful result of setting a value. Looking closer at how the event is raised brings us some ideas about what this event can be used for.

```
if (IntSetEvent != null)
{
    IntSetEvent(privateInt);
}
```

When the event is raised, we're passing in the value of the privateInt. This means that anytime privateInt is set, we're passing the new value to the event. Therefore, if privateInt is set to 7, the event is raised knowing the new value 7. If the value is set to a negative value, then the event is raised again with a value of 0. Once a proper accessor to a protected variable has been created, we're able to do a few more tricks with our new setup.

7.5.3 Read-Only Accessor

When writing a class, it's often a good idea to prevent some values from getting set inadvertently. It's not possible to set a variable if its value has been calculated by a function. In these cases, we need to make that variable a read only accessor.

```
class GetSetReadOnly
{
    public int Int;
    // Read only value
    public int doubleInt
    {
        get
        {
            return Int * 2;
        }
    }
}
```

The above code in the GetSetReadOnly class has a simple system to get a value that's two times the Int value. Notice too that there's no set; included in the accessor. If we try to set doubleInt with something like doubleInt = 2;, we get the following error:

```
getset.doubleInt = 2;
```

int GetSetReadOnly.doubleInt { get; }

Property or indexer 'Accessors.GetSetReadOnly.doubleInt' cannot be assigned to -- it is read only

By omitting set, we've turned doubleInt into a read-only variable. This has a similar effect to the variable as the readonly accessor. The difference is that the class can still make changes internally to the value after the class has been initialized.

```
GetSetReadOnly getset = new GetSetReadOnly();
getset.Int = 7;
Debug.Log("getset.doubleInt: " + getset.doubleInt);
```

This set of code produces the following output:

> ⚠ getset.doubleInt: 14
> UnityEngine.Debug:Log(Object)

These examples with `get;set;` should expand to quite a variety of useful tricks. We can guard the internal value from bad values. We can raise events when a value is changed. And we can make the value read-only by omitting set; from the accessor.

7.5.4 Simplification

We have several options for getting information from a class. With accessors, we are spared the use of parentheses when we ask for a value from a class or struct.

```csharp
struct AccessorStruct
{
    private int privateInt;
    public int publicInt
    {
        get
        {
            return privateInt;
        }
        set
        {
            privateInt = value;
        }
    }
    public int GetInt()
    {
        return privateInt;
    }
    public void SetInt(int i)
    {
        privateInt = i;
    }
}
```

We have a couple of options here with the above struct. We can set the value of the `privateInt` variable in the struct by the accessor or a pair of functions. We can set the value of `privateInt` to 3 with `SetInt(3);` or `publicInt = 3`.

How does this look in practice?

```csharp
AccessorStruct accessorStruct = new AccessorStruct();
accessorStruct.publicInt = 3;
Debug.Log("accessorStruct.publicInt: " + accessorStruct.publicInt);
// accessorStruct.publicInt: 3
accessorStruct.SetInt(7);
Debug.Log("accessorStruct.GetInt(): " + accessorStruct.GetInt());
// accessorStruct.GetInt(): 7
```

The simplicity of publicInt = 3; means quite a lot. It's a notation that we're used to seeing; however, by the nature of the accessor, we have a great deal of control over what can be done in the accessor's logic.

7.5.5 What We've Learned

Accessors are useful for so many reasons. They provide functionality that has already been covered quite a lot, though in a simpler system. There are many powers which the accessor provides us. We'll be exploring some of the other tricks that make coding easier.

Many tricks in C# are made to make your work easier. Convenience offers more than just simplicity. If a trick makes things easier, then you're allowed to make more important decisions. Rather than dwelling on function names and parameters, you're allowed to focus on game play. After all, if you're making a game, the last thing you want to do is spend all your time rewriting code.

7.6 Base Classes: Another Look

When we begin to use inheritance and add keywords such as virtual and override onto functions, we begin to add many new layers of complexity onto the use of a class. How we write these class members greatly depends on how we want them to be used.

Depending on who you work with, you might find yourself seeing your code being used in unexpected ways. Often this is the case when you've written functions that have similar-sounding identifiers. Perhaps even misleading function names can be the cause for a great deal of confusion.

It's up to you to keep your code organized to begin with; however, given tight deadlines and poor sleeping habits, this can't always be the case. You can add descriptive comments, but these are all too often ignored. Your best option is to just disallow other code from seeing the variables and functions at all and prevent bugs from sneaking in.

This topic brings into question why any of these techniques is necessary. Inheritance is a system in which you can write a base class and have variations of that class extend functionality. The intent is to make a system that allows for a common set of base-level functions sharable. Based on what's been written, you make additions to, or variations of, that functionality.

To begin we'll look at building up some classes not derived or based on MonoBehaviour. This makes them regular C# classes outside of the influence of the normal Update() and Start() behaviors which we commonly see in most C# classes in Unity 3D.

The Unity 3D MonoBehaviour is not an abstract class, which means that we cannot make an abstract class based on it. An abstract class determines the necessary collections of data that every derived class will need to implement and use. To see how a base class can be used to do some work for us, we'll look at the BaseClassesAnotherLook script in the BaseClassesAnotherLook_Scene attached to the game object of the same name.

7.6.1 Generalization—Base Classes

Generalization allows us to make some wide-use cases for a class and then allow for more specific cases later. In general, if you were working on a game with a compendium of monsters there would still be plenty of shared attributes. If our behavior was nothing more than moving forward and turning left or right, we can add some variables that allow for this and name them appropriately.

A good base class will include some primitive variables, but at the same time provide a system for building up the types of behaviors we'll want. This is almost like writing code before it's written, but at least you can jump between classes and make changes when necessary. For our next behavior, we want some generic shapes driven by two numbers: a forward speed and a turn speed. Aside from that, the objects should have a very minimal set of instructions to prevent any unnecessary meddling in their activity.

```
public abstract class BaseClass
{
    BaseProperties
    BaseFunctions
}
```

The BaseClassesAnotherLook.cs script is a detailed class. This data was necessary since we didn't have the usual objects inherited from MonoBehaviour. You can see its completion in the source code, collapsed here. Since we had to generate a great deal of this information from scratch, we needed to add in some accessors and other protections around the different data members to ensure that nothing unexpected might happen.

```
public virtual void Speak()
{
    Debug.Log("Base Hello.");
}
```

As an abstract class, nothing has been implemented. We have one function called Speak(), which says "Base Hello." Everything else has been stubbed in to ensure that any class inheriting from BaseClass will have a great deal of work to do. The first region has been set up for many protected and private variables.

In the above class, we use the abstract keyword as well as virtual. In many cases, we might add many variables in anticipation of what we might need. These can be declared as we need or we might just leave in a bunch of place holders, thinking that we might need them later. Often, it's far better to create them as they are needed and decide if it's specific to a child class and move them into a parent class afterward. However, in this example, it's good to see that any number of variables can be added to this class for later use even if they're not necessary for all child classes to use them.

By making accessors for these variables, we've created a barrier between how the variables are set and who can set them. The protected variables are accessible only to siblings of the class. Other classes that might be trying to change these classes' movement patterns have to go through functions to change these variables. They won't be able to access them directly through a dot operator.

Following the base class, we have a ChildA class that inherits from the base class. Shown here in brief:

```
public class ChildA : BaseClass
{
    #region ChildA_Properties
    protected GameObject Me;
    protected Mesh m_Mesh;
    protected MeshRenderer m_MeshRenderer;

    public override bool Equals(object obj)[...]
    public override int GetHashCode()[...]
    #endregion
    public override void Initialize(MeshFilter meshFilter, Material material)[...]
    public override void MoveForward(float speed, float turn)[...]
    public override void Speak()[...]
    public override string ToString()[...]
    public override void UpdateChild()[...]
}
```

This class has two important functions: MoveForward() and ChildUpdate(). Since we have bypassed the MonoBehaviour class, we don't get to have either of these. Just as important, we have the Initialize() function that replaces the Start() functionality.

7.6.2 Specialization

```
public override void Initialize(MeshFilter meshFilter, Material material)
{
    MeshFilter = meshFilter;
    Material = material;
    Me = new GameObject(this.ToString());
    Mesh = meshFilter.mesh;
    MeshRenderer = Me.AddComponent<MeshRenderer>();
    MeshRenderer.material = Material;
    MeshFilter = Me.AddComponent<MeshFilter>();
    MeshFilter.mesh = Mesh;
}
```

The `Initialize()` function has two arguments: `meshFilter` and `material`. These are then applied to a new `GameObject` Me. Here is where the `ChildA` starts to add layers of specialization on top of the BaseClass. The term *specialization* comes in whenever we add new properties or behaviors that were not present in the base class. The base class should be as generalized as possible. In our case, our base class is called `BaseClass`, just so we don't forget.

When we add additional behavior to a second `ChildB`, we have another opportunity to add another layer of specialization. In the following case, we add a color to the `Material` property.

```
public class ChildB : ChildA
{
    #region ChildB_properties
    private Color mColor;
    public Color MyColor
    {
        get { return mColor; }
        set { mColor = value; }
    }
    #endregion

    public override void Initialize(MeshFilter meshFilter, Material material)
    {
        base.Initialize(meshFilter, material);
        this.MyColor = new Color(1, 0, 0, 1);
        m_MeshRenderer.material.color = this.MyColor;
    }
}
```

7.6.3 Base

As new classes derive from each other, they require only smaller and smaller adjustments to gain added functionality. The specialization adds only thin layers of additional code on top of the base class and any class below. There are some important changes that need to be noted when deriving from a class that has some important functions already in place.

```
public override void Initialize(MeshFilter meshFilter, Material material)
{
    base.Initialize(meshFilter, material);
    this.MyColor = new Color(1, 0, 0, 1);
    m_MeshRenderer.material.color = this.MyColor;
}
```

The first line in the override void Initialize() function is base.Initialize(mesh, material);. Here we have some important new tricks to inspect. When the keyword base is invoked within a function, it's an indication that we're informing C# that we want to do what's already been done in the previous layer of that code. We can explore what the code looks like with what base. Initialize() is doing.

The base keyword tells C# to execute the parent classes' version of the function after the dot operator. The above code is what the function would look like to Unity 3D. Thanks to the base. Initialize, we've done the equivalent of this work without having to worry about any typos. Without invoking base. Initialize() we'd lose the mesh material and gameObject creation and setup process.

ChildB is based on ChildA and ChildA is based on BaseClass. This means that both ChildB and ChildA are related to one another because they both are also derived from BaseClass. This means that we can address them both as BaseClass objects. If we look at the ManageChildren.cs class, we'll have the following code:

```
public MeshFilter ChildMesh;
public Material ChildMaterial;
BaseClass[] children;

public void Initialize()
{
    children = new BaseClass[2];
    children[0] = new ChildA();
    children[0].Initialize(ChildMesh, ChildMaterial);
    children[1] = new ChildB();
    children[1].Initialize(ChildMesh, ChildMaterial);
}
//Update is called once per frame
private void Update()
{
    for (int i = 0; i < children.Length; i++)
    {
        children[i].MoveForward(i * 0.1f + 0.1f, i * 3.0f + 1.5f);
        children[i].UpdateChild();
        children[i].Speak();
    }
}
```

This class is derived from MonoBehavior and we have the benefit of the Start() and Update() functions to use. It's worth noting that this is the only class based on MonoBehavior active in the scene in which we've added any code to. In ManageChildren class, we have a BaseClass[] array and an identifier children. This means that the array can accept any number of BaseClass type objects.

In the Start() function, we instantiate ChildA() and ChildB() and assign both of them to the BaseClass[] array. This is valid since they both derive BaseClass. Because BaseClass had the abstract functions MoveForward() and ChildUpdate(), they can be called in the Update() function in the Manager. This for loop provides some motivation to make the two little guys move around.

This also provides a system for them to speak. What's important here is how both the ChildA() and ChildB() classes are locked down. Only the exposed functions are available to outside classes.

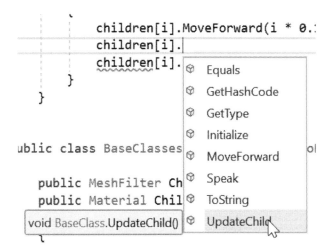

```
            children[i].MoveForward(i * 0.:
            children[i].|
            children[i].
        }
    }
}

ublic class BaseClasses                              ol

    public MeshFilter Ch
    public Material Chil
   ┌──────────────────────────┐
   │ void BaseClass.UpdateChild() │
   └──────────────────────────┘
```

Autocomplete list:
- Equals
- GetHashCode
- GetType
- Initialize
- MoveForward
- Speak
- ToString
- UpdateChild

Inside the Manager, they have just a few exposed functions or variables. Aside from `Child-Update()`, `Initialize()`, `MoveForward()`, and `Speak()`, the rest of the functions derive from the object. This is great for a few different reasons. The first is the fact that once the code starts working, it's hard to break.

Code turns into spaghetti when variables are accessed by many too many objects. Because options are now limited, your code must make changes to the internals of a class and therefore it's less likely your code will fall apart. Should we not have a BaseClass for the two child objects, we'd have to write our code more like the following:

```
if (FirstChild != null)
{
    FirstChild.MoveForward(0.1f, 3.0f);
    FirstChild.UpdateChild();
    FirstChild.Speak();
}

if (SecondChild != null)
{
    SecondChild.MoveForward(0.05f, -3.0f);
    SecondChild.UpdateChild();
    SecondChild.Speak();
}
```

Each one would have to be initialized and updated separately. This defeats the purpose of the base class entirely. There are still clever and dangerous tricks that we can use to add functionality to ChildA without needing to expand how much bigger that class might want to be.

7.6.4 Partial

If we're expanding on a class enough that our functions begin to feel crowded, we can split the work into different partial classes. One possible reason is to store all the accessors and properties in one partial class. Another partial class can store protected functions. Yet another could store the

Unity specific functions. Each partial class can live in a different .cs script. When working with a team, complex code merges can cause minor problems. One way to avoid this is splitting the work across multiple files.

```
public partial class ChildC : ChildA
{

}
public partial class ChildC : ChildA
{

}
```

In the ChildC class, we could go in and extend ChildA: BaseClass with the prefix partial before class so that we have public partial class ChildA: BaseClass. This gives us the ability to tack on last-minute functionality to the ChildA class.

```
// ChildCProperties.cs
public partial class ChildC : ChildA
{
    private float _scale;
    protected float Scale
    {
        get { return _scale; }
        set { _scale = value; }
    }
}
```

```
// ChildCFunctions.cs
public partial class ChildC : ChildA
{
    protected void SetScale(float scale)
    {
        Scale = scale;
        Me.transform.localScale = Vector3.one * Scale;
    }
    public override void Initialize(MeshFilter meshFilter, Material material)
    {
        base.Initialize(meshFilter, material);
        SetScale(2.0f);
    }
}
```

Therefore, say we needed a system for ChildB to set its scale to some arbitrary new size, we can do that by adding the code locally to ChildB, or we can make sure that anything else deriving from ChildA will also have this ability. This also means that ChildA has that new ability as well.

The result of using partial classes like this tends to scatter code all over the place. This quickly leads to angry nights debugging code. Although there are some cases in which this can be quite helpful, it's best to start with the best use case for partial in mind.

```
// ShapeProperties.cs
public abstract partial class BaseShape
{
    public enum Shapes
    {
        Cube,
        Sphere
    };
    Shapes Shape;
}
```

```
// ShapeFunctions.cs
public abstract partial class BaseShape
{
    public abstract void SetShape(Shapes shape);
}
```

To facilitate separation of duty the `BaseShape` has been split into different partial classes. The concept here would be to store properties in one abstract class and the abstract functions in another class. When the partial classes are implemented the separation is invisible to the class inheriting from the abstract partial class.

```
public class SomeShape : BaseShape
{
    public GameObject Me;
    public override void SetShape(Shapes shape)
    {
        switch(shape)
        {
            case Shapes.Cube:
                Me = GameObject.CreatePrimitive(PrimitiveType.Cube);
                break;
            case Shapes.Sphere:
                Me = GameObject.CreatePrimitive(PrimitiveType.Sphere);
                break;
        }
    }
}
```

Setting up both the base class and the immediate child at the same time reduces the number of places you might have to go in order to find any problem areas in the code. This still isn't the best use case; however, when implementing various interfaces, you can have a different class as a helper for each interface being implemented. This certainly helps separate the different tasks. Suppose, for instance, that the BaseClass looked something like the following:

```
// ShapeICollection.cs
public abstract partial class BaseShape : System.Collections.ICollection
{
    public void CopyTo(Array array, int index)[...]

    public int Count => throw new NotImplementedException();

    public bool IsSynchronized => throw new NotImplementedException();

    public object SyncRoot => throw new NotImplementedException();

    public IEnumerator GetEnumerator()
    {
        throw new NotImplementedException();
    }
}
```

Both the IEnumerator and the ICollection interfaces are rather complicated. Having ShapeIEnumerator.cs and ShapeICollection.cs would help. Each one would start the same as Shape, but the contents of each would be related to the interface they are implementing. Thanks to Visual Studio, we have a quick way to generate the code we need.

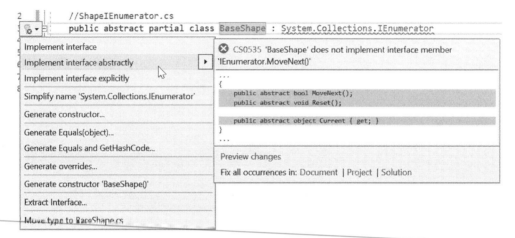

To the left of the function in the margins is a little lightbulb icon, this is a code helper where we can select various menu options to write in the required placeholders or abstract functions required to fulfill the interface.

By adding the different partial classes to each one of these different files, the Shape is already getting to be quite big. However, the original file has not increased in complexity. Each partial addition has only added complexity to its own portion of the class. The new behaviors we've been adding are all being inherited by ChildA and ChildB. This is a remarkable amount of work that can be done with less effort, thanks to our simplifying how classes can be merged as needed.

Normally, Unity 3D would complain that the class name doesn't match the file name. This exception is made for classes not deriving from MonoBehaviour. By avoiding MonoBehaviour, we're more able to take some liberties with the C# language. The partial, abstract, and virtual functions and classes offer a great deal of flexibility not allowed when deriving from MonoBehaviour.

7.6.5 Protected, Private, and Public

The accessibility keywords include protected to help shield your code from influence from other classes. The only classes allowed to see a protected member are related classes. Below we show a Base class that has a private protected and public string. The Child class inheriting from Base can only see the protected and public string,

```
class Base : System.Object
{
    private string MyPrivateString;
    protected string MyProtectedString;
    public string MyPublicString;
}
class Child : Base
{
    void VisibleProperties()
    {
        My
    }
}
```

MyProtectedString
MyPublicString

For a class to hide any properties from any other class the private keyword is used to shield a member from outside influence. The `protected` accessibility attribute ensures that only inheriting members can see the variable. Once a property is made `public` anyone can see the variable.

```
partial class Half : System.Object
{
    private string MyPrivateString;
}

partial class Half : System.Object
{
    void SeesPrivates()
    {
        MyPrivateString = "";
    }
}
```

A `partial` class can see `private` members of the other portions of themselves. A partial class is still the same class, so `private` members are members of all parts of a partial class. The `private public` and `protected` accessor attributes can be applied to variables and functions of a class.

7.6.6 What We've Learned

It's difficult to set strict rules for breaking a class apart into base and child members. The reasons for this design behavior are three-fold. The first is to enable faster development by reducing the necessity for rewriting code. The second is for maintenance. If you fix code in one place you've fixed it for everyone inheriting the fix. The third is for reusing code. Working code should be used everywhere.

If you find a situation where multiple classes are looking for a specific object, make a base class that finds the object, then every child of that base class will inherit that code. Splitting a class into multiple parts can take a while as you'll re-write several functions to suit multiple specializations. Each class may need to inherit code differently.

This is often painful, but it's worth it. The second time, though, is almost always faster than the first time. Organizing everything into a clean simple group and branching with more reliable behaviors always comes once you've got a better understanding of what you wanted to do to begin with.

7.7 Optional Parameters

We've been putting a great deal of thought into how functions work and how we can make them more flexible through inheritance and overrides. The different features are not to add complications; they are meant to add flexibility. Once you get used to how the features work, you're allowed to do more things with less work. It's just a matter of understanding how the features work.

Hopefully, you're able to keep up with the break-neck speed at which we've been adding these features. If not, then it's time to practice what you know before going on. This is a pretty simple chapter that adds a pretty simple feature to our C# toolbox. Adding optional features is a pretty simple trick to our functions that often comes up. Normally, when we declare a function, we use syntax like the following:

```
void MyFunction()
{
    // some code here...
}
```

Therefore, we've used a few different variations on how to manipulate the argument list of a function to get a few different uses out of a single function. We're allowed to use a few other tricks that can help make things a bit easier to deal with when making many changes. When the process of writing code gets to a fevered pitch, you're going to be needing to write a great deal of code fast and finding yourself going back to fix things quite a lot.

Say for a moment that you've written a function that appears in many different places but you want to change it. This would mean spending the time to fix it everywhere it's used, and this can be a boring time-consuming chore.

Therefore, you wrote a function that might look something like the following:

```
GameObject CreateACube(string name, Vector3 position)
{
    GameObject cube = GameObject.CreatePrimitive(PrimitiveType.Cube);
    cube.name = name;
    cube.transform.position = position;
    return cube;
}
```

In use you might do something like this to use the function:

```
GameObject bobCube = CreateACube("bob", new Vector3(10, 0, 0));
Debug.Log("Created a cube named + " + bobCube.name + "At:" + bobCube.transform.position);
// "Created a cube named + bobAt:(10.0, 0.0, 0.0)"
```

For a moment, let's pretend that the function making use of `CreateACube()` is far too much work to change and we are incredibly lazy. What happens when we need to make some changes to the argument list, but we don't feel like making many changes everywhere the function appears? For a moment, we want all of the current uses of the function to use the same code, which means that an override will not work.

Suppose there is a request to make a fundamental change to the `CreateACube()` function, which tells us that we need to make a third parameter set the scale of the cube; we have a few options that we've been introduced to. The simple option is to simply make a new function with a new name. We're missing the point of using C#'s features if we do that.

The better option is to make a second version of the `CreateACube()` function with a different signature that might look like the following:

```
GameObject CreateACube(string name, Vector3 position, float scale)
{
    GameObject cube = GameObject.CreatePrimitive(PrimitiveType.Cube);
    cube.name = name;
    cube.transform.position = position;
    cube.transform.localScale = new Vector3(scale, scale, scale);
    return cube;
}
```

This would mean that we have two different versions of the same function, only the second one has some additional statements, to take care of the third parameter. This should bring up the question, Isn't there a cleaner way to take care of any additional parameters without making more than one version of the same function? The answer is an optional parameter.

7.7.1 Using Optionals

When a function is used the parameter list allows for default values. There are some simple rules to follow if you want to make some of the arguments in the parameter list optional.

```
GameObject CreateACubeWithOptions(string name = "bob", Vector3 position = new Vector3(), float scale = 1.0f)
{
    GameObject cube = GameObject.CreatePrimitive(PrimitiveType.Cube);
    cube.name = name;
    cube.transform.position = position;
    cube.transform.localScale = new Vector3(scale, scale, scale);
    return cube;
}
```

The third parameter is float scale = 1.0f. The addition of the = 1.0f predefines the incoming value unless it's overridden by a third parameter's value. In short, if there's no third parameter given, then the float scale parameter is defaulted at 1.0f, and fulfilling all three parameters is not necessary. The same goes for the first and second parameter so long as they have a default assignment set in the parameter list.

Without any modifications to the Start() function's use of CreateACube, we've added a simple override that handles both cases with little additional work. There are, however, some restrictions to how optional parameters are used.

Setting variables in case they're not used in the argument list is an easy way to skip writing several versions of the same function; in case there are different ways, you intend the function to be used. Even with one loss with a predefined parameter, they will retain their order and value types.

```
void ParamUsage(int i)
{
    Debug.Log("using an int " + i);
    // "using an int 5"
}

void ParamUsage(string words)
{
    Debug.Log("using a string " + words);
    // "using a string not a number"
}
```

For instance, we should remember that using two different signatures altogether can be used without any additional fuss.

This would result with two different types being used with predictable results. This works for situations in which this was expected and different types were used from the beginning since there was a predefined reason for the behavior of function's differences. However, does this mean we can add an optional parameter to either of these functions?

7.7.1.1 A Basic Example

Let's start with the OptionalParameters scene in the Chapter7 Unity Project and look at the OptionalParameters script of the game object with the same name.

```
void MoreParamUsage(int i)
{
    Debug.Log("using int i, " + i + " no optional floats here.");
}

void MoreParamUsage(int i, float optionalFloat = 1f)
{
    Debug.Log("using an int " + i + " and a float " + optionalFloat);
}
```

The option exists only because the parameter has an assignment in the parameter list. This does not mean that we cannot use regular overrides along with the regular use of the function. You're not actually required to write an override of any kind to begin with, though we're adding one just to show that it is possible to do so without any adverse or unexpected results.

The two functions above show a behavior which comes with the use of the optionalFloat parameter being given the default value. The override will never be called.

```
MoreParamUsage(7);
// using int i, 7 no optional floats here.
MoreParamUsage(5, Mathf.PI);
// using an int 5 and a float 3.141593
```

The function without the second parameter will be preferred over the override with the optional parameter. The most suitable version will take priority. In all cases where the second parameter is given a value, the default value for the optionalFloat will never be used.

7.7.2 Optional Arguments

We should check to see if the optional parameter can be made unoptional in a different version of the same function; this would look something like the following:

```
void MoreParamUsage(int i, float requiredFloat)
{
    Debug.Log("using an int " + i + " and a float " + requiredFloat);
}
```

Unity 3D gives us the following error:

> ❌ CS0111 Type 'OptionalParameters' already defines a member called 'MoreParamUsage' with the same parameter types

The signature combination for the function (int, float) is the same with both versions of the function. Therefore, no, we are not allowed to redefine the function with one using an optional parameter and another using a required parameter of the same type. This should make sense: When you're using the function, the appearance of the use would look the same. Why stop with just one optional parameter?

```
void UsingOptionals(int i = 1, float f = 1f)
{
    Debug.Log("using an int " + i + " using a float " + f);
}
```

We can set all of the parameters in a version of the function with defined values, which means that we're allowed to do the following in the Start() function:

```
void UsingUsingOptionals()
{
    UsingOptionals();
    // "using an int 1 using a float 1"
    UsingOptionals(7);
    // "using an int 7 using a float 1"
    UsingOptionals(9, 13f);
    // "using an int 9 using a float 13"

    /* the following are not valid uses */
    /* of optionals                     */
    UsingOptionals(23f);
    UsingOptionals(,31f);
}
```

The first use has no arguments, the second has an int for the first int, the third has an int and a float. The last two uses of the function are not valid. There is no version of the UsingOptionals() function that has one float argument. The empty int space followed by a float is also invalid since all parameter fields require some form of input before the list is usable.

To prevent further complication, use of the prefixes *ref* and *out* as we've used before in a parameter are also disallowed when assigning a default value to a parameter. The behavior of requiring a value in each parameter from left to right also means default values can only be assigned after required values are assigned.

```
void UsingOptionals(int i = 1, int j)
{
    Debug.Log("using an int " + i + "   Optional parameters must appear after all required parameters
}
```

7.7.3 Named Parameters

Naming the arguments can be an easy way to make the parameters easier to read. In the case of CreateACube (string name, vector3 position), it's pretty clear what the two parameters are for. And thanks to helpful pop-ups in MonoDevelop, we can get useful reminders telling us what each parameter is for.

```
CreateACube()
```

▲ 2 of 2 ▼ GameObject OptionalParameters.CreateACube(**string name**, Vector3 position, float scale)

A less commonly used feature which gives us additional flexibility is the named parameter. If we consider a function that might have several different parameters, some of which might be optional, it's easy to forget the order in which they are expected. Furthermore, if you want to use only one of the optional parameters but don't necessarily want to override any of the others, then we'd have a problem trying to express this.

Consider the following function's signature:

```
void LotsOfParams(int a = 0, int b = 1, int c = 2, int d = 3)
{
    Debug.Log("a: " + a + " b: " + b + " c: " + c + " d: " + d);
}

void UseLotsOfParams()
{
    LotsOfParams();
    //"a: 0 b: 1 c: 2 d: 3"
}
```

All the parameters are optional, and not using any of them prints the following line of output to the Console.

```
⚠ a: 0 b: 1 c: 2 d: 3
   UnityEngine.Debug:Log(Object)
```

This should be expected, but if we simply want b to be 99 and leave the rest of the parameters set to the provided default value, what then?

```
LotsOfParams(0, 99);
//"a: 0 b: 99 c: 2 d: 3"
```

From this result, we infer that a isn't an optional argument. Unfortunately, LotsOfParams(null,99); isn't even an option. We are missing out by not using named parameters. If the parameters from LotsOfParams had names, in this case a, b, c, and d, we can use them in the following manner.

7.7.3.1 A Basic Example

Named parameters follow a bit of a different look. Once there are a great deal of parameters, it's easy to forget which is which. By using a named parameter, it's more clear what the value is for and what the assignment is.

```
LotsOfParams(b:99)

void OptionalParameters.LotsOfParams([int a = 0], [int b = 1], [int c = 2], [int d = 3])
```

Just use the name of the argument you want to assign a value to followed by a: and the value you want to assign to it. The order is also ignored so long as the identifiers are used.

```
LotsOfParams(b: 99, a: 88, d: 777, c: 1234);
//"a: 88 b: 99 c: 1234 d: 777"
```

The b followed by a and then d before c should look rather confusing, and in practice, it's not the best form to mix arguments so badly. However, there's nothing preventing you from confusing anyone else when reading your code. From the previous CreateACube example, we're allowed to do the following:

```
CreateACube(scale: 6.0f, name: "Henry", position: new Vector3(2f, z: 0, y: 1));
```

Furthermore, the named parameters also work in the Unity 3D's own data types like Vector3 where we name z and y out of order.

Starting off with named parameters, we're going to have to use the rest of the names. They can be in any order, but once we start off with naming parameters before assigning them, we're stuck with naming all of them before finishing the function. Once the order is messed up, we're unable to tell the function our intent for the data going into the different slots in the argument list. For instance, consider the following three statements:

```
CreateACube("Bob", new Vector3(3f, 0, 0));
CreateACube("Henry", position: new Vector3(4f, 0, 0));
CreateACube(position: new Vector3(5f, 0, 0), "Jack");
```

> [●] (parameter) Vector3 position
>
> Named argument 'position' is used out-of-position but is followed by an unnamed argument

We created a cube named Bob in the first statement, as we have before; we didn't use the name in the second parameter. When we created Henry, we didn't use a name in the first parameter where the string is expected.

This works fine since the order has been retained. However, if we use position: as the first parameter but then use "Jack" to assign the string to an out-of-order position, we get the following error:

> ⊗ CS8323 Named argument 'position' is used out-of-position but is followed by an unnamed argument

Basically, the position or order of the unnamed arguments must line up with the function's signature. After that names can be used for any remaining arguments in the list.

7.7.4 Combining What We've Learned

We've looked at the out and ref parameters, and now we've covered both optional and named parameters in relation to the arguments and functions. We should know a bit about how they should be used together.

If we write a strange combination of out, ref, and some optional parameters, we might come up with something like the following:

```
void Variations(ref float a, out float b, float c = 10.0f, float d = 11.0f)
{
    b = c / a;
    a = c / d;
}
```

There are a couple of important notes about this: First is the fact that ref cannot have a default value. It might look something like the following:

```
void Bad(ref int a = 1)
{

}
```

The logic that results in this error is simple. The ref keyword is reserved to tell the parameter that it's going to assume the place of another variable that already exists. This means that the value that's in the argument list can't be defined as the ref tells the value that it must be modifying something that exists outside of the function.

> ⊗ CS1741 A ref or out parameter cannot have a default value

7.7.5 What We've Learned

We've got many options. At this point, there are very few things which you might come across in a function's parameter list that will come as a surprise. Keeping your code under control is largely dependent on your discretion and your team's decision making. Coming up with standards may or may not include using named or optional arguments, which are not too common.

Optional arguments are certainly clever, and when used properly, they're readable and easy to understand. Life can continue with or without these types of parameters appearing in your code. There's certainly nothing you can't do without them.

Optional parameters alleviate the necessity of writing additional overloaded functions, which saves some time. This is possibly best suited for a longer function that spans a heavy number of lines of code. In these cases, a repeated block of code is more likely to have errors.

Any time you need to write code again is another chance for a bug to creep in. Overloaded functions, in which one version works and another version doesn't, can lead to long nights searching for which version is being called and why it's broken.

Even in bug fixing, we learn how to write better code. Often having others check your work is a good practice to keep you in line with the rest of the team. Code reviews are a common practice among large companies, especially on high-profile projects in which a small bug can cause big problems.

7.8 Delegate Functions

A delegate acts like a data type; just like how both int and double are number types, a delegate is a type of function. The idea of a delegate is a bit weird. So far we've been thinking of functions as a construct that processes data.

A delegate allows us to use a function in a variable. If you're able to assign a variable to a function, you can use it like data. This means passing it between functions, structs, or classes through a parameter or assignment.

7.8.1 Delegates

A clever trick that C# has the ability to do is to store a function into a variable just like it was data. There are a few rules for doing this. The first important step is to ensure that the signature of the variable you're storing a function in and the function you're about to delegate match.

7.8.1.1 A Basic Example

Starting with the Delegates project, we'll look at the DelegateFunctions.cs class. First we need to write a new delegate function, which is a sort of a template signature for any function that is to be delegated. This is easier to see in code than to explain. At the class level, add in the following code statement:

```
delegate void MyDelegate();
```

We've defined a delegate, which is pretty simple; but if you look at the signature, there's not a whole lot going on. We defined the MyDelegate() with return type void and assigned no arguments in the parentheses. However, we'll go with this as a basic example and look at more complex delegates in a moment.

Now that we have a defined delegate, we need to make some functions that match the signature.

```
void FirstDelegate()
{
    Debug.Log("First Delegate Called.");
}

void SecondDelegate()
{
    Debug.Log("Second Delegate Called.");
}
```

It's important that any functions that are going to be used with MyDelegate() have matching signatures. If not, then you'll get an error before the code compiles. To make use of a delegate, you need to make an instance of the function like you would if it were a class object.

```
void UseDelegates()
{
    MyDelegate myDelegate = new MyDelegate(FirstDelegate);
}
```

Looking at the statement added to UseDelegates(), you should notice a couple of things. MyDelegate() is the name of the delegate we defined at the class scope. This defines not only the signature we're going to be matching but also the identifier of the delegate we're going to be using. To make an instance of that delegate, we use it's defined name.

This is followed by an identifier that is defined like any other variable. In this we're using a short identifier *del* to identify the MyDelegate function. This is then followed by an assignment. We use the new keyword to create an instance of the delegate function MyDelegate(), but then we add in a parameter to a set of parentheses.

We wrote two functions with matching signatures: FirstDelegate() and SecondDelegate(). Choose FirstDelegate() and add its name to the delegate parameter. This is a bit weird, but it's an overloaded use of parentheses for delegates. After the assignment, del is now a FirstDelegate(). To use it, simply add the following statement:

```
//call on function assigned to delegate
myDelegate();
// "First Delegate Called."
```

When the computer runs myDelegate();, we get "First Delegate Called." printed to our Console. Now here comes the interesting part.

```
// reassign who is assigned to myDelegate
myDelegate = SecondDelegate;

// call on function assigned to delegate
myDelegate();
// "Second Delegate Called."
```

We can give myDelegate a new assignment. To do this, we add myDelegate = SecondDelegate; to change what function has been assigned to the delegate myDelegate. When myDelegate(); is used again, we'll get "Second Delegate Called." printed to the Console of Unity 3D.

7.8.2 Delegate Signatures

Now for a more interesting example, let's add a delegate with a more interesting signature.

```
delegate int OtherDelegate(int a, int b);

public int ThirdDelegate(int a, int b)
{
    return a + b;
}

public int FourthDelegate(int a, int b)
{
    return a - b;
}
```

Here we have assigned a return value and two arguments to the delegate `MyDelegate()`. To make use of this signature, we wrote two different functions using the same signature: The first function returns a + b and the second function returns a − b, as you might expect.

```
OtherDelegate myDelegate = new OtherDelegate(ThirdDelegate);
int added = myDelegate(1, 2);
Debug.Log("added: " + added);
// "added: 3"

myDelegate = FourthDelegate;
int subtracted = myDelegate(5, 6);
Debug.Log("subtracted: " + subtracted);
// "subtracted: -1"
```

When del is assigned the duty of being the delegate to a function, it should be treated like a function. The clever trick is that now we're allowed to change which function `myDelegate` is delegating. There's a more important underlying use for delegates, but it's important to understand the basic setup and use of a delegate first.

The use of delegates involves first matching up all the signatures to ensure type safety. Once this is done, you're allowed some leeway to make changes, but only under some strict rules. We'll come back to that in a later chapter. We've got plenty to work with before we get there.

So far we've used del = SecondDelegate to assign a delegate that was created within the `Start()` function. There's a much more interesting way to assign and use a delegate function.

7.8.3 Stacking Delegates

When the delegate is first declared, it's useful to add a variable to store it in at the class scope. This allows other objects in the scene to have access to the delegate.

```
delegate void StackedDelegates(int i);
StackedDelegates stacked;

void FifthDelegate(int i)
{
    Debug.Log("FifthDelegate: " + i);
}
```

The default initialization of a delegate is null. The first assignment can be done as we have before with stacked = FifthDelegate; syntax. You can use the += notation to assign more than one function to the delegate. When the stack is called, the assigned functions are called. As we write more functions that fit the delegates' signature, we can chain more functions for del to execute when called.

```
void SixthDelegate(int i)
{
    Debug.Log("SixthDelegate: " + i);
}

void UseStackedDelegates()
{
    stacked = FifthDelegate;
    stacked += FifthDelegate;
    stacked(5);
    // "FifthDelegate: 5"
    // "FifthDelegate: 5"
    stacked += SixthDelegate;
    stacked += SixthDelegate;
    stacked(6);
    // "FifthDelegate: 6"
    // "FifthDelegate: 6"
    // "FifthDelegate: 6"
    // "FifthDelegate: 6"
}
```

This code stacks more functions onto our delegate. When this code is run, we get FifthDelegate: 5 followed by FifthDelegate: 6 twice then SixthDelegate twice printed to the Console panel in Unity 3D. The feature sounds cool, but when is it used? More importantly, how does this feature make C# more useful?

Once we get into events and event management, we'll get a clearer picture of what delegate functions are really used for, but it's important to understand how to create and assign delegates before we get to events. Events are basically functions that call other functions when something specific is triggered. Usually collision events and input events need to trigger user-defined events.

This is where delegates become important. The event that was initially written by the Unity 3D programmers doesn't have a specific task, because they don't know what you have in mind when a key is pressed or a collision occurs on a game object. They leave the definition of what to do on the event up to you to define in your own function. To use the event, we need to match the signature of the event with our own function. Then we assign the function we wrote to the event written by the Unity 3D programmers.

7.8.4 Using Delegates

A delegate is basically a type, like any other int or float. The functions GetSeven and GetThree do different things, but they both match the signature provided with IntDelegate(); as both return an integer value with no parameters.

```
delegate int IntDelegate();
int GetSeven()
{
    return 7;
}
int GetThree()
{
    return 3;
}
```

This also means we're allowed to pass them to functions as though they were variables as well. UseDelegate ignores the contents of the IntDelegate so long as they return an int.

```
void UseDelegate(IntDelegate intDelegate)
{
    IntDelegate intFromDelegate = intDelegate;
    int i = intFromDelegate();
    Debug.Log("int from intDelegate: " + i);
}
```

When GetSeven or GetThree are passed into UseDelegate they return a value and it's printed out.

```
void UseIntDelegates()
{
    UseDelegate(GetSeven);
    UseDelegate(GetThree);
}
```

The log produces the following results:

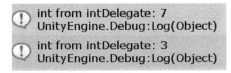

7.8.5 Updating Delegates

Delegates are often used to update multiple objects from a central function. In a basic form a Counter class would get an update from a single function. Given a class Counter as in the following:

```
class Counter
{
    private int Count;
    private int Limit;
    public Counter(int countLimit)
    {
        Limit = countLimit;
    }

    public void UpdateCount()
    {
        if(Count < Limit)
            Count++;
        if (Count >= Limit)
            ReportCount();
    }

    void ReportCount()
    {
        Debug.Log("Counts: " + Count + " Limit: " + Limit);
    }
}
```

We have a function called UpdateCount() where we increment the internal Count value and check if it's reached a limit, then we report that the limit has been reached. Without a delegate function we could use the following notation to call the update on a number of counters.

```
foreach (Counter c in Counters)
{
    c.UpdateCount();
}
```

Delegates give us an option to update them with a single call to a delegate of the function:

```
bool CountersInitalized = false;
Counter[] Counters = new Counter[10];
delegate void UpdateCounters();
UpdateCounters CounterUpdate;
void CreateAndUpdateCounters()
{
    if (!CountersInitalized)
    {
        for (int i = 0; i < 10; i++)
        {
            Counters[i] = new Counter(Random.Range(10, 30));
            CounterUpdate += Counters[i].UpdateCount;
        }
        CountersInitalized = true;
    }
    CounterUpdate();
}
```

After the Counter is created with a random number to count up to, we assign the Counter's UpdateCount() function to a CounterUpdate() delegate. Then when the CounterUpdate() delegate is called every assigned Counter.UpdateCount() function is called at once.

The function CreateAndUpdateCounters() is called in the script's Update() method called once per frame. This effectively becomes a system where we get a Debug.Log(); called after a random count has been reached.

7.8.6 What We've Learned

In Unity 3D, delegates are often used to update the state of an object that has been created in the scene. Unity 3D as a framework often leads to MonoBehaviour objects, getting Start() and Update() called in a non-specified order.

This means you can't rely on a specific function before or after another function as you might expect. To be more specific, you could check on a value during an update and make decisions that will effect the game on the following update. You can't ensure you can check a value at the start of an update and expect to effect the scene before the end of the update.

This is best done via events. We'll find out more about that in a few chapters. I'll leave you to play with some delegates for now; using events is going to take up a chapter, so we'll leave that for later.

7.9 Interface

An interface is a promise that your new class will implement a function from its base class. The implementation of an interface can be made for any method, event, or delegate. Anything that has a signature with an identifier and argument list can be turned into an interface for a base class. This promise of a new class implementing an interface is not unlike that of a class implementing an abstract class.

```
abstract class ThisClass
{
    public abstract void DoAThing();
}

abstract class ThatClass
{
    public abstract void DoAThing();
}
```

C# does not support multiple inheritance to avoid confusion with how behaviors may overlap. Consider the above two classes, if you were to implement both at the same time then which version of DoAThing() would be inherited?

The structure of your code depends on having a plan. With every new function and every new data structure, you're adding to the overall complexity of your game or software. The more people you collaborate with, the more complex it will get, necessitating some way to stay organized and maintain some sort of consistency. Your game's chance of success is based on your code remaining consistent and stable.

An interface provides a framework for derived classes to implement. An interface is an organizational tool that helps us when sweeping changes are made. Say you decide that all your zombies now need to have a new feature, for example, their arms needing to be cut off; it will help out in the end if you made an interface for building the body of the zombie when you started.

7.9.1 Early Planning

Using an interface could be considered early on. Creating them after many classes have already been written can turn into a nightmare if your different monsters took on a wide variety of implementations, but therein lies the strength of the interface.

An interface is a construct that helps other programmers understand what you've written. These tools are intended to provide a basis for understanding without needing to hover around the rest of your team to explain what your code does. Interfaces provide a system for constructing a class that implements your code.

When we consider why object-oriented programming helps us rather than hinders us, we need to remember a few things. First, we need to think of each new class as a progressive evolutionary process to a previous class. Every fundamental change we make to our game has to be reflected on as wide a scale as possible. Second, we need to remember that every object should share as much data as possible. Finally, we need to make sure that all our objects interact with one another as closely as possible.

To communicate this interaction and to solidify this unity between characters and properties in our game world, you need to set up some base rules. These rules are best communicated by using an interface. For an interface to make sense, we should create a class that the rest of the objects in our game should follow as their base, a common foundation for all objects in our game to share. Once we begin with some basic design patterns, we'll really understand why interfaces are important, but for now, we'll just look at a basic implementation.

7.9.1.1 A Basic Example

We'll start with the Interface_scene, in which we have an Interfaces.cs attached to the similarly named game object. Unlike many other classes, an interface isn't directly used in Unity 3D. The naming convention always starts with an I to indicate that the class is an interface and not necessarily an object for use in the game.

```
interface IThis
{
    string ThisName
    {
        get;
        set;
    }

    void ThisFunction();
}
```

As a common practice, we prefix the interface with an uppercase I, though it's not necessary. Inside our interface we added an arbitrary string called `ThisName` as well as a function `ThisFunction`. Everything needs a name, doesn't it? Of course, you can use any type inside the interface as an example, but a string is something easy to test, so we'll start with string `ThisName` in our example.

The new syntax we're seeing is called an *interface property,* and the format we're seeing is how a property is created in an interface. Interface properties are consistent identifiers, which all classes that implement the interface will have. Often you might see this done with the following style:

```
string ThisName { get; set; }
```

This looks cleaner, so we should get used to seeing the `get; set;` syntax, as in the above statement. The interface property is used as a system to allow each implementation of the interface to change how the property is used. We can change how the get and set work, depending on the goal for each implementation. Interface implementations need to be made public.

Until we fully implement the `IThis` interface, Unity 3D will be telling us that there are some errors because it doesn't implement all of IThing. This is corrected by adding in members of the interface.

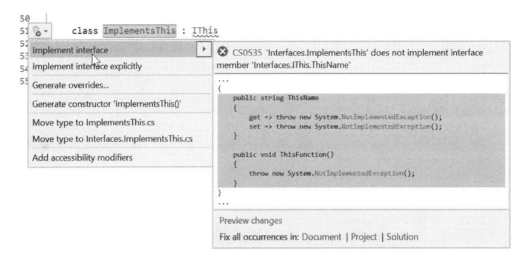

This can automatically be stubbed out by using the helper icon in VisualStudio. Selecting Implement interface will generate the following code:

```csharp
class ImplementsThis : IThis
{
    public string ThisName
    {
        get => throw new System.NotImplementedException();
        set => throw new System.NotImplementedException();
    }

    public void ThisFunction()
    {
        throw new System.NotImplementedException();
    }
}
```

This shouldn't be the final code, but it's telling us what we need to provide to complete the implementation.

```csharp
class ImplementsThis : IThis
{
    private string thisName;
    public string ThisName
    {
        get
        {
            return thisName;
        }
        set
        {
            thisName = value;
        }
    }

    public void ThisFunction()
    {
        Debug.Log("Hello, my name is " + thisName);
    }
}
```

We need a private local variable specific to the class to store in the class that holds onto string `ThisName`, which was supplied in the interface. In this case, we use `thisName` in the Toaster class. This isolates the local data, but uses the interface property for the variable `ThisName` that was created in the `IThis` interface.

How do we know what `ThisFunction()` is supposed to do? In most cases the naming of the function should be more clear. In many cases the name can't describe enough what the intent of the function is. In most cases a base implementation is provided as an example as to what is expected from the interface. With the class `ImplementsThis`, we could consider this to be an example of how `IThis` is to be implemented.

7.9.1.2 Using Accessors

The keyword value is used in the `get;` `set;` `{}` function to access the interface's variable. The `get;` `set;` statement is called an accessor statement and is used for interface implementation. The appearance of `get;` `set;` in a class implementing the interface now requires code to be complete. Finally, we can use an interface of the object in the `Start()` function of the Interfaces.cs script in the Interfaces scene.

```
void UseToaster()
{
    Toaster toaster = new Toaster();
    toaster.ThisName = "Talkie";
    toaster.ThisFunction();
    // Howdy, my name is Talkie
}
```

As an example, we create a new Toaster T, assign its name to "Talkie," and then print out the name to double check that the accessor is correctly implemented. Notice that we're not using ToasterName that was made private in the Toaster class. The use of This Name and not ToasterName is the key reason for why interfaces are important. For every class that implements the IThis interface, we must have a system to set a ThisName.

If you have programmers adding new monsters, they should be instructed to implement the IThis interface. With this rule, their code will not work unless their monster has a ThisName. If you make a rule to never check-in code that's broken, you should always confirm your code works before checking it in. Needing to implement an interface to every new object ensures that every object has a ThisName. Therefore, if we were to create a new zombie with the same interface, we'd need to do something like in the following example:

```
class Zombie : MonoBehaviour, IThis
{
    private string ZombieName;
    public string ThisName
    {
        get { return ZombieName; }
        set { ZombieName = value; }
    }

    public void ThisFunction()
    {
    }
}
```

This is a new zombie class that is based on MonoBehaviour. This means that we're creating a new ZombieGame object since we're inheriting from MonoBehaviour. We've also implemented the name accessor to follow the IThis interface. Without public string ThisName{get;set;} defined, we get the following error:

```
class Zombie : MonoBehaviour, IThis
{
    private string ZombieName;
    //public string ThisName
    //{
    //    get { return ZombieName
    //    set { ZombieName = value;
    //}
```

interface Chapter7_9.Interfaces.IThis

'Interfaces.Zombie' does not implement interface member 'Interfaces.IThis.ThisName'

Show potential fixes (Alt+Enter or Ctrl+.)

A programmer needs to know quickly when an error has occurred. I've heard people say "fail fast and fail often" to describe rapid development in small game studios. There are many reasons for this, and finding bugs in your code is one of them. Interfaces ensure that new game objects follow the proper setup you might want to use in your game. We should be careful when instancing a class that is based on MonoBehaviour. Using the following code fragment will give us an error:

```
void UseZombie()
{
    Zombie zombie = new Zombie();
}
```

The error looks like the following:

⚠ **You are trying to create a MonoBehaviour using the 'new' keyword.**
UnityEngine.MonoBehaviour:.ctor()

```
UnityEngine.MonoBehaviour:.ctor()
Zombie:.ctor()
Example:Start () (at Assets/Example.cs:11)
```

To remedy the error that this produces, we'll have to use `gameObject.AddComponent();`. Therefore, the code should look a bit more like the following:

```
void UseZombie()
{
    //Zombie zombie = new Zombie();
    Zombie zombie = gameObject.AddComponent<Zombie>();
}
```

Now with the Zombie MonoBehaviour added to the gameObject, we can also fill in the Zombie's `ThisFunction()`."

```
public void ThisFunction()
{
    Debug.Log("mmmmuh name is " + ZombieName);
}
```

Now we've created a gameObject that uses the IThis interface. Both Toaster and Zombie implement the same interface. Therefore, we can assign both a name and get that name to print. If you check the Unity attribute editor while running the code, you'll notice that a new component has been added to the Interfaces game object.

7.9.2 Multiple Interfaces

In C# we do not have the ability to inherit from multiple classes. We can however implement more than one interface.

```
interface FirstInterface
{
    string FirstString { get;set; }
    void FirstFunction();
    void SameFunction();
}

interface SecondInterface
{
    string SecondString { get; set; }
    void SecondFunction();
    void SameFunction();
}
```

A special case appears when multiple interfaces use a function with the same name. Both interfaces suggest a SameFunction() needs to be implemented, but how to we tell which is which?

```
class ImplementsFirstAndSecond : FirstInterface, SecondInterface
{
    private string firstString;
    public string FirstString
    {
        get { return firstString; }
        set { firstString = value; }
    }

    public void FirstFunction()
    {
        Debug.Log("First Function Called");
    }
    private string secondString;
    public string SecondString
    {
        get { return secondString; }
        set { secondString = value; }
    }

    public void SecondFunction()
    {
        Debug.Log("Second Function Called");
    }

    public void SameFunction()
    {
        Debug.Log("Which version is Called?");
    }
}
```

The explicit declaration of the interface is required to inform the class which of the two interface you're implementing.

```
void FirstInterface.SameFunction()
{
    Debug.Log("First SameFunction Called.");
}
void SecondInterface.SameFunction()
{
    Debug.Log("Second SameFunction Called.");
}
```

The explicit declaration is used by the interface name followed by the dot operator and the function name in the function declaration. To follow this up, each interface function needs to be called.

```
public virtual void SameFunction()
{
    Debug.Log("Which version is Called?");
    ((FirstInterface)this).SameFunction();
    ((SecondInterface)this).SameFunction();
}
```

The non-explicit implementation needs to call the explicit forms of the function call by casting to the interface within the class implementing them. The reference to the class itself is done with the this keyword. A cast from the class itself is done to the specific interface using the (FirstInterface) or (SecondInterface) syntax. This provides the connection to the specific interface in the class implementing that interface. The dot operator is used to call the function from the specific interface after the cast.

```
((SecondInterface)this).SameFunction();
/*         ↑            ↑           ↑        */
/*         |            |           |        */
/*         |      _____|_____     |        */
/*         |     |             |    |        */
/*         |     |reference    |    |        */
/*         |     |to this class|    |        */
/*         |     |which implements||         */
/*         |     |the interfaces|   |        */
/*         |     |_____|    |        */
/*      ___|___              ____|____        */
/*     |the interface to|   |the function in|  */
/*     |cast into from  |   |the interface  |  */
/*     |this class      |   |to call        |  */
/*     |_____|   |_____|  */
```

When the implementing class marks the SameFunction() as virtual, any implementing class will then call all three versions of the function.

```
class ImplementsBoth : ImplementsFirstAndSecond
{
    public override void SameFunction()
    {
        base.SameFunction();
    }
}
```

The `ImplementsBoth` class inherits from `ImplementsFirstAndSecond`. This becomes a class which brings the two interfaces into a single implementation.

```
void UsingMultipleInterfaces()
{
    ImplementsBoth fromBoth = new ImplementsBoth();
    fromBoth.SameFunction();
}
```

Calling on the `SameFunction()` from the class which implements the two interfaces which were called in the `SameFunction()` from the previous class produces the following output in the Unity 3D Console:

```
(!) Which version is Called?
    UnityEngine.Debug:Log(Object)

(!) First SameFunction Called.
    UnityEngine.Debug:Log(Object)

(!) Second SameFunction Called.
    UnityEngine.Debug:Log(Object)
```

We call every version of the `SameFunction()` when we inherit from a class which implements the `SameFunction()` and then references two more functions, one from each interface. It's uncommon, but it's an edge case you should be aware of.

Most interfaces are written as a system to comply with various systems already implemented. Often an interface can be used to allow commonly used C# constructs to work with your custom script classes.

7.9.3 IComparer

Building a collection of interfaces makes sense so long as the interfaces provide necessary functionality. The interfaces provided by C# offer more interesting possibilities in that they can be customized for any suited purpose.

The System.Collections library built into C# has a class called the `ArrayList`. Starting with a list populated with int values ranging from 0 to 1000.

```
ArrayList numberList = new ArrayList();
for (int i = 0; i < 100; i++)
{
    numberList.Add(UnityEngine.Random.Range(0, 1000));
}
```

To show this list we simply read them out one at a time to the Unity 3D Console with a `Debug.Log()` command.

```
Debug.Log("Unsorted list.");
foreach (int i in numberList)
{
    // show list as generated by
    // a random number generator
    Debug.Log(i);
}
```

The fragment here prints out a hundred random numbers between 0 and 1000. The `ArrayList` has a function to rearrange the values stored in it called `Sort()`. After the `Sort()` function is used in the `ArrayList`, the values are rearranged from lowest to highest.

```
numberList.Sort();
Debug.Log("Sorted list.");
foreach (int i in numberList)
{
    // show list sorted
    Debug.Log(i);
}
```

The ArrayList isn't complete without having our own object to sort. The sort requires a customized version of the IComparer interface. The ArrayList has a built in comparison to sort the integer type. To enable sorting of a new type we need to create one.

```
class CompareDistance : IComparer
{
    public int Compare(object x, object y)
    {
        throw new System.NotImplementedException();
    }
}
```

In this interface, the public int Compare() function takes two objects.

We can extend this CompareDistance class with another object to compare against. We've added a third term called Target. This can be assigned after the DistanceComparer has been instanced. Therefore, after DistanceComparer dc; has been created with the new keyword, we assign the Target to another GameObject in the scene.

```
class DistanceComparer : IComparer
{
    public object Target;
    public int Compare(object x, object y)
    {
        GameObject xObj = (GameObject)x;
        GameObject yObj = (GameObject)y;
        GameObject target = (GameObject)Target;
        Vector3 tPos = target.transform.position;
        Vector3 xPos = xObj.transform.position;
        Vector3 yPos = yObj.transform.position;
        float distanceX = (tPos - xPos).magnitude;
        float distanceY = (tPos - yPos).magnitude;
        if (distanceX > distanceY)
        {
            return 1;
        }
        else
        {
            return -1;
        }
    }
}
```

The above code has the added Target GameObject and some math to check the distance from object x to the Target and the distance to object y. Once these two values are found, we compare them. If the distance to the first object is greater, then we return 1; if the value is less, we return −1. If neither of these two cases is fulfilled, then we return 0, inferring that x and y are equal.

The `ArrayList.Sort()` function uses the different 1, −1, and 0 values to move the objects it's comparing. 1 means to move the x object up one in the array, −1 down one in the array, and finally 0 means don't move any objects. Depending on the length of the list, the `Sort()` uses what is often referred to as a *quicksort* algorithm.

7.9.4 Using IComparer

In the scene we have several cubes placed around our game object with the Interfaces script. The first fragment of code collects an array and adds them to an ArrayList.

```
GameObject[] allObjects = FindObjectsOfType<GameObject>();
//get all game objects in the scene

ArrayList objectList = new ArrayList();
//make an arrayList to copy all of the game objects to

foreach (GameObject go in allObjects)
{
    objectList.Add(go);
}
```

This is followed by creating an instance of the `DistanceComparer` class which implements the IComparer interface.

```
DistanceComparer comparer = new DistanceComparer();
// create a distance comparer

comparer.Target = this.gameObject;
// assign the comparer a target

objectList.Sort(comparer);
// sort the list with the comparer
```

We then copy the sorted list to a public GameObject array we can observe in the editor.

```
SortedByDistance = new GameObject[objectList.Count];
objectList.CopyTo(SortedByDistance, 0);
// copy to Array we can observe in the Editor.
```

By adding the code to the `Update()` in the Interfaces script we can watch the SortedByDistance array change as we move the GameObject with the script attached.

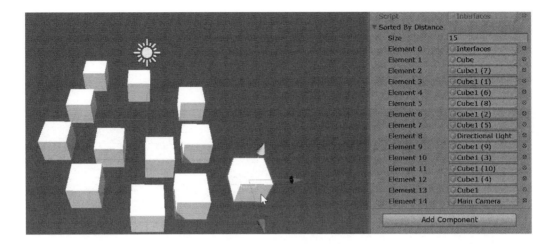

The SortedByDistance array is now rearranged not by the order in the scene but by distance! Very quick and easy.

7.9.5 What We've Learned

There has already been a great deal of material in this chapter. Interfaces are sort of like promises to reuse both the same identifier and the same signature that were created in the interface.

This ensures that you always get the same implementation for each class that uses the same interface. It would be a good idea to have as few interfaces as necessary. You shouldn't implement a IMedPack interface and an IShieldPowerup interface. What should be implemented is an IPickup interface. An IPickup would cover anything that your player could pick up. An interface should be less specific, not more specific.

Likewise, an IWeapon would be fine to cover anything that shoots, needs to hold ammo, and does anything that a weapon is used for. The IPickup could hold information for incrementing ammo, health, armor, or anything else. Classes implementing the IPickup interface could decide which they are incrementing, allowing for one or all of the stats to be adjusted when the item is picked up.

We'll get into a few common-looking setups later on when we look at game design patterns. For now try to think on your own what sort of interfaces you'll be implementing.

7.10 Class Constructors Revisited

Interfaces provide a system to ensure that a class is talked to in a specific way. When we start building more complex classes, we need to use an apparatus to ensure a consistent creation of the class. When starting a game where zombies are spawned and chase after the player, we might begin with a single zombie type. Later, we'd want to change this up for more variety. Modifying the amount of damage to destroy a zombie or change its size, shape, and model would all need to be modified according to specific parameters.

When working with a team, you're going to be needing to make sure that the class you're writing is created consistently. If you allow one programmer to directly set the hit points and another one to modify its armor instead, then you might get some unexpected behavior between the two monsters. This could be mitigated by enforcing a specific interface. You set up a specific set of parameters that must be used to properly modify a zombie.

A class *constructor* is used to set up an initial set of parameters required to instance a new object. The constructor can include several parameters, including references to the object creating them.

7.10.1 A Basic Example

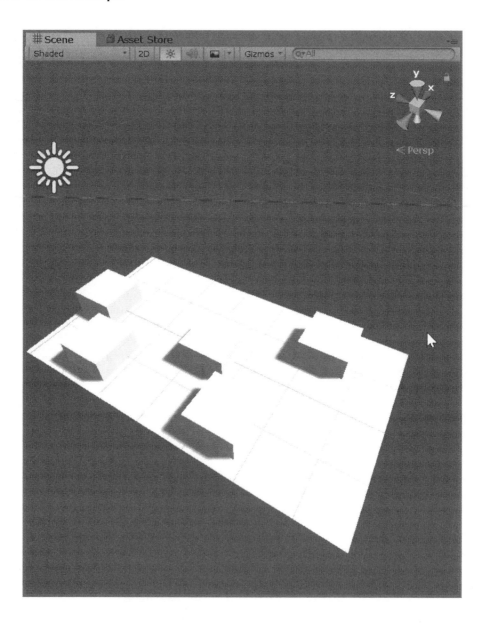

In the following code sample in the ClassConstructors_Scene in the Chapter 7 Unity Project, find the class ClassConstructors script on the game object of the same name. Within the ClassConstructor class is a nested class used to create a treadmill; a system useful for an endless runner style game.

```
class TreadmillSegment
{
    static int Segments;
    private float Speed;
    private int StepSize;
    private int Step;
    private GameObject Segment;

    public TreadmillSegment(float speed, ObstacleType obstacle, ref TreadmillUpdate treadmillUpdater)
    {
        Speed = speed;
        Segment = Instantiate(Resources.Load(obstacle.ToString()) as GameObject);
        treadmillUpdater += TreadmillUpdated;

        StepSize = (int)(1 / Speed);
        Step = Segments * StepSize;
        Segments++;
    }

    void TreadmillUpdated()
    {
        int totalSteps = Segments * StepSize;
        Segment.transform.position = new Vector3()
        {
            z = -(float)(Step++ % totalSteps) * Speed
        };
    }
}
```

The `TreadmillSegment` constructor takes three parameters. The first is a `float` used to designate how quickly the treadmill moves. The second is an `enum` to pick which shape the treadmill will use, and the last is a reference to a delegate.

```
enum ObstacleType
{
    Treadmill_Empty,
    Treadmill_Center,
    Treadmill_Left,
    Treadmill_Right
}
```

A Closer look at the `ObstacleType` enum shows four options. These coincide with the names of four prefabs found in the Resources directory of the Unity 3D project. Objects found in the Resources directory can be loaded by Unity 3D at run-time. This means after the game has started, a file located on disk can be loaded into the scene through script.

The last parameter is the reference to the `TreadmillUpdate` delegate. The delegate lives in the MonoBehaviour script that gets the `Update()` function called on every frame.

```
private delegate void TreadmillUpdate();
private TreadmillUpdate UpdateTreadmill;
```

This is used to ensure that classes, like the `TreadmillSegment` will be able to receive an `Update()` call even though they are not inheriting from MonoBehaviour.

```
int numSegments = 7;
for (int i = 0; i < numSegments; i++)
{
    ObstacleType obstacle = (ObstacleType)(i%4);
    new TreadmillSegment(0.015f, obstacle, ref UpdateTreadmill);
}
```

To use the `TreadmillSegment` class we create an arbitrary number of segments, in this case 7. This value could be anything. An `ObstacleType` is necessary to assign to the `TreadMillSegment` in the constructor. Using the i from the for loop cast from `int` to the `ObstacleType` enum. This approach is used to create a simple pattern quickly. More interesting logic aside, the cast from int to enum is possible since C# understands that an enum is a clever use of an int. Modulo 4 is used since there are only 4 values in the ObstacleType. The last ref `UpdateTreadmill` makes a reference to the delegate. The ref is necessary so the value of the delegate going in can retain an assignment.

```
public TreadmillSegment(float speed, ObstacleType obstacle, ref TreadmillUpdate treadmillUpdater)
{
    Speed = speed;
    Segment = Instantiate(Resources.Load(obstacle.ToString()) as GameObject);
    treadmillUpdater += TreadmillUpdated;

    StepSize = (int)(1 / Speed);
    Step = Segments * StepSize;
    Segments++;
}
```

A closer look at the constructor of the `TreadmillSegment` shows we store the `Speed` value. The enum is converted to a string. The `string` is then used to load a resource from disk with the same name as the enum's value. We cast from an `int` to enum to `string` to load a file from disk. Then the incoming `ref` to the delegate `TreadmillUpdate` is assigned `TreadmillUpdated` function found inside of the `TreadmillSegment` class. After that we make and store a calculation for how much the segment will move on each update, where the treadmill starts, and how many treadmill segments there are in total.

```
void TreadmillUpdated()
{
    int totalSteps = Segments * StepSize;
    Segment.transform.position = new Vector3()
    {
        z = -(float)(Step++ % totalSteps) * Speed
    };
}
```

The update function that gets assigned to the `ClassConstructors` delegate looks at how many steps there are in total. This is calculated by how many segments there are by how far they move per update. The `Step` value is incremented with every call. The position is reset to 0 by `Step` modulo `totalSteps` value. An integer value is used to keep track of the position since floating point values can begin to multiply small rounding errors over time.

```
void Update()
{
    if (UpdateTreadmill != null)
    {
        UpdateTreadmill();
    }
}
```

The last thing to do to update the segments is call the `UpdateTreadmill()` delegate in the `Update()` function of the `ClassConstuctors` class. There are only points in code in contact with the TreadmillSegment. The only contact with the `TreadmillSegment` is made through the constructor.

7.10.2 When to Create a New Class

Now that we've been working with classes for a few chapters, you might begin to wonder how often you'll need to write a new class. It's a good idea to separate groups of related functions into separate class. The pattern in which the treadmill appears should be something we can have more control over. Comment out the use of the first Treadmill system and uncomment the `UseTreadmillManager()` function.

```
void Start()
{
    //UseTreadmillSegments();

    UseTreadmillManger();
}
```

This deactivates the first test of the treadmill setup to allow us to inspect how a file can be used to store the pattern of our treadmill. We start at the beginning of the `TreadmillManager` class.

```
public readonly static string ProjectPath = System.IO.Directory.GetCurrentDirectory();
```

A `readonly static string` with the `ProjectPath` ensures that we cannot change this value once the game has started. The static keyword here also allows us to access the value more globally.

```
public static void WritePatternExample()
{
    string filePath = ProjectPath + "\\pattern.txt";
    // filePath = C:\Users\[user name]\Documents\BookContents\Chapters\Chapter7\pattern.txt

    StreamWriter writer = new StreamWriter(filePath);
    string defaultPattern =
        "Treadmill_Left\n" +
        "Treadmill_Center\n" +
        "Treadmill_Right\n" +
        "Treadmill_Right\n" +
        "Treadmill_Center\n" +
        "Treadmill_Left";
    // easier to read than a really long string.

    writer.Write(defaultPattern);
    writer.Close();
}
```

Also included in the header of this class is using System.IO, one of the many useful C# libraries
that have been included with .NET giving Unity 3D plenty of tools to work with. This provides us with
StreamWriter, a file utility that can write a file to disk so long as it's got a file path. In this case we used
ProjectPath and added a file name. The ProjectPath leads to the directory where the Project is stored on
your computer so your path may differ from the one indicated in the comment.

We then take a long string with '\n' between each value. This will allow us to break the string into
usable parts later. Then we give the StringWriter the defaultPattern string to write to disk. The writer
needs to be closed to finish writing the file.

```
public static string ReadPattern()
{
    string filePath = ProjectPath + "\\pattern.txt";
    // filePath = C:\Users\[user name]\Documents\BookContents\Chapters\Chapter7\pattern.txt

    StreamReader reader = new StreamReader(filePath);
    string readPattern = reader.ReadToEnd();
    /* reads something like "Treadmill_Left\nTreadmill_Center\nTreadmill_Right\n */
    /* until it reaches the end of the file.                                  */
    reader.Close();
    return readPattern;
}
```

We see a very similar pattern with reading that file. A StreamReader is given the same path. Then
ReadToEnd() is used to consume the contents of the file into a string. Once that's done then we close
the reader before returning the string.

```
public static string[] PatternToArray(string pattern)
{
    //remove trailing '\n'
    pattern.TrimEnd(new char[] { '\n' });
    /* if there was a "Treadmill_Center\n" at the end this will */
    /* cut it off.                                              */

    string[] patternArray = pattern.Split('\n');
    /* breaks this into string[]{ "Treadmill_Center", "Treadmill_Left"} */
    /* an array with each string part between the \n chars.             */

    return patternArray;
}
```

To break the string into an array we look for the "\n" characters to break the string into smaller parts.
This does a few things at once. First we have a bunch of smaller strings to work with, each object in the
string[] array is one of the values written in the string. Second we know how many segments were
written to the string.

```
string pattern = TreadmillManager.ReadPattern();
// gets the pattern of segments from disk

string[] obstacleArray = TreadmillManager.PatternToArray(pattern);
// gets the converted string to string[]{ "Treadmill_Left", "Treadmill_Center" } etc...

int numSegments = obstacleArray.Length;
// get the number of segments in the array

for (int i = 0; i < numSegments; i++)
{
    switch (obstacleArray[i])
    {
        case "Treadmill_Empty":
            new TreadmillSegment(0.015f, ObstacleType.Treadmill_Empty, ref UpdateTreadmill);
            break;
        case "Treadmill_Center":
            new TreadmillSegment(0.015f, ObstacleType.Treadmill_Center, ref UpdateTreadmill);
            break;
        case "Treadmill_Left":
            new TreadmillSegment(0.015f, ObstacleType.Treadmill_Left, ref UpdateTreadmill);
            break;
        case "Treadmill_Right":
            new TreadmillSegment(0.015f, ObstacleType.Treadmill_Right, ref UpdateTreadmill);
            break;
    }
}
```

To use this we read the pattern from the TreadmillManager.ReadPattern() which returns the contents of the pattern.txt file. Then we convert that into an array with TreadmillManager.PatternToArray() which returns a string[] array. We know how many segments to create so a for loop using the numSegments value allows us to check each object in the array for a string. The switch statement uses case "Treadmill _ Empty," "Treadmill _ Center," "Treadmill _ Left" and "Treadmill _ Right" to supply the TreadmillSegment() constructor with its proper ObstacleType.

```
public static void AppendPattern(ObstacleType obstacle)
{
    string previousPattern = ReadPattern();
    /* previous string might be like "Treadmill_Center" since we    */
    /* trim the trailing \n                                          */

    string newPattern = previousPattern + "\n" + obstacle.ToString();
    /* this adds a new "Treadmill_Left + "\nTreadmill_Center"        */
    /* to the end of the previous string                            */

    string filePath = ProjectPath + "\\pattern.txt";
    // filePath = C:\Users\[user name]\Documents\BookContents\Chapters\Chapter7\pattern.txt
    StreamWriter writer = new StreamWriter(filePath);
    writer.Write(newPattern);
    writer.Close();
}
```

To make things more interesting, we can add additional functions to the `TreadmillManager` like a system to append more obstacles to the text file. Here we convert the `ObstacleType` into a string preceded by a `'\n'` character to create each appended object on a new line.

When we use the `TreadmillManager` in the following manner:

```
TreadmillManager.WritePatternExample();

TreadmillManager.AppendPattern(ObstacleType.Treadmill_Center);
TreadmillManager.AppendPattern(ObstacleType.Treadmill_Center);
TreadmillManager.AppendPattern(ObstacleType.Treadmill_Center);
TreadmillManager.AppendPattern(ObstacleType.Treadmill_Empty);
TreadmillManager.AppendPattern(ObstacleType.Treadmill_Empty);
TreadmillManager.AppendPattern(ObstacleType.Treadmill_Empty);
```

The text file generated appears as such:

```
 1  Treadmill_Left
 2  Treadmill_Center
 3  Treadmill_Right
 4  Treadmill_Right
 5  Treadmill_Center
 6  Treadmill_Left
 7  Treadmill_Center
 8  Treadmill_Center
 9  Treadmill_Center
10  Treadmill_Empty
11  Treadmill_Empty
12  Treadmill_Empty
```

Tools that allow you to read and write to disk will need to use some additional tricks to avoid interrupting your game while it's playing. Large files can cause your game to stall or glitch and you'll lose a frame or two. We'll learn a few tricks in Section 7.18 when we cover a system where your game can continue to run with new tasks running in the background.

7.10.3 What We've Learned

As we add new tricks to our bag, we need to consider how to use them. Even though the tricks are no more than organizational or even for practice, it's important that we use them. Practice is the only way we will get better at the craft of code. With each new tool we learn we should use it.

This might not always work out for the better. In many cases, inappropriate uses of some of these tricks can cause problems for other programmers when they come across your use of some interesting new programming trick. Only after some experience will you be more able to deploy these tricks in an appropriate manner. Until then, use them often until you find a case where you're in need of using a different trick.

7.11 Preprocessor Directives

We live in a computer-diverse age where PCs and mobile devices share code. More important to our everyday lives as a game developer, we must consider the differences between the Unity 3D Editor and the game that the editor produces on Windows, OSX, iOS and Android. To further complicate the development process, each platform may include many differences with how to address local storage or graphics.

The system in place to enable or disable blocks of code is called a *preprocessor directive*, which acts somewhat like a comment that can use logic to bypass or enable blocks of code. Many directives are already defined by the Unity 3D Editor; these include directives that are enabled specifically when targeting specific platforms like mobile or console.

7.11.1 A Basic Example

To follow along use the Chapter 7 unity Project, open the PreprocessorDirectives_Scene and find the PreprocessorDirectives script attached to the like-named game object. Preprocessors are placed above the usual header of the file. PreprocessorDirectives are created by using the hash tag define (#define) followed by an identifier.

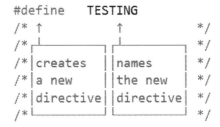

The definition of the directive comes before the using UnityEngine and other usings that are included in your new C# file. This also provides the use of the preprocessor directives to define whether or not usings are included in the file.

```
#if TESTING
using DOTNET = System.Diagnostics;
#endif
using UnityEngine;
```

This means we could include a diagnostics library from the dot net libraries just for testing. To keep specific blocks of code limited to specific tasks or scope the definition of TESTING is used by #if and #endif to create a scope of enabled code where TESTING allows. To make things a bit more simple to use, System.Diagnostics is renamed DOTNET to

```
    void Start()
    {
        Debug.Log("UNITY DEBUG TEST");
#if TESTING
        DOTNET.Debug.WriteLine("DOT NET TEST");
#endif
    }
```

Looking further down, we see the #if TESTING in the Start() function followed by the DOTNET. Debug.Log("DOT NET TEST");, which is followed by #endif to end the statements scoped by the directive. The result of this code allows us to easily pick chunks of code to switch on and off. In Visual Studio click on the Attach to Unity button, or go into the Debug menu and select Start Debugging. Then go back to Unity to start the game.

UNITY DEBUG TEST
UnityEngine.Debug:Log(Object)

We see the above output in the Unity Console. In the Visual Studio Output we get the following output:

```
DOT NET TEST
```

The `System.Diagnostics` version of `Debug` will send output exclusively to the Visual Studio output window and the Unity's version of `Debug` will send output to the Unity Console window.

The above code is enabled with #define TESTING located at the top of the class. If we comment out `//#define TESTING` and leave the rest of the code alone, The Visual Studio output is excluded.

```
#if !TESTING
        Debug.Log("Not using TESTING");
#endif
```

When the code is run, the second "Not using TESTING" log will not be sent to the console as TESTING is defined. Once TESTING is commented out, the directive `#if !TESTING` or "if not testing" enables the `Debug.Log()` with `Not using TESTING` and we'll get Unity's output with the second log. Preprocessors like this can be used to completely omit code from compiling, depending on whether or not the code it's around is needed. This is why it's called a preprocessor directive. Based on how the directives are set up, you can have entire sections of code omitted from various versions of the code. It's worth noting that you have to put all of your #define directive statements before any other token appears in the class, so all of the #define statements must appear at the top of the class file.

Using the #if preprocessor is a clever way to manage what code gets executed based on the programmer adding in or taking out various #define directives. In Unity 3D, however, we get a very useful predefined set of directives.

7.11.2 UNITY_EDITOR

Continuing in PreprocessorDirectives.cs file, take a look at the line where #if UNITY_EDITOR appears.

```
    void EditorOnly()
    {
#if UNITY_EDITOR
        Debug.Log("im an only editor message");
#endif
    }
```

The `UNITY_EDITOR` directive is defined only when the code is being run in the editor. A complete listing of the different symbols that have been defined can be found on the Unity 3D website. The other defined symbols include Unity 3D version number and the platform that the game is running on.

```
    public int Health;
    /* define not allowed in body of  */
    /* the class                      */
#define START_LOW_HEALTH
```

It's important to remember that you cannot define a new directive in the body of the code.

When the game is run in stand-alone mode or on a mobile device, the `UNITY_EDITOR` directive doesn't exist, so any code inside of any `#if UNITY_EDITOR` preprocessor directives will skip being compiled into the game. It's often useful to have specific behaviors when running in the editor. This can speed up testing if you find yourself changing numbers while testing in the editor.

```
      public int Health = 10;
      void EditorCheats()
      {
#if UNITY_EDITOR
          Health = 1000;
#endif


      }
```

With something like this, we can easily just skip over changing the numbers every time we start the game in the editor. This also prevents us from accidentally checking in code that might affect the final release of the game. We can add on some layers of complexity onto the use of directives.

```
#if UNITY_EDITOR && START_LOW_HEALTH
      Health = 1;
#elif UNITY_EDITOR
      Health = 1000;
#endif
```

Here we can comment in and out the directive definition at the top and switch between Low_Health and Unity_Editor testing. The first preprocessor statement #if UNITY_EDITOR && START_LOW_HEALTH only sets when we're running in the editor and we've uncommented out the //#define LOWHEALTH directive at the beginning of the class. The && operator works the same as though we were using it in an if statement.

To make things more clear, we can use parentheses around the preprocessor's condition #if (UNITY_EDITOR && START_LOW_HEALTH), which will produce the same result. This isn't required; however, programming style might dictate that you use parentheses anyway. To switch between the two statements, we use #elif, which is a preprocessor version of else if normally found in the rest of your code.

The difference comes from an old habit that originated from an older less integrated system. An external text editing software went through each file and deleted text before it was compiled. Each # command had to be one word for the macro to work properly. The macro has been incorporated into the parser now, but the formatting hasn't changed. We're also looking at #endif rather than a closing parenthesis or curly brace.

It's a whole different language, and to that there are some benefits. It's much more obvious that there's a secondary set of actions taking place on the code. Rather than using something that looks like the following:

```
public bool unityEditor = false;
public bool startLowHealth = false;

void UsingBools()
{
    if (unityEditor && startLowHealth)
    {
        Health = 1;
    }
    else if (unityEditor)
    {
        Health = 1000;
    }
}
```

Here it's not so clear if these are directives. The real problem here is that this code will be compiled into the shipping game and it's more likely someone might accidentally leave a check box turned on before checking in. Of course, the real issue is the fact that there is extra code being checked into the shipping version of the game that doesn't need to be there.

```
public bool unityEditor = false;
```

Of course, we could actually leave these check boxes on or off based on how they are being used. However, the automation provided by simply adding #if UNITY_EDITOR is preferable, and also less prone to mistakes. Before moving on, it should be mentioned that along with #define there's also #undef.

```
#undef UNITY_EDITOR
/* hides the UNITY_EDITOR define from this file */
```

This immediately undefines the UNITY_EDITOR directive and anything relying on this will deactivate.

7.11.3 Mobile Development

In a previous exercise we wrote a file to the project directory. In the code a StreamWriter was used to create and write text to a file.

```
// something like this doesn't work for Android!?
string filePath = System.IO.Directory.GetCurrentDirectory();
filePath += "\\fileData.txt";
string contents = "Editor File Data.";
```

We use the System.IO.Directory.GetCurrentDirectory() function to find where the Assets directory is located that Unity is currently using. With this the Unity 3D Editor is able to locate and write to the file, in this case we're writing "Editor File Data." However, if we used this in a mobile device we'd run into a few problems.

Unfortunately, iOS requires several hurdles to jump to become a developer and some of them are financial. Android doesn't offer as many blockades to development, so if you are an Android phone user, you'll be able to try this out yourself.

If you don't have access to an Android device don't worry, we'll cover the most important parts, which include how directives work in a mobile platform.

If you're not an Android developer, follow the link below to switch your phone over to enable developer options. Every phone is a bit different, so it's best to get the how to from the creators of Android—Google.

https://developer.android.com/studio/debug/dev-options#enable

Android is included in the different target platforms that Unity can produce a build. In short you'll need to do the following:

1. Open Settings
2. Scroll down to System, (Android 8 or newer)
3. Scroll down to Build number and tap on it 7 times.
4. Go back one screen and you'll see the Developer Options
5. Select that and enable USB Debugging.

Now you're officially an Android Developer. Plug your phone into your computer's USB port and allow your computer to talk to your phone.

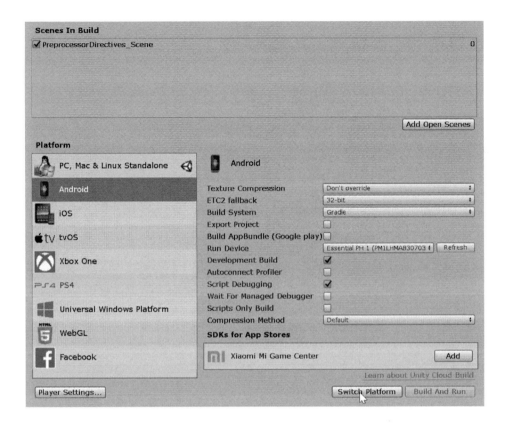

The list for building projects is extensive. Android, iOS, Xbox and web browsers are all targets for Unity 3D. Selecting Android and pressing the Switching Platform button changes which directives are enabled.

Once switched the preprocessor logic changes which blocks of code are enabled. Simply adding `#if UNITY_ANDROID` will not be enough to include code for that platform.

Running this code on an Android device will not work. Running the Android development tools and peeking at the log from the Console will show that `GetCurrentDirectory()` function doesn't do what we'd expect.

```
        Debug.Log(filePath);

// /\fileData.txt
// UnityEngine.DebugLogHandler:Internal_Log(LogType, String, Object)
// UnityEngine.DebugLogHandler:LogFormat(LogType, Object, String, Object[])
// UnityEngine.Logger:Log(LogType, Object)
// UnityEngine.Debug:Log(Object)
// PreprocessorDirectives: WriteToDevice()
// PreprocessorDirectives: Start()
```

The debug outout from the device looks a bit like the above. The file path looks like `"/\fileData.txt"` and lacks any directory structure. To get the proper directory path we need to use a different approach. This is followed by the StreamWriter running into problems as well.

```
UnauthorizedAccessException: Access to the path "/\fileData.txt" is denied.
  at System.IO.FileStream..ctor (System.String path, System.IO.FileMode mode,
```

The path to the `fileData.txt` leads to nowhere, so there's nowhere for the file to be written.

```
#if UNITY_EDITOR
        // something like this doesn't work for Android!?
        string filePath = System.IO.Directory.GetCurrentDirectory();
        filePath += "\\fileData.txt";
        string contents = "Editor File Data.";
#if UNITY_ANDROID
        // Required or the path looks like "/"
        string filePath = Application.persistentDataPath;
        filePath += "/fileData.txt";
        string contents = "Device File Data.";
#endif
```

Including `&& !UNITY_EDITOR` will hide the code when running in the editor, but the code will be included when running on Android.

```
#if UNITY_ANDROID && !UNITY_EDITOR
        // Required or the path looks like "/"
        string filePath = Application.persistentDataPath;
        filePath += "/fileData.txt";
        string contents = "Device File Data.";
#endif
```

Once the proper directives separate the editor's version of the function from the Android version of the function, both can operate as expected.

```
/storage/emulated/0/Android/data/com.CSharp.Project/files/fileData.txt
UnityEngine.DebugLogHandler:Internal_Log(LogType, String, Object)
UnityEngine.DebugLogHandler:LogFormat(LogType, Object, String, Object[])
UnityEngine.Logger:Log(LogType, Object)
UnityEngine.Debug:Log(Object)
PreprocessorDirectives:ReadbackPath() (at C:\Users\alexokita\Documents\BookContents\Chapters\Chapter7\Assets\PreprocessorDirectives.cs:68)
PreprocessorDirectives:Start() (at C:\Users\alexokita\Documents\BookContents\Chapters\Chapter7\Assets\PreprocessorDirectives.cs:79)
```

On Android the path assigned using `Application.persistentDataPath` looks quite different. The same path assignment works in the editor, but leads to a hidden directory in your user's folder, far less convenient than the project directory.

In some ways, the preprocessor directives means supporting multiple codebases. A block of code working in the editor, and another for your target platform. Imagine for a moment having to support multiple code projects, one in Objective-C or Swift, which is what iOS natively runs in XCode, another project written in Kotlin in Android Studio, and possibly something like C++ for Windows, etc. The list can go on and on for every platform.

Using preprocessor directives in Unity 3D can certainly add some complexity. Without preprocessor directives, you would use if else statements in your code for each operating system you might target. Preprocessor directives are a preferable alternative.

7.11.4 Warning

When using `#define` for debug purposes, it's often important to remind yourself that some directives are enabled. It's useful to add a reminder that a directive is active. In Unity the UNITY_EDITOR directive is useful; however, if you find it necessary it's possible to hide it in the class you're working in.

As a self-serving reminder, #warning can be added after an #if as a reminder in Unity 3D that there are modifications going on with your directives.

```
    void UseWarning()
    {
#if UNITY_EDITOR && TESTING
#warning TESTING MODE ACTIVE
#endif
    }
```

After adding this to the code, you'll get a warning once the script has been interpreted by Unity 3D that 'TESTING MODE ACTIVE':

⚠ Assets\PreprocessorDirectives.cs(130,10): warning CS1030: #warning: 'TESTING MODE ACTIVE'

This text can be anything you like, so long as the warning message you're giving to yourself makes sense. The warning message has no special formatting. Whatever appears on the line after the #warning is what will appear in the Unity 3D Console.

So your messages need to stay on the line where the #warning appears. The same goes for the rest of the #define preprocessor directives. As a rule of thumb, these should be short and in all caps. The all caps notation isn't enforced, although it is common practice. This helps point out where any of these special case definitions are happening in the code.

7.11.5 Organizing

Organization is a constant struggle. In a Visual Studio, you have little boxes for folding code. #region NAME is a useful directive that is used to help keep your development environment sane.

```
#region FirstSection
void FirstFunctionInFirstSection()
{
    //Do things here
}
void InFirstSection()
{
    //Do other things here
}
#endregion
```

Adding regions to your code can help collapse sections of code. Adding too many different #ifdef and #region tags might work against you. Having more hash tags in your code than actual functions defeats the purpose of why these are used to begin with.

Though used wisely in a long class, a few regions can help. A #region can be nested inside of another region. Once inside of a region you're able to collapse sections of a long function to help you observe relations between variables that might be far apart.

7.11.6 What We've Learned

We will be coming back to some of the preprocessor directives again once we've covered some error handling concepts. In general, preprocessors work on the code in a manner closer to how comments work. Because of this, we can use preprocessor directives to manage different chunks of code based on a single #define at the beginning of a class.

Directives are used for many different things: One of the most common is to manage work with multiple platforms. Using preprocessor directives, you can set different settings for screen resolutions based on make or model.

7.12 Try Catch Finally

Working with a few warnings such as unused variables is simple enough; having too many of these can create situations where an important warning might be missed. In general, it's best to keep your warnings to an absolute minimum, or at least, no unexpected warnings at all.

There are situations where we might want to get specific warnings. In situations where we try to read a uniform resource locator (URL) from a web page and the server is down, we don't want our game to simply crash or freeze.

There are also situations where you might expect some values to be incorrect. When dealing with a user, you might expect a numeric value and get a letter instead. Rather than freeze and crash the game, you can ignore the input until a correction is made.

7.12.1 A Basic Example

Starting in the TryCatchFinally_Scene in the Chapter 7 Unity Project, open the TryCatchFinally script on the like-named game object. In the function `DontUseTryCatch()`, `int.Parse()` is used to read a string and extract an integer value.

```
void DontUseTryCatch()
{
    int i = 0;
    i = int.Parse("1");
    // this does work, and we get 1
    Debug.Log("i is " + i);

    int j = 0;
    j = int.Parse("One");
    //throws an error

    Debug.Log("j is " + j);
    // never gets called, the game stopped.
}
```

In the first block of code we parse a string containing "1" and the `int` i is assigned an `int` 1. In the second block of code we parse the string "One" and Unity, or rather C# errors and the game stops.

Your game, mobile or otherwise, would have crashed. To keep Unity 3D from crashing, using the try-catch pattern will help prevent bad input from crashing the game.

```
void UseTryCatch()
{
    int i = 0;
    try
    {
        i = int.Parse("One");
    }
    catch
    {
        i = 1;
    }
    Debug.Log("i is " + i);
}
```

With the above we get "i is 1" printed to the Console. The attempt to parse the string "One" to a 1 failed, but we didn't error, and the game didn't stop. The code assigned 1 to i using the catch which only executes if the try block fails. How do we know it failed? There wasn't any warning, debug log, or any indication that the Parse("One") failed.

```
void UseTryCatchWithException()
{
    int i = 0;
    try
    {
        i = int.Parse("One");
    }
    catch (Exception e)
    {
        Debug.Log(e.Message);
        i = 1;
    }
    Debug.Log("i is " + i);
}
```

Adding (Exception e) to the catch block leaves an input variable for try to assign an exception. The Exception type comes from using System, a core .NET library. The output from e.Message can inform us as to what didn't work with the Parse function when reading the string.

> ⓘ Input string was not in a correct format.
> UnityEngine.Debug:Log(Object)

The try{} statement makes an attempt to process to the input value. If it succeeds i is assigned a valid number. If it fails the catch{} statement picks up what failed. From here you can make a decision as to how to work around the error.

```
void UseCheckExceptions()
{
    object[] objs = new object[] { 7.0, "23", null, "Seventeen"};
    Debug.Log("Check for Exception.");
    foreach (object o in objs)
    {
        CheckException(o);
    }
}

void CheckException(object o)
{
    int i = 0;
    try
    {
        i = (int)o;
        Debug.Log("I guess it wasn't an int.");
    }
    catch (Exception e)
    {
        Debug.Log(e.Message);
    }
}
```

From a given object we can try to cast to int to unbox a value. In the above we have four objects, none of which are int, and each one may or may not be able to be converted to an int by C#. We can give ourselves more information about what is going wrong with some parameters going into the catch{}. To start, we'll want to add a new directive at the beginning of the class. This means that we know not only that try{} failed, but why it failed. We can create a specific response to the failure. When the failure occurs for different reasons, we can create different catches for each situation.

7.12.2 Exception Messages

The Exception is a generic catch all for all varieties of exception types. The more specific NullReferenceException and InvalidCastException are the two that are brought up with the above example.

```
void CheckExceptionType(object o)
{
    int i = 0;
    try
    {
        Debug.Log("Got: " + o);
        i = (int)o;
    }
    catch (NullReferenceException e)
    {
        Debug.Log("NullReferenceException " + e.Message);
    }
    catch (InvalidCastException e)
    {
        Debug.Log("InvalidCastException " + e.Message);
    }
    catch (Exception e)
    {
        Debug.Log("Unexpected Exception " + e.Message);
    }
}
```

The CheckExceptionType() function can check for different types of input problems from object. When casting the different types to an int we usually get an InvalidCastException. In the case where we catch the null in the array we get the NullReferenceException. In all the cases, the cast doesn't halt the game as it usually would. This provides a bit of a safety net if we're dealing with an unreliable data source. Something like a text input field to be filled in by the player or calling a web URL could return an unexpected data type. Because we were able to catch this problem and make a decision on how to handle it, we can save our game from an execution error. In the Scene an InputText field sits centered in the Game view.

The field is connected to a function called TextInputChanged() where the field's text is sent to the functions parameter for evaluation. The text is then sent to a function to parse into an int value.

```
void ConvertFromStringToInt(string input)
{
    int i = 0;
    try
    {
        i = int.Parse(input);
        Debug.Log("int parse successful, got " + i);
    }
    catch (Exception e)
    {
        Debug.Log(e);
        try
        {
            i = (int)float.Parse(input);
            Debug.Log("float parse successful, got " + i);
        }
        catch{
            Debug.Log("input wasn't a float or an int.");
        }
    }
}
```

The first try{} block uses int.Parse() to check the string for an integer value. If that fails then we try to look for a float value, something like 1.0. The nested try catch try catch will give us two ways to convert the string to an integer value.

Even if the input isn't a numeric value we'll get an exception not a crash. We could simply ask the player to try to provide a numeric input if that's what we're expecting. Rather than using Debug.Log, we could open an information pop-up and ask for a different input and have the player try again.

7.12.3 Custom Exceptions

Working with many different conditions complicates debugging. Finding and dealing with a specific error condition is best dealt with by using custom exception code.

```
public class MyException : Exception
{
    public MyException()
    {
    }
    public MyException(string message) : base(message)
    {
    }
    public MyException(string message, Exception innerException)
    : base(message, innerException)
    {
    }
}
```

Classes like int and float have a `Parse()` function. This function tries to read a string and interpret the characters in the string as a number value. If this fails, it creates a new exception and throws it. In a simple range example we'll do the following to check an array of numbers for integer values between 0 and 100 with a `ValidateRange()` function.

```
void ValidateRange(int i)
{
    if (i > 100)
    {
        MyException e = new MyException(i + " is above range.");
        e.Number = 100;
        throw e;
    }
    else if (i < 0)
    {
        MyException e = new MyException(i + " is below range.");
        e.Number = 0;
        throw e;
    }
}
```

The above function checks the incoming value for a number higher than 100 or a value below 0. If either case is true a new MyException is created and the keyword throw is followed by the created MyException. Visually, there's no connection between the `ValidateRange()` function and the `catch{}` block.

```
try
{
    ValidateRange(i);
    Debug.Log("input: " + i + " is in range.");
    /* this works a little bit like this    */
    /*      MyException e;                   */
    /*          └────────→┐                  */
    /*      ValidateRange(i, out e);         */
}   /*          ┌─────────←┘                 */
catch (MyException e)
{
    Debug.Log(e.Message + "value bypassed:" + e.Number);
}
```

In some of the C# syntax we've seen before we might expect that the Exception needs to go into a function before it comes out. When we use throw, the Exception appears without any visible variable to acknowledge its presence before it's used in the catch parameter. In addition, the only catch block that will execute is the one with the matching Exception type.

```
void UseCustomExceptions()
{
    int[] inputs = new int[] { 0, 1, -10, 50, 100, 3000 };
    foreach (int i in inputs)
    {
        try
        {
            ValidateRange(i);
            Debug.Log("input: " + i + " is in range.");
        }
        catch (MyException e)
        {
            Debug.Log(e.Message + "value bypassed:" + e.Number);
        }
    }
}
```

If the value throws an exception then the `try{}` block exits and we jump to the `catch{}` block. Once in the `catch{}` block we read back the message and the value that was passed by the input value. If the ValidateRange doesn't throw any Exceptions, then we get the `Debug.Log()` in the try block indicating that the input value passes the validation.

> (!) input: 0 is in range.
>   UnityEngine.Debug:Log(Object)
>
> (!) input: 1 is in range.
>   UnityEngine.Debug:Log(Object)
>
> (!) -10 is below range.value bypassed:0
>   UnityEngine.Debug:Log(Object)
>
> (!) input: 50 is in range.
>   UnityEngine.Debug:Log(Object)
>
> (!) input: 100 is in range.
>   UnityEngine.Debug:Log(Object)
>
> (!) 3000 is above range.value bypassed:100
>   UnityEngine.Debug:Log(Object)

We could add any number of possible catches to an Exception. However we can throw different types of Exceptions, not just MyException. For validating scene objects we could throw a NullReferenceException if an object provided isn't a gameObject.

Now once the Exception is caught, we can check what situation threw the message, and then react appropriately. In cases where we can't possibly come up with every imaginable situation, we have one last keyword to help us.

7.12.4 Finally

To complete our try{}-catch{} statement, we can add a finally{} statement. Since we're not doing anything complex here, all we need is the following:

```
void UseFinally()
{
    try
    {
        ValidateRange(101);
    }
    catch (MyException e)
    {
        Debug.Log(e.Message);
    }
    finally
    {
        Debug.Log("Done.");
    }
}
```

In this situation, the finally{} statement is unnecessary. Where finally comes in handy is with functions that require some clean up afterward. After parsing player input we might want to clear lock the input field, or perhaps switch UI (user interface) panels to a new screen. The finally{} block only runs once try and catch have finished their tasks.

7.12.5 Try-Catch and Finally in Use

When working with System.IO and the StreamWriter function we often get a few UnauthorizedAccessExceptions. This is often because we've got the path wrong.

```
void UseWriteToFile()
{
    string path = System.IO.Directory.GetCurrentDirectory();
    FileStream file = null;
    FileInfo info = null;
    try
    {
        info = new FileInfo(path + "//FinalFile.txt");
        file = info.OpenWrite();
        for (int i = 0; i < 255; i++)
        {
            file.WriteByte((byte)i);
        }
    }
    catch (FileNotFoundException e)
    {
        Debug.Log(e.Message);
    }
    catch (UnauthorizedAccessException e)
    {
        Debug.Log(e.Message);
    }
    finally
    {
        if (file != null)
        {
            file.Close();
        }
    }
}
```

With this in mind, we use the try{} to create a new file called FinalFile.txt in our project directory. Once it's created, we open it for writing, and then add in a bunch of characters with file.WriteByte(). If we're not allowed to write to this directory, we catch that problem with UnauthorizedAccessException and have Unity 3D let us know if there was a problem. If the file has been written, it's closed with the finally{} block.

7.12.6 What We've Learned

The notation used here creates a clean and tidy way to create a file, check for problems, and finish the file writing process. The blocks are clear and the proper procedures are followed. We also get an interesting look at all of the different characters in a font.

In the file.txt, we get many weird characters before we start to see letters and numbers. Aside from unusual characters, it's important to know how the try-catch-finally process works for using network connections.

When setting up a connection through hypertext transfer protocol (HTTP) to get an image from the internet or models from a web server, we'll want to make sure that the connection didn't disconnect halfway through. Possibly a user name or password was incorrect. All of these situations will need to be caught before we reach a `finally{}` block and pretend that everything went as expected.

After the file.txt was written, you can get properties on the file and change it to read only. This will throw the exception and you'll get the following error:

Access to the path "C:\file.txt" is denied.

UnityEngine. Debug:LogWarning(Object)

Warnings:Start () (at Assets/Warnings.cs:26)

This means that the `try{}` block failed and the `catch{}` block was activated. When the `finally{}` block is reached, the file is null and doesn't need to be closed.

There are many different types of exceptions that Unity 3D will often be throwing. It's likely that you might need to move an object and want to catch if a number gets out of hand or you suspect a divide by zero exception might be thrown. These situations are easier to work with if you use `try{}` and `catch{}`.

7.13 IEnumerator

C# has several built-in interfaces, IEnumerator is just one of them. We used the IComparer interface to sort through distances to gameObjects. The utility of an interface is a means to reduce work. Any task coming up more than a few times should lead toward simplification of work.

An enumerator is a system that is used to iterate through an array. The prefixed letter is an I, so it's an interface, but what does that even mean? An IEnumerator is something that we use on an array of an object with an enumerator interface.

The problem begins as a long list of items. The usual `for(int i = 0; i < array.Length; i++)` works fine for most situations, and in fact you can get by with just that. There are cases in which some data is not presented as an array but as an IEnumerator. Extended markup language, which looks a lot like a web page for data, doesn't always present its data to you in the form of an array. We'll find out more about that in a later chapter about reading and writing data.

With cases like this, we are forced to use either a foreach or a while loop. However, the way these loops are used aren't as simple as you might expect. Once you understand how it works, you will find that a large array is really easy to iterate through.

7.13.1 Enumeration

Before we make our own enumerator, it's easier to see how it's used. The IEnumerator is an interface with one property and two methods. The only property is called Current, and the two methods we can use are called Reset and MoveNext.

7.13.1.1 A Basic Example

Let's find the Enums class in the Assets directory of the Enums project.

```
int[] intArray = new int[] { 10, 20, 30, 40, 50, 60, 70, 80, 90, 100 };
void UseIntEnumerator()
{
    IEnumerator intEnumerator = intArray.GetEnumerator();
    while (intEnumerator.MoveNext())
    {
        Debug.Log("Current int: " + intEnumerator.Current);
    }
    // Current int: 10
    // Current int: 20
    // Current int: 30
    // Current int: 40
    // Current int: 50
    // Current int: 60
    // Current int: 70
    // Current int: 80
    // Current int: 90
    // Current int: 100

}
```

This is a pretty short example of what an IEnumerator does. First we get an array of integers, though the array can be of anything. We're calling the array `intArray`, just to keep things simple. Arrays have a method called `GetEnumerator()` that returns a type `IEnumerator`. To use this we can assign a variable, in this case o as a type `IEnumerator` to `intArray.GetEnumerator();`.

The variable `intEnumerator` is an `IEnumerator`, has a few simple functions. Peeking at the IEnumerator in Visual Studio will reveal the following:

```
namespace System.Collections
{
    public interface IEnumerator
    {
        object Current
        {
            get;
        }

        bool MoveNext();
        void Reset();
    }
}
```

It's important to note that the IEnumerator intEnumerator is an object. To use it for something else, we'll need to cast it to whatever it is we're expecting. We will need to remember this later on. We can use the IEnumerator o outside of a while loop.

```
void UseWithoutLoop()
{
    IEnumerator intEnumerator = intArray.GetEnumerator();

    intEnumerator.MoveNext();
    Debug.Log("Current int: " + intEnumerator.Current);
    // Current int: 10

    intEnumerator.MoveNext();
    Debug.Log("Current int: " + intEnumerator.Current);
    // Current int: 20

    intEnumerator.MoveNext();
    Debug.Log("Current int: " + intEnumerator.Current);
    // Current int: 30

    intEnumerator.MoveNext();
    Debug.Log("Current int: " + intEnumerator.Current);
    // Current int: 40
}
```

This might not be the most efficient way to use an IEnumerator, but this is a good approximation of what's happening inside of the while loop. The intEnumerator.MoveNext(); function call tells intEnumerator to change the value of intEnumerator.Current. To make this more clear, we'll add in why the while loop works.

```
void UseIfToIterate()
{
    int[] someInts = new int[] { 1, 3, 7 };
    IEnumerator intEnumerator = someInts.GetEnumerator();
    if (intEnumerator.MoveNext())
    {
        Debug.Log("Current int: " + intEnumerator.Current);
    }
    if (intEnumerator.MoveNext())
    {
        Debug.Log("Current int: " + intEnumerator.Current);
    }
    if (intEnumerator.MoveNext())
    {
        Debug.Log("Current int: " + intEnumerator.Current);
    }
    if (intEnumerator.MoveNext())
    {
        Debug.Log("I won't get called.");
    }
}
```

After shortening the array of ints to only three items, we'll see what happens if we use if `intEnumerator.MoveNext()` past the length of the array. Does `intEnumerator.Current` have a value? The array is three items long, so the fourth if statement returns false, and a fourth Current value won't be printed. The `IEnumerator` function of an array returns a useful little trick to use for tasks involving arrays.

7.13.1.2 What Doesn't Work

For many of the basic tasks involving arrays, you might use the foreach statement. The following code fragment could work on its own if you didn't use a foreach statement.

```
void UseStringArray()
{
    string[] strings = new string[] { "A", "B", "C" };
    IEnumerator strEnumerator = strings.GetEnumerator();
    foreach (string s in strEnumerator)
    {
        Debug.Log(s);
    }
}
```

With a foreach statement, we might expect the IEstring to contain something useful as though it were a simple array. However, this is not the case. The IEumerator type doesn't actually give access to its contents without providing it though Current. Just as interestingly enough, if you were to ask for IEString. Current, the first value found has nothing in it.

```
string[] strings = new string[] { "A", "B", "C" };
IEnumerator strEnumerator = strings.GetEnumerator();
Debug.Log(strEnumerator.Current);
```

Try doing the above code sample and you'll get a run-time error message:

```
InvalidOperationException: Enumeration has not started. Call MoveNext.
System.Array+ArrayEnumerator.get_Current () (at <ac823e2bb42b41bda67924a45a0173c3>:0)
```

The enumeration process has not started, it seems. This requires at least one use of `MoveNext()` before the IEnumerator variable's. Current object has a value of some kind. As we've seen, there are various ways to use `MoveNext()` to get a value from the `Current` property in the IEnumerable data type.

Take a moment to think about what's going on. The IEnumerator is an interface class written by C# programmers. It was created to provide you, the programmer, a method to make a consistent interface that can be incorporated into your code smoothly. Once implemented, other programmers can use your class as they would use any other IEnumerator. You can think of it as adding a handy feature to your class. However, to fully implement the feature and make sure that it does what you want it to, you'll need to understand how it's expected to work.

7.13.2 Implementing IEnumerator

The implementation of an enumerator comes in two new additions to your starting class. This means you can take any existing class and add an enumerator to it. So you could take any zombie, and make an array of that zombie enumerable. In this example we'll look at AZombie class which is simply a wrapper for a zombie's name.

To enumerate through the AZombie class we'll need the two additional classes. A ZombieEnumerator which inherits from the IEnumerator and an interfacing class that inherits from IEnumerable. The IEnumerable provides the GetEnumerator() function through an array of AZombie objects.

We're starting in the ZombieEnumerator class that implements the IEnumerator interface. This is an interface that is found in the System.Collections .NET library. We store two things in the ZombieEnumerator: a reference to the array that's going to be enumerated and an int that keeps track of where we are in the array.

```csharp
class ZombieEnumerator : IEnumerator
{
    private AZombie[] AZombieArray;
    private int index;
```

To instantiate the IEnumerator object we assign it an array.

```csharp
/* constructor saves the incoming array    */
public ZombieEnumerator(AZombie[] zombieArray)
{
    AZombieArray = zombieArray;
}
```

The locally stored array is assigned in the constructor. This is followed by the three functions that are required in the IEnumerator interface. The MoveNext(), Reset(), and the Current accessor.

```csharp
/* MoveNext increments the locally stored  */
/* index of the array and returns true     */
/* so long as the index doesn't exceed     */
/* the length of the stored array          */
public bool MoveNext()
{
    index++;
    return index >= AZombieArray.Length;
}


/* put the array index back ahead of 0      */
public void Reset()
{
    index = -1;
}


/* return the object from the array at the  */
/* index                                    */
object IEnumerator.Current
{
    get
    {
        return AZombieArray[index];
    }
}
}
```

The MoveNext() increments the index value and returns true so long as the index is either less than or equal to the length of the stored array of enumerable objects. The Reset() function simply sets the index value to −1 so when MoveNext() is called after a reset it returns the 0th, or zeroth, object in the stored array. The object IEnumerable.Current explicitly implements the IEnumerable's interface for the Current value. This only provides get{} since we don't want anything to change what is stored in the array.

When implementing an interface or any class inheriting from another class, you can use an explicit declarator. We will see this again when implementing the IEnumerable interface.

```
/* you then make an IEnumerable object where     */
/* an array of the enumerated object lives.      */
class Zombies : IEnumerable
{
    // the array to iterate through.
    private AZombie[] AZombieArray;

    // constructor to assign to the new Enumerator
    public Zombies(AZombie[] zombieArray)
    {
        AZombieArray = zombieArray;
    }

    // the explicit method which returns the IEnumerator
    // object to start enumeration
    IEnumerator IEnumerable.GetEnumerator()
    {
        return (IEnumerator)GetEnumerator();
    }

    // the actual Enumerator that's returned
    public ZombieEnumerator GetEnumerator()
    {
        return new ZombieEnumerator(AZombieArray);
    }
}
```

The Zombies class acts as the generator to the ZombieEnumerator class we just looked at. The IEnumerator IEnumerable.GetEnumerator() is the explicit declaration to fulfill the IEnumerable interface. The class stores an array of AZombie so it can assign it to the created ZombieEnumerator.

```
// the explicit method which returns the IEnumerator
// object to start enumeration
IEnumerator IEnumerable.GetEnumerator() /*→┐❶    */
{                                        /*  │    */
    return (IEnumerator)GetEnumerator();/*←┘❷    */
}                                        /*  │    */
                                         /*  ↓❸   */
public ZombieEnumerator GetEnumerator()
{
    return new ZombieEnumerator(AZombieArray);
}                                        /*←❸ returned    */
                                         /* after initalized    */
```

To more clearly see how the chain of calls is made to GetEnumerator(), we start with the first interface version of IEnumerator IEnumerable.GetEnumerator(). This is how the first call is made; this then looks for the local GetEnumerator, which is a public ZombieEnumerator GetEnumerator(). The second function returns the populated ZombieEnumerator().

To use the new Enumerator, an array of different AZombie objects is created and a new IEnumerator is made from the array.

```
AZombie Stubbs = new AZombie("Stubbs");
AZombie Bob = new AZombie("Bob");
AZombie Rob = new AZombie("Rob");
AZombie Freddy = new AZombie("Freddy");
AZombie Jason = new AZombie("Jason");
AZombie[] zombies = new AZombie[] { Stubbs, Bob, Rob, Freddy, Jason };
IEnumerator zombieEnumerator = zombies.GetEnumerator();
```

The new IEnumerator works as we created from the array of strings or ints. To enumerate through the zombieEnumerator we use the same syntax with the while loop.

```
while (zombieEnumerator.MoveNext())
{
    Debug.Log(zombieEnumerator.Current);
}
// Enumerations+AZombie
// Enumerations+AZombie
// Enumerations+AZombie
// Enumerations+AZombie
// Enumerations+AZombie
// Enumerations+AZombie
```

The catch here is that we need to cast or unbox the contained object in the Current value.

```
// reset the enumerator after you've used it
zombieEnumerator.Reset();

while (zombieEnumerator.MoveNext())
{
    // don't forget to cast!
    AZombie z = (AZombie)zombieEnumerator.Current;
    Debug.Log(z.Name);
}
// Stubbs
// Bob
// Rob
// Freddy
// Jason
```

Before using the zombieEnumerator again we need to Reset() the object. This sets the Current value of the Enumerator to −1 so the next time we see MoveNext() in a while loop there will be an object to assign to Current.

Take care to notice how Enumerator and Enumerable are used. It's easy to get mixed up between the two interfaces.

7.13.3 What We've Learned

This has been a pretty heavy chapter about implementing the IEnumerator and IEnumerable interface. It's great practice and it's important to know how to go about implementing an interface from the C# library.

There are many cool tricks that can be added to your classes to make them more feature complete. This does require more thought and time, but in the end your classes will be more useful to the rest of the team of programmers you might be working with.

When to decide to implement one of these programming features is up to you and your team. Sometimes adding a feature might make a simple class too complex. If you're fine with using simple code to avoid the complexity, then you're free to do so. Thankfully, C# allows you to do pretty much anything that's allowed within the language. There aren't any hard and fast rules in the language that limit how it's used.

Interfaces not only tell you what is expected out of your class but also how to get it done. You're allowed to provide the data in any way you feel fit, but it's important to not provide something to start testing with.

On your own you should figure out how to add and remove items in a dynamic array in the IZombieEnumerator. You've implemented the required functions and properties to make the IEnumerator interface happy, but there's nothing limiting you from adding more features to the class beyond the IEnumerator interface.

7.14 Generics

When you create a new data structure, you're creating a strict organization and naming of your new data. This begins to run into problems when you need to make small modifications to that structure to suit multiple tasks. As your project gets more complex, your data will become more complex as well.

Thankfully as of C# version 2.0, generics were included to make data flow a bit more easily. In Unity 3D, we get used to doing casts with the following syntax where (float) takes the int 1 and converts it into the expected type to assign to f.

```
void UseCastTypes()
{
    float f = (float)1.0d;
    Debug.Log(f);
    // 1
}
```

Of course, this can be avoided if we start off with the correct type to assign by using 1.0f to indicate that we're using 1.0d as a float and not a double. Although many conversions are automatic between int and float, for example, not all conversions can be done for you.

When faced with making different data structures for different needs, you'll end up with more and more new data types. This leads to more and more mismatching of data. New data types diminish your object's ability to inherit from other objects; therefore, we lose the power of an object oriented programming language.

All forms of data we create are based on the Object class, and as such we're able to use Object as a common ground to cast them from. However, we run into problems when casting incorrectly or not knowing what to cast a value to. This is the problem with type-safe programming languages; using an object is an unfortunate work-around to which we should have a better method, to ensure that we don't run into mismatching data.

There is a way to make your data more flexible, and to do this we need generic types.

7.14.1 Generic Functions

Generics finally make sense now that we've looked at and used delegates and lambda expressions. Generics allow a function to adhere to the type-safe nature of C# but also allow you to pretend that it matters a little less. In the case of building a game involving a variety of monsters, we could quite readily use a system to organize various items we're using in our game. If we were to think in a world without generics, we'd have to make a few different systems for storing and categorizing items and monsters.

Generics are indicated by a function followed by an identifier to be used to indicate the type expected in the function.

7.14.1.1 A Basic Example

The following code produces a debug output of what was put into it.

```
/*   ┌──────────────────────┐   */
/*   │ the "generic"        │   */
/*   │ type is indicated    │   */
/*   │ starting with <T>    │   */
/*   │ which is used again  │   */
/*   │ in the parameter     │   */
/*   └──────────────────────┘   */
/*            ┌──┴──┐           */
/*            ↓     ↓           */
void Log<T>(T thing)
{
    string s = "thing is: " + thing.ToString();
    s += " type: " + thing.GetType().ToString();
    Debug.Log(s);
}
```

To indicate the use of a generic, the <T> follows the identifier for the function where T is used again in the parameter list. With this we are able to use an int a GameObject or Vector3 in the log<T> function. Rather, we can use any object that has a ToString() function and a type. The function log<T> (T thing), where T indicates a placeholder for a type, accepts both ints and GameObjects. Without the <T>, how would this work for various other data types? Let's look at a simple alteration that would instantly create a great deal of additional work.

```
void LogInt(int i)
{
    string s = "int is: " + i.ToString();
    Debug.Log(s);
}

void UseLogInt()
{
    LogInt(13);
    LogInt(new GameObject("Zombie"));
    LogInt((int)new GameObject("Zombie"));
}
```

Suppose we wrote a `LogInt` for the `int` type; it might look something like the above code. The function won't work even if we cast `GameObject` to `int` first. Zombies aren't just numbers after all.

Okay, so `LogInt` doesn't like `GameObjects` mixed in with its ints; that's fair enough. We should know not to mix types by now. Without generics we'd have to write a different function for every type that can be converted to a string and logged to the Console panel. To attempt this would be a huge waste of time, impractical at best. Thanks to `<T>` we don't need to.

7.14.1.2 Why *T*?

We use the identifier `T` to denote a use of the type expected to be reused elsewhere in the function. This is just a convention and not a strict rule. We could break the convention and traditionally trained programmers' brains by writing the same function again with another type identifier.

```
void LogCat<LOL>(LOL cat)
{
    Debug.Log("I can has " + cat.GetType().ToString());
}

 void UseLogCat()
{
    LogCat(new GameObject("GameObject"));
    // I can has UnityEngine.GameObject
}
```

This works just fine, but it's hardly appropriate. The `T` is purely a convention that has stuck around since it was first implemented. This is somewhat like how the for loop is always taught with `for (int i; i < 10; i++)`; in this case, `int i` just seemed appropriate. My best guess is `i` is either from integer or possibly index, which can be defined as a list of items.

Therefore, in this case, generic type `T` seemed to match well. Unlike so much of mathematics, the letters we use in programming have much less intrinsic meaning. If this were not the case, then we'd need a whole lot more letters. Therefore, in the end, sticking to the convention `T` will make any other programmer more easily understand what you're trying to do.

The applied cases often require specific reasons in which no other solution could be found. Creating and assigning delegates like this are often avoided due to the uncommon nature of needing to write specific code for the same function call. However, that is the entire reason for the anonymous expressions for being in use.

On occasion, when you have several classes inheriting behaviors from one another, you'll want one class to react differently than other classes when a function is called. Shoving a wooden stake through the heart of a vampire has a very different effect on a zombie. Calling the same `OnStakedThroughHeart()` function on both should result in different code being executed.

Normally, you'd just want to have both zombie and vampire use an interface which includes an `OnStakedThroughHeart` event; however, your player's character might not necessarily care into what monster he's pushing the pointy end of the stake, through. This is where the problem begins.

The code running the player will probably not want to check for each type and decide what to do based on the different types encountered.

7.14.2 Making Use of Generic Functions

One benefit of a generic type is the fact that you can write your own types of data, vampires or zombies, to use as generic types. To begin with a simple example, we'll build a simple zombie class. After that we'll look at using a generic function to swap data between two variables. What should be a simple task will prove to be an interesting use of what we've learned so far. We'll start with the generic function and then observe how it can be used for more than one type of data.

```
void Swap<T>(ref T first, ref T second)
{
    T temp = second;
    second = first;
    first = temp;
}
```

Create a simple generic function in your code that looks like the above. We have a function called Swap<T>, where T can be any sort of data. We use the ref T to indicate that we're making a reference to the data stored in the variable that's being used in the argument list directly, rather than making a copy of it. Then we make a T temp that holds onto the value of second. After that we tell second to take on the value stored at first. Then we tell first to take on the value that was stored locally in temp. Here's what the function looks like when in use.

```
void UseSwap()
{
    int[] ints = new int[] { 7, 13 };
    foreach (int i in ints)
        Log(i);
    //thing is: 7 type: System.Int32
    //thing is: 13 type: System.Int32
    Swap(ref ints[0], ref ints[1]);
    foreach (int i in ints)
        Log(i);
    //thing is: 13 type: System.Int32
    //thing is: 7 type: System.Int32

    string[] strings = new string[] { "First", "Second" };
    foreach (string s in strings)
        Log(s);
    //thing is: First type: System.String
    //thing is: Second type: System.String
    Swap(ref strings[0], ref strings[1]);
    foreach (string s in strings)
        Log(s);
    //thing is: Second type: System.String
    //thing is: First type: System.String
}
```

This prints out 7 and 13, followed by 13 and then 7 after the swap has been applied. Then we apply Swap(ref first, ref second); that swaps the values stored in the array. Without making any additional changes to the swap generic function, we're allowed to pass in an array of strings. This sends First and Second followed by Second and First in the Console, as you might expect. To make this more interesting, we'll create our own form of data.

```
class GenericHumanoid
{
    public string Name;
    public GenericHumanoid(string name)
    {
        Name = name;
    }
}

class GenericZombie : GenericHumanoid
{
    public GenericZombie(string name) : base(name)
    {
    }

    public override string ToString()
    {
        return "A Zombie named " + Name;
    }
}
class GenericVampire : GenericHumanoid
{
    public GenericVampire(string name) : base(name)
    {
    }

    public override string ToString()
    {
        return "A Vampire named " + Name;
    }
}
```

Using a GenericHumanoid class that stores a Name variable we'll want a constructor with a string argument to accept a name. Then, to make the class return a more useful value when it's translated to a string, the ToString() function is overridden to return A Zombie or Vampire named Name.

```
void UseSwapGenerics()
{
    GenericHumanoid[] humanoids = new GenericHumanoid[2];
    humanoids[0] = new GenericZombie("Stubbs");
    humanoids[1] = new GenericVampire("D");
    Swap(ref humanoids[0], ref humanoids[1]);
    foreach (GenericHumanoid humanoid in humanoids)
        Debug.Log(humanoid);
    // A Vampire named D
    // A Zombie named Stubbs
}
```

The UseSwapGenerics() function, as in the above code, will print out A Vampire named D and A Zombie named Stubbs. This brings up a few questions about how the <T> works. What happens when we mix data types?

```
GenericZombie first = new GenericZombie("Rob");
string second = "Jackson";
Debug.Log(first + " " + second);
Swap(ref first, ref second);
// Error CS0411
// The type arguments for method 'Generics.Swap<T>(ref T, ref T)'
// cannot be inferred from the usage.
// Try specifying the type arguments explicitly.Assembly
```

For instance, if we try to use the above code with a string and a GenericZombie, we'll get an error. The type arguments for method 'Generics.Swap<T>(ref T, ref T)' cannot be inferred from the usage. Try specifying the type arguments explicitly.

When we try to mix different types, we won't be able to infer what we want to happen. When we tell a zombie that it's now a word, it's not likely to turn into anything comprehensible. This is very important for a C# to be able to parse your code. In the end there's no simple way to convert between different types that have very little in common. It's up to you to keep things organized in such a ways you won't have to worry about swapping types that don't match.

7.14.3 Generic Types

Speaking of types, a generic type can be created. You can make a data type that has no specific type to start off with. In particular, these come in handy when we want to organize data in a particular fashion. For instance, if we wanted to create a short list of three zombies, we might want to create new data, that is, three zombies, but why restrict this data type to just zombies?

```
class ThreeThings<T>
{
    public T FirstThing;
    public T SecondThing;
    public T ThirdThing;
    public ThreeThings(T first, T second, T third)
    {
        FirstThing = first;
        SecondThing = second;
        ThirdThing = third;
    }
    public override string ToString()
    {
        return "1:" + FirstThing + " 2:" + SecondThing + " 3:" + ThirdThing;
    }
}
```

Start off with a new class with a constructor for holding onto three different things of the same type. The declaration of ThreeThings<T> infers that we're going to have an object that has objects of a single generic type. We'll be able to create a new class ThreeThings to hold three ints, floats, strings, or even GenericZombies.

Next we'll want to create a new ThreeThings object in our Start() function and assign three different zombies to it using its constructor.

```
ThreeThings things = new ThreeThings(
//Using the generic type 'Generics.ThreeThings<T>' requires 1 type arguments
```

But wait; we're getting an error! So using the class constructor for a generic type involves a type argument. What does this mean? A <GenericsZombie> is required to declare the type of generic. This means that when we deal with generic types, we need to inform ThreeThings what it's going to be. Therefore, to fix this, we need to tell <T> what it is.

```
ThreeThings<GenericZombie> things = new ThreeThings<GenericZombie>(
new GenericZombie("Bob"),
new GenericZombie("Rob"),
new GenericZombie("White"));
Debug.Log(things.ToString());
// 1:A Zombie named Bob 2:A Zombie named Rob 3:A Zombie named White
```

We need to tell ThreeThings that it's going to be dealing with <GenericZombie> as the generic type. However, there's a more clever trick to dealing with generic types.

7.14.4 Var

Normally, when we use types, we'd create a type by assigning it explicitly. For instance, zombie first-Zombie = new zombie("stubs") is an explicit type. It's a zombie and we knew that as it was created because it's a zombie class object. This is the same int a = 10;, which means that a is an int and it's assigned 10 as a value. This changes when the type can be anything and we don't necessarily know what it's going to be ahead of time.

To the computer, it's saying "The thing that SomeThings might turn into is going to be a generic of what ThreeThings is about to be assigned." We have to remind ourselves that computers aren't clever enough to figure this out. However, we can work with generics in a more straightforward way with the var keyword.

```
GenericZombie first = new GenericZombie("Stubbs");
GenericZombie second = new GenericZombie("Frankenstein");
GenericZombie third = new GenericZombie("Michael");
/*    ┌───────────────────────────────┐    */
/* ┌─┤ Assumes the type after assigned │    */
/* └─┘└───────────────────────────────┘    */
var someThings = new ThreeThings<GenericZombie>(first, second, third);
Debug.Log(someThings);
// 1:A Zombie named Stubbs 2:A Zombie named Frankenstein 3:A Zombie named Michael
```

Here we use var someThings to tell the computer to expect any data type to store into someThings. That's right, *any* data type. There are some limitations, as one might expect with anything to do with computers, but var is a very open keyword. The var keyword means to implicitly get a type once it's been assigned. Only after the actual object is created and assigned to the identifier that was created with var will the identifier turn into a type. For instance, we can test this with a simple integer.

```
var whatAmI = 1;
Debug.Log(whatAmI.GetType());
// System.Int32
```

Every object has a GetType() function that returns the data type of the variable in question. Therefore, when we create var whatAmI and assign it 1, which is an integer, we get the following output to the Unity's Console panel:

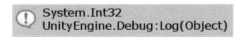

As it turns out, System.Int32 is the integer that we've been using all this time. What happens when we do the same with someThings?

```
Debug.Log(someThings.GetType());
// Generics+ThreeThings`1[Generics+GenericZombie]
```

Well, it's a bit less clear, but we do know that it involves a Generics class, ThreeThings, and a 1, which indicates how many different types are involved along with a Zombie. Quite informative. Therefore, if var allows us to deal with any different type, why don't we use it more often? To be honest, the best reason is not because of code efficiency. The main reason why we don't want to use var so often is because of clarity. For instance, we can use the following code and give horrible nightmares to any programmer trying to follow our code.

```
int TellMeLies(float f)
{
    return (int)f;
}

void UseTellMeLies()
{
    var imAFloat - TellMeLies(11.8f);
    Debug.Log(imAFloat);
    // 11
}
```

This sends 11 to the Console panel; 11.8f is certainly not 11, and as such the var imAFloat is indeed telling lies. Were we to tell the truth from the beginning and use int imAFloat, we might have a clue right away that something is amiss with the naming of the integer imAFloat. This should prompt a meeting with the programmer concerned about naming variables clearly.

This can get a bit murky with generic classes, which don't have a specific constructor, but luckily the compiler will catch things for us.

```
class Stuff<T>
{
    T thing;
    public void AssignThing(T something)
    {
        thing = something;
    }
}
```

Here we can start with a generic class called Stuff<T>, that holds onto T thing. Then we make an available function afterward to assign T thing after the class has been instanced.

```
var what = new Stuff<int>();
what.AssignThing(1.0f);
// cannot convert from 'float' to 'int'
```

If we try the following assignment to assign a float value 1.0f to the Stuff<int>, we get an appropriate error telling us that we can't assign a float to an int.

Assets\Generics.cs(256,26): error CS1503: Argument 1: cannot convert from 'float' to 'int'

This is a good thing as we'd be losing any numbers when converting a float to an int value. Therefore, there are some limitations indeed when it comes to dealing with generic types. They start off being generic, but once assigned they change into the assigned type and must be used accordingly. When Stuff or any generic class is created, it's referred to as an open type. Once it's been assigned with <type>, it's then considered a closed type. Once a generic has been assigned, it can't be reassigned.

7.14.5 Multiple Generic Values

This is all fine and dandy, but what if we have more than one type that might be assigned later on?

```
class TwoThings<T, U>
{
    public T FirstThing;
    public U SecondThing;
    public void AssignThings(T first, U second)
    {
        FirstThing = first;
        SecondThing = second;
    }
}
```

As a good programmer, flexibility and forthought should anticipate using more than a single type in a generic class. The above code uses <T, U> to assign the first and second types. You might consider a zombie followed by its rank in the zombie army or a glass of water and its percentage of fullness. These tasks can be completed in any way you feel needed.

```
var twoThings = new TwoThings<int, double>();
twoThings.AssignThings(3, 30.0);
var differetThings = new TwoThings<GenericZombie, float>();
differetThings.AssignThings(new GenericZombie("Stubbs"), 1.0f);
```

Once one instance of TwoThings has been assigned; you're able to assign the next instance of TwoThings to two different types. Each one stands on its own, but after they have been assigned, they can't necessarily interact with one another in any expected way. This feature should not detract from the overall usefulness of a generic type or function.

This works in a similar way for a generic function.

```
void LogTwoThings<T, U>(T firstThing, U secondThing)
{
    string log = "FirstThing is a " + firstThing.GetType();
    log += " SecondThing is a " + secondThing.GetType();
    Debug.Log(log);
}
```

The function shown simply takes two of any time and then prints them out to the Console log.

```
void UseLogTwoThings()
{
    LogTwoThings(3, new GenericVampire("Vlad"));
    // FirstThing is a System.Int32 SecondThing is a Generics+GenericVampire
}
```

The first argument takes on the type of T and the second is assigned to the type of U. We can combine the examples in this chapter to fully demonstrate how generics can avoid type confusion.

```
class GetTwoThings<T, U> : TwoThings<T, U>
{
    public T GetFirstThing()
    {
        return FirstThing;
    }

    public U GetSecondThing()
    {
        return SecondThing;
    }
}
```

Here we use T and U as return values for the GetTwoThings<T, U> class. We can also see that inheriting from TwoThings we need to include the <T, U> type declarations. The public T GetFirstThing() returns the FirstThing, and public U GetSecondThing() returns the value stored in SecondThing. We can use LogTwoThings<T, U> to log the types of the objects that were used in the GetTwoThings class.

```
var gotTwoThings = new GetTwoThings<GenericZombie, float>();
gotTwoThings.AssignThings(new GenericZombie("White"), 3.0f);
LogTwoThings(gotTwoThings.GetFirstThing(), gotTwoThings.GetSecondThing());
// FirstThing is a Generics+GenericZombie SecondThing is a System.Single
```

We should get used to where the T appears throughout the function or class in which it makes its appearance. Once the type for T is assigned in the declaration of the class or function, T becomes whatever type it was assigned.

It might be tempting to use var as a return type. The convenience of being inspecific when passing data around could be used to get data from a function. However, C# has other mechanisms in place that allow for this and var isn't one of them.

```
var ReturnAVar()
{
    The contextual keyword 'var' may only appear within a local variable declaration or in script code
}
```

7.14.6 Anonymous Objects

In a practical sense, you should always know the data types you're working with. When bundling data to pass between objects it's sometimes easier to skip the work of writing a struct or class and use something more convenient.

```
var things = new { someInt = 3, someClass = this };
Debug.Log("What is things?" + things);
// What is things?{ someInt = 3, someClass = Generics (Chapter7_14.Generics) }
```

An anonymous object can be assigned to a var with the notation new {}; syntax. Objects in the var are named with identifiers without a type. From the example seen above someInt = 3 skips it's type declaration.

```
var moreThings = new
{
    someIntArray = new int[] { 1, 2, 3 },
    someZombie = new GenericZombie("Stubbs"),
    someQueue = new System.Collections.Queue()
};
Debug.Log("MoreThings: " + moreThings);
// MoreThings: { someIntArray = System.Int32[],
// someZombie = A Zombie named Stubbs,
// someQueue = System.Collections.Queue }
```

Any sort of data can be packed into an anonymous object. This includes other anonymous objects.

```
void acceptAThing(object thing)
{
    Debug.Log(thing);
}

acceptAThing(new { things, moreThings });

/* formatted for readability:
 *
 * { things = {
 *     someInt = 3,
 *     someClass = Generics(Chapter7_14.Generics)
 *   },
 *   moreThings = {
 *     someIntArray = System.Int32[],
 *     someZombie = A Zombie named Stubbs,
 *     someQueue = System.Collections.Queue
 *   }
 * }
 */
```

The anonymous object can be passed to a function through a system.object type. Not knowing what each type in the anonymous object can lead to errors when unboxing the data. Aside from the name, it's easy to handle the anonymous data with functions that don't necessarily know what the variable is. Using a function in this way is unrecommended and may lead to bad habits, but it's interesting to know.

```
object returnsAThing()
{
    return new { things, moreThings };
}

Debug.Log("Can't use var, so lets try object:" + returnsAThing());
/* formatted for readability:
 * "Can't use var, so lets try object:"
 * { things = {
 *   someInt = 3,
 *   someClass = Generics(Chapter7_14.Generics)
 *   },
 *   moreThings = {
 *   someIntArray = System.Int32[],
 *   someZombie = A Zombie named Stubbs,
 *   someQueue = System.Collections.Queue
 *   }
 * }
 */
```

This may lead you to think that you can use object as a return type. This is possible and there isn't anything that disallows this abuse of object. In practice this should be avoided; strong typing is one of the strengths of C# and abusing object acts as a work around. It's preferable to avoid awkward code like the above, but again, it's interesting to know it's possible.

```
things.someInt++;
// properties of the anonymous object are
// read only.
```

The anonymous object might seem to have a lot of flexibility, however the properties in the anonymous object are read-only and cannot be changed once the object has been created. Not all properties in the anonymous object are read-only.

```
moreThings.someQueue.Enqueue(30);
moreThings.someQueue.Enqueue(20);
moreThings.someQueue.Enqueue(10);
Debug.Log(moreThings.someQueue.Peek());
// 30
moreThings.someQueue.Dequeue();
Debug.Log(moreThings.someQueue.Peek());
// 20
moreThings.someQueue.Dequeue();
Debug.Log(moreThings.someQueue.Peek());
// 10
```

The queue can be used as usual. Only POD (plain old data) types become read-only. Reference type objects are usable as expected.

```
things.someClass.LogInt(10);
// int is: 10
```

```
var readOnlyThings = new { floatThing = 1.0f, intThing = 1 };
readOnlyThings.floatThing = 10f;
readOnlyThings.intThing = 10;
```

The float and int type values cannot be modified once assigned. Anonymous objects have a place in very limited situations where a declared type may be cumbersome. When a multitude of data needs to be passed between two functions near one another an anonymous object may prove to be more convenient. Just make sure to leave clear comments when using one to enlighten others as to why the object was necessary.

7.14.7 What We've Learned

This chapter has covered a great deal about generics. In short, "generic" is the term given to a type that can be assigned once the function or the class it appears in is used.

```
void LogTwoThings<T, U>(T firstThing, U secondThing)
```

We can change the order in the signature from the declaration of the generic identifiers. Of course, this leads to confusion, so it's best to use them in order, although technically there are no adverse behaviors. The var keyword is handy, but mainly when dealing with generic types. It's important to try to use explicitly typed variables where possible. Generics should only be used when there are no other alternatives. It's good to know that you have options available to you when you find yourself cornered by your own data types.

Making collections of data by writing classes for each type is inefficient and excludes the ability to reuse code. When you need to make different functions for different situations that seem to behave in practically the same way, it's a good opportunity to look at a generic method to take care of the task at hand.

The main drawback of the generic methods is that once you start using them, it's difficult to break the habit. If your code begins with too many generic types, you'll end up writing code that depends on var and <T> in a myriad of different places.

This leads to type conflicts that are hard to track down. Debugging code with many generic classes and methods is difficult and can lead to a great deal of wasted time. In short, use them only when you have to.

Unity's GameObject describes a function as GetComponent<T>();, where <T> is a generic type.

```
var t = GetComponent<Transform>();
if (t is Transform)
{
    t.localPosition = new Vector3(1, 0, 0);
}
```

We might use the GetComponent function in a script to get a component in the game object our script is attached to. After we get the Transform component, it can be set. The alternative use is GetComponent(typeof (Transform));, which is a bit more verbose, but does the same thing.

7.15 Events

For many simple tasks, Unity 3D has provided some useful functions that update objects and execute when the object is first created in a world. There are event handlers in place ready for any mouse clicks which take place in the UI.

When an object receives a condition to act upon, any actions are usually limited to that object. With the tools we already know, we can probably find some way to spread out a message pretty easily, but they'd be awkward and use various static functions. This leads to spaghetti code: interdependent function calls leading to difficult debugging and long nights wondering why everything is broken.

Having a single large set of code that acts as the central switching board for the entire game becomes very cumbersome very quickly.

Delegates allow for many different cool tricks. Delegates with generic types allow for even more cool things, most notably, the event. An event acts as a container or a handy place to put any number of functions. When the event is called, all of the functions assigned to it are then called. It's a great system to notify another function that something has occurred that you were waiting for.

We identify a function using a declaration such as `public void functionName() {//code statements}`, something we've been doing already. Delegates are declared using `delegate void delegateName();` depending on what you're trying to accomplish. First we'll start with the minimal parts to explain what's required, and then we'll go into an example of why it's useful.

7.15.1 A Basic Example

Starting the Events_Scene in unity, locate the Events script on the like-named game object.

Normally the EventHandler is named based on what sort of event it will be handling. We'll decide on better names after we know how they're used.

```csharp
class Dispatcher
{
    /*   indicates type of method */
    /*   we are declaring         */
    /*           ↓                 */
    public delegate void Handler();
    /*                      ↓      */
    /*        ┌──────────────┘     */
    /*      Handler is the type    */
    /*          ┌┘                 */
    /*          ↓                  */
    public Handler HandleDelegate;
    public event Handler HandleEvent;

    public void CallHandlers()
    {
        /*   check if handle delegate */
        /*   has an assignment        */
        /*          ↓                 */
        if (HandleDelegate != null)
        {
            /* call function assigned */
            /* to the delegate handler */
            HandleDelegate();
        }

        /*   check if handle delegate */
        /*   has an assignment        */
        /*          ↓                 */
        if (HandleEvent != null)
        {
            /* call function assigned */
            /* to the event handler   */
            HandleEvent();
        }
    }
}
```

The statement public delegate void Handler(); is a type declaration. After creating the type, the variable HandleDelegate is created. To wait for the delegate to be handled we'll create a new Listener class that has a function that will be assigned to the HandleDelegate variable. The event is declared using similar syntax to the delegate with the addition of the event keyword.

In many cases we assumed we can only assign data to a variable. Delegates have functions assigned to them. When the delegate is called, the functions assigned are called. The assignment comes with one condition: the signatures must match. Both the delegate's declaration and the function assigned to the delegate must have matching signatures. Let's create another new class called Listener, which should look like the following:

```
class Listener
{
    private string Name;

    public Listener(string name)
    {
        Name = name;
    }

    public void OnDelegateHandled()
    {
        Debug.Log(Name + "'s Delegate Was Handled");
    }
}
```

When Listener is created, we assign the OnDelegateHandled() event to the Dispatcher's HandleDelegate and HandleEvent variables.

```
/* attach the dispatcher to ourself. */
Dispatcher dispatcher = new Dispatcher();
/* make a couple of listeners to wait for the delegate or event */
Listener sigmond = new Listener("Sigmund");
Listener frasier = new Listener("Frasier");

dispatcher.HandleDelegate += sigmond.OnDelegateHandled;
dispatcher.HandleDelegate = new Dispatcher.Handler(frasier.OnDelegateHandled);
```

Once the dispatcher and the listeners are created, we can assign delegates in one of two ways. The first is using the += operator, the other is with a new Dispatcher.Handler() function initializer. However, something interesting happens with the second assignment.

```
dispatcher.CallHandlers();
// Frasier's Delegate Was Handled
```

Only Frasier's Delegate Was Handled, Sigmond didn't have his OnDelegateHandled function called when the dispatcher has its CallHandlers() function invoked. The HandleDelegate lost any previous assignments when new Dispatcher.Handler() was called. Clearing out a delegate is something allowed.

```
dispatcher.HandleDelegate = null;
dispatcher.CallHandlers();
// nothing is called.
```

We can assign null to the `HandleDelegate` handler, and when `CallHandlers()` is invoked, nothing happens. The `HandleDelegate` has been cleared of any functions to call. By marking the `HandleEvent` handler with the event keyword we prevent misuse of the `HandleEvent` variable.

```
dispatcher.HandleEvent = new Dispatcher.Handler(sigmond.OnDelegateHandled);
// The event 'Events.Dispatcher.HandleEvent' can only appear on the
// left hand side of += or -= (except when used from within the type 'Events.Dispatcher')
```

The error tells us we can only use the += or -= operators when making assignments to an event. So the event keyword is more like a special case accessor keyword for delegates. We see the same error when trying to set the `HandleEvent` to null.

```
dispatcher.HandleEvent = null;
```

The event protected delegate can only have += or −= used to assign functions.

```
dispatcher.HandleEvent += sigmond.OnDelegateHandled;
dispatcher.HandleEvent += new Dispatcher.Handler(frasier.OnDelegateHandled);
dispatcher.CallHandlers();
// Sigmund's Delegate Was Handled
// Frasier's Delegate Was Handled
```

This protects the variable from mishandling or accidentally clearing anything already assigned to the event handler. To remove a function from the handler, the −= operator is used.

```
dispatcher.HandleEvent -= frasier.OnDelegateHandled;
dispatcher.CallHandlers();
// Sigmund's Delegate Was Handled
```

By removing `Frasier.OnDelegateHandled` from the `HandleEvent` with -=, only Sigmund's delegate handler is called. Delegates and events operate in essentially the same way. The main difference is related to the protection level at which delegates and events are allowed.

7.15.2 A Proper Event

The .NET Framework has many conformant procedures to which your code needs to comply. Microsoft has described many different best practices that cover everything from variable names to events. Therefore, it's somewhat necessitated by Microsoft that we look at how we should be writing our events should we want to comply with proper code procedures.

```
public delegate void ProperEventHandler(object sender, EventArgs args);

class ProperDispatcher
{
    public delegate void ProperEventHandler(object sender, EventArgs args);
    public event ProperEventHandler ProperEvent;
    public void CallProperEvent()
    {
        ProperEvent?.Invoke(this, new EventArgs());
    }
}
```

Let's add the above delegate to our `EventDispatcher` class just after the old `EventHandler`. This has the addition of object sender and `EventArgs` args. We'll get into what these are in a moment.

After the delegate has been declared outside of the class scope, add in a handler for the delegate in the scope of the class.

```
class ProperListener
{
    private string Name;

    public ProperListener(string name)
    {
        Name = name;
    }

    public void OnProperEvent(object sender, EventArgs args)
    {
        Debug.Log(Name + "'s event from " + sender + " " + args);
    }
}

public event ProperEventHandler ProperEvent;
```

The above code should follow our MyEvent; just for sake of consistency. Next we'll want to make our event more useful by adding EventArgs, or rather Event Arguments, so our new event can have some additional functionality. EventArgs are used to pass parameters to anyone listening to the event. Before we can create a custom EventArg, we need to add in a new directive.

```
ProperDispatcher dispatcher = new ProperDispatcher();
ProperListener listener = new ProperListener("Sigmund");
dispatcher.ProperEvent += listener.OnProperEvent;
dispatcher.CallProperEvent();
// Sigmund's event from Events+ProperDispatcher System.EventArgs
```

The arguments object and EventArgs are a part of a conformant .NET event, but what are we supposed to do with them?

7.15.3 EventArgs

The system directive gives us access to a new class called an EventArg.

```
using System;
using UnityEngine;
```

The EventArg type comes from System, so to make a class based in it, we need to add the using System; at the class scope. Once this is done, we'll want to create a new class at the global scope of the EventDispatcher.

```
class MessageEventArgs : EventArgs
{
    public string Message;

    public MessageEventArgs(string message)
    {
        Message = message;
    }
}
```

This is a pretty simple class. Once the new `MessageEventArgs` class is created or instanced, we should assign string message in the constructor. It's important to note here is that the customized event arguments allow for specific event information to be passed to anyone who is listening for the event.

To dispatch an event with the new `MessageEventArgs` object we change the delegate signature to emit the `MessageEventArgs` type.

```
class ProperEventArgDispatcher
{
    public delegate void ProperEventHandler(object sender, MessageEventArgs args);
    public event ProperEventHandler ProperEvent;
    public void CallProperEvent()
    {
        ProperEvent?.Invoke(this, new MessageEventArgs("Listen to me."));
    }
}
```

Inside of the `ProperEventArgListener` class, the `OnProperEvent` function called by the event must match the signature of the `ProperEventHandler`.

```
class ProperEventArgListener
{
    private string Name;

    public ProperEventArgListener(string name)
    {
        Name = name;
    }

    public void OnProperEvent(object sender, MessageEventArgs args)
    {
        Debug.Log(Name + "'s event from " + sender + " said: " + args.Message);
    }
}
```

Now dispatcher has MyEvent calling the EventListeners CallMeMaybe function and ProperEvent calls the CallMePlease function. Finally, in the EventDispatcher, we need to add the ProperEvent to the if statement that makes calls.

```
ProperEventArgDispatcher dispatcher = new ProperEventArgDispatcher();
ProperEventArgListener listener = new ProperEventArgListener("Frasier");
dispatcher.ProperEvent += listener.OnProperEvent;
dispatcher.CallProperEvent();
// Frasier's event from Events+ProperEventArgDispatcher said: Listen to me.
```

The `MessageEventArgs()` object is a class, so it needs to be instanced with new before it's used. In the `ProperEvent` argument list, we use this as the sender and new `MessageEventArgs()` as the second argument. These two values are passed to the listener.

We've got some interesting concepts here that we can use. The best situation is to have a clean event-driven game. Rather than wait for conditions to be met and perform some sort of task, it's better to do nothing until an event happens. This approach ensures we avoid having too many scripts updating all at once. On a PC this might not be an issue; however, you'll have a much lower processor ceiling once you want to put your game on a mobile device.

7.15.4 Generic EventArgs

We can have multiple events derive from the single delegate type. To do this we need to use a generic type to declare the delegate.

```
public delegate void EventHandler<TEventArgs>(object sender, TEventArgs args);
public event EventHandler<MessageEventArgs> MessageEvent;
public event EventHandler<NumerEventArgs> NumberEvent;
```

Once the EventHandler delegate is created with <TEventArgs> in the description we use the generic type in place of a strong type for the arguments list. This means a MessageEvent and a NumberEvent can both derive from the delegate EventHandler. Each one replaces the TEventArgs with its own specific EventArg type. But why stop there?

```
public event EventHandler<GenericEventArgs<string>> StringEvent;
public event EventHandler<GenericEventArgs<int>> IntEvent;
public class GenericEventArgs<T> : EventArgs
{
    public T Value;
    public GenericEventArgs(T arg)
    {
        Value = arg;
    }
}
```

Using a generic value in the GenericEventArgs allows us to interface with the delegate EventHandler with a GenericEventArg. A type does need to be specified when the event is created. The matching type must also be included when creating the argument.

```
public void CallGenericString()
{
    StringEvent?.Invoke(this, new GenericEventArgs<string>("Generic generic arg!"));
}

public void CallGenericInt()
{
    IntEvent?.Invoke(this, new GenericEventArgs<int>(42));
}
```

Likewise, the listener for the generic types must also include event listeners with matching signatures.

```
public void OnGenericMessage(object sender, MessageEventArgs message)
{
    Debug.Log(Name + " got message " + message.Message + " from " + sender);
}

public void OnGenericNumber(object sender, GenericEventDispatcher.NumerEventArgs number)
{
    Debug.Log(Name + " got number " + number.Number + " from " + sender);
}

public void OnGenericEvent(object sender, GenericEventDispatcher.GenericEventArgs<string> args)
{
    Debug.Log(Name + " got value " + args.Value + " from " + sender);
}

public void OnGenericEvent(object sender, GenericEventDispatcher.GenericEventArgs<int> args)
{
    Debug.Log(Name + " got value " + args.Value + " from " + sender);
}
```

When using the events we get quite a lot of flexibility from just a few type definitions.

```
GenericEventDispatcher dispatcher = new GenericEventDispatcher();
GenericListener sigmund = new GenericListener("Sigmund");
dispatcher.MessageEvent += sigmund.OnGenericMessage;
dispatcher.NumberEvent += sigmund.OnGenericNumber;
dispatcher.IntEvent += sigmund.OnGenericEvent;
dispatcher.StringEvent += sigmund.OnGenericEvent;

dispatcher.CallMessageEvent();
// Sigmund got message Generic Message from Events+GenericEventDispatcher

dispatcher.CallNumberEvent();
// Sigmund got number 3 from Events+GenericEventDispatcher

dispatcher.CallGenericInt();
// Sigmund got value 42 from Events+GenericEventDispatcher

dispatcher.CallGenericString();
// Sigmund got value Generic generic arg! from Events+GenericEventDispatcher
```

The `sigmund.OnGenericEvent` is assigned to both `IntEvent` and `StringEvent`. Proper overloaded functions are provided for each. The `GenericEventArgs<int>` and `GenericEventArgs <string>` allow the assignment to find which function is invoked when the different events are called.

7.15.5 What We've Learned

It's important to use events in an intuitive manner. Generics add flexibility when we create an event based on a flexible delegate declaration. The use of the event over a delegate is two main reasons. First events add a level of protection, the second is to allow multiple derivatives from a single delegate type.

7.16 Extension Functions

When writing new classes, a classic programmer's mentality would be to write a single monolithic class that handles many different tasks in a single complex algorithm. As a programmer, you might approach many different problems with a single complex solution. The better, more Unity-friendly approach is quite the opposite.

When we think about building a solution for a complex problem, it's sometimes easier to start with a generalized solution. For instance, should we want to build a complex behavior for managing a group of zombies and humans chasing and eating one another, the first thought might be to write a crowd manager class that keeps track of each zombie and human, and then moves each one around based on a set of parameters.

This approach leads to what might be a single solution, since we know everything about everyone in a scene. Writing this might be a difficult task, but getting it right would be quite an accomplishment; unfortunately, there are a few drawbacks. First off, now you have a single complex algorithm to debug, should small problems arise.

Next you run into an inflexibility problem. Rewriting anything to gain different behaviors turns into adding additional layers of complexity. Additional layers in an already complex class easily introduces more bugs and makes fixing those bugs more and more difficult.

The worst part of the monolithic approach comes when someone else needs to open your class and interpret what's going on. The more complex your code is, the more difficult it is to explain. What makes things worse, the longer your algorithm, the more the explanation that is required. Usually nobody likes to read every little comment, even if you wrote detailed comments throughout your code.

7.16.1 Extensions

When we're working with the built-in Unity 3D types such as GameObject, we're unable to extend those classes. If we try to use the following code, we'll get an interesting error:

```
public class MyGameObject : GameObject
{
}
```

> ⬧ class MyGameObject
>
> 'MyGameObject': cannot derive from sealed type 'GameObject'

This produces the following output: `'MyGameObject'`: cannot derive from sealed type `'GameObject'`

A `sealed` class means that its final, and no one is allowed to extend or make further modifications to the `GameObject` class. However, it doesn't mean that we can't give the GameObject new functions. For instance, if we wanted `gameObject.NewTrick();`, we're able to do this through Extensions methods.

7.16.2 A Basic Example

Let's start with the ExtensionFunctions_Scene and open the ExtensionFunctions.cs script on the object of the same name class.

At the top we add `using Tricks;` to enable the `ExtensionFunctions: MonoBehaviour` class to use the contents of the namespace tacked to the bottom of this class. In a more regular case, you should put the namespace into another file, but for clarity we're just going to merge these two objects together in this file.

In the namespace, we need to add a new class where we're going to be making use of our GameObject class.

```
namespace Tricks
{
    using UnityEngine;
    public static class GameObjectExtensions
    {
        public static void NewTrick(this GameObject gameObject)
        {   /*                                              ↓    */
            /*          reference this gameObject           ┘    */
            /*                  ↓                                */
            Debug.Log(gameObject.name + " has a new trick!");
        }
    }
}
```

Here we use `static class GameObjectExtensions`, but this could be anything. So long as the name is descriptive as to what it's going to be doing. The `namespace Tricks` indicates a new group of functions or objects. The .NET library contains many namespaces already: `System`, `System.Collections`, and Unity 3D's `UnityEngine` namespace. Inside of the static `GameObjectExtensions` class, we add a new `static` function that will extend the sealed `GameObject` class.

The public static void NewTrick() is our extension function. To extend the GameObject, we use the argument this GameObject gameObject where the this keyword informs C# that we're writing an extension method. In the argument list, we use the identifier gameObject that appears in the function as gameObject.name. This NewTrick() simply prints the name of the gameObject and "has a new trick!" to the Console.

```
GameObject go = new GameObject("Penn");
go.NewTrick();
// Penn has a new trick!
```

Back in the MonoBehaviour attached to the ExtensionFunctions game object in the ExtensionFunctions_Scene we are shown (Extension) void NewTrick() in the list of functions available to the gameObject type. Perhaps NewTrick() is not the most exciting trick for gameObject to have, but it is a good beginning. Selecting the NewTrick(); and running the game prints "Penn has a new trick!" to the Console.

Any additional arguments must come after the argument where the keyword this is used. Depending on the type that follows this in the first argument, you can change the function to extend a different sealed class.

```
public static void Move(this GameObject gameObject, Vector3 position)
{
    gameObject.transform.position = position;
}
```

Adding Vector3 position as a second parameter and then using gameObject.transform.position = position; will tell the gameObject to update its position. In use, we can use the following code to move gameObject to Vector3(0, 1, 0); when the Move() extension function is used. Even though the first parameter is the gameObject itself, it doesn't show up when it's used. The syntax using the first parameter referring to the object changes the function into an extension function for the object following the keyword this in the first parameter of the function.

```
go.Move(new Vector3(0, 1, 0));
// changes position to 0, 1, 0
```

Extension functions can be applied to any sealed class. When working with third-party libraries, it's often useful to add your own functions to classes which you don't have source code for.

The static keyword is necessary to make the function appear in any context. The same goes for the class in which the Extension function appears. The static class that the function is written in is a side effect of a function not being able live on its own. A function is always a member of a class, even though it might not be related to the class in which it's written in.

An extension function can technically be written into any static class, though it would be confusing if they appeared in an unrelated class. Clear naming practices are just as important as ever, when naming functions unrelated to the class they exist in.

Because of extensions, it's easy to keep adding to a sealed class. Often if you're able to do, it's far better to add the functions to the class itself. This sidesteps the necessity of writing any number of extension functions. This doesn't just have to work on a gameObject.

```
public static void Reset(this Transform transform)
{
    transform.position = Vector3.zero;
    transform.rotation = Quaternion.identity;
    transform.localScale = Vector3.one;
}
```

In the above example, we can use gameObject.transform.Reset(); to move the gameObject or any other object in the scene that has a transform to the origin as well as reset it's rotation and scale. However, this does highlight the fact that Reset() should probably appear in a different class called TransformExtensions, or should it?

Functions can be overloaded, so we can have more than one Reset() extension function in the class.

```
public static void Reset(this GameObject gameObject)
{
    gameObject.transform.position = Vector3.zero;
    gameObject.transform.rotation = Quaternion.identity;
    gameObject.transform.localScale = Vector3.one;
}
```

Here we have a Reset() function that works on both the GameObject and the Transform types. Perhaps we should rename GameObjectExtension to something more like GameExtensions. Naming classes and functions is such a big part of writing code. Going back into your code only to rename a class or function is called refactoring.

7.16.3 Overloading with Extensions

In addition to adding new functions to the Transform or gameObject through extensions, you're also able to create new overloads to functions already in place. When the new Reset() extension is invoked, the gameObject moves to the origin of the scene. This includes if it's parented to an object that's moved away from the origin.

```
public static void SetParent(this Transform child, Transform parent, bool resetToWorldPosition = true)
{
    child.SetParent(parent);
    if (resetToWorldPosition)
    {
        child.Reset();
    }
}
```

The Transform object has a SetParent() function which has a few overloads in place. The first option sets the parent, but retains the child's local position rotation and scale. The second set parent retains the world position after parenting. The function shown above sets the child to the origin of the scene after the parent is set.

```
GameObject go = new GameObject("Child");
Debug.Log(go.transform.localPosition);
// (0.0, 0.0, 0.0)
go.transform.position = Vector3.one;
Debug.Log(go.transform.localPosition);
// (1.0, 1.0, 1.0)
GameObject parent = new GameObject("Parent");
parent.transform.position = new Vector3(0,0,1);
go.transform.SetParent(parent.transform, resetToWorldPosition: true);
Debug.Log(go.transform.localPosition);
// (0.0, 0.0, -1.0)
```

The code fragment above shows a new Child gameObject created at the origin. After it's created, it's repositioned to 1.0 1.0 1.0. Now the object is no longer at the scene's origin. A "Parent" object is created then moved to 0,0,1, a single unit above the origin. When we set the parent we use our overloaded version of `SetParent` on the `Transform` and write out `resetToWorldPosition: true` as the second parameter. When we check the local position of the child it reports 0.0 0.0 −1.0, which is −1 from the position of the parent putting the child back at the origin of the scene.

```
parent.transform.position = new Vector3(0,0,1);
//go.transform.SetParent(parent.transform, resetToWorldPosition: true);
go.transform.SetParent(parent.transform, true);
Debug.Log(go.transform.localPosition);
// (1.0, 1.0, 0.0)
```

There are two overloads that use the signature `(Transform, bool)` pattern. The built-in version uses the bool to indicate whether or not the child will retain its relative world position. Using that option will report 1.0, 1.0, 0.0 for its localPosition after parenting. By writing out the name of the bool parameter name `resetToWorldPosition:true` we tell C# that we want to use our extension function instead of the built-in version.

7.16.4 Magic Mirror

A lot of what programmers do is write code to write less code. Seems paradoxical, but most programming time is spent writing large functions that are called by short functions. In the ultimate goal of reduced complexity, complexity is unavoidable.

```
GameObject original = GameObject.Instantiate(Resources.Load<GameObject>("TransformPrimitive"));
original.Mirror(new Vector3(-1, 1, 1));
```

Here we use an extension function on GameObject that's called Mirror, which takes a `Vector3` value to give it an axis of mirroring. In this case, we're reflecting the x axis.

```
public static GameObject Mirror(this GameObject original, Vector3 reflection)
{
    GameObject mirror = GameObject.Instantiate(original, original.transform.position, original.transform.rotation);
    Vector3 reflected = new Vector3()
    {
        x = original.transform.localScale.x * reflection.x,
        y = original.transform.localScale.y * reflection.y,
        z = original.transform.localScale.z * reflection.z
    };
    mirror.transform.localScale = reflected;
    mirror.name = original.name + "_Mirrored";
    UpdateReflection reflector = new UpdateReflection(original, mirror, reflection);
    return mirror;
}
```

The Mirror function takes the original object and creates a clone. The clone is then set to the size and position of the original. A mirrored scale is calculated and then it's applied to the mirrored object. Then a system to update the mirrored object is created which is assigned the original object, the mirrored object and the reflection value used to create the mirror.

```
public class UpdateReflection
{
    GameObject Mirror;
    Vector3 Reflection;

    public UpdateReflection(GameObject original, GameObject mirror, Vector3 reflection)
    {
        UpdatesReflected reflector = original.AddComponent<UpdatesReflected>();
        reflector.ReflectionUpdateEvent += OnReflectionUpdated;
        Mirror = mirror;
        Reflection = reflection;
    }

    public void OnReflectionUpdated(Transform t)
    {
        // update the mirrored position
        Vector3 reflectedPosition = new Vector3()
        {
            x = t.position.x * Reflection.x,
            y = t.position.y * Reflection.y,
            z = t.position.z * Reflection.z
        };
        Mirror.transform.position = reflectedPosition;

        // now update the mirrored rotation
        Vector3 reflectedRotation = new Vector3()
        {
            x = t.localEulerAngles.x * -Reflection.x,
            y = t.localEulerAngles.y * -Reflection.y,
            z = t.localEulerAngles.z * -Reflection.z
        };
        Mirror.transform.localEulerAngles = reflectedRotation;
    }
}
```

The UpdateReflection class keeps track of two things, the mirrored object and the reflection vector. When it's created it adds a component called UpdatesReflected to the original object. The UpdatesReflected object has an update event which calls on the OnReflectionUpdated function. The updates set the mirrored object's position and rotation based on the reflection axis value.

```
public class UpdatesReflected : MonoBehaviour
{
    public delegate void UpdateReflected(Transform transform);
    public event UpdateReflected ReflectionUpdateEvent;
    private void Update()
    {
        ReflectionUpdateEvent?.Invoke(transform);
    }
}
```

The original object gets the MonoBehaviour UpdatesReflected attached to it where the Reflection-UpdateEvent calls the OnReflectionUpdated function in the UpdateReflection class. The event sends along the originals transform so the mirrored object can know what the original's transforms have updated to.

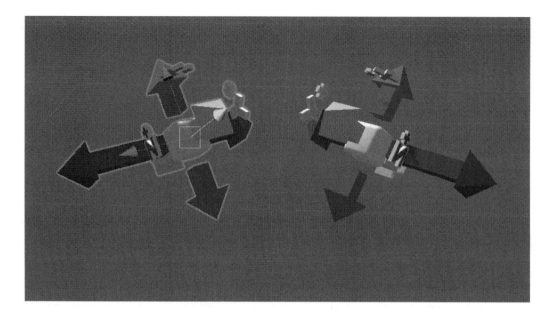

As update events are sent to the Mirror object through the `UpdateReflection` class, we get an object that mirrors the originals position and rotation.

A simplified `gameObject.Mirror()` function call performs quite a lot of steps behind the scene to create what seems like a simple task. The reality of this means that what might seem like a simple task hides a large scope of complexity.

7.16.5 What We've Learned

Other interesting tricks that often come up in a small C# class in Unity 3D is limiting how much of a library is used. When you add directives such as using `System;`, you're including a heavy amount of memory that needs to be accessed. This memory isn't necessarily used when you're running the game; however, this is used when your code is compiled.

For ease of use, it's a simple matter to have a simple case like the following:

```
using Vect3 = UnityEngine.Vector3;
```

This shortens `Vector3` into `Vect3`. Doing so helps to reduce namespace conflicts as well as speeds up picking names in the Autocomplete feature in MonoDevelop. The normal behavior always has Vector2 above Vector3 in the pop-up list. After a while, this behavior can easily be replaced if you get used to using Vect3 instead.

The usual practice is to use the regular name, in case the rest of the library is needed. However, it's good to know that tricks like this are possible, in case you come across something strange. Working in Unity 3D places specific constraints around what code will and will not work when it comes to the full feature set that the .NET Foundation has to offer.

The developers at Unity 3D are hard set on supporting many different platforms, and the lowest common denominator sets the height of the bar. Getting to know a language with a focus is great; this is why Unity 3D is a great stage for learning C#. Once you've gotten into how the language works, it's a good idea to explore other development environments where you can make games with the full .NET Framework. Never limit yourself.

7.17 Destructors

While you're busy creating objects, Unity 3D is busy cleaning them up. If you clean them up quickly, you limit how often and how long it takes Unity 3D to do this for you.

We've looked at the constructor in Chapters 5 and 6. Destructors are the opposite construct from the constructor. C# is a garbage-collected language, so in most instances, you're not in need of a specific cleanup of your own data when your object is no longer referenced. However, when you begin to use unsafe code, some cleanup might be more necessary.

Unity 3D provides the OnDestroy() event after any object based on MonoBehaviour has been destroyed. If you want to destroy an object that isn't based on MonoBehaviour, you don't have an OnDestroy() event. Therefore, what else is there to do?

7.17.1 A Basic Example

In the Destructors project, open the Example.cs component attached to the Main Camera and also open the DestroyMe.cs file. The DestroyMe has both a constructor and a destructor.

```
public class SelfDestructor : Object
{
    string Name;

    // Constructor
    public SelfDestructor(string name)
    {
        Name = name;
        Debug.Log(Name + " says hello.");
    }

    // Destructor
    ~SelfDestructor()
    {
        Debug.Log(Name + " says goodbye.");
    }
}
```

The destructor can be identified by the ~, or tilde, preceding the class identifier. Somewhat like a very simple-looking constructor, the destructor is called any time the object is garbage collected. C# is a garbage-collected environment. Specific destructors aren't specifically written into the language. If several seconds pass and there's nothing going on in the class and there's nothing accessing the class, the unused class is destroyed automatically.

```
void UseSelfDestructor()
{
    SelfDestructor bomb = new SelfDestructor("Bob-omb");
    // Bob-omb says hello.
    // after ~5 seconds
    // Bob-omb says goodbye.
}
```

In the Destructors.cs attached to the Destructors game object in the Destructors_Scene, we create an instance of the SelfDestructor() class. When we create a new SelfDestructor we give it a name so we can know what is being cleaned out and when. If we run the game scene, we see "Bob-omb says hello." printed to the Console when the game starts.

Several seconds later we see "Bob-omb says goodbye." There are other ways to destroy objects.

```
private UnityEngine.Object Bomber;
void UseDestroyBomber()
{
    Bomber = new SelfDestructor("Bomber");
    do
    {
        Bomber = null;
        GC.Collect(GC.MaxGeneration, GCCollectionMode.Forced, true);
    }
    while (Bomber != null);
}
```

In this code function we assign and destroy the SelfDestructor Bomber. The log shows the hello and goodbye immediately.

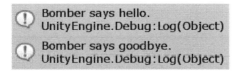

Bomber inherits from Object, so we can store a variable Bomber as UnityEngine.Object. A strange side effect of creating class wide variables is that they are sometimes created while the editor is running. This can be observed when the Bomber variable is changed to a SelfDestructor type.

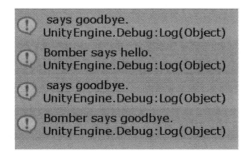

A mysterious "says goodbye." appears in the first line and again after the "Bomber says hello." lines. The general practice with Unity is to let Unity, or rather .NET, run its own garbage-collection (GC) cycles in the background untouched.

In general, GC in C# works automatically. For objects such as a struct, GC should be done very quickly. Only when you need to work with many class objects do you need to pay close attention to the number of objects that are being created.

The automatic GC is done in random intervals. Usually there is little consequence of the GC on a PC. The memory and CPU are running so fast that it's imperceptible when the GC takes place.

On a mobile device, the GC can lead to a sudden loss in frame rate once every few seconds. The interval between GC cycles can be longer or shorter depending on how often objects are created. Because of this, it's important to build some sort of scheme to track and destroy objects on your own. Forcing garbage collection is generally shunned upon. In the above log, does this mean we had three SelfDestructor objects in memory? It's hard to say for sure, but it certainly seems that way. Because of these weird behaviors in the editor, it's difficult to say exactly how things will react when garbage collection is forced.

For reasons of unpredictability, it's better to create an object pool, this avoids the issue with creating and destroying many dozens or even hundreds of objects in the scene.

7.17.2 Clearing Events or Delegates

One important function the destructor does have a purpose for when being cleared is to clear an event or a delegate. With a simple delegate and event dispatcher we'll add in a couple of Debug.Log functions to announce when the dispatcher class is created and destroyed.

```
class EventDispatcher
{
    public EventDispatcher()
    {
        Debug.Log("Hello! from dispatcher");
    }

    public delegate void SomeDelegate();
    public event SomeDelegate SomeEvent;
    public void CallSomeEvent()
    {
        SomeEvent?.Invoke();
    }

    ~EventDispatcher()
    {
        Debug.Log("Goodbye from dispatcher");
    }
}
```

Then to make use of the function, we'll create a class which accepts the dispatcher as an argument in its constructor.

```
class SelfCleaning
{
    public int CountDown = 3;
    private EventDispatcher Dispatcher;
    public SelfCleaning(EventDispatcher dispatcher)
    {
        Dispatcher = dispatcher;
        Dispatcher.SomeEvent += OnSomeEvent;
        Debug.Log("Hello!, connecting to dispatcher");
    }

    public void OnSomeEvent()
    {
        Debug.Log("I should be destroyed in " + CountDown--);
    }

    ~SelfCleaning()
    {
        Dispatcher.SomeEvent -= OnSomeEvent;
        Debug.Log("Goodbye!, cleaning up dispatcher");
    }
}
```

In this class, the dispatcher's event gets assigned in the constructor, in the destructor we use the −= operator to remove the reference from the `SelfCleaning` class to the event dispatcher.

```
SelfCleaning Cleaner;
void UseDispatcherAndSelfCleaner()
{
    EventDispatcher dispatcher = new EventDispatcher();
    Cleaner = new SelfCleaning(dispatcher);
    while (Cleaner.CountDown > 0)
    {
        dispatcher.CallSomeEvent();
    }
    Cleaner = null;
}
```

The `Cleaner` class is updated for a count of three, then the variable is set to `null`. The dispatcher runs the event till the Cleaner's CountDown value reaches 0, so we've called the event which connects both the cleaner and the dispatcher.

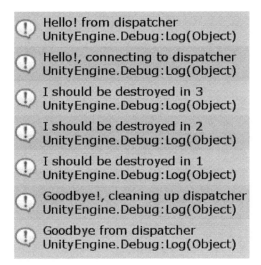

In the log we see the dispatcher is created followed by the cleaner being created and connecting itself to the dispatcher. We see the CountDown decrement, and then the logging stops for a moment. A few seconds later, the cleaner says Goodbye where it also removes its function from the dispatcher's event. After that, we see the dispatcher say Goodbye as well.

So this works well with very simple classes, but how do we handle GameObjects and MonoBehaviours?

7.17.3 OnDestroy

Classes which derive from `MonoBehaviour` use a slightly different function to destroy themselves. With a similar setup to a class which doesn't derive from `MonoBehaviour`, a class which does uses `void OnDestroy()` and not `~ClassName()` to clean its own memory.

In a very simple example, we'll have the `OnDestroy()` function in the MonoBehaviour derived class.

```
class DestroyMe : MonoBehaviour
{
    private void OnDestroy()
    {
        Debug.Log("I've been destroyed.");
    }
}

void DestroyDestroyMe()
{
    DestroyMe destroyMe = gameObject.AddComponent<DestroyMe>();
    Destroy(destroyMe);
}
```

As soon as the MonoBehaviour is destroyed the OnDestroy() function is called and "I've been destroyed." is printed to the Console. With a similar setup as before, we store a variable for the event dispatcher. Instead of a constructor assigning the dispatcher's event to a function, we use a separate function where we assign the event dispatcher.

```
class UsesOnDestroy : MonoBehaviour
{
    DestroyEventDispatcher Dispatcher;
    private int CountDown = 3;
    public void AssignListenerUpdater(DestroyEventDispatcher dispatcher)
    {
        Dispatcher = dispatcher;
        Dispatcher.UpdateListenerEvent += OnUpdateListener;
    }

    public void OnUpdateListener()
    {
        Debug.Log("Got Updated");
        gameObject.transform.localScale = Vector3.one * CountDown;
        if (CountDown-- < 0)
        {
            Debug.Log("CountDown less than 0");
            Destroy(this);
        }
    }

    // One of the built-in MonoBehaviour functions
    private void OnDestroy()
    {
        Debug.Log("OnDestroy Called.");
        // similar to ~Destroy() function.
        Dispatcher.UpdateListenerEvent -= OnUpdateListener;
    }
}
```

When we call the event dispatcher's event we send the listeners events until they are ready to destroy themselves.

```
class DestroyEventDispatcher
{
    public delegate void UpdateListeners();
    public event UpdateListeners UpdateListenerEvent;

    public void CallUpdateListenerEvent()
    {
        int count = 0;
        while(count++ < 5)
        {
            UpdateListenerEvent?.Invoke();
        }
    }
}
```

The class that sends the MonoBehaviour holds, calls the event a few times to make the MonoBehaviour decrement the CountDown value.

```
// cube primitive is created.
GameObject gameCube = GameObject.CreatePrimitive(PrimitiveType.Cube);
// the MonoBehaviour that scales the cube when the event is called
// then destroys itself once countdown is less than 0
UsesOnDestroy monoDestroyer = gameCube.AddComponent<UsesOnDestroy>();

// dispatcher will call the event that the self destroying MonoBehaviour
// is listening to.
DestroyEventDispatcher destroyDispatcher = new DestroyEventDispatcher();
// the event dispatcher is assigned to the MonoBehaviour
monoDestroyer.AssignListenerUpdater(destroyDispatcher);

// there will be a cube for a moment after start
// but it's destroyed almost right away.
destroyDispatcher.CallUpdateListenerEvent();
```

A cube primitive is created and the MonoBehaviour is attached to the cube gameObject. Following the creation of the class, an event dispatcher is created. The MonoBehaviour derived class gets the assignment to the dispatcher where it assigns the event listener to the dispatcher's event.

We call the dispatcher's event which then raises the event enough times to trigger the UsesOnDestroy self destruction call Destroy(this). The final product is a scene with a cube with scale of −1 on the *x*, *y*, and *z* axis without any scripts attached to it. The only evidence that there was a script attached is the scale and the "OnDestroy Called." printed to the Console.

7.17.4 The Ugly Truth

The unfortunate, or maybe fortunate truth to how garbage collection really works is a bit murky.

```
void UseDestroyTooMuch()
{
    GameObject gameCube = GameObject.CreatePrimitive(PrimitiveType.Cube);
    UsesOnDestroy monoDestroyer = gameCube.AddComponent<UsesOnDestroy>();
    DestroyEventDispatcher destroyDispatcher = new DestroyEventDispatcher();
    monoDestroyer.AssignListenerUpdater(destroyDispatcher);

    // Calling the event 100 times.
    destroyDispatcher.CallUpdateListenerEventTooManyTimes();
    // it should be gone, but it's still listening?
    destroyDispatcher.UpdateListenerEvent -= monoDestroyer.OnUpdateListener;
    // lets disconnect the event listener.

    Debug.Log("Calling event again");
    // Calling the event 100 times.
    destroyDispatcher.CallUpdateListenerEventTooManyTimes();

    Debug.Log("When will the UseOnDestroy script actually destroy itself?");
}
```

So with a different system to call the event the UsesOnDestroy class we call it 100 times.

```
public void CallUpdateListenerEventTooManyTimes()
{
    int count = 0;
    while (count++ < 100)
    {
        Debug.Log("Calling Update Event.");
        UpdateListenerEvent?.Invoke();
    }
}
```

In theory, this should not actually get a response from the object listening to it, after the CountDown is less than 0 the object should destroy itself.

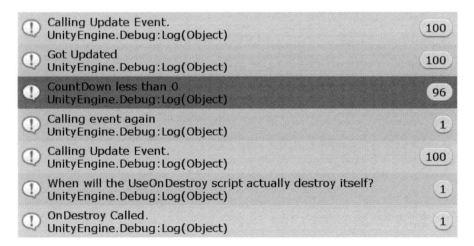

The UsesOnDestroy gets the call to destroy itself 96 more times after it should have destroyed itself. Then we call the event again after removing it from the dispatcher. So it doesn't get any additional calls.

So disconnecting the listener from the dispatcher is working, but the script hasn't destroyed itself. It's not until after the function is finished that the OnDestroy is called.

It's important to be aware that garbage collection is lazy. Objects are usually still resident in memory for a few seconds after they've been destroyed. For this reason, after many objects are instanced it's unclear as to when memory will freed up. Once it does, it's usually all at once, and quite often causes a frame or two to be lost.

7.17.5 What We've Learned

Destructors are used when manual clean up of a class is needed. When using classes based on any of the Unity 3D class objects, it's not recommended you use the OnDetroy() function to clear any extra data created by the class. It's recommended that any class not based on a Unity 3D class use a destructor, though it's not a common practice to create classes not based on Unity 3D.

When classes add a delegate to an event, the destructor can be used to remove the delegate. Unfortunately, we can't use the −= operator to remove the reference to the event listener. This still leaves behind some traces to the created class in the memory and prevents GC from cleaning out the object.

Garbage collection happens in regular intervals, usually about a second between each pass through the heap. The heap is a pile of memory that can become disorganized. When an object is removed, it leaves behind a gap. After many hundreds of objects are created and destroyed, the heap can become a cube of Swiss cheese of usable and unusable spaces. Garbage collection tries to mitigate and clean the heap as often as it can. If the heap were processed any more, then performance in maintaining clean memory would take over your CPU cycles.

The balance between performance and memory management isn't always to your benefit. As improvements are made, there may be speed gains, but it's up to you to keep your use of memory as slim as possible to allow for quick GC passes.

This is one of the reasons why a struct is preferable over a class. Structs are allocated to a different section of memory for your game and, thus, don't need to be garbage collected at all. This isn't true if a struct is stored as a part of a class. A struct doesn't have a ~Destroy() function, so any clean-up needs to be done before clearing a struct.

```
struct SomeStruct
{
    public int MyInt;
    public SomeStruct(int myInt)
    {
        MyInt = myInt;
    }
}

void UseSomeStruct()
{
    SomeStruct[] LotsOfStructs = new SomeStruct[1000000];
    //allocates a bunch of memory.
    for(int i = 0; i < 1000000; i++)
    {
        LotsOfStructs[i] = new SomeStruct(i);
    }
    //as soon as we exit this function they're all gone.
}
```

In the end, C# allows for so many different ways to use the language; the benefit far outreaches the limitation of memory management. Your task of creating a game shouldn't be hindered by the nitty-gritty of poking holes in memory and trying to fill them in manually. This sort of stuff isn't fun and should be left to the folks writing C# to figure out for you.

7.18 Concurrency or Co-Routines

So far, everything that has been talked about has been for writing code that is executed in order. As the code is executed, each statement must wait until the preceding statement has completed its task. For the most part, this is done exceedingly fast.

7.18.1 Yield

We've gone over the use of IEnumerator earlier; it's a handy interface for more than one reason. The IEnumerator type is notable for iterating over an array; in addition, in Unity 3D it also allows the use of yield. The primary reason for the yield keyword was to allow a computer to continue with a function and allow something like our Update() loop to come back to the function using the yield statement.

For instance, if we had a task that might take more than a single update frame to complete, we could use a function with a yield; this works only with a function that is an IEnumerator. This means that the function starts when it's called, but then allows us to come back to it again and check on how it's doing.

For instance, a really slow function, which fills the scene with 40,000 randomly placed cubes, might take a long time to complete.

```
private bool UsedFillupObjects;
void FillUpObjects()
{
    if (!UsedFillupObjects)
    {
        UsedFillupObjects = true;
        int numObjects = 50000;
        GameObject[] lotsOfObjects = new GameObject[numObjects];
        for (int i = 0; i < numObjects; i++)
        {
            GameObject g = GameObject.CreatePrimitive(PrimitiveType.Cube);
            g.name = i.ToString() + "_Cube";
            g.transform.position = new Vector3()
            {
                x = Random.Range(-1000, 1000),
                y = Random.Range(-1000, 1000),
                z = Random.Range(-1000, 1000)
            };
            g.transform.localScale = new Vector3()
            {
                x = Random.Range(1, 10),
                y = Random.Range(1, 10),
                z = Random.Range(1, 10)
            };
            lotsOfObjects[i] = g;
        }
        Debug.Log("Finished at:" + Time.fixedUnscaledTime);
    }
}
```

Unity 3D will lock up for a few seconds waiting for this function to finish before the game begins. To measure the time passed, we'll have a log in the script's Start and we'll run another log once the function finishes in the first Update() loop.

```
private void Start()
{
    Debug.Log("Started at:" + Time.fixedUnscaledTime);
}

void Update()
{
    FillUpObjects();
}
```

Depending on the speed of your computer, the time elapsed from the Start() of the script to the end of the FillUpObjects script will be different.

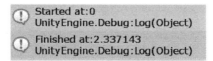

One way to get around this is to use a co-routine. In the System.Collections library is the IEnumerator. This is the same sort of class that enables the foreach(thing in stuff) enumerator type.

```
private bool UsedFillWithYield;
IEnumerator FillWithYield()
{
    if (!UsedFillWithYield)
    {
        UsedFillWithYield = true;
        int numObjects = 1000;
        GameObject[] lotsOfObjects = new GameObject[numObjects];
        for (int i = 0; i < numObjects; i++)
        {
            GameObject g = GameObject.CreatePrimitive(PrimitiveType.Cube);
            g.name = i.ToString() + "_Cube";
            g.transform.position = new Vector3()
            {
                x = Random.Range(-1000, 1000),
                y = Random.Range(-1000, 1000),
                z = Random.Range(-1000, 1000)
            };
            g.transform.localScale = new Vector3()
            {
                x = Random.Range(1, 10),
                y = Random.Range(1, 10),
                z = Random.Range(1, 10)
            };
            lotsOfObjects[i] = g;
            /* Yield goes after an interation  */
            /* through the for loop.           */
            yield return null;
        }
        Debug.Log("Finished at:" + Time.fixedUnscaledTime);
    }

}
```

Rather than `void`, `IEnumerator` is used, then at the end of the for loop, and add yield return null; so that the `IEnumerator` interface has something to return. The new sort function is called differently from a regular function as we see in the following call:

```
StartCoroutine(FillWithYield());
```

`StartCoroutine()` calls the `IEnumerator` as a co-routine. When the game is started, we don't experience a lock, but we do get to watch cubes fill in the world. This is a simple example on how a co-routine is usually used. It's a great method to start an unusually long function and not have to wait for its completion before the rest of some code is executed. There's one drawback to using this method. To generate merely 1000 objects it takes considerably longer to create the field of cubes.

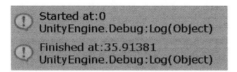

When using a co-routine, the Update() loop continues to run.

```
int count;
void Update()
{
    /*
     * Section 7.18.1 Yield
     */
    //FillUpObjects();
    StartCoroutine(FillWithYield());
    Debug.Log(count++);
}
```

The `Debug.Log(count++);` after the start of the co-routine continues to print out numbers even with the `FillWithYield()` running. Contrast this with the same function without using a coroutine. You'd simply wait until the function is finished before the `Debug.Log()` gets called.

7.18.1.1 A Basic Example

In terms of a usable function in a game, there are more interesting uses for the co-routine. To see how this works, we'll start a Unity 3D Scene with a new script called Concurrent attached to the Main Camera.

```
void UseDelayAStatement()
{
    StartCoroutine(DelayAStatement());
}       /*                 ↑               */
        /*      ┌──────────┴──────────┐    */
        /*      │the function and parameter list│ */
        /*      │is added as a parameter to the │ */
        /*      │StartCoroutine function │    */
        /*      └──────────┬──────────┘    */
        /*                 ↑               */
IEnumerator DelayAStatement()
{
    Debug.Log("DelayAStatement Started at:" + Time.fixedTime);
    yield return new WaitForSeconds(3.0f);
    Debug.Log("DelayAStatement Finished at:" + Time.fixedTime);
}
```

With the above, we can see the statement `StartCoroutine(DelayAStatement());`. This starts the `IEnumerator` function. Functions defined with the `IEnumerator` return type and is identified must have a `yield return` somewhere in the body of the function.

In the DelayAStatement code block, we see that it starts with `Debug.Log("Started at:" + Time.fixedTime);` followed by the `yield` statement.

The `yield` statement `return new WaitForSeconds();` creates a concurrent task that then pauses the DelayAStatement code block at the yield. Once the yield is done, it releases the function's operation and allows it to move to the next statement. It's also worth looking at starting multiple Concurrent co-routines.

```
void UseMultipleDelayAStatements()
{
    for (int i = 0; i < 3; i++)
    {
        StartCoroutine(MultiDelayAStatement(i));
    }
}


IEnumerator MultiDelayAStatement(int i)
{
    Debug.Log(i + ") DelayAStatement Started at:" + Time.fixedTime);
    yield return new WaitForSeconds(3.0f);
    Debug.Log(i + ") DelayAStatement Finished at:" + Time.fixedTime);
}
```

With the above code, we have the following output. Note that we're changing the `Debug.Log()` to include an index to identify each of the `MultiDelayAStatement()` functions as they are executed.

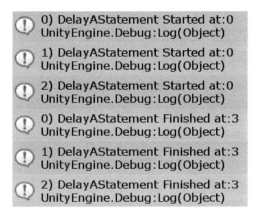

The three concurrent tasks 0, 1, and 2 started in order. After their WaitForSeconds(), they finish in the same order. Concurrent co-routines are useful for a good number of tasks including setup with events and timings.

7.18.2 Setting Up Timers

So as a game play engineer, you're going to write a lot of code. Writing a timing function should be something you do once. With that in mind, you'll want it to be flexible; what you write should be easy to reuse. A good timing function should be something you can use to time explosions in a game, separate waves of monsters, or even just count down some numbers on screen. What each of these have in common, is a flexible amount of time, so we'll use a float for that. And some sort of action when the time has run out.

```
void TheAction()                            /*  ┌─────────────┐      */
{                                           /*  │this function│      */
    Debug.Log("Doing the thing!");/*        │gets assigned│      */
}                                           /*  │as a variable│      */
                                            /*  └─────────────┘      */
void UseTimedAction()                       /*         |             */
{                                           /*         ↓             */
    StartCoroutine(TimedAction(3f, TheAction));/*                    */
}                                           /*         ↓             */
                                            /*         └─────────────┐ */
private IEnumerator TimedAction(float time, Action action)
{                                                   /*         ↓     */
    yield return new WaitForSeconds(time);/*                   |     */
    action?.Invoke();/* ←──────────────────────────────────────┘     */
}                          /* then gets called here after wait */
```

The UseTimedAction() is called in the Start() of the script in the scene. A function named TheAction() which does a thing, is assigned as a variable to the TimedAction() function in the Coroutine. The Action type comes from System, as do many useful base types. In this case TheAction just prints out "Doing the thing!" to the Unity 3D debug Console. However, this could just as easy call on a script to set off an explosion, start a race, or let loose a horde of zombies.

```
/*
 * we have two parts here, a delegate
 * and the IEnumerator ValueUpdater
 */
delegate void UpdateValue(float value);

IEnumerator ValueUpdater(float start, float finish, float time, UpdateValue valueUpdated)
{
    /* starting at 0      */
    /* we increment this */
    /* toward 1           */
    float t = 0;
    while (t < 1)
    {
        /* Lerp goes from start value to    */
        /* the finish value using a range   */
        /* from 0 to 1                      */
        float v = Mathf.Lerp(start, finish, t);

        /* increment the t value from       */
        /* 0 to 1                          */
        t += Time.deltaTime / time;

        /* call the event assigned          */
        valueUpdated?.Invoke(v);

        /* wait till the end of the frame   */
        /* before starting the while loop   */
        /* again.                           */
        yield return new WaitForEndOfFrame();
    }
}
```

We can make our timers more useful by adding a repeated event to a loop within the coroutine. A Mathf. Lerp takes two values and interprets a value between them using a value from 0 to 1. For instance, you can use the function to quickly get the value half way between 6 and 9 and see it's 7.5.

```
Debug.Log(Mathf.Lerp(6f, 9f, 0.5f));
// 7.5
```

We call our `lerp` co-routine using the same `StartCoroutine()` function calling the value updater.

```
/* starting at a value of 3, we go to 7 in 3 seconds */
StartCoroutine(ValueUpdater(6f, 9f, 3f, GetUpdatedValue));
```

The `GetUpdateValue` function starts with 6 and increments toward 9 in 3 seconds. A linear interpolation, or Lerp, isn't the only option. There's also `LerpAngle`, `SmoothStep`, and `LerpUnclamped` available in the `Mathf` library. These share similar parameters with `Lerp` and can be interchanged quite easily.

Containing a timer within a single function keeps the work contained. A co-routine encapsulates the work in a single function. With the following code, you can have a repeating timer that uses a co-routine instead.

```
float delayTime = 2.0f;
int repeatCount = 5;

StartCoroutine(RepeatTimer(delayTime, repeatCount));

IEnumerator RepeatTimer(float delay, int repeats)
{
    while (repeats > 0)
    {
        Debug.Log("Starting timer");
        yield return new WaitForSeconds(delay);
        Debug.Log("Restarting Timer");
        repeats--;
    }
}
```

This uses a while loop in `IEnumerator RepeatTimer()`. The `WaitForSeconds()` uses an incoming parameter `delay` to give us some flexibility to decide how long to wait till the `RepeatTimer()` restarts. When this while loop is restarted, the first statement `Debug.Log("Starting timer");` is executed immediately.

Any code found before the `yield return new WaitForSeconds();` statement will be executed normally. This means that you can set up new GameObjects, add components, and build any number of systems before the yield. Once the `WaitForSeconds()` statement is finished, all the following lines are then executed normally. Therefore, anything that needs to happen before the timer is reset should happen here.

A Coroutine can control another co-routine as well. A variable visible to both can be setup as a kill switch. A co-routine checks if the live bool is true to continue executing the while loop. Another co-routine is set to set that bool to false.

```
bool live = true;

StartCoroutine(KillCoRoutineIn(5f));
StartCoroutine(RepeatTimer(0.2f));

IEnumerator KillCoRoutineIn(float delay)
{
    Debug.Log("Kill Switch To hit in " + delay + " seconds");
    yield return new WaitForSeconds(delay);
    live = false;
    Debug.Log("Coroutine killed.");
}

IEnumerator RepeatTimer(float delay)
{
    while (live)
    {
        Debug.Log("Repeating...");
        yield return new WaitForSeconds(delay);
    }
}
```

7.18.3 Arrays of Delegates

Timers that call a function when they're finished are useful in many ways. We could make a modification to the co-routine to accept an array of delegates. In addition, the delegates can also have a return type to change the behavior of the coroutine.

```
delegate float ThingsToDo(string thing);
IEnumerator DoingTheThings(ThingsToDo[] things)
{
    Debug.Log("Doing the things:" + Time.fixedTime);

    foreach (ThingsToDo thing in things)
    {
        float nextTime = thing.Invoke("Doing the thing.");
        yield return new WaitForSeconds(nextTime);
    }

    Debug.Log("Things done:" + Time.fixedTime);
}
```

In this IEnumerator called DoingTheThings() we have a parameter which is an array of ThingsToDo. As we've seen before, delegate functions can be useful in many different situations. For this we'll use them to some very basic tasks. A delegate is simply a redirection of a function as a variable.

```
float FirstThing(string thing)
{
    Debug.Log("First thing is:" + thing + " at " + Time.fixedTime);
    return 3f;
}

float SecondThing(string thing)
{
    Debug.Log("Second thing is:" + thing + " at " + Time.fixedTime);
    return 3f;
}
```

We could have more variations, but in this case two different functions that match the signature of the ThingsToDo delegate are FirstThing and SecondThing. The functions themselves are not very complex, but this doesn't mean your functions couldn't do much more.

```
void UseThingsToDo()
{
    ThingsToDo[] someThings = new ThingsToDo[2] { FirstThing, SecondThing };
    StartCoroutine(DoingTheThings(someThings));
}
```

The delegate ThingsToDo as a type can be used as an array. In this example we're populating the some-Things variable with the two functions matching the delegate signature. Then we start the co-routine DoingTheThings with the ThingsToDo array.

When the co-routine is started we get the FirstThing and SecondThing functions are invoked by the same co-routine. The functions are invoked in the order they were added to the delegate array. Each returns a float value which is used to delay calling any following delegate. The system here allows you to set up a queue of actions. Each action can provide its own time before the next function is called.

7.18.4 Stopping a Co-Routine

To terminate all co-routines, the StopAllCoroutines(); function will terminate any co-routine in process. In some cases where co-routines aren't used often, stopping anything in process might not have any unexpected side effects.

```
void UseStopAllCoroutines()
{
    StartCoroutine(GetsInterrupted());
    StartCoroutine(StopsAllCoRoutines());
}

IEnumerator GetsInterrupted()
{
    Debug.Log("Started");
    yield return new WaitForSeconds(10f);

    Debug.Log("Stopped.");
    // never gets called.
}

IEnumerator StopsAllCoRoutines()
{
    yield return new WaitForSeconds(2f);
    Debug.Log("Stopping all coroutines");
    StopAllCoroutines();
}
```

With the above example, we start a co-routine which will log "Stopped." after 10 seconds. Before that is printed we start another co-routine that uses the StopAllCoroutines() function after 2 seconds. When the co-routine is interrupted "Stopped." is never printed to the Console.

```
void UseStopCoroutine()
{
    IEnumerator counter = Counter();
    /*              ↓              create and        */
    /*             └──┐            store the Counter()  */
    /*              ↓             as a variable and pass */
    StartCoroutine(counter);/* the variable to be    */
    /*              ↓             used to stop it      */
    /*             └───────────┐                        */
    /*                         ↓                        */
    StartCoroutine(StopCounter(counter));
}
```

We can also pass an IEnumerator variable to start and stop a specific co-routine. The Counter() function is used to print a number to the Console every second.

```
IEnumerator Counter()
{
    int i = 0;
    while (true)
    {
        yield return new WaitForSeconds(1);
        Debug.Log("Counting:" + i++);
    }
}
```

This co-routine will continue to count so long as StopAllCoroutines() is not called. To stop this specific co-routine without stopping any others, we need to pass the IEnumerator counter to the StopCoroutine() function. The second co-routine started in the above example calls on the following:

```
IEnumerator StopCounter(IEnumerator counter)
{
    yield return new WaitForSeconds(3f);
    Debug.Log("Stopping Coroutine Counter()");
    StopCoroutine(counter);
}
```

This stops the counter after 3 seconds. The StopCoroutine can stop a specific co-routine given it's able to access as a variable. In some cases, it's not always convenient to stop a co-routine with this method. In some cases, it's easier for a co-routine to check a variable to see if it should continue to execute.

```
bool ContinueToDoTheThing = true;
IEnumerator ChecksToKeepGoing()
{
    Debug.Log("Starting to do the thing.");
    int i = 0;
    while (ContinueToDoTheThing)
    {
        yield return new WaitForSeconds(1f);
        Debug.Log("Continuing to do the thing " + i++ + " times.");
    }
    Debug.Log("Finished the things.");
}
```

A simple bool can be used in the co-routine to allow it to continue to execute. The condition to allow a co-routine to continue is checked before any yield return values are calculated.

```
IEnumerator StopDoingTheThing()
{
    yield return new WaitForSeconds(5f);
    Debug.Log("Setting ContinueToDoTheThing to false");
    ContinueToDoTheThing = false;
}

void UseExternalInterrupt()
{
    StartCoroutine(ChecksToKeepGoing());
    StartCoroutine(StopDoingTheThing());
}
```

To use the co-routine we start both co-routines at the same time. The first one checks a bool value to continue. If the value is true it waits for a second before printing out how many times it's run. The second co-routine sets the bool value the first co-routine used to continue to false.

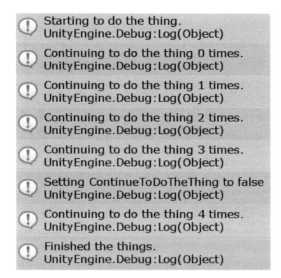

If you read the log carefully you'll see there was a 4th log printed to the Console after the dependent bool was set to false. In the ChecksToKeepGoing co-routine notice that the while loop only checks at the beginning to see if it should keep going. The co-routine continues through the while statements until the while loop checks the bool again to repeat.

7.18.5 What We've Learned

Co-routines are useful in games to manage various aspects of timing. Complex behaviors often involve movement, logic, and awareness. Creatures in general do not continuously move without pause. It's possible to use regular Update ()–style timers, but this gets cumbersome.

With co-routines, we're free to make interesting combinations of behaviors with interesting decisions. The co-routines we looked at earlier could execute maneuvers and strategic behaviors. A co-routine can also call other functions, so it doesn't have to contain all of the logic in one block.

It's also possible for an IEnumerator to start its own co-routine. This can create overlapping behaviors, each one with its own timing. Combined with event handlers, you could trigger functions when a co-routine is started and when it is complete. If the event is raised before or after the yield, you can trigger an event when the co-routine begins or ends.

7.19 Dictionary, Stacks, and Queues

A dictionary type is an interesting version of an array. One basic use is setting up a list of items, say, zombies, vampires, and werewolves. Then we can give each one a value: 10 zombies, 13 vampires, and 7 werewolves. If we want to know the number of zombies, we can ask the dictionary what "Zombies?" and we'll get the value stored at "Zombies" as 10.

The system works in a fairly similar way to an ArrayList, only we'll want to assign some specific types. The Dictionary data type is found under `System.Collections.Generic;`. We'll start a new Dictionary project. We'll assign a simple Dictionaries.cs component to the Main Camera in the scene.

7.19.1 A Basic Example

This example starts with the DictionariesStacksAndQueues scene and the corresponding script in the scene.

```
Dictionary<string, int> MyDictionary = new Dictionary<string, int>();
MyDictionary.Add("Zombies", 10);
Debug.Log(MyDictionary["Zombies"]);
// 10

int[] UnnamedInts = new int[1] { 10 };
Debug.Log(UnnamedInts[0]);
// 10
```

The directive named Systems.Collections.Generic has the Dictionary data type in it. We can use it any number of ways, but one of the most common is the Dictionary<string,int> combination. This allows us to use a string to find a value in the dictionary. Similar to an array of int[], you can recall a value in the array by its index in the array. Rather than using a number to recall a stored value, you use a string as a name for the value. Dictionaries are organized as Key and Value. The string "Zombie" is the key, it's value is 10 as assigned in the example above.

The structure of the declaration of a Dictionary is <first type, second type>, where the first type you use is called a key and the second type is the value that is associated with that key. The key, or the first value, must all be unique throughout the dictionary.

```
MyDictionary.Add("Zombies", 7);
// ArgumentException: An item with the same key has already been added. Key: Zombies
```

If we try to use the above code, we'll get an error that the same key has already been added.

When a dictionary is used, the key is the value that is used to find the association to the second type. Therefore, in the above code, if you asked for "Zombies," the dictionary would not be able to tell you 10 or 7.

To add dictionary entries to the dictionary, we use the MyDictionary.Add("Zombies",10); to push strings with associated values into the variable. To retrieve them, we use what looks like addressing an array.

MyDictionary["Zombies"] acts as though it were the value assigned when using the .Add() statement. We can use different types in the dictionary as well.

```
Dictionary<int, Object> intObjectPair = new Dictionary<int, Object>();
Object[] allObjects = FindObjectsOfType<Object>();
for (int i = 0; i < allObjects.Length; i++)
{
    intObjectPair.Add(i, allObjects[i]);
}

foreach (int i in intObjectPair.Keys)
{
    Debug.Log("Number:" + i + " is " + intObjectPair[i]);
}
// finds 22 objects in the scene.
```

The above code will print out every Object found in the scene. The specific line obs[i] is all it takes to extract an object found in the scene by using an int. To make this a bit more clear, we can use the following three statements:

```
Debug.Log(intObjectPair[0]);
// NavMeshSettings (UnityEngine.NavMeshSettings)
Debug.Log(intObjectPair[8]);
// DictionariesStacksAndQueues (DictionariesStacksAndQueues)
Debug.Log(intObjectPair[13]);
// Directional Light (UnityEngine.GameObject)
```

Using an <int, object> key value pair isn't very different from using a regular array. Dictionaries use generics to help make any combination of types to map from one type to another, not just referencing objects by a number. These can be used for any number of data systems. Usually, when addressing a number of similar associations, we can use dictionaries to a great degree.

With this sort of data structure, we're allowed to ask how many zombies there are in the scene, with int numZombies = MyDictionary["zombies"];. Using a dictionary in this way adds a simple interface for storing an arbitrary number of values and things in the scene.

7.19.2 ContainsKey

To put a Dictionary to some use, we'll count how many GameObjects have the same name in the scene.

```
Dictionary<string, int> objectIntPair = new Dictionary<string, int>();
GameObject[] allObjects = FindObjectsOfType<GameObject>();
for (int i = 0; i < allObjects.Length; i++)
{
    // get the name of the object
    string name = allObjects[i].name;

    // check if we have a key with matching name
    if (objectIntPair.ContainsKey(name))
    {
        // found another, add 1
        objectIntPair[name]++;
    }
    else
    {
        // found at least 1
        objectIntPair.Add(name, 1);
    }
}
```

A dictionary called objectIntPair stores a string for the name of an object and an int to count how many objects have that name. Then we get an array of all the GameObjects in the scene called allObjects.

A foreach loop iterates through each object in the allObjects array. A check is made with ContainsKey() on the objectIntPair. The ContainsKey() function checks the dictionary if the string passed to it has already been added to the dictionary.

The if-else statement uses objectIntPair.Add(name, 1); to both add a new key to the dictionary and increment the value for that key to 1. If the name is already in use the value store there is incremented.

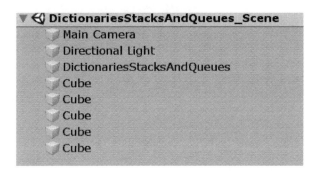

The scene reveals that there are 5 cubes in the scene and one Main Camera, one Directional Light and one DictionariesStacksAndQueues object.

7.19.3 Stacks

A stack is basically an array with some added features. You get a Push(), a Pop(), and a Peek() function when you use a stack. The names of the functions might not mean a lot, but they can act as a clue as to what they do.

A stack is basically an array which you can mentally imagine as an actual stack of books. The top of the stack is where all of the functions perform their operations. Pushing an object onto the stack loads another book on the top of the stack. Peeking at it means to look at the contents of the book on the top of the stack. Popping the stack means to take the top item on the stack off, not that popping a book makes all that much sense.

7.19.3.1 A Basic Example

A stack is an array with a specific order. To maintain the order of the stack you're only able to use three commands to access the contents of the stack. The first function is Push() which adds a new object to the top of the stack. To see what's on the top of the stack you use Peek(). To take the top object from the stack you use Pop().

```
Stack stack = new Stack();
stack.Push("First"); /* "First"┐                 ┌──────────────┐  */
stack.Push("Second");/*        [↓]               │pushes "First"│  */
stack.Push("Third"); /*        ●["First"]←●───────┤into the top  │  */
                     /*                           │of the stack  │  */
                     /*                           └──────────────┘  */
                     /*"Second"┐                  ┌──────────────┐  */
                     /*        [↓]                │"Second" pushes│ */
                     /*        ●["Second"]←●───────┤"First" down  │  */
                     /*        ●["First"]          │into the Stack│  */
                     /*                           └──────────────┘  */
                     /* "Third"┐                  ┌──────────────┐  */
                     /*        [↓]                │"Third" pushes │ */
                     /*    ┌──●["Third"]←●─────────┤"Second" down │  */
                     /*    │   ●["Second"]         │into the Stack│  */
                     /*    │   ●["First"]          └──────────────┘  */
                     /*    ↓                                         */
object peeked = stack.Peek();/* ┌──────────────┐                    */
/*     ↑   ┌─────────┐    ↓      │Peek returns  │                    */
/*     └───┤"Third"├←──────┴─────┤what is on top│                    */
/*         └─────────┘           │of the stack  │                    */
Debug.Log(peeked);/*             └──────────────┘                    */
// Third
```

Push() makes the size of the stack longer. Objects down in the stack are not accessible using Peek() or Pop(). This enforces the fact that the Stack is meant to be accessed in a specific manner. This behavior is called "Last in first out" ordering. Peek() will return the value of the object on the top of the stack, but will not remove it.

```
object popped = stack.Pop();
/*       ↑               ↓                              */
/*       └─┤"Third"│←────┴─┤Pop() pulls the│            */
/*         └───────┘       │top off of the │            */
/*         [↑]             │the Stack      │            */
/*         ●["Second"]→─┐  └───────────────┘            */
/*         ●["First"]   │                               */
/*                      ├─┤"Second" is now │            */
Debug.Log(popped);/*    │ │top of the stack│            */
// Third          /*  ↓ └────────────────┘              */
object secondPeek = stack.Peek();
Debug.Log(secondPeek);
// Second
```

To get the value of the object at the top of the stack and remove it use Pop(). By popping the stack you shorten the stack and the item before the top is promoted.

7.19.4 Movement Stack

Movement systems are often best managed by abstracting how something moves from asking it to move. This is best illustrated with the following:

```
public enum Moves
{
    None,
    Left,
    Right,
    Forward,
    Backward
}
```

You should limit your tasks to basic parameters. Let complex behavior do its work on its own. With a short set of Moves in the enum above we could move an object around with a short set of commands using a stack.

```
public void Move()
{
    if (Movements.Count > 0)
    {
        StartCoroutine(Movements.Pop());
    }
}

private IEnumerator MoveTo(Vector3 direction)
{
    Vector3 start = transform.position;
    Vector3 finish = transform.position + direction;
    float t = 0;
    while (t < 1)
    {
        transform.position = Vector3.Lerp(start, finish, t);
        t += Time.deltaTime;
        yield return new WaitForEndOfFrame();
    }
    Move();
}
```

A MonoBehaviour called MoveStack has the above two statements. The public function Move() simply looks at a stack of IEnumerators called Movements and Starts the co-routine at the top of the stack. The Movement stack has a property called Count which is greater than 0 so long as there's something to Pop from the top of the stack.

The MoveTo co-routine it starts is the same sort of co-routine we saw in the previous chapter. At the end of the co-routine we call on Move again to check if there's another object in the stack to execute.

```
private Stack<IEnumerator> Movements;

public void AddMove(Moves move)
{
    if (Movements == null)
        Movements = new Stack<IEnumerator>();

    switch (move)
    {
        case Moves.None:
            Movements.Push(MoveTo(Vector3.zero));
            break;
        case Moves.Left:
            Movements.Push(MoveTo(Vector3.left));
            break;
        case Moves.Right:
            Movements.Push(MoveTo(Vector3.right));
            break;
        case Moves.Forward:
            Movements.Push(MoveTo(Vector3.forward));
            break;
        case Moves.Backward:
            Movements.Push(MoveTo(Vector3.back));
            break;
    }
}
```

To add movements to the `MonoBehaviour MoveStack`, we have the `AddMove()` function which accepts the `Moves` enum. The switch statement pushes the `IEnumerator MoveTo()` with different `Vector3` values based on the incoming `Moves` enum into the `Movements` stack.

```
GameObject capsule = GameObject.CreatePrimitive(PrimitiveType.Capsule);
MoveStack mover = capsule.AddComponent<MoveStack>();
mover.AddMove(Moves.None);
mover.AddMove(Moves.Forward);
mover.AddMove(Moves.None);
mover.AddMove(Moves.None);
mover.AddMove(Moves.Right);
mover.AddMove(Moves.None);
mover.AddMove(Moves.Right);
mover.Move();
```

This simplifies moving around a game object. Simply `AddMove()` and then tell the script to `Move()`. In the scene a capsule appears and begins moving around based on the stack of Movement commands.

Stacks aren't as intuitive since the ordering is "last in first out." The last command you add to the stack is the first command to be executed. An undo list is often a stack, since you want to keep the most recent command at the top of the stack. To have a better sense of execution order a Queue is more often used.

7.19.5 Queues

A Queue is first in first out. So by adding objects at the start of the queue, they're the first go come back out of a queue. So in the code fragment below we add first second and third in that order to the queue.

```
Queue queue = new Queue();
queue.Enqueue("First");
queue.Enqueue("Second");
queue.Enqueue("Third");
Debug.Log(queue.Peek());
// First
Debug.Log(queue.Dequeue());
// First
Debug.Log(queue.Dequeue());
// Second
Debug.Log(queue.Dequeue());
// Third
```

When we dequeue we get first second and third in the same order we added them. Rather than `Push()` and `Pop()` to add and remove from a stack we use `Enqueue()` and `Dequeue()` to add and remove from the `Queue` type. The `Peek()` function remains the same between the `Stack` and `Queue` types.

A modification to the MoveStack MonoBehaviour to a MoveQueue MonoBehaviour swaps the Stack for a Queue. Likewise, the commands in the `AddMove()` function change from `Push()` to `Enqueue()`.

```csharp
private Queue<IEnumerator> Movements;

public void AddMove(Moves move)
{
    if (Movements == null)
        Movements = new Queue<IEnumerator>();

    switch (move)
    {
        case Moves.None:
            Movements.Enqueue(MoveTo(Vector3.zero));
            break;
        case Moves.Left:
            Movements.Enqueue(MoveTo(Vector3.left));
            break;
        case Moves.Right:
            Movements.Enqueue(MoveTo(Vector3.right));
            break;
        case Moves.Forward:
            Movements.Enqueue(MoveTo(Vector3.forward));
            break;
        case Moves.Backward:
            Movements.Enqueue(MoveTo(Vector3.back));
            break;
    }
}
```

The co-routine is also changed from `Pop()` to `Dequeue()` to execute the IEnumerator co-routine from the queue of Movements.

```csharp
public void Move()
{
    if (Movements.Count > 0)
    {
        StartCoroutine(Movements.Dequeue());
    }
}
```

The Movements.Count works the same on both the Queue and Stack.

The MoveQueue can be used in the same way as the MoveStack, only we might have a better idea on how it will move using a Queue rather than a Stack.

```csharp
GameObject capsule = GameObject.CreatePrimitive(PrimitiveType.Capsule);
MoveQueue mover = capsule.AddComponent<MoveQueue>();
mover.AddMove(Moves.None);
mover.AddMove(Moves.Forward);
mover.AddMove(Moves.None);
mover.AddMove(Moves.Left);
mover.AddMove(Moves.Right);
mover.AddMove(Moves.None);
mover.AddMove(Moves.Backward);
mover.Move();
```

7.19.6 What We've Learned

Organizing and referencing data is an important part of programming. Therefore, much of programming is collecting, organizing, and reorganizing data; there are already many mechanisms in place for use in your own code.

Learning every system in C# isn't our goal. What is important is remembering that there is a system that might be useful for many different situations. As you begin to remember them, you can look them up later to see how they're used.

The most important part of learning any language is the fact that there are words such as queue, stack, and dictionary, which all manage data differently. When you come across something that looks like a list of things that need to be handled, then you should look up what system might best suit your needs at the time.

It's impossible to learn everything at once. It's difficult to remember even half of the features that any programming language has. What's not difficult is looking things up on the Internet and remembering how they're used by reading some examples.

The best thing to do is observing how these constructs have been used here. When you're working on your own and come across something that seems familiar, it's a good idea to go looking around and try to remember what you learned here as a refresher. Then apply the discovery to your current task.

7.20 Lambda Expressions

Now that we're iterating through arrays, it's time to put those arrays to some work for you. Lambda expressions are relatively new to C#. The concept finds its origin in lambda calculus, an invention of the 1930s. The calculus form uses arrows with notation that looks a bit like the following:

$$(x) \to x \cdot x$$

Unity 3D now updates with the latest version of C#. Lambda expressions were first introduced with C# 3.5. Lambda expressions were an upgrade from what is called an anonymous function. Anonymous functions were basically clips of code that could be stored as a variable. This sounds a bit like a delegate, and in some ways it is.

To clarify, we've made some uses of delegates with some basic uses in previous chapters. When we create a delegate, we need to do a bit of setup ahead of time to use them. We can use a delegate only if it's been created and a variable defined to hold onto the delegated tasks. Lambda expressions allow for creating and using a delegate in a single line.

The major difference is that an anonymous function can appear in the middle of your `Start()` or `Update()` function. Then be set to a variable before being used. After the anonymous function is declared, its arguments are assigned in the same statement where it's used. Because anonymous expressions still work in C#, it's good to know how they work and why lambdas replaced them.

One strange syntactical situation that needs to be seen is the fact you can declare a function inside of a function.

```
void UseFunctionInAFunction()
{
    /* this function is hidden outside    */
    /* of this function.                  */
    void FunctionInAFunction()
    {
        Debug.Log("Im a function in a function.");
    };
    FunctionInAFunction();
    // Im a function in a function.
}
```

The immediate utility of something like this might not be readily apparent, but when it comes to keeping code portable this might come into play. A complex situation where you're able to protect and hide the inner workings of a function might benefit from using a complex function as a base for abstract classes to inherit.

Where these weird situations do come up are where delegates and events might require a special case.

7.20.1 Anonymous Expressions

Anonymous expressions are basically short functions that can appear in the middle of a function. This seems a bit weird, but this will make more sense once we see what the code looks like.

```
delegate void SomeDelegate();
void NamedExpression()
{
    Debug.Log("Named Expression called.");
}
void UseAnonymousExpression()
{
    // un named function assigned to SomeDelegate();
    SomeDelegate del = () => Debug.Log("Anonymous Expression called.");
    del += NamedExpression;
    del.Invoke();
    // Anonymous Expression called.
    // Named Expression called.
}
```

In most cases you'll declare a delegate as a template to follow. In this case a very simple delegate called `SomeDelegate()` returns void and has no parameters. As delegates can accept more than one function assigned to them, the above code shows del being assigned a `Debug.Log()` call as assigned through the `= () => Debug.Log();` syntax. This is followed by the more common `+= NamedExpression()` syntax as we've seen before. When the `Invoke()` function is called on the delegate both the anonymous assignment and the named function are called in the order in which they were assigned.

```
delegate int Multiply(int a, int b);
void UseAnotherAnonymousExpression()
{
    Multiply m = (a, b) => a * b;
    Debug.Log("m = " + m.Invoke(5, 6));
    // m = 30

}
```

Depending on the complexity of the delegate definition, the anonymous expression would look different. The above delegate returns an int value and accepts two parameters. In the body of the function we assign m the values `(a, b) => a * b;` where the debut prints out the result of the math. This of course doesn't mean we must follow any rules when making the assignment.

```
m = (a, b) => a / b;
Debug.Log("m = " + m.Invoke(50, 5));
// m = 10
```

The name of the delegate is Multiply, but we can fib, and assign any use of the delegate we want. This allows quite a lot of flexibility, though we should keep in mind what's expected from a delegate named Multiply to do what it says.

```
/*                                          */
/*              ┌─────────────────┐         */
/*              │ input parameters│         */
/*              └─────────────────┘         */
/*                      │                    */
SomeDelegate del = ( ) => { };
/*                       │                   */
/*                       │                   */
/*              ┌─────────────────┐         */
/*              │lambda expression│         */
/*              └─────────────────┘         */

/*                                          */
/*              ┌─────────────────┐         */
/*              │ input parameters│         */
/*              └─────────────────┘         */
/*                      │                    */
Multiply mult = (a, b) => a + b;
/*                        │                  */
/*                        │                  */
/*              ┌─────────────────┐         */
/*              │lambda expression│         */
/*              └─────────────────┘         */
```

The syntax involves two main parts, a set of input parameters indicated with () the => operator followed by an expression. The expression can be encapsulated with a set of curly braces, or if it's simple enough the expression can appear in the same line with the => operator. Lambda expressions are intended to be short quick statements so in most cases a single line is often used without curly braces.

These are called anonymous expressions since the expression section of the assignment has no name. With a delegate assigned to a function we use a name pointing at a function. Something like void SomeDelegatedTask() can be assigned to a delegate. When using an anonymous expression there's no named function assigned, it's just the code without a named function around it.

7.20.1.1 A Basic Example—Action Func and Expression

Functions are meant to be reused. In many cases, writing a delegate type that's used once can feel a bit verbose. In the same way, functions written to assign to a delegate that's called once may also feel overwritten. To avoid unnecessary code being written lambda functions can reduce the amount of excess code to accomplish a complex behavior.

```csharp
void UseAction()
{
    IEnumerator delayedCall(Action del)
    {
        Debug.Log("Delayed Call Started.");
        yield return new WaitForSeconds(3f);
        Debug.Log("Delayed Call Finished.");
        del.DynamicInvoke();
    }
    StartCoroutine(delayedCall(() => Debug.Log("A Basic Action.")));
    // Delayed Call Started.
    // (3 seconds)
    // Delayed Call Finished.
    // A Basic Action.
}
```

The unusual use of an inner function can also be used to create an IEnumerator function to use as a co-routine. This can allow this one function to remain self contained. In previous examples the functions used in a coroutine were all separate functions.

The parameter of the delayedCall is an Action which is a type of Delegate. To start the coroutine, we assign a lambda function in the delayedCall parameter in the StartCoroutine() function. An Action is a type of Delegate. Remember that we normally have to define a delegates signature before we can use it. An Action is basically a collection of predefined delegate functions.

```
void UseMoreActions()
{
    int delay = 0;
    IEnumerator delayedCall(Action<int, int> action, int a, int b, float delayTime)
    {
        yield return new WaitForSeconds(delayTime);
        action.DynamicInvoke(a, b);
    }
    Action<int, int> mult = (a, b) =>
    {
        Debug.Log("a * b = " + (a * b));
    };
    Action<int, int> add = (a, b) =>
    {
        Debug.Log("a + b = " + (a + b));
    };
    Action<int, int> sub = (a, b) =>
    {
        Debug.Log("a - b = " + (a - b));
    };

    StartCoroutine(delayedCall((a, b) => Debug.Log("a:" + a + " b:" + b), 2, 3, delay++));
    // a: 2 b: 3
    StartCoroutine(delayedCall(mult, 3, 5, delay++));
    // a * b = 15
    StartCoroutine(delayedCall(add, 7, 13, delay++));
    // a + b = 20
    StartCoroutine(delayedCall(sub, 23, 7, delay++));
    // a - b = 16
}
```

Some of the fun here is the reusing of code inside of a function. Three specific Actions are used in the above example: a mult, add, and sub. These print out a result after a delay provided by a co-routine. Without writing any additional code the above could continue to print many more lines of math once a second.

The Action has many pre-defined variations for incomint parameters. Func is another type of delegate that has a return value. The Func is an Action with a return value. When defining a Func you may notice that the auto-complete provided by Visual Studio has some additional notation.

```
Func<int, >
▲ 2 of 17 ▼  Func<in T, out TResult>
```

One of the options includes out TResult as one of the many provided overrides.

```
Func<int, int> intOutFunc = (x) => x * x;
int result = intOutFunc(3);
Debug.Log(result);
// 9
```

Assigning the Func the above code returns the value to `int result` after processing 3. The Func uses generic types for both input and output. Generics allow for a great deal of flexibility.

7.20.2 Lambda Expressions

Lambda expressions are best recognized by the => operator. This is sometimes called either the *becomes* or the *points to* operator. This wording is used because the left side becomes the expression to the right side of the => operator. This works the same as the assignment operator =, only we're assigning a variable the result of an expression. The following code sample simply takes out some of the extra syntax used by the anonymous expression.

7.20.3 A Queue of Lambdas

Lambdas expand your ability to create different uses for events from within your code. Without writing many dozens of class functions you're able to assign unique behaviors to an object without needing to write hard-coded functions.

In a previous exercise we wrote a function that would start a co-routine based on a Movement enum. We'd then push different vectors into a queue to move an object around in the scene. Rather than a queue of co-routines, we can also create a queue of Lambdas expressions.

```
class DoesThings : MonoBehaviour
{
    // stored list of Delegates
    public Queue<Delegate> ThingsToDo;

    /* a single function to start      */
    /* and execute the generate        */
    /* task list.                      */
    public void StartDoingThings()
    {
        IEnumerator DoSomeThings()
        {
            int thing = 0;
            while (ThingsToDo.Count > 0)
            {
                yield return new WaitForSeconds(1);
                ThingsToDo.Dequeue().DynamicInvoke(thing++);
            }
            Debug.Log("Done doing things.");
        }
        StartCoroutine(DoSomeThings());
    }
}
```

In the function where we start doing the things we include an inner function. The innerfunction is a simple IEnumerator that's called immediately after it's defined. The `ThingsToDo` Queue is a collection of delegates where we use `DynamicInvoke()` to call the code contained in the Queue.

```
GameObject capsule = GameObject.CreatePrimitive(PrimitiveType.Capsule);
DoesThings doerOfThings = capsule.AddComponent<DoesThings>();

// assign procedural task list
doerOfThings.ThingsToDo = new Queue<Delegate>();
for (int i = 0; i < 7; i++)
{
    // Delegate functions generated
    Action<int> action = (x) =>
    {
        Debug.Log("doing #" + x);
    };
    // assign them to the MonoBehaviour
    doerOfThings.ThingsToDo.Enqueue(action);
}
// start the task list
doerOfThings.StartDoingThings();
```

The `Action<int>` is added to the `ThingsToDo` Queue. The Lambda here is static, but it's possible to pick different Lambda functions to assign to the queue in the MonoBehaviour attached to the capsule. Running the code above will execute doing #1 to #6 as the functions in the queue are invoked.

7.20.4 What We've Learned

Lambda expressions are more useful than simply printing to the Console; they're often used to sort through arrays of data. The same goes for anonymous expressions, but it's more important that we use a lambda expression to do this.

7.21 Leveling Up

We've reached the end of a very difficult chapter. One of the most important topics that have been covered more than once is inheritance. We looked at several different systems about controlling the inheritance of a class. Special classes such as the abstract class and the interface control how inheritance is managed.

We've been working to become a functional programmer, or at least being able to talk to one. At this point, it should be plausible that you would be able to build some interesting behaviors and write something compelling.

When talking about special programming tricks and learning new idioms and patterns, a great deal of work can be done by reading code. Finding interesting projects on GitHub or any other open-source code sharing site is a good place to start.

Studying code is more than trying to just understand what each statement is trying to do. The hard part is to interpret what an entire function is doing, determine how it works, and check if it's doing something you haven't seen before.

If the code contains a new trick, learn how it works. If the structure looks interesting, try to understand why it was built in that way. If there is new syntax, look it up and figure out how it works. The more code you read, the more you'll learn.

In Chapter 8, we'll look at some more interesting tricks and some common patterns, and syntax that is often used by more skilled programmers. Of course, not everything will be covered in as much depth as it deserves, but it's a starting point.

8

Extended

8.1 What We'll Be Covering in This Chapter

If we've got this far together, we're in a good position to learn some of the more interesting aspects of the C# language. Not everything in this chapter is common in everyday programming, but it's all good to know, or at least know about.

We'll cover a few new tricks that include some style, some interesting syntax with LINQ, and more obscure number of tricks. A few design patterns and structure ideas will also be introduced. It's easy to get carried away with the new tricks and use them everywhere. It's important to remember when these tricks are useful and to use them in moderation.

- Readability
- Source control, revisited
- Debugging techniques
- Recursion
- Reflection
- LINQ
- Bitwise operations
- Attributes
- Architectures
- Design patterns

This chapter is relatively short in comparison to the Chapters 2 through 7. At this point, it should only act as a launch pad to start you on your own into further study. Many of the basic concepts that will be covered have a wider scope into themselves than can be covered in this book.

Concepts like architecture and their related systems often cover entire volumes of text that dive deep into topics about optimizations and use cases. In this chapter, we'll cover the topics only in a very superficial way.

There are some important tricks here: Bitwise operations are useful for enums and dealing with what are called flags. We'll also be covering some of the trickier topics of attributes and reflection. We'll also cover the last looping system called recursion in which a function calls itself.

8.2 Review

Previously we looked over the topics of events and some interfaces. There are hundreds of other common interfaces, but thanks to implementing a few of them and making our own interfaces, we should be able to understand what interfaces are and how they're used.

Delegate functions and anonymous functions are useful abbreviations of a named function. When you need to deal with delays and call backs, delegates and concurrent functions work together to wait for data without holding up your other functions.

Accessors, also known as properties, are also very useful to catch bugs early on. As a creative engineer you can decide how your code communicates. You decide to use `MyClass.property = data;` or `MyClass.SetProperty(data);`. Because properties can be so flexible, it's good to know a bit about how to best think about them.

```csharp
public class Review : MonoBehaviour
{
    void UseHasProperties()
    {
        CanIHasProperties hasProperties = new CanIHasProperties();
        hasProperties.IHasFloat = 5f;
        Debug.Log(hasProperties.IHasFloat);
        // 5
        Debug.Log(hasProperties.IHasHalfFloat);
        // 2.5
        hasProperties.IHasHalfFloat = 9f;
        Debug.Log(hasProperties.IHasFloat);
        // 18
    }
}

class CanIHasProperties
{
    protected float hasFloat;
    public float IHasFloat
    {
        get { return hasFloat; }
        set { hasFloat = value; }
    }
    public float IHasHalfFloat
    {
        get { return hasFloat * 0.5f; }
        set { hasFloat = value * 2; }
    }
}
```

In the above code, we have a `IHasFloat` and `IHasHalfFloat` exposed to the public. We can get and set either one and get predictable values set by using either one. The `Debug.Log()` files return half and can set them at half. Whether or not these values make sense is determined by how you intend them to be used. Should setting `IHasHalfFloat` mean that you are giving a half value or giving it a value to be halved?

Like so many things, how the accessors are implemented is up to you; they're flexible in that you're allowed to write any form of logic into them. This power also opens the opportunity for problems. Expecting one thing and getting another means only a miscommunication or a bug in the code.

Like so many things, writing code that makes sense means communication not only by your code to the reader but also between engineers. When you are working on your projects alone at home, you might be moving between different side projects. The systems you write should be portable and usable between your projects.

If you write a useful character controller, it's a shame to have to write another one for a different project that has a similar behavior. Any time you can reuse good code, you're saving time and effort and making advancements in your game's progress. Make enough parts for a game; eventually you'll be able to assemble an entire game by copying and pasting code from your other projects!

8.3 Readability

Reducing complexity and keeping the notation short is a simple way to make your code easier to read. Some of these notations follow specific patterns. For example, the `foreach()` loop is a more simple version of the `for(;;)` loop without an internally scoped int. There are other optimizations that you can use to make your code more brief, but in some cases the code becomes a bit less clear.

Some of these optimizations have become common enough to be called idioms, or commonly used programming patterns. C# idioms have been inherited from other programming languages like C and C++, which have had a longer history and more time to develop common patterns.

8.3.1 ?: Notation

A simple system to change a value based on a single comparison is the ?: notation.

```
var result = condition ? true: false;
```

The above notation is a truncation of the following code:

```
string result;
bool condition = true;
if (condition)
{
    result = "True";
}
else
{
    result = "False";
}
Debug.Log("Result of condition = " + result);
// Result of condition = True
```

The first notation might be confusing the first time you see it; however, its compactness is its advantage. There are many cases where keeping a simple "if true do this, else do that" to a single line makes sense.

```
bool condition = true;
/*                                            */
/*                                            */
string result = condition ? "True" : "False";
/*                                            */
/*                                            */
/*                 first statement returned   */
/*                 if condition is true else  */
/*                 second statement is returned*/
/*                                            */
Debug.Log("Result of condition = " + result);
// Result of condition = True
```

The ternary is made of three parts a condition followed by a true statement then a false statement. In practice a ternary is usually used for short statements.

```
int greaterThan(int a, int b)
{
    return a > b ? a : b;
}
Debug.Log("Greater:" + greaterThan(5, 7));
// Greater:7
```

The above code simply returns the value of which int is greater than the other; it's simple and has only one line of code. If a is greater than b, return a; otherwise return b. The code is very simple and elegant and, more important, very hard to break. The above notation becomes less clear if you nest conditions.

```
int greaterThan(int a, int b, int c)
{
    return (a > b) ? ((a > c) ? a : c) : ((b > c) ? b : c);
}
Debug.Log("Greater:" + greaterThan(5, 7, 11));
// Greater:11
```

The above code compares all three values and returns the greatest, though from looking at the code it's not clear that this will do. The parentheses help, but they're not necessary. The above code could look like the following:

```
int greaterThan(int a, int b, int c)
{
    return a > b ? a > c ? a : c : b > c ? b : c;
}
Debug.Log("Greater:" + greaterThan(5, 7, 11));
// Greater:11
```

Even though the above code is perfectly valid, it's less readable.

8.3.2 If

Another common strategy to keep code clean is to ignore curly braces {} when an if statement controls only one line of code.

```
if (true)
    Debug.Log("No curly braces needed");
else
    Debug.Log("Doesn't do much for me.");
Debug.Log("done with if.");
```

The above code uses only tabs to determine the execution of each line. You're allowed to omit curly braces {} if each statement is only one line long. This works for a single if statement as well.

```
int i = 0;
while (i < 3)
    Debug.Log("No curly braces needed: " + i++);
Debug.Log("while done.");


int i = 0;
do
    Debug.Log("No curly braces here either:" + i++);
while (i < 3);
Debug.Log("do done.");


for (int i = 0; i < 3; i++)
    Debug.Log("still no curly braces:" + i);
Debug.Log("for done.");
```

The above code shows other statements without the regular curly braces. The readability of each form changes with the exclusion of the formatting afforded by the curly brace placements.

8.3.3 Smell

Programming style is sometimes referred to as either flavor or smell. As such there are good smells and bad smells. A bad smell doesn't necessarily mean that the code is broken and buggy. However, bad smelling code usually leads to problems later.

This programming style is categorized into several groups.

8.3.3.1 Comments

Comments are descriptive but useless. They make up a part of your code as much as functions and variables. They're used to inform fellow programmers as to what a function or code block is used for. Poorly commented code smells bad, and such bad smells cause many headaches.

The real problems begin once any major overhaul of the code is required. Poorly formatted or organized code can become more problematic when finding and replacing field names or function names. Code that conforms to an expected formatting can more quickly and easily be updated, whereas bad smelling code will often result in botched renaming and replacing in a process called refactoring that will be covered in Section 8.12.5.

8.3.3.2 One Responsibility Rule

Long extremely complex functions often exude a certain bad smell. When a function gets too long, it's often a source for many different problems. Here, bad smell means that finding a problem in the function can take a long time to fix. Short functions are easier to debug as there are only fewer lines of code to fix.

The problem usually comes about when a single function tries to do too many different tasks. In other words, a function should have enough statements to complete a specific task and nothing more. Once a function completes more than necessary, it's time to split the function into two or more different functions.

A function should ever take care of only a single task. If there's a repeated task that needs to happen, then another new function should be written to take on that responsibility. This means that many different functions can also make use of a function that has that one task.

8.3.3.3 Duplicated Code

Long functions often have many repeated sections of code, leading to more problems. If one block of code needs a fix, the same fix will need to be applied to every other block that looks and acts in a similar fashion. Repeated code means repeated effort in fixing bugs.

Long functions often use too many parameters; more than two or three arguments in a function's list can also lead to bad smelling code. Often these long parameter lists can feed into longer logical chains.

A long ladder of if-else statements can become very difficult to decode and interpret. Too many conditions in a single if statement also lead to bad smelling code. In some cases, they're difficult to avoid, but they will leave a bad smell even if the code works.

There are always more simple and clever ways to solve problems like too many arguments and conditions. Clever solutions come once you've accumulated experience. To gain this experience, you need to expose yourself to a lot of clever code and read and understand how it all works.

We're not seeing many clever examples in this book, only pragmatic examples to explain basic concepts. There are programmers who are quite clever and willing to share their wisdom on the internet. Forums are a great way to seek clever solutions to complex problems.

8.3.3.4 Naming

Both variables and functions should follow a simple naming convention. When a name becomes too long and cumbersome, it's difficult to read statements that use long identifiers. Programming shouldn't feel like a restrictive set of rules that confine what you're allowed to do. However, there are some general concepts that help keep code readable and easy to understand.

For true false data types like bools, it's often useful to prefix the variable with "is" such as bool isActive; or bool isEnabled. If the prefixing is consistent throughout your own code, you'll be able to identify a variable as a bool simply by its name.

Classes and structs should be named as nouns. A Zombie class is a perfect example. A classZombie is a horrible name for a Zombie class. If it's a noun, you already know it's a class object, and having a type in the name of the variable is redundant.

Classes that inherit from certain interfaces should start with an uppercase I, so, for example, a Graveyard which inherits from IEnumerable should be an IGraveyard. In most cases, a naming standard should be followed. Usually, when you join a company or group of programmers, you'll want to come to agree on a shared set of coding standards.

8.3.4 What We've Learned

Coding standards are commonly thought about and shared, so there are many references on the internet. General concepts can easily be followed to avoid bad smelling code and inconsistent identifier names. It's important to discover on your own why these rules have been written. This comes about only through practice and reading code on your own.

8.4 Git Revisited

Working in a team means more than one person might modify a file. When changes overlap, picking how the changes come together is called merging. In the best case your change will modify code in a different part of a file from someone else's change.

In the general case when you get started at the beginning of your day, you start with coffee, maybe a doughnut, boot up your computer and open Unity. However, if you're working with a team you missed a step. The first thing before opening Unity is Git. Since Git serves as a repository for everyone's work the first thing is to catch up with the work anyone else has contributed.

8.4.1 Git Branch and Merge

In the Git Bash shell start by creating what's called a branch. A Branch in Git is a system to isolate changes you're about to make. When a branch is created you've created a special save point. This can be better visualized with a graph created in the Git Bash console. Open the Git Bash and enter the command:

```
git log
```

This displays in text the last several check-ins with the most recent at the top. You can scroll through the log with the up and down arrow keys. The Q key quits the log view and you're free to type commands again.

```
commit 6d822783ef4adac0cac8b0ddb2f300e624a71703 (HEAD -> AddingReadMe, origin/develop, develop)
Merge: 64ce5bc e34f565
Author:        Alex Okita <           @           >
Date:    Tue Dec 11 22:17:20 2018 -0800

    Merge remote-tracking branch 'origin/master' into develop

commit e34f5654931beb37d15a4deb41ed1e267640d253 (origin/master, origin/HEAD)
Author: alexokita <            @         >
Date:    Tue Dec 11 22:16:59 2018 -0800

    Update README.md
```

Another way to check out what's going on is with the following command:

```
git log --graph
```

That's two dashes followed by "graph."

```
* commit 6d822783ef4adac0cac8b0ddb2f300e624a71703 (HEAD -> AddingReadMe, origin/develop, develop)
|\  Merge: 64ce5bc e34f565
| | Author:        \Alex Okita <           @           >
| | Date:    Tue Dec 11 22:17:20 2018 -0800
| |
| |     Merge remote-tracking branch 'origin/master' into develop
| |
| * commit e34f5654931beb37d15a4deb41ed1e267640d253 (origin/master, origin/HEAD)
| | Author: alexokita <            @         >
| | Date:    Tue Dec 11 22:16:59 2018 -0800
| |
| |     Update README.md
```

This shows the most detail for the `log` command. The string of numbers and letters after the commit is a unique hash creating an identifier for the check-in. To the right of the hash is the branch on which the check-in was made. The comment, date, and the author are also included with the check-in information. Another way to more clearly see the dots and lines is to hide the added information leaving only the comments with:

```
git log --graph --oneline
```

The above is git log space, followed by dash dash graph space, dash dash oneline.

```
*   6d82278 (HEAD -> AddingReadMe, origin/develop, develop) Merge remote-tracking branch 'origin/master
' into develop
|\
| * e34f565 (origin/master, origin/HEAD) Update README.md
* |   64ce5bc Merge branch 'master' into develop
|\ \
| |/
| * 2ff49d5 (master) Create README.md
* | 8c55836 added some more stuff to chapter 8
* | ac4c636 more stuff for chapter 7
* | f008904 adding some more stuff to ch7
* | 57f32f5 more last minute additions
:█
```

The `--oneline` command tells the graph to hide extra information making the dots and lines more visible. Each dot in the vertical time line is a check-in of changes. Not to a single file, but to everything that was committed and pushed. Each vertical line is a branch, imagine the branches as timelines with unique events. When branches come back together, they merge combining the changes from each timeline. When starting out you'll be working in the master branch. To observe how branches work, we'll make one with the command:

```
git branch NewReadme
```

This creates a branch called `NewReadme`. After this we'll need to jump to the branch we made. This is done with the command:

```
git checkout NewReadme
```

nothing to commit, working tree clean

alexokita@Buggy MINGW64 ~/Documents/BookContents/Chapters/Chapter8
(master)
$ git branch NewReadme

alexokita@Buggy MINGW64 ~/Documents/BookContents/Chapters/Chapter8
(master)
$ git checkout NewReadme
Switched to branch 'NewReadme'

alexokita@Buggy MINGW64 ~/Documents/BookContents/Chapters/Chapter8
(NewReadme)
$ ▉

The name of the branch you're in is indicated at the end of the line in the parenthesis (`NewReadme`) changes, based on the branch you're working in. Now the changes we make will take place in the `NewReadme` branch. The changes we make here are now in a new timeline. So when we add the following to a README.md text file in Chapter 8 we only effect the `NewReadme` timeline.

```
#Chapter8
- - -
Welcome to the Chapter8 project.
```

A regular text file called README.md is added with the text seen above. The command:
`git status` shows the following:

(NewReadme)
$ git status
On branch NewReadme
Untracked files:
** (use "git add <file>..." to include in what will be committed)**

**   README.md**

nothing added to commit but untracked files present (use "git add"
to track)

alexokita@Buggy MINGW64 ~/Documents/BookContents/Chapters/Chapter8
(NewReadme)
$ ▉

With the new README.md file created we should check it. As we had done before we add

```
$ git checkout master
Switched to branch 'master'
Your branch is up to date with 'origin/master'.
```

```
$ git push
fatal: The current branch NewReadme has no upstream branch.
To push the current branch and set the remote as upstream, use

    git push --set-upstream origin NewReadme
```

So we enter the command it suggests and we can push the new branch to our fork on GitHub.

```
 * [new branch]      NewReadme -> NewReadme
Branch 'NewReadme' set up to track remote branch 'NewReadme' from '
origin'.
```

So now the content is pushed and saved. We can continue to make changes on this branch without fear of losing work, or interfering with other people work. Branches are often used to add features or fix bugs.

Once everything works, we can then merge the work into the master branch. The idea here is to save work in progress, and when the feature is done, we can contribute our work to the main timeline and not break the build.

To merge the new README.md into the master branch we first jump back into the master branch with the command:

```
git checkout master
```

```
$ git checkout master
Switched to branch 'master'
Your branch is up to date with 'origin/master'.
```

This is followed by the git merge command:

```
git merge NewReadme
```

```
git merge NewReadme
$ git merge NewReadme
Updating e34f565..4835c5e
Fast-forward
 Chapters/Chapter8/README.md | 3 +++
 1 file changed, 3 insertions(+)
 create mode 100644 Chapters/Chapter8/README.md
```

To see the work, we can read the log. In this case, we didn't do a whole lot of changes, so the log doesn't look very interesting. In a case where multiple check-ins occurred, the log would have more interesting details. Our goal shouldn't be to make interesting looking git graphs, perhaps not in this chapter anyway.

Branches can be managed as a feature/NewMonster or perhaps bugfix/FixingScoreChart. Adding a slash makes the branches easier to differentiate. To facilitate this, an add on to Git called Git flow was created. Release versions and development branches are used to separate work.

It's not always necessary to merge branches. This is an important feature of Git. Branches can be used as an experimental divergence from the main timeline. You could for instance test a concept which might not work. This means that you can very easily check in work, test, and fail. Should your experiment not bear fruit, that's okay. You can checkout master and your experiment will have never touched the master branch.

8.4.2 Merge Conflicts

Not everything goes as planned. Merging code can often result in a merge conflict. A conflict occurs when changes from one branch do not match changes in another branch.

```
/* original function */
void FirstFunction()
{
    // doing things here
}
/*            | original                                              */
/*            ┌──────────────────────────────────┐                    */
/*            ↓ changed in Branch A                ↓ changed in Branch B */
/* void FirstFunction()                    void FirstFunction()        */
/* {                                       {                           */
/*     // doing things here                    // doing things here    */
/*     // This line changed in Branch A        // Same line changed in Branch B */
/* }                                       }                           */
/*                                                                     */
```

In the above we see a line changed in both Branch A and Branch B. When we are working in Branch A and we merge changes in from Branch B we'd get the following conflict:

```
    void FirstFunction()
    {
        // doing things here
<<<<<<< HEAD
        // This line changed in Branch A
=======
        // Same line changed in Branch B
>>>>>>> origin/BranchB
    }
```

The changes you're working on are at the HEAD or the latest you have. When merging, the changes appear after yours. From here you'll need to determine which line to keep and which to discard. For this you'll want to try out which version works better or is more important, or maybe you'll keep both lines. The result is your decision.

```
void FirstFunction()
{
    // doing things here
    // This line changed in Branch A (I like mine more)
}
```

Before pushing your code, always check that everything works. After you finish your changes commit and push. To use Unity as an example we'll look at the following:

```
// Start is called before the first frame update
void Start()
{
    Debug.Log("Player 1 Start");
}
```

Simple and to the point. This gets added this to a check-in and you commit the code. Then you merge from Git and get this message.

```
$ git merge origin/FirstBranch
Auto-merging Chapters/Chapter8/Assets/GitRevisited.cs
CONFLICT (content): Merge conflict in Chapters/Chapter8/Assets/GitRevisited.cs
Automatic merge failed; fix conflicts and then commit the result.
```

Git has changed the branch title from (develop) to (develop|MERGING) just to remind you there are conflicts that need resolution before you can push your code. At least we know what file needs merge. The CONFLICT points to the file where the content needs attention.

```
          // Start is called before the first frame update
          void Start()
          {
<<<<<<< HEAD
              Debug.Log("Player 1 Start");

              Debug.Log("Player Two Start");
>>>>>>> origin/FirstBranch
          }
```

To help you see the conflict, you get some characters which will not let your C# compile. There is also text indicating where and what changed. The HEAD indicates what you've changed, the text below indicates the branch from which the code conflict came from. In most cases it might be easy to talk to the author of the conflicting code. Discuss which change to keep, clean up the code, and check it all in.

This is a simple case, and there are sure to be larger, more severe conflicts in the real world. To help resolve these issues it's often useful to find a stand-alone diff-merge app. These won't be covered in this book since there are so many to choose from. However, the tools do the same thing, they look for the <<<<<<< and >>>>>>> to identify where the conflict came from. Then the ======= is used to find which block came from what source.

After the conflict is resolved, add, commit, and push as usual. There are times when you may have changed a file and forgot to add and commit before pulling. This results in the following:

```
$ git merge origin/SecondBranch
error: Your local changes to the following files would be overwritten by merge:
        Chapters/Chapter8/Assets/GitRevisited.cs
Please commit your changes or stash them before you merge.
Aborting
```

This tells you that you need to commit changes or stash them before merging. Git aborts the pull and you can choose to do either.

Stashing is a way to temporarily undo the changes to a file. To do this enter:

```
git stash
```

This creates a local check-in with a hash id. Now you're able to pull or merge as though none of the files you were working on had any changes. To un-stash the changes enter:

```
git stash pop
```

The pop command after stash infers a stack. And yes, stashes can be stacked. And as you pop stashed changes, the changes come out in order. However, if you pull and pop a stash you may still run into merge conflicts.

```
        // Start is called before the first frame update
        void Start()
        {
<<<<<<< HEAD
            Debug.Log("Change From Second Branch");

=======
            Debug.Log("Merge ahead of stash pop");
>>>>>>> bcc91fb3303769cee3d942d023b4af38f3437cb9
```

When you pop a stash after a pull you'll get a hash rather than a branch indicating where the conflict came from. After all this branching, merging, and stashing, the git graph is starting to look a bit more interesting:

```
* 43f6d41 (HEAD -> develop) Merge branch 'develop' of https://github.com/CSharpWithUnity/BookContents into develop
|\
| * bcc91fb (origin/develop) before unstashing
* | cccc327 Merge remote-tracking branch 'origin/SecondBranch' into develop
|\ \
| * | bd9cbeb (origin/SecondBranch) Second Branch Change.
| |/
* | 2db04ae my code
* | d4100bf Merge remote-tracking branch 'origin/FirstBranch' into develop
|\ \
| * | 7e10323 (origin/FirstBranch) changes 1 to Three
* | | 2398359 fixed
|\ \ \
| |/ /
| * | 59202ba Update GitRevisited.cs
* | | f526b43 changed 1 to Two
| |/
|/|
* | b46d1d4 (SecondBranch) Second Change
|/
* 500fcd1 (FirstBranch) change to one
```

If something seems to have changed and you remember a line acting differently from a different check-in, you're able to checkout a file from a specific hash. Each node in the graph is preceded by a 7-digit hash. This helps identify specific check-ins in the git repos history.

```
git checkout <hash> <path to file>
```

```
alexokita@Buggy MINGW64 ~/Documents/BookContents (develop)
$ git checkout 2398359 Chapters/Chapter8/Assets/GitRevisited.cs
```

The command above takes the version of the file indicated from that point in time and checks it out to your directory. The file replaces the one currently in the directory. The checkout also ignores any changes that are currently in progress. To read the history related to a specific file use:

```
git log --oneline <file name>
```

```
alexokita@Buggy MINGW64 ~/Documents/BookContents (develop)
$ git log --oneline Chapters/Chapter8/Assets/GitRevisited.cs
bcc91fb (origin/develop) before unstashing
b46d1d4 (SecondBranch) Second Change
500fcd1 (FirstBranch) change to one
30d7302 added git stuff
```

This shows the hash IDs for the file at each change. This will help when you want to pick a specific version of a file knowing the specific hash to use to check out the file will help.

8.4.3 What We've Learned

Once all the merges have been made and you've tested your code to make sure that everything still works as intended, it's time to push your changes back up to the server. At this point, it's a good idea to remind your fellow programmers to get the latest version before they make too many more changes.

Communication remains the best form of code conflict resolution. Making sure that your code integrates well involves talking to everyone to make sure your changes don't stomp on something others have been working on. Everyone has his or her own coding style. C# is flexible enough to allow different philosophies to work together.

Knowing your way around git is important. Even when working independently, using Git helps a great deal every step of the way. All too often the phrase, "This was working a few minutes ago; what did I break?" will be saved by reverting a file to a previous version. Using checkout with a hash can save a lot of time.

Git diff can show you what changed between check-ins, so if you checkout a specific file at a specific hash:

```
alexokita@Buggy MINGW64 ~/Documents/BookContents/Chapters/Chapter8/Assets (develop)
$ git checkout 3b87392 GitRevisited.cs
```

You can see what's different between that version and another with the following git diff command:

```
alexokita@Buggy MINGW64 ~/Documents/BookContents/Chapters/Chapter8/Assets (develop)
$ git diff 500fcd1 GitRevisited.cs
diff --git a/Chapters/Chapter8/Assets/GitRevisited.cs b/Chapters/Chapter8/Assets/GitRevisited.cs
index 1946902..c3ec366 100644
--- a/Chapters/Chapter8/Assets/GitRevisited.cs
+++ b/Chapters/Chapter8/Assets/GitRevisited.cs
@@ -9,7 +9,8 @@ namespace Chapter8_4
        // Start is called before the first frame update
        void Start()
        {
-            Debug.Log("Player One Start");
+            Debug.Log("Player 1 Start");
+            Debug.Log("Stashed Line");
        }

        // Update is called once per frame
```

In your Console, the + indicates added lines and the – indicates removed lines. Lines above and below the change are visible to help identify the context where the changes were made. You can also use `git diff` at any time to see what your current changes are.

The scenarios here are basic, but the commands are the same. There are still plenty of git commands that have not been revealed, but to do so would require an entire new book. Git is popular enough, that most questions have several answers findable through a quick internet search.

8.5 Recursion

> "To understand recursion, you must first understand recursion."
>
> **—James Teal**

We've studied most of the basic iteration loops. The for, while, do while, foreach, and even goto can be used to iterate through a task. Of all these options, we're left to adding them to the body of a function.

The for loop:

```
//for loop
for (int i = 0; i < 10; i++)
{
    Debug.Log("for:" + i);
}
```

The while loop:

```
// while loop
int i = 0;
while (i < 10)
{
    Debug.Log("while:" + i);
    i++;
}
```

The do loop:

```
// do loop
int i = 0;
do
{
    Debug.Log("do:" + i);
    i++;
} while (i < 10);
```

The foreach:

```
// foreach loop
int[] ints = { 0, 1, 2, 3, 4, 5, 6, 7, 8, 9 };
foreach (int i in ints)
{
    Debug.Log("foreach:" + i);
}
```

Enumerators:

```
// enumerator
int[] ints = { 0, 1, 2, 3, 4, 5, 6, 7, 8, 9 };
IEnumerator enumerator = ints.GetEnumerator();
while (enumerator.MoveNext())
{
    Debug.Log("enumerator:" + enumerator.Current);
}
```

And the unlikely goto:

```
{   // goto
    int i = 0;
BEGIN:
    if (i < 10)
    {
        Debug.Log("goto:" + i);
        i++;
        goto BEGIN;
    }
}
```

Each one of these loops will count from 0 to 9, and all of them operate within the UseLoops() func-tion. However, if we wanted to create a self-contained function, we might want to consider a recursive function. A recursive function, or method, is any method that calls upon itself.

Recursion is often used to deal with complex sets of data. If we're not sure how many layers of data are buried within a set of parameters, we need to have a flexible system to deal with what we're given.

8.5.1 A Basic Example

In the Recursion_Scene the Recursion script attached to the game object of the same name has the following:

```
// begin function  /*                                    */
recurse(0);           /* ↓ start recurse                 */
void recurse(int i)/* ←  ─────────────┐                  */
{                     /*               │                  */
    if (i < 10)       /* ↓ check i     │                  */
    {                 /*          ┌─────┤ start over       */
        Debug.Log("recurse:" + i);/*   └──────┘           */
        i++;          /* ↓ iterate i   │                  */
        recurse(i);/* →  ──────────────┘                  */
    }                 /*                                    */
}                     /*                                    */
```

8.5.2 Understanding Recursion

Using a recursive function can be a bit mind-bending at first. It's all too easy to set yourself up for a loop that never breaks. It's important that we understand why recursion works in order to use it more effectively. The first rule for a recursive function is to have a clear condition where the function returns without calling on itself. This is how the function breaks out of itself. If we look at the above example, the if statement has a clear escape condition where the recurse function will not call on itself.

```
int i = 11;

if (i > 10)
{
    Debug.Log(i);
    i++;
    // code isn't
    // reached.
}
```

This statement does not call on the recurse() function again, so the recursion stops here. The reason recursion repeats itself is that the function calls on itself at some point. Once the function stops calling itself, the recursion terminates. To observe this with another example consider the following:

```
CountDownRecursion(10);

void CountDownRecursion(int i)
{
    Debug.Log(i);
    if(i > 0)
    {
        i--;
        // Only called when
        // the if statement
        // is true.
        CountDownRecursion(i);
    }
}
```

Here we can see that int i is decremented just before recurring. Once i is no longer greater than 0, the function doesn't call on itself. Once the function stops calling on itself, the function ends, we've reached the end of the recursive loop.

8.5.3 In Practice

When dealing with a set of data with many child objects, we might have to use for loops within for loops to get through all the data. If there's another tier of data underneath that, then we might pass over it without even knowing. To get started, building a simple blob of game objects will be our first goal. This way we'll have something to sort through.

```
GameObject top = new GameObject("6_0");
CreateHierarchy(top, 5);
void CreateHierarchy(GameObject parent, int a)
{
    GameObject[] subObjs = new GameObject[a];
    int b = 0;
    while (b < a)
    {
        subObjs[b] = new GameObject(a + "_" + b);
        subObjs[b].transform.SetParent(parent.transform);
        b++;
    }

    // decrease the iterations
    a--;
    foreach (GameObject sub in subObjs)
    {
        CreateHierarchy(sub, a);
    }
}
```

The above code will produce a hierarchy of game objects in the scene. Some of the game objects were left collapsed. The above code is a recursive function to create a number of objects under a parent object. Each iteration is one less than the previous iteration. Once in the scene they're parented in such a way that they create the nested game object you see in the following hierarchy:

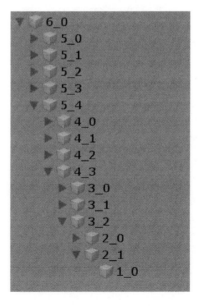

Now we'll want to make our recursive function that calls on itself to iterate through the whole lot of the game objects with a single call. After the recursive function is added, we just need to call it after the hierarchy of objects has been created.

```
LogObjects(top.transform);
void LogObjects(Transform a)
{
    Debug.Log(a.gameObject.name);
    foreach (Transform b in a)
    {
        LogObjects(b);
    }
}
```

With a complex hierarchy in the scene, we want to see each one of the game object's names printed to the Console panel with the recursive function LogObjects() by passing it a game object. It looks pretty simple, but there's a very interesting behavior that's going on with this simple function LogObjects(); in the Console panel.

```
1_0
UnityEngine.Debug:Log(Object)

1_0
UnityEngine.Debug:Log(Object)
Recursion:<UseHierarchy>g__ListObjects|3_1(Transform) (at Assets/Recursion.cs:155)
Recursion:<UseHierarchy>g__ListObjects|3_1(Transform) (at Assets/Recursion.cs:158)
Recursion:<UseHierarchy>g__ListObjects|3_1(Transform) (at Assets/Recursion.cs:158)
Recursion:<UseHierarchy>g__ListObjects|3_1(Transform) (at Assets/Recursion.cs:158)
Recursion:<UseHierarchy>g__ListObjects|3_1(Transform) (at Assets/Recursion.cs:158)
Recursion:<UseHierarchy>g__ListObjects|3_1(Transform) (at Assets/Recursion.cs:158)
Recursion:UseHierarchy() (at Assets/Recursion.cs:152)
Recursion:Start() (at Assets/Recursion.cs:195)
```

If you look at the log, you'll notice a single function is listed more than once! The first part of this log Recursion: indicates the class where the call is originating. It tells us what file is sending the Console output command.

After that we get the function name where a call is being made, UseHierarchy, which indicates what function has created the Debug:Log, highlighted in the Console panel.

The function has called several times! This is proof that the recursion is calling itself correctly. Also, it's quite interesting to see this behavior in action in the Console panel. Rather than just printing out the names of each game object in the hierarchy, we'd make something more useful with the information we're iterating through.

To build something more interesting to look at, we'll add in some GameObject primitives that spawned rather empty GameObjects with a name in the hierarchy. We'll add in some simple transforms and rotations to some primitives. To set a goal, we're going to build a set of objects parented to one another; like in the hierarchy, we're going to have them orbit around one another.

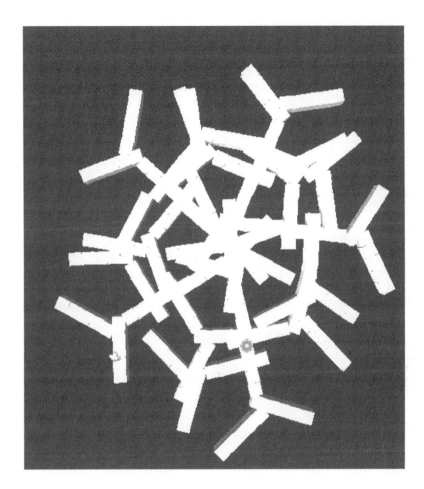

The above example will clearly show us a rotational relationship connected through the hierarchy. We'll start off with the following GameObject:

```
GameObject hub;
void UseObjectHieararchy()
{
    hub = new GameObject("hub");
    CreateHierarchy(hub, 5);
    void CreateHierarchy(GameObject parent, int a)
    {
        GameObject[] subObjs = new GameObject[a];
        int b = 0;
        while (b < a)
        {
            subObjs[b] = GameObject.CreatePrimitive(PrimitiveType.Cube);
            subObjs[b].name = a + "_" + b;
            subObjs[b].transform.SetParent(parent.transform);
            subObjs[b].transform.localEulerAngles = new Vector3()
            {
                x = 0,
                y = (360 / a) * b,
                z = 0
            };
            subObjs[b].transform.localPosition = new Vector3()
            {
                x = 1 * a + b,
            };
            b++;
        }

        // decrease the iterations
        a--;
        foreach (GameObject sub in subObjs)
        {
            CreateHierarchy(sub, a);
        }
    }
}
```

The GameObject hub is used at the class scope to begin. From here we'll try to stick to the same operation as we did before. However, after this we'll want to set some local offsets and rotations.

```
subObjs[b] = GameObject.CreatePrimitive(PrimitiveType.Cube);
subObjs[b].name = a + "_" + b;
subObjs[b].transform.SetParent(parent.transform);
subObjs[b].transform.localEulerAngles = new Vector3()
{
    x = 0,
    y = (360 / a) * b,
    z = 0
};
subObjs[b].transform.localPosition = new Vector3()
{
    x = 1 * a + b,
};
b++;
```

The above code takes over the construction of the hierarchy that we created before. Notice here that the parent object from the previous for loop has its localEulerAngles set before the child is parented. This makes it critical to get the rotation to affect the child. Without this function the child object rotates in place rather than having an orbit set.

In addition, I've also created each set of objects to different PrimitiveTypes; this gives some variety to the final solution to make different levels of hierarchy more clear. Then we'll add in a simple recursive function that rotates objects in the hierarchy.

```
void RotateHierarchy(Transform a)
{
    a.transform.Rotate(new Vector3()
    {
        y = 0.5f
    });
    foreach (Transform b in a)
    {
        RotateHierarchy(b);
    }
}
```

Rather than Debug.Log(), we'll use transform.Rotate and slowly rotate each object's *y* axis. Using the first command go.transform.Rotate(new Vector3(0, 0.5f, 0));, we'll simply grab the object and add some rotation to it. Now it's only a matter of adding the RotateHierarchy() function to the Update() function.

As programmers have a knack for giving clever names for systems, we've experienced what is commonly called linear recursion or sometimes single recursion. This is a recursive function that calls itself only once as a condition is met.

Linear recursion is the simplest type of recursive function. Basically, if we need to recurse then we do; otherwise we end the recursion. Because the linear recursion we wrote has the call to itself at the end of the function, it's in a subcategory of linear recursion functions called tail recursion.

Another common type of recursion is called indirect recursion. This occurs when two or more functions call on one another before ending. Indirect recursion is often useful for one function to be called that returns a completed set of data from the recursive function.

```csharp
ArrayList arrayList = GetList(hub);
ArrayList GetList(GameObject go)
{
    ArrayList list = new ArrayList();
    BuildList(go, list);
    return list;
}

void BuildList(GameObject go, ArrayList list)
{
    list.Add(go);
    foreach (Transform t in go.transform)
    {
        BuildList(t.gameObject, list);
    }
}

Debug.Log(arrayList.Count);
```

The first function called `GetList()` calls the recursive function and gives it a list to fill in. This function is commonly referred to as a wrapper function. The task in the recursive function adds the incoming game object to the list given by the wrapper function. Then if there are children, it repeats the process for every child. Once it's done, the recursion ends and the function which called it gets the completed list. For instance, can use these two functions with the following call:

```csharp
ArrayList arrayList = GetList(hub);
Debug.Log(arrayList.Count);
foreach (GameObject g in arrayList)
{
    Debug.Log(g);
}
```

The above code fragment creates a list, then iterates through the list, and logs the names of each object in the `arrayList` that was returned from the `GetList()` function. There are similarities between simple iterative loops like the one that created the original hierarchy of primitives and the recursive systems that look through them.

However, there are more differences at play than the superficial appearance of the code. In many cases, recursion functions often operate faster in the computer's memory than iterative functions. With increased complexity, the iterative function will slowdown more. Without going too far into how a computer's memory is managed, it's good to know that by using a recursive function you might be speeding things up, even if just by a tiny bit.

8.5.4 What We've Learned

As you might have guessed, there's a lot of information on recursion out on the vast sea of the internet. It's one of those topics that people tend to write about to prove their competence. Aside from the somewhat confusing nature of a function calling on itself, the more important part of the recursion function is when the function *doesn't* call on itself.

The programmers writing Unity must know that recursion is a tricky topic. Many functions provided like `GetComponentsInChildren()` do some recursion to iterate through all of the components in the gameObject's hierarchy. These functions supplant the necessity of writing your own function to do the same thing. That being said, at least now you know how the inner workings of the `GetComponent()` functions work.

8.6 LINQ

LINQ (language-integrated query) sorts objects and data.

Let's think for a moment about a data driven game in Unity 3D. A game where statistics, like hit points, magic, abilities, skills and the like are tracked and updated. You'll likely store a mass of data in either a spreadsheet, XML, Json file or database. This generates a long list of items with respective stats.

How then will we need to find and organize the items? One simple method is using LINQ, pronounced "link." LINQ stands for *language-integrated query,* something Microsoft introduced to C# and the .NET Framework several years ago. LINQ draws techniques created for database query systems like SQL. A database is a collection of information grouped and organized for searching and retrieval.

8.6.1 Lambdas and Arrays

Wading through a vast database of information can be intimidating. Writing a loop to search through an array and acting on each bit of data could be a verbose long-winded task. LINQ to the rescue. Instead of what might have been a rather tedious manual task of sifting through a scene with a bunch of monsters looking for the ones with the most hit points, you can now use the Linq library to sift through that data for you.

8.6.1.1 A Basic Example

We'll start with a simple way to find even numbers in an array of ints. This is found in the Chapter 8 Unity Project in the Linq_Scene in the Linq script on the game object of the same name.

```
int[] numbers = { 0, 1, 2, 3, 4, 5, 6, 7, 8, 9, 10 };
var evenNums = from n in numbers
               where (n % 2) == 0
               select n;
// Linq adds the keywords, from
// where and select.
foreach (int n in evenNums)
{
    Debug.Log(n);
}
// 0
// 2
// 4
// 6
// 8
// 10
```

The above code will produce the even numbers output when the game is run. The syntax involves the from keyword. The following n becomes a reused variable. Much like a foreach statement. Syntax in a Linq statement appears different, but the more it's seen the more sense it makes.

```
int[] numbers = { 0, 1, 2, 3, 4, 5, 6, 7, 8, 9, 10 };
/*         ┌──────────────●─────┐ numbers is an array     */
/*                   ┌──●─┐  ↓ n is each object in         */
/*                   ↓      ↑  ↓ the number array.         */
var evenNums = from n in numbers
/*       ↑ the result  ↓                                   */
/*       ● is added to └●┐ an operation is performed       */
/*       │ evenNums       ↓ on each object in the array    */
/*       │      */where (n % 2) == 0                       */
/*       │                ↓ if this operation is true      */
/*       │                ● the value is added to          */
/*       │                ↓ the result of the statement    */
/*       └────────←*/select n;
```

The value n represents each element in an array. Operations follow the extraction of each element. The where statement is a Boolean operation, if the statement is true, n is added to the result output array.

8.6.2 Var

The System.Linq library introduces many new keywords, the depth to which Linq can be used may actually surpass the scope of this book. We will cover the basics and a few cases in which Linq can be applied.

If we look at the variable we created called evenNums, we'll see that it's an IEnumerable<int> of values. Though the var can be different everywhere, it's used in your code as the type is assigned dynamically depending on how it's used.

```
int[] numbers = { 0, 1, 2, 3, 4, 5, 6, 7, 8, 9, 10 };
var evenNums = from n in numbers
```

[✪] (local variable) IEnumerable<int> evenNums

Hovering over each variable in Visual Studio can reveal quite a lot, especially when working with Linq where the result output type might not always be obvious. For instance, if we create a few different things assigned to var, we can see how C# sees the types being assigned to var.

```
var aThingHere = 7;
var anotherThingThere = (object)19;
var aDifferetThing = (float)23;

System.Type firstType = aThingHere.GetType();
System.Type secondType = anotherThingThere.GetType();
System.Type thirdType = aDifferetThing.GetType();

Debug.Log(firstType);
// System.Int32
Debug.Log(secondType);
// System.Int32
Debug.Log(thirdType);
// System.Single
```

The first is seen as int, the second as an object, and the third as a float. The var type is fine with any type of assignment, even arrays. The GetType is assigned based on the value it is first assigned. Once var has a type, it cannot change.

```
var someThing = 1;
var anotherThing = new GameObject();
someThing = anotherThing;
```

In the above, someThing has become an int. The other value anotherThing is a GameObject type. Once assigned, the int type someThing cannot accept GameObject type anotherThing.

8.6.3 LINQ From

For a more informative use for Linq, we'll add more detail to the operation of the Linq expression in a manner which might actually come up in use.

```
class Zombie
{
    public int hitPoints;
    public Zombie()
    {
        hitPoints = UnityEngine.Random.Range(1, 100);
    }
}
```

A nested class called zombie has some hit points that will be randomly assigned between 1 and 100 when a new Zombie is instanced. Then in we create a hundred zombie objects with the following block of code:

```
// make a bunch of zombies
Zombie[] zombieArray = new Zombie[100];
for (int i = 0; i < 100; i++)
{
    zombieArray[i] = new Zombie();
}
```

After the array is populated with some Zombie objects, we can find zombies with less than 50 hit points, with the following Linq expression.

```
// select weak zombies;
var weakZombies = from z in zombieArray
                  where z.hitPoints < 50
                  select z;
```

Then to prove that we've got a list of zombies with less than 50 hit points, we'll print out the hitPoints of each zombie in the new weakZombies var.

```
foreach (Zombie z in weakZombies)
{
    Debug.Log(z.hitPoints);
}
// a bunch of numbers < 50!
```

From this little exercise, we'll get the following output to the Console panel.

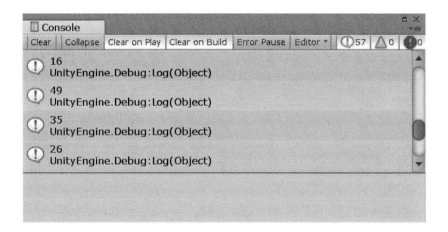

The multitude of tricks you can deploy using Linq can fill a book on its own. When dealing with a large number of objects to sort through, Linq is often the most flexible option. Another bonus is that it's surprisingly fast.

8.6.4 Strange Behaviors in LINQ

When a Linq query is created, it's not immediately executed. We can see the numbers array that we started with and observe some interesting behaviors by adding to the list after the Linq statement is used.

```
//declare an array
int[] numbers = { 0, 1, 2, 3, 4, 5, 6, 7, 8, 9, 10 };
var divisibleByThree = from n in numbers
            /*    └──┐ */where (n % 3) == 0
            /*       │ */select n;
numbers[0] = 1;/*    │ */
numbers[3] = 1;/*    │  changes made to numbers not to        */
numbers[6] = 30;/*   │  divisibleByThree but divisibleByThree */
numbers[9] = 300;/*↓  still knows it's function               */
foreach (int i in divisibleByThree)
{
    Debug.Log(i);
}
// 30
// 300
```

After the `divisibleByThree` Linq query is created, we can change the numbers in the array to new values after the Linq operation. After the `divisibleByThree` var is created, it's source data can be modified. It's only when the foreach statement uses the var from the Linq statement the actual query is made.

The above code prints out 30 and 300 values which were not in the numbers array when the Linq query was applied to the array. The operation applied to the variable assigned by the Linq operation remains alive.

```
numbers[0] = 3000;
numbers[1] = 30000;
Debug.Log("look again!");
foreach (int i in divisibleByThree)
{
    Debug.Log(i);
}
// 3000
// 30000
// 30
// 300
```

Even after the first foreach statement we can make changes to the numbers array again, log the items in the array, and get the new values in the output.

8.6.5 LINQ on Lists

The Linq statements offer additional functionality through the dot operator as well. Here we have an array of numbers where the `.Where()` function can be used with a lambda instead of the previous `where select` statement. After the statement an additional function can be applied to change the result to an array.

```
int[] setA = { 1, 2, 3, 4 };
int[] setB = setA.Where(x => x % 2 == 0).ToArray();
foreach (int i in setB)
{
    Debug.Log(i);
}
// 2
// 4
```

The last `ToArray()` function avoids the strange behaviors by converting the query into an array by using what is called a greedy operator. If we encapsulate the Linq statement in () and add.ToList() afterward, we can force the Linq statement to fulfill the var into an array.

This tells us that the `divisibleByThree` query is set before the numbers array is modified. This becomes a very important change to the operation of this query. The var type is important to the query, but not to how it's used. Because var is flexible, we don't have to figure out what we're getting back from the query.

```
int[] setA = { 1, 2, 3, 4 };

// Lambda
Func<int, bool> even = (x) => { return x % 2 == 0; };
int[] setB = setA.Where(even).ToArray();
foreach (int i in setB)
{
    Debug.Log(i);
}
// 2
// 4
```

In the case were we used different lambda statements, we can also use a Func type to assign to the `Where()` function on the array. The `Func<int, bool>` even can be used to satisfy the `Where()` function. In addition to Where we can also use a function called `Distinct()` on an array.

```
int[] setA = { 1, 1, 2, 2, 3, 3, 4, 4 };
// Distinct removes repeated values
List<int> setB = setA.Distinct().ToList();
foreach (int i in setB)
{
    Debug.Log(i);
}
// 1
// 2
// 3
// 4
```

The `Distinct()` function removes repeated values. Adding the `ToList()`, rather than `ToArray()` function at the end creates a `List<int>`. So what else can we use Linq to do?

```
int[] setA = { 1, 2, 3, 4 };
int[] setB = { 3, 4, 5, 6 };

// union merges the two lists together
// distinct removes duplicates
int[] setC = setA.Union(setB).Distinct().ToArray();
foreach (int i in setC)
{
    Debug.Log(i);
}
// 1
// 2
// 3
// 4
// 5
// 6
```

Here we take two arrays and use Union() to merge them together. The values 3 and 4 are repeated. To remove repeated values we chain Distinct() and then finally ToArray() at the end. The result is a single array with all of the unique values of both arrays.

```
int[] setA = { 1, 2, 3, 4 };
int[] setB = { 3, 4, 5, 6 };

// only shows things unique to setA
int[] setC = setA.Except(setB).Distinct().ToArray();
foreach (int i in setC)
{
    Debug.Log(i);
}
// 1
// 2

// only shows objects unique to setB
int[] setD = setB.Except(setA).Distinct().ToArray();
foreach (int i in setD)
{
    Debug.Log(i);
}
// 5
// 6
```

Functions like Except can take values seen in one array from the other. This can show you what was added or what values were taken away.

8.6.6 Monsters Linq

Starting with some definitions of a monster class we begin with an Alignment enum. We also give the monster class a few attributes for a name, Alignment, HP, and Position. Each monster is likely to be unique when it's created. Functions like `Distinct()` will take into consideration all attributes when filtering an array of these objects.

```
public enum Alignments
{
    Good,
    Neutral,
    Evil
}

class Monster
{
    public string Name;
    public int HP;
    public Alignments Alignment;
    public Vector3 Position;
    public Monster()
    {
        string[] nameParts = { "Ba", "Ga", "Da", "Wa", "Pa", "Na", "La", "Ta", "Fa" };
        Name = "";
        for (int i = 0; i < 2; i++)
        {
            int p = UnityEngine.Random.Range(0, nameParts.Length);
            Name += nameParts[p];
        }
        Alignment = (Alignments)UnityEngine.Random.Range(0, 3);
        HP = UnityEngine.Random.Range(1, 11);
        Position = new Vector3()
        {
            x = UnityEngine.Random.Range(-1f, 1f),
            y = UnityEngine.Random.Range(-1f, 1f),
            z = UnityEngine.Random.Range(-1f, 1f)
        };
    }
}
```

To customize how Linq is used we have several options. Linq and C# are very flexible in that regard. Lambda functions interface classes and Linq all diverge the C# syntax for better or for worse. Not to get too confused, we can still pick a syntax that's comfortable, however it's also important to be able to read code if someone else writes in a different style than you are accustomed to.

```
int numMonsters = 100;
Monster[] monsters = new Monster[numMonsters];
for (int i = 0; i < numMonsters; i++)
{
    monsters[i] = new Monster();
}
{
    var distinct = monsters.Distinct();
    string log = "Distinct default: \n";
    int count = 1;
    foreach (Monster m in distinct)
    {
        log += count++ + ") name: " + m.Name + " " + m.Alignment + "\n";
    }
    // odds are that all 100 are still in the list.
    Debug.Log(log);
}
```

In this array of monsters, we have 100 objects. Using the default `Distinct()` parameter, we find that there have been no monsters taken out of the array. We can use an `IEqualityComparer` interface for the `Monster` type object and write a custom parameter for the `Distinct()` function.

```
class MonsterNameEqualityComparer : IEqualityComparer<Monster>
{
    public bool Equals(Monster x, Monster y)
    {
        return x.Name.Equals(y.Name);
    }

    public int GetHashCode(Monster obj)
    {
        return obj.Name.GetHashCode();
    }
}
```

To take two monster objects and only use the name to qualify the two objects are equal we name the class a `MonsterNameEqualityComparer`. This allows us to use the `Distinct()` function using only names as a comparison rather than all properties of each monster.

```
/* this will use the Name Comparer to filter out
 * monsters with the same name
 */
MonsterNameEqualityComparer nameEqualer = new MonsterNameEqualityComparer();
var unique = monsters.Distinct(nameEqualer).ToArray();
//about a third of the names will be removed.
string log = "";
int count = 1;
foreach (Monster m in unique)
{
    log += count++ + ") name: " + m.Name + " " + m.Alignment + "\n";
}
Debug.Log(log);
```

The `nameEqualer` object is given to the `Distinct()` function and now about a third of the objects in the array have been removed. No two monsters have the same name in the array. We can also make a custom sort. We could rearrange the array in alphabetical order based on the name.

```
class MonsterNameComparer : IComparer<Monster>
{
    public int Compare(Monster x, Monster y)
    {
        return string.Compare(x.Name, y.Name);
    }
}
```

The name is isolated from each monster to make the comparison rather than equality check. A list that's both ordered alphabetically and only contains unique names can be generated.

```
MonsterNameComparer compareNames = new MonsterNameComparer();
MonsterNameEqualityComparer nameEqualer = new MonsterNameEqualityComparer();
var distinctOrdered = monsters.OrderBy(m => m, compareNames).Distinct(nameEqualer);

string log = "using classes to compare and filter: \n";
int count = 1;
foreach (Monster m in distinctOrdered)
{
    log += count++ + ") name: " + m.Name + " " + m.Alignment + "\n";
}
Debug.Log(log);
```

To get here we had to write two classes, one to compare name equality and another to compare name ordering. We can avoid extra code by using a lambda function instead.

```
/* this uses lambdas to sort the names
 * then we filter out repeated names but ignores
 * alignments.
 */
var distinctOrdered - monsters.OrderBy(m => m.Name)
                               .GroupBy(m => m.Name)
                               .Select(group => group.First());

string log = "using lambda to compare and filter: \n";
int count = 1;
foreach (Monster m in distinctOrdered)
{
    log += count++ + ") name: " + m.Name + " " + m.Alignment + "\n";
}
Debug.Log(log);
```

With the function `OrderBy` we can arrange an array of monsters alphabetically. Follow this with `GroupBy` unique names are selected. The last statement `.Select()` uses `group` which is a keyword for the values inside of the Linq statement. This might seem to appear out of nowhere, and to be honest, it kind of does. But this behavior is similar to how `value` appears in a get set property. The `.First()` function on the group selects the isolated group we just created using the `GroupBy()` function.

```
/* this does the same name sorting and
 * also filters out repeats, but ignores
 * alignment.
 */
var distinctOrdered =  from monster in monsters
                       orderby monster.Name ascending
                       group monster by monster.Name into uniqueNames
                       select uniqueNames.First();

string log = "using linq to compare and filter \n";
int count = 1;
foreach (Monster m in distinctOrdered)
{
    log += count++ + ") name: " + m.Name + " " + m.Alignment + "\n";
}
Debug.Log(log);
```

Another form of the same function is using only Linq commands. This last version uses a few more key-words unique to Linq. We have `orderby` as a keyword and not a function. We see `group monster by` and `into` appear as well.

The `into` keyword creates a new group of objects and again we see `.First()` appear on the uniqueNames object. This should raise the question, Is there a `.Second()` function as well?

So what else is hiding in the Linq statement?

```
var distinctOrdered = from monster in monsters
                      orderby monster.Name ascending
                      group monster by monster.Name into uniqueNames
                      select uniqueNames;

string log = "What is in uniqueNames \n";
int count = 1;
foreach (var group in distinctOrdered)
{
    var groupKey = group.Key;
    foreach (Monster m in group)
    {
        log += count++ + ")" + groupKey +" " + m.Alignment + "\n";
    }
}
Debug.Log(log);
```

The value `uniqueNames` without the `.First()` function returns a group of items with a Key, much like a Dictionary. Then each object in the new group can be accessed like a dictionary. What's going on here is that all 100 objects are still in the `uniqueNames` object, but the `.First()` gives you the unique names and not the whole array.

8.6.7 What We've Learned

The Linq library is a powerful tool made available through System.Linq. For sorting through and finding bits of information, we are able to use Linq to find and use data quickly and easily. Rather than using for loops and complex foreach loops for inspecting each object in an array, we're better able to use Linq to find what we're looking for.

Practically any data type can be sorted out with a Linq expression, even if it's a list of zombies, weap-ons, or colors. A Linq expression can use an external function to provide additional logic or a lambda or even some built in functions.

```
/* This produces a list of all 100 monsters
 * they are grouped together based on their
 * names and alignments.
 */
var sorted = monsters.OrderBy
(
    m =>
    m.Alignment.GetHashCode() + m.Name.GetHashCode()
);

string log = "Sorted Monsters using lambda \n";
int n = 1;
foreach (Monster m in sorted)
{
    log += n++ + ") name: " + m.Name + " " + m.Alignment + "\n";
}
Debug.Log(log);
```

The flexibility of C# really begins to show when we start to use lambdas mixed in with other function types with Linq.

```
/* This picks out monsters with HP above 9
 * then lists them out.
 */
var strongMonsters = monsters.Where
(
    monster =>
    monster.HP > 9
);
string log = "Strong Monsters: \n";
int n = 1;
foreach (Monster m in strongMonsters)
{
    log += n++ + ") " + m.Name + " " + m.HP + "\n";
}
Debug.Log(log);
```

We can continue to explore many different variations of the same thing with the Monsters Linq experiment.

```
/* This picks out monsters with HP above 9
 * then lists them out. This and the above
 * statements are equivalent. The only difference
 * is the syntax and use of keywords in place
 * of anonymous lambda like syntax.
 */
var strongMonsters = from monster in monsters
                     where monster.HP > 9
                     select monster;

string log = "Strong Monsters: \n";
int n = 1;
foreach (Monster m in strongMonsters)
{
    log += n++ + ") " + m.Name + " " + m.HP + "\n";
}
Debug.Log(log);
```

One of the most important lessons here is the use of a local lambda and LINQ allow for capturing local variables.

```
/* Objects in the linq statement can see
 * variables in its immediate scope
 */
Monster ComparedTo = new Monster();/* ─────┐      ComparedTo can  */
var weakerThan = from monster in monsters/* ↓       be used in the  */
                    where monster.HP < ComparedTo.HP/* where statement */
                    select monster;

string log = "Weaker than " + ComparedTo.Name + ":" + ComparedTo.HP + "\n";
int n = 1;
foreach (Monster m in weakerThan)
{
    log += n++ + ") " + m.Name + " " + m.HP + "\n";
}
Debug.Log(log);
```

When using the open natural version of Linq, you're more able to integrate local variables into the function statement easily. The above function shows a local variable `ComparedTo` being used to against `monster.HP` in the `where` statement. The topic of Linq allows for a fun variety of uses when it comes to sorting through data. We could spend more time on the subject, but it's time to move on!

8.7 Reflection

A type like `int` or `string` is a clearly defined type of data. To that point, when you create your own class, you're also define a new type. While you're busy writing new classes, it's often the case that you'll want to check for attributes of an object.

It's important to start with clearly defined sets of parameters. All classes of characters should have matching parameters. Constraining parameters with a base class can help. Making changes to different parameters depending on different combinations can mean writing a function for every possible combination. This could end up a cumbersome process. One way to avoid writing many special case functions, inspecting properties and making decisions based on what a class has can vastly improve the flexibility of the code you write.

```
class Stuff
{
    public float PubFloat;
    public int PubInt;
    public void AFunction()
    {
    }
    public int IntFunction()
    {
        return 1;
    }
}
```

Code can read code. You're able to make decisions based on the members of a class. Reflection enables you to see into a class and read the variables it contains. When you look at a class, you can normally get its name; from its name, you might be able to assume what it contains. Something like MyZombieMonster() might be fairly clear, but what does the zombie monster do?

```
Stuff stuff = new Stuff();
Type type = stuff.GetType();
foreach (MemberInfo member in type.GetMembers())
{
    Debug.Log(member);
}
```

With System.Reflection MemberInfo allows you to read the public contents of a class. In this case, the Type Stuff has a float an int and two public functions.

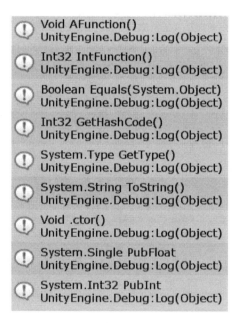

Along with Object's inherited functions like ToString() or GetType() the AFunction() IntFunction() and PubFloat and PubInt are printed out to the console. These members are all publicly visible. Private functions, if present, will not be presented as MemberInfo properties.

8.7.1 A Basic Example

In the Reflection_Scene the Reflection script attached to the game object of the same name has a very simple string comparison to find a function:

```
class HasAFunction
{
    public void TheFunction()
    {
        Debug.Log("You found me");
    }
}


void UseHasAFunction()
{
    Type hasAFunctionType = typeof(HasAFunction);
    HasAFunction hasAFunction = new HasAFunction();
    foreach(MemberInfo info in hasAFunctionType.GetMembers())
    {
        if (info.Name.Equals("TheFunction"))
        {
            hasAFunction.TheFunction();
        }
    }
}
```

This simply searches for a function with a name we're looking for. As a superficial example, this doesn't accomplish much if we already knew what the function was named. If we knew that much, we could just call it. However, this does illustrate the use of the type of object and not the object itself. Reflection uses the type definition of an object to discover the object's properties.

8.7.2 Reflection MethodInfo

Aside from the fields found in a class, it's also possible to inspect a function. The complexity of a class grows over time. With that growth comes added a growing number of functions to act on the class.

If your game has powerups which all act in a specific manner, it's often cumbersome to write into a character functions like "ActivateExtraDamage" or "EnableHealthRecovery", etc. In cases where you want the powerup.

In a MonoBehaviour we have an enumerator that processes a queue of delegate tasks.

```csharp
public void DoTheThings()
{
    IEnumerator DoesThings()
    {
        while (ThingsToDo.Count > 0)
        {
            Delegate thing = ThingsToDo.Dequeue();
            string thingName = thing.Method.Name;
            // figure out which function is in the Queue.
            MethodInfo methodInfo = thing.GetMethodInfo();

            // read the name of the incoming parameter
            ParameterInfo[] paramInfos = methodInfo.GetParameters();
            switch (paramInfos[0].Name)
            {
                case "life":
                    Func<int, int> life = (Func<int, int>)thing;
                    Life = life.Invoke(Life);
                    break;
                case "money":
                    Func<int, int> money = (Func<int, int>)thing;
                    Money = money.Invoke(Money);
                    break;
            }
            Debug.Log("Did " + thingName + " Life:" + Life + " Money:" + Money);

            yield return new WaitForSeconds(1f);
            if (Life <= 0)
                Destroy(this.gameObject);
        }
    }
    StartCoroutine(DoesThings());
}
```

The delegate pulls out a task from the queue and gets its name. Then we pull out the method's information with GetMethodInfo(). This returns everything we'd ever want to know about the method assigned in the queue. One of the values in the MethodInfo is a list of names in the parameters of the function.

For this exercise we can assume that every function assigned to the queue has at least one parameter and it's named either life or money. The Person : MonoBheaviour has three parameters,

```csharp
class Person : MonoBehaviour
{
    public Queue<Delegate> ThingsToDo;
    public int Life = 0;
    public int Money = 0;
    private void Awake()
    {
        ThingsToDo = new Queue<Delegate>();
    }
}
```

Life, Money, and ThingsToDo, reflecting on this Person reveals a very simple existence. When Person is created it initializes a Queue of things to do. This person is unaware of what will become of its life or money. One thing is for sure, with each loop through the switch statement we wait for a second, then we check if life is <= 0 and we destroy the gameObject.

When we look at the parameter of the incoming delegate function we check the name and assign the function either Life or Money. This could be expanded to any number of properties your class might have.

```
int BeBorn(int life)
{
    Debug.Log("You've got one life...");
    return life + 10;
}

int GoToWork(int money)
{
    Debug.Log("You're Welcome.");
    return money + 10;
}

int Accident(int life)
{
    Debug.Log("Oops.");
    return life - 5;
}

int PayTaxes(int money)
{
    Debug.Log("Thankyou come again.");
    return money / 2;
}

int Die(int life)
{
    return life - life;
}
```

Person has instore the above functions. Each one acts on the parameter as you might expect. The different functions are assigned to Persons ToDo list using enqueue.

```
GameObject capsule = GameObject.CreatePrimitive(PrimitiveType.Capsule);
Person bob = capsule.AddComponent<Person>();
Func<int, int> born = BeBorn;
Func<int, int> work = GoToWork;
Func<int, int> accident = Accident;
Func<int, int> taxes = PayTaxes;
Func<int, int> death = Die;
bob.ThingsToDo.Enqueue(born);
bob.ThingsToDo.Enqueue(work);
bob.ThingsToDo.Enqueue(accident);
bob.ThingsToDo.Enqueue(taxes);
bob.ThingsToDo.Enqueue(death);
bob.DoTheThings();
```

Once the person's queue is populated, the Function `DoTheThings()` is called and the queue begins its invocation process.

With each process of the queue we step through the short and dismal life of Person. As unassuming as what's happened here, we can take for granted we know what happens to life and money, aside from death and taxes. Person had no idea what the function was going to do. We only had the information of what the incoming parameter was asking for, and Person assigned its life and money to the incoming function not knowing what it would do.

The outcome is still clear, we saw the name of the incoming function and that's something we could have processed. But if we didn't know ahead of time what to expect then that wouldn't have mattered. The important take away is that we only knew the name of the parameter of the function.

```csharp
void LifeInMoneyOut(int life, out int outMoney)
{
    outMoney = life * 2;
}

delegate void InOutDelegate<T, U>(T input, out U output);
InOutDelegate<int, int> lifeInMoneyOut;
```

Additional parameters named in the function can be assigned to change how a function can be discovered and used from the assigned function.

8.7.3 What We've Learned

To explore the idea that a class might have a list of properties and a delegate coming in might want to modify those properties we could do so by reflection alone.

```csharp
class HasStuff
{
    public int number = 0;
    public Vector3 position = Vector3.one;
    public GameObject gameObject = new GameObject();
```

In the `HasStuff` class we have a few class members, a number position, and a gameObject. These are names of members which reflection can find. To match this, a delegate is setup that mirrors the property names.

```
delegate void ThreeInputs<T, U, V>(T A, U B, V C);
ThreeInputs<int, Vector3, GameObject> GiveThreeInputs;
void TheThreeThings(int number, Vector3 position, GameObject gameObject)
{
    Debug.Log("Got called!");
    Debug.Log(number + " " + position + " " + gameObject);
}
```

The input parameters number position and gameObject can also be seen through reflection. We can iterate through the properties of the class and compare them to the properties of the delegate.

```
public void CheckOnStuff()
{
    GiveThreeInputs = TheThreeThings;
    Delegate threeIns = GiveThreeInputs;

    var delegateMethodInfo = threeIns.GetMethodInfo().GetParameters();
    var myFields = this.GetType().GetFields();
    object[] pars = new object[delegateMethodInfo.Length];

    for (int i = 0; i < delegateMethodInfo.Length; i++)
    {
        for (int j = 0; j < myFields.Length; j++)
        {
            if (delegateMethodInfo[i].Name.Equals(myFields[j].Name))
            {
                pars[i] = myFields[i].GetValue(this);
            }
        }
    }

    threeIns.DynamicInvoke(pars);
}
```

A small touch of magic here seems to happen. The array `object [] pars` gets populated through getting the classes property by name. The class properties are turned into an object in an array. The `threeIns` delegate is assigned the array of parameters in the `DynamicInvoke` call. The fields in the class that match the names of the parameters in the delegate are assembled and called.

```
HasStuff hasStuff = new HasStuff();
hasStuff.number = 42;
hasStuff.position = new Vector3(3, 5, 7);
hasStuff.gameObject = new GameObject("magic");
hasStuff.CheckOnStuff();
```

The values of hasStuff get set to something unique. Then the delegate gets assigned. The delegate's values are name checked against the fields of the class. When matching string names are found the values are added to an array. The delegate is called with the object array populated with the classes properties.

By using Reflection, the class was able to identify parameters and assign a function values from its own members. Add this functionality to incoming delegates and you'll be able to assign any variety of modifications to a game character or object.

8.8 Dynamic

C# is a strong typed language, usually. As we've seen with var, the type of data that can be stored in a variable isn't always clearly defined. The var type gets defined after it receives a value. This is useful when the value assigned is assumed to be changing, as with the case with Linq values. The dynamic type is a bit different.

Opening the Dynamic_Scene find the Dynamic script attached to the game object of the same name. The dynamic type, unlike var can be reassigned at any time to anything. This defies what it means to be a string typed language. Especially since the GetType() function returns no clue that the variable is being stored in a type that isn't set.

```
dynamic d = "im a string";
Debug.Log(d.GetType());
// System.String

d = 1;
Debug.Log(d.GetType());
// System.Int32

d = (Action)(() => { });
Debug.Log(d.GetType());
// System.Action
```

The dynamic isn't commonly used, and for clarity it shouldn't be used very often. The practice of defining a type is important. Type definition and use restricts a variable from changing accidentally. Even with generic types, the <T> becomes a type when it's assigned and after assignment the type can't change.

Variables in most cases remain static or unchanged once assigned or created. The dynamic type can change. The chaos this may introduce allows for errors Visual Studio might have been able to catch. Compile-time error checks are skipped on the dynamic variables; use with caution.

```
d = 1;
d++;
Debug.Log(d.GetType() + " " + d);
// System.Int32 2

d = d / Mathf.PI;
Debug.Log(d.GetType() + " " + d);
// System.Single 0.6366197
```

In some cases, the dynamic can change types even without a specific assignment. By dividing an int by a float, the type gets reassigned. The type mutation occurs without error or warning. This behavior mimics that of other languages like LUA or Python where a variable's type changes as the assignment changes.

```
/* in Visual Studio we don't get an error    */
/* only when you run the game, will an error  */
/* be produced!                               */
d = 1;
d = "im a string again!";
d++;
// RuntimeBinderException:
// Operator '++' cannot be applied to operand of type 'string'
```

Where the dynamic type causes problems is when the variable is used in an unexpected way. The data stored in the dynamic variable still functions as a specific type, so operations like ++ cannot function on a string. Though in most cases the error would have been caught in Visual Studio before the game is played.

8.8.1 ExpandoObject

The unique ability of dynamic to change type can be expanded upon. The `System.Dynamic` name space includes a strange object called the ExpandoObject.

```
dynamic expando = new System.Dynamic.ExpandoObject();
expando.thing = "im a thing";
expando.dodad = 1;
expando.widget = 1.0f;
expando.gizmo = (Action)(()=>{ Debug.Log(expando.thing);});

Debug.Log(expando.thing.GetType() + " " + expando.thing);
// System.String im a thing
Debug.Log(expando.dodad.GetType() + " " + expando.dodad);
// System.Int32 1
Debug.Log(expando.widget.GetType() + " " + expando.widget);
// System.Single 1
expando.gizmo();
// im a thing
```

The dot operator allows a new ExpandoObject() to create add name and define a type of a member dynamically. The near magic powers of the ExpandoObject() should be used with caution. Once assigned, the type and function of each member of an ExpandoObject cannot be debugged before it's used.

The expando object can reference itself, as we can see in the Action assigned to the expando.gizmo object. And a value in the ExpandoObject can be a delegate of some kind as well, not just a plain old data type. The ExpandoObject can also be used as different types.

8.8.2 Expando Reader

Data is quite often stored as text. Properties for game objects are parsed from string values into an expected data type for use elsewhere in the Scene of the game. A Zombie could have a name, some hit points, and a position in the world. These would be stored as a string, int, and a Vector3, but in text form there's no type other than string.

```
/* some data in string format */
string data = "" +
    "Name:Rob\n" +
    "HP:10\n" +
    "Position:1.23,4.56,7.89";
```

The data could originate from anywhere, but we begin with a few lines of data separated with the \n character and put together with a + character. We'll forgoe reading and writing a text file to disk since we've already done that before.

```
dynamic expando = new System.Dynamic.ExpandoObject();
// convert expando to a dictionary!
var expandoAsDictionary = (IDictionary<string, object>)expando;
```

To make the ExpandoObject into a type we can dynamically add new members to convert the ExpandoObject() into an IDictionary<string, object>. In this form we can use the Dictionary's interface member Add() to create new members.

```
var parts = data.Split('\n');
foreach(string part in parts)
{
    var pair = part.Split(':');
    // ExpandoObject doesn't have Add
    // but Dictionary does!
    expandoAsDictionary.Add(pair[0], pair[1]);
}
```

The data string gets turned into three strings when it's split with the \n char. The result is Name:Rob, HP:10, and Position:1.23,4.56,7.89. These three strings are then split at the : character into a string object key value pair. Each key value pair is added to the expandoAsDictionary var.

```
expando = expandoAsDictionary;
Debug.Log(expando.Name + ":" + expando.Name.GetType());
// Rob:System.String
```

The `expando` value is then assigned the expandoAsDictionary to convert the dictionary back into an ExpandoObject. The `expando` object now has a `Name`, `HP`, and `Position` property. For the first pair Name we didn't have to convert the value. So `expando.Name` is the string Rob.

```
expando.HP = int.Parse(expando.HP);
Debug.Log(expando.HP + ":" + expando.HP.GetType());
// Rob:System.Int32
```

The values of a ExpandoObject object are also dynamic, so the string "10" can be parsed and to itself and become an int. Now `expando.HP` is an `int 10` after the Parse function has been applied to itself.

```
Vector3 toVector3(string s)
{
    var v = s.Split(',');
    return new Vector3()
    {
        x = System.Single.Parse(v[0]),
        y = System.Single.Parse(v[1]),
        z = System.Single.Parse(v[2])
    };
}
expando.Position = toVector3(expando.Position);
Debug.Log(expando.Position + ":" + expando.Position.GetType());
// (1.2, 4.6, 7.9):UnityEngine.Vector3
```

The `expando.Position` gets converted with a split and more parsing. This also shows that dynamic can be assigned types from Unity as well.

The example shown here has no error checking. There's no guarantee that a text file from disk won't have an unexpected character or an extra space. The interesting effect though is converting a string to an int without jumping through any tricky conversions or type assignments. The dynamic type is suited for situations like the one shown.

8.8.3 What We've Learned

The dynamic type was added to C# to add compatibility with languages like LUA or Python. In LUA variables were all just names. The only definition added to a LUA variable was it's scope, either Local or Global. Python did the same thing were you simply wrote "bob = 10" and now bob is a value of 10.

By using dynamic you can use variables in a similar fashion. This does open more opportunity for unexpected behavior with fewer safeguards in place. The dynamic is also useful for parsing more complex types like Json or XML. With C# on a web server, dynamic is often used to read and build complex HTML web pages. Each <ELEMENT> becomes a new expando.object with values.

```
expando.Transform.Position = expando.Position;
expando.Transform.Rotation = Quaternion.identity;
expando.Transform.Scale = Vector3.one;
```

It doesn't stop there. Each object in an ExpandoObject can have members with values with members and more values as well. ExpandoObject lives up to it's name and it's quite expansive.

8.9 Bitwise Operators

When you are taught to count, you're learning the decimal system. The decimal system is a base-10 numeral system, but there are many other systems as well. Your computer uses binary or a base-2 numeral system. The transistors in your computer have only two states; they are either on or off. To be more technically correct, they are in either a charged state or a ground state.

Manipulating individual bits seems a bit low level for the common game-building tasks, but once you get the hang of flipping individual bits, they can be used for many different tricks. Going back to the basics, we'll review about how numbers are stored in the computer's memory.

```
ShowBits(1);
// bits in 1:
// 10000000

ShowBits(128);
// bits in 128:
// 00000001

ShowBits(255);
// bits in 255:
// 11111111
```

A byte is a collection of eight 1s and 0s. Therefore, the binary 0000 0000 represents the decimal 0. The binary representation is what is stored in the computer's memory. A decimal 1 is stored as binary 1000 0000, and a computer represents decimal 2 as 0100 0000. The second place is a decimal 2. Therefore, decimal 128 is binary 0000 0001.

```
bool isLittleEndian = System.BitConverter.IsLittleEndian;
Debug.Log("Is Little Endian?: " + (isLittleEndian?"Yes":"No"));
// Is Little Endian?: Yes
```

8.9.1 Big Endian and Little Endian

The arrangement of the digits we're looking at is called *little endian*. The name comes from the position in the line of 1s and 0s where the biggest value is stored at the far end of the stream of ones and zeros. Since the lowest value is stored at the start of the number, it's called little endian. If we were to represent 128 in binary as 10000000, where the largest values are stored first, then we're looking at a big-endian number.

Each digit is a value of a power of 2. The first number is either 0 or 1; the first value is either 0 or 1 to the power of 0. The second digit is either 0 or 2 to the power of 1, which is 2. The third digit is 0 or 2 to the power of 2, which is 4. The pattern repeats for each digit in the binary number.

To explain how binary works and what the 1s and 0s represent, consider first that binary is made up of 1s and 0s. If each represents a power of 2, then 1, 2, 4, 8, and then 16, 32, 64, 128 are what each digit in a byte means. With these we're able to represent each number between 0 and 255.

As a simplified example, we'll look at a 2-bit number. To count to 3, we'd start with 00, 10, 01, and then 11. The first digit is 0 or 1 followed by 0 or 2. To count 0, we use 00. The combination 10 counts 1. To count to 2, we use 01. Last, the number 3 is indicated with a 10 and a 01, added together as 11. If you add 1 and 2, you get 3. This is how your computer counts.

This arrangement comes from backward compatibility with older processors that go back to the 8008 made by Intel in 1972. This was a tiny processor which used little endian byte storage to more easily communicate with a serial bus, a computer interface to send bytes between systems. This dictated that the lower values needed to be calculated first.

Today most modern CPUs are big endian since, as humans, we read the largest values first, not last. A million one hundred eleven thousand one hundred and eleven begins with the large value and works down to the smallest value. Modern assembly is organized in the same way.

8.9.2 Signed or Unsigned

The same system as above works for a byte that is eight 1s and 0s. An int stores 32 1s and 0s, but there's a catch. The words signed and unsigned indicate if a number is allowed to have negative values. If the number is signed, then you lose a bit to indicate a plus + or minus – sign; though you don't usually see a plus + symbol in front of a positive number, it is inferred.

To go back to our 2-bit number, we'd only be able to count to three values again. To begin we can start with 10 that would translate into −1. When the first bit represents a value, the second bit indicates a sign.

We can use 00 to indicate a 0 and 11 to indicate a +1. We still have three usable values: −1, 0, and +1. Whether or not a bit is used to indicate a plus + or minus – sign is called signed or unsigned. When we have only positive values, we consider that an unsigned number; if we can show both positive and negative numbers, programmers call this signed.

```
sbyte sbite = (sbyte)-127;
ShowBits(sbite);
// bits in -127:
// 10000001
```

A signed `byte` or `sbyte` is a number from -127 to +127. Using little endian bits, the last bit is 1 if the value is negative and 0 if the value is positive. In the case with -1 we get a lot of 1s. The reason for this is that with negative numbers we change how we use the value of the bits. The system is more like, what value do you subtract from 128 to reach the value in the signed byte?

```
ShowBits((sbyte)-1);
// bits in -1:
// 11111111
```

```
ShowBits((sbyte)1);
// bits in 1:
// 10000000
```

```
ShowBits((sbyte) 0);
// bits in 0:
// 00000000
```

```
ShowBits((sbyte)127);
// bits in -127:
// 10000000
```

```
ShowBits((sbyte)-127);
// bits in -127:
// 10000001
```

An int is a number between –2,147,483,648 and 2,147,483,647. Notice that the number reaches one more negative than positive; we will see why in a moment. A uint or an unsigned int is a number from 0 to 4,294,967,295. To get these numbers, the last bit is the only one that controls the sign of the number.

So the regular math operators work as we'd expect, but we get an interesting behavior when we reach the limit of these numbers.

```
int max = 2147483647;
Debug.Log(max);
// 2147483647
```

```
max += 1;
Debug.Log(max);
// -2147483648
```

Normally, you might expect c to print out 2147483648; however, we get -2147483648, a negative number. There's also an unsigned version of int called the uint where the u means unsigned.

```
uint umax = 4294967295;
Debug.Log(umax);
// 4294967295
```

```
umax += 1;
Debug.Log(umax);
// 0
```

The increment of 1 on the unsigned int starting at 4294967295 results with 0. When umax is assigned 4294967295, you can imagine 32 1s filling up the 32-bit number. When we add 1, they're rolled over and the result turns into 32 0s instead. Therefore, the numbers in the computer, because they are binary, act weird. This is a simple awkward fact of computing. In a small example, rather than looking at 32 numbers, we'll look at just a few digits.

A 4-bit number, 0000, sometimes called a nibble, starts off as a collection of four digits. If we add 1, we get the following result 0001, which is then pushed to the left; when we add another 1, we get 0010 to get 2. Remember that the second digit is 2^1.

Adding another 1, we get 0011 to get $1 + 2$ or $2^0 + 2^1$, so we have 3. By adding another 1, we get 0100; the first two numbers are reset and the 1 is pushed to the left again, so we have 4. Adding another 1, we get 0101 to get $1 + 4$. To continue we add another 1 and we get 0110; then we add another 1 and we get 0111 or $1 + 2 + 4$ to get 7.

Finally, by adding another 1, we get 1000, which is the last digit for 8. The process continues until we have 1111, and following the pattern of adding another 1 will push the 1 to the right, but there's no space left, so we get 0000. The 4-bit number has rolled over. With a 4-bit number, we get a range from 0 to 15. If we have a signed 4-bit number, we get a range from –7 to 7.

This whole business of counting with $2^0 + 2^1 + 2^2 +...$ was invented in 1679. A mathematician named Gottfried Wilhelm von Leibniz concocted the system. He also happened to invent calculus, so if you're having trouble in math class, you can blame Gottfried.

Though without him we wouldn't have computers. After he created the system, he said, "When numbers are reduced to 0 and 1, a beautiful order prevails everywhere." Indeed, computers have led to many beautiful things.

The system works for larger numbers. In the case of a 32-bit number, we'd be counting till we hit the 4294967296 number before we roll the number. When we use a signed number, we lose either the first or last digit to store the sign, either + or –. Technically, it's a 31-bit number with a sign whose range is either $+2^{31}(-1$ for holding a 0) or -2^{31}, which means 2147483647 to -2147483648. Even though computers are limited by the bits per number, we can work with this, so long as we keep these limitations in mind.

8.9.3 Bitwise Or |

The bitwise operators |, &, ^, and ~ are used to manipulate numbers on the bit level rather than on the math level. These are referred to as "Bar" where we assume $1 + 2 = 3$. We can also use $1 | 2 = 3$, though this is not working in the way you might think it is. The or operator | is used to merge bits together. Looking at the previous 4-bit number, we can use the following notation:

```
  1248
  1001 =   9
  1010 =   5
|  _____
  1011 = 13
```

Or in C# we can use the following notation:

```
uint a = 5;      // 1 + 0 + 4 = 5
uint b = 6;      // 0 + 2 + 4 = 6
uint c = a | b; // 1 + 2 + 4 = 7
Debug.Log(c);
```

The above example looks at the 1s, and if either bit is 1, then the resulting bit is set to 1. If both numbers are 1s, then the result is only another 1. Therefore, in the above example, we get the result 7, not 11 as you might imagine.

At first glance, we might not immediately see the advantage of using numbers by the bits that they are made of. However, programmers like to think in strange ways, and to learn how to write code is to think like a programmer, which is never an easy task.

8.9.4 Enums and Numbers

If we use an enum, we can set each value to a number.

```
enum CharacterClasses
{
    Farmer  = 0x00,
    Fighter = 0x01,
    Thief   = 0x02,
    Wizard  = 0x04,
    Archer  = 0x08
}
```

If we use the above enum, you can see some assignments to number values. You should also notice that they are being assigned the same values that are used when counting in binary. Therefore, if 0000 is a farmer, then 0001 is a fighter. This means 0010 is a thief, 0100 is a wizard, and 1000 is the archer. What should happen if we want to have a multiclass character who is a fighter wizard?

```
CharacterClasses fighter = CharacterClasses.Fighter;
ShowBits((byte)fighter);
// bits in 1:
// 10000000

CharacterClasses wizard = CharacterClasses.Wizard;
ShowBits((byte)wizard);
// bits in 4:
// 00100000

CharacterClasses multiClass = fighter | wizard;
ShowBits((byte)multiClass);
// bits in 4:
// 10100000
```

Therefore, we can use the statement multiClass = fighter | wizard; to merge both values into the enum. Hidden on the inside of the multiclass value is a 01010000 from using 0001 | 0100 to combine the bits. This might seem strange, since the result is 5, and there is no numeric value in the CharacterClasses enum assigned 5. However, that's assuming we're using the enums as numbers, not bits, or in this case, we're using them as flags. We'll read more into what this means in the following section.

8.9.5 Bitwise And &

To find out which bits are in use, we use the bitwise operator and, &. Therefore, to see if the bits match up, we can use the & operator to compare two sets of bits.

```
  1248
  1001 = 9
  1010 = 5
& _____
  1000 = 1
```

This shows the value for each bit, then using the & operator we can see how the bits are modified in the result of the operation. With an enum we get the following result.

```
CharacterClasses fighter = CharacterClasses.Fighter;
ShowBits((byte)fighter);
// bits in 1:
// 10000000

CharacterClasses wizard = CharacterClasses.Wizard;
ShowBits((byte)wizard);
// bits in 4:
// 00100000

CharacterClasses fighterAndWizard = fighter & wizard;
ShowBits((byte)fighterAndWizard);
// bits in 0:
// 00000000
```

The above notation returns a 1 only when bits in both values match 1. To use this to check what classes our character is, we can use the following fragment:

```
CharacterClasses multiClass = fighter | wizard;
ShowBits((byte)multiClass);
// bits in 5:
// 10100000

byte andFighter = (byte)(multiClass & CharacterClasses.Fighter);
ShowBits(andFighter);
// bits in 1:
// 10000000

byte andWizard = (byte)(multiClass & CharacterClasses.Wizard);
ShowBits(andWizard);
// bits in 4:
// 00100000
```

The multiclass has a 1 in the first and third place of the byte. Using & CharacterClasses.Fighter we can see if multiClass has a value in the first place. The same works for checking if multiClass has a value in the third place.

```
byte andArcher = (byte)(multiClass & CharacterClasses.Archer);
ShowBits(andArcher);
// bits in 0:
// 00000000
```

The check of multiClass is an Archer that we check with & CharacterClasses.Archer and we see that there are no bits that match.

8.9.6 Bitwise Exclusive Or ^ (xor)

We can also see which bits are mismatching.

```
  1248
  1001 =   9
  1010 =   5
^ _____
  0011 = 12
```

The ^ operator in the following fragment shows us where two sets of bits misaligned. The 0s are ignored, but if there are 1s, then we take action. In this case, we get the first and second bits mismatching. The following bits are the same, so they are left at 0.

```
// ^ "Xor" also known as caret
uint a = 5;     // 1 + 0 + 4 = 5
uint b = 6;     // 0 + 2 + 4 = 6
uint c = a ^ b; // 1 + 2 + 0 = 3
Debug.Log(c);
// 3
```

To go back to the enum we were just using, we have a multiclass fighter and wizard, but how do we take the fighter out from the enum? This is what the xor operator is for. MultiClass is a combination of the bits from the fighter and the bits from the wizard. The fighter was 10000000 and the wizard was 00100000, so multiClass is 10100000. To remove the wizard, we want to end up with 10000000 again.

```
/* using | we add in a wizard to the fighter
 * to take the wizard flag back out use ^
 */
CharacterClasses wizard = CharacterClasses.Wizard;
CharacterClasses fighter = CharacterClasses.Fighter;
CharacterClasses multiClass = wizard | fighter;
ShowBits((byte)multiClass);
// bits in 5:
// 10100000

CharacterClasses result = multiClass ^ CharacterClasses.Fighter;
ShowBits((byte)result);
// bits in 4:
// 00100000
```

Using the ^ on multiClass, we get remove the 10000000 from 10100000 and the result is 00100000.

To add bits we use the or operator |, to check for bits we use the and operator &, and to remove bits we use the exclusive or operator ^. In the above case, we'll be looking at the multiClass and we get fighter sent to the Console. This works with any number of classes.

```
multiClass = CharacterClasses.Fighter | CharacterClasses.Thief | CharacterClasses.Wizard;
ShowBits((byte)multiClass);
// bits in 7:
// 11100000
```

The | operator can compound as many values as there are bits to work with. In the above code, the multiClass is now a fighter, a wizard, and thief. To check which of these classes multiClass is, we use the same statement as we did earlier. To check if multiClass contains the bits required to be a thief, we use the same statement:

```
bool isThief = (multiClass & CharacterClasses.Thief) == CharacterClasses.Thief;
Debug.Log("multiClass is Thief:" + isThief);
// multiClass is Thief:True
```

Therefore, isThief in this case is true. However, now we're starting to repeat ourselves, and as any programmer should do, we should make our lives easier by writing a function to do all this stuff for us. So where do we start? Logically, we'll want to begin with the same processes. We started with adding bits to a value, so we should begin there.

8.9.7 Setting Bitwise Flags

After assigning a characterClass, it's time to add one. The enum isn't something we can extend, so we'll want to use something like addClass(my current class, class im adding) that would look like the following:

```
CharacterClasses addClass(CharacterClasses a, CharacterClasses b)
{
    return a | b;
}
CharacterClasses newbie = CharacterClasses.Farmer;
newbie = addClass(newbie, CharacterClasses.Wizard);
```

Now newbie is a wizard. To continue, we can use the following.

```
newbie = addClass(newbie, CharacterClasses.Archer);
```

By using newbie in the addClass() function, we're adding a second value to the newbie enum. To remove a class, we'll want to do something similar.

```
CharacterClasses removeClass(CharacterClasses a, CharacterClasses b)
{
    return a ^ b;
}
newbie = removeClass(newbie, CharacterClasses.Wizard);
```

This means that if we use removeClass(newbie, characterClass.archer);, we'll take the archer flags back out.

Of course, we could use a bool to check if a class contains a value with the following function:

```
bool hasClass(CharacterClasses a, CharacterClasses b)
{
    return (a & b) == b;
}
bool isFarmer = hasClass(newbie, CharacterClasses.Farmer);
Debug.Log("newbie is a farmer:" + isFarmer);
// newbie is a farmer:True
```

This simply checks if the flag is present, and if it is then our return is true; otherwise it's false. This can be used to check if a character, given its characterClass, can be allowed to fire a bow or pick a lock. This changes the nature of the enum that is usually intended to be fixed at a single value. Of course, it would be easy to store these as boolean values, but where's the fun in that?

8.9.8 Bitwise Shortcuts | = and ^ =

When assigning these enums, we can shorten some of the assignments by using the same operators. If we want to assign a = a | b;, we can use a |= b;. Similar looking syntax appears when adding a value to a where a = a + b; and a += b; from Section 5.6. The same goes for a = a ^ b;, which can be replaced with a ^= b;.

```
CharacterClasses character = CharacterClasses.Farmer;
character |= CharacterClasses.Fighter;
character |= CharacterClasses.Wizard;
character |= CharacterClasses.Archer;
character |= CharacterClasses.Thief;
ShowBits((byte)character);
// bits in 15:
// 11110000

character ^= CharacterClasses.Fighter;
ShowBits((byte)character);
// bits in 14:
// 01110000
```

8.9.9 Bits in Numbers

Remember that we're still dealing with numbers, not just bits. Being numbers, we can use this to check for odd or even numbers with a simple & operator. Odd numbers always have a 1 in them, but even numbers do not. What does that mean? We can use `bool even = (number & 1) == 0;` to check if a value is odd or even.

This system has the same result as checking `number % 2 == 0`.

```
int number = 758;
bool even = (number & 1) == 0;
Debug.Log("number:" + number + " is even:" + even);

bool evenMod = number % 2 == 0;
Debug.Log("number:" + number + " is even:" + evenMod);
```

This returns `true`, quick and easy. In addition, performing checks like this happens very quickly on most CPUs. We'll want to keep this in mind for some later math tricks in C#.

8.9.10 Bit Shifting >> and <<

Our enum was written in the form `farmer = 0X00`, `fighter = 0X01`, through `archer = 0X08`, and so on. However, if you had many different classes, we might easily miscalculate one of the numbers. It's not too easy to remember what 37^2 is; your higher numbers turn into—rather difficult to remember—power of two values. Therefore, again bitwise operators can help here as well. We can add the >> and the << between numbers to indicate a movement of bits.

```
enum Alignments
{
    Neutral          = 0,
    CrazyNeutral     = 1 << 0,
    NormalNeutral    = 1 << 1,
    CrazyGood        = 1 << 2,
    NormalGood       = 1 << 3,
    ReallyGood       = 1 << 4,
    CrazyEvil        = 1 << 5,
    NormalEvil       = 1 << 6,
    ReallyEvil       = 1 << 7,
    Unknown          = 1 << 8 //is this valid?
}
```

The above code is simply numbered 0–8, and if we need a ninth class, we simply add `monk = 1<<9` at the end. What does the << do? It's taking the value of 1 and moving it over to the right the number of digits indicated by the number following the operator. Therefore, in the bits we start off as 1000, which is 1. Then if we look at fighter, we shift the bits 0 places, and we still get 1.

The opposite works in a similar way: 0011 or 3 turns into something else altogether when shifted one space. Looking at 3 or 0011 << 1 = 0110, which is 6. Then, 6 << 1 = 12 or 1100, so there is a pattern! This is the same as multiplying by 2—altogether another useful math operation that can be done by shifting bits!

Of course, we're just looking at the little end of the value range of a 32-bit int; it's just as simple as writing out 0011 0000 0000 0000 0000 0000 0000 0000 to show 12. Shifting the values << can happen many times before we run out of digits.

```
Alignments neutral = Alignments.Neutral;
ShowBits((byte)neutral);
// bits in 0:
// 00000000

/* 1 << 0
 * remember, 0 is the first index! or zeroth index
 */
Alignments crazyNeutral = Alignments.CrazyNeutral;
ShowBits((byte)crazyNeutral);
// bits in 1:
// 10000000

/* 1 << 1
 * shifted skipping the 0th index into the first
 * index, which is the second from the zeroth
 * position.
 */
Alignments normalNeutral = Alignments.NormalNeutral;
ShowBits((byte)normalNeutral);
// bits in 2:
// 01000000
```

When using the bit shifted enum we can see how the bits are shifting around in the bits themselves. Things are easy to understand, though conceptually the direction of the << and >> might seem a bit off. It's important that << is pushing into higher values and ignores the little or big endian direction. The bit we're pushing seems to be traveling to the right even though the arrows << point to the left to shift the bits. The enum for Alignments has not been set to a specific type. It's an enum. What happens when we push the bit past the range of a byte?

```
/* 1 << 7
 * in a byte there are only 0 to 7 positions
 * the last position for a 8 bit byte.
 */
Alignments reallyEvil = Alignments.ReallyEvil;
ShowBits((byte)reallyEvil);
// bits in 128:
// 00000001

/* 1 << 8
 * in a byte there are only 0 to 7 positions
 * past the last bit, we've rolled a byte!
 */
Alignments unknown = Alignments.Unknown;
ShowBits((byte)unknown);
// bits in 0:
// 00000000
```

The last unknown value in the enum has rolled the byte over and shows a 0 when printing out the bits as a byte. The same enum for alignments given to ShowBits produces an int with a value of 256, with one bit beyond the byte range.

```
/* 1 << 8
 * in a byte there are only 0 to 7 positions
 * past the last bit, we've rolled a byte!
 */
Alignments unknown = Alignments.Unknown;
ShowBits((byte)unknown);
// bits in 0:
// 00000000

Debug.Log("use an int?");
ShowBitInt((int)unknown);
// bits in int:256
// 00000000100000000000000000000000

void ShowBitInt(int number)
{
    int bitLen = 32;
    string log = "bits in int:" + number + "\n";
    for (int i = 0; i < bitLen; i++)
    {
        int mask = 1 << i;
        if ((number & mask) == mask)
        {
            log += "1";
        }
        else
        {
            log += "0";
        }
    }
    Debug.Log(log);
}
```

An int is 32 bits long and we can still count the values in each position by using a bit mask. Shifting over each value to check what bit is turned on in the number.

8.9.11 What We've Learned

Computers do math in a unique way, different from what we are accustomed to. Thinking in 1s and 0s requires a fundamental restart in learning how to do math. Multiplication, addition, subtraction, and even counting require a whole unique system.

Some of these systems have effects outside of math. Using the binary system as a collection of flags or using them as enums allows for a greater ability to control a breadth of information in a single value. A 64-bit integer allows for 64 unique boolean values to be stored.

So why study how bits work? In classic video games top scores are usually stored as some number form where 65,575 was the maximal limit. Score one more point and the score was reset to 0 or "The score was rolled." Knowing the limitations of numbers will help avoid bugs or, at the very least, you'll know what to expect when using some number types.

Even today many pieces of hardware that communicate over Bluetooth use number types with very limited ranges. Game controllers can often send analog joystick values using a single int with bits masked for each axis.

A wireless controller may send a single 16-bit value as an orientation. The first 5 bits are used as pitch, the following 6 as yaw, then the last 5 as roll. Color can also be compressed into a single 16-bit number using similar encoding for red blue and green.

Knowing how to mask values, shift bits, and decode a usable number can greatly extend your game development beyond the built-in controllers and types in Unity. Devices like Arduinos can send custom inputs to your game if you know what the bits are doing.

8.10 Attributes

When working with the editor, we can add new menu items, windows, and other useful tools for helping with the level design. Many of the new menu items are done through Unity 3D-specific attributes. Attributes is another layer added to the C# language that augment how the code is read by the computer.

Attributes in some ways look out of place; like preprocessor directives, they have their own set of rules and uses. They use the square brackets [] to indicate their use and function. Attributes allow your code to read additional information about your code. Reflection occurs when your code can look up additional information on a function or type. This includes any field in a class as well as any function or the class itself.

Often in Unity 3D we use [Serializable] to indicate a field or value which you want to have saved by the game. For instance, you've created custom data structures and other public settings that show up in the editor; normally any form of plain old data (POD) will be automatically serialized. However, in times where you've written your own data, you need to tell Unity 3D that your new data types must also be serialized to be saved.

In many cases, you might be getting used to using a struct or class to store a complex assortment of different types of data. This is fine; however, it's better to consider using a class to hold data rather than a struct.

This serves two purposes: first, you're better able to handle data coming in and going out of each variable, and second, you're able to use the class in Unity 3D as a clever container for your variables which you can edit in the Inspector panel.

8.10.1 A Basic Example

We'll need to add the using System; directive to start. This will give us the [Serializable] attribute for use in the editor. Our code will start off like the following:

```
[Serializable]
public class DataParameters
{
    public int Players;
    public int MinRange, MaxRange;
}

public DataParameters ParameterData;
```

This gives us a simple public class DataParameters to which we'll add a some data fields. The public int Players will serve as our basic example of serialization. After this is public DataParameters ParameterData; where we can hold data we just set up in DataParameters class. Without the [Serializable] attribute, the editor's Inspector panel doesn't show any new information.

To get the `ParameterData` to show up, we simply add a single attribute to the class, not the variable.

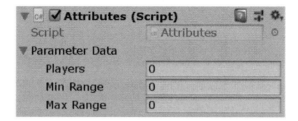

After the Serializable attribute was added to the `DataParameters` class, the public members of the class become visible under the `ParameterData` object in the Unity 3D Inspector panel. The result in the editor is our DataParameter information in the editor.

Adding the Serializable attribute makes the data stored inside of the class savable. Once we make changes to the values in the serialized class, the editor can save them with the scene. The attribute tells Unity 3D to look at the class as a chunk of information which it needs to both expose to the Inspector panel and save with the scene.

The other attributes that System gives us are also useful for different reasons.

Should we add an int to the class outside of the nested class, we'd get what you'd normally expect to see in the Inspector panel.

```
public int PlainOldInt;
```

This shows up as an int value in the editor as we have seen earlier.

```
▼ Parameter Data
    Players        0
    Min Range      0
    Max Range      0
  Plain Old Int    0
```

However, we can add an attribute to keep this out of the editor, but also maintain the variable's public accessor selling.

```
[NonSerialized]
public int PlainOldInt;
```

Adding the attribute magically hides the value from the Inspector panel. This has two effects: first, any values assigned to the PlainOldInt variable will not be saved with the scene, and second, the value cannot be set from the editor. The variable still acts as any normal public int, only that we're not able to manipulate it from within the editor.

Adding serialized attributes for the Inspector is handy, however for a game to have some additional features it's useful to enable the serialization of that data for saving to file.

```
[Serializable]
class CharacterData
{
    public string Name;
    public int HitPoints;
    public int Defense;
    public int Offsense;
}

class GameData
{
    public CharacterData[] Characters;
    public string Town;
    public int players;
    private int GameID;
}
```

By adding the [Serializable] attribute to the CharacterData class you allow GameData to save the Characters array. Let's see how this works.

```
// make some data
GameData data = new GameData();
data.players = ParameterData.Players;
data.Characters = new CharacterData[data.players];
data.Town = "Someville";
for (int i = 0; i < data.players; i++)
{
    data.Characters[i] = new CharacterData();
    // give the character some random name.
    string[] nameParts = { "La", "Da", "Fa", "Ma" };
    for (int j = 0; j < 2; j++)
    {
        data.Characters[i].Name += nameParts[UnityEngine.Random.Range(0, 4)];
    }
    // populate the rest of the player's data with random values
    int min = ParameterData.MinRange;
    int max = ParameterData.MaxRange;
    data.Characters[i].HitPoints = UnityEngine.Random.Range(min, max);
    data.Characters[i].Defense   = UnityEngine.Random.Range(min, max);
    data.Characters[i].Offsense  = UnityEngine.Random.Range(min, max);
}

// store the data to file!
string path = Directory.GetCurrentDirectory() + "/Data.json";
string text = JsonUtility.ToJson(data);
Debug.Log(text);
File.WriteAllText(path, text);
```

In the fragment we create a new set of data to save. In here we create a number of characters. The `ParameterData` settings in the Inspector panel in the editor will make modifications to the data being saved.

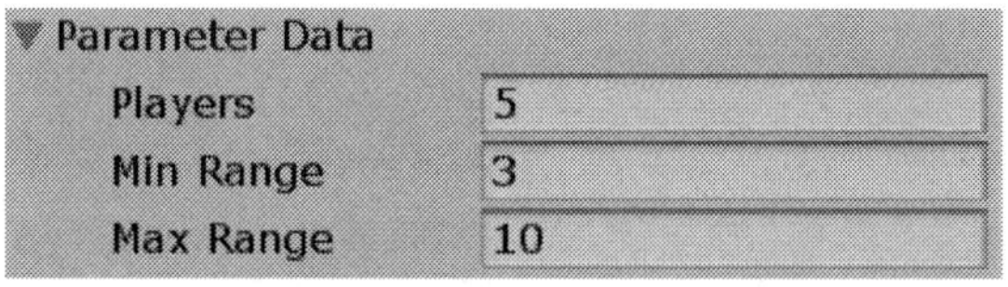

```
▼ Parameter Data
      Players          5
      Min Range        3
      Max Range        10
```

The data here turns into settings to be saved in the data.

```json
{
  "Characters": [
    {
      "Name": "FaFa",
      "HitPoints": 9,
      "Defense": 5,
      "Offsense": 9
    },
    {
      "Name": "MaFa",
      "HitPoints": 8,
      "Defense": 9,
      "Offsense": 8
    },
    {
      "Name": "LaLa",
      "HitPoints": 4,
      "Defense": 8,
      "Offsense": 3
    },
    {
      "Name": "MaMa",
      "HitPoints": 8,
      "Defense": 3,
      "Offsense": 3
    },
    {
      "Name": "LaDa",
      "HitPoints": 7,
      "Defense": 9,
      "Offsense": 7
    }
  ],
  "Town": "Someville",
  "players": 5
}
```

Characters are saved and written to a Data.json file in the Chapter 8 Unity Project directory. When the file is first opened it'll be a long unbroken stream of text. In Visual Studio you can reformat the Json file into what is seen above. If the [Serializable] tag is left out, then the array of characters gets omitted from being written to the data file being saved.

```
// to read the file back again
GameData ReadData(string dataPath)
{
    string dataText = File.ReadAllText(path);
    return JsonUtility.FromJson<GameData>(dataText);
}

data = ReadData(path);
```

To read the data that was written to the Data.json file we simply use the `JsonUtility.FromJson()` once the text from the data is read back. The combination of [`Serializable`] and writing data to Json is a useful combination. With this it's possible to save game data between sessions.

8.10.2 Custom Attributes

A custom attribute allows us to prepare information we'd like to apply to an object. The setup appears quite simple, but allows us to create a tag of our own creation.

```
[AttributeUsage(AttributeTargets.All)]
class CustomAttribute : Attribute
{
    public string customString = "A Custom Attribute";
}

[CustomAttribute]
class Something
{
}
```

Once created and assigned over an object we can look for the specific attribute with Reflection.

```
// using Reflection, get the custom attributes of the
// Something class.
var memberInfos = typeof(Something).GetCustomAttributes(true);
foreach (var i in memberInfos)
{
    CustomAttribute custom = i  as CustomAttribute;
    Debug.Log(custom.customString);
}
// A Custom Attribute
```

The `GetCustomAttributes()` function returns any tag given to the class type. We can create categories of objects we'd like to process for any number of classes. This gives us a system to highlight some objects as special. What makes the attribute usable on the class or any other specific type is that the attribute tag is applied to the custom attribute. In this case, the `AttributeTargets.All` is provided.

8.10.3 Custom Attributes for Default Values

Setting default values for fields in Unity is usually something set up in a Prefab or setting values in the Inspector. The values become difficult to retrieve in runtime.

```
[AttributeUsage(AttributeTargets.Field)]
class DefaultValue : Attribute
{
    public object Value;
    public string Name;
    public DefaultValue(string name, object value)
    {
        Name = name;
        Value = value;
    }
}
```

Another example for Attributes is to hold a value for a class value. Attributes can only hold onto values that inherit directly from object. This means that most of Unity's specific data types like Vector3 and GameObject cannot be stored in an attribute. Attribute constructors are limited to storing simple type literals or POD types.

```
class Character
{

    [DefaultValue("Health", 10)]
    public int HP;
    [DefaultValue("Magic", 10)]
    public int MP;
    // excluded from default settings
    public int XP;
    public float Time;


}
```

The field tagged by the attribute shows the constructor creating the attribute. The syntax reveals the values the attribute will store when it's created.

```
Character character = new Character();

var fields = typeof(Character).GetFields();
foreach (var f in fields)
{
    DefaultValue d = f.GetCustomAttribute(typeof(DefaultValue)) as DefaultValue;
    if (d != null)
    {
        f.SetValue(character, d.Value);
    }
}
Debug.Log("character.HP " + character.HP);
// character.HP 10
Debug.Log("character.MP " + character.MP);
// character.MP 10
Debug.Log("character.XP " + character.XP);
// character.XP 0
Debug.Log("character.Time " + character.Time);
// character.Time 0
```

The `GetFields()` function is provided by `System.Reflection`. The character type reveals a list of the available fields in the class. A simple search through each field allows us to check and set values if the tag exists.

As a human reading a function like `int AddInts(int a, int b);`, you're able to understand that it's a function with two arguments and an `int` return type. Reflection gives us the ability to read the function's arguments, return type, and its name. However, this might not be enough information to work with.

Reflection allows your code to make decisions based on attributes assigned to struct or class members. Once your code can read these attributes, you're able to apply logic and make decisions on which function to use. If we were able to assign additional information to a function or field, we would be able to better scheme up new ways to make our code smarter.

Attributes need to be prepared before they are used. A custom attribute is a class that inherits from the System.Attributes class. The class itself is also labeled as a special class that is used to define custom attributes.

8.10.4 Multiple Attributes

Each custom attribute should be specific. The special instructions or hint which you mark a field or function with should be for a specific use. If you need to add multiple attributes to a class member, then you can stack them.

[AttributeUsage(AttributeTargets. All, AllowMultiple = true, Inherited = true)]

The addition of `AllowMultiple = true` tells the attribute that you can stack different attributes over a class member. In addition, we can add the `Inherited = true` option to this attribute as well. This code tells anything inspecting this attribute that any child class inheriting the member will also have the accompanying attribute.

```
[AttributeUsage(AttributeTargets.All, AllowMultiple = true, Inherited = true)]
class SpecialAttribute : Attribute
{
}
[AttributeUsage(AttributeTargets.All, AllowMultiple = true, Inherited = false)]
class SuperficialAttribute : Attribute
{
}

[Special, Superficial]
class BaseThing
{                    ⚙ SuperficialAttribute.SuperficialAttribute()
}

class SuperThing : BaseThing
{
}
```

In use, the above `BaseThing` class has both Special and SuperficialAttributes tagged. The superficial attribute has Inherited = false. This means that `SuperThing`, which inherits from `BaseThing`, will not have the superficial attribute.

```
Debug.Log("BaseThing's Attributes:");
var attribs = typeof(BaseThing).GetCustomAttributes(true);
foreach (var attrib in attribs)
{
    Debug.Log(attrib);
}
// BaseThing's Attributes:
// Attributes+SpecialAttribute
// Attributes+SuperficialAttribute
```

Logging the custom attributes on the BaseThing reveals both the Special and SuperficialAttributes. The SuperThing only has the special attribute.

```
Debug.Log("SuperThing's Attributes:");
var attribs = typeof(SuperThing).GetCustomAttributes(true);
foreach (var attrib in attribs)
{
    Debug.Log(attrib);
}
// SuperThing's Attributes:
// Attributes+SpecialAttribute
```

The attributes are also applied to the BaseThing as [Special, Superficial] where the Attribute part of the name has been omitted. A simple feature of the Attribute class has allowed trimming the end of the name of the attribute. You're still allowed to use SpecialAttribute, but C# has allowed the obvious part of the name to be used alone.

To make things simple, we can check the types of attributes and cast them as they are found. Once they have been cast, we can extract the expected information and make use of it. In this example, we're just looking at simple casts to find the attributes. Once the attribute is found, we have both the information from the attribute and the member of the class the attribute is associated with.

8.10.5 Putting Attributes to Work

To make an attribute useful, we can make special classes that don't rely on an active Update() function. The MonoBehavior base class makes them considerably more controllable. To make these classes controllable we use a MonoBehaviour class to inspect and start co-routines for more simple classes.

```
[AttributeUsage(AttributeTargets.Method |
                AttributeTargets.Event |
                AttributeTargets.Delegate,
                AllowMultiple = true,
                Inherited = true)]
class UpdateAttribute : Attribute
{
    public float Delay;
    public UpdateAttribute(float delay)
    {
        Delay = delay;
    }
}
```

This attribute is named `UpdateAttribute` and it's got a `Delay float` value. In a simple class we can use this to tag functions for updating with a frequency.

```
class HasUpdates
{
    // updates every half a second
    [Update(0.5f)]
    public void RequiresUpdateOften()
    {
        Debug.Log("Got Updated");
    }
    // updates every three seconds
    [Update(3f)]
    public void AlsoRequiresUpdateSlowly()
    {
        Debug.Log("Also Got Updated");
    }

    // doesn't get updated.
    public void DontUpdate()
    {
        Debug.Log("Exclude me.");
    }
}
```

A simple class named `HasUpdates` contains two tagged functions and one that's not tagged. The first has a frequency of `0.5f` or an update every half a second. The second function has `Update(3f)`, which means to update every three seconds. To serve as a starting point we simply print out either `Got Updated` or `Also Got Updated` when the functions are actually called.

```
// this class has methods
// that need updating.
HasUpdates needsUpdates = new HasUpdates();

// now we know what method has the attribute
// in the class type
var updateMethods = from m in needsUpdates.GetType().GetMethods()
                    where m.GetCustomAttribute<UpdateAttribute>() is UpdateAttribute
                    select m;
```

To start we'll make an instance of the class. The instance could occur anywhere as long as we can find the variable referencing the object. After that, we need a list of methods based on the object type. This contains the method names and if the method has the `UpdateAttribute` then we'll add it to the `updateMethods` from the Linq statement.

```
/* hold onto the coroutines incase
 * we want to kill them later.
 */
List<IEnumerator> routineList = new List<IEnumerator>();

// has methods with update attribute
foreach (var method in updateMethods)
{
    /* inner function for each
     * method with custom attribute
     * inner function can pretty much
     * appear anywhere.
     */
    IEnumerator updater()
    {
        while (true)
        {
            UpdateAttribute upa = method.GetCustomAttribute<UpdateAttribute>() as UpdateAttribute;
            method.Invoke(needsUpdates, new object[] { });
            yield return new WaitForSeconds(upa.Delay);
        }
    }
    routineList.Add(updater());
}
```

Once the LINQ statement has filtered out and selected the tagged methods, a new co-routine is made for each one. The `updater()` inner function appears inside of the foreach loop. This means that for each instance of an `updateMethod` in the class we create a new `IEnumerator` function. A `List<IEnumerator>` stores each function after it's been populated with the method info data.

To find the `Delay` value we use the `method.GetCustomAttribute()` function to get to the `Delay` value in the attribute the function was tagged with. Then we add that value to the `yield return WaitForSeconds` function in the while loop in the `updater()` function. Once that's setup, the `Updater()` is added to `routineList`.

```
foreach (IEnumerator e in routineList)
{
    StartCoroutine(e);
}
```

Once we finish the `updateMethods` foreach loop we iterate through any items that were added to the `routineList` and start the co-routine. The result makes Got Updated and Also Got Updated appear in the Unity console window. Twice a second we get "Got Updated" and every three seconds we get "Also Got Update" as expected.

By storing the `routineList` we can also go through the list and stop the co-routines. This makes the system a bit more robust. By keeping the co-routine around we can start them up again if they're needed. This could be handy when switching scenes or pausing the game, etc.

8.10.6 Attribute Flags

Attributes can be applied to classes, functions, and variables. We should also consider keeping track of what an attribute should be applied to, limiting where an attribute can be used to prevent an attribute being applied to an object for which you don't want to have a specific attribute assigned.

When declaring the new attribute class, we've got several options we can apply.

```
[AttributeUsage(AttributeTargets.Method |
                AttributeTargets.Event |
                AttributeTargets.Delegate,
                AllowMultiple = true,
                Inherited = true)]
```

Additional AttributeTargets can be added using the bitwise operator | to add multiple flags. Such flags were covered in Section 8.9.

```
[Flags]
public enum AttributeTargets
{
    Assembly = 1,
    Module = 2,
    Class = 4,
    Struct = 8,
    Enum = 16,
    Constructor = 32,
    Method = 64,
    Property = 128,
    Field = 256,
    Event = 512,
    Interface = 1024,
    Parameter = 2048,
    Delegate = 4096,
    ReturnValue = 8192,
    GenericParameter = 16384,
    All = 32767
}
```

This changes the option to include both functions and variables. As we've just seen the bitwise operator | in Section 8.9.3, we know that the AttributeTargets enum is set up for bitwise checks.

8.10.7 What We've Learned

With a custom attribute, we can simplify with many tasks. An Update attribute with a time delay [UpdateAttribute (3.0f)] helps functions update at their own pace. Not all functions need to be updated at the beginning of each frame.

Each monster could have a different parts of their behavior update at different time values. Smarter, faster monsters can update more often than slower, dumber monsters that have long delays between updates.

If you revive a character, various stats may need to be reset to their default values. If each different character had a different set of stats, the bookkeeping might get more difficult. A [DefaultAttribute(int restoredAmount)] attribute would make the bookkeeping automatic. Just get all the fields that need to be restored and restore them to the indicated restored amount.

Custom attributes provides an easy readable system to attach important information to a function or variable.

8.11 Bitwise Math

The strange thing about bits is that they are numbers that operate with a system different from what we've been taught in your usual math class. If you wanted to make 10 into -10, you might normally think to simply multiply 10 by -1. However, the usual tricks don't work in the context of the computer's binary world.

Remember what happens when we add 1 to a number at the limit of the binary range. For a nibble of a 4-bit number, that would be 1111 or 15. However, the nibble we're looking at is unsigned, or rather the four digits are all used for counting. If we use a signed nibble, or perhaps a snibble, our limit would be either -8 or 7, which is either 1000 or 0111. Maybe we're talking about a unibble, or unsigned nibble that can count to 15. In any case nibbles, snibbles, and unibbles don't exist in C# so let's move on.

The interesting fact going on binary numbers is that it's a range from 0 to a limit. Often we observe the values as hexadecimal. You come across this term often when making colors for a web page.

When we're in base 10, we start at 0 up to 9. To count to 10, we add another digit to fill in the 10s' place. When we count past 99, we add another digit for hundreds, and so on. When computers count, they use 16, or a nibble; we've come back to that again. To represent each hexadecimal, we use a few letters to fill in the extra digits.

To count like a computer, we use the sequence 0, 1, 2, 3, 4, 5, 6, 7, 8, 9, a, b, c, d, e, f, before getting to another digit. For the computer to count from 0 to 255, it uses eight binary digits, but if we use two nibbles we can represent that with two digits. This is two nibbles, not one nibble, or a byte. A byte is a specific number of bits in a computer's memory. This can tell the computer to store a 1 in decimal it actually thinks "0x01" in hexadecimal. Where the computer uses ff in hex we see 255 in decimal.

```
byte ff = 0xff;
Debug.Log("ff: " + ff);
// ff: 255
```

The above code prints "ff: 255" to the Console panel in Unity. Here the prefix 0x informs C# that we are representing a byte followed by two digits in hexadecimal. The syntax is used to avoid something like "byte b = 11111111;". If we want to use a signed byte or an sbyte, we can represent negative numbers with the following:

```
sbyte sff = -0x80;
Debug.Log("sff: " + sff);
// sff: -128
```

This shows us -0x80 in hex is -128 in decimal. If we try to assign a value outside of the range of the sbyte, we get an error reminding us that we can't assign 255 to an sbyte. However, after a valid assignment, anything can happen.

```
sff--;
Debug.Log("sff--: " + sff);
// sff--: 127
```

If we decrement sff by 1 from -0x80, we get 127 printed to the Unity's Console panel, not -129. Again, we roll numbers even though we're using a different notation. The difference in notation hasn't changed the nature of how the data is stored or calculated. Not surprisingly, the int type has a larger range.

```
int hexMax = 0x7fffffff;
Debug.Log("max in hex:" + hexMax);
// max in hex:2147483647

int intMax = int.MaxValue;
Debug.Log("max from int:" + intMax);
// max from int:2147483647
```

The int is 8 nibbles long. Or rather 8 hexadecimal digits long. The max value of which is 0x7fffffff. The max value is also stored in the int.MaxValue accessor. Smaller values, like 0xff will fit into an int, so assignments using fewer hex digits are perfectly valid.

8.11.1 Two's Complement Unary Operator ~

The unary operator ~ referred to as a tilde works on int values, and if you use byte b = 0 × 01;, then ~b; C# will automatically up-cast the byte to an int before performing the operation. In general, the int type is the more universal of the different integer numbers used in C#. It's just 8 nibbles long, or 4 bytes.

Aside from the casting implications of using the ~ operator, this operator does an interesting trick. If we have 0001, the ~ operator applied to this nibble gives us 1110. This two's complement is used for many different things, including addition.

To change an int from 10 to -10 using binary operations, we use a method known as two's complement. If we wanted to use multiplication, we could go that route; however, by using a bitwise operation, we can speed up the process. Starting with a value, say an int -1 that would look like binary 32 1s.

```
int negOne = -1;
ShowBits(negOne);
// bits in int:-1
// 11111111111111111111111111111111
```

With a slightly more interesting number like 10 which in hex is 0x0a have 0101 followed by a bunch of 0s.

```
int ten = 0x0a;
ShowBits(ten);
// bits in int:10
// 01010000000000000000000000000000
```

We can use the complement bitwise operator ~ to flip the bits. Therefore, if we look at the important value after ~ we see the following:

```
int nTen = ~ten;
ShowBits(nTen);
// bits in int:-11
// 10101111111111111111111111111111
```

Therefore, to get the correct value, add 1 to ~n and assign that to p.

```
int nTenOne = ~ten+1;
ShowBits(nTenOne);
// bits in int:-10
// 01101111111111111111111111111111
```

In a very simple form rather than `int a = 100; a = a*-1;` we can instead use the following:

```
int complement = 100;
complement = ~complement + 1;
ShowBits(complement);
// bits in int:-100
// 00111001111111111111111111111111
```

And we get the same as if we had used `int p = -n;` on the value. So why do things this way? In short, bitwise operations are fast. Because bitwise operations are fast, we often see them in optimized code seen in some C++ projects. The syntax looks unusual, and it is. By seeing this here, you'll have a better chance of reading code written by programmers in other fields.

8.11.2 Bitwise Addition and Subtraction

The computer's CPU has no + and − circuits built into it. It's a collection of these bitwise operators. Because of this reason, it's an interesting exercise to understand what is actually going on when you do something simple like 7 + 3.

Looking at the nibble again, we have the decimal 7 represented as 1110 and 3 being 1100; adding these together makes the bits look like 1010 or 10. There isn't a direct process by which 0111 and 0011 can be added together in one operation. To add we need to move bits from one number into the other.

```
int a = 7;
int b = 3;
int c = a & b;
int r = a ^ b;
while (c != 0)
{
    int s = c << 1;
    c = r & s;
    r = r ^ s;
}
Debug.Log(r);
```

Where `while (c != 0)`, we are done taking all of the bits from the carry `c` and adding them to the result `r`. A breakdown of the code, one line at a time, shows what's happening to the bits and their decimal values. There are only three significant lines we need to observe. The first line `int s = c << 1;` is temporary storage for clarity.

The loop begins by finding all the digits that match. This loop will tell us which digits need to be carried over. The carried-over digits are the ones where 1s appear in both numbers. So, `a & b` shows us where 1s appear in both numbers, and we get 0111 & 0011 = 0011. After this we need to find where the digits are mismatched with 0111 ^ 0011 = 0100.

```
int c = a & b;
//a  1110 0000
//b &1100 0000
//  =1100 0000

int r = a ^ b;
//a  1110 0000
//b ^1100 0000
//  =0010 0000
```

In the first line where we begin adding the numbers, we start with a shifted digit.

```
int s = c << 1;
//[ s = 0110 0000 << 1]
```

We move the digits over by one space and find the next digit to carry over.

```
c = r & s;
//[ r   0010 0000     ]
//[ s & 0110 0000     ]
//[ c = 0010 0000     ]
```

After shifting the digit and finding the one that needs to be carried over, we need to reassign r to the next digit to carry.

```
r = r ^ s;
//[ r   0010 0000     ]
//[ s ^ 0110 0000     ]
//[ r = 0100 0000     ]
```

We've reduced the number of carry digits by 1. However, we still have one digit to merge in, so we go back to the beginning of the loop.

```
int s = c << 1;
[ s = 0001 0000 << 1] → actual direction
```

We have a digit carried over from the previous loop that needs to be merged back into the result. But we need to check whether there are any digits overlapping to check if we need to do the loop again.

```
c = r & s;
[ r   0100 0000     ]
[ s & 0001 0000     ]
[ c = 0000 0000     ](c == 0)
```

Here we see that 0010 & 1000 has no overlapping digits. Therefore, we can merge to our final result.

```
r = r ^ s;
[ r   0100 0000     ]
[ s ^ 0001 0000     ]
[ r = 0101 0000     ](final result)
```

Now our result is a correct merging of 0100 and 0001, which is 0101 or decimal 10. Inside the computer's CPU, there is a section of circuits called an adder that does the same thing. When you have a computer running several billion operations per second, this operation happens incredibly fast. However, if you need to do this operation a hundred million times, then you'll see a performance difference between this operation and perhaps a more complex operation.

To turn the above code into a function, we'll use the following:

```
int BitwiseAdd(int a, int b)
{
    int c = a & b;
    int r = a ^ b;
    while (c != 0)
    {
        int s = c << 1; //shift digits to add
        c = r & s;       //find overlapping digits
        r = r ^ s;       //merge digits that don't overlap
    }
    return r;
}
```

Subtraction is an addition with a negative number. To get the negative number, we use the previous two's complement. So, in the case of the following

```
int a = 7;
int b = 3;
int c = BitwiseSub(a, b);
```

subtraction involves flipping the b into a negative number using two's complement and then adding them together. To use this feature, we can simply reuse the BitwiseAdd() function a couple of times. The first one is basically two's complement without using a + 1 to get the negative version of b, and then we use BitwiseAdd() again to get a result.

```
int BitwiseSub(int a, int b)
{
    b = BitwiseAdd(~b, 1);
    return BitwiseAdd(a, b);
}
```

8.11.3 Bitwise Multiplication

The bitshift operators can be used to multiply by 2: $4 << 1 = 8$ or $0100 << 1 = 1000$; this is rather handy when finding a specific half or double of a value. However, when multiplying, we need to do something like that of addition. We need to find out how many times we can multiply by 2, and then to an odd number we add the last number. So, in the case of $7 * 3$, we use $(7 * 2) + 7$; the code that can do this operation is shown below.

```
int BitwiseMultiplication(int a, int b)
{
    int r = 0;
    while (b != 0)
    {
        if ((b & 1) != 0)
        {
            r = BitwiseAdd(r, a);
        }
        a = a << 1;
        if (b == 0)
        {
            r = a;
            break;
        }
        b = b >> 1;
    }
    return r;
}
```

The above code shifts a `<< 1` for each multiple of 2 we find in b. Each time b is shifted `>> 1`, it's moved toward 0. When we check if b is odd using `(b & 1) != 0`, we add to int r whatever is at int a before it's shifted again. When we're done shifting and thus done multiplying by 2, our while loop exits, and we're done.

Division can be simplified to the number of times b can be subtracted from a.

```
int BitwiseDiv(int a, int b)
{
    int divideStart = a;
    int timesDivided = 1;
    while (true)
    {
        divideStart = BitwiseSub(divideStart, b);
        if (divideStart <= 0)
            break;
        timesDivided = BitwiseAdd(timesDivided, 1);
    }
    return timesDivided;
}
```

The above code is a very simple version of an integer division solution using our `BitwiseAdd()` and `BitwiseSub()` functions. Multiplication can also be a simple addition of a to a by b times. Though not as efficient as the system used in the multiplication function, the division system is a very rudimentary example of how the most basic bitwise operators can be used to do mundane math functions. The problem with an integer is that you're not allowed any fractions, so division will end up with an incorrect value unless a is evenly divided by b.

8.11.4 Bitwise Tricks

Now that we know how bits work on a more fundamental level, we can use them to our advantage to perform quick operations. Rather than checking if an int is odd or even by using n % 2 == 0, we can use the faster n & 1 == 1 to check for an odd number. We can tell if a number is negative using a bit; if (someNumber & (1<<31)) != 0, then we have a positive number. This checks for the last digit, which is at 1<<31 and looks to see if it's a 1 or a 0. If it's 1, then it's negative; otherwise it's positive.

Not all these tricks are necessarily faster than using more regular math functions. We can check the 1<<31 bit. But perhaps it's just easier to check if someNumber > 0 to see if it's positive or not. However, knowing how bits work is interesting.

If you need to know whether two values are both negative, both positive, or different, then you can check with the following:

```
int a = 20;
int b = 1;
bool same = ((a ^ b) > 0);
Debug.Log(same);
```

If a and b are positive, the same is true; otherwise if a and b are different signs, then the same is false. This condition works only when the bit at 1 holds a sign for positive or negative. Simple tricks like this can be used in various situations.

The following function will help with the above examples by printing out each digit.

```
string BitsToString(int number, int digits)
{
    char[] binary = new char[digits];
    int digit = digits - 1;
    int place = 0;
    while (place < digits)
    {
        int d = number & (1 << place);
        if (d != 0)
        {
            binary[digit] = '1';
        }
        else
        {
            binary[digit] = '0';
        }
        digit--;
        place++;
    }
    return new string(binary);
}

Debug.Log(BitsToString(42, 8));
// 00101010
```

The above code uses int d, which is a check for a 1 or a 0 at the place in the given number. Each iteration of the while loop increments the place and decrements which digit we're looking at. If d is 0, then we add a 0 to the char[] array; otherwise we add a 1. With the above code, we can check out the first 4 bits or all 32 bits of an int.

8.11.5 What We've Learned

These tutorials got into quite low-level concepts. Finding practical game play applications for these concepts may not be readily evident. However, the concepts do provide an important foundation for your understanding of C#.

The ability to create complex algorithms means being able to create more complex and more interesting game play scenarios. Adding in various logical parameters and making use of them in creative ways means providing more interesting puzzles.

Outside of games, many of these concepts are also useful for processing data. A modern game requires many different tasks, from collecting and analyzing data from users to sorting through databases for building leader boards.

8.12 Architectures and Organization

So far in this book we've focused on writing individual classes or inheriting one class to another. This is fine to learn the mechanics of the language, but it doesn't help toward building a larger project. Take a moment, step back, and think about how all your classes fit together to build an entire project. This takes another frame of mind altogether.

When you're building a structure for your game, it's important to keep C# files separated by task. Tasks can be added or merged as needed far easier when separated into different files. The more separation you keep, the less often files will have to be merged when working in a team of engineers.

If each class is limited in scope to just a few related tasks, you also decrease the number of places you need to look to fix bugs. This also helps when using the debugger; if the file isn't long and the scope is limited, you can find a problem and fix it in a smaller file.

When you're working by yourself, it's easy to claim ownership over your code base. You know where everything is, and you have a better idea of what it's doing. However, when it comes to working in a team, each person needs to focus on smaller, more specialized part of the code base. When you're able to focus on a specific task, you're better able to limit your scope and build a more thoughtfully crafted class.

Once each task lives in its own file, it's unlikely that too many people will have to touch the file while you're working on it. This reduces the number of merging you'll need to do when using version control systems like Git. If a single C# script file spans many different operations, then more and more people will need to make changes to the file. When you check in the file, having to merge your changes with many other changes can create problems if the merge isn't done correctly.

Approaching a project with the intent to build a complex game involves a great amount of thought; luckily, if you've written functions that have little or no side effects, then you're better able to rearrange and separate the classes and functions into different files much more easily.

The following work is seen in the GameCo directory in the Assets of the Chapter 8 unity Project.

8.12.1 Planning Structure: Namespaces and Directories

Even the smallest project can grow into a huge undertaking. There's almost no such thing as overly organized when it comes to programming. When programming is well organized, it also becomes much easier to both read and write. Your specific tasks become precise and sometimes easier.

In the root of Assets should be a directory for either your game company or the game title. This serves as a container for the most generic functions and classes for your project. We'll come back to what sort of classes should live in this namespace.

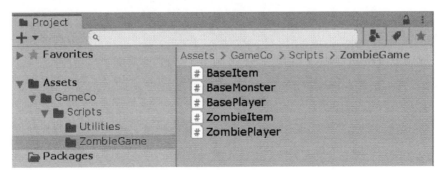

If you intend to make only one game ever, then a game-specific namespace may not be necessary, but I'm sure that you've got bigger visions than that. After a broad namespace, a slightly more specific namespace for your game should be considered. So we might be looking at `AwesomeGameCo.ZombieGame` that would contain classes that are particularly useful for a zombie game.

Directories and namespaces should match. The scripts running in the game should live in your game scripts `ZombieGame`. The `GameCo.ZombieGame` namespace should implement game behaviors. This could be further divided into `GameCo.ZombieGame.Player` or `GameCo.ZombieGame.Monster` to further isolate and encapsulate specific functions.

The purpose of a namespace and the following directory structure is to divide the different tasks in your game. A namespace for the player, the environment, effects, monsters, and weapons will ensure focus and specialization.

Tools that help debugging tasks can be fit into a GameCo.Utilities. Repeated functions and methods can be moved into lower level base class functions so implementations further up the inheritance hierarchy can implement them.

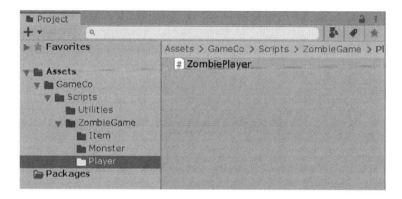

In the `ZombieGame` directory lives the `BasePlayer` for implementation in the `ZombieGame`. `ZombiePlayer` object. The specialization also divides how many files need to be checked into Git. By separating classes, the engineer can also find a bug and fix it in relative isolation from other bugs.

8.12.2 Divide and Conquer

The use of partial comes into play when needing to extend a specific class with different Interface classes. Consider something like a pick-up item. Various Interface classes like the `IComparer` and `IEnumerable` allow for LINQ to compare items in the scene or in the player inventory.

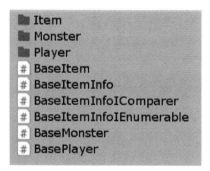

The using partial in a class allows you to break up a single file across multiple appropriately named files. This ensures that a bug in an Interface is contained to a specific file. Naming files also serves as a system to divide work.

You may have noticed that `MonoBehaviour` uses a particular spelling which isn't common in American English. If this bothers you, it can easily be fixed with a starting namespace for your own game company. Here we can create a simple renaming of `MonoBehaviour` to `Behavior`.

```
using UnityEngine;
namespace GameCo
{
    public class Behavior : MonoBehaviour
    {
    }
}
```

8.12.3 Refactoring

When you've decided that a class or type name needs to change, the work to change it has multiplied once the name has spread across many different files. Searching for every place that a specific name appears isn't always so easy.

```
namespace GameCo.ZombieGame
{
    public class Damage
    {
        public DamageInfo Info;
    }

    public class DamageInfo
    {
        public DamageTypes DamageType;
        public int DamageAmount;
    }

    public enum DamageTypes
    {
        Projectile  = 0,
        Poison      = 1,
        Fire        = 2,
        Explisove   = 4,
        Cutting     = 8,
        Dimensional = 16,
        Freezing    = 32,
        Crushing    = 64,
        Falling     = 128
    }
}
```

A Find and Replace may find something like Damage in DamageType and DamageInfo. This means inspecting each instance and deciding whether it should be changed. So long as the name only appears in a few places, this might not be too bad. If the word were more common, then you might be looking at many dozen instances that can easily lead to creating bugs.

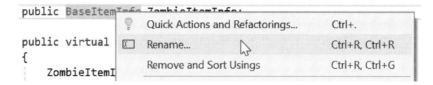

```
public BaseItem
           Quick Actions and Refactorings...        Ctrl+.
public virtual     Rename...                        Ctrl+R, Ctrl+R
{
    ZombieItemI    Remove and Sort Usings           Ctrl+R, Ctrl+G
```

The Rename tool in Visual Studio as well as many other IDEs was created to help this process. The rename tool is aware of the name's use and where it appears. In addition, conflicts will also be pointed out as you change the name.

```
public class Damage
{
    public Damage Info;
}


public class Damage
{
    public DamageTypes DamageType;
    public int DamageAmount;
}
```

The Rename tool helps redefine identifiers throughout the project. It's important to avoid conflicting with names already in use. If the conflicts are ignored, Visual Studio will not remember how the classes were separated. The tool is also aware of namespace and will not change identifiers in another namespace that has the same identifier.

8.12.4 What We've Learned

Creating and using a structure for your game takes a lot of experience and practice. Coming to a final decision on structure before you've started writing the code for your game is unlikely. By creating namespaces and writing small classes in each one, you're also giving yourself a much easier way to reorganize the files into new namespaces and new directories.

Even after things get established, it's not so difficult to make widespread changes. One of the best ways for making these changes is by keeping categories and types clearly separated. Ensuring that the crossover between classes is limited to only specific functions is difficult, but no less important.

The less each class needs to depend on another class to operate, the less chance you have of one object causing a cascade of errors. If each function can act on its own, then you have a better chance of preventing bugs. If a class can be fragmented into many different parts, then assigning work to different team members is easier.

By splitting off functions to different people, you've also made decisions that make the design more clear. If the design is still undecided to make clear tasks for a given project, then it might be a good idea to spend more time thinking about what you're building before writing any code.

8.13 Design Patterns

We can't get the feeling that we've learned how to speak the same language as a programmer unless we've studied something called a design pattern. Computer programmers have been solving the same problems time and again, so it should come as no surprise that some common solutions for similar problems have been discovered and shared.

The solutions to these re-occurring problems became known as design patterns. With the long history of programming, many complex problems are solved with known patterns. The more common the problem, the more likely there's already a known pattern. These solutions are described by how the problem has been solved.

Design patterns are reusable solutions. The patterns become established when they are reusable, and they are proven to work. They are also general enough to be modified to suit the situation you need it for.

Often the patterns have been tested enough and optimized to the smallest fastest code required for a solution to the problem. When properly understood and applied, the pattern will often prevent edge cases from escaping the solution. If a pattern stands the test of time, it becomes established and relied upon.

Learning patterns means you get to build up your vocabulary and overall ability as a programmer. There are a great number of established design patterns. The list of design patterns is extensive and the topic concerns many matters beyond the scope of this book. However, we can still talk to some of the main points behind why the design patterns matter.

There are three categories of design patterns in computing: creational, structural, and behavioral. When writing software for the first time, you're going to be coming across tasks thinking that they're all new. In fact, they're the same problems which everyone has had to solve many times before you.

8.13.1 Creational Design Patterns

Creational design patterns are named so because they relate to how an object is created and later used. These systems are often used in games to instance new creatures and items. When you start a game, it's a good idea that you're starting one game and referencing the one game that was started. Other patterns are useful for creating a variety of similar objects.

Creational design patterns represent the idea of creating and setting up any object from a class using a consistent system. To list a few common creational design patterns, we can start with the Factory, Prototype, Singleton, and Builder.

8.13.1.1 Singleton Pattern

A singleton pattern is a creational pattern which limits the number of instanced objects to one instance. If a problem comes up like "I'd like to make ensure there's only one instance of an object," then you might look on the internet to how someone has solved this particular problem. After a few searches, you'll come across a "Singleton pattern" which ensures that only once instance of an object is ever created.

The first time the object is asked for like CommandCenter MyCommander = CommandCenter. Commander;, you can use an accessor to create and return the commander. If the commander has already been created, then you can pass him along, and not create a new one.

The Singleton pattern is useful to ensure that a game only has a single game state controller. If you want to keep track of the player's navigation through your menus and into your game, it's better to have a single class instructing the rest of your game to start, stop, and post results through one class.

The reason why we don't simply use a lot of static fields and functions is more an effect to memory. If everything was static, then they're never be cleared out of memory. If you're managing a lot of data, then the static field storing them will never be freed, and your game's memory will bloat and take up all the room left for the rest of your game.

Like the "Singleton pattern," many different patterns have a specific role and description. The "factory pattern" uses a class whose only purpose is to instance and create objects. Much like a candy factory produces various sweets. The "builder pattern" is similar to the "factory pattern," but requires another class called a director to control its activity. The "prototype pattern" is another variation on the factory pattern, but copies from a pre-existing copy of a class to create a new object.

8.13.2 Structural Design Patterns

Structural design patterns help consolidate how data and functions are organized and arranged in a class. In this category, we've got the Decorator, Facade, Flyweight, Adapter, and Proxy. Of these the Decorator pattern comes up often in games.

The Decorator pattern is used when instancing objects into a scene. We use this pattern extensively in Unity 3D. For each component you attach to a gameObject, you're decorating it with new behaviors. See that you've been using design patterns all this time and didn't even know it.

When you create a template for creating a zombie or a vampire, you're creating a system to decorate a gameObject with the appropriate components. By keeping movement, armor, attack patterns, and other behaviors separated into different components, you're allowing yourself more freedom to create new objects with different decorations.

Add a blood-sucking component to a Plymouth Fury and you've got a 1980s movie car. Add a talking component to a toaster and you've got a British situation comedy in space. Various components allow for unexpected and sometimes fun results.

8.13.3 Behavioral Design Patterns

Behavioral design patterns focus on communication between objects in a system. Some behavioral patterns include Iterator, Mediator, Observer, and Visitor. In this section, we'll take a close look at the Iterator and Observer patterns.

The Observer pattern is a common system of behavioral design. Combine this with the Singleton, and you've got a game state manager. Combine this with a character, and you've got a level boss. The Observer pattern means that a single class orchestrates the behavior of many child classes.

The children are actually the observers; they watch a central class for changes in the game. Based on the events in the game, a condition will change, and they'll all change their behavior, or rather they observe a state change and react accordingly.

When building your game, it's often a good idea to make sure that data isn't duplicated anywhere it's not necessary. If every child had a record of the player's health, then you're wasting space on redundant data. The player's health should only ever be located in the player object.

When new conditions are met, an event can be raised to tell the game state that the player's health is low. When this event is raised, anyone observing this change should be notified. Then the observing objects can rush in to finish off the player.

8.13.4 What We've Learned

It's unfortunate that we don't have another few hundred pages for this book to go into more depth on the different design patterns. Each one has not only benefits but also some interesting drawbacks. A Singleton pattern is great for centralizing all of your object management. The main problem here is the fact that the Singleton tends to get very big once it's managing a lot of different things.

There's no perfect answer for which pattern any situation should use. In the end, a blend of a few different patterns is usually how the final implementation ends up. Holding too close to any single pattern will only accomplish slowing down overall development time and limit what your game can do.

The final product should be something fun for your player. Even if the code is a little bit awkward in some places, your player isn't reading your code. So long as the code runs fast, reliable, and is easy to read, you're on the right track.

8.14 Continuing on Your Own

Where to go from here? You'll want to explore more of the different function calls that are found within .NET and the Unity 3D application programming interfaces. Google and Bing are both great to help search for answers. Also, now that you know a lot of different programmer jargons, you're less likely to be ignored when asking questions on forums.

One of the hardest lessons to learn is less about code and more about time management. The time management I speak of is not the amount of work any given task is going to take. The amount of time your work takes up of your life is more about what I'm speaking of.

After talking to many vets in the games and software industry is the amount of time left after work and dedicated to living *away* from your keyboard. When first getting into any new topic, it's natural to want to dedicate a large portion of your life to learning more and getting better. However, when this becomes the majority of your life to the degradation of your health, it's time to pull back.

Only after experience can one clearly see that overzealous dedication was a mistake. Of course, getting to that point leads to the experience necessary to see where things went wrong, a horrible catch-22 if there ever was one. Because of this, I'll just leave you with a final word of caution to not let your computer take over your life.

Personally, I've realized that I don't draw as often as I used to. I appreciate my weekends more, and I'm learning a wider variety of things, trying not to focus so heavily on a single topic any more. This comes after realizing that putting your life's work into a single project can all too easily lead to disaster. Though I haven't really had any giant plans crushed by being over-focused, I have seen friends and co-workers having family problems and personal issues grow due to lack of a life outside of work.

Anything can happen, and a project can get canceled before it sees the light of day. The end result can be months or, worse yet, years invested into a lost cause. Nothing is worse than walking away from a gigantic project with nothing to show for your work.

The games industry is volatile; it's filled with politics and instability. The more you know, the easier it is to remain relevant. The more skills you have, the wider your opportunities. Eventually, once you've accumulated enough skill, it's time to work on personal projects that mean more to you.

9

Stuff We Couldn't Cover

Writing in C# means being able to write software for many platforms. This includes embedded systems like the Arduino. Although the C# for Arduino is limited to older versions of .NET and thus older features of C#, a lot of the basic C# functionality is available. You can build software to drive little affordable processors for building robots or internet connected sensors.

You also can build stand alone software applications for the Windows Store, Linux, OSX. You can build for both Android and iOS using Xamarin and Visual Studio. You can write stand-alone apps that aren't necessarily games. The boundaries for where C# has reached span far past the bounds of this book.

Really interesting bits like writing assembly with C# is also possible.

9.1 The Extern Keyword

We could inspect a simple dynamically linked library (DLL) project in Visual Studio. The included project can also build an external library for osX and Linux as well. UnityEngine is a DLL. A DLL is a pre-built binary file that contains any one of the constructs that were covered in this book.

Open the MyUnityLibrary.sln in Visual Studio. Until now, most of the projects in the BookContents repository were created by Unity. This Visual Studio project was created in Visual Studio from a DLL template.

```
using System;
public static class MyUnityLibrary
{
    public static string MyString()
    {
        return "Hello World.";
    }
}
```

The one C# file in the Solution Explorer has a static class and a static function. This is just a simple starting point, but the project isn't to serve as anything more than a simple example of how to import methods from a DLL.

From looking at the content of the DLL you could imagine that you're able to get a "Hello World." string from the MyString() function. To build the DLL, you'll find the "Build" command in the Visual Studio menu as Build -> Build Solution.

Learning C# Programming with Unity 3D

A DLL is created and stored in the project directory MyUnityLibrary\MyUnityLibrary\bin\Debug\, where you'll find MyUnityLibrary.dll. To use the library, copy the dll file into a Plugins directory in Unity's Assets directory.

```
using System.Runtime.InteropServices;
using UnityEngine;

public class TestLibrary : MonoBehaviour
{
    [DllImport("MyUnityLibrary")]
    public static extern string MyString();

    void Start()
    {
        Debug.Log(MyUnityLibrary.MyString());
    }
}
```

Once Unity is aware that there's a DLL in the Plugins directory, the project is updated with some additional files reflecting how the DLL is to be used. Cross platform compatibility is also allowed when writing a plugin with C#. A C# library built with .NET can conveniently run on any platform that runs Unity.

The classes in Unity need to know how to operate with an external library. The System.Runtime.InteropServices enables the external library connection. The [DLLImport()] attribute searches for a DLL with the MyUnityLibrary name. The MyString() function has an extern accessor assigned telling C# to look outside of the class and into external sources for the MyString() function. When the game is played, the "Hello World." string is pulled from the DLL and printed to the Unity console.

This is a very simplified example of an external Library. A DLL can also be written in C++, C, or any other language, assuming that the target platform matches the target of your Unity game project. Special optimizations can be built into a DLL that cannot be built in C# with Unity. This allows for heavy calculations to be done with faster optimizations and packed into a DLL using C++ or assembly language.

If some code is special and you're not willing or able to share the code with a project, this can also be built into a DLL and only an interface to the code needs to be exposed in Unity.

10

Good Luck

If you've gotten this far, thank you. Even though you've read through miles of material, you've still got a long way to go to be a full-fledged game engineer. However, don't let this dull your motivation.

The most important advice I can give you is to remain focused on learning with your first few projects rather than finishing that massively multiplayer online role-playing, first-person World War II zombie shooter game. It's important that you understand what you're capable of, and to do this, you need to learn your own limitations.

Your strengths aren't just about what you're able to do, but how long it takes to do them. Eventually, you'll be able to write a fairly complex multiplayer game. It might take a few years, but it'll eventually get done. If you think you'll still be interested in working on one project for many thousands of hours, then I commend your focus and dedication.

For many people, a weekend or an evening project should remain fairly simple and small. A puzzle game, an endless runner, or a simple adventure game can still be done by one person. Once your game requires several hundred assets, sounds, effects, and the like, you're now looking at a product requiring a large-scale effort.

Such efforts require teams of people simply because of the hours involved to finish the product. Even a team of less than a dozen people means that there is several times more hours dedicated to a project than you can dedicate alone. Even if you dedicate 2000 hours a month to a project, it would not be enough, as many large-scale projects require tens of millions of hours to complete.

Finishing a project, even a small one, means you have something to show for your effort. You may well start down the path of a super cool game that no one has ever seen before, but is it something you can stay focused on for a few million hours? It's likely that even after a few hundred hours into the project, you'll realize that you need to start over anyway.

Learning how to write code is an ongoing process. Halfway through a large project, you'll learn that the beginning of your project had many mistakes because of bad programming habits. Usually, fixing all of the problems means throwing everything out and starting over. Don't let this discourage you. You've learned something, and you've become a better programmer!

Index